Also by Herbert Weinstock

CHOPIN

HANDEL

MUSIC AS AN ART

TCHAIKOVSKY

MEN OF MUSIC
(with Wallace Brockway)

THE WORLD OF OPERA
(with Wallace Brockway)

DONIZETTI

DONIZETTI

AND

*the World of Opera
in Italy, Paris, and Vienna
in the First Half of the
Nineteenth Century*

BY

HERBERT WEINSTOCK

Pantheon Books / *New York*

A DIVISION OF RANDOM HOUSE

FIRST PRINTING

© Copyright, 1963, by Herbert Weinstock
All rights reserved under International and Pan-
American Copyright Conventions. Published in
New York by Pantheon Books, a division of
Random House, Inc., and simultaneously in To-
ronto, Canada, by Random House of Canada,
Limited. Manufactured in the United States of
America by The Haddon Craftsmen, Inc.,
Scranton, Pa.
Library of Congress catalog card number: 63-13703

DESIGN BY HERBERT H. JOHNSON

"*Luce, luce! O quella di Dio, o quella
dell'olio e della cera!*"
(Light, light! Either that of God
or that of oil and wax!)

—Donizetti, *October 7, 1845,*
in a letter to Tommaso Persico

Note

THE working Bibliography (pp. 405–10) lists books and articles in alphabetic order, by the names of their authors or editors. The list is numbered, and individual titles are referred to throughout the text by these numbers, thus: (27), which a glance at the Bibliography will show to be the number there of Alberto Cametti's *Donizetti a Roma,* or (54), that item in the Bibliography being Francesco Florimo's *La Scuola musicale di Napoli.* The page reference numbers are set in roman type following the italic bibliographical entry number; thus: (27, 1–13).

H. W.

Foreword

My special interest in Donizetti dates from the evening of April 13, 1958, when I heard his *Anna Bolena* for the first time. That stupendous performance, at La Scala, Milan, was under the direction of Donizetti's fellow-townsman Gianandrea Gavazzeni, and was produced by Luchino Visconti, with scenery and costumes by Nicola Benois. It starred Maria Meneghini Callas, Giulietta Simionato, Gabriella Carturan, Gianni Raimondi, and Cesare Siepi. One of the most profoundly moving operatic experiences of my life, *Anna Bolena* suddenly showed me that Donizetti was a musicodramatic creator of far greater power and importance than any of my earlier contacts with others of his operas had led me to believe. I began to understand then that he was a bridge between Rossini and Verdi and to wonder about his life and career.

In 1961, my friend Wallace Brockway invited me to contribute an article on Donizetti to a musical encyclopedia that he was editing. Turning to bibliographies and the card catalogue of the Music Division of the New York Public Library, I at once discovered that no full-length biography of Donizetti was available in English. My friend Ben Meiselman was traveling in Italy at the time, and I persuaded him to go for me to the Museo Donizettiano at Bergamo and to G. Ricordi & C., Milan, obtaining for me all the Italian, French, and other books, pamphlets, and catalogues relating to Donizetti which he could find, and ordering others.

I was unaware at that juncture—and indeed until this book was in semifinal draft—that Mr. William Ashbrook was also at work on a book about Donizetti. When I finally learned of his plans, both of us were too far advanced in actual writing for either of us to be able to withdraw and leave the field open for the other. We established an amiable friendship-in-competition by letter, and I know that Mr. Ashbrook's book will deal at some length in analyses of Donizetti scores, a valuable contribution that never was part of my own plan, largely because I wanted to fill a longish book entirely with a historical account of his life and works.

I have examined and collected, however, as many Donizetti opera scores as I have been able to locate and afford. Familiarity with them has served both to increase my respect for Donizetti the dramatic composer and to multiply my regret that he so often was a frantically rushed and slipshod craftsman. No musical work of any sort, I feel certain, can be judged relevantly apart from adequate performance. An opera, furthermore, is not purely music, being in effect a verbal-musical scenario for a performance, for which reason it can be judged apart from such performance even less meaningfully than a sonata or a symphony. The Italian operas of the early nineteenth century, finally, are perhaps, of all operas, those least likely to reveal their complete potentialities by study, however careful, of the engraved score. They need staging, acting, the full resources of the most imaginative production, need them more drastically than any other group of operas of like or greater intrinsic purely musical quality.

The early-nineteenth-century world of Italian opera in Italy, Paris, and Vienna—the three arenas of Donizetti's activity—cannot be understood without full realization that it was the golden era of the impresario. Librettists, composers, and the titular managers of opera houses—including La Scala at Milan, the San Carlo at Naples, the Théâtre-Italien at Paris, and the Kärnthnertortheater at Vienna—preponderantly bowed to the dictates of such men as Domenico Barbaja, Vincenzo Jacovacci, Alessandro Lanari, Bartolomeo Merelli, and Giovanni Paterni. The impresarios either leased theaters or hired themselves out to managers. Then they themselves signed up (usually in this order) singers, composers, and librettists. Most often, for example, Donizetti did not deal with the manager of the theater for which he was composing, but with its current impresario: his dealings with Duke Carlo Visconti di Modrone at La Scala only seem exceptional, for Visconti was at least as much impresario as manager. Otherwise, Donizetti's only important negotiations with house managers were for operas to be sung at the Paris theaters: the directors of the Opéra, Opéra-Comique, and Théâtre-Italien exercised much more authority than their counterparts in Italy. At times, of course, impresarios temporarily became house managers as well.

Except where attributed to others, all of the translations in this book are my own. Some words must be said about the quotations and translations of Donizetti's letters. His handwriting, often difficult to decipher at all, became less legible as he grew older. It very often invites several widely varying interpretations. His spelling and punctuation remained insouciant, and he was addicted to dots and dashes.[1] I have tried to translate exactly what I have understood to be exactly what he wrote. But my determination to do that has not been easy to carry out, and I certainly have no ethical quarrel with others who occasionally have interpreted some of his squiggles differently.

Some conception of the problems involved can be gleaned from a single instance. The letter to Mayr cited on page 204 of the text contains a passage that Federico Alborghetti and Michelangelo Galli (5) transcribed in 1875 as:*"Vidi con Ahiblinger [sic] in vettura il paese dov'ei nacque e la casa; mi ha fatto sommo piacere. . . ."* Translated literally, that would be: "I saw with Aiblinger in [a] carriage the village where you were born and the house; this has given me the highest pleasure. . . ." That reading of Donizetti's script permitted Alborghetti and Galli (and therefore the numerous writers who thereafter depended upon their reading) to state that Donizetti had visited the upper Bavarian village of Mendorf and there had seen the house in which Mayr had been born.

But, as Ciro Caversazzi pointed out (31), the passage in Donizetti's letter almost certainly reads: *"Vidi da Ahiblinger [sic] in pittura il paese dov'ei nacque, e la cosa mi ha fatto sommo piacere. . . ."* That in literal translation would be: "I saw at Aiblinger's in [a] painting the village where you were born, and the thing has given me the highest pleasure. . . ." The difference between Donizetti's having stopped outside Mayr's birthplace at Mendorf in a carriage and his having seen a painting of that house at Munich is already a matter of some importance, at least to a biographer. But passages of far greater importance have been misread similarly, misinterpreted, and therefore misused—and then trustingly cited from book to book for so many decades that trying to unsnarl the resulting misinformation has become one nerve-frazzling part of a Donizetti biographer's labor.

Nor can all such problems be solved by deciding that someone excusably misinterpreted Donizetti's handwriting. In a letter to his father on January 10, 1830, Donizetti mentioned *"Gli Amori degli Angeli di Lord Bijron [Bayron?],"* and Giuliano Donati-Petténi (39, 81), aware that Byron did not write *The Loves of the Angels*, whereas Thomas Moore did, asserts that what Donizetti in fact wrote was *"Gli Amori*

---

[1] Regretfully, in the cause of not cluttering up these pages with cabalistic symbols, I have decided to make no distinction between Donizetti's widely strewn dots and the points of suspension that I have introduced to indicate omissions. Any careful students wishing to establish the complete texts of almost all of the letters from which I have quoted will find the Italian text, completely—and for the most part accurately—transcribed in *138*.

degli Angeli di Moore." For proof that this is not a question of misreading a difficult script, but conscious "editing," see the reproduction of this page from Donizetti's letter of January 10, 1830, Plate 5.

Then there is the extremely involved and fascinating question of who wrote the libretto of *Don Pasquale*. A text issued for sale at the Metropolitan Opera House, New York, in December 1955—and containing an English translation copyrighted that year—confidently says "Libretto by Camerano," the name probably being a misprint[2] for that of Salvatore Cammarano. Now, Cammarano wrote eight librettos that were set by Donizetti, but he had nothing whatever to do with the text of *Don Pasquale*, though *Kobbé's Complete Opera Book* (1954, "edited and revised by the Earl of Harewood") lends its weight to the statement that he did. Most Italian and other sources,[3] however, state accurately that the earliest printed librettos of *Don Pasquale* gave the author as "M. A.," and then add, incorrectly, that those initials stood for " 'Michele Accursi,' pseudonym of Giovanni [some even say Giacomo] Ruffini." A few sources state that the libretto was Donizetti's own work—which, in part, it was.

Incorrect attributions of the *Don Pasquale* libretto occur in a variety of sources that would appear to be trustworthy. These include, besides those already mentioned, the 1843 La Scala libretto (*"poesia di Angelo Anelli, Michele Accursi e Gaetano Donizetti"*), Ulderico Rolandi's *Il Libretto per musica attraverso i tempi* ("M. *Accursi ed altri*"), the *Enciclopedia dello Spettacolo* ("M. *Accursi scrisse il Don Pasquale per Donizetti*"), Pompeo Cambiasi's *Rappresentazioni date nei Reali Teatri di Milano, 1778–1872*, and almost every book on Donizetti, as well as the fifth edition of *Grove's Dictionary of Music and Musicians*.

And yet as early as 1941, Guido Zavadini (*139*) stated correctly that the libretto of *Don Pasquale* had been written by Giovanni Ruffini. He stood all but alone then, as he did when he repeated the statement seven years later in his monumental *Donizetti: Vita—Musiche—Epistolario* (1948). But the correct information had been published in 1915, if not earlier. As the late Frank Walker pointed out ("The Librettist of 'Don Pasquale,'" in *The Monthly Musical Record*, November-December 1958), the fact that Giovanni Ruffini had written the libretto had been established beyond doubt by Alfonso Lazzari in an article (*"Giovanni*

---

[2] For many years, the official Metropolitan libretto of *Aïda* carried its author's name as Ghislandoni instead of Ghislanzoni.

[3] Including, I am very unhappy to say, *The World of Opera* by Wallace Brockway and Herbert Weinstock (New York, 1962).

Ruffini, Gaetano Donizetti e il 'Don Pasquale' ") published in the *Rassegna musicale* (October 1 and 16, 1915).

Nor was Michele Accursi a pseudonym for Giovanni Ruffini. If Donizetti's correspondence were not sufficient proof that these were two different men, then Arturo Codignola's *I Fratelli Ruffini* (Genoa, 1925–31) established beyond doubt that Ruffini was deviled into writing the libretto of *Don Pasquale* by Michele Accursi—and deviled while writing it by their mutual friend, Donizetti. There, in Codignola's book, are letters from Ruffini to his mother which tell the whole story in detail.

Michele Accursi was a renegade member of Giuseppe Mazzini's Giovine Italia movement. His writing activity seems to have been confined almost wholly to reports that he sent to Gregory XVI, in whose pay he served as an informer on the activities of Mazzini and his friends and colleagues, including the Ruffini brothers. Ilario Rinieri reprinted more than three hundred of these communications—which he had located in the Vatican archives—in *Le Cospirazioni Mazziniane nel carteggio di un trasfuga* (Milan, 1923–28), and apparently stopped at that number only because he had become weary.

In the article mentioned above, Frank Walker wrote of Accursi: "After Pio Nono's amnesty of 1846, Accursi returned to Rome and on April 21, 1848 [five days after Donizetti's death], was given high office under the Minister of Police, Giuseppe Galletti. Astonishingly, he survived to take office also in Mazzini's Republican Government of 1849. After the fall of the Roman Republic [1849], he went again into exile, having exhausted all the possibilities of betrayal, of one side as of the other." He was, then, not a convinced reactionary, but an unflinching opportunist. Accursi's dishonesty extended to his dealings with money, considerable amounts of which he extracted from Donizetti, among others, on the most suspect promises of repayment. He seems to have squandered these borrowed sums while trying to become rich quickly through an unbeatable system of gambling which he had worked out.

Giovanni Ruffini and his brothers Agostino,[4] Jacopo, and Ottavio were friends of the young Mazzini. From 1834 on (Jacopo Ruffini having committed suicide in prison after being arrested for subversive activities), at least Giovanni and Agostino lived outside Italy. Indeed, Giovanni's extremely popular novel of the Risorgimento, *Il Dottor' Antonio*, was

---

[4] Agostino Ruffini helped Donizetti by some patching work on the libretto of *Marin Faliero* when that opera was to be sung at Paris. He also agreed, in Paris early in 1833, to write for Donizetti a libretto based on Goethe's *Faust*, but this project fell through. Somewhat later, too, Donizetti rejected a libretto that Agostino Ruffini had derived from a comedy by his brother Giovanni.

published first in London. He remained an active Mazzinian until 1849, after which he wrote prolifically and was in the diplomatic service; he died in 1881.

Almost the only thing that can be said in favor of Michele Accursi is that he was helpful to Donizetti in Paris, and not least when persuading Giovanni Ruffini to write the libretto of *Don Pasquale*. He also earned some credit for having recognized the quality of the opera itself: in a letter to Giovanni Ricordi he described it as "Donizetti's *Barbiere di Siviglia*." Giovanni Ruffini, however, deserves better even of musical history than to be mistaken for Accursi. Fortunately, his place in Italian history is secure wholly apart from his literary productions—which were not inconsiderable—as one of the *"fratelli Ruffini,"* those four heroes of the Risorgimento memorialized by a monument at Taggia, their birthplace about five miles northeast of San Remo.

These are but a very few of the fascinating problems involved in writing a biography of Gaetano Donizetti. I do not need my critics to tell me that I have not solved them all. What I do need them for, urgently, is to tell me more about those which I have failed to solve and any that I may have solved incorrectly.

For example, I am satisfied that the retrospective diagnosis of Donizetti's mortal disease is correct. But I am not satisfied by the best guess that I have been able to make as to the time and place of the inception of that disease. Frankly, too, I have not known what to do with the facts that Francesco Donizetti was mentally peculiar, that Giuseppe Donizetti's son, Andrea, died in an insane asylum, that Virginia Vasselli Donizetti had a mentally deficient brother, described by Antonio Vasselli in a letter of April 27, 1848, to Andrea Donizetti as *"mio fratello mentecatto"* (my dim-witted—or even insane—brother). The possibility certainly exists that Donizetti did not contract during his student days that syphilitic infection which was to have such terrible results. But evidence to support other suppositions—many of which I have entertained—simply does not exist.

Finally, there is the Marianna Donizetti problem. An eleven-part article entitled *"Donizetti et l'Opéra italien"* was published in the *Revue de la Méditerranée*, Nos. 73–83 inclusive (May–June 1956, through January–February 1958). It was by Maurice-Pierre Boyé, a poet and writer on Romantic art and various regions of France. It carried a dedication that raised a perhaps unimportant, but teasing problem that I have been unable to solve. That dedication reads: *"A la tendre et mélancolique mémoire/ de/ Marienna DONIZETTI/ fille de Joseph et nièce de Gae-*

tano DONIZETTI/ dont le portrait n'aura pas quitté mes yeux/ pendant que j'écrivais ces pages./ Son arrière-petit-fils/ M.-P. B." (To the tender and melancholy memory of Marienna Donizetti, daughter of Giuseppe and niece of Gaetano Donizetti, whose portrait never has been out of my sight while I was writing these pages. Her great-grandson, M.-P. B.).

To the best of my knowledge—and to the best of that of everyone I have consulted—Giuseppe Donizetti had no daughter, Gaetano Donizetti no niece, or at least, no niece whose last name was Donizetti or whose first name was Marienna. The carefully prepared genealogical table in Ciro Caversazzi's book (*31*), which I have drawn upon (see page 275) with some editorial emendations, but without the deletion of a single individual, shows no trace of such a person. Did she exist? Was she, perhaps, an illegitimate daughter whose existence the Donizetti family combined to hide? The good men at the Museo Donizettiano, Bergamo, deny all awareness of her.

Through the kindness of friends in Paris, I succeeded in getting into direct correspondence with Maurice-Pierre Boyé, who very generously sent me a family document stating that Marianna Donizetti ("Marienna" had been a typographical error), who had married his great-grandfather, Guglielmo Comelati, indeed had been the daughter of Giuseppe Donizetti. Further, M. Boyé generously sent me a photograph of the water-color portrait of Marianna, a charming-looking girl in whose features I found no difficulty in detecting some resemblance to portraits of Giuseppe Donizetti. The family paper, copied from a statement by Georgina Alish, M. Boyé's great-aunt, shows his mother's family as having been Campbells from Scotland whose name, after emigration to Italy, changed first to Cambellati and then to Comelati. It shows the Comelatis as having included British officials in Hong Kong; it shows Marianna Donizetti as having married Guglielmo Comelati at Constantinople when she was scarcely sixteen years old. M. Boyé wrote me that Marianna died at Hong Kong on December 1, 1858, when "she was forty years old."

Marianna's date of birth thus would be established as 1818 or December 1817. On that basis, her marriage at Constantinople in 1833 or 1834 would be natural, as Giuseppe Donizetti settled in that city in 1828. But her birth in either December 1817 or during 1818 raised an apparently insurmountable obstacle to acceptance of these vital statistics. Giuseppe's son Andrea was born on April 29, 1818, and it is extremely unlikely that Giuseppe's wife, Angela Tondi Donizetti, could have had another child during the implied period of Marianna's birth. If Marianna was born in 1818, she must have been either a twin sister of Andrea or Giuseppe's daughter by a woman other than his wife. And it is credible only by straining that the existence of a twin sister of Andrea Donizetti should have gone unmentioned anywhere in the surviving correspondence of the Donizetti family.

With the information supplied me by M. Boyé in hand, I turned for assistance to the Information Services of the Hong Kong Government and—in London—to the Public Record Office, the Colonial Office, the Department of the Chief of Naval Information, the Westminster Public Reference Library, and Somerset House. Although several of these offices replied quickly and with the greatest courtesy and expressed desire to be helpful, all that I was able to establish in months of correspondence and research was that a man named J. G. Comelate (not Comelati) served at Hong Kong as Cashier of the Colonial Treasury and Revenue Office in 1849 and was promoted in 1850 to the post of Chief Clerk and Cashier of that department, and that a William Comelate, who was twenty-eight years old in 1827, entered Admiral Sir Edward Codrington's flagship *Asia* at Smyrna on July 29 of that year as Clerk, giving his birthplace as Ancona. This latter is the man who is said to have married Marianna Donizetti—and who certainly was M. Boyé's great-grandfather.

Teasingly, that was all. Then, as this book was about to go into page proof, Mr. A. E. H. Sammons of the Colonial Office sent me from London the following literal translation of an entry in the *Liber Defunctorum* of the Catholic Cathedral in Hong Kong: "Mariana [*sic*] Donizetti Comelatte [*sic*] from Italy. In the year of the Lord 1858, on the 1st December, in Victoria, Island of Hongkong, MARIANA DONIZETTI, wife of William Comelatte, professor of literature, legitimate daughter of deceased Joseph and Angela Donizetti, at the age of about 43 years, after having received all the Sacraments from Rev. Paul Reina, Vice-Prefect of this Mission, passed away, and her body, on the following day 2nd Dec., was by me accompanied to the grave, according to the rites of the Church. F. Angelus Vandagna, Apostolic missionary in Hong Kong." If Marianna was forty-three in 1858, she was born in 1815, the very year of Giuseppe Donizetti's marriage to Angela Tondi, a possibility that raises new problems that at present remain insoluble.

My hope is that in time I may be able to establish the actual identity of M. Boyé's great-grandmother and perhaps to publish my findings in a periodical. But on the basis of the data I have succeeded in collecting thus far, the most that I can say is that M. Boyé and other members of his family have believed that their Comelati ancestress was Giuseppe Donizetti's daughter Marianna. They may be correct or incorrect, but their sincerity is beyond question, and Marianna Donizetti continues to be a side-issue of compelling fascination to a biographer of the composer of *Lucia di Lammermoor*.

HERBERT WEINSTOCK

New York, 1963

Acknowledgments

For many invaluable acts of kindness and for essential assistance in assembling the materials for this book, and then in writing it, I want especially to thank Signora Luisa Ambrosini, Rome; Mr. William Ashbrook, Terre Haute, Indiana; the Ateneo di Scienze, Lettere ed Arti, Bergamo; Signor G. Balzani, formerly of G. Ricordi & C., Milan; Mr. Harold M. Barnes, Paris; Dottore Carlo Betha, Naples; M. J. Bourcier, Secrétaire-Archiviste de l'Académie des Beaux-Arts, Paris; M. Maurice-Pierre Boyé, Neuilly-sur-Seine; Mr. Wallace Brockway, New York; Signor Giorgio Camici, Paris; Signor G. Cella of G. Ricordi & C., Milan; Maestro Giuseppe Cesati of the Museo Donizettiano, Bergamo; Professore Napoleone Fanti, Bibliotecario del Conservatorio Musicale G. B. Martini, Bologna; M. V. Fédorov, Conservateur de la Bibliothèque du Conservatoire de Musique, Paris; Mr. Gerald Gross, New York; Mr. Ben Meiselman, New York; Dr. Hans Moldenhauer, Spokane, Washington; the Museo Donizettiano, Bergamo; the Museo Teatrale alla Scala, Milan; Mrs. Lionello Perera, New York; G. Ricordi & C., Milan; Dr. Victor de Sabata, Jr., Milan; the heirs of the late Senatore Conte Giovanni Treccani degli Alfieri, Milan; Miss Paula Van Doren of Pantheon Books, New York; Dottoressa Maria Vismara of the Società per l'Organizzazione Internazionale, Rome; Mr. A. G. Walker, Chandlers Ford, Hants., England; Mr. William Weaver, Rome; The Reverend Anthony S. Woods, S.J., New York; and Professoressa Dina Zanetti Masiello, Rome. To many other friends and correspondents, as well as to many (but not all) of my predecessors in Donizettian studies, my gratitude is no less sincere because necessarily expressed without the publication—except in part in a bibliography—of their very numerous names.

HERBERT WEINSTOCK

Contents

xx) *Contents*

(xxi)

Illustrations

(FOLLOWING PAGE 230)

DONIZETTI

CHAPTER I

1797-1821

SOME thirty miles east and a little north of Milan lies Bergamo. The present city of more than one hundred thousand inhabitants consists of the large lower town sprawled over this northern edge of the Lombard plain and, in smaller part, of the tortuous *città alta*. The old upper town, incorporating the site of ancient Bergomum, clambers high above the northwestern zone of the modern city and contains what has endured of the medieval-Renaissance town that grew over the foothills of the Bergamese Alps.

The modern lower city of Bergamo holds little to attract a passing visitor, but the intensely evocative upper town can detain even a tourist hurrying between Milan to the west and Verona or Venice to the east. At its center, the abutting Piazza Vecchia and Piazza del Duomo strongly and handsomely pronounce the past. On the Piazza Vecchia, made gracious by an eighteenth-century fountain, stands the twelfth-century Palazzo della Ragione and, to its right as one faces its façade, the powerful Torre del Comune. Opening out of the Piazza Vecchia is the Piazza del Duomo, more picturesque because of its lordly asymmetry. Here the relatively modern and undistinguished cathedral competes for attention with the fourteenth-century Baptistery, the twelfth-century Romanesque Church of Santa Maria Maggiore, and the fifteenth-century Cappella Colleoni. This last, the masterwork of Giovanni Battista Amadei, contains the impressive tombs of Bartolomeo Colleoni (the great *condottiere* memorialized by Verrocchio's equestrian statue in Venice) and of his daughter Medea. It is ornamented with Tiepolo frescoes dealing with incidents in the life of St. John the Baptist.

Should the traveler in Bergamo be familiar with the lore of Italian literature, he will remember the city's connections with Bernardo Tasso and his more famous son, Torquato. Should he be a music lover and opera enthusiast, he may recall some of Bergamo's musical history and stop in the cool interior of Santa Maria Maggiore to see the tombs of Gaetano Donizetti and of his teacher and lifelong friend, the adoptive *bergamasco* Johann Simon Mayr. He will note, too, that Bergamo was the birthplace of Pietro Locatelli in 1695, as well as of a whole chorus of renowned nineteenth-century opera singers, mostly male, headed by Giovanni Battista Rubini. And he will persist in finding his way to the Museo Donizettiano, which houses a painstakingly assembled collection of scores, documents, and relics connected with Donizetti, his colleagues, his family, his interpreters, and his friends. In its way, the Museo Donizettiano is as evocative as the Cappella Colleoni.

In February 1786, Andrea Donizetti, a twenty-year-old son of a family of poor Bergamo artisans,[1] took his bride—who had been Domenica Nava—to live with him in two cramped, dark rooms in the Codazzi house at No. 10 (later renumbered 14) Borgo Canale, an area just outside the high walls of the upper town. Andrea Donizetti somewhat improved his financial status in 1800 by becoming janitor (and, in 1804, usher) of the Monte de' Pegni, or pawnshop. From 1808 on, his perquisites included two rooms and a kitchen in the Palazzo della Misericordia, in which the Monte de' Pegni was housed. But twenty years were to pass after his marriage before he would feel able to remove his family to brighter quarters inside the walls of the upper town, at No. 35 Piazza Nova.[2] Before that improvement, Domenica Donizetti would have given birth to six children—three boys and three girls, two of the latter dying in infancy—in the hovel in Borgo Canale.

The eldest of the Donizettis' three sons, born on November 6, 1788, was to become the most important musician-functionary at the faraway court of Mahmud II, sultan of Turkey, at Constantinople.[3] Much more of a figure was to be cut in the world by the last but one—and last surviving—of their children, the son born on November 29, 1797, and baptized

---

[1] For the Donizetti family tree, see Appendixes, pp. 275–77. Those interested in the heredity and psychopathology of genius will note that Andrea Donizetti's parents had thirteen children, including two sets of twins, both sets consisting of a boy and a girl.

[2] Now designated as No. 8 Piazza Mascheroni. The Donizettis later moved again, this time to No. 130 Via Santa Grata, a street now called Arena.

[3] See Appendixes, pp. 308–10, for some details of Giuseppe Donizetti's variegated and interesting career.

Domenico Gaetano Maria.[4] Forty-five years later, on July 15, 1843, Gaetano Donizetti, by then internationally famous as a composer of operas, would write from Munich to his teacher and friend Giovanni Simone Mayr: "I was born underground in Borgo Canale—you went down by a cellar stairs to which no suspicion of light ever penetrated. . . ." The stairway is as dark as Donizetti painted it, and in relation to the front elevation of the building, the corridor and two rooms indeed were subterranean. But on the back they opened onto a small orchard-garden from which the ground sloped down to the Via di Sotto Gli Orti and, beyond it, to the vast openness of the Lombard plain.

At least since the Renaissance, and very probably from earlier times, Bergamo has preserved the reputation of being a musical city inhabited by people inclined to decorative gaiety, clownish play acting, and some provincial slowness of everyday wit. The Italian *bergamasco* and the French *bergamasque* both came to refer to a buffoonish dance and to one or another of the masks in the *commedia dell'arte* and other theatrical entertainments. That the town's musical traditions had not lapsed late in the eighteenth century was proved when a young Bavarian, Johann Simon Mayr, leaving the Ingolstadt Jesuit Seminary at which he had been educated and visiting Italy to further his musical training, went to Bergamo to study before continuing on to Venice. In 1802, then thirty-nine, Mayr —whose first names soon were Italianized permanently as Giovanni Simone—was back in Bergamo, where he was appointed *maestro di cappella* at Santa Maria Maggiore.[5] Three years later, he reconstituted the local training school for church choristers as the Lezioni caritatevoli di musica, a charity institution depending from the local Pii luoghi della Misericordia. The decree founding the school was issued on March 18, 1805.

The music school itself had existed for centuries, but formerly had served exclusively for training boys to sing in the chapel of Santa Maria Maggiore, which itself dated from the twelfth century. What Mayr added in 1805 was chiefly instrumental training on violin and cembalo and some primary courses in literature, his aim being in part to enable talented boys to continue their musical education after change of voice had terminated their usefulness as trebles and altos. When the reconsti-

[4] See Appendixes, p. 276, for the record of his birth.
[5] An extraordinary number of nineteenth-century singers of considerable renown also emerged from Bergamo and its immediate surroundings. They included Giovanni David (whose father, Giacomo, had been a famous tenor), Domenico Donzelli, Ignazio Marini, Andrea Nozzari, Giovanni Battista Rubini, and Giuseppe Viganoni, several of whom sang in Donizetti's operas.

tuted school was prepared to accept pupils, Andrea Donizetti thought it a sensible idea to enroll two of his sons—Giuseppe, the eldest, aged eighteen, and Gaetano, the youngest, aged nine—in the Lezioni caritatevoli. Giuseppe was refused admission because he already was too mature to serve as a choirboy. But Gaetano was accepted in the first of the new classes, twelve boys in all, for lessons in singing and on the cembalo, his admission being for a trial period of three months.

Notice was at once taken that Gaetano suffered from a "throat defect" that would prevent him from being useful as a member of the chapel choir. Exactly what the condition of Donizetti's voice may have been cannot now be determined. References were to be made in the school reports to a *difetto di gola* (throat defect) and to a *voce difettosa* (defective voice). Yet, as will be told, he sang roles in public or semi-public theatrical performances on several occasions during his school years, and on more than one occasion was borrowed from the school for that purpose. In April 1807, Mayr informed the administrators of the school that the nine-year-old Gaetano Donizetti "surpasses all the others in musical progress," but he was forced to add that "it has not been altogether possible to do away with the defect in his voice." Almost identical reports on the boy's progress and condition were turned in during 1808 and 1809, and for a time it seemed inevitable that he would be forced to leave the school. From 1809 on, however, his studies were enlarged to include harmony and counterpoint, for by then Mayr had become certain that in young Donizetti he had come upon a genuine talent. He therefore petitioned the administrators to permit the boy to continue his lessons provisionally for a short period, adding that Donizetti could make himself extremely useful to the chapel by playing in its instrumental ensemble.

Two curious documents of 1810 were reproduced in facsimile by Aristide Dragoni (*46*) in 1897. The first of them, dated October 6, is an application signed (twice) by Donizetti, who begs to be admitted among the amateurs who attend the Accademia Carrara, specifying that he wishes to interest himself "in the study of decorative design and the [human] figure." The second, dated October 15, is an order from Count Francesco Colleoni, President of the Noble Commissariat of the Accademia, to its Professor Bianconi, instructing him to admit among his pupils six youths, one of them "Gaetano Donizetti, son of Andrea, living in the City at Number 35 [Piazza Nova]." It is possible, then, that Donizetti did take lessons in drawing and design at the Accademia Carrara. His later modest skill in caricature suggests that he might have had some training, but no other documentation of these possible lessons has been found.

Donizetti remained in Mayr's school until 1815, during those nine years conceiving an unwavering appreciation of and attachment to Mayr. That now largely neglected composer was not only a man of encompassing human warmth and sympathy, but also a very considerable figure in the musical life of his completely adopted country. His position in the evolution of Italian music and of opera in general was summarized well by Paul Henry Láng (74): "Everything he learned from the great classic school in his homeland he transmitted to his adopted country, especially the newly won technique of the pliable symphony orchestra, which he transplanted to the opera and developed to a degree that fascinated every composer in Europe. Neither Spontini nor Meyerbeer could have arisen without his school,[6] and the supposed inventor of the modern orchestra, Berlioz, owed him the lion's share." By the time of Donizetti's departure from the Lezioni caritatevoli, Mayr had composed all of his most successful operas, including the one generally looked upon as his culminating work, *La Rosa bianca e la rosa rossa,* first sung at the Teatro San Agostino, Genoa, on February 21, 1813.

During 1808, Donizetti sang the contralto role in *Alcide al bivio,* Mayr's setting of a Metastasio *"fiesta teatrale"*[7] as performed by pupils of the Lezioni caritatevoli. During 1811, Mayr prepared for that year's final student performance a two-act *farsa giocosa* entitled *Il Piccolo Compositore di musica.* The text was his own and may well have been written with Donizetti in mind; the music was a *pasticcio* of numbers by several composers. When this light entertainment was presented on September 13, 1811, Donizetti sang the title role, the "little composer." At one point in the performance he was required to take out a manuscript, place it on the music stand of the piano, glance at it, begin to improvise, and then— having hit upon a motive—write while singing what he was supposed to be writing. What he played was in fact a waltz of his own devising, perhaps the first of his compositions to be accorded a semipublic hearing. Proudly, once he had completed the singing, he was required to exclaim:

[6] Dr. Láng might well have included Rossini, for there seems to be no doubt that—as Giovanni Pacini pointed out in his *Le Mie Memorie artistiche*—Mayr preceded him in the use of the crescendo that came to be regarded as one of Rossini's trademarks.

[7] As part of the festivities attending the marriage of the Archduke Joseph (later Joseph II, Holy Roman Emperor), Johann Adolf Hasse's setting of *Alcide al bivio* had been sung at Vienna in 1760. The text also had been composed by Nicola Conforto, Luciano Saverio dos Santos, Giovanni Paisiello, Nicola Zingarelli, and Vincenzo Righini.

Ah! perbacco con quest'aria	Ah! by Bacchus, with this aria
Avrò un plauso universale.	I'll have universal applause.
Mi diran:—Bravo Maestro!—	They'll say to me: Bravo, Maestro!
Io con aria assai modesta	I, with a sufficiently modest air,
Inchinando andrò la testa. . . .	Will go around with my head bent. . . .
Avrò elogi nel giornale,	I'll have eulogies in the newspaper,
Saprò rendermi immortale.	I'll know how to make myself immortal.

The little composer also remarked: "I have a vast mind, swift talent, ready fantasy—and I'm a thunderbolt at composing." As Guido Zavadini remarked in *Donizetti: Vita—Musiche—Epistolario*, a basic and highly useful book (*138*): "Here the librettist [Mayr], without knowing it, put into the young protagonist's mouth truly prophetic words." The rapidity with which the adult Donizetti would compose some seventy operas and hundreds of other pieces was to become one of the most frequently discussed of his characteristics, to guarantee his worldly success, and to contribute very largely to the unevenness of quality which at last led to the silence in which all but a few of his operas now subsist.

Donizetti's vocal condition cannot have been severely disaffecting, for in 1812 one Angelo Micheli addressed the authorities of the music school to ask that two of its pupils, Gaetano Donizetti and Antonio Tavecchi, be permitted to sing in a performance at the local Teatro Riccardi on September 23. By the next year, however, Donizetti's voice had begun to show clear signs of deepening to a bass, as Mayr noted in reports dated May and November, 1813. During the pre-Lenten season of 1813–14, Donizetti had the opportunity of hearing two of Mayr's operas: *Amor non ha ritegno* and *La Roccia di Frauenstein* were sung at the Teatro della Società (or Sociale) di Bergamo. On January 27, 1814, Donizetti himself asked for permission to sing a *secondo buffo* part at the Teatro della Società, perhaps in one of Mayr's operas. An endorsement of this letter indicates that this request was granted on January 29.

The extent of young Donizetti's extracurricular activities led to his neglecting his duties as teacher for the youngest pupils in the school. On April 15, 1814, a note criticized him for that neglect, as well as for irregular conduct outside school hours. A little later, another warning was issued to him, and finally, some corrective punishment was prescribed. But his obvious talent and abilities won out: on the following September 3, Antonio Capuzzi, the school's teacher of violin, asked to be granted the services of the pupils Gaetano Donizetti and Giovanni

Manghenoni as singers, those of Antonio Piatti[8] and Vailati as instrumentalists, for a concert to be given nine days later. Finally, on August 6, 1815, Donizetti, Tavecchi, and Manghenoni appeared during a concert at the Teatro Riccardi. One day short of twelve weeks after that *accademia*, the seventeen-year-old Donizetti was to leave Bergamo for the first of his adventures in the great world outside.

That Donizetti had begun to compose music while still in the Bergamo school is testified to not only by the little waltz inserted into Mayr's *pasticcio, Il Piccolo Compositore di musica*, but also by the survival of several of his dated juvenilia.[9] Of these, a set of piano variations on the *"Canzon del bardo"* from Mayr's *Alfredo il grande* was published in 1820 by the Milanese music publisher Giovanni Ricordi, probably the first of Donizetti's compositions to be issued.

On November 29, 1815, Donizetti would be eighteen years old. Mayr, realizing that it now was time for the talented young man to obtain more advanced musical education than was available in Bergamo, had decided that his deep-voiced pupil deserved to attend what he himself considered the best music school in Italy, the Liceo Filarmonico Comunale at Bologna, then presided over by the legendarily learned Bolognese priest-musician, Padre Stanislao Mattei.[10] There Donizetti

[8] Piatti later became the father of the internationally famous cellist Alfredo Carlo Piatti (1822–1901). See p. 267.

[9] To 1813 belong a *pastorale* for piano or organ and a *sinfonia* for piano. A three-voice *Gloria in excelsis*, in D, scored for small orchestra with organ, and a *Qui tollis*, for tenor and orchestra with clarinet obbligato—dated "September 7, 1814"—belong to 1814. A sextet for two sopranos, two tenors, and two basses, with text beginning *"Ah! quel Guglielmo,"* bears this notation in the youth's script: "Done before the studies at Bologna followed in 1816–1817." To 1815 belong a bass aria with orchestra, its text beginning, *"Ognun dice che le donne"* (the autograph score in the Paris Conservatory Library bears this notation: *"Quand mai l'ò tirada a mà. Bergamo a dì 20 marzo 1815 ad uso di G. D."*—roughly, "How did I ever get into this? Bergamo, March 20, 1815, for use by G. D."); an anacreontic for voice and orchestra set to a text by Jacopo Vittorelli beginning *"Guarda che bianca luna"* (the autograph score in the Paris Conservatory Library contains this notation: *"Post'n musica da me Gaetano Donizetti per il Sig. Gian. Batt. Capitanio a dì 30 marzo 1815"*—"Set to music by me, Gaetano Donizetti, for Mr. Giovanni Battista Capitanio on March 30, 1815"); and (if it indeed survives or ever existed) a set of variations on a melody from a duet in Mayr's opera *La Rosa bianca e la rosa rossa*.

[10] Stanislao Mattei was born at Bologna on February 10, 1750. He studied with—and became assistant to—the internationally famous Padre Giovanni Battista Martini, whose pupils also included Johann Christian Bach, Mozart, Grétry, and Niccolò Jommelli. Mattei served as *maestro di cappella* at the Bolognese churches of San Francesco and San Petronio. On the foundation of the Liceo in 1804, he became its professor of counterpoint, which he taught to Rossini, Francesco Morlacchi, Donizetti, Giuseppe Pilotti, Giovanni Pacini, and Giovanni Tadolini, among others. President of the Filarmonici in 1790 and 1794, Mattei was elected

was to take strict courses in counterpoint and fugue. From that same school and the hands of that same great (if strict and uncommunicative) pedagogue had emerged only recently a young man from Pesaro who already was well advanced upon a conquest—hard fought by conservative musicians and critics—of the opera houses of Italy: Gioacchino Antonio Rossini, almost six years Donizetti's senior. By 1815 Rossini had composed a dozen operas, including *La Scala di seta*, *La Pietra del paragone*, *Il Signor Bruschino*, *Tancredi*, *L'Italiana in Algeri*, and *Il Turco in Italia*.

So strict was Mattei in upholding the "classical rules of music" that when Rossini's first operas began to be staged, he said that they dishonored his school. On June 10, 1865, Rossini, in reporting to Francesco Florimo that, on the basis of his *Petite Messe solennelle*, the "Parisian doctors" had begun to class him among the learned and the classical, wrote: "Rossini learned! Rossini classical! Now laugh, good friend, and with you too will smile Mercadante and Conti (whom I embrace with affection). If my poor Maestro Mattei were alive, he would say: Well, well, this time Gioacchino has not dishonored my school. When you come here, I'll show you my work, and you can decide whether Mattei judged better at the beginning or would have judged better later."

Mayr was a man of generous impulses. His decision that Donizetti should study under Padre Mattei led him to act. In late October, 1815, he wrote to Mattei, to the Marchese Francesco Sampieri, a wealthy young Bolognese composer whom he had met the preceding summer and who was a friend of Rossini's, to the Milanese music publisher Giovanni Ricordi, and to the administrative organism of his own school, the Congregazione di Carità di Bergamo. He doubtless told Padre Mattei of young Donizetti's unquestionable talent and remarkable industriousness. To Sampieri he merely recommended his pupil, speaking in laudatory but not excessive terms of his talent, his eagerness, his quickness to learn, his moral character. He also remarked on the young man's indigence, implicitly asking for the Marchese's help. To Ricordi, whom Donizetti was to seek out en route from Bergamo to Bologna—and who later became his publisher and lifelong friend—he recommended the young man and requested Ricordi's assistance in finding him a seat— "but as cheaply as possible"—in a carriage leaving Milan for Bologna.

---

to the Académie des Beaux-Arts in 1824. Besides composing eight Masses, a Passion, and much other church music, he wrote a three-volume text in harmony. He died at Bologna on May 12, 1825.

The most interesting of these Mayr letters is that to the Congregazione di Carità. Writing on October 28, 1815, he said:

If in the establishment of the Lezioni caritatevoli di musica, an institution that often has enjoyed the approval of the Superiors, the First Magistrates, and the public, there was especially taken into consideration the cultivation of nascent geniuses in the art of music, who, lacking the means of fortune, would remain buried, and who, thanks only to the generosity of the Congregazione, could be placed in a position to obtain by means of the art a subsistence for themselves along with their families—certainly supported on the basis foreseen in the establishment of this Institution and on those philanthropic feelings which always guide the illustrious Members and Rectors of the Pii luoghi to go to the assistance of needy families in various ways, and in relation to their needs—I permit myself to hope that the Illustrious Congregazione will allow me to advance my humble prayers in favor of Gaetano Donizetti, a young student who is about to leave the school, and who, not well favored by the nature of the change in a clear voice, is, however, gifted with propensity, talent, and genius for composition, not least in the swift fantasy and facility with which he conceives musical ideas not unadapted to words, leaving the best-founded hope of certain success in the study of counterpoint. It would be a shame if this not mediocre talent should be unable to be cultivated in the most proficient way and through the most solid and nearly perfect instruction that Italy can boast today, which is that of the excellent Padre Maestro Stanislao Mattei of Bologna. However, the young man referred to being without the means by which to aspire to such an advantage, and likewise calculating the good that could result for him and for his parents—who, deprived of two other sons serving in the army,[11] must base their only hope of aid in their declining years wholly on this son —and the honor that could redound to the fatherland itself for having shaped in that one a distinguished musical composer, some generous souls[12] have been pleased to offer openhanded subventions for the upkeep of this young man for two years. But these not being wholly sufficient, I venture to beg the Illustrious Congregazione that, as an act of true charity directed toward the most praiseworthy ends, it also be pleased to join in that subvention, that you will contribute your noted generosity to the contemplated result. The certificate of his good conduct and good attendance given him by his teachers leaves the most solidly founded hope that he will be able to profit by such generous treatment with untiring study, the most efficacious means of demonstrating gratitude to his benefactors, while I myself will have an immense obligation to the Illustrious Congregazione for the many repeated favors with which it constantly has deigned to heap him who, full

[11] Donizetti's two brothers mentioned as in military service were Giuseppe (1788–1856) and Francesco (1790–1848). By 1816, Andrea, their father, had been caretaker of the local pawnshop for some years, but both their mother and their twenty-year-old sister Maria Antonia were listed in the public records of vital statistics as *cucitrice* [seamstresses].

[12] These "generous souls" almost certainly included Mayr himself.

of the feeling of gratitude and respect, has the honor to profess himself

Humble, devoted, obedient Servant
Gio. Simone Mayr.

Mayr's campaign to enlist support for young Gaetano was crowned with success. On October 28, 1815, one month before his eighteenth birthday, Donizetti left Bergamo by diligence[13] for Milan and Bologna, the latter city restored that year to the States of the Church after the dissolution of the Napoleonic Cispadine Republic. In Bologna, he found lodging in the home of a *maestro di musica*, Tommaso Marchesi, on the third floor of a building at No. 1333 Viario Pepoli, now No. 1 Via Pepoli. On his arrival, he at once began to study counterpoint: the Museo Donizettiano at Bergamo has a volume on the outside of which is inscribed, in Donizetti's script, "Study of Counterpoint,/ made by Gaetano Donizetti of Bergamo/ under the direction of the Celebrated Signor Maestro Dn Stanislao Mattei./ In Bologna the years 1815 and 1816/ begun on the day 22 November 1815." The first of the sixty-one student exercises that the volume contains, then, was written out on November 22. Of this lesson book, Guido Zavadini said (*138*): "A small autograph volume, fallen into our hands by chance, and containing in very diligent order his sixty-one scholastic works, from the end of 1815 to March 1817, provides a way to follow, almost day by day, what were his daily occupations in study."

During 1816, Donizetti wrote out forty-nine of the examples of counterpoint and fugue which the student notebook contains. The first of the fugal studies is dated March 14 and bears this autograph inscription: "From March 14 to here 23 [the number of this exercise in the volume] there was vacation. The Maestro went to Cesena. First fugue in two voices." From No. 29 to No. 41, the fugues and fughettas are in three voices; thenceforward they are in four. In the margin of the forty-ninth exercise, Donizetti wrote: "On the day 5 of September 1816, ten-thirty in the evening. My instructor [Mayr] ought to arrive during this month. *Evviva!*" And on the next page, alongside No. 50, a fugue, he wrote: "Mayr has come. In this period I did: the year '1817' in fugue—*In gloria* for four voices—*Il Pigmalione*." The fugal exercises in three and four voices end with No. 58, the last of 1816.

As far as is known, *Il Pigmalione* was the first of Donizetti's approximately seventy operas. The author of its one-act libretto remains undetermined, but it is notable that both Giambattista Cimadoro (1790)

---

[13] Biographers formerly presented as factual a purely fictitious tale of Donizetti's going on foot from Bergamo to Bologna.

and Luigi Cherubini (1809) had composed one-act operas to Antonio Simone Sografi's Italian rendition of Jean-Jacques Rousseau's *Pygmalion*.[14] The autograph score of 105 pages, now in the Paris Conservatory Library, contains this notation in Donizetti's script at the end: "Begun September 25, finished October 1, 1816, at almost 2 o'clock in the morning of Tuesday, arrival of the new Legate." No record of any performance of this opera during Donizetti's lifetime survives. The *In gloria* composed during this period is an unaccompanied four-voice *In gloria Dei patris* in C minor, dated September 17, 1816.[15] That all of Donizetti's time was not taken up in working out exercises in counterpoint and fugue is proved by the existence of several other pieces from 1816. These include a four-voice *Kyrie* with orchestra, which appears to have been sung under Mattei's direction; a *concertino* for English horn and orchestra, dedicated to "Giovanni Catolfi, student at the Liceo Filarmonico" and performed by him during the school examinations on June 19, 1817;[16] a *Tantum ergo* for voices and orchestra, sung in the Bolognese Church of San Giacomo on St. Cecilia's Day (November 8), 1816; a *sinfonia* dated November 19, 1816, "composed in an hour and a quarter at the order of Padre Maestro Mattei" and "completed at the hour of dinner"; and another *sinfonia* (C major) for orchestra "played at the Casino dei Filarmonici in Bologna on November 24, 1816."

Two Bergamese physicians, Federico Alborghetti and Michelangelo Galli, in their invaluable—if sentimentalized—pioneering book (5), first put into the form in which later it became familiar as truth about Donizetti an anecdote that requires comment:

While Gaetano was a student at the Bologna school, we believe during the Carnival of 1817, there was performed at the Teatro Comunale of that city the opera *La Rosa bianca e la rosa rossa*, one of the best, if not perhaps the very best, of the many that were written by Simone Mayr.[17] The impresario

[14] Cherubini's little opera was composed for performance in Napoleon's private theater at the Tuileries, and apparently had few other stagings. But Cimadoro's, after its first performance at Venice in either 1788 or 1790, had been very widely performed.

[15] From this point onward, Donizetti's nonoperatic compositions will be mentioned only when some special interest or importance attaches to them. They will be found listed as comprehensively as possible in Appendixes, pp. 371–404.

[16] Donizetti's name figured in the program of June 19—at which that term's prizes were awarded—as the composer of this *concertino*, a *Sinfonia a piena orchestra concertata*, and a *Scena ed Aria* sung by Giovanna Albertini of Faenza.

[17] *La Rosa bianca e la rosa rossa*, first sung at the Teatro San Agostino at Genoa in 1813, and *Medea in Corinto*, given its *première* at the Teatro San Carlo, Naples, on November 28 of the same year, were widely regarded as the best of Mayr's operas. The libretto for the former, based on a French libretto by

of the theater, for some reason—but certainly one that cannot have been honorable, as it abused Mayr's good faith—had refused to return not only the manuscript of the original score, but also the copy; for that reason the Maestro was not a little vexed and worried, the more so because he could see no way to get back his property without serious sacrifice.

Learning about this matter, Donizetti, who adored his Maestro, thought of consoling him and getting the better of the rascally speculator. To think was to act. For three evenings in succession, he went to the theater, where —in part assisting himself with notations written down at top speed, but more with the aid of his prodigious memory—he was able to put the whole opera together exactly, from the first note to the last, and when he saw the Maestro in Bergamo again, he presented the voluminous manuscript to him, saying: "I wanted to exert my memory for you, and I hope that I have succeeded in doing something that pleases you."

Such were the Maestro's surprise and joy that, moved almost to tears, he placed his arm on the pupil's shoulders; then, taking his watch from his pocket, he answered: "And you take this. That way, we'll have a mutual souvenir."

At Paris twenty years later, Donizetti showed this watch to his friends as a precious relic that he religiously guarded among his dearest objects.

This anecdote belongs to a recognizable class of legends dealing with feats of copying and memory by young composers—including that of the fourteen-year-old Mozart hearing Gregorio Allegri's *Miserere* (a four- and five-voice work with a final nine-part chorus) once in the Sistine Chapel and then writing it out whole from memory. The story is certainly inexact in detail. Corrado Ricci showed by careful research that neither *La Rosa bianca e la rosa rossa* nor any other opera by Mayr was sung at the Teatro Comunale or any other Bolognese theater between 1815 and 1819, a period that included all of Donizetti's stay at the Liceo there. The watch, however, seems to have existed: the 1897 catalogue of memorabilia from the collections of Giuseppe and Gaetano Donizetti (grandsons of Donizetti's brother Giuseppe) which were exhibited in Bergamo in August and September of that year includes a "gold repeater watch, a gift from Maestro S. Mayr," and appended to this catalogue entry is the Alborghetti-Galli telling of the story as quoted above.

Except for a visit to Bergamo in July and August 1817,[18] Donizetti remained in Bologna until the end of November of that year. The amount of work that he accomplished during 1817 is staggering to con-

---

René-Charles-Guilbert de Pixérécourt and set to music in 1809 by Pierre Gaveaux, was the first of many operatic texts by Felice Romani, who was to prepare several librettos for Donizetti. See p. 34.

[18] The manuscript of a *Cum sancto* for voices and orchestra is dated at Bergamo on July 16, 1817; that of a four-voice *Kyrie* with orchestra is dated there on August 1, 1817.

template—or would be staggering from a composer less prolific than he was to show himself. In addition to continuing the exercises in fugue,[19] he composed at least four *sinfonie* for orchestra and one, in G minor, for wind instruments alone; one or more of these probably were played at the Casino dei Filarmonici. In 1817, Donizetti also composed his first surviving string quartet, dated December 26. The Paris Conservatory Library has the score of a second opera composed in Bologna during this year: *L'Ira d'Achille*, to a one-act libretto of undetermined provenance. Like *Il Pigmalione*, it is nowhere listed as having been performed at that time. Donizetti composed still another unperformed opera—*L'Olimpiade* —in Bologna in 1817, to a text that may have been by Metastasio, whose *L'Olimpiade* was extremely popular.[20] The manuscript of this opera is lost, but the Museo Donizettiano has a *scena e duetto* from it— not in Donizetti's autograph—with separate parts for singers and orchestra: the characters are Aristea and Megacle, the lovers in Metastasio's *dramma*. Several pieces for piano and others for solo and concerted voices likewise date from 1817.

When Donizetti returned to Bergamo in the summer of 1817, he no doubt proudly took with him the following letter from the Bologna school:

To the Scholar Gaetano Donizetti:
    The progress that you have made in the study of counterpoint and the diligence with which you have attended the school have led to the determination to assign to you one of the prizes established by His Excellency the Signor Senator and by the Council of the Wise Men [*Signori Savj*] for encouraging the studious youth of this establishment.
    This merited distinction will add to the virtuous efforts that you will make to justify your reputation, of which you happily now have laid the foundation, and to fulfill the hopes that the homeland has placed on your later development.
    While assuring you of all our assistance, so that you may be able to attain your goal, we have the pleasure to send you distinguished salutations.
                                    For the Office.
                            Ott. Malvezzi Ranuzzi Cons. Dep.
                                L. Segretario.

[19] The student exercise book mentioned above starts 1817 off with a fugue and countersubject dated January 10 (No. 59) and continues through No. 62, which carries this autograph notation: "On the day 2 March Bologna." The rest of the exercises are on many half-pages, now in the Museo Donizettiano, where they have been collected into volumes, and in the Library of the Naples Conservatory. They include fugal studies for four, five, and six voices.
[20] In *Tutte le Opere di Pietro Metastasio* (1953), Bruno Brunelli listed some fifty settings of *L'Olimpiade* between the first one—by Antonio Caldara, 1733— and 1829. Beethoven's "*Oh, care selve*," opus 267 B (1794), is a setting of the first part of its Act I, scene 4.

Although Donizetti provided no surviving indications of being unhappy in Bologna, he notably did not form for any of his teachers or fellow students there the sort of close, enduring attachment that he formed in Bergamo for Mayr and several of his own contemporaries, who were to remain his friends for life. One of the most interesting of his companions at the Liceo Filarmonico was Piero Maroncelli of Forlì, his senior by two years, who was to become a writer, a musician, and a revolutionary. Some time later, Maroncelli was arrested in Rome: a Sacred Hymn that he had written was condemned by the papal police as inciting to rebellion. Sent into exile at Milan, he was arrested there in 1820 as a *carbonaro* in company with Silvio Pellico. Sentenced to death at first, he later was condemned to twenty years at hard labor in the notorious Austrian state prison of the Spielberg at Brünn. There he was tortured; one of his legs had to be amputated. Finally freed in 1830, Maroncelli emigrated, first to France and then to New York, where he became blind and, eventually, insane, dying in 1846.

On July 30, 1843, Maroncelli gave to an oboist named Paggi, who was leaving New York for Europe, a letter of introduction to Donizetti:

You will not have forgotten the beautiful years of our youth, spent together at Bologna, you at the Liceo Musicale, I at it and at the University; and, furthermore, the dear conversations at the home of the Antoni. And, emerged from captivity, it had to be through that enchanting Clementina[21] that I was able to see you for the first, and up to now the last, time. I hope that it will not be the last time in my life. . . . My wife went to Paris last year for about six months, and had the fortune to encounter you: how much I have envied her! Enough, I have not yet lost the hope of seeing you once more before dying; in the meanwhile, believe me always your most sincere admirer as well as your dearest friend.

Piero Maroncelli.

On October 18, 1817, Donizetti wrote to Mayr to thank him for having made it possible for him to remain longer in Bologna: Mayr had paid his board and lodging for an additional month. Probably alluding to the possibility of obtaining paid musical work after leaving Bologna, he wrote: "I shan't fail to write to my brother [Giuseppe] to ask him if he can do something for me in Turin, though I think that that will be very hard, as he never has been in that city except passing through." Nine days later, Donizetti dated at Bologna a *sinfonia* for orchestra entitled *La Partenza*. But his own departure did not take place then, for on November 16 he still was writing from Bologna, this time

[21] Clementina degli Antoni sang in Rossini's *Stabat Mater* under Donizetti's direction at Bologna in March 1842. See p. 174.

to ask Mayr's advice about accepting a position at the Adriatic port of Ancona as piano teacher to five families, to each of which he would give two lessons per week.

The honorarium suggested for the proffered position was only ten scudi[22] per month, plus room and meals. Donizetti had told his prospective employers that he could not be in Ancona before the beginning of March 1818: he explained to Mayr that his reason for this proviso was the possibility of composing for an opera house during the Lenten season. Mayr must have advised him to accept the offer, for Donizetti wrote to him again on November 30 to say that, though he had taken Mayr's advice, he again had insisted upon the Lenten leave—his desire to compose an opera for performance was strong. He was awaiting a reply from Ancona. Either the Anconese refused his request or something else went awry during the negotiations, for he dated at Bergamo on December 17, 1817, a *sinfonia* in D major for orchestra, and he never went to Ancona.

Early biographers of Donizetti, worshipful nineteenth-century men, several of them fellow *bergamaschi* and one a member of his wife's family, used to picture Donizetti during his three years at Bologna as, in the words of Corrado Ricci,[23] an "emaciated little saint, a grind" who stayed constantly at Padre Mattei's side in church, recited the rosary with him, played innocent games of *briscola* with Mattei's mother (who would have been over eighty at the time), and devoted himself undeviatingly to young-manly purity and the good opinion of the authorities at the Liceo. But, as Ricci wrote: "That this, and this alone, was Donizetti's life between his eighteenth and twentieth years, especially in a city like Bologna, where a spirit of gaiety suggested diversions of every sort, we have difficulty in believing. Certainly he would have been in the Maestro's company voluntarily; probably he would have gone with him to say the rosary or to bore himself with playing cards

[22] Approximately twenty-five dollars in the values of 1963. See Appendixes, pp. 311–12, "A Note on Present-Day Values of Some Currencies Mentioned in This Book."

[23] In the so-called *Numero Unico (18)*, an oversized paperbound memorial volume issued at Bergamo in 1897 under the editorship of Parmenio Bettòli, illustrated and containing contributions and letters from, among many others, Jules Barbier, Maurice Barrès, Sarah Bernhardt, Arrigo Boito, Paul Bourget, Alfred Bruneau, François Coppée, Ernest Daudet, José María de Heredia, Eleanora Duse, Antonio Fogazzaro, Alberto Franchetti, Eduard Hanslick, Engelbert Humperdinck, Charles Lenepveu, Adelina Patti, Arthur Pougin, Ernest Reyer, Corrado Ricci, Giulio Ricordi, Adelaide Ristori, Camille Saint-Saëns, Marcella Sembrich, Francesco Tamagno, Giuseppina Strepponi Verdi, Jean-Baptiste Weckerlin, and Émile Zola. The full title of the publication was *Gaetano Donizetti/Numero Unico nel Primo Centenario della sua Nascita 1797–1897.*

with an old lady, but there is a great difference between that and making him out an emaciated little saint, a grind, as happens in the old biographies. At Bologna he certainly studied, but he will also have diverted himself with his companions, with the university students, and with—" Ricci's sentence breaks off mockingly. And in truth, in view of everything that can be learned about Donizetti's passionate nature, his good looks, and his future private life, it can be assumed without doubt that he had sexual experiences during those Bolognese years, the first of his young manhood. It may very well have been during his stay in Bologna, in fact, that he contracted the syphilis that, apparently never diagnosed firmly or properly treated, was to lead to his physical and mental disintegration thirty years later.

Back at Bergamo, Donizetti seems at first to have formed no clear plans for a future. He agreed to teach his friend Marco Bonesi[24] the mysteries of figured bass in return for instruction in playing the viola. After a few of these lessons, Donizetti took part as violist in playing a quintet of his own composition.[25] This may well have been in the hospitable home of Alessandro Bertoli, an excellent amateur violinist who had taught Donizetti some theory at the Lezioni caritatevoli, and who held weekly sessions of chamber music.[26] Knowing that Mayr, who also played the viola, often attended these friendly music makings, Donizetti asked to be introduced into them. In manuscript notes that Bonesi left for a biography of Donizetti, he said that his friend listened voraciously to the playing of classical chamber pieces, as if trying to solve the mystery of composing in that style. And Bonesi adds that in fact Donizetti brought to their very first session together a quartet "composed alla Haydn." This must have been the First String Quartet, dated December 26, 1817. Donizetti composed all or parts of nineteen string quartets, seventeen of them between 1817 and 1821, one in 1825, and one in 1826.

[24] In 1838, Marco Bonesi was appointed professor of violin at the Bergamo Conservatory and first violinist of the chapel at Santa Maria Maggiore. He also became an opera conductor, leading many performances of Donizetti's operas at Bergamo's Teatro della Società and Teatro Riccardi (later renamed Teatro Donizetti).

[25] Undated fragments of two string quintets survive in autograph. A complete quintet in six movements, also undated, is in the Library of the Naples Conservatory; it is for violin, two violas, cello, and guitar.

[26] Writing to Antonio Dolci from Vienna on May 15, 1842, Donizetti would say: "I have felt the death of our Bertoli with infinite pain. I shall never forget that it was through him that I began to know all the quartets of Haydn, Beethoven, Mozart, Reicha, Mayseder, etc., which then were so useful to me for husbanding my fantasy and constructing a piece with few ideas. But that's the way things go!"

Of Donizetti at about the period of the music making at Bertoli's, Dr. Federico Alborghetti and Dr. Michelangelo Galli, who well may have seen him in his later years—and who knew many *bergamaschi* friends of his—wrote (*5*, 43–44): "He then was entering upon the full development of adolescence. He had become a handsome young man, tall and slender in figure, with certain gestures between the frank and the elegant, and with certain manners that thus had characteristics both of good-fellowship and of reserve which could fill with envy one of those more detached types of the aristocratic class. . . . The shape of his head was long and bold, with an ensemble of facial lines somewhat soft as compared with the form of his nose, and with an amply domed head that had a Roman rather than a Lombard appearance; he had a thick mass of hair shading to dark brown, in part curly, and two fascinating eyes." Of a portrait of Donizetti lithographed on wood almost twenty years later,[27] Ciro Caversazzi rightly wrote (*31*, 12): "One sees him animated by an intense expression, with very beautiful eyes, electrifying, but gazing within as though to dominate a rising uneasiness." This likeness shows him with a moustache and short side whiskers.

A brief season of opera was presented in Bergamo at the Teatro della Società during the 1817–18 Carnival. The stars of the company were Giuseppe de Begnis, a bass, and his wife, the soprano known as "Beppa" Ronzi de Begnis,[28] who later would create roles in five of Donizetti's operas. The little season offered Ferdinando Paër's very popular *Agnese* and Rossini's *La Cenerentola*. Donizetti became friendly with the singers, naturally being eager to learn what he could from professionals about operatic performance and the possibilities of an operatic career for himself. The Begnis couple became interested in the good-looking, vivacious, talented young *bergamasco* and advised him to go to Verona, where they were booked to sing during the next spring season. Perhaps he would be able to obtain a *scrittura*—engagement—to com-

[27] This is a portrait in miniature which serves as part of the decoration of a small table given Donizetti by a group of his friends and admirers in 1836. It is in the Museo Donizettiano at Bergamo. Reproduced as Plate 11.

[28] Giuseppina Ronzi de Begnis, even more than most other operatic sopranos of her era, attracted to herself the reputation of very free sexual habits. Thus, without the citation of proofs of any sort, it has been asserted that she was the mistress of several very young men. These included Donizetti himself and the twenty-two-year-old King Ferdinando II of the Two Sicilies (notably when, in 1832, she sang the leading female role in Donizetti's *L'Esule di Roma* at the Teatro San Carlo, Naples). Her amatory exploits aside, she was a much-admired interpreter of several Donizettian roles as well as of roles in Rossini's *Otello*, *La Cenerentola*, and *La Gazza ladra*. Her husband, a somewhat less celebrated singer, nonetheless created the role of Dandini in Rossini's *La Cenerentola* (Rome, 1817).

pose an opera for the impresario, a Sicilian named Paolo Zancla. Verona
is only about seventy-five miles from Bergamo, and Donizetti decided to
try his luck.

Before Donizetti had left the Liceo in Bologna, the authorities there
had asked him to compose and forward to them a cantata that might be
sung in the examination performances at the end of the next term.
A reminder of this duty reached him at Verona, whence he wrote on
April 11, 1818, that the piece would be completed and sent off before
the end of that month. Using a poetic text by Gaetano Morandi, he
completed *Il Ritorno di primavera*, a cantata for three voices and full
orchestra, and dispatched it to Bologna. In Verona, meanwhile, luck
was not with him: he accomplished nothing there beyond writing some
pieces used in recital by members of Zancla's company. So he returned
once more to Bergamo. Learning there that Antonio Capuzzi, the music
school violin teacher, had died, he sat down and with typical Donizettian speed composed an orchestral *sinfonia* in D major in memory of
the dead man. Mayr copied out the parts and conducted the memorial
performance.

At about this time, Bartolomeo Merelli, one of Donizetti's childhood friends and co-students at the Bergamo music school—he was to
become a renowned impresario and librettist and something more than
an amateur composer (a cantata with text and music both by him, *Un
Viaggio a Vienna*, was performed in Vienna in April 1854 as part of the
celebrations of the marriage of the Emperor Franz Joseph to Elisabeth
of Bavaria)—handed him a two-act libretto for an *opera semiseria*,[29]
Enrico di Borgogna. If Donizetti could not obtain a commission to
compose an opera, then he would compose an opera first and later
persuade an impresario to stage it. When he had completed *Enrico di
Borgogna*, Zancla, who was planning a season at the Teatro San Luca
in Venice,[30] accepted it. Donizetti traveled to Venice (about one hundred
and fifty miles from Bergamo) in October 1818. On his arrival, he found
announcements of his opera listing him as "Maestro Donzelletti," but
this error cannot have damaged his pleasure over the first public performance of one of his operas in the city in which Mayr had initiated
his operatic career in 1794 (with *Saffo*), Rossini his in 1810 (with *La
Cambiale di matrimonio*). On October 13, he wrote to Mayr from

[29] Lighter than a full-fledged *opera seria*, an *opera semiseria* typically mixed
the serious and the comic.
[30] One of the oldest, if not the oldest, of Venetian theaters (1629), the San
Luca later became the Teatro Apollo; still later, it was renamed again, becoming
the Teatro Goldoni.

Venice to say that "La Petrali," the expected prima donna, having proved unavailable, the leading female role in *Enrico di Borgogna* would be sung by "*la Catalani iuniore*,[31] who has a large, beautiful voice, and I am hoping for a happier outcome. I have had to recompose some things because of this soprano, but that doesn't matter to me, seeing that I'll have a donna so much better than the first one."

Enrico di Borgogna duly received its *première* at the Teatro San Luca on November 14, 1818.[32] Unhappily the audience was more interested in inspecting the redecorated theater—the Vendramin family, who owned it, just had had it restored—than in Donizetti's *opera semiseria*, which was received with indifference and was repeated only on December 15 and 16. The *Gazzetta privilegiata di Venezia*, reporting the *première* on November 19, said: "Superb spectacle for the redecoration of the theater. Fresh, if not new, the so-called poet; new in fact the composer, who, provided with good talents, now exposes himself for the first time in these arduous labors." Donizetti's debut had been anything but brilliant.

It is particularly unfortunate that no letter from Donizetti survives from the period between October 18, 1818, and June 17, 1821. While it is known, for example, that one month after the unimpressive first singing of *Enrico di Borgogna*, he was represented again on the boards of the Teatro San Luca, this time with a one-act *farsa* entitled *Una Follia*, probably also to a Merelli libretto—it shared a double bill with a revival of Rossini's six-year-old first success, the one-act *L'Inganno felice*—no trace ever has been found of this score. It has also been reported that on the date of its performance—December 15, 1818—a one-act opera entitled *Il Ritratto parlante* was sung at the San Luca. Could this have been an alternate title for *Una Follia?* Nothing certain is known.

Back to Bergamo Donizetti went, his career advanced but little beyond the point at which it had stood when he had left there to travel to Venice. On December 26, however, he made his professional debut before his townspeople: *Enrico di Borgogna* was sung at the Teatro

---

[31] Guido Zavadini (*138*, 228, n. 1) wrote that this was Angelica Catalani, though there would have been no reason for referring to that internationally famous singer as "junior." The substitute soprano at Venice was, in fact, Adele Catalani, who had a secondary career in several Italian opera houses and who was listed as on the roster at La Scala, Milan, as late as 1832.

[32] It would be interesting to know whether or not the young composer realized that he thus was making his professional debut in the theater in which, about seventy years before, some of the brilliant comedies of Carlo Goldoni first had been staged.

Sociale under the direction of his friend Pietro Rovelli,[33] with much the same cast that had sung it in Venice. More of a local sensation seems to have been created in Bergamo early in 1819 by a conflagration that not only left several families homeless, but also forced a woman to stand with one child in her arms and watch two other small children die in the flames. When an evening benefit concert for the victims of this disaster was arranged, Donizetti composed a *sinfonia* for orchestra "after an ode in blank verse" by Ferdinando Arrivabene, a Mantuan lawyer-writer. This was performed on March 19 at the Teatro della Società. Also, for the annual student concert at the music school he composed a one-act *opera buffa* to a libretto by Merelli, *Piccioli Virtuosi ambulanti*, sometimes referred to as *Piccoli Virtuosi di musica ambulanti*. Into it (Scene 5), he inserted a recitative and aria with chorus taken from *Le Nozze in villa*, still another *opera buffa* to a Merelli text, which he had composed earlier in 1819.

Piccioli Virtuosi ambulanti first reached performance early in the summer of 1819. Some chroniclers have doubted the production of *Le Nozze in villa*; others have said that its *première* occurred at the Teatro Vecchio, Mantua, during the Carnival season of 1820–21, again under the aegis of the itinerant impresario Paolo Zancla and with a leading role taken by Fanny Eckerlin, who had sung in *Enrico di Borgogna*. Mayr, writing a letter of introduction for Donizetti on October 1, 1821, mentioned "the practice that he has acquired in some theaters at Venice and Mantua," thus making the production of *Le Nozze in villa* at Mantua very likely. Donizetti presumably was referring to its lack of success—Giuliano Donati-Petténi (*39*) wrote that it won only two performances—when, in a letter to Count Ottavio Tasca eighteen years later, he wrote: "Mantua! Historic city for you . . . for me!!!"[34]

More important for Donizetti's future was a third 1819 opera, *Il Falegname di Livonia, ossia Pietro il grande, czar delle Russie*, to a

[33] Pietro Rovelli (1793–1838) was a native of Bergamo. He had studied the violin with Rodolphe Kreutzer (to whom Beethoven had dedicated his Violin Sonata in A major, opus 47), and while at Munich he himself had taught the noted German violinist Wilhelm Bernhard Molique. In 1819, he became professor of violin at the Bergamo conservatory, teaching there until his death. From 1820 to 1832, he conducted most of the operatic performances at the Teatro Riccardi, Bergamo, being succeeded in that position by another of Donizetti's friends, Michele Rachelle.

[34] Francesco Florimo assigned to a Mantua performance in 1821 the first singing of Donizetti's cantata *Teresa e Gianfaldoni*, for two voices and orchestra, which later was published at Rome with a dedication to ex-Queen Maria Luisa of Etruria, Duchess of Lucca, the unfortunate daughter of Charles IV of Spain. Mantua was "historic" for Count Tasca because there he had met his future wife, the soprano Elisa Taccani, who sang at Bergamo. See p. 134.

libretto by Gherardo Bevilacqua-Aldovrandini.[35] The conditions under which he composed it remain obscure, but it was mounted for the first time at the Teatro San Samuele, Venice, on December 26, 1819. Some early writers on Donizetti placed in doubt even the existence of *Il Falegname di Livonia*, Edoardo Clemente Verzino (*132*), for example, proposing that what had been staged at the San Samuele in 1819 was Giovanni Pacini's opera of the same title.[36] But Donizetti's score survives, as does the libretto published at the time of its first performance. Donizetti was in Venice at the time of its staging: a four-voice *Miserere* for contraltos, tenors, and basses, which he composed for the orchestral players Grassi and Orlandini, is dated "*Venezia, gennaio 1820.*" Final proof that the performance took place is the report that the Milanese periodical *I Teatri* published, quoting its Venetian correspondent: "A company of singers gathered together in the greatest haste by the Teatro San Samuele has produced, to begin with, operas rather improvised than prepared. The *opera buffa* of Maestro Donizetti, *Pietro il grande*, was received coldly."

Operatically inactive, Donizetti remained in Bergamo through the rest of 1820. His first flights into the operatic world at Venice, Mantua, and Bergamo had not been sufficiently successful to bring him commissions from eager impresarios. So he unloosed the swiftness of his pen on the only sort of music for which life in Bergamo made much demand: sacred pieces. Interspersed among the year's settings of sacred texts are a few instrumental pieces, including a *sinfonia* for piano duet; two four-hand piano sonatas; four complete and two incomplete string quartets;[37] and an aria for soprano, English horn obbligato, and orchestra which Donizetti composed especially for a singer named Carolina Magni, who sang it at the Teatro Riccardi, Bergamo, on September 11, 1820. The other nonsacred music certainly was composed for performance by his friends and himself at informal musical gatherings.

In December 1820, the Austrian authorities at Milan issued a call

[35] The romantic legend about Peter the Great upon which the libretto of *Il Falegname di Livonia* was based (via a comedy by Alexandre Duval) was to become much more enduringly famous as supplying the subject of Gustav Albert Lortzing's text for his own opera, *Czaar und Zimmermann* (Leipzig, 1837). That legend would turn up again in the libretto of another Donizetti opera, *Il Borgomastro di Saardam* (Naples, 1827). Tsars seem to have fascinated Donizetti: one also appears in another of his operas, *Otto Mesi in due ore* (Naples, 1827).

[36] *Il Falegname di Livonia*, by the lively Pacini, to a libretto by Felice Romani, was staged at La Scala, Milan, on April 15, 1819. Four years later, it was staged at the Teatro San Carlo, Naples, with a cast that included Fanny Eckerlin, Giovanni Battista Rubini, and Pio Botticelli.

[37] These are not dated, but Guido Zavadini assigned them to 1820 with good reason.

to arms for five classes of young men born between 1795 and 1799, ordering them to sign up for service between December 15 and 24 in their home communities. This would have included Donizetti, but that in fact he never served in the army is proved by the autograph datings on music that he composed during the period in which he would have been called to serve. Also, it is known that he avoided military service because someone paid for him the sum by which it then was possible to purchase exemption from conscription. Who that person was is established by a letter that he wrote from Paris on July 26, 1839, to his Bergamo friend Antonio Dolci. In it he mentions a "fine woman" who had done a favor for Dolci and himself when they both had needed money to avoid conscription and for whom he had composed many pieces at the time. During 1819 and 1820, in fact, Donizetti dedicated many pieces to Marianna Pezzoli-Grattaroli—the "fine woman" who had saved him from service in the Austrian army.

Except for the probable trip to Mantua at the time of the staging of *Le Nozze in villa*, Donizetti appears to have remained in Bergamo until the beginning of October 1821. In June of that year, he somehow entered into negotiations with Giovanni Paterni, then impresario of the Teatro Argentina at Rome, about the possibility of composing an opera for the forthcoming Carnival season. These negotiations prospered, possibly with help from Mayr: on June 17, Donizetti returned the signed contract, in which he agreed to compose an opera to a Merelli libretto, his fee to be five hundred Roman scudi. In the letter accompanying the contract, he asked Paterni "to grant me lodgings, [I] being sure of not putting the smallest burden upon you."

On August 9, Donizetti was able to write Paterni that Merelli had started to write the libretto, some part of which he hoped to see soon. It is interesting to note that the lengthening list of Donizetti's religious and secular vocal and instrumental pieces was cut off for the time being in May of this year: once stimulated by the prospect of composing an opera, he had no compelling urge to any other sort of composition. On October 1, Mayr wrote out for Donizetti a handsome letter of introduction to the Roman poet and librettist Jacopo Ferretti.[38] Armed

[38] Jacopo Ferretti (1784–1852), a Roman, was, except for Felice Romani, the most accomplished Italian librettist of his era. Among the very numerous composers whom he supplied with texts were Pier'Antonio Coppola (*La Pazza per amore, Enrichetta Baienfeld*), Donizetti (*L'Ajo nell'imbarazzo, Olivo e Pasquale, Il Furioso all'isola di San Domingo, Torquato Tasso*), Filippo Grazioli (*La Festa della riconoscenza*), Luigi Ricci (*Il Nuovo Figaro, Gli Esposti, Chi dura vince*), Lauro Rossi (*La Casa disabitata*), Rossini (*La Cenerentola, Mathilde di Shabran*), and Nicola Antonio Zingarelli (*Berenice, regina d'Armenia*).

with it, his contract with Paterni, and a partially completed *opera seria* entitled *Zoraide di Granata*, the twenty-four-year-old Donizetti reached the Rome of Pius VII on October 21. He was on the verge of his first unequivocal metropolitan success, a success that was to launch him at last upon one of the most fecund, variegated, and finally tragic careers in the annals of opera.

CHAPTER II

1822-1826

"Well, I have known from the beginning that the profession of the poor composer of operas is of the unhappiest, and only necessity keeps me tied to it." —DONIZETTI, in a letter to MAYR, December 25, 1825

THE rehearsals of *Zoraide di Granata* at the Teatro Argentina were marred by a sad incident that required Donizetti to recast the music he had provided for the character of Abenamet, the victorious general of the Abencerrages. The role had been adapted to a second tenor named Americo Sbigoli, who also was singing in the opera that had opened the Argentina's season on Santo Stefano's Day (December 26) 1821, Giovanni Pacini's *Cesare in Egitto*, in which the *bergamasco* tenor Domenico Donzelli had the first tenor role. The second act of Pacini's opera included a quintet in which Sbigoli was required to sing a phrase closely resembling one sung just previously by Donzelli. Wanting not to be overshadowed by the force of the noted Donzelli, Sbigoli strained himself at this point in the quintet, rupturing a blood vessel and dying several days later, leaving a pregnant wife and a small son.[1] No tenor with whom to replace him in Donizetti's opera appears to have been at hand, for Donizetti recomposed this notably

---

[1] On February 15, during the run of *Zoraide di Granata*, a benefit for the widow and child of Sbigoli was held at the Argentina. Prince Agostino Chigi noted in his diary that six thousand lire were collected.

male and military role for a female singer named Mazzanti, a change that necessitated the omission of three numbers.

While rehearsals were proceeding amid hubbub, tragedy, and alarms at the Argentina,[2] Donizetti found time, on January 18, to compose—for what purpose is not known—a four-voice C major *Miserere*. Ten days later, his great night arrived: on January 28, *Zoraide di Granata* was sung for the first time. Prince Agostino Chigi wrote in his diary that it was an *"incontro straboccivole,"* an "overwhelming success," and the reaction of that first-night audience in truth had boiled up to a degree just below hysteria. At once Donizetti was recognized as a leading claimant to the throne of Rossini, whose *Zelmira* was staged at the Teatro San Carlo, Naples, nineteen days after Donizetti's first Roman success. But Rossini was nearing the end of his Italian career. After *Semiramide*, which received its *première* at the Teatro La Fenice, Venice, on February 3, 1823, no more of his operas were composed for Italy: from that time on, he became in effect a Parisian composer, writing both *Le Comte Ory* and *Guillaume Tell*—his last opera—to French texts.

As was the custom of the era, Donizetti was required to supervise and attend the first three performances of his new opera. On the third night of *Zoraide*, he and Donzelli left the Argentina in a carriage and proceeded as far as the Trattoria di Monte Citorio to the accompaniment of a loud military band along a route illuminated with torches in his honor.

In the weekly *Notizie del giorno* of January 31, 1822, the remarks on *Zoraide di Granata* were the work of the *abate* Celli:

A new and very happy hope is rising for the Italian musical theater. The young maestro Gaetano Donizetti, a pupil of the most famous professors of music, has launched himself strongly in his *opera* truly *seria, Zoraide di Granata*. Unanimous, sincere, universal was the applause that he justly collected from the capacity audience, which decreed a triumph for his work. Every piece was received with particular pleasure; with enthusiasm, however,

[2] The Argentina was housing only *opera seria; opera buffa* was being staged temporarily at the Teatro Apollo (ex-Tordinona) because the Teatro Valle, meant to be its regular house, was being reconstructed out of the former Teatro Valadier. Both the Apollo and the Argentina had begun the season of 1821–22 on the traditional opening day, December 26, the former with Michele Carafa's *La Capricciosa ed il soldato*, the latter with Pacini's *Cesare in Egitto*. The Pacini was received well; it ran at the Argentina for about a month, and was followed by Donizetti's *Zoraide di Granata*, the libretto of which Merelli had based on a story by Florian Gonzales which Luigi Romanelli had transmuted into a libretto for setting by Giuseppe Niccolini. Niccolini's opera had been staged at La Scala, Milan, in 1807.

the introduction, the duet and quartet of the first act, and the romanza, the tenor's big aria, and the finale of the second act. What would have happened if the other pieces had not been deprived of the performance by the person for whom they were composed [Sbigoli] and if an unhappy combination had not deprived us of the pleasure of hearing three other pieces of music worthy of the highest praise in the opinion of those who have heard them played on a pianoforte? Donzelli, an excellent singer and a very able actor, draws to himself at will the affections of those who hear him; La [Ester] Mombelli, always equal to herself, ravishes with the sweetness of her singing and the pathetic expression of her emotion. All minds, however, turned to the young composer and tacitly called upon him not to stop along the road he has taken and not to deviate

> *Dal bel stil che gli fece onore.*
> *Macte animo, generose puer, sic itur ad astra.*[3]
> (From the fine style that does him honor.
> Take heart, generous boy, thus the way to the stars.)

Giovanni Pacini, two years before his death in 1867, published a book entitled *Le Mie Memorie artistiche*. In it he said: "After my above mentioned opera [*Cesare in Egitto*] Donizetti also had a very splendid success with *Zoraide di Granata*, and under that circumstance, two parties came into being—one Pacinian, the other Donizettian—but we held out our hands to one another, and from that time forward we always were good colleagues, each esteemed and loved by the other." With regard to the public's acceptance of *Zoraide*, Donizetti contented himself, in writing to Mayr on January 30, with saying: "I won't waste time telling you about the fate of the opera, as you will have heard of it from a thousand reports; I'll limit myself to saying that it was very happy."[4]

Donizetti naturally conceived a great affection for Rome and the Roman opera audiences, but he was making no plans to remain. He already had asked Mayr to supply him with a letter of introduction to someone in Naples, and he left Rome shortly after February 19. On February 28, the *Giornale del Regno delle Due Sicilie*, announcing that

---

[3] The writer of this critique, the Abbé Celli, was a noted character in Rome, and was referred to by the famous *romanesco* poet Giuseppe Gioacchino Belli as "*er sor abbate Urtica*," roughly "Mister Abbé Nettle," with allusion to his sharp pen. Neither of the poetic lines quoted was given in its original form. The first (*Inferno*, Canto I, verse 87) reads: "*Lo bello stile che m'ha fatto onore.*" The second line is an adaptation by Publius Papinius Statius of one from the *Aeneid* (IX, 641): "*Macte nova virtute, puer; sic itur ad astra.*"

[4] This letter also includes the following sentence: "My father's letter will tell you (if you wish) about the great disasters that befell me beforehand." Unless this refers to the death of Americo Sbigoli, the "great disasters" remain unexplained, as the mentioned letter to Andrea Donizetti appears not to have survived.

the forthcoming summer season at the Teatro Nuovo would include operas by Pasquale Sogner, Valentino Fioravanti, and Giuseppe Mosca,[5] also stated that another opera to be played was "a production of Signor Gaetano Donizetti, [who] is a young pupil of one of the most valued Maestros of the century, Mayer [*sic*], a large part of whose glory might be called ours, he having modeled his style on that of the great luminaries of the musical art sprung up among us. Judging by what we hear, this pupil of Mayer does not show himself to be unworthy of such a preceptor. A specimen by him produced in Rome on the stage of the Teatro Argentina was accepted with the most flattering applause." Guglielmo Barblan (*12*) pointed out that in the eyes of the Neapolitans, to be a pupil of Mayr—whose operas often were staged in Naples— was much more impressive than to have studied with the erudite but nonoperatic Padre Mattei at Bologna.

Writing from Naples on March 4, 1822, Donizetti chided Mayr for not having written to him, and then reported on a performance of Mayr's oratorio *Atalia* at the Teatro San Carlo under Rossini's direction.[6] The liveliness of Donizetti's epistolary manner—elliptical, allusive, often jocular—is in early bloom in this letter:[7] "It will be enough for you to know that the role of David is being done by [Domenico] Donzelli, that of Natan by Cicimarra, and that of Atalia by Fabbré [Flora Fabbri], who has not sung for two years and who is not good enough: she has a very dark contralto voice, for which reason Signor Rossini has had to edit the whole part. At the rehearsals, he lazes along Jesuitically with the singers, who don't follow him well, and then at the orchestral rehearsals, there he is, gossiping with the *prime donne* instead of conducting. . . . I think that this will suffice, and if it

---

[5] The operas were Sogner's *Amare per finzione*, Fioravanti's *Il Ciabattino*, and Mosca's *La Poetessa errante*.

[6] Rossini, who had been serving the impresario Domenico Barbaja as director of the orchestra at the San Carlo under a contract by which he also was bound to compose three operas each year—his stipend was nine thousand francs per annum—was to leave Naples during this year.

[7] A psychological study of Donizetti's letters, of which about eight hundred now are available, could produce fascinating results. They suggest a manic-depressive personality, and they assuredly show an attractive, lively, intelligent, and humorous mind. In his later years they become more and more ejaculatory and frantic, and they are larded not only with insistent scatological and obscene phrases, but also with excessive displays (not always correct) of foreign phrases, notably in French and German, in addition to passages in *bergamasco*. Frank Walker well said (*137*, 98): "Half a dozen indecencies are monotonously repeated. It is the automatic, humourless swearing of the weary conscript soldier. Must the campaign go on for ever? Will peace never come?" It is possible to follow the onset of Donizetti's final mental breakdown in the letters he wrote during the months preceding it—and to be present as it happens in his last pitiful screeds.

doesn't suffice, I'll tell you that [Girolama] Dardanelli doesn't sing the first-act aria, that they have deleted recitatives, choruses, the little finale of the second act after Atalia's aria, etc., etc. Really, I don't know whether by doing this they are doing well or badly, for they are such dogs that they should be out hunting bones rather than performing this music . . . ; that is the gratitude of La Colbran[8] after you favored her so. As for me, I don't care to watch any more of this, and that's what I told myself this morning. But Barbaja says that he will give it later at Vienna, and there it will be what it really is."

By March 26, Donizetti had entered into an arrangement with the impresario of the Teatro Nuovo; on that date he wrote to his "very dear friend" Jacopo Ferretti: "I am writing *precipitevolissimevolmente* in order to accelerate the staging of my opera, which will be after the novena of San Gennaro,[9] toward the middle of May." The opera he was composing in a hurry, to a libretto by the Neapolitan poetaster Andrea Leone Tottola, was *La Zingara*. His letter to Ferretti contains his first surviving mention of Antonio Vasselli, later to become his brother-in-law and lifelong confidant, a military surgeon whom he apparently had met in Rome through Ferretti. It also contains the remark "Naples doesn't please me," surprising in view of the fact that Naples quickly was to become his choice of residence—and was, in fact, to be the nearest approximation to a real home which he was to have for the rest of his active life. In a postscript, Donizetti added: "But tell me, is it true that in Rome they are saying that I composed the new *sinfonia* for Mayr's oratorio [*Atalia*]? I beg you to contradict this gossip because, among other things, the *sinfonia* doesn't even please me, for the work is long enough."

Donizetti, having been presented to Prince Leopoldo of Salerno, a brother of Ferdinando I, King of the Two Sicilies, dated at Naples on April 6, 1822, a cantata beginning *"Questo il suolo, l'aura è questa,"* which he had composed to signalize the birth of Prince Leopoldo's daughter Maria Carolina Augusta, who later was his pupil. This curious composition, with piano accompaniment, is for two sopranos ceremoniously representing the Genius of Parthenope (Naples) and the Genius of the Danube (the little Princess's mother being an Austrian archduchess).

---

[8] Isabella Angela Colbran, a Spanish soprano who probably had been the mistress of the impresario Domenico Barbaja and certainly had been Rossini's, was to marry Rossini eleven days after Donizetti wrote this letter.

[9] Neapolitan theaters remained closed during the nine days leading up to the annual liquefaction of the blood of St. Januarius and the nine days thereafter.

Tottola's libretto for *La Zingara* was abjectly bad. Francesco Pastura, a biographer of Vincenzo Bellini—for whose 1825 student opera *Adelson e Salvini* a Tottola libretto was used—says (*91*) of that persistent librettist of operas by (among others) Donizetti, Mayr, Saverio Mercadante, Pacini, and Rossini: "The career of the theatrical poet had begun in 1804. His first work was *La Riedificazione di Gerusalemme*, a sacred tragedy with music composed by Domenico Cimarosa given at the Teatro dei Fiorentini. His activity lasted until 1830 and ended with the libretto of the opera *Imelda de' Lambertazzi*, set to music by Donizetti and performed at the San Carlo. In all that is known of this activity of the poet Andrea Leone Tottola, spread over twenty-six years, one never is able to find a single libretto that recommends itself either as a subject or as workmanship. He was one of the numerous librettists by profession who, during that period, lived poorly in the shadow of the theater, elaborating intolerable stage texts and putting together words and rhymes that pretended to follow the Metastasian manner. Tottola did not particularly stand out from among them, and if he was held to be the best of them—to the point of becoming official poet of the largest theater [the San Carlo] of the Parthenopean capital—one can leave to the imagination what the rest of his colleagues can have been." An epigrammatist of the era happily discovered that Tottola rhymed with *nottola*, a word with several meanings, including "screech owl" and "bat." Rossini referred to him as "Torototela."

Despite the ineptnesses of Tottola's libretto, *La Zingara*, first of the many operas that Donizetti was to compose for Naples, was greeted with hot enthusiasm by the audience at the Teatro Nuovo when it was sung there for the first time on May 12, 1832. Writing two days later to Anna Carnevali[10] in Rome, Donizetti said:

[10] Donizetti had become acquainted with the Carnevali family while in Rome, probably introduced to them by Antonio Vasselli. The family then consisted of the husband, Paolo, his wife, Anna, and two daughters, Clementina and Edvige, both of whom were good amateur singers. Eighteen of Donizetti's letters to Anna Carnevali (and one to Clementina) survive (*138*, *43a*). Guglielmo Barblan wrote (*43a*, *7) that the letters allow one "to suspect that between the mature Anna, by then the mother of a newly married daughter, and the twenty-seven-year-old Gaetano there blossomed a feeling more profound and tender" than friendship. Signor Barblan, however, seems prone to discovering these "more profound and tender" feelings in most relationships between Donizetti and women; also, he says that a letter of Donizetti's (*43a*, 116), "probably of September 1833," shows Donizetti freeing himself "and forever" from his Roman friend—though in fact he was writing to her in terms of warm friendship as late as November 9, 1834 (*138*, 366). One's decision about the intimate nature of this relationship, as about that of several others of Donizetti's friendships with women, depends upon the amount of emphasis placed on isolated phrases in existing letters.

The fortunate Donizetti, then, went on stage Sunday with *La Zingara*, and certainly the audience was not miserly with compliments, inasmuch as I might almost say that they abounded—the more fortunate in that at Naples they applaud very little. Those who contributed most to this happy result, however, were the *signori* [Carlo] Moncada and [Giuseppe] Fioravanti, and I assure you that they sang their numbers divinely, even though the former had not been persuaded about his aria (and saw later that he had been mistaken), whereas the latter had to carry off a very tiring scene. La [Giacinta] Canonici,[11] though she almost had been overlooked in the preceding opera, garnered uncommon applause in this one, this time not because of any excellence of mine, but rather because of that of the poet, who knew how to clothe her in a very brilliant character, which she sustained happily.[12] Yesterday, at the second performance, the audience did not overlook a single number that had slipped by unnoticed the first evening, and again I was called out to accept the plaudits that the performers perhaps deserved more than I did. This evening, His Majesty [Ferdinando I] is coming to us for the first time. Yesterday's papers confirmed the Romans' judgment of my ability . . . and there you have a new source from which I drink eternal gratitude to that people, who decided so favorably for my reputation. It seems to me that I have said enough, and all that remains is for me to note that my colleagues at the theater immediately presented me with a copy of the score and that if the good Signora Clementina [one of Anna Carnevali's daughters] finds in it something that does not displease her, she will honor me by singing it. In the meantime, I beg you to tell the very good Signor Dottore [Antonio Vasselli?] and all your household about this, paying my respects also to the wonderful friends who frequent your good home.

P.S. I know that you will have received my *Angelica e Medoro*,[13] and for that reason I beg the Signora Clementina to let me hear it on my return, which will be soon. A thousand greetings to your husband, many kisses for your delightful children.

The continuing performances of *La Zingara* at the Teatro Nuovo occasioned the first meeting of Donizetti and Vincenzo Bellini, then a twenty-one-year-old student of music at Naples. The story was told by Francesco Florimo (*53*, 129–30):

[11] Giacinta Canonici was much admired by Stendhal. He referred to her, however, as Graciata Canonici. And, as Giuseppe Radiciotti wrote (*96*, 1, 86, n. 1): "Stendhal mistakenly wrote *Graciata Canonici* in place of Giacinta Canonici, and the error, as usual, has been repeated by many—and even aggravated because some have transmuted this single person into two separate artists: *La Graciata* and *La Canonici!*"

[12] It is, of course, possible that Tottola had provided the excellence Donizetti described. But this is much more likely to be an example of Donizetti's persistent modesty about his own creations, a modesty that he forsook only on a few occasions, and then under the pressure of extreme exasperation.

[13] Perhaps a solo cantata composed in Naples in honor of Anna Carnevali, this composition seems not to have survived.

Preceded by great fame because trained in the severe school of Mattei and that of the wise Simone Mayr, [Donizetti] came to Naples in 1822 to compose for the Teatro Nuovo. *La Zingara* was his first—and happy—production, announcing and revealing this future great talent to the Neapolitans. The success was splendid and complete: it was given for a year, and always to the increasing delight of the public, never weary of hearing it. As is natural, it was eagerly attended by—along with the rest of the public—those young men who meant to enter the same musical arena, not the least among whom was the very distinguished composer Carlo Conti, who one day said to Bellini and me: "Go to hear Donizetti's *La Zingara*, which I enjoy every evening, and with increasing effect; and among the other pieces you will find a septet that only a pupil of Mayr would be able and would know how to create." We hastened to go, and the septet mentioned, the culminating number of the opera, was what caught the attention and admiration of Bellini, who soon obtained a copy of it, studying it and playing it every day, so that it remained stationary on the stand of his cembalo. Shortly thereafter, he begged and urged Conti to introduce him to Donizetti; and I remember that the day when that introduction occurred was a red-letter day for Bellini, who, returning from the meeting still in a state of enthusiasm, told me: "Aside from the great talent that this Lombard has, he is also a big, handsome man, and his noble physiognomy, sweet and at the same time imposing, inspires sympathy and respect." They are his precise words, which I still remember.[14]

On June 29, 1822, *La Lettera anonima*, a one-act *farsa* by Donizetti, the libretto by Giulio Genoino, reached the stage of another Neapolitan theater, the Teatro del Fondo (later renamed the Teatro Mercadante). This too was accepted eagerly, but was attended by problems. Writing to Mayr on July 22, Donizetti reported:

On the 29th of last month, my *farsa* was given at the Fondo, and even though with a *donna* half in ruins [Flora Fabbri], it did not have the unhappiest outcome. Strange that these *prime donne* declare war on my products without even knowing me. The one mentioned above came in person, begging me to let her sing (and in fact she has an excellent voice), and then the bitch was the one who did not sing; the Direction, however, has suspended her pay for the time being, and if she doesn't sing, she'll be turned over to the police. It's lucky for me that her wickedness has been recognized by the public! I send you the newspaper article, not to call your attention to the praise, but rather to show you how hard I am trying not to deviate from the good style, and that at least if I haven't the ability to restore music to its first luster, I am at least not blemished by being one of those who deprave it. I'm leaving

[14] Writing sixty years after the event, Florimo certainly could not have remembered Bellini's "precise words." Nor is he a writer to be trusted without careful consideration. But that Donizetti and Bellini met in 1822 and that at first Bellini greatly admired and respected Donizetti are facts. Bellini's disaffecting jealousy of Donizetti came into being years later.

here Friday night and will be in Milan about the 20th and hope to see you again there.

Of *La Lettera anonima*, a writer in the *Giornale del Regno delle Due Sicilie* of July 1, 1822, said: "What pleases in the quartet is to see made fresh again the oldtime procedure of our so-called concerted pieces without those cabalettas and that symmetry of motives which obliges all the actors to repeat the same musical phrases no matter what the very different emotions agitating them may be. This is a good step toward that school of dramatic music which made the name 'Neapolitan' famous in all the theaters of Europe and to which we hope to be able to see it finally returned." Of the little *farsa*, Guglielmo Barblan (*12*) wrote: "And that the attempt to recover 'the first luster' was part of Gaetano's intentions is proved by the fact that one discovers in this score a tendency to shun, in the concerted numbers, rigorous melodic symmetries, whatever the feeling they may be meant to signify, and to turn toward freer and psychologically more elaborated forms in which differing melodic lines correspond to various feelings. This was not a novelty: Rossini had tried it in his juvenile operas and affirmed it luminously in the *Barbiere;* before him, Cimarosa had realized it exquisitely in the *Matrimonio segreto.* But current practice and the slovenly indifference of singers and public too often had led to forgetfulness of the composers of the 'first luster.'"

Shortly after the production of *La Lettera anonima*, Donizetti probably visited Bergamo. In Milan, on August 3, he accepted the challenge of composing an opera for the premier Italian theater, the Teatro alla Scala. On that day he signed a contract with the Royal Theaters of Milan, an agreement to which Felice Romani, foremost Italian librettist of the time, also was a party. Romani, a Genoese, had abandoned the practice of law to devote himself to writing, and he became the best Italian opera poet of the nineteenth century before Arrigo Boito. The list of his works includes some hundred librettos.[15]

[15] For operas by such composers as Francesco Basilj (*Gl'Illinesi*), Bellini (*Il Pirata, La Straniera, Zaira, I Capuletti ed i Montecchi, La Sonnambula, Norma, Beatrice di Tenda*), Michele Carafa (*Adele di Lusignano, I Due Figaro*), Carlo Coccia (*Caterina di Guisa*), Giacomo Cordella (*Gli Avventurieri*), Donizetti (*Chiara e Serafina, Alina, regina di Golconda, Anna Bolena, Ugo, conte di Parigi, L'Elisir d'amore, Parisina, Lucrezia Borgia, Rosmonda d'Inghilterra, Adelia*), Adalbert Gyrowetz (*Il Finto Stanislao*, a libretto used later by Verdi), Mayr (*La Rosa bianca e la rosa rossa, Medea in Corinto*), Mercadante (*I Normanni a Parigi, Ismailia*), Meyerbeer (*Margherita d'Anjou*), Francesco Morlacchi (*Gianni di Parigi, Colombo*), Pacini (*Il Barone di Dolsheim*), Luigi Ricci (*Un'Avventura di Scaramuccia*), Rossini (*Bianca e Falliero, Aureliano in Palmira, Il Turco in Italia*), Joseph Hartmann Stuntz (*La Rappreseglia*), Niccola Vaccaj (*Giulietta e Romeo*), and Peter von Winter (*Maometto II*).

The biography of Romani by his wife, Emilia Branca (*23*), supplies rich and fascinating reading, though it is extremely unreliable in its handling of facts. Romani now agreed to supply Donizetti with a libretto in seven weeks, by September 20. The opera was to be staged as the third attraction of the season at La Scala.

Romani's almost unparalleled gift for delay, tergiversation, and keeping composers on tenterhooks intervened. On October 3, only the first act of the opera had been completed, though the *première* was scheduled for that month. Romani finally delayed so long that Donizetti was driven to improvising numbers to be rehearsed. The rehearsals began on October 15, when he still had to complete the orchestration. His easily understandable agitation over this turn of events temporarily earned him the nickname *Maestro Orgasmo* (Maestro Excitement). On October 16, he wrote to Mayr: "I must tell you that unfortunately the *première* will be on the 26th because the first little rehearsal was held only yesterday. I hope, however, that I'll have the pleasure of seeing you, if not on the first evening, then at least on the third. I recommend that you bring a Requiem, as I'll be murdered, and thus the exequies can be carried out . . . *donne* who do so much grunting, buffos who disdain the music, [singers of] secondary parts who complain. I have only La [Isabella] Fabbrica; she is the best leading lady, therefore rejoice. . . . I say no more so as not to tire you out and so as to finish orchestrating a bitchery of a sextet."

In the midst of local excitement over the trial of a group of patriots accused of high treason,[16] Donizetti's *Chiara e Serafina*, an *opera semiseria* in two acts, was heard at La Scala on October 26, 1822, on a triple program with two ballets by Gaetano Gioja: *Gabriella di Vergy* and *Il Merciajuolo in angustie*, all this for a ticket price in the orchestra of two lire, about $1.75 in 1963 values. Although nobody seems to have considered *Chiara e Serafina* a success, it ran for twelve nights. An idea of what was demanded of performers in 1822 can be gleaned from the dates of these twelve singings at La Scala. The opera was sung on October 26, 27, 28, 29, 30, and 31, and November 2. Then Mercadante's *Adele ed Emerico* was put on for some performances and there was a concert, after which *Chiara e Serafina* was heard again on November 21, 23, 24, 25, and 26.

[16] The men on trial included Giovanni Arrivabene, a notable Mantuan senator; the Marchese Giuseppe Arconati-Visconti, a Milanese patriot; and the *carbonaro* leader Giuseppe Pecchio. Giuliano Donati-Pettèni (*39*) wrote that many liberals, knowing that the theater, and particularly the best seats in it, was under police surveillance—including spies—stayed away out of self-protection.

Donizetti, who had written to Mayr ten days before the *première* of *Chiara e Serafina* that he himself held out small hope for its success, fully understood that his first assault on the central temple of Italian opera, undertaken in a maddening rush and under adverse circumstances, had been thrown back. But he was not the sort of young man to retire, sulking in defeat, to Bergamo. Instead, he set out again for Naples. En route, he once more stopped off at Rome, probably in joyful reunion with the Carnevalis, the Vassellis, and Ferretti. On November 27, 1822, he was created a Knight of the Golden Spur, and Pius VII may have received him in audience in order to confer the decoration upon him. He dated at Rome on December 19 a soprano-tenor duet with piano accompaniment, composed for Clementina Carnevali and Nicola Cartoni,[17] and he seems to have remained in Rome until late in March 1823. It was very probably during this sojourn that he composed the three *canzonette* for soprano with piano accompaniment—"*Bei labbri che amore formò*," "*Non giova il sospirar*," and "*Rendimi il core o Barbara*"—which were published by Giovanni Battista Cencetti, a Roman music copyist and publisher.

Some conception of the young Donizetti's capacity and need for work can be gained from a letter that he wrote to Ferretti from Naples on April 1, 1823:

Then let's talk about the poor *Zoraide* [*di Granata*], which is going to be skinned alive: Ferretti! leave as much as you can of the second act, I tell you no more; what matters to me is that the musician's rondo be tender and terrible; amen. Also, the first-act cavatina is in need of renovation. What I implore you most of all is that the most beautiful of all the subjects that you have in mind must be for the [opera for the Teatro] Valle. You know that we have an excellent company, and for that reason it's up to you, and to me, both for self-esteem and out of gratitude to the good Romans, to do as well as possible. . . . Out of pity, Ferretti, no more children, as poetry and children don't go together very well.[18] I go on May 30 with the one-act opera of [Giovanni Federico] Schmidt[19]. . . then with Tottola's *Alfredo il grande*. Later at the Teatro Nuovo, and then at Rome.

[17] A composer and singer, Cartoni died at Rome in 1837.
[18] Ferretti's wife had borne him one child and was to have another in September.
[19] Giovanni Federico Schmidt (1775?–1835?), a Neapolitan, wrote more than one hundred librettos and translated numerous others into Italian. He provided Rossini with the texts of *Elisabetta regina d'Inghilterra* and *Armida*, and was the original author of the text revised for the Rossini *pasticcio* called *Edoardo e Cristina*. This last he originally had written for Stefano Pavesi, who had set it in 1810 as *Odoardo e Cristina;* for the purposes of the *pasticcio* of music by Rossini, it was revised by Andrea Leone Tottola and Gherardo Bevilacqua-Aldovrandini. Schmidt's translations included those used for Spontini's *La Vestale* (Naples, 1811), Gluck's *Iphigénie en Aulide* (Naples, 1812), Spontini's *Fernand Cortez* (Naples, 1820), and Hérold's *Zampa* (Milan, 1835). Donizetti set his *Elvida* in 1826.

This passage requires exegesis When the Teatro Argentina at Rome had expressed the intention of staging Donizetti's *Zoraide di Granata* a second time, Donizetti, who was sufficiently conscious of the low quality of Tottola's libretto to refer to it as a "great barking," persuaded Ferretti to rework it. Now he was ready to begin the recomposition demanded by Ferretti's revision. The "one-act opera of Schmidt" with which he was to "go on" on May 30 was by strict definition not an opera at all, but an *azione pastorale* or pastoral cantata in one act entitled *Aristea*. He was composing it. Tottola's *Alfredo il grande* was the *opera seria* libretto for the work that he had promised the San Carlo; he was ready to begin composing that. "Later at the Teatro Nuovo" meant that he had promised that Naples theater that he would set still another Tottola libretto for them: this was to become *Il Fortunato inganno*, a one-act *opera buffa*, produced on September 3, 1823. And "then at Rome" reminded Ferretti that he had promised still another opera to the Teatro Valle: this would turn out to be the one of the best and most interesting of Donizetti's early operas, *L'Ajo nell'imbarazzo*, a two-act *opera buffa* staged at the Valle on February 4, 1824. In April 1823, that is, Donizetti was involved in the refashioning of an opera, the composition of an *azione pastorale*—and thoughts and plans concerning three new operas.

Why did Donizetti spread his energy and talent so thinly over so many compositions and continue to set librettos by Tottola and Schmidt while conscious of their abysmal quality? In part, he was driven by the simple need for money, which in that era—as now—meant either creating highly successful works that would spread from theater to theater, and thus continue to bring in revenue, or—lacking that stroke of fortune—the continual turning-out of new operas that would earn small amounts before, much too quickly, they sank into desuetude. Donizetti was twenty-four, and it was now more than five years since his first professionally staged opera, *Enrico di Borgogna*, had been heard at Venice. None of the operas he had composed up to 1823 had been picked up by other opera houses after their *premières* (the extra-Venetian career of *Il Falegname di Livonia* did not begin until 1825), and he was undoubtedly pressed for funds, in part because he had to contribute to the support of his parents and perhaps to that of his brother Francesco, in part because he already was considering marriage. And it was this need to earn more money by constantly composing new operas which left him willing to accept the abject texts of Tottola, Schmidt, and their peers as offered him by impresarios and directors. They were the best that Naples then had to offer—and though no

ironclad rule prevented "outside" librettists from writing librettos for
local theaters, a strong custom connected certain writers with certain
theaters: Tottola and Schmidt, for example, with the Fondo, Nuovo,
and San Carlo at Naples, Ferretti with Rome, Romani, eventually, with
Milan. Donizetti knew the differences between a good libretto and a
bad one and was aware that a bad one very seldom meant a good or
a successful opera. But he was caught up in a self-inflicted producing
schedule that made it absolutely necessary for him to set bad librettos
rather than no librettos at all.

Stylistic and psychological elements doubtless also influenced Donizetti toward the frenetic overproduction that doomed many of his
operas to almost immediate death. He composed, most of the time,
with terrible ease and was most attuned to himself when composing.
He seems very often to have been driven by an unconscious, almost
frantic urge to compose, compose, compose, too seldom by the conscious intention of slowing down, taking a long, searching look at
what he just had composed, then deciding upon its merits, reworking,
discarding, and beginning again. Stylistically, especially in the transi-
tional period between the adapted eighteenth-century styles of Rossini
and the first overtly Romantic Italian operas—those of Bellini—Donizetti, who was not an intellectually decisive innovator or remoulder,
had difficulty in defining his own musical personality and operatic
methods. And so he largely remained an artisan, practicing his craft
honestly and to the best of his very considerable ability, but always in
a hurry, and therefore only on occasion—notably when just fortunate
enough to find one good libretto in the grab bag—composing an entire
opera at the top of his creative dramatic ability.

Early in 1823, Donizetti seemed momentarily to have lost his touchstone. When *Aristea*, the *azione pastorale* to a Tottola text, was sung
at the San Carlo on May 30, it dishearteningly failed to please: it was
repeated only once.[20] The same sort of reception and history awaited
Alfredo il grande, which had its *première* at the San Carlo (then, as
now, the second opera house of peninsular Italy) on July 2. Little better

[20] The cast included Girolama Dardanelli (Filinto), De Bernardis (Corinna),
the *bergamasco* tenor Andrea Nozzari (Licisco), Michele Benedetti (Comone),
Gaetano Chizzola (Erasto), and, in the title role, Elisabetta Ferron. Some of the
cool reception of *Aristea*, as of the opera *Alfredo il grande* that followed it, may
have been owing to Ferron's being out of voice: on April 23, Donizetti had written
to Anna Carnevali in Rome that in a performance of Rossini's *La Donna del lago*
which he had heard, everyone sang excellently "except the *donna* [Ferron], who
performed everything very badly, and for whom, Heaven be praised, I am writing
a cantata and an opera." He was to have further difficulties with Ferron during
his stay in Palermo in 1825-26.

was in store for *Il Fortunato inganno* when it reached the boards of the Teatro Nuovo on September 3: it was heard on only three nights. Clearly, Donizetti was composing too much at too frantic a speed even for his own purposes.

Despite these disappointments, which perhaps he saw as more financial than artistic, and despite his commitments at Rome, Donizetti lingered in Naples until mid-October. He remained there in part because life in that city had come to attract him, in part because Pius VII had died on August 20, for which reason all Roman theaters were closed during the resulting conclave, which was stretching out week after week with the cardinals unable to agree upon a new pope.[21] On September 23, Donizetti wrote to Giovanni Paterni, impresario of the Teatro Argentina:

In another letter of mine I begged Ferretti to send me in the meantime the cavatina and aria to be done for La Pisaroni[22] in *Zoraide* because—in the hope that this pope will be made quickly—I too will shortly have to start my labors. But I haven't had an answer. A few days more or less don't matter, but that was only my eagerness to begin quickly so as to be able to reflect more on the thing, as well as to be forehanded, so that if fortune should have it that the Holy Father should not be made by Christmas, we would have the *serioso* score [the new version of *Zoraide di Granata*] ready. That, then, will make me decide to leave [here] as soon as possible even though uncertain about the date when the theaters can be opened. I want to think that our contract will take its course as soon as the pope is elected—is that right, for the coming Carnival? Because it is only counting on your friendship that I shall make the trip. Here the theatrical regulations merely suspend contracts, but don't cancel them, and for that reason I suppose that it will be the same in Rome.

Once having reached Rome, Donizetti settled down to earning the five hundred Roman scudi that Paterni had contracted to pay him for revising *Zoraide di Granata* and composing a new opera. The revised opera, first heard at the Argentina on January 6, 1824,[23] was received

[21] This contentious conclave lasted one hundred and four days, finally ending with the election of Annibale della Genga, who took the pontifical name of Leo XII.

[22] Rosamunda Pisaroni-Carrara, a singer greatly admired by Stendhal, who said in a letter to Mareste: "La Pisaroni is really a singer of the first order, perhaps the second or the third of the impoverished musical Parnassus as it is at present. This is a superb contralto voice that executes the greatest difficulties with ease and which, from time to time, appears to be in a rage and then carries off a number."

[23] The cast included as Almuzir, the role he had created two years before, Domenico Donzelli, of whom Stendhal wrote: "The tenor Donzelli, very good. His voice, however, doesn't please me at all; it is veiled, and in the upper register resembles a cry."

less well than the original version had been received nearly two years before at the same theater, and that despite the fact that it now contained new numbers as expressive and attractive as any that Donizetti yet had composed, most notably the once-popular second-act duet that begins "*Là nel tempio, innanzi al nume.*" Stendhal, who attended this second *première* of *Zoraide di Granata*, did not care for the opera—or for Donizetti, of whom he wrote: "Donizetti is a large, handsome, cold young man without any sort of talent. It seems to me that he was applauded two years ago to spite Princess Pauline [Borghese], who was patronizing the young Pacini." A curious pronouncement in view of the fact that Donizetti was neither unusually large nor in any sense cold, and that Stendhal was attributing to Roman operatic audiences motives more likely to occur to him or to one of the characters in his novels than to them.

But Donizetti refound his touchstone at last, largely because this time he had set a good libretto by Ferretti, a text that awoke the peculiar combination of melancholy and buffoonery which he perhaps had first encountered (and found native to himself) in Rossini's *La Cenerentola* and was to transform into an operatic texture all his own. On February 4, 1824, at the Teatro Valle, *L'Ajo nell'imbarazzo*, to the Ferretti text, was an unmistakable—in fact, a smashing—success; it was to hold the boards for the rest of that season and to be staged many times throughout Italy and abroad. This was by all odds the best-achieved of his operas to that date. Still a trifle Rossinian in texture, *L'Ajo* nonetheless was marked by especially Donizettian pathos, by convincing sensuous melodies, by an individual quality of farcical movement which was to blossom more fully in *L'Elisir d'amore*, *La Fille du régiment*, and—above all—*Don Pasquale*. The day after its first performance, the periodical *Il Pirata* justly referred to it as having "spontaneity, fecundity, clarity, and originality of ideas; light, elegant phrasing, full of grace; an accompaniment modeled on the words, and fascinating for its sweet attractions, good taste, a flash of genius—all to be found in it."

In the flush of this extremely heartening endorsement by both audiences and critics, Donizetti went "home"—back to Naples. There he shortly signed a contract with Francesco Tortoli, impresario of the Teatro Nuovo, for a new *opera semiseria* and a revision of *L'Ajo nell'imbarazzo* which would suit it to the resources of the Nuovo's roster of singers and the special taste of its audiences. New numbers were to be added to it, and the *buffo* role of the protagonist was to be translated into Neapolitan dialect by Andrea Leone Tottola. For these two pieces of work, Donizetti was to be paid three hundred ducati, half on delivery of the first act of the new opera, half after having attended its first three performances.[24] To a libretto by Giuseppe Chec-cherini, he at once began to work on *Emilia di Liverpool*, sometimes referred to as *Emilia o L'Eremetaggio di Liverpool*. While composing it, he received from Bergamo word that he had been elected an Honorary Member of the Unione Filarmonica there.

First heard at the Teatro Nuovo on July 28, 1824, *Emilia di Liverpool* failed to please; it never was to establish a claim to popularity anywhere. Its disappointing reception, following upon the success of *L'Ajo nell'imbarazzo* at Rome, was succeeded by one of the least productive periods of Donizetti's early professional life.

Writing to Ferretti on August 21, 1824, Donizetti said that he stood ready to place himself at the disposition of the impresario Giovanni Paterni for another opera to be staged in Rome. Paterni had visited Donizetti in Naples for at least a preliminary discussion, but an additional meeting had not taken place because Donizetti had been ill with what he referred to simply but ominously as "the fever." This is the last Donizetti letter that appears to have been preserved from 1824. Only one of his letters seems to have survived from 1825 (December 21, from Palermo to Mayr), and the earliest known letter of 1826— again to Mayr, but from Naples—is dated May 30. Outside evidence— notably files of the Palermitan newspapers of the period and Ottavio Tiby's *Gaetano Donizetti a Palermo*[25]—fills in many details; others are supplied by newspaper and other accounts in Naples and by datings on compositions.

On October 15, 1824, for example, Donizetti dated and dedicated to the Marchesa Sofia de' Medici di Marignano a cantata for soprano with piano accompaniment, *La Fuga di Tisbe*. And during late 1824 he also composed a four-voice *Credo* in D major for the annual celebration honoring Saint Cecilia which Mayr had instituted at Bergamo, where it was held each November 24 in Santa Maria Maggiore. That Donizetti

[24] The proposed Neapolitan restaging of *L'Ajo nell'imbarazzo* (as *Don Gregorio*) was delayed until 1826. Like most other mountings of this opera, it was a joyful success. When the opera was sung at La Scala in that same year, it received the accolade of twenty performances, to which five more were added in 1829, twenty-five in 1837.

[25] An excellent example of original scholarship on a small scale, Tiby's account of "a lyric season of one hundred and twenty-five years ago" originally appeared in the *Annuario dell'Accademia Nazionale di Santa Cecilia*, 1949–51. It was issued as a pamphlet in Rome in 1951.

was still in Naples during the early months of 1825 is proved by his having dated "*Napoli Febbraio 1825*" a piano rondo also dedicated to the Marchesa de' Medici di Marignano, as well as by the performance of his cantata—really a five-scene *azione pastorale*—entitled *I Voti dei suddi* (The Prayers of the Subjects). Ferdinando I, King of the Two Sicilies, had died on January 4, 1825, and the customary period of public mourning had followed. It was suspended on March 5, 6, and 7, however, for celebrations of the enthronement of his son, Francesco I. On the evening of March 6, the new sovereign, accompanied by the entire court, attended a gala at the Teatro San Carlo. Before the singing of Nicola Vaccaj's opera *Zadig e Astartea*, Donizetti's setting of Giovanni Federico Schmidt's *I Voti dei suddi* was sung—apparently to full royal satisfaction: *La Cerere*, the official court journal, said that Donizetti "had clothed the *melodramma* in expressive harmonies" that had "beautifully symbolized the feelings that all Neapolitans nourish today for a Neapolitan King."

Guido Zavadini stated that Donizetti left Naples for Palermo on March 15, 1825[26]—but if indeed he left Naples on that date, he must have proceeded elsewhere first, as he did not reach Palermo until April 6. Somewhat recklessly, he had contracted to serve as musical director of the Teatro Carolino[27] for the 1825–26 lyric season there. He probably was drawn into his unhappy venture by financial necessity and possibly was assisted in obtaining the position by either Mayr or Domenico Barbaja. His duties evidently included some teaching at the Conservatorio del Buon Pastore (a *convitto*, or charity boarding school), for on December 2, 1825, he would write in a letter to Mayr:

Would you like to know about the establishment of this musical college? Ah, *misericordia,* horrors: ragged boys, terrible voices, no teachers of *bel canto;* ah, in short, a synagogue, a perfect synagogue.[28] Some among the instrumentalists give promise, but they have teaching dogs like myself. . . . They look upon the theater people as abject beings, and because no one

[26] *138*, 26. The basis for Zavadini's statement was a letter written by Mayr to Marco Bonesi.

[27] The old Palermitan Teatro di Santa Lucia had been renamed in honor of Queen Carolina, wife of Ferdinando I, in 1809. After Garibaldi's entry into Palermo, its name was to be changed again—to Teatro Bellini. But it already had begun by then to lose its leading position.

[28] Ottavio Tiby wrote: "Neglected by the Bourbon government, which furnished funds in insufficient measure for the progress of the studies and the maintenance of the students . . . in 1825 the institute even was watched by the police because it seemed to be infiltrated by *carboneria*. During the years when Donizetti was in Palermo, the Conservatory, of which the director was an obscure Isidoro Gatti, composer of a little sacred music, had in fact reached the lowest point on its parabola."

takes any trouble about us, we don't take any trouble at all about them. Well, I have known from the beginning that the profession of the poor composer of operas is of the unhappiest, and only necessity keeps me tied to it. But I assure you, dear Maestro, that I suffer plenty from the kind of animals we must have to carry out our tasks. . . . I have put on Spontini's *La Vestale* in nineteen days—or, to say it better, nineteen mornings, for during the evenings there are performances; I doubt that more can be done, but *perbacco*, one's arms fail; there are dancers who in two months have twenty-five hundred ducati for trilling with their feet, and we poor devils are humiliated—we are cornered; ah, when I consider all this, I sweat. In all, dear Maestro, throughout the summer you and I have attracted people with the *Originali*[29] and *L'Ajo nell'imbarazzo*, and now their trills don't help to bring in another ducat. I'm supposed to give my new opera[30] now, but because of the illness of La Ferron,[31] it will be put forward to the first of the year. I feel more than a little scared. . . . They don't want to hear La Ferron. . . . Tamburini's wife (daughter of Gioja)[32] is a dog, the tenor Winter, etc., etc., etc., and in the midst of all this I have wanted each day to dally with music demanding some intelligence.

The company for the 1825–26 season at the Teatro Carolino was supposed to have consisted, as of the promised opening on April 11, 1825, of three *prime donne* (Elisabetta Ferron, Caterina Liparini, Marietta Gioja-Tamburini), a single *primo tenore* (Berardo Winter), a *primo basso cantante* (Antonio Tamburini), a *basso comico* (Nicola Tacci), a *secondo basso cantante* (Antonio De Rosa), a *seconda donna* (Carlotta Tomasetti), a *terza donna* (Antonietta Sciambran), and two *ultime parti* (Celso Alberti and Filippo D'Urso). Additionally, a list of understudies and singers who could be called in when needed was published: *prima donna*—Irene Cerioli; *primo basso cantante*—Giovanni Sardo; *seconda donna*—Teresa Fabiani; and *secondo tenore*—Salvatore

[29] Mayr's first widely popular opera, *Che originali!*, a one-act *farsa* to a text by Gaetano Rossi, had been given its *première* at the Teatro San Benedetto, Venice, on October 18, 1798; it is said to have been the first Italian opera performed in Philadelphia (May 5, 1829). No record of its having been sung in Palermo during Donizetti's term there ever has been found, but Ottavio Tiby, rejecting the possibility that in this letter Donizetti merely was flattering Mayr with an outright falsehood, reasonably suggested that a large part of the music from *Che originali!* probably was used in a *farsa-pasticcio* entitled *Il Trionfo della musica*, which was staged at the Carolino on July 6, 1825, and was repeated there several times during the rest of the season.

[30] To a libretto listed as being by "M. A.,' Donizetti had composed a two-act *opera seria* entitled *Alahor di Granata* for production at the Teatro Carolino.

[31] Elisabetta Ferron, the wife of Giuseppe [Joseph?] Glossop—an Englishman who temporarily succeeded Domenico Barbaja as impresario of the Royal Neapolitan Theaters—had sung in the Naples *première* of *Alfredo il grande* in 1823. Her "illness" was an advanced pregnancy, but she would have the child in time to get to Palermo and sing the leading soprano roles in *Il Trionfo della musica* and *Alahor di Granata*.

[32] A pun on the Italian equivalent of *fille de joie?*

Patti, future father of the great Adelina. In view of Donizetti's being named officially as *"Maestro di cappella,* director of the music, and composer of the new operas" from March 15, 1825, to March 15, 1826, the fact that he was to receive only forty-five ducati per month, plus round-trip transportation to Palermo from Naples and one month of vacation, is interesting: even a *seconda donna* like Tomasetti was booked at sixty ducati per month and a reigning star like Ferron at 517.50 ducati per month, exactly eleven and one half times the director's stipend.

No possibility existed of opening the season at the Carolino on the announced date, April 11. Donizetti did not reach Palermo on the steam packet *San Ferdinando* until April 6—and both Caterina Liparini and Berardo Winter disembarked with him. More of the company arrived the next day, still more of it on April 9. As there was no expectation that Ferron could arrive before June 15, an opera that would slide by satisfactorily without a star had to be selected. The choice fell on Giovanni Pacini's *Il Barone di Dolsheim,* which had scored a major success after its first performance at La Scala, Milan, in 1818, and the season actually got under way with it on May 4, 1825, a little more than three weeks late.

Nine days later, the Marchese Ugo delle Favare, Lieutenant-General of Sicily—in effect, the viceroy—addressed sharp words to the authorities of the Teatro Carolino on the subject of the theater's orchestra,[33] which had been arousing rabid disapproval among the public. This was only the beginning of the troubles that were to surge up and down the corridors and in and out of the auditorium of the Carolino during that season, which had started off badly and would end in a near catastrophe. Matters began to look up a little when the Tamburinis arrived and it became possible (May 30) to put on, as the second offering of the season, Rossini's *L'Italiana in Algeri.* Still no sign of Elisabetta Ferron—and it was decided that Donizetti himself must go to Naples to find her.

Early in June, Donizetti made the round trip to Naples. He caught up with Ferron in a small village where she was recovering from her labor. She promised to go to Palermo, however, and kept her promise, arriving on June 28, by which time the management of the Carolino was taking advantage of Tamburini's being on hand to stage Rossini's

[33] It consisted of thirteen violins, two violas, three cellos, five double basses, one piccolo, two flutes, two oboes, two clarinets, two bassoons, three horns, two trumpets, two trombones, one bass serpent, and three-desk percussion, a total of forty-three players. The chorus consisted of eight women and eleven men.

Il Barbiere di Siviglia to grateful audiences. By this juncture, the Duca Giuseppe Branciforti, who was superintendent of the Carolino in fact, was trying to get the topmost authorities to throw out of office the titular superintendent—his own puppet—one Francesco Morabito. The court refused to support his request, and the infuriated Duke had to continue suffering the bad results of his own selection.

With Ferron finally on Sicilian soil, rehearsals of Rossini's *opera seria* of 1813, *Aureliano in Palmira*, were begun. When, however, that first serious opera of the season could not be made ready for the gala of July 6—the Queen's birthday—Cimarosa's *Il Matrimonio segreto* was rushed in to fill the gap. Being too brief, it did not fill the gap completely, and *Il Trionfo della musica*, a *farsa-pasticcio* which, as re-marked earlier, may have contained largely music from Mayr's *Che originali!*, was added to it, being made sufficiently gala by the fact that Ferron used it as the vehicle of her belated Palermitan debut. Still not enough music for a royal gala—and so an occasional cantata, *Il Tempio di Minerva* by Pietro Generali, filled out the bill.

Another official occasion, this time the departure for Naples of the Marchese Ugo delle Favare, required another gala at the Carolino on July 23. The program was made up of one act of *Il Matrimonio segreto*, of the continuingly popular *Il Trionfo della musica*, and of a *licenza*, or occasional cantata, composed, according to *La Cerere* of two days later, by Maestro "Dorizetti." This appears to have been the first music by the director of the theater to be heard during that season. *La Cerere* added: "This extemporaneous work, applauded by the public, has given us the first sample of his talents and has acquainted us, in him, with a professor full of genius, of inspiration, of vivacity."

Then, of course, the Marchese Ugo delle Favare returned from Naples to Palermo, and another gala evening was in order. Donizetti may or may not have "extemporized" another occasional piece for that event, as he certainly prepared one for the gala of August 14—the King's birthday—when it was sung with the first performance of the much-delayed *Aureliano in Palmira*. Then, suddenly, hell broke loose. Public dissatisfaction with all of the company's singers but Tamburini became acute, and audiences began to dwindle; the singers complained of protracted delays in the receipt of their stipends; poor Morabito was arrested and kept in prison for twenty-four hours for what clearly was beyond his power to put right; then the *secondo basso cantante*, Antonio De Rosa, insulted Donizetti for having criticized him at a rehearsal, and he was also imprisoned for a day. Much of the worst of the complicated contretemps that was behind this trouble had to do with ballets rather than with operas, but that cannot have been true consolation to Donizetti.

On September 5, however, Donizetti's Roman success of 1824, *L'Ajo nell'imbarazzo,* with a cast including Caterina Liparini, Carlotta Tomasetti, Berardo Winter, Antonio Tamburini, Nicola Tacci, and Salvatore Patti, was put on the boards at the Carolino to the pleasure of audiences and praise from *La Cerere*—which, however, continued to refer to its composer as Donnizzetti. But a week later, the Superintendent of Public Spectacles and of Theaters, Domenico Lo Faso Pietrasanta, Duca di Serradifalco, suggested to the Marchese delle Favare that the management of the Carolino be discharged on the ground that it had not been carrying out its contractual obligations. It should have given, for example, eighty-nine performances by September 12 but had given only sixty-six, and the ballets still had not made their first appearance. The management owed enormous sums to the personnel of the theater, the chorus, and the publisher of the librettos— and almost two and one half months' salary to Donizetti. A receiver should be appointed, Serradifalco insisted, and he suggested Prince Diego Pignatelli for the position.

The viceroy agreed, but appointed a committee of three receivers, who at once had to face the task of getting a program ready for October 4. The plan had been to stage Rossini's *L'Inganno felice* and a ballet by Domenico Serpo entitled *Le Nozze di Figaro.* But no *corps de ballet,* no ballet; and *L'Inganno felice* would not by itself fill out an evening. So Rossini's *Mosè* was suggested. But the viceroy said no: not only had *Mosè* been heard in Palermo earlier, but also it seemed to him more an oratorio than an opera. So the triumvirate suggested Giovanni Pacini's opera *La Gioventù di Enrico V* and a danced divertissement with music by Serpo, *La Festa di Terpsicore.* The choreographer was Tamburini's father-in-law, they said, and besides, it could be staged without a *corps de ballet.*

Now the Duca Branciforti and his puppet, Morabito, succeeded in persuading the viceroy to free them from their five-year contract for the Carolino, largely on Branciforti's promise to pay the theater's debts and finish out that season in a decent manner. Finish it he did, but the decency of manner remains questionable. On October 31, *L'Inganno felice* was heard at last; eight days later it even was accompanied by a Serpo ballet, *Nina pazza per amore.* Spontini's *La Vestale* received its Sicilian *première*—eighteen years after its first performance in Paris—on November 24. The full-length ballet *Le Nozze di Figaro* finally was managed on a late November evening. And on December 8, Saverio Mercadante's opera *Elisa e Claudio*, with at least one substitute aria by Donizetti, was badly received. The *Mercurio siculo* commented: "A final aria by Maestro Donizetti replaced that of Mercadante, but certainly without greater success, and neither the former nor the latter ever will provide a maestro with reputation or the public with diversion."

Only after New Year's Day—on January 6, 1826—did the Teatro Carolino finally house a new opera by Donizetti, *Alahor di Granata*, with Ferron, Gioja-Tamburini, Tomasetti, Winter, Tamburini, and Patti. It received a favorable press, but apparently was not sung many times. On January 25, it was replaced by Rossini's *Tancredi*, and a number of full-length ballets dotted the schedule. On January 26, Elisabetta Ferron sailed for Naples on the packet *Arturo*, accompanied, it was noted, by her baby and by four servants. The year 1825 had been a Holy Year, and on the day before Christmas, Pope Leo XII had issued a bull prolonging the Jubilee outside Rome. Soon thereafter, Francesco I ordered all theaters throughout the Kingdom of the Two Sicilies closed for a month, to begin on the first Sunday in Lent. And so it fell out that on February 19, 1826, the tempestuous, unhappy season at the Teatro Carolino would have had to end. Five days before that, however, Donizetti had boarded the royal packet *Leone* and started back for Naples.

Guido Zavadini (*138*) and others have stated that another opera by Donizetti, a one-act *farsa* entitled *Il Castello degli invalidi*, was sung at the Teatro Carolino during the spring of 1826. This assertion is based on a passage in a letter (October 24, 1841) that Donizetti wrote to his brother-in-law, Antonio Vasselli, in which he mentions this farce as having been staged at Palermo. But Ottavio Tiby, who did careful research in the Palermitan archives and libraries for the entire period of Donizetti's stay in Sicily, found no mention whatever of this title. Neither the score nor any copy of its libretto ever has come to light. It being extremely unlikely that Donizetti would have claimed authorship and production of an opera that he in fact never had composed, possible explanations suggest themselves: (1) he did compose *Il Castello degli invalidi* for Palermo, but not during his own term at the Teatro Carolino; (2) this is an alternative title for another opera. In any case, Tiby's conclusion—"All these reasons together induce me, therefore, to strong doubts, even against the composer's affirmation, that this *Castello* ever was erected—or at least, that it was erected during the 1825–56 [*sic*] season"—seems to me unassailable.

While Donizetti had been absorbing the irritations and discourage-
ments of his Sicilian engagement, the members of the Unione Filarmonica di Bergamo, of which he was an honorary member, had been
preparing to install in their meetingplace a portrait of him which they
had commissioned from Morigia. On February 13, the day before his
departure from Palermo, a concert of his compositions had been given
to signalize installation of the picture. Understanding that Mayr must
have been the instigator of this honor, Donizetti wrote to him from
Naples on May 30: "I have learned about events of the other world,
[what was] done for me at the Accademia. . . . How this world exists
on illusions! There they celebrate and honor one who has no merit
other than that of having been away from home for a few years, while
that man lives under another sky, with the very qualities—or perhaps
worse qualities—than he had at home! . . . It is enough that Mayr
loves me, and a thousand times more of all the rest never will make
me conceited."

On the evening of the day on which he wrote this letter to Mayr,
Donizetti went to the Teatro San Carlo to hear the first performance
of a new opera by a new Sicilian composer: Vincenzo Bellini's *Bianca e
Gernando*.[34] He had been an onlooker at at least one rehearsal of it, for
in the letter to Mayr he said: "This evening there will be given at the
San Carlo the *Bianca e Gernando* (not *Fernando*, because that is a sin)
of our Bellini, his first production—beautiful, beautiful, beautiful, and
especially because it is the first time that he writes. It is unhappily
beautiful, as I shall find out with my [opera] two weeks from now. I
have been rehearsing my beloved *Don Gregorio* [an alternative title for
L'Ajo nell'imbarazzo] at the Teatro Nuovo since yesterday, with a new
number added. Thursday I shall begin at the San Carlo, and then, on
July 6, the other one in one act.[35] Not many pennies, plenty of

[34] This was the first fully public performance of an opera by the twenty-four-
year-old Bellini, though his *Adelson e Salvini* had been sung by students in 1825
at the theater in the Conservatorio di San Sebastiano during the Carnival season.
The curious name "Gernando" originally had been "Fernando" in Domenico
Gilardoni's libretto, but because the *première* of the opera was in honor of Fernando,
Duke of Calabria, heir to the throne of the Two Sicilies, the censors refused to
allow his name to be used for an operatic character. The one-letter change
was solemnly agreed to. In a much-revised version of this opera which was used
to inaugurate the Teatro Carlo Felice at Genoa in 1828, the title was restored as
Bianca e Fernando. At the San Carlo *première* the remarkable series of Bellini
first casts was begun: this one included Henriette-Clémentine Méric-Lalande,
Giovanni Battista Rubini, and Luigi Lablache.
[35] Donizetti had composed a one-act *opera seria* entitled *Elvida*, to a libretto
by Giovanni Federico Schmidt, and it was scheduled for production at the San
Carlo.

weariness—patience; if I am to have much honor, I shall be well paid."

The performance of *Don Gregorio* at the Nuovo took place on June 11, 1826. Four days later, Donizetti reported to Mayr: "Last Sunday, the poor *Don Gregorio* went on at the Teatro Nuovo; it had the luck of a more than happy success. Every number was much applauded, and I earned honors at least, if not money." Then, after retailing the difficulties being encountered over a performance of *Alahor di Granata* which had been scheduled for June 21, he added: "On Monday we shall rehearse the one-act *Elvida*. To tell you the truth, it's not any great shakes, but if I take them with Rubini's cavatina and the quartet, that will be enough for me. On gala evenings, no one pays much attention." Donizetti may at times be accused accurately of cynicism—writing operas and having them staged was his business—but scarcely ever of incorrectly judging or overvaluing the operas resulting from that cynicism.

In the same letter to Mayr, Donizetti announced that for his own pleasure he was composing "the *Gabriella* of Carafa," meaning—as Mayr would have understood—that he was writing an opera, *Gabriella di Vergy*, to the two-act *opera seria* libretto by Tottola which Michele Carafa had set a decade earlier.[36] This opera never was to be produced during Donizetti's lifetime, which fact easily may have contributed to his writing so seldom to please himself rather than in answer to demands by an impresario and to fit the exigencies of particular star singers or companies of singers. He had not the high romantic notion of composing as a form of self-expression. Opera in his eyes was preponderantly the commodity that he supplied to order and fitted to the purchasers' and users' potentialities and requirements.

Twenty-one years after Donizetti's death, what was announced as his *Gabriella di Vergy* was staged at the San Carlo. But neither of the two versions of its libretto which were published for that production bears the name of the librettist, and this fact added to discrepancies between the autograph score (now in the Museo Donizettiano at Bergamo) and the manuscript score, by other hands, of the opera staged in 1869 (now in the Ricordi archives in Milan), makes almost certain that the 1869 opera was so much revised as to be very unlike what Donizetti had composed for his own pleasure forty-three years before. Even though *Gabriella di Vergy* was early Donizetti and was composed before the sudden maturity represented by *Anna Bolena*

[36] Carafa's *Gabriella di Vergy* was heard for the first time at the Teatro del Fondo, Naples, on July 3, 1816, with Isabella Colbran in the title role.

four years later, its revival as he created it would at least tell us what Donizetti composed to please himself and might perhaps tell us much more. Donizetti was an intensely theatrical composer, and his operas can be judged pertinently only in performance.

On July 6, 1826, *Elvida* was staged at the San Carlo in honor of the birthday of Queen Maria Clementina—and therefore with the sovereigns attending in state. What the presence of the court might mean to the performance of an opera, and particularly to a first performance, is suggested by what Giovanni Pacini wrote (*88*) concerning the *première* of his *Niobe*: "It was court etiquette never to applaud singers who belonged to the royal *cappella*, for which reason Rubini and Lablache, being of the category of those who enjoyed that honor, most of the time remained unapplauded. But under such circumstances, the court ought to have deviated from standard procedures."

Whether because the court was present and the applause therefore constrained or because of probable lacks in the opera itself, *Elvida* has left few traces in the annals of performance, despite the presence in that first cast of three of the foremost singers of the era: Henriette-Clémentine Méric-Lalande, Giovanni Battista Rubini, and Luigi Lablache. Writing to his father on July 21, Donizetti said:

L'Ajo nell'imbarazzo, which was put on at the Teatro Nuovo, pleased well enough. . . . On July 6, at the San Carlo, I gave the one-act opera *Elvida*, and it was applauded by the King [Francesco I] and Queen [Maria Clementina], and on the second evening[37] I was called out with Rubini, Lalande, and all the others; on the 19th I gave *Alahor*, the Palermo opera, and this produced no great effect: only the *sinfonia*, the donna's cavatina, the tenor's aria, and the final rondo pleased. But for Naples that is not enough:[38] here they want everything excellent, so it's plenty that there was applause. . . . You are looking about for money? Alas! I would be honored to give you some, but cash . . . behold, that at the Teatro Nuovo, to which I sold the score [of *L'Ajo nell'imbarazzo*], I have received forty ducati for the rehearsals and everything, two hundred from the San Carlo for *Elvida*, but for the other opera I don't know if they'll even thank me. It's enough that I'll find a way to help you as much as possible in any case. The opportunity is difficult to come by, but then, you'll see.

Donizetti told his father, too, that he planned to divide the next month, August, between Naples and Rome. Not only had he agreed

[37] Royalty conventionally applauded in a token manner to indicate appreciation and approval of what was being offered. But it is notable that Donizetti should record that he was called out with the singers not at the *première*, but on the second night: the restraining presence of the sovereigns shows again.

[38] Donizetti's implicit claim that three numbers applauded would have sufficed elsewhere to gain support for *Alahor di Granata* is beyond denial or any accusation of pride: dozens of operas by himself and by other composers had triumphed and were triumphing on less.

to write another opera for the Teatro Valle in Rome, but also he had fallen in love. The girl was Virginia Vasselli,[39] the sister of his friend Antonio ("Totò"). Rome, then, to which he still felt grateful for his first appreciable success, strongly called him. From there, on September 30, he wrote to Mayr: "I am at work here, and am up almost to the middle of the second act, but not orchestrated. . . ." The opera that he was elaborating for Aniceto Pistoni, then impresario at the Teatro Valle, was to be a two-act *opera buffa, Olivo e Pasquale, ovvero Gli Opposti caratteri,* to a libretto by Ferretti, who had derived it from a comedy by the Paduan writer Antonio Simone Sografi. He completed it while at Rome late in 1826.

A violin-and-piano piece that Donizetti compiled during this stay in Rome and dedicated *"Alla Signora Virginia Vasselli, Roma,"* is of special interest. A type of potpourri-scherzo, the piece houses twenty-seven themes from the operas that Donizetti had composed up to that time. The last page of the autograph score, now in the Museo Donizettiano at Bergamo, contains a list of the operas from which he had extracted these melodies. The operas in the list are numbered to correspond with numbers that appear throughout the piece itself to indicate the presence of themes as they are introduced. Number 17 reads: *"La Bella Prigioniera, farsa non rappresentata."* Nothing further is known of *La Bella Prigioniera* except that the Museo Donizettiano has two autograph fragments of it for voice and piano.[40] Also dedicated to Virginia Vasselli is a duet, *"Sarà più fida Irene,"* for two sopranos, the inscription on which reads: *"Per la Sig. Virginia Vasselli, nell'anniversario suo D. D. D.—Sono 29—30 Nov. 1826."* Donizetti presented this manuscript to Virginia, then, on his twenty-ninth birthday, six months before she formally became his fiancée, though official announcement of the betrothal appears not to have been made until early in 1828.

Two letters that Antonio Vasselli wrote to Donizetti in August 1837, immediately after Virginia's death, raise problems presently soluble only by extensive supposition. On August 15, 1837, he wrote:

[39] Virginia Vasselli was born at Rome on November 27, 1808, a daughter of Luigi Vasselli, a lawyer of some prominence, and his wife, Rosa Costanti. The father, in 1818, had codified the procedural acts of the civil code of Rome in line with the wishes of Pius VII, publishing the results as *Formolario di tutti gli atti di procedura analogamente al Codice pubblicato con Motu proprio del 22 novembre 1817* (Poggioli, 1818).

[40] These are a recitative and duet for characters named Amina and Everardo (soprano and bass), *"Ella parlar me vuole,"* and a recitative and duet for Amina and Carlo (soprano and tenor), *"Olà . . . tosto discenda e a me si guidi Amina."*

"Remember the evening in July 1826 in the Piazza Colonna when I promised you Virginia." Why he rather than his father—who lived until January 2, 1832—should have been the member of the family to promise Virginia to Donizetti is far from clear. Also, Donizetti is very unlikely to have been in Rome in July 1826. His opera *Elvida* had its *première* at the Teatro San Carlo in Naples on July 6, 1826: he wrote letters from Naples to both his father and Anna Carnevali on July 21, 1826, and one to Mario Aspa, musical director of the opera at Messina, on August 11, 1826. We know that he went from Naples to Rome early in the second week of September 1826 and remained there until January 1827. All of this makes an additional trip to Rome in July 1826 extremely unlikely, though not impossible. Additionally, Donizetti as early as May 1827 was planning to marry Virginia, as is proved by a letter of May 25, 1827, to his father in which he mentions "the young girl whom I perhaps shall marry," but the possibility exists that his engagement to her was not formal until much later in 1827 (Zavadini, *138*, 255, n. 3 to letter 36, assumed that the sentence "I hope soon to give you some good news" referred to a formal announcement of the engagement, though it well may have referred to something else). Might Antonio Vasselli's "evening in July, 1826, in the Piazza Colonna" have been an error for "evening in July, 1827"? No indication that Donizetti was in Rome then can be found. The evidence for his not having been in Rome then is negative: Once his opera *Otto Mesi in due ore* had been staged at the Teatro Nuovo, Naples, on May 13, 1827, he continued to fulfill his contract with Domenico Barbaja—which required him to compose twelve operas in three years for the Nuovo, San Carlo, and Fondo—by setting to work on *Il Borgomastro di Saardam*, for which preparations must have been under way in July 1827, as it received its first performance at the Nuovo on August 19, 1827. The likelihood of Donizetti's having been in Rome to receive Vasselli's promise in the Piazza Colonna in July 1827 is as small as that of his having been there in July 1826. But that he did indeed receive that promise some time in 1827 is likely.

The second of Antonio Vasselli's 1837 letters referred to above (Zavadini, *138*, 871–72, letter 12) suggests that Donizetti come to live with him for a time and continues: "We loved one another in 1817, and I gave you at that time proof of eternal friendship." With the exception of two brief visits to Bergamo, Donizetti spent all of 1817 in Bologna at the Liceo. Where Vasselli was during that year is not known. He almost certainly had no musical training, however, and if he was in Bologna in 1817, it is likely to have been as a student at the University rather than as a fellow pupil of Donizetti's at the Liceo. In 1817, however, Vasselli was twenty-two years old, Donizetti nineteen until his birthday on November 29. The possibility that Vasselli, who became a military surgeon, was studying medicine in Bologna cannot be overlooked. But what is much more likely is that the "1817" in his letter of August 26, 1837, was a slip of memory or pen for 1827. For then the "proof of eternal friendship" of which he wrote could have been his agreement to give his sister to Donizetti as a wife.

Donizetti certainly knew Antonio Vasselli before March 26, 1822, on which date he mentioned Vasselli in a letter from Naples to Jacopo Ferretti in Rome, and surviving evidence strongly suggests that the two young men met for the first time in Rome during the rehearsals of *Zoraide di Granata* late in 1821, very possibly introduced by Ferretti. The best supposition in view of surviving documents and other evidence, then, is that Vasselli promised Virginia to his friend Donizetti not in July 1826, but in January 1827, when Donizetti was there for the production of his opera *Olivo e Pasquale* (Teatro Valle, January 7, 1827) or just possibly in February 1828, when Donizetti spent some time in Rome en route from Naples to Genoa for the production there of *Alina, regina di Golconda*. But this is, as remarked above, all extensive supposition.

CHAPTER III

1827-1830

A MONG Donizetti's many astonishingly productive years, 1827 and
   1828 proved two of the most abundant. In those twenty-four
   months, he composed eight operas, a cantata, a royal hymn, and
—for insertion into another composer's opera— a cabaletta that became
and remained extraordinarily popular.

At Rome during the closing months of 1826, Donizetti had completed to Ferretti's libretto the two-act *opera buffa* entitled *Olivo e
Pasquale.* This was staged on January 7, 1827, at the Teatro Valle,
winning the sort of reception that guaranteed it stagings throughout
Italy and soon resulted in productions abroad. After a production of
Olivo e Pasquale at the Teatro della Canobbiana, Milan, on June 19,
1830, the *Gazzetta privilegiata di Milano* said:

Music that always is brilliant, though not always new, an exact performance,
comic situations well sustained by the singers, assure the success of this opera.
The composition of the exit number for the bass, [Luciano] Mariani, who
portrays the character of Olivo—a gruff, prattling man—was found by the
intelligentsia to be well done, and it would have succeeded even better if
Mariani, profiting more from the gifts of nature and wise advice, had restrained the sometimes disgusting outbursts of his too-voluminous voice. A
quartet that can be cited as among the best pieces of the first act was greatly
applauded. In the second act, a duet between [Vincenzo] Galli and Mariani
did not provide full satisfaction; the music seemed somewhat trivial and not
fully thought out. Another duet, between [Elisa] Orlandi and [Giovanni
Battista] Verger, all *brio,* all expressiveness, was very much to the audience's
taste. We have observed that some pieces of the music strike us as a little

trivial, and we repeat this with the more frankness in view of the fact that all the rest indicates that the composer has in him taste, understanding, and that *brio* which is proper for *opera buffa*.

A few days after the successful Roman *première* of *Olivo e Pasquale*, Donizetti returned to Naples. There he shortly signed an agreement with Domenico Barbaja by which he was bound not only to compose twelve new operas for that powerful impresario (they were to be parceled out among the Fondo, the Nuovo, and the San Carlo), but also to conduct at the Teatro Nuovo. By this contract, Donizetti was to earn two hundred ducati per month, plus fifty scudi per month for his labors at the Nuovo. This promise of a relatively dependable income permitted him to consider marriage seriously: he was to become engaged to Virginia Vasselli in May 1827 and to marry her in June 1828.

Donizetti was soon hard at work on the first of these new operas, this one destined for the Teatro Nuovo. To a libretto by Domenico Gilardoni,[1] this was *Otto Mesi in due ore, ossia Gli Esiliati in Siberia*. Gilardoni had borrowed the central idea of *Otto Mesi in due ore* from a French play, *La Fille de l'exilé ou Huit Mois en deux heures*, by "the father of the melodrama," René-Charles-Guilbert de Pixérécourt, who in turn had borrowed the coils of its central entanglement from a novel (1806) by Sophie Cottin, *Elisabeth ou Les Exilés en Sibérie*.[2]

As *Otto Mesi in due ore*, the opera was given its first staging at the

---

[1] Domenico Gilardoni had provided Bellini with the text for his *Bianca e Gernando*. He was to supply Donizetti with eleven librettos: *Otto Mesi in due ore, Il Borgomastro di Saardam, L'Esule di Roma, Gianni di Calais, Il Giovedì grasso, Elisabetta al Castello di Kenilworth, I Pazzi per progetto, Il Diluvio universale, Francesca di Foix, La Romanziera e l'uomo nero,* and *Fausta* (this last completed by Donizetti when Gilardoni died leaving it incomplete). He also based on Goldini's *Il Ventaglio* the libretto of the opera by that name composed by Pietro Raimondi and produced at the Teatro del Fondo in 1831. In the pioneering book *Il Libretto per musica attraverso i tempi (105)*, Ulderico Rolandi evoked the crushing banality and crudity of many operatic texts of the first half of the nineteenth century; doing so, he cited the following "notably ugly and disconnected verses" from Gilardoni's text for Donizetti's *L'Esule di Roma*, Act I, Scene 1:

> *Ahi che di calma un'ombra*
> *Nemmen mert'io goder*
> *Per lui . . . nel mentre . . . avea . . .*
> *Lustro! Splendor! Senato!*

The lines might be translated crudely as "Ah, whereas I do not deserve to enjoy even the ghost of peace, for him . . . at this moment . . . there have been . . . Fame! Splendor! The Senate!" In fact, Gilardoni appears to have been small improvement over the traditionally incompetent Tottola.

[2] The Italian writer Luigi Marchionni also had adapted Mme Cottin's novel for the Italian stage, and Gaetano Gioja had used its story as the scenario for a ballet. Marchionni's comedy had been played at Rome in the summer of 1820 by the Vestris-Venier company, as *La Figlia dell'esiliato*.

Teatro Nuovo on May 13, 1827. Like most of Donizetti's other operas of this period, it was enjoyed enough so that reports about it won it stagings elsewhere in Italy, after which—beginning in 1829—it also was sung abroad. Edoardo Clemente Verzino (*133*, 44–45) stated that it was sung more than fifty times at the Nuovo, failed to please in Milan, but captured the Romans in 1832.

The *romanesco* poet Giuseppe Gioacchino Belli made that Roman performance the subject of one of his comic sonnets, a poor example of his poetry. In it, a simple fellow is supposed to be narrating his impressions of the opera after returning home:

Io, pe nun perdeme, Anna de Pumpara	I—[first] so as not to overlook myself, [with] Anna de Pumpara
La Spaccata, Chiafò, Cuccio e Luterio	La Spaccata, Chiafò, Cuccio, and Luterio,
Annasimo a la Valle in piccionara	Went to the pigeon-loft [gallery] of the Valle,
Che c'è la melodramma e 'r semeserio[a]	Where there is a *melodramma semiserio.[a']*
È un certo Pugnatoschi[b] che de Zara[c]	There is a certain Pugnatoschi[b'] who by the tsar
Lo mannorno in esijo in ner Zibberio:	Was sent into exile in Siberia:
E c'è un Unghera[d] c'è, che la pianara	And there's a Hungarian woman[c'] who by the flooded stream
La porta a galla drent'a un cimiterio.	Is carried straight into a cemetery.
Uscì er Bazzarro de Moscovia, poi,	Then the Ba-tsar of Muscovy[d'] came out,
Che se cibbò una sarva de fishchietti[e]	Who was greeted by a salvo of whistling,[e']
E li primi a fischià fussimo noi.	And we were the first to whistle.
Ogni tanto però da li parchetti	Every once in a while, however, from the loges
Se sentiva a ripete un tibbidoi[f]	A din was heard
D'apprausi ar machinista e a Donizetti.[3]	Of applause for the stage-mechanic and for Donizetti.

[3] The Italian notes, supplied by Belli's editor, read [a]*Melodramma semiserio* Gli Esiliati in Siberia. [b]*Il conte Poniatowski.* [c]*Czar.* [d]*Carolina Ungher.* [e]*Vi furono fischi pel modo di vestire.* [f]*Un strepito.* The sonnet, dated February 6, 1832, was published at Rome in *Poesie inedite di G. G. Belli* (1865). Notes to the rough translation: [a']*Otto Mesi in due ore, o Gli Esiliati in Siberia.* [b']A pun on Poniatowski, *pugnato* being the past participle of the Italian verb *pugnare*, to fight. [c']Caroline Ung(h)er—a pun on her name, she being Hungarian. [d']This complex pun probably involves reference to "bizarre" and to a bumpkin. [e']The whistling expressed disapproval of the way the tsar was costumed. The proper names in Belli's first two lines, typical Roman appellations, well may have referred to either real or imaginary people familiar to Belli's regular readers.

At about the time of the Naples *première* of *Otto Mesi in due ore*, Donizetti formally became engaged to marry Virginia Vasselli. Writing to his father on May 25, 1827, he said: "I hope to find you less displeased, now when you know the name of the young girl whom perhaps I shall marry, as I would not have found a better one than she is with regard to character. I do not say beauty because that endures only a short time." Andrea Donizetti clearly had not been overjoyed by the first intimation that his increasingly famous and prosperous son was considering marriage. Perhaps he feared both a rash choice and the cutting-off of the funds that Gaetano had been forwarding to Bergamo. This, at least, is suggested by Donizetti's sly insistence on her admirable character (which she had) rather than on her beauty and attractiveness (which both he and others considered notable). And in truth theirs was to be a very happy marriage. Although their life together was to last only a little more than nine years and was to be marred by terrible domestic tragedies, the passion that Donizetti had conceived for this vivacious, good-looking, devoted Roman girl was romantically so intense that proofs of it would survive her early death, haunting his memory and his letters for many years thereafter. His loss of her when he was only thirty-nine very probably contributed to his own subsequent decay.

Otherwise, throughout 1827, Donizetti was bound to his workshop in Naples. With *Otto Mesi in due ore* promisingly launched, he next turned to the second new opera for the Teatro Nuovo, again to a Gilardoni text. Its libretto, like that of Donizetti's *Il Falegname di Livonia*, was based on the legend[4] about Peter the Great which Gustav Albert Lortzing was to use exactly ten years later for his much more popular (indeed, in German-speaking countries, apparently eternal) *Czaar und Zimmermann, oder Die Zwei Peter*. This two-act *opera buffa*, entitled *Il Borgomastro di Saardam*, reached the stage of the Nuovo on August 19, 1827, and at first seemed to win a less enthusiastic welcome than had been accorded *Otto Mesi in due ore*. But on February 2, 1828, Donizetti was able to write Mayr that "*Il Borgomastro* has been done for more than thirty-five performances, and still is being done," and it too was to have an ample history both in Italy and elsewhere.

The libretto of Donizetti's next opera, a one-act *farsa* called *Le Convenienze ed inconvenienze teatrali*, emerged out of a long lineage of burlesques on the foibles and follies of impresarios, singers, singers'

---

[4] As found in a play by Anne-Honoré-Joseph Mélesville, Jean-Toussaint Merle, and Eugène Cantiran de Boirie (1818).

mothers, composers, and opera in general. A renowned early exemplar of the type had been Benedetto Marcello's *Il Teatro alla moda* (1720).[5] Although the punningly named text of Donizetti's gleaming little farce sometimes has been attributed to Jacopo Ferretti, Donizetti himself was largely, if not completely, responsible for writing it. It was based on two comedies by Antonio Simone Sografi (1794 and 1800). The *convenienze* of the adapted title were the conventional libretto requirements that Giuseppe Mazzini also mocked in his *Filosofia della musica* (*82*, 309–10): "An opera can be defined only by enumeration of its parts, a series of cavatinas, choruses, duets, trios, and finales, interrupted—not joined—by recitative to which no one listens: a mosaic, a gallery, a medley." Exactly who, from the *prima donna* and *primo uomo* down, was to have a solo number, and when, and the junctures at which certain among the singers were to be heard in duet, trio, or other concerted number—all this was a tactical matter established by long experiment and custom. The rules governing this structural pattern could be set aside only under extraordinary circumstances, and even then at considerable peril. The central personages of the little Donizetti opera are a mindlessly conceited, pushing prima donna who makes life wildly difficult for her colleagues, and her chief opponent, an older woman named Agata (played by a *basso comico* in travesty) who has been outraged, as she proclaims in a tempest of fury. Through both text and music, Donizetti's special gift for light farce, for the sweeter forms of satire, is evident, as it was to be notably in *L'Elisir d'amore* (1832), *La Fille du régiment* (1840), and *Don Pasquale* (1843), and had been in *L'Ajo nell'imbarazzo* (1824). The opera was staged at the Teatro Nuovo on November 21, 1827, and Eduardo Clemente Verzino stated (*132*, 44) that it then was sung more than fifty times. Berlioz wrote (*15*) of his visit to Naples in 1831: "*Opera buffa* is performed at the [Teatro del] Fondo with such fire, spirit, and *brio* as to raise it above almost every other theater of its sort. While I was in Naples, they were playing a most amusing farce of Donizetti's, *Le Convenienzi* [*sic*] *teatrali*."

During the last part of 1827, Donizetti (who wrote to his father

---

[5] Among the very numerous operas making use of librettos of this satirical nature were Domenico Sarro's *L'Impresario,* with a text by Metastasio (actually an intermezzo in Sarro's setting of the *opera seria* libretto *Didone,* 1724); Mozart's *Der Schauspieldirektor,* to a text by Gottlieb Stephanie the younger, 1786; Domenico Cimarosa's *L'Impresario in angustie,* with a libretto by Giuseppe Maria Diodati, 1786; Antonio Salieri's *Prima la musica e poi le parole* (a direct ancestor of Richard Strauss's *Capriccio*), with a text by Giovanni Battista Casti, 1786; Francesco Gnecco's *La Prova d'un opera seria,* to a libretto by Giulio Artusi and Gaetano Rossi, 1803; Vincenzo Fioravanti's *Don Procopio,* to a text by Carlo Cambiaggio, 1844. There have been many others.

on October 23 that he had been well up to that day, but then seemed to have a little fever) composed, to a Gilardoni libretto with scenes laid in the age of Tiberius, the two-act *opera seria* entitled *L'Esule di Roma, ossia Il Proscritto* (often played as *Settimio il proscritto*). The first-act trio finale of this opera was to garner some of the sort of extensive popularity later attracted by the sextet from *Lucia di Lammermoor*. Donizetti himself, in a letter to Mayr on February 2, 1828, said: "The finale of *Il Proscritto*, which is a trio, is very effective on the stage" and Rossini was quoted as saying that this trio by itself would suffice to earn fame for its composer. Rehearsals of *L'Esule di Roma* were under way in December, and its first singing occurred at the San Carlo on New Year's Day, 1828, when it was greeted so enthusiastically that Barbaja at once asked Donizetti to compose two more operas for that theater. By this resulting new contract, dated January 16, 1828, his remuneration was to be five hundred ducati per opera.

While *L'Esule di Roma* remained on the stage of the San Carlo, Donizetti showed his appreciation of the excellence of Luigi Lablache's performance in it by composing for the great *basso*[6] a cantata with piano accompaniment, taking the text from the Conte Ugolino episode in Canto XXXIII of the *Divina Commedia*. Either about this cantata or about another Donizettian setting of Dante (of lines from the Francesca da Rimini episode in Canto V), Rossini wrote, in a letter to Giacomo Pedroni: "I have heard that the melancholy idea has occurred to Donizetti to set a canto of Dante to music. *This seems to me too much pride*: at such an undertaking I don't believe that the Eternal Father could succeed, supposing that he were a composer of music."[7]

The city of Genoa was planning a protracted celebration for the inauguration of its splendid new opera house, the Teatro Carlo Felice, named after the reigning King of Sardinia and Piedmont. Operas had been ordered from Bellini, Donizetti, and Francesco Morlacchi, and the prospectus of the inaugural festival was filled out with the promise

---

[6] Lablache (1794–1858), by all descriptions a sort of Fyodor Chaliapin of his era, had several curious distinctions. As a boy contralto, he had sung in the Mozart Requiem at the funeral of Haydn in 1809; as a bass, he had sung in the same work at the funeral of Beethoven in 1827. Schubert dedicated to him in 1827 his *Drei italienische Lieder*—and he was to be a pallbearer at Schubert's funeral in November 1828.

[7] Yet Rossini himself, wanting to please his friend the Dante enthusiast Lord Vernon (Sir William Vernon Harcourt), set the Francesca da Rimini episode, as is proved by the survival at the Liceo Musicale, Pesaro, of the autograph inscribed: "*Recitativo ritmato sui versi di Dante: 'Farò come colui che piange e dice'—A Milord Vernon il suo candido estimatore G. Rossini.*" The piece was published by Ricordi as *Racconto di Francesca da Rimini nella Divina Commedia.*

of one or more operas by Rossini.[8] Donizetti agreed to set a text by Felice Romani entitled *Alina, regina di Golconda* (very often called simply *La Regina di Golconda*), which he was to have the most debilitating difficulties extracting from the overworked, procrastinating Romani.[9] At the end of January 1828, Donizetti decided to go to Genoa. He stopped over in Rome for about three weeks beginning on February 2, staying with the Vassellis, who lived on the second floor of the Palazzo Gavotti in the Via delle Muratte, between the Corso and the Piazza di Trevi. He reached Genoa on February 28, writing to his father on that day: "I happily arrived this morning, though with broken bones. In April, I'll go on the boards, and then I'll leave for Naples at once." His belief that *Alina, regina di Golconda* was going to be staged in April soon was dispelled; actually, it was not to be heard until May 12. The splendid Carlo Felice opened on April 7, with Bellini present to hear his *Bianca e Fernando*. Also part of that inaugural evening was an *Inno reale* that Donizetti had composed for voices and orchestra to a Romani text, as well as a ballet, *La Disfatta dei Guebri*, by Giovanni Galzerani.

During the succeeding, continuingly festive days, Rossini's *Il Barbiere di Siviglia* and *L'Assedio di Corinto* filled the boards. Someone —either one of the two leading singers in *L'Assedio di Corinto* or the impresario of the Carlo Felice—asked Donizetti to supply a cabaletta to be inserted into the second-act duet of that opera (Rossini had stayed in Paris), and he complied by composing it on the spot—not, as confidently stated in early books on Donizetti, during a sea trip from Genoa to Naples. This *"Pietosa all'amor mio"* duly was sung—and evoked frenetic enthusiasm from the audience. In fact, Donizetti's cabaletta thereupon became an integral part of *L'Assedio di Corinto*: when the opera was sung at the Teatro Apollo in Rome in 1830, the cabaletta again was fervently applauded. At that time, the Bolognese periodical *Teatro, Arti e Letteratura* published some correspondence concerning Donizetti's piece, including this sentence: "This bold issue of Donizetti is such that, by universal consensus, nothing better could be desired

[8] Bellini's opera was *Bianca e Fernando*, a drastic rewriting, with nine new numbers, of his *Bianca e Gernando* (1826). Morlacchi's was *Colombo*. Two operas by Rossini were sung: *Il Barbiere di Siviglia* and *L'Assedio di Corinto*, this latter an Italian version of *Le Siège de Corinthe* (Opéra, Paris, October 8, 1826), which in turn had been a revision and translation of his *Maometto II* (Teatro San Carlo, Naples, December 3, 1820).

[9] From Rome on February 2, 1828, Donizetti wrote to Mayr: "That Romani, who promises everything, keeps no promises; I wrote to him, he doesn't answer; he chooses a subject, and it doesn't please me very much. Enough. I'm going to leave for Genoa in a few days, and I'll turn sky, sea, and land upside down."

from the immense genius of the *pesarese* [Pesaro was Rossini's birthplace]; and if it was an audacity on his part to place it in contact with those divine harmonies, no audacity ever was crowned with greater success; the proof is that during the second performance, the enthusiasm stirred up was such that for a full half hour the audience insisted that it be repeated, which, given the regulations in effect, was not permitted."

On January 11, 1842, Donizetti, in a letter to Antonio Vasselli, referred to this famous cabaletta as *"Vieni Pamira all'ara,"* in reality the third of the eight lines of its text. Maometto II (Antonio Tamburini in the Genoa performance) sings:

Pietosa all 'amor mio	Taking pity on my love,
Alfin t'arrendi o cara,	At last surrender yourself, my dear,
Vieni Pamira all'ara	Come, Pamira, to the altar,
Vieni a regnar con me.	Come and reign with me.

Pamira (Adelaide Tosi at Genoa) replies:

Fatale è l'amor mio!	My love is ill-fated!
Pena crudele e amara;	A cruel and bitter pain;
Vorrei seguirlo all'ara,	I want to follow you to the altar,
Ma onor m'arresta il piè.	But honor holds fast my feet.

Alina, regina di Golconda finally was heard at the Carlo Felice on May 12, the first new opera to be given there. Donizetti had had to rush it to completion to the tardily delivered Romani libretto, and it was not entirely to his satisfaction, as is proved by the fact that when it was staged in Rome in October 1833, he revised it more than would have been required by the customary adaptation to a new company of singers. That it was received warmly nonetheless is indicated by a critique in the *Gazzetta di Genova*: "To Their Majesties' august suffrage was united acclamation by the public, and the authors and singers were repeatedly called to the stage, but the poet did not wish to appear. All the pieces in the score, and especially those concerted with chorus, prove the lofty ability of the young Lombard composer; and in them all there shines a joyful festivity of thoughts which always stirs and pleasantly entertains."

Donizetti himself was not pleased. Three days after the *première*, in a letter to Mayr, he reported:

I was obliged to go on the stage in seven days [of rehearsals] because the *Signori* directors had told His Majesty [Carlo Felice, King of Sardinia and Piedmont] that it would be given on Monday and they were constantly giving operas in the evenings. Enough! When Heaven wants to protect you,

you can go on even without rehearsals, and my *Alina* emerged as the happiest success. His Majesty was pleased to applaud its cavatina, the tenor's aria, the duet of the basso and the donna, and the final variations. . . . The tenor was bad, the donna was . . . enough . . . with all that, up to the end of the performance, the singers were called out twice and the composer twice. I swear to you that after the disorder of the final rehearsal, held that morning and completed at three o'clock, I thought that I'd be slaughtered. Yesterday evening, [Rossini's] *Otello* was given because of the illness of my tenor, Verzé [Verger], and perhaps this evening will be mine, but *il poveretto Dio* knows what will occur.

He dedicated *Alina* to his lifelong Bergamo friend, Antonio Dolci.

Donizetti apologized to Mayr for not being able to visit Bergamo, where he had been named an Honorary Member of the Accademia Filarmonica della Fenice di Bergamo on March 27, 1828. He explained that he must hurry back to Naples, where he had to compose an opera in time for August staging. But by May 12 he very probably was even more eager to leave Genoa for another reason: he was about to get married. He left Genoa on May 19, going directly to Rome. There, on June 1, 1828, he and Virginia Vasselli were married at the Church of Santa Maria in Via.[10]

No suggestion that Andrea and Domenica Donizetti should attend the wedding seems to have been raised, and in fact Donizetti's parents and his wife never were to meet.[11] Andrea undoubtedly had opposed his son's marriage. Dr. Federico Alborghetti and Dr. Michelangelo Galli, writing at Bergamo in 1875 (5), made statements and insinuations that it now is impossible to document, but which are to be considered seriously because the two physicians had had access to surviving relatives and friends of Donizetti, and therefore to sources of oral information which long since have vanished. Of Donizetti's peculiar brother, Francesco, for example, they wrote: "Francesco too was a little learned in music, and we remember him very well when, during the final years of his life, he marched, his chest stuck out, clashing the cymbals in the town band of Bergamo. It was as though he wanted to say: One is not a Donizetti for nothing!" This suggests that they probably also knew— or at least saw—Donizetti himself, as Francesco survived his famous

---

[10] For text of the record of Donizetti's marriage, see Appendixes, p. 278.

[11] In a letter of July 19, 1828, from Naples, Donizetti urged his father to come there on a visit, and Virginia added warm words of invitation. In another letter from Rome, of August 20, 1829, Donizetti again urged his father to visit Rome and Naples. By then, his mother was unwell, and he told his father that a visit from him would be particularly welcome because it would indicate improvement in her condition. But Andrea Donizetti seems never to have traveled far from his native Bergamo.

brother only a little longer than eight months. The pages of their book exude scrupulous fidelity to fact as then available and unclouded by conscious mythmaking. What they said about Andrea Donizetti's opposition to Gaetano's marriage is worthy of careful notice:

We have reasons for believing that his marriage to the Vasselli girl, which took place in the next year, 1827,[12] did not occur without the displeasure of Signor Andrea, his father, who, if he had not refused to give his consent to that marriage, in any case had let him know that it did not please him at all. Gaetano's parents' objection certainly had nothing to do with his fiancée, whom they did not know even by name, but rather with the subject in the abstract.

Nothing more natural than that the good old people, their spirits now happily restored by joyful hopes aroused by the good start made by their son, should be terrified by the mere notion of his taking a wife, and in a city so far away. The matter resolved itself in their eyes into nothing less than the loss of that son on whom, by then, they had come to rely for their old age, as they no doubt supposed that once he became entangled with new relations and settled down, there at the bottom of Italy, he would have a growing family around him, and as a result would end up by forgetting completely Bergamo and those who lived there. Therefore the groans and wry faces of Signor Andrea, who was destined, with regard to his predictions concerning his Gaetano, not to hit the mark even by mistake.

Gaetano, on the other hand, foreseeing everything very clearly, hastened to calm his parents' apprehensions, writing first to Mayr about the good qualities of the girl whom he wished to marry, and then to his father, this time insisting chiefly on clarifying the economic conditions attached to the marriage contract.[13] He wanted to make them understand that his marriage would not cut off his help to them, at the same time letting them anticipate as a possibility that one day or another, provided with a little of God's goods, he would bring his wife with him to Bergamo to live.

If this final promise was a vague one ventured for the sole purpose of pacifying his father, the other—that of not neglecting his family's needs—was a firm decision of his noble heart. And here we ought to say so in his honor, once and for always. Beginning with those hoarded ducati which he had been in the habit of sending his father from Naples, it can be seen in his letters that contributions to his family were constantly, gradually in-

[12] A typographical error for 1828.
[13] This refers to Donizetti's letter of May 25, 1827, quoted from above. The passage indicated here reads: "Now, understand that they give two thousand colonati, payable in three years, which means that for three more years I shall have the use only of the six per cent, after which I shall become master, to transport the sum wherever it seems good and pleases me; not earlier, because the contract that the father made up was for six years, and became three only with the banker. She has, for another thing, thousands of scudi worth of goods in the house, for herself, and silverware; so, it seems to me, a man without a single scudo could marry her. In the final analysis, then, what more would others have? And so, who knows if I may not come to live with you? The girl does what I wish; therefore?—"

creasing in number and amount as his own resources were growing, so that, long before his brother Giuseppe began sending his contributions of money from Constantinople, their parents were abundantly provided with everything by Gaetano.

Almost immediately after their wedding, Donizetti and Virginia went to Naples, where they moved into an apartment on the third floor at No. 6 Vico Nardones, not far from the Teatro San Carlo. There Donizetti worked at a new opera in the familiar atmospheric pressure created by a nearing deadline. On July 19, in the letter in which he and Virginia both pressed his father to visit them, he also said: "Now I have paid the tribute to the climate with a little fever of two or three days; now it is cured." He turned out the promised score in less than two months, using a three-act *opera semiseria* libretto by Gilardoni, *Gianni di Calais*. The opera was staged at the Teatro del Fondo, Naples, on August 2, and proved a very satisfying success, as it was to prove in Milan when it was mounted there at the Teatro Carcano during the Carnival of 1830–31. Of the Naples *première*, a correspondent of the *Gazzetta privilegiata di Milano* wrote: "The situations that the libretto offers are truly ingenious and do honor to the poet, Gilardoni. Maestro Donizetti has known how to take advantage of them, and what the *melodramma* has of comic grace he has clothed with charming character-istic music. Particularly outstanding is a sailor's aria, masterfully handled by [Antonio] Tamburini, who, like the Rubini couple [Giovanni Bat-tista Rubini and Adelaide Comelli-Rubini], had a large part in the success. Several pieces were honored by the applause of Their Royal Highnesses the Prince and Princess of Salerno, present at the perform-ance, and the public, echoing these plaudits, called the artists and the Maestro onto the proscenium."

And when *Gianni di Calais* was sung in Milan, the *Gazzetta privilegiata* critic wrote:

The music is by Donizetti, the composer of *Anna Bolena*.[14] This Maestro has given us two examples in two classes—tragic and comic—very close together. The former wins incomparably over the latter. In *Gianni di Calais*, we find in the first act a sea song that pleases, and which [Giuseppe] Frez-zolini declaims rather than sings, with that elegance familiar to everybody. A bass aria recalling too clearly that of Don Magnifico in [Rossini's] *La Cen-erentola* at the same time records the difference that occurs between com-position and composition, performance and performance. Then Rubini appears; this luminous star of music, welcomed and rewelcomed with inde-

---

[14] *Anna Bolena* had received its *première* at the Teatro Carcano, Milan, on December 26, 1830.

scribable enthusiasm, ravishes us with those smooth modulations by which even the most colorless harmonies are beautified. Charming, pretty, spontaneous, the young [Elisa] Orlandi by her singing gives to the Maestro's conceptions in her role all the outstanding quality that it is possible to give; but she could not be what she was in the opera *Anna Bolena*[15] .... During the rest of the opera, another triumph was won by Rubini's final aria, which he sang in a manner superior from every point of view, but which is, in the context, a collection of scraps of a baroque sort, made up of little fragmented phrases that prevent this great singer from developing those full sounds, agile and extremely smooth, which give ineffable delicacy to melodies. . . . Many times during the performance itself—and at the fall of the final curtain with Orlandi, with Frezzolini, and with the Maestro—Rubini appeared on the proscenium to receive from the audience proofs of that pleasure which it showed that it had experienced.

After the reception of *Gianni di Calais* at the Teatro del Fondo, Barbaja, more than ever impressed by Donizetti's gift for pleasing, his fecundity, his ability to meet deadlines under difficult conditions, and his mastery of operatic procedures, offered him the position of Director of Music of the Royal Theaters of Naples for the year 1829. Donizetti was not entirely eager to accept. In a letter to his father on October 21, 1828, he explained: "The public says that the Director does badly by [*mande a soqquadro*] the operas of other composers so that he himself may stand alone, and for that reason I don't know whether I'll accept." He finally took the position, however, and held it without stirring up any known complaints of self-favoritism from other composers. Somewhat confused records appear to indicate that Donizetti occupied this exposed post for at least ten years, or until some time in 1838.

On an undetermined date in the autumn of 1828, a one-act *farsa* that Donizetti had composed to a Gilardoni text entitled *Il Giovedì grasso* (sometimes called *Il Nuovo Pourceaugnac*) also was mounted at the Teatro del Fondo. It was not, however, the opera that Donizetti mentioned in a letter of October 21 to his father, when he said: "I am writing, but don't know for when, perhaps the end of December." This referred to an *opera seria* to still another Gilardoni libretto, *Il Paria*, in two acts. He labored over this late into December, and it was not to be staged until early in January 1829. On December 30, evidently writing in a depressed mood, he told his father that he hoped that Giuseppe's son Andrea—then ten years old—who had displayed some talent for music, but now seemed destined for some other career, would not "remain mediocre like me."

Rehearsals of *Il Paria* began late in December and went on into the

---

[15] Orlandi created the role of Giovanna Seymour.

early days of 1829. The first performance took place at the Teatro San Carlo on January 12, 1829, and though Donizetti was called to the stage to take applause, he was not happy with the opera. To his father, on January 19, he wrote: "I have given the opera, and was called out; nonetheless, I say that I made a mistake at some spot, and I'll try to fix this." But *Il Paria*, which never turned into any sort of success, began a poor year poorly for him.

Late in April or early in May 1829, Donizetti was seriously ill. Reading what he wrote to his father about this illness on May 7, one can only speculate that in reality it may have given, if not the first, then the first ominous indication of the malady that was to cripple him physically and mentally by 1845: "I write you after the storm; I have been very ill, with convulsions and bile and internal hemorrhoids; therefore bleedings, baths, purgatives, treatments. And afterwards . . . I had a relapse." At the bottom of this letter, Virginia added some lines; after referring to the fact that her mother-in-law was unwell, she said: "Gaetano already has told you the reason why we have not written up to now; I assure you that this illness of poor Gaetano's has made me suffer much, but much. Now, however, I thank God that He has showed His grace, and I hope that he will be perfectly recovered in a short time."

Two weeks later, perhaps still depressed by the aftereffects of the attack, Donizetti wrote to his father: "I hear that the position of singing master is open at the [Bergamo] Liceo; have them give me two piastres per day, and the Cappella secure after Mayr (who will live a thousand years after me), and then I'll come." This must have been written less than half in earnest. For his illness had seized upon him while he was at work on an opera for the San Carlo, a three-act *opera seria* to a text by Tottola, *Elisabetta al Castello di Kenilworth* (often called *Il Castello di Kenilworth*), which had been billed for a *première* on May 30, but which now had to be postponed until July 6. That performance was a gala in honor of Queen Isabella Maria, and the audience therefore of necessity reacted coolly to its new Donizetti opera. He wrote to Mayr on July 24 that it had been "almost disapproved of at its first performance," but added that court etiquette, as always on such occasions, had restrained the audience from applauding. "The opera was neither very well performed nor very well listened to," he wrote. "Then La [Adelaide] Tosi was taken ill, and it was repeated only on the 12th. It was a Sunday, a beautiful day, the theater crowded, the singers happy.

. . . I alone trembled. Their Majesties of Piedmont[16] came and applauded. Prince Leopoldo [of Salerno] did as much. The King and Queen of Naples[17] came and did as much. Therefore, with the singers animated, an audience that could let itself go—and the result was continuous applause! Everyone was called out, and the evening was very brilliant." Although *Elisabetta* was not the total failure that it sometimes has been painted, Donizetti was not tempted to overrate it. At the end of his July 24 letter to Mayr, he said: "(Between us) I'd not give one piece of *Il Paria* for the whole *Castello di Kenilworth* . . . but, in the meantime . . . luck is bizarre."

Still wanting to win back some of the strength that his recent attack of illness had cost him—and also because Virginia was well-advanced in her first pregnancy—Donizetti obtained a six-week leave of absence from his Neapolitan duties. On July 28, he and Virginia were in Rome, where, they hoped, she would benefit from the care that her family could supply. The next day, however, she was prematurely taken in labor and gave birth to a boy, who was named Filippo Francesco and lived less than two weeks. Having received word of the arrival of this grandson, Andrea Donizetti wrote to congratulate Virginia and Gaetano on the birth of their first child. His letter arrived after the baby had died, and Donizetti replied from Rome on August 29 to give his father details of the sorrowful event:

Your congratulations have been most pleasant to me even though they arrived late. I say late because the baby left for Heaven after the twelfth day. The uncertainty of the pregnancy and the visit to her made by the best doctors in Naples, who decided against any disease of the uterus, led her to adopt the remedies prescribed by those beasts, but the child nonetheless came to light at seven months. But it had a very long vein on top of its head, crossing over the head and reaching from one ear to the other. The fact is that after seven days of life it began to have convulsions, its eyes were twisted, it ate no more, and after the little life kept in it by spoon-feeding it milk, it remained for two days with its mouth shut, and died. Better that way than to have a boy marred by illness, for they say that if it had been cured, it would at best have remained crippled. Let's not talk about it any more!

Now Virginia's condition gave cause for worry to those near her. So when Barbaja sent urgent demands that his Director of Music of the Royal Theaters return to Naples, Donizetti found himself in a very painful position. On August 11, he wrote to Barbaja:

[16] King Carlo Felice and Queen Maria Cristina of Sardinia and Piedmont.
[17] King Francesco I and Queen Isabella Maria.

As regards the stones you have been hurling at me about my leave, dear Barbaja, you are too cruel. You granted me a month and a half. I have been here only two weeks. You know that my wife requires at least six weeks, and the more so because the boy died last night—and you want me to leave! Pity, my Barbaja, pity! If you really were in need of me, I would want to help you. But seeing that on the 19th you have Guglielmi,[18] that on October 4 there is Pacini,[19] that Gilardoni is exhausted and cannot work for me, why force me to travel to Naples? I have just given birth [to *Elisabetta al Castello di Kenilworth*], and now you want to make me pregnant? You are too barbarous. And so that I shall not be deprived of everything, I hope to put an opera of mine on the boards here. If, however, you really need me, then here I am—but if you can allow me a little rest, I'll work with more spirit after my return.

Barbaja did not prove inexorable: on August 29, Donizetti wrote to his father that he would not be returning to Naples until mid-September.

Aside from *Il Paria*, which had been completed in 1828, and *Elisabetta al Castello di Kenilworth*, the only new music by Donizetti performed during 1829 seems to have been that in a cantata for voices and orchestra, *Il Genio dell'armonia*, which he composed in Rome in collaboration with the Marchese Vincenzo Costaguti and the Marchese Domenico Capranica, to a text by the Cavaliere E. Visconti. This was sung on December 20, 1829, in celebration of the enthronement of the new pope: Leo XII had died in February 1829, and Francesco Xavier Castiglione had been elected as his successor, taking the pontifical name of Pius VIII.

As 1830 began, Donizetti was under contract to provide the San Carlo with two new operas. The first of them, to be staged during the coming Lenten season, was to be a full-length opera-oratorio on a Biblical subject, and therefore without ballet, dancing on the stage being forbidden during Lent. Donizetti therefore required a libretto that in itself would provide reasonably for stage spectacle. The Flood struck him as exactly the right subject, and he therefore elaborated a scenario for a libretto,[20] turning it over to Gilardoni (evidently re-

[18] *Teresa Navagero*, by the Sicilian composer Pasquale Guglielmi, was staged at the San Carlo on August 19, 1829.

[19] Giovanni Pacini's *Margherita, regina d'Inghilterra* was staged at the San Carlo on October 4, 1829.

[20] In a letter to his father headed "What rain . . . what cold . . . what snow/Naples, January 10, 1830," Donizetti said: "I have the writing of *Sassy*, of *Calmet, The Loves of the Angels* of Lord Bijron [*sic*], *Il Diluvio*, tragedy of Father Ringhieri, and if I find it, I'll also read the poem on the same subject of *Bernardino Baldi*." "*Sassy*" probably was Louis-Isaac Lemaistre de Sacy, a seventeenth-century converted Jew who became a Jansenist translator of the Bible. Agostino Calmet was a seventeenth-century writer of Biblical commentary, notably a *Storia dell'antico e nuovo testamento*. Padre Francesco Ringhieri (1721-87), an Olivetan monk,

covered from his exhaustion) for development and versification. The
result was a three-act libretto entitled *Il Diluvio universale*, character-
ized as an *azione tragico-sacra*, which Donizetti at once began to compose, consciously devising a musical style of relative simplicity and lofty
severity as required.

In the midst of these preliminaries for a large opera, Donizetti,
with his by then accustomed versatility and energy, set still another
Gilardoni text, this one a one-act *farsa* entitled *I Pazzi per progetto*.
Composing it for the unusual cast of two sopranos and five basses, he
had it ready for its first singing at the Teatro del Fondo on the night
of his own benefit, February 7, 1830. Writing to his father on February
13, he reacted briskly to the news that *L'Ajo nell'imbarazzo* had been
a fiasco at Bergamo on New Year's Day[21] and reported on the reception of *I Pazzi per progetto*:

Bravo, bravo, bravo! I really experience a sort of mad delight that *L'Ajo*
has been a fiasco; only the tiring efforts on the part of the good, even the
excellent, Mayr displease me. But I laugh at the rest. There people hiss, and
here I receive applause; in fact, this time I could have wished for less applause and more money, but because of a ball given by the Russian minister
on the very night of my gala, the theater was only half filled. For my evening
I had composed a little comedy-farce, *I Pazzi per progetto*, and it went off
very brilliantly: that may be because I am well regarded, but everything
goes well here with everything that I do. And you other people, in Lombardy, never should do my things—never, never; the newspapers have dis-
credited me too much. . . . Today I begin rehearsals of the oratorio *Il
Diluvio*, and I hope to God that it will go well. . . . And the weather continues cloudy. Everyone even says that since I began to compose *Il Diluvio*,
I have brought the real scourge upon Naples.

On February 13, with *I Pazzi per progetto* and his benefit gala
out of the way, Donizetti turned to placing the final touches on, and

---

from 1746 on wrote poetic tragedies and *azioni sacre* that won considerable public
suffrage but were deprecated by critics because of the somewhat lurid liberties he
took with his stories. Among his best-known works was *Il Diluvio universale*.
Bernardino Baldi of Urbino was a didactic poet of the late sixteenth and early
seventeenth centuries. As for Donizetti's curious attribution to Byron of *The
Loves of the Angels*, an examination of Gilardoni's libretto shows that either
Donizetti or he had read both Thomas Moore's *The Loves of the Angels* and
Byron's *Cain*, and the two evidently had coalesced into one in his mind as he wrote
rapidly to his father. As remarked in the Foreword, p. ix, it is fascinating to note
that Giuliano Donati-Pettèni (*39, 81*) misquoted this passage, apparently in a desire
to save face for Donizetti. At the same time, he introduced three new errors
for which Donizetti cannot be blamed: "*Ho letto la scrittura del Sossi* [sic], *di
Colmet* [sic], *gli Amori degli Angeli di Moore, il Diluvio tragedia di Padre Righini*
[sic], *e se lo trovava leggea pure il poema sullo stesso soggetto di Bernardino Baldi.*"
[21] See p. 318.

then to rehearsing at the San Carlo, the three-act *azione tragico-sacra*, *Il Diluvio universale*. It was sung for the first time on February 28, 1830. The audience's reaction was preponderantly favorable: performances of the solemn opera-oratorio continued throughout Lent.

Belatedly reporting to his father on the reception of *Il Diluvio universale*, Donizetti wrote him on May 4: "The oratorio—on the first night there were many votes in favor and many against, but it appears that in the end the favorable party has won, not because I was called out on the stage, but because it was sung throughout all of Lent. In this music, I take this opportunity to tell you, I worked very hard, and I find myself satisfied with it. If you believed that you would find cabalettas in it, then don't try to hear it, but if you want to understand how I intended to separate the type of profane music from the sacred, then suffer, listen, and hiss if you're not pleased."

The tone and content of many of Donizetti's letters to his father indicate both that he felt very close to him (much closer than to his mother, who remains a shadowy figure at best) and that he had very considerable respect for the older man's native intelligence and ability to understand matters that must, in fact, have been outside his experience. In a letter from Naples dated June 24, 1830, after speaking of financial matters and of a gold box that perhaps Barbaja was going to give him, whereupon he would give it to his father, Donizetti added: "Here it is very hot, and working as I do, I suffer plenty between the ache in my head and the hemorrhoids in my —" Donizetti was only thirty-three, and the rhythmically repetitive references to headaches were perhaps, therefore, the more ominous.

In August 1830, Donizetti composed a ceremonial cantata in honor of the return of King Francesco I and Queen Isabella Maria from a ten-month visit to Spain. This was *Il Fausto Ritorno*, to a text by Gilardoni. Writing to Mayr about it on August 7, in a letter headed "San Gaetano's [Day] . . . and I am full of little presents," Donizetti said: "I wrote the cantata for the return of Their Majesties, and it suffered the usual fate of cantatas. The final hymn was not mine, but of godfather Simone [Mayr], and it was that '*Viva ognor Francesco primo*' in 3/4 time which I myself sang at the Liceo. My memory served me, and I served myself by adding the band—a thousand excuses."

Before performing this courtier's duty, Donizetti had been deep into the planning of his second new opera for the San Carlo. On May 4, writing to his father, he had said: "In a few days I shall start composing the other opera, that is, *Imelda de' Lambertazzi*." During a hot Neapolitan June, all the while complaining of weariness, the crushing heat, and persistent headaches, he slaved away at this setting of Tottola's two-act *opera seria* libretto (his last), dealing with events at Bologna during the thirteenth-century Guelph-Ghibelline struggle. Nonetheless, he completed *Imelda* in a few weeks. It was staged for the first time at the San Carlo on August 23, when it was greeted with every sign of approval. The usually worshipful Guido Zavadini, writing of the fact that this successful opera, like most of its Donizettian predecessors, long has remained unheard, said (*138*): "It must be admitted, however, that this, like all of its predecessors, smelled too much of the Rossinian influence, and for that reason, more or less undeservedly, and in the measure of the others, also was forced into oblivion. The composer from that moment on was obliged to recover his own personality, and to our great good fortune, he found it in the very next opera [*Anna Bolena*]." This is, perhaps, to accept too unquestioningly the temporary verdict of fashion—and is surely unfair to, among a few others of Donizetti's early operas, *L'Ajo nell'imbarazzo*.

While rehearsals of *Imelda de' Lambertazzi* had been proceeding at the San Carlo, Donizetti had written to Mayr on August 7: "After my *Imelda* is got onto the stage, I shall fly to the bosom of *risotto* and that of *polenta e uccelli*." These gustatory references meant that he intended to go to Milan, where *risotto* (a dish of rice, meat, and other ingredients) was and is a specialty, and to Bergamo, where whole small birds were and are eaten with *polenta* (a maize- or chestnut-flour pudding). His reason for going to Milan was that, his contract with Barbaja for composing operas for the Neapolitan opera houses having run out, he had signed a contract (for a fee of six hundred and fifty colonati) to write a two-act *opera seria* for the Teatro Carcano there, the libretto to be by Felice Romani.

Donizetti and Virginia left Naples early in September, going to stay with the Vassellis in Rome. Then, leaving her behind, Donizetti set out alone for the north. He was in Bologna from October 3 to 6, and from there,[22] on October 5, he wrote his father to say that he intended to be in Bergamo the following Sunday, October 10, but that work with Romani might delay him in Milan. He reached Bergamo as fore-

---

[22] On June 24, 1830, writing to Mayr, Donizetti had said that if *Imelda de' Lambertazzi* proved successful, he wanted to present a copy of it to the Liceo at Bologna, "in which city, I am told, I am not very well accepted (even though *L'Ajo* has pleased sufficiently) because it is believed that I refused to write an opera [for Bologna], whereas no one has thought of [asking] me." But see the list of Donizetti operas performed in Bologna, p. 315.

seen, however, visiting with his parents and others of his family (not including his brother Giuseppe, who had been in Constantinople since 1828). Although this was his first trip to Bergamo in nine years, time pressed him and he could remain only a few days. He had to return to the world of opera.

This time the proverbially dilatory Romani was so captured by the subject of the new libretto for Donizetti that he wrote swiftly and without major interruptions, producing *Anna Bolena*, one of the best of his texts and one of the best-achieved librettos of the era, getting it into Donizetti's hands, it seems, by November 10. A story that there is no valid reason to doubt has had it that he composed this tragic opera about Anne Boleyn at the Lake Como villa of the great singer who was to create its title role, Giuditta Pasta.[23] The score was completed in one month, and rehearsals began at the Teatro Carcano on December 10.

Virginia Donizetti, left behind in Rome, wrote to her father-in-law from there on December 21, five days before the Milan *première* of *Anna Bolena*: "As soon as my Gaetano shall have come out on the stage, I pray you to be willing to give me exact news of the result. For, to tell you the truth, I don't trust him; for that reason, I turn to you, and thus assure myself of lessening my sufferings, as you can imagine the agitation in which I live, the more so because I know the sensitivity of his character; for that reason, I commend myself to you so that you may keep me company during the days when he is about to go on the stage." Virginia was right not to trust her husband's reports on the success or failure of one of his operas. Even in writing to Mayr and to his father, Donizetti often demonstrated curious reticence when reporting the reception given one of his operas by its first audiences, a mixture of natural modesty and something not far removed from godly indifference.

The *première* of *Anna Bolena*, more fateful for Donizetti than even the first performance of *Enrico di Borgogna* at Venice in 1818 or that of *Zoraide di Granata* at Rome in 1822, took place at the small Teatro

[23] Born Giuditta Negri at Saronno, near Milan, on April 9, 1798, of Jewish parents, Pasta made her debut in 1815, but after further studies she reappeared in Paris in 1822 and was recognized as a great singing actress, though not possessing perfect equalization of tone throughout the very wide range of her voice. Her extremely brilliant career (she sang most of the leading soprano roles in the Italian operas of her day—roles created especially for her, in addition to Anna Bolena, included the title roles in Bellini's *La Sonnambula* and Pacini's *Niobe*) was of even shorter duration than Maria Malibran's, though for a different reason: whereas Malibran died young, Pasta's vocal powers untimely deteriorated. She sang infrequently after 1835, but lived until April 1, 1865, dying at her villa on Lake Como. Besides Malibran, her chief rival was Giulia Grisi, whose phenomenal career extended from 1828 to 1861.

Carcano on December 26, 1830. The result was an overwhelming success whether measured by the reactions of the audience or by the writings of the critics, though some news reports suggested that much of the applause went to the singers rather than to the opera itself. *Anna Bolena* solidified Donizetti's previously oscillating fame. Significantly, it was only after the production of *Anna Bolena* that Mayr began to address his former pupil as Maestro.

More than half a century after the first performance of *Anna Bolena* at the Carcano, the biography (*23*) of Felice Romani by his wife, Emilia Branca, was published. It is a fascinating but unreliable book, and nowhere less reliable than in its handling of operatic events in Milan in the winter of 1830–31. Branca states, for example, that Vincenzo Bellini, who was under contract to supply the Teatro Carcano with an opera for that season, was a member of that first wildly applauding audience for *Anna Bolena*. He was not. On the night of that *première* at the Carcano, Bellini was at La Scala, which opened its season on that Santo Stefano with the first Milanese performance of his own opera *I Capuletti ed i Montecchi*, with a cast including Giuditta Grisi, Amalia Schütz, and Lorenzo Bonfigli.[24] Branca also wrote that Bellini had begun to compose an opera to a text by Romani derived from Victor Hugo's *Hernani*, which was correct—Bellini later drew on that incomplete score for parts of *La Sonnambula* and *Norma*—but then added that he had been so impressed by *Anna Bolena*[25] that he had decided suddenly to drop *Ernani* because he did not wish to compose a historical opera that might appear to be trying to compete with Donizetti's.[26] Instead,

[24] On January 3, 1831, Bellini wrote to his Venetian friend Giovanni Battista Perucchini: "I did not write you after the first evening because they could not have performed my poor opera worse—which, even though it made some effect and the audience wanted me on the stage, so enraged me that I did not want to go out."

[25] According to Branca, Bellini attributed the success of *Anna Bolena* above all to the "extremely harmonious verses" of her husband's "model drama, full of intimate, strong, and affecting passion."

[26] Had Bellini composed his *Ernani*, Verdi almost certainly would not have set Francesco Maria Piave's treatment of that subject fourteen years later. Verdi only twice knowingly set as operas texts that already had been used by other prominent composers: in *Un Giorno di regno* (1840), which was based on a libretto, then called *Il Finto Stanislao*, which Adalbert Gyrowetz had set in 1818, and in *Un Ballo in maschera*, based on a text by Scribe which Auber had set in 1833 as *Gustave III, ou Le Bal masqué*, a text, coincidentally, that Bellini in 1834 had decided to compose for the San Carlo, Naples, but which he never even began to set. True, Verdi also used for *Les Vêpres siciliennes* a libretto adapted by Scribe from that which he had written for Donizetti's *Le Duc d'Albe*. But he seems to have done so unawares, Donizetti's then unproduced opera having been forgotten by 1855. By the time of Verdi's maturity, that is, and partly through his influence, operatic customs had changed. In deciding to use a text derived from Hugo's *Hernani*, Verdi was willing to ignore the fact that texts based on it had been set by Vincenzo Gabussi (Théâtre-Italien, Paris, November 25, 1834), and by Albert Mazzucato (Teatro Carlo Felice, Genoa, December 26, 1843), operas that remained of almost

she asserted, Bellini had begged Romani to prepare for him, in a rush, an entirely different type of story, on a rustic or pastoral subject, saying that to come out with another *opera seria* after Donizetti's splendid one would be a temerity. "And Romani," Emilia Branca continued, "by then extremely weary, having prepared four *melodrammi* for other composers during the Carnival season, had to bow to the irresistible prayers of the *catanese*[27] and prepare very quickly the libretto of *La Sonnambula*."

This circumstantial anecdote, presented though it be with many sorts of apparently substantiating detail, will not bear the test of careful examination. *Anna Bolena* received its *première* on December 26, 1830. And, as Eugenio Gara wrote,[28] "It is only a pity that in the announcement of the Carcano [season] published by the Milanese journals on December 23, 1830, the two operas already were announced by their definitive titles: on the one hand, *Anna Bolena*, 'expressly written by Maestro Donizetti,' on the other, *La Sonnambula*, 'new music by Maestro Bellini.' A sign that the change of direction that had been made in the Bellinian program did not depend upon the success of the rival (*Anna Bolena* went on the boards on December 26), but upon other causes, not excluding encounters with the censorship which Vincenzo mentioned in a letter to his friend [Giovanni Battista] Perucchini."

And in fact, Bellini wrote to Perucchini, in the letter already cited: "You should know that I no longer am writing *Ernani* because the subject would have to undergo certain modifications because of the police, wherefore Romani, so as not to become involved, has given it up and now is writing *La Sonnambula, ossia I Due Fidanzati svizzeri*, and I began the introduction only yesterday." Bellini more than once referred to the projected *Ernani* as having been "prohibited." Branca's anecdote, then, was largely fiction. But Bellini's *La Sonnambula* did begin its long career at the Teatro Carcano on March 6, 1831, only two and a half months after the *première* of *Anna Bolena* there.[29]

purely local interest. But the originality of a libretto and of its subject matter nonetheless had come to be as desirable as originality in the music. It is altogether probable that some of the diminution in the production of viable operas in more recent times has resulted from this refusal to adapt and re-use suitable librettos from the past.

[27] Catania, in Sicily, was Bellini's birthplace.

[28] In "*La seconda moglie di Re Barbablu*," published in the program of the 1958–59 performances of *Anna Bolena* at La Scala.

[29] The first cast of *La Sonnambula* included two of the leading singers from that of *Anna Bolena*: Giuditta Pasta and Giovanni Battista Rubini, as well as Luciano Mariani, who was to sing in the *première* of Donizetti's *Lucrezia Borgia* at La Scala in 1833.

With *Anna Bolena*, thus heard for the first time the year before the Paris *première* of Rossini's final opera, *Guillaume Tell,* and on the threshhold of the four years during which Bellini was to cap his career by composing *La Sonnambula, Norma, Beatrice di Tenda,* and *I Puritani,* Donizetti began to emerge as one of the three most luminous names in the world of Italian opera.[30] *Anna Bolena* began very quickly to shed some of that luminosity over the opera stages of other countries. In Italy itself, the opera quickly became so popular that the fine French tenor Gilbert-Louis Duprez and his wife (assuming the roles of Percy and Anna Bolena) were able, under the aegis of the impresario Alessandro Lanari, to make a large part of their careers for two years and more (1832–34) out of touring in it: they played it in, among other Italian cities and towns, Foligno, Leghorn, Lucca, Siena, and Sinigaglia. In his *Souvenirs* (47), Duprez wrote: "Almost everywhere we sang our eternal *Anna Bolena,* which always was enjoyed."[31]

For Donizetti, then, 1830 closed in a professionally successful, if personally lonely atmosphere of achievement in the very capital of Italian opera, an aura of swiftly spreading fame and apparently unlimited future. Already he was one of the two foremost active composers of opera in Italy, and he had witnessed the triumph of his most recent work, of which the great republican leader Giuseppe Mazzini was to write (*82,* II, 313):

The individuality of the characters, so barbarously neglected by the servile imitators of Rossini's lyricism, is painted with rare energy and religiously observed in many of Donizetti's works. Who has not felt in the musical expression of Henry VIII the severe, tyrannical, and artificial language required by the story at that point? And when [Luigi] Lablache fulminates these words:

> Salirà d' Inghilterra sul trono
> Altra donna più degna d'affetto, etc.
> (There will come to the throne of England
> Another woman more worthy of affection. . .)

who has not felt his spirit shrink, who has not understood all of tyranny in that moment, who has not seen all the trickery of that Court, which has showed that Anne Boleyn will die? And Anne, furthermore, is the chosen

---

[30] When *Anna Bolena* was staged in 1830, Verdi's first opera, *Oberto, conte di San Bonifacio,* lay nine years in the future.

[31] It is interesting to notice that for the overture to *Anna Bolena*—a symphonic piece intended to establish the atmosphere for the action—Donizetti borrowed a theme from his 1828 opera *Alina, regina di Golconda.* The theme for the allegro of the *Anna Bolena* overture was taken over, almost intact, from the *sinfonia* that had preceded the earlier opera.

victim, whom the libretto—and history too, whatever others may say—depicts, and her song is a swan song that foresees death, the song of a tired person touched by a sweet memory of love.

Anna Bolena is such a thing that it approaches the character of the musical epic. Smeton's *romanza*, the duet of the two rivals [Anna Bolena and Giovanna Seymour], Percy's "*Vivi tu,*" etc., Anna's divine "*Al dolce guidami,*" and, in general, the concerted pieces, irrevocably place this opera among the first in the repertoire. The orchestration, if not yet equal to the melodic inspiration, nonetheless goes along fully, continuously, majestically. The choruses, among which must be noted especially the "*Dove mai n'andarono,*" etc., give the work a finish that, within the limits of our discussion, leaves nothing to be desired.

CHAPTER IV

1831-1834

A FTER Donizetti's successes of 1830, and despite his rapidly increasing fame, 1831 was to be a relatively inactive year for him. Publicly, it was a year marked by revolutionary outbreaks and a widespread cholera epidemic. For Donizetti personally it began, amid continuing performances of *Anna Bolena* at the Carcano, with the composition of a ceremonial cantata for the festivities attending the marriage of the Archduke Ferdinand of Austria (later the Emperor Ferdinand I) and the Princess Maria Anna Carolina of Sardinia and Piedmont, daughter of King Carlo Felice.[1] This cantata probably had a determining effect upon Donizetti's future: some years after the royal couple had become Emperor and Empress of Austria in 1835, he was to be summoned to Vienna, where, befriended by them both, he was to become a court official and an important figure in the city's musical life.

Political events now began to influence the tenor and activity of Donizetti's life. At Marseille in 1831, the young *carbonaro* Giuseppe

[1] Filippo Cicconnetti *(33)* said that this cantata was composed in Turin. Giuliano Donati-Petténi *(39)* suggested that Donizetti went from Bergamo to Turin—but he seems to have believed that Donizetti was in Bergamo after the *première* of *Anna Bolena* (a visit that is possible but undocumented) rather than before that *première* (a visit that is documented). No direct evidence survives that Donizetti was in Turin in 1831, and though it is possible that he went there in October 1830, or even in January or early February 1831, it is difficult to believe that he would have made the trip there merely to *compose* a cantata the first performance of which he could neither conduct nor attend. He was back in Naples by February 19 or 20, 1831; the royal marriage did not occur until February 27. Unless further documents come to light, it will continue to seem likely that he composed the royal wedding cantata in Milan in January 1831.

Mazzini founded the secret revolutionary society called Giovine Italia, dedicated to the unification of Italy.[2] The effects of its underground labors and of the diffusion of its propaganda and proposals, added to the continuing ferment brought about by the *carbonari*, became evident in outbreaks of violence, riots in several Italian cities, and consequent acts of governmental repression. In Rome, for example, to which Donizetti returned early in February 1831 (he was in Bologna, en route from Milan, on February 4), the new pope, Gregory XVI, had instituted stringent police measures.[3] These included (order of February 12) the boarding-up of all theaters: audiences tended to become patriotically —which then meant rebelliously—inflamed and to get out of hand.

From Rome, Donizetti wrote on February 15 to his father:

I'm writing to you so that you may not think that I may be dead among the fusillades. I am a man who worries about few things, even about only one thing—that is, if my work goes badly. I don't pay much attention to other things. I live because they let me live. I'll want to live even when I shan't be able to live any longer, etc. The fact is that I am well, that I shall leave Sunday for Naples, but there are assassins because the government there provisionally has recalled the soldiers who garrison the roads in the Pontine Marshes, and scarcely had that happened when the carriage of the very courier who came with me from Bologna to Rome was riddled with bullets on the way from Terracina.[4] I'm waiting for the militiamen to take up their posts, and then I'll go.

Donizetti and Virginia left Rome on February 19 for Naples. There, before 1831 had run its course, he was to compose four operas, only two of which—the *opera semiseria* called *Francesca di Foix* and the *opera buffa* entitled *La Romanziera e l'uomo nero*—reached performance during that year.[5] Both were in one act; neither made much impression on the public or procured a prolonged career. Donizetti does not refer to either of them in any of his known surviving letters. *Francesca di Foix*,

[2] Among its earliest members were Giuseppe Garibaldi and three of the Ruffini brothers—Jacopo, Ottavio, and Giovanni Domenico, this last, particularly during his political exile in Paris, being Donizetti's friend.

[3] Pius VIII had died in November 1830. Bartolomeo Alberto Cappellari was elected as his successor, taking the pontifical name of Gregory XVI, and was consecrated on February 6, 1831.

[4] A town on the Gulf of Gaeta, little more than halfway from Rome to Naples.

[5] *Gianni di Parigi*, a two-act *opera comica* to a libretto by Felice Romani which Francesco Morlacchi had set in 1818 (La Scala, Milan, May 30, 1818), was composed by Donizetti in 1831 as a starring vehicle for Giovanni Battista Rubini. But Rubini never sang in it. It reached production eight years later (La Scala, September 10, 1839). *Fausta*, a two-act *opera seria* to a Gilardoni libretto that Donizetti himself completed (Gilardoni having died), was composed in 1831 and heard for the first time at the Teatro San Carlo, Naples, on January 12, 1832.

to a Gilardoni libretto, was staged at the San Carlo on May 30, 1831; *La Romanziera e l'uomo nero*, also to a Gilardoni text, received its *première* at the Teatro del Fondo on an undetermined date during the summer. The two operas appear, in effect, to have sunk from sight thereafter without further trace or echo.

From April 11 or 12 to the end of May, Felix Mendelssohn visited Naples, which had become an intensely attractive place to visitors from the north. While there, he worked at *Die erste Walpurgisnacht,* which he had begun in Rome. The very proper, sometimes even prissy, German had a low opinion of Neapolitan *dolce far niente,* of music in Italy generally speaking, and of Donizetti in particular. "There is therefore so little industry or competition," Mendelssohn wrote, "and it is therefore that Donizetti finishes an opera in ten days; to be sure, it may be hissed, but that doesn't matter, as it is paid for all the same, and he then can go about amusing himself. If in the end his reputation should be endangered, however, in that case he would be compelled to labor in real earnest, which he would find by no means agreeable. Therefore he sometimes spends as much as three weeks on an opera, taking considerable pains with a couple of arias in it so that they may please the public and he then can afford to amuse himself once more, and once more write trash." Donizetti's opinion of Mendelssohn's music, unhappily, has not survived.

In Milan during 1830, Donizetti had become friendly with Count and Countess Gaetano Melzi, and through the summer and fall of 1831 he corresponded with the Count.[6] On July 30, he mentioned to Melzi the spreading of the cholera epidemic: "By two posts we have had fumigated letters from Rome, etc., and the poor traveler must stay at Terracina for three weeks before introducing himself into the Kingdom [of the Two Sicilies]." In another letter to Melzi (September 8), Donizetti said: "This evening is the second performance of Mercadante's *Zaira,* which was loaded with applause the first evening. In reality, it is very beautiful music and deserves a good success. Tamburini sang excellently, even though he was applauded less than Signora [Giuseppina] Ronzi de Begnis (I speak of the Court). Now we embark on the novena of San Gennaro, and during the eighteen days of silence there will be rehearsals of [Rossini's] *Tancredi* for the debut of Sophie Löwe,[7] of *Le*

---

[6] Count Gaetano Melzi (1793–1852) was a noted bibliophile and the compiler of a dictionary of anonymous and pseudonymous writings by Italian authors.

[7] Johanna Sophie Löwe (1816–66), a German soprano, was to marry Prince Friedrich Lichtenstein, a brother of the reigning prince, Aloys Joseph, in 1848, thereafter retiring from the stage.

Convenienze ed inconvenienze teatrali [Donizetti's 1827 *farsa*], of Ricci's *Ginevra*, of [Pietro] Generali's *La Scarpara*, etc., etc." And on November 26: "You will have learned that I shall be returning to Milan. The management has agreed to the fine company [of singers] in the hope of being equally indulged. It wants the sky! My *Fausta* will be put on on the twelfth day of 1832."

Before leaving Naples for Milan, that is, Donizetti had to supervise the staging of *Fausta*, the two-act *opera seria* that he had composed in 1831 to a text begun by Gilardoni which he himself had completed after that writer's sudden death. It was staged at the San Carlo on January 12, 1832, and was a success. Unhappily, no indubitably authentic letters from Donizetti are available for the period between November 9, 1831, and April 24, 1832, for which reason his own reactions to the first performance of *Fausta* and detailed information on his movements and activities between those dates cannot be determined. The absence of authenticatable letters from Donizetti at this time is regrettable also because the aged and ailing Sir Walter Scott visited Naples during this period and was greatly feted there. Donizetti well may have met him—and any reaction to a meeting of the author of *The Bride of Lammermoor* and the future composer of *Lucia di Lammermoor* would be fascinating to have. Also, Bellini was visiting in Naples from January 11 to February 25, 1832,[8] and as he too, like Donizetti, was to bring out his "Scottish" opera in 1835, the bare possibility exists that a meeting of Scott and the two composers may have occurred and may have influenced their future choice of subject matter for *Lucia di Lammermoor* and *I Puritani di Scozia*.

A frequently reprinted letter from Donizetti to a Maestro Rebotti of Pesaro, dated as from Milan on December 31, 1831, is spurious.[9] Donizetti would not have left Naples for Milan before the *première* of his *Fausta* at the San Carlo, which did not take place until twelve days after the date on the Rebotti letter. Then, in a long passage of praise for

[8] The Museo Belliniano at Catania has a letter dated January 18, 1832, from an otherwise unidentified "Giovanni" to his uncle—identified by Francesco Pastura (*91*, 312) as Ignazio Giuffrida-Moschetti, one of Bellini's close friends—in which the writer speaks of recently having encountered both Bellini and Scott in Naples.

[9] Guido Zavadini (*138*, 287–88) mistranscribed the name Rebotti as "Rubetti," but his scrupulous footnote to the letter itself clearly expresses his uncomfortable doubt of its authenticity: "Published in the *Voce di Bergamo* on November 13, 1931, which in turn took it from the *Rassegna artistica*, and this, I was told, was taken from a book by Carlo Nava published at Genoa in 1854." The book by Carlo Nava, sometimes described as a biography of Donizetti, seems never to have existed.

Bellini's *Norma*—which was sung for the first time at La Scala on December 26, 1831—the letter presents Donizetti as writing: "The duet (Verdi expresses the same opinion) *'In mia mano alfin tu sei'* is an admirable example of dramatic melody." But in December 1831, Verdi was an unknown youth of eighteen whose opinion of an operatic duet would have meant very little, if anything, to a "Maestro Rebotti" of Pesaro even if Donizetti had been aware of it. Actually, the spurious letter appears to have been the invention of Vincenzo Ricca, who in 1932 published at Catania a book entitled *Vincenzo Bellini: Impresssioni e ricordi* which includes it and numerous other forgeries.

It is impossible not to underwrite Guido Zavadini's implied doubt about another supposed Donizetti letter, this one to his Neapolitan friend the painter and publisher's agent Teodoro Ghezzi. It is dated at Milan on December 27, 1831, and was published first by Francesco Florimo (*53*, 132), who asserted that it had been communicated to him by Ghezzi. Florimo was not a charlatan like Ricca, but his love for Bellini more than once led him to the creation of desired documents, and this fragment, like the spurious letter to "Maestro Rebotti," purports to give Donizetti's enthusiastic reaction to the first performance of *Norma*. Possibly Florimo believed in its authenticity. But apart from the fact that its style is drastically un-Donizettian as coming from a letter to an intimate friend, it also is gravely suspect for the reason given above: Donizetti almost certainly was not in Milan for the *première* of *Norma* on December 26, 1831. The doubtful quotation reads: "*Norma* yesterday evening on the stage of La Scala was not understood and was inopportunely judged by the Milanese. As for me, I should be very content to have composed it, and I would willingly put my name under this music. Just the introduction and the last finale of the second act are enough to constitute the greatest of musical reputations; and the Milanese very quickly will realize with what rashness they rushed into a premature judgment of the merit of this opera." Donizetti might well have expressed these feelings—but it must be added that they are precisely the feelings that Florimo would have liked him to express about a work of his adored friend and idol, Bellini.

Alberto Cametti stated in his *Donizetti a Roma* (*27*), an almost wholly reliable—and extremely diverting and useful—book, that on January 27, 1832, Donizetti stopped off in Bologna en route to Milan. Whence he derived this information it now seems impossible to determine. Donizetti certainly was in Milan for some time before April 24, as he himself indicated clearly by the tone and contents of a letter that he sent his father from there on that date. In it, he says that he will begin rehearsals the next week even though his new opera is not yet entirely finished. The opera was *Ugo, conte di Parigi*, to a two-act *opera seria* text by Romani. It was staged at the Teatro alla Scala on March 13, 1832, after very protracted difficulties with the censors over its libretto, difficulties that had necessitated deletions calculated to cause Donizetti interminable irritation and added fatigue. Not one of his happiest works, *Ugo, conte di Parigi* was received so coldly by the Scala audience that only four additional performances of it were sung.

The impresario of the Teatro della Canobbiana, another Milanese lyric theater, was not discouraged by the insuccess of *Ugo*: during its brief run, he signed Donizetti to a contract for an *opera giocosa* for staging during the impending spring season. Already it was mid-April, and no time was to be lost. Romani turned out a two-act libretto in record time,[10] and Donizetti set it to warm, sparkling music in two weeks. It was named *L'Elisir d'amore*. Rushed into rehearsal, it was sung for the first time at the Canobbiana on May 12, 1832, and became an instant and enduring delight. Its first run at the Canobbiana was for thirty-two performances.[11] Yet Donizetti, writing to Mayr on May 16, four days after the *première*, merely said: "The *Gazzetta* [*privilegiata di Milano*] judges *L'Elisir d'amore* and speaks of it too well, too well, believe me . . . too well."[12] Writing to Giovanni Ricordi on July 31, he said: "Seeing that through your thoughtfulness the dedication of *L'Elisir d'amore* is left up to me, I am very grateful to you, and let it be 'To the Milanese fair sex.' Who more than they would know how to distill it? Who better than they how to dispense it?"

L'Elisir d'amore, that touching tomfoolery which still is delighting opera audiences of another century, thus seems to have been one of the

[10] The libretto was based on Eugène Scribe's *Le Philtre*—the work of a man of whom Donizetti was to hear much more—and had been set as an opera by Auber (Opéra, Paris, June 20, 1831). Scribe, in turn, had based his libretto for Auber on Silvio Malaperta's *Il Filtro*, of which Stendhal had published an adaptation in the *Revue de Paris* in 1830. Auber's *Le Philtre* became a notably popular opera, reaching its two-hundred-forty-third performance at the Opéra by 1862. After Donizetti's *L'Elisir d'amore* also became very popular, the inevitable happened: At St. Petersburg in 1836, music from the two operas was mixed in a *pasticcio*—which was sung in German.

[11] Berlioz (*16*) mentioned having attended one of these performances (he was in Milan on May 20–21, 1832). He wrote that he had strained to overhear the music through the din in the theater. "The people talk," he wrote, "gamble, sup, and succeed in drowning out the orchestra."

[12] In this letter, Donizetti asked Mayr to convey his thanks to Count Pietro Moroni, who on April 14 had signed the diploma certifying that Donizetti had been named a Corresponding Member of the Ateneo di Scienze, Lettere ed Arti di Bergamo.

best results of Donizetti's ability to compose under pressure. There is no reason to doubt the substantial accuracy of a conversation attributed to Donizetti by Alborghetti and Galli (*5*, 77–78), according to whom the management of the Teatro della Canobbiana found itself in grave difficulties because a composer who had promised it an opera had failed to deliver it—and only two weeks remained to produce a substitute for it. The manager approached Donizetti, begging him, under these depressing circumstances, to rework an old score and make it presentable to the public:

"Who is making fun of me?" the Maestro answered. "I am not in the habit of patching up an opera of my own—and never that of other composers. You'll see, rather, that I have enough energy to make you a brand new opera in fourteen days! I give you my word. Now send Felice Romani to me here."[13]

"I am obliged," the Maestro said with a smile to the poet, "to set a poem to music in fourteen days. I give you one week to prepare it for me. We'll see which of us two has the more guts!"

According to Emilia Branca (*23*, 217–18), he went on jokingly:[14] " 'It bodes well, my friend, that we have a German prima donna [Clara Sabina Heinefetter], a tenor who stammers [Giovanni Battista Genero], a buffo who has the voice of a goat [Giuseppe Frezzolini], a French basso who isn't worth much [Henry-Bernard Dabadie]—and still we must do them honor. Dear Romani, courage, march on.' " The marvel is that what Romani and Donizetti produced during the succeeding two weeks was *L'Elisir d'amore*.

On May 4, Donizetti wrote his father that he would be in Bergamo shortly. Twelve days later, however, in the above-mentioned letter to Mayr, he wrote: "I leave this evening [for Rome and Naples]. Signor Andrea will be displeased, but what can I do?" En route, he stopped off at Florence, where he signed a contract with Alessandro Lanari,[15] impresario of the Teatro della Pergola in that city and of La Fenice at Venice, agreeing to supply one new opera for each theater, both to have librettos by Romani. The opera for Florence was to be produced dur-

---

[13] It is amusing to notice that when Emilia Branca quoted this last sentence (*23*, 217), purportedly verbatim, from Alborghetti and Galli, she altered it to read: " 'But only if Romani backs me up! . . . I'll speak to him'—and at once went to find him." Evidently she did not like the picture of Donizetti's asking to have Romani brought to him.

[14] This part of the conversation does not appear in Alborghetti and Galli, but it sounds characteristic.

[15] Verdi was to compose both *Attila* (1846) and *Macbeth* (1847) for Lanari, who also had played a part in the negotiations leading to the composition of Bellini's *Norma* (1831).

ing Lent, 1833, that for Venice during the Carnival of 1832–33; the fee stipulated was ten thousand five hundred francs. Moving southward to Rome, Donizetti signed another contract there, this one with Giovanni Paterni, impresario of the Teatro Valle. By this he undertook to provide an opera for the 1832–33 season, to a Ferretti libretto, for a fee of five hundred seventy scudi romani. Shortly after June 14, he was back in Naples.

On August 2, Donizetti wrote to Ferretti: "Bravo, bravo, Ferretti! The first act pleases me very well, and therefore the second will be very beautiful!" This referred to the libretto for the Teatro Valle opera, *Il Furioso all'isola di San Domingo*, derived from *Don Quixote* (part I, chap. xxvii *et seq.*). Here and in succeeding letters to Ferretti up to November 6, we find Donizetti attending both to large matters of action in the libretto and (sometimes not altogether to the librettist's pleasure) to small details of diction, even of punctuation; in a letter of early September, for example, he said that he had recast four lines in one scene so that the buffo might have "verses that end in *a*." But he had to interrupt work on *Il Furioso* to compose another opera, this the one for the forthcoming season at the San Carlo.

Donizetti's friend Pietro Salatino of Palermo had supplied the libretto, a two-act "Spanish" *opera seria* text entitled *Sancia di Castiglia*. Working under forced steam (in mid-August he still did not have the text), Donizetti finished this score in time to institute rehearsals in October; the first performance took place on November 4, 1832. *La Rivista teatrale* on November 15 reported: "First appearance of *Sancia di Castiglia*, new music by G. Donizetti, singers [Giuseppina] Ronzi [de Begnis], [Luigi] Lablache, [Giovanni] Basadonna. Decided, fanatic success. Repeated plaudits. Summonings-out onto the stage of the Maestro and the virtuosos amid tumultuous acclamations." Writing to Ferretti on November 6, Donizetti said: "My *Sancia di Castiglia* was performed marvelously, and the applause was such as to bring out the singers and, in company with them, the Maestro, among shouts of joy! . . . How La Ronzi sang . . . how Lablache, and how Basadonna . . . oh, my happiness! Second performance today. Friday, the third—and goodbye or until I see you."

But now a new opera, even a hysterically approved new opera, could be no more than a passing incident in Donizetti's driven life. At once he had to compose a ceremonial hymn: King Francesco I of the Two Sicilies had died in 1830, and his son, the new King Ferdinando II, was to be married to Princess Maria Cristina of Sardinia and Piedmont at Voltri, near Genoa, on November 21. The required *Inno* duly was composed and sung, but Donizetti was not present to conduct or hear it. For on November 10, six days after the first performance of *Sancia di Castiglia,* he left Naples with Virginia, reaching Rome two days later and staying with the Vassellis.[16] With him he had brought the partially completed score of *Il Furioso all'isola di San Domingo,* the title role of which was being tailored to fit the baritone Giorgio Ronconi. Rehearsals at the Valle were to begin in December, and the first performance was scheduled for January 2, 1833.

The day after Donizetti reached Rome, Ferretti sent him the following note, on the outside of which was written "The writer of the enclosed bows to the composer of *Anna Bolena,* of *Fausta,* of *Il Furioso,* and of *Parisina*":

If you can, send back to me the recitative and aria for [Lorenzo] Salvi so that I can have them copied into the big book for the censorship. I am at work on [text to be sung by Elisa] Orlandi, and am about to finish, as I am up to the rondo and will send it to you tomorrow.

I am and will be
hot with verses and immortal sentiments,
the asthmatic Ferretti.

Replying, Donizetti employed rhyme:

"*Se asmatico è Ferretti*	(If Ferretti is asthmatic,
C'è pure Donizetti	Donizetti is also
In letto coricato	Confined to bed
Con un dolore al lato.	With a pain in the side.
Compagni ne' malori. . .	Companions in illness. . .
Amici ne' furori. . .	Friends in frenzies. . .
T'aspetto col rondò. . .	I await you with the rondo. . .
Or m'addormento un po'.	Now I'll sleep a little.
Ché il mal di testa torna,	The headache returns,
Per causa della corna!"	Because of the horn!)

To this, referring to the "dedication" on the outside of Ferretti's note, he added: "It is the composer of *Anna Bolena,* of *Sancia* and *L'Elisir,* who comes to honor you (that 'comes' isn't correct, as I'm in bed, but there it is, and let it remain there)."

While the rehearsals at the Teatro Valle were proceeding, Donizetti wrote a unique letter to his father on December 18, 1832:

I don't know which is worse for [a certain] one of my compatriots—if I write little or if I write a lot, if I am paid much or little—that he should

[16] Virginia's father, Luigi Vasselli, had died of an apoplectic stroke on January 2, 1832. At this time the Vassellis lived at No. 78 Via delle Muratte, on the second floor of the Palazzo Gavotti.

reach as far as Rome to break my balls . . . with anonymous letters giving me advice that is more insolent than anything else. How does he know whether I am paid little or enough? What difference does it make to him if I want to write twelve scores per year? Should I, for that reason, be called the "day laborer" among composers, the man who writes incorrectly, the man full of reminiscences, the man who composes without criteria and philosophy? . . . I don't know of anyone who doesn't use reminiscences, and if he wants to have the kindness to reveal himself, I'll take him for a short amble through the scores of someone whom he doesn't name [Bellini?] and make him, with his own hand, pick out, in whichever one of them he selects, not reminiscences, but whole pieces taken from I know where. He advises me to compose for the best theaters, and yet I move only from the San Carlo of Naples to La Scala at Milan, and next year to La Fenice at Venice. . . . The Valle at Rome certainly is not among the secondary ones, as Rossini composed all of his most beautiful operas there. What, then, does he want of me? He says that I should compose to better librettos. Let him give them to me; let him find a theatrical poet who is less of a rascal than Romani about keeping his word, and I'll offer him one hundred scudi for whoever will write a good book. He has a lovely speech in that key. I don't live at no expense in the homes of beautiful women who can present me with the poet and who belittle others in order to satisfy their protégé, as is happening now,[17] and which I have protested to Florence because of the libretto that I should have had in October, and which I still don't have today. As for the rest, then, not that I despise bits of advice from anyone, but when they are like these—which with good right I can call more insolence than anything else—I detest the writer and the counsellor as one; that anyone who loves my glory doesn't come to give opinions anonymously, but says 'I am so-and-so, etc.,' I am your friend, etc., and then I'll thank him exactly as much as I now despise and detest this zealot.

Reacting protectively to this sustained outburst of anger, one of the few of its sort in Donizetti's more than eight hundred surviving letters, the good Guido Zavadini said (*138, 46*): "Here the allusion to the composer of *Norma* is evident enough to anyone aware of the events of that time and of the extraconjugal relations[18] between the 'beautiful woman' and the composer alluded to. But it must be made clear, to vindicate the truth, that this is *the only time* in his writings that Donizetti makes so discourteous a reference to a colleague in art, whose name he has the extreme delicacy not to mention." This entirely misses the point.

[17] Bellini was living in the home of his mistress, Giuditta Turina. The poet he was being "given" was Romani; the opera in question was *Beatrice di Tenda*. Giuditta Turina's mother was related to the Appiani family—and Bellini also had composed *La Sonnambula* in the home of a beautiful woman: that remarkable friend of Donizetti and Verdi, the Countess Giuseppina Appiani, in whose home Donizetti himself was to compose *Linda di Chamounix* in 1841–42. Bellini was a guest in the Appiani home from November 1830 through all of 1831.

[18] Giuditta Turina was a married woman living with her husband.

While it is true that Donizetti nearly always showed himself to have a generous and equable disposition, devoid of envy and jealousy and protected by humor, Zavadini glides over the fact that Donizetti's anger had been aroused, not by Bellini's living without expense in Giuditta Turina's home, but by the anonymous letter writer. It is impossible, what is more, not to believe that Donizetti's reaction was furious precisely because the critic had charged him with at least some of the failings with which, in private, he had been charging himself.

Donizetti was indeed composing too much too rapidly; he was indeed often composing to inferior librettos. Nor could the obvious fact that, given the circumstances of the period and the pressures of his own life and personality, he could not alter his course take the sting out of being told the truth so flatly by an anonymous "outsider." Also, despite whatever very high value Donizetti placed on Bellini's operas, he could not have felt much sympathy for the personality of Bellini himself, who was vain, haughty, devouringly egocentric, and more than a little affected.

On January 2, 1833, *Il Furioso all'isola di San Domingo*, Donizetti's new three-act *opera semiseria*, was given its first singing at the Teatro Valle.[19] It scored an immediate success, was repeated for several weeks, and within a decade was to be staged in about one hundred Italian and foreign opera houses. It is one of the Donizetti operas that would repay revival most interestingly: it is "peculiar" among them all, not least in that its title role is that of a Spaniard who goes insane when he discovers that his Portuguese wife is unfaithful, flees to a West Indian island, and becomes a savage in the forest, living on plants and rejecting all human company. Ferretti's libretto certainly has structural faults—and Donizetti's score does not, on the page, look like a cumulating unity. But it seems equally certain that, with the right singers, a tremendous series of moving effects would be evoked by exactly those numbers which produced the greatest emotional effect in the 1830s and 1840s: the introductory duet *"Freme il mar lontan lontano,"* the first appearance of Kaidamà, the baritone aria *"Raggio d'amor parea,"* the cavatina for Eleonora—*"Ah lasciatemi, tiranni"*—the first-act Cardenio-Kaidamà duet —*"Di begli occhi i lampi ardenti"*—the second-act Cardenio-Eleonora duet—*"Apri il ciglio"*—and the chorus *"Oh sciagura!"*

The performance of *Anna Bolena* presented by the Modenese impresario Pietro Camuri at the Teatro Apollo on the very night of the

---

[19] *Anna Bolena* was being sung at another Roman theater, the Apollo, on that same night.

première of *Il Furioso all'isola di San Domingo* was a pirated version arranged by one Carlo Valentini. The cast included[20] only one singer— the tenor Giovanni Basadonna—who met with the audience's approval, and the *Rivista teatrale* said that in Valentini's version the score had been "vandalistically slashed, castrated, profaned, against the canons of the musical code of good manners," adding that what was offered was nothing "but a bloodstained corpse" and that "cadavers always arouse pity, but horrible pity." Donizetti could do nothing to prevent this maltreatment of his opera. But four days later he himself conducted at the Palazzo Lancellotti the first of four performances of *Anna Bolena* given under the aegis of the Filarmonici romani.[21] As these performances were presented during the run of *Il Furioso* at the Valle, Donizetti may well have felt that Rome was repaying his devotion with devotion.

But Donizetti's other commitments would not allow him to linger in Rome. His contract with the Teatro della Pergola summoned him first to Florence. He had no libretto as yet: Romani, writing too many texts for too many composers, was physically and mentally unable to supply this one at the promised time. It was to be called *Parisina*, and its central situations were borrowed from Byron's poem of the same name, which he, in turn, had based on an account by Gibbon of a fifteenth-century tragedy of incest. Donizetti had promised Lanari a completed opera by January 10, however, and so he doggedly went to Florence. From there on January 13, he wrote to his father: "Tell Maestro Mayr that Noè has written me . . . he asks me for a piece by which he can judge . . . . This is an embarrassment to me because if by chance the piece should be weak, I would be rejected, and then perhaps someone worse than me would be accepted. He wants a *Tantum ergo*, but I don't think that I have one. Enough: discuss it with [Antonio] Quarenghi, and then he can work out with Mayr what I can do." This referred to Mayr's efforts to procure for Donizetti the vacant position of *maestro di cappella* of the cathedral at Novara, efforts that were to prove unavailing. The position finally went to Saverio Mercadante, who later was to be appointed to another position that Donizetti coveted more— that of permanent director of the Naples Conservatory. To this period of anxious waiting at Florence belongs one of the very few anecdotes of Donizetti involved in a passing love affair which can be documented in any way. The Florentine impresario Giulio Piccini, who wrote

[20] See Appendixes, p. 325, for details of this performance.
[21] See Appendixes, pp. 325–26, for details of this production.

under the pen name of Jarro, reported (*70*, 133) that on August 1, 1833, Alessandro Lanari wrote a letter to Felice Romani in which he mentioned a contralto by the name of Giuseppina Merola, "who has a beautiful figure, is pretty and able, with whom Donizetti cuckolded me. . . ." On the basis of this reference, and perhaps with other information not now available, Alberto Cametti (*27*, 111) wrote: "During the enforced waiting, the composer did not waste time, but rather occupied himself with the contralto of the company, Giuseppina Merola, in a way that certainly would not have satisfied his distant wife." Nothing about this story is intrinsically unbelievable. But nothing about it is sufficiently circumstantial to justify the very positive statements about it that have been made with Jarro and Cametti as sources.[22]

The delay lengthened out to a point at which Donizetti and Lanari discussed the possibility of substituting for the unwritten new opera a mounting of *Fausta*, which had not yet been heard at Florence. But Lanari decided to gamble on Donizetti's famed ability to compose at very high speed, and so held out until the libretto finally arrived from Romani. By the end of February, the completed *Parisina*, an *opera seria* in three acts, was ready for rehearsals, which lasted two weeks. On March 17, at the Pergola, *Parisina* was performed for the first time. It was liked very well, but could be played only nine times because the season was ending. When Lanari complained to Donizetti that as a result of the short run, he had lost eleven thousand lire, Donizetti replied in a letter dated August 6, 1833, from Rome: "If then you have lost 11,000 in Florence, these are things to say to the poet [Romani] and not to Donizetti, who finished the opera for you in such a few days, who staged it, who even corrected the printing of the librettos. . . ."

For a long time, *Parisina* remained Donizetti's favorite among his operas. He doubtless would have been disturbed if he had known that when it was staged at the Teatro La Fenice in Venice for the second time, in March 1838, no less a person than Daniel Stern—that is, the Countess Marie d'Agoult—visiting Venice with her lover, Franz Liszt, did not like it. She wrote in her diary: "They gave Donizetti's *Parisina*, music as amusing as it is bad." The Countess greatly admired Caroline Unger in the title role, finding her "an admirable singer, pathetic, full

---

[22] Giuliano Donati-Pettèni, for example (*39*), made the incident into a veritable cautionary tale: "At Florence, he had formed close relationships with illustrious men: [Innocenzo] Giampietro, librarian of the Palatine [Library], [Giambattista] Niccolini, and [Gino] Capponi. Also he had a fleeting adventure there with the contralto of the company, Giuseppina Merula [*sic*]. The adventure certainly would not have satisfied his distant wife, who alone, furthermore, would have had the right to throw the evangelical stone."

of intelligence," who had succeeded in moving her listeners "in the stupidest of roles, with the most insipid music." Her opinion of *Parisina*, which well may have reflected Liszt's, was not shared by the over-whelming majority of operagoers among her contemporaries. Gilbert-Louis Duprez, who had sung in the opera's *première*, wrote of it in his *Souvenirs d'un chanteur*: "Composed especially for me, it united the grace and elegance of the light genre, in which I had performed at the beginning of my career, with the elevated qualities of *opera seria*, which produced such good results for me after eighteen months, and it seemed to be the act of union between the two genres."

Late in April or early in May, Donizetti was in Rome in discussion with Giovanni Paterni about an opera to be staged at the Teatro Valle in September. By the terms of the resulting contract, signed on June 6, Donizetti's fee was to be six hundred scudi romani, the opera was to deal with Torquato Tasso, and the libretto was to be by Ferretti. On May 27, in a letter to Mayr, Donizetti had said: "Have you divined what I am composing? *Tasso!* I have read Goethe, [Giovanni] Rosini, Goldoni, [Alexandre] Duval, [Pietro Antonio] Serassi, [Giovanni] Zuccala, and the latest things of [Melchiorre] Missirini, which he should have given to Italy by means of the suppressed anthology; and from so many men and so many things—to which I now add those of Signor [Giovanni] Colleoni[23]—I am forming a plan, and from that an opera. The company is weak, but I can make something out of Ronconi, who played the *Furioso* for me excellently. For many years I have wanted to do some-thing about so great a poet, and I have wanted a Rubini as the pro-tagonist, but, whether it's an effect of chance or I don't know what, all my tenors have showed me only the one-thousandth part of the friendliness of the foreigners. So I threw myself into the arms of an outsider, and Ronconi will be the Tasso." By "my tenors," Donizetti evidently meant tenors from Bergamo—Domenico Donzelli, for one,

[23] Earlier in this letter, Donizetti had asked Mayr to thank Colleoni some of whose "very beautiful poems" Mayr evidently had sent him. The other authors to whom Donizetti referred in connection with his reading about Tasso were—in addition to Goethe and Goldoni—Giovanni Rosini (1776-1855), a critic and historian of art, novelist, and poet; Alexandre Duval (1767-1842), an antiromanticist who was the playwright brother of the noted archaeologist Amaury Duval; Pietro Antonio Serassi (1721-91) of Bergamo, a student of Tasso and the author of somewhat confused writings about him; Giovanni Zuccala (1778-1836), a Venetian who taught at the University of Pavia and in 1818 published *Lettere sulla solitudine e la vita di Torquato Tasso*, derived largely from Serassi; and Melchiorre Missirini (1773-1849) of Forlì, a priest who lived mostly in Rome and Florence, who wrote numerous lives of illustrious men, and whose *Sulla prigionia di Torquato Tasso* was published posthumously at Pisa in 1883.

and Giovanni Battista Rubini, who had been born at Romano, near Bergamo, whereas Giorgio Ronconi, a baritone, was from Milan.

The advantages of being in Rome, with Ferretti at hand, soon showed in the swiftness with which Donizetti was able to obtain the libretto and start composing it. *Torquato Tasso*, in fact, begun by June 1, was complete by July 11, and at the end of the score, Donizetti put this dedication: "To Bergamo, Sorrento, and Rome—the city that conceived him [Tasso], the one in which he saw the light, and the one that has his body." Curiously, as Nando Bennati pointed out (*14*, 10), *Torquato Tasso*, following upon *Parisina* and preceding *Lucrezia Borgia*, was one of three operas produced by Donizetti in 1833 which had all or most of their action set in still another Italian city, Ferrara.

But Donizetti's thoughts had begun to veer away from his homeland and toward Paris, then looked upon as the world center of opera even by Italians (and not least because Rossini was there and because the Théâtre-Italien staged Italian operas in Italian with casts of the most accomplished singers available). On June 15, 1833, he had written to Giovanni Ricordi: "The success of *Parisina* has not had any influence in facilitating the way to Paris with the impresarios, who say 'Rossini being here, it is unnecessary for us to seek out others in order to put performances on the stage' (almost as if that colossus were jealous of the insects). My misfortune!" And in another letter (July 2) to Ricordi, referring to a visit to Rome by the co-directors of the Théâtre-Italien —Édouard Robert and Carlo Severini—he said: "M. Robert and Severini have been to see me, and on their return from Naples in ten days (they say) they want to arrange with me for an opera for Paris during the coming year—saying that this year they will do *Gianni di Calais* and perhaps also *Gianni di Parigi*.[24] As for *Parisina*, they don't mean to pay that much, and in fact it is too much, it is too much—this displeases me, and God knows how much; but they have reason on their side, and too much!" By this last, Donizetti meant that Alessandro Lanari, who owned the score of *Parisina*, was forcing Ricordi to demand an exorbitant price for it from the French impresarios, to Donizetti's despair.

Difficulties with Lanari kept simmering throughout July and August. These were chiefly over settling upon a date for the new opera for the Teatro della Pergola at Florence, the opera that was to turn out to be *Rosmonda d'Inghilterra*. Donizetti's letters to the impresario ran

[24] Donizetti's *Gianni di Calais* was presented at the Théâtre-Italien on January 3, 1834. *Gianni di Parigi*, however, was not to be heard anywhere until it was staged at La Scala, Milan, on September 10, 1839.

the gamut from determined common sense to rage to blasting irony, as when (August 6), in insisting that Lanari did not understand the meaning of "to agree," he listed from a dictionary all the synonyms for that verb and the noun "agreement." Detailing these imbroglios to Ricordi in a letter of August 13, Donizetti also wrote: "For Heaven's sake, Paris, Paris, Paris, and Romani the librettist." By that time, too, the complexities of the arrangements with Lanari had begun to be smoothed down. On August 15, still from Rome, Donizetti wrote him:

Ahead! I'll serve you very willingly either in this Carnival or during Lent or even during the spring, but I see that you cannot give me a firm answer as to when; and therefore I hope that you'll not find it unjust now that I too should look for an assignment elsewhere; I mean to say that if your firm arrangement reaches me in time, you will always be my good employer, but if not, we'll shift our contract to another season. I believe that you'll not find it irregular if I try to take an assignment for the Carnival. . . . I want to be with you, and it is very true that you mount the spectacles extremely well and that this is an attraction; but that is for your own honor and you do it for old operas as much as for the new ones; still, it's truly a seductive thing for me to have your excellent performance and the magnificence of your stagings.

Lanari had told him that a libretto had been ordered from Romani and evidently had sent him the roster of available singers. On August 22, Donizetti complained that the company seemed imperfect, especially as contrasted with that of the past Lent. He begged for Domenico Cosselli or—lacking him—Giuseppe Frezzolini "if you have him, and we'll make a *semiserio*." In fact, he was to have neither of them, but, instead, Fanny Tacchinardi-Persiani, Gilbert-Louis Duprez, and Carlo Porto, and *Rosmonda* was to be an *opera seria*. But now he had to forget the future for a time because, as he told Lanari in the letter of August 22, "This evening the rehearsals of *Torquato* [*Tasso*] began."

The first performance of *Torquato Tasso*, as had been foreseen in the contract, occurred at the Teatro Valle on September 9. Four days later, in a letter to Duprez, then with a touring company at Foligno, Donizetti reported: "My *Torquato* has been very happy, and each evening more so."[25] The Roman audiences liked the opera well enough so that it remained on view at the Valle for more than fifteen performances during three weeks.

In an article entitled "Tasso in the Theater," Parmenio Bettòli

[25] Quoted from one of five letters to Duprez which do not appear in *138*, but which were prepared for publication by Zavadini before his death and are included in *43a*. They were given to the Museo Donizettiano by Dr. René Duvernoy, a descendant of Duprez.

wrote: "The *bergamasco* Ferretti[26] took his inspiration from Goldoni's comedy to write the not very happy *libretto semiserio* [*sic*] of *Torquato Tasso*, which, set to music by Gaetano Donizetti, was staged for the first time in the autumn of 1833 at the Teatro Valle in Rome, where it did not please very well because of 'lack of spontaneity and unification.' In fact, if exception be made of some inspired pieces put in the mouth of the protagonist and the stupendous *concertato* that ends the second act, the opera as an entity is not very worthy of its very lofty subject or of Donizetti's genius." Short of an unlikely revival of *Torquato Tasso* with adequate singers, it is not now possible, even by studying the score, to argue with Bettòli's judgment of the opera as a work of musical art. To agree with his poor opinion of the libretto—which on September 7 Donizetti told his friend Innocenzo Giampieri (*43a*, 18) not to bother reading "*per pietà, per pietà*"—is not difficult. But that the canny penny-scrounging impresarios of the 1830s and 1840s would have continued staging an opera that "did not please very well"—or that such an opera would have been kept on over three weeks at the Teatro Valle—appears extremely unlikely. Bettòli would seem to have made the mistake of reading some, but not enough, of the contemporary reviews.

In the letter to Giampieri, Donizetti himself said of *Torquato Tasso*: "It could have been forty times better, but I, proud to sing (or make sing) he who sang of arms and loves, threw myself desperately on the prosaic libretto and, singing and re-singing, made an opera sing by means of singers who do not sing too much except for the protagonist (Ronconi)." As news of interest to Giampieri, he added: "The body of Raphael has been found. I saw it. Only bones among the earth, the head with the beautiful teeth intact. Everything is being exposed. I almost cried (what a ninny)."

After the third singing of *Torquato Tasso*, Donizetti went to Milan, where he was to supervise a production at La Scala of *Il Furioso all'isola di San Domingo*. The first performance occurred on October 1, evoking such tremendous enthusiasm that thirty-five more singings followed. Donizetti wrote Jacopo Ferretti on October 9 that at the fourth performance, nine hundred tickets had been sold in addition to the subscriptions. The new director-impresario of La Scala, Duke Carlo Visconti di Modrone,[27] thereupon signed (October 10) a contract with Donizetti by

---

[26] Ferretti, of course, was not *bergamasco* but Roman.

[27] The Visconti family, prominent in Milanese life since the thirteenth century, has been represented more recently on the stage of La Scala by Count Luchino Visconti, whose production (1957) of *Anna Bolena* was perhaps the finest Donizetti restoration of recent decades.

which the composer promised to provide the house with two new operas at the rate of six thousand five hundred Austrian lire per opera. The first of these was to be staged during the Carnival of 1833–34, the second in the autumn of 1834. The libretto of the first opera, *Lucrezia Borgia*, was to be written by Felice Romani and was to be delivered to Donizetti not later than October 25. The reason for this very short period of preparation was that Romani already had been working on this text in the belief that it would be composed by Saverio Mercadante.[28] He was deriving the outlines of the action from Victor Hugo's *Lucrèce Borgia* (at first entitled *Souper à Ferrare*), which had been staged in Paris at the Théâtre Porte Saint-Martin on February 3, 1833, with Mlle George in the title role, Frédérick Lemaître as Gennaro, and Juliette Drouet (who soon became Hugo's mistress) as the Princess Negroni. Hugo, in turn, had based his drama on an incident in Louis-Antoine-François de Marchangy's *Gaule poétique*.

Once again Romani delayed delivery of the promised text, this time with more reasonable excuse. Not only the protracted negotiations with Visconti, Mercadante, and Donizetti, but also numerous infuriating interpositions by the censors—alarmed by an opera that would present Borgias on the stage—delayed him. Only toward the end of November[29] did Donizetti begin to receive the text act by act. For that reason, he found himself lashed into composing each act in a few days. As soon as Henriette-Clémentine Méric-Lalande, who was to portray Lucrezia Borgia, had read her role through, she began to demand that a bravura number for her be added at the close of the opera, after the death of Lucrezia's son Gennaro. Romani joined Donizetti in opposing this preposterous suggestion, but it soon became a question of no cabaletta, no Méric-Lalande. Librettist and composer at last had to produce the added number. This cabaletta, beginning *"Era desso il figlio mio,"* appeared in all the early scores of *Lucrezia Borgia*, as Donizetti himself remarked in 1841 in a letter to Antonio Vasselli. Nonetheless, he continued to disapprove of it, finding it ridiculous that a mother should launch into such a display of vocal agility in the presence of her son's body. When the opera was to be revived at Rome in 1841, he expressed

[28] For the story of the negotiations over this libretto among Visconti, Romani, Mercadante, and Donizetti, see Appendixes, pp. 294–96.

[29] On November 29, 1833, Donizetti's thirty-sixth birthday, the Marchese Brancaccio, administrative majordomo to Prince Leopoldo of Salerno, wrote to tell him that he had been appointed "Honorary *Maestro di Cappella*" to the Prince's household. Earlier in this year (March 2), Donizetti also had been named Honorary *Maestro di Cappella* to the Royal College of Music Professors of Florence.

the wish that if the cabaletta had to be sung, it be placed elsewhere in the action.

Lucrezia Borgia opened the Carnival season at La Scala on December 26, 1833, the first of thirty-three consecutive performances. In that first audience was Giovanni Ricordi's twenty-two-year-old son Tito, who, inheriting his father's business in 1853, was to build it into the largest music-publishing firm in Italy and, as Verdi's publisher, was to make very large sums of money for both the composer and G. Ricordi & C. before his retirement in 1887.[30] Although critical reaction to *Lucrezia Borgia* was by no means unanimously favorable, this opera played a determining role in the establishment of Donizetti's position in foreign countries. Since its *première* in 1833, it never has left the active repertoire entirely.

When *Lucrezia Borgia* was staged at Venice for the first time—at the Teatro La Fenice in the autumn of 1838—Napoleon's widow, the ex-Empress Marie-Louise, attended a performance. In a letter dated October 4, she wrote: "Last evening I heard at the Fenice the prologue and first act of *Lucrezia Borgia*, which in my opinion is Donizetti's *chef d'oeuvre.*" This opera, too, won over Eugène Delacroix, who usually had found nothing to admire in Donizetti or his operas. Writing in his journal on November 26, 1853, Delacroix said:

Last evening, *Lucrezia Borgia.* I was entertained from one end to the other, even more than the other day at [Rossini's] *Cenerentola.* The music, the actors, the scenery, the costumes—all that interested me. On that evening I made amends to the unhappy Donizetti, now dead, and to whom I render justice—in that, alas, imitating the generality of mortals, and even the first among them. All of them are unfair toward contemporary talent. I was enthralled by the chorus of cloaked men in the charming setting of the garden stairs under the moon. There are reminiscences of Meyerbeer amid that Italian elegance,[31] and they mate very well with the rest. Especially delighted with the next aria, sung by Mario in his delicious manner; another injustice made up for—today I find him charming. This is like the way one suddenly falls in love, years later, with a person one has been used to seeing every day and to whom one has thought oneself indifferent. Here we have the good school of Rossini; among the best things that Donizetti has bor-

[30] Tito Ricordi (1811–88) was, in turn, succeeded by his son, Giulio (1840–1912), who bought out the important competing house of Francesco Lucca and became to Giacomo Puccini much what his father had been to Verdi. Giulio Ricordi was succeeded by his son Tito (1865–1933), after whose death the management of the firm no longer was headed by a Ricordi.

[31] Here Delacroix either was referring to the pomp of this particular staging of *Lucrezia Borgia* or had forgotten that the opera itself dated from 1833, when Meyerbeer had composed, of his big French operas, only *Robert le Diable*—*Les Huguenots* not having been staged until 1836.

rowed from him are those introductions which bring the listener's spirit to the state desired by the musician. Like Bellini, he also owes to Rossini those mysterious choruses of the sort I have mentioned, nor does he spoil them (I think back upon the chorus of priests in *Semiramide*, etc.).

The libretto of *Lucrezia Borgia* acquired a strange history. When the opera was staged in Paris for the first time, at the Théâtre-Italien on October 27, 1840, the accompanying translation of the Romani text into French was by Étienne Monnier. Hugo objected strenuously to the publication of this translation (not, as is stated so often, to the performance of the opera itself in the Italian original), but Monnier paid no heed. The score, as published together with the Monnier translation by Bernard Latte, was played at Metz. Hugo then sued for plagiarism. Both Monnier and Latte were found guilty as charged. Then it became necessary, if Donizetti's score was to go on being played in France, to disguise the source and change the plot and title of the original libretto. The scene was transplanted from Venice and Ferrara to Granada, and the resulting patchwork was staged at the Théâtre de Versailles on March 31, 1842, as *Nizza di Grenade*, and at the Théâtre-Italien, Paris, on January 16, 1845, as *La Rinnegata*. Hugo's anathema would appear to have extended to Italy, where *Lucrezia Borgia* became *Eustorgia da Romano* in the opera houses of Tuscany and the Grand Duchy of Modena, *Alfonso, duca di Ferrara* in Trieste, *Giovanna I di Napoli* in Ferrara, and *Elisa da Fosco* at Rome.

Writing of Verdi's life in Milan at the time of the first performance of *Lucrezia Borgia*, Franco Abbiati said (*1*, 1, 124-25): "In what form Peppino satisfied his longing for life it is difficult to conjecture. Certainly, one escape, like a valve for everything churning in his breast, was the evenings he spent at La Scala, which seemed to him platters of epicurean fruits: Donizetti's *Fausta*, [Spontini's] *Fernand Cortez*, and Luigi Ricci's *Il Nuovo Figaro*, [Carlo] Coccia's *Caterina di Guisa*, Ricci's *I Due Sergenti*, Donizetti's *Il Furioso all'isola di San Domingo*. And again Donizetti, the evening of Santo Stefano of the direction-indicating 1833, unloosed upon him the fantasy of Romanticism, with the Victor Hugoesque *Lucrezia Borgia*, for which the composer had asked the librettist Romani for particularly strong scenes that would arouse 'emotions to make one shudder.'" And certainly the shift in the texture of Italian opera from the classical Romanticism of Rossini's *opere serie* and all of Bellini to the controlled blood-and-thunder of Verdi nowhere is prefigured better than in the strongest scenes of *Anna Bolena* and *Lucrezia Borgia*: in them Donizetti has moved a long distance away from the sort of dawntide Romanticism—so well represented in literature by Manzoni's *I Promessi Sposi* and in opera by *La Sonnambula* and *Lucia di Lammermoor*—with which his name so long has been connected.

Donizetti left Milan on December 29, 1833. He went first to Turin, where his *Fausta* was being staged: in a P.S. to a letter that he wrote from Genoa on January 17, 1834, to Duke Carlo Visconti, he reported that it had been a "fortunate success." His purpose in visiting Genoa was to spend some time with his nephew, Andrea, the son of his brother Giuseppe. The boy, who was fifteen years old at this time, had been sent from Constantinople to the Real Collegio at Genoa to begin the long course of studies leading toward a career at law. This appears to have been the first meeting between Donizetti and this boy, who, twelve years later, was to become the chief companion of his last long illness. During this stay in Genoa, which lasted at least until January 17, the Turin impresario Giuseppe Consul sent him (January 14) an offer to compose an *opera buffa* for the Teatro Carignano, the opera to be completed not later than October 15, 1834, and an *opera seria* for the Teatro Regio for the Carnival of 1834-35. Nothing whatever was to come of all this.

While in Milan, Donizetti had suggested to Visconti a change in the seating arrangement of the orchestra in La Scala. His letter of January 17 from Genoa to Visconti, referred to above, both alludes to this question interestingly and throws a light on Donizetti's attitude toward performances of his operas—even at La Scala—by rosters of singers not fully adapted to them:

I hear from friends who have been writing me that you are a little disturbed about the new disposition of the orchestra in the R. Teatro della [*sic*] Scala . . . in all the leading theaters it is disposed in this way and this way of dividing (a little more, a little less) the instruments is not without its reason; if a true advantage did not result, we would then have wished to go back to the first plan. The principal quartet of the orchestra being brought together at the center, it can at will lead the rest of the instruments, and the composer who finds himself in its midst, and next to the first violin, has (whenever he wishes) the advantage of giving the principal, both with his voice and with his gestures, the indication of the tempos that he wishes, a very advantageous thing by present taste.

In any case, the inspiration for the happy change was yours, and if you have enough philosophy to laugh at those who talk, as well as enough conviction of the advantage, leave the orchestra this way, and in the final analysis the followers of antediluvian manners will realize that our age too has its understanding of improvement for the fine arts.

De hoc satis.

They write me furthermore that it is desired to give my *Parisina.* For Heaven's sake no, Signor Duca. I don't at all see the company as adapted, and now Your Excellency would do nothing but place in a bad light before the public poor Donizetti, who, what is more, must write for them during the coming Carnival. If, however, Your Excellency wishes to give this opera, wait until next year, when I'll be there and the company will, at that time, be better adapted. For you it will be extremely easy to replace it with something better, and thus to save me the pain of having to say to the newspapers what Pacini has had to say about [his] *Ivanhoé.*

Today I leave for Florence, and there I hope to have the consoling news that I have been able to dissuade you from giving an opera not suitable to the company.

In fact, the proposed performance of *Parisina* never took place, and that opera was heard at La Scala for the first time during the Carnival season of 1838–39.

In Florence, Donizetti completed, to a two-act *opera seria* text by Romani, the opera *Rosmonda d'Inghilterra,* which during the preceding summer had caused him to carry on the protracted, painful exchange of letters with Alessandro Lanari, then impresario of the Teatro della Pergola. During that period, too, Romani had sent him a few verses for the text. On the back of that letter, Donizetti had addressed Romani as follows (capitalization and division into lines his):

> Remove Arturo altogether.
> Magnify Rosmonda and give her
> Cavatina not interrupted by anyone.
> Finish the opera with the tenor's aria.
> Make into a duet the trio of Act
> I among Ros., Clifford, and Arturo.
> Do not slight Ros. in the finale,
> or at least in the *stretta.*
> The introduction shorter, if that is
> possible.
> And everything that it pleases the friend
> Romani to make or to remove.
>
> DONIZETTI.

Given at the Pergola on the first night of the 1834 Lenten season, February 27, this Romani-Donizetti opera about the Fair Rosamond[32]—

---

[32] Rosamond Clifford, very probably the mistress of Henry II of England, died about 1176. What seems to have been the first opera libretto to deal with the legend about her was written by Joseph Addison and set by Thomas Clayton as *Rosamond* (Drury Lane Theatre, London, March 15, 1707). The music was attacked as execrable, and the opera failed, attaining only three performances, thus ending Clayton's efforts to establish opera in England as a going concern.

Rosmonda d'Inghilterra—pleased the Florentine audience without at all stirring up the sort of enthusiasm that had followed *Lucrezia Borgia* at La Scala some months earlier.

His duties carried out, Donizetti bade farewell to Florence and his friends there and continued on to Rome. There he picked up Virginia, and they went to Naples. On April 12, he signed a contract with Prince Torrella, promising to compose a new opera for the Teatro San Carlo for a fee of twelve hundred piastres (about six thousand lire). And on April 24, writing to Mayr, he announced that the Prince of Salerno had named him *maestro di camera* for the purpose of teaching singing to his daughter[33] and that he had accepted an invitation from Rossini to go to Paris and—at last—compose an opera for the Théâtre-Italien. Actually, he would not reach Paris for the first time until January 1835. That same letter to Mayr also stated that King Ferdinando II wanted to appoint him to a professorship in the Royal College of Music, "and when I placed before him [the fact] that I am now under various contracts elsewhere, he replied to that: 'It is altogether just that I should give you leaves'—and what is to be answered to that?" He explained that Rossini's very flattering letter of invitation to compose an opera for Paris led him to hope that his opera for La Scala (*Gemma di Vergy*, La Scala, December 26, 1834) could be the first of the coming Carnival season so that he could "fly" to Paris. Giuseppina Ronzi de Begnis, for whom the title role of that opera was being designed, already had requested that the opera be staged to open the season, but Donizetti asked Mayr not to mention any of these details lest the Scala management get its back up and relegate him to the second position. "I'll be writing here in August," he commented, meaning that he would be composing an opera then for the San Carlo. But this opera, *Maria Stuarda*, was not to be produced until October 18—and then, under peculiar circumstances, as *Buondelmonte*.

Numerous writers on Donizetti have stated that his appointment to a professorship at the Neapolitan Conservatorio di San Pietro a Maiella (then under the direction of Nicola Antonio Zingarelli, who had occupied this position since 1813) followed upon the extraordinary first success of *Lucia di Lammermoor* in 1835. But as the remark to Mayr quoted above shows—and as is proved by the autograph letter,

---

Addison's text was used again by Thomas Augustine Arne, whose *Rosamond* (Lincoln's Inn Fields Theatre, London, March 18, 1733) was much more successful, being played throughout the British Isles for about twenty-five years.

[33] Princess Maria Carolina Augusta, in honor of whose birth in 1822 Donizetti had composed a cantata. See p. 30.

dated June 28, 1834, in which Nicola Santangeli of the Ministerio e Regio Segretario di Stato degli Affari Interni at Naples informs Donizetti officially of this appointment—he became a professor there before *Lucia di Lammermoor* even had been considered. Santangeli's letter specifies that King Ferdinando II has deigned to appoint Donizetti as professor of counterpoint and composition at a monthly salary of four hundred ducati.[34] The autograph of the contract that Donizetti had signed shortly before (May 9, 1834) with the Théâtre-Italien, Paris, also survives in the Posony Manuscript Archive, Vienna. By its terms, Édouard Robert, director of the company, placed at Donizetti's disposition the singers Giulia Grisi, Giovanni Battista Rubini, Nicholas Ivanoff, Antonio Tamburini, Luigi Lablache, and Santini. He was to compose a two-act opera for eight thousand francs, to which four thousand more were to be added for Austrian and Italian performance rights.

Meanwhile, Donizetti worried about carrying out his contract to provide the San Carlo with an opera. Giuseppe Bardari (not, as stated in many places, Leone Emmanuele Bardare) was preparing for him a three-act *opera seria* libretto under the title *Maria Stuarda*. On June 7, Donizetti had not composed a measure of it; on July 18, he was writing to his father that the opera would be staged about the middle of the next month; on September 6, he wrote his friend Andrea Monteleone in Palermo that it would go on the following Saturday. As matters evolved, however, rehearsals continued into late September, when Donizetti suffered one of his attacks of "bilious fever" (*43a, 26*). Thereafter the new opera ran into strange difficulties, not receiving its *première* until October 18—and then under another title. In the interim, as Donizetti informed his father in the letter cited above, *Parisina* and *Anna Bolena* had been sung at the San Carlo and he had taken up his new position at the Conservatory, only to learn that he was expected to serve there without pay during the first six months. On the first night of *Parisina* at the San Carlo, the performance had been interrupted by efforts to locate the composer and induce him to come to the theater to accept the audience's enthusiastic acclaim. When he finally was found elsewhere in the city, he was taken to the San Carlo, led to a box, and given a prolonged ovation.

To Innocenzo Giampieri on September 30 (*43a, 26*) Donizetti reported in the liveliest terms what had happened to *Maria Stuarda:*

[34] Donizetti's predecessor in this post had been Pietro Raimondi, who had left Naples that year to become director of the Teatro Carolino at Palermo, where Donizetti had been the unhappy musical director in 1825-26.

I wrote *la Stuarda,* it was prepared, and we gave the dress rehearsal with (excuse me) fanatical success. What happened? It was prohibited! How? Why? The Queen [Maria Cristina] does not like such sad subjects.[35] Order: the music already having been judged good, it was to be rearranged in small details by the Society, or by me at the Society's orders, and given as *Giovanna Grey.* Worse. Her Majesty does not wish it, there shall be no more deaths on the stage. We'll sell it to Milan, then. . . . First, I said, the Duke [Visconti di Modrone] will believe that the opera has been prohibited not because of the subject, but for a musical reason. . . . Finally, thought, excogitation . . . and a third attempt. We'll adapt it to *Bondelmonte.*[36] Do it in eight or ten days on the same situations, changing nothing but the metrical recitative. Who? Eh, cobblers aren't lacking. Behold, in fact, the cobbling accomplished . . . *ho res magna, oh l'horreur.* It is done! Between the fifteenth and the twentieth of this October, this triform birth will see the light, and God knows how. If I had not done it myself, others would have done it after my departure.

Having adapted the music of *Maria Stuarda* to a *Bondelmonte* by his Sicilian friend Pietro Salatino, Donizetti saw it into rehearsal on October 7. It received its first hearing at the San Carlo on October 18.[37]

As Donizetti's letters of this period to Giovanni Ricordi show, until May 1834 he was able to hope that he should obtain from Romani the librettos for the San Carlo opera, the opera for the Théâtre-Italien, and that for the next Carnival season at La Scala. But Romani, though for the Paris libretto he had been offered one thousand francs, had "remained deaf." That was why Donizetti had had to turn to the inferior Giuseppe Bardari for the *Maria Stuarda* text, as later he was to turn to a Greco-Italian hack named Giovanni Emmanuele Bidera for the text of the Paris and Milan operas. Not being able to collaborate with Romani delayed him considerably. On October 7, he wrote to Ferretti that *Marino Faliero* [often called *Marin Faliero*], the three-act

[35] During the confession duet in Act III (*"Delle mie colpe lo squallido fantasma"*), Her Majesty had been so overcome by the emotions it generated that she fainted. This reaction undoubtedly strikes modern operagoers as hysterically exaggerated. But which of them has experienced a like scene from the highly special point of view of a reigning queen?

[36] Buondelmonte, a Florentine, had promised to marry a daughter of the Amidei. When he broke this promise, he touched off the first Florentine episodes of the Guelph-Ghibelline struggles. He was assassinated in 1215, and is mentioned by Dante (*Paradiso,* XVI). Another libretto dealing with him, the work of Salvatore Cammarano, was to be composed by Giovanni Pacini and presented at the Teatro della Pergola, Florence, on June 18, 1845. Both Donizetti's opera and Pacini's are referred to in Italian books as both *Bondelmonte* and *Buondelmonte.*

[37] For the text of the revelatory contract between Donizetti and La Scala for the production of *Maria Stuarda* seen there first on December 30, 1835, see Appendixes, p. 297.

opera seria to a text by Bidera, derived from one of the less classicizing tragedies of Casimir Delavigne (1793–1843),[38] was almost finished. As for the Milan opera, Donizetti wrote Visconti one week later that he still had some hope of enlisting Romani, for which reason he was not planning to start work before October 21. If nothing had arrived from Romani by then, he would put Bidera to work on that libretto too. Nothing came from Romani, and so Bidera tumbled out a two-act *opera seria* libretto entitled *Gemma di Vergy*, basing it on *Charles VII chez ses grands vassaux*, a drama by Alexandre Dumas *père* (1831).

On November 9, 1834, Donizetti signed with Prince Ottajano and Cavaliere Antonio Santorelli, representing the Royal Theaters of Naples, a contract by which he was to provide the Neapolitan opera houses with three more operas, the first of them to be staged in July 1835, the date to be selected by the management. Article vii of this agreement, which must have seemed welcome assurance (however illusory) to Donizetti, specified that the authorities must hand him the approved libretto, already passed by the censors, at least four months before a given production. The first opera that he would compose under this contract, as it turned out, was not heard until September 26, 1835. It was *Lucia di Lammermoor*.

In mid-November, with *Gemma di Vergy* on the way to completion, Donizetti sent Virginia to the Vassellis in Rome and himself embarked for Genoa to meet his brother Giuseppe, who was en route there from Constantinople to pick up his son Andrea. With them Donizetti went on to Milan and thence to Bergamo, where he spent at least November 21 and 22 with his family. Then, as though running a race with time itself, he rushed back to Milan and the rehearsals of *Gemma di Vergy*, which opened the Carnival season of 1834–35 at La Scala on December 26 and ran for twenty-six performances. Giuseppe Verdi, who just had returned to Milan from Busseto, was present at this *première*. Abbiati wrote (*1*, i, 182) that he was not "exactly disappointed. But inside himself he felt that from the Dumas story . . . he would have been able to carve out something different. How, where,

---

[38] Not, as often stated, directly from Byron's *Marino Faliero*. Delavigne's tragedy—about the fourteenth-century Doge of Venice who plotted to restore absolutism and was put to death on the grand staircase of the Doges' Palace—had been presented for the first time at the Théâtre Porte Saint-Martin, Paris, on May 30, 1820, with its leading female role acted by Marie Dorval. More than fourteen years later, when a benefit program for the unfortunate Dorval was presented at the Opéra-Comique (October 22, 1843)—attracting a box office of six thousand eight hundred and eighty-one francs, the largest of that year—one special attraction of the event was Act iv of Donizetti's *La Favorite*.

he himself did not know precisely. But that internally he dreamed of having to—and of being able to—attempt what Donizetti had not entirely achieved is certain." The production of his own first opera still was almost five years off.

What Verdi must have approved of without qualification, if he learned of it, was the patriotic demonstration that occurred nearly fourteen years later during a performance of *Gemma di Vergy* at the Teatro Carolino, Palermo. What happened then was described by Harold Acton thus (*3*, 189):

When the "faithful slave" sang the moving aria:
> *Mi togliesti e core e mente*
> *Patria, Numi, e libertà*
> (You took away my heart and soul,
> Country, gods, and liberty)

the whole audience rose automatically, waving handkerchiefs and shouting: "Long live the Pope, the King, and the Italian League!" Again, when the prima donna Parodi appeared on the stage with a tri-colored flag to sing "It is already the first dawn of the new year," a shower of leaflets fluttered over the pit and there were frantic cries of *Viva l'Italia!* "Though universally and eagerly joined in by all classes from the highest to the lowest, they both quickly terminated without the slightest violation of order," wrote Lord Mount-Edgcumbe* who was present—"unless indeed the act of pelting with cushions one in authority at the theatre till he joined in the cry (having locked him up in his box), may be so termed; which it hardly can be, as immediately on his doing so, the greatest good humour was restored. A more violent spirit was undoubtedly displayed the following day at the theatre, and a paper was signed by many, demanding a national guard."

To return to 1834, no surviving documents can be used to date Donizetti's departure from Milan on his first journey outside Italy and Sicily. However, the predominantly trustworthy Cametti said (*27*, 150): "Assured of the fate of *Gemma*, the indefatigable composer left Milan on the last day of the year, and by way of Genoa and Marseille started for the so-much-desired goal, Paris." During the first days of 1835, Donizetti reached Louis-Philippe's capital—which he, like most other musicians, then regarded, and with justice, as also the capital of music.

---

* *Acton's footnote:* Extracts from a Journal kept during the commencement of the Revolution at Palermo in the year 1848. London, 1850.

CHAPTER V

1835-1837

"*Donizetti wrote quickly; to such an extent that, when I saw him write for the first time, I did not think he was writing music. He had a knack of covering the staff with dots like a telegraph strip, and when he had done so he added the tails and lines.*"
—Louis Engel, in *From Mozart to Mario: Reminiscences of Half a Century* (49)

O N January 24, 1835, at the Théâtre-Italien in Paris, Donizetti heard the starry cast of Giulia Grisi, Giovanni Battista Rubini, Antonio Tamburini, and Luigi Lablache in the first performance of Bellini's last opera, *I Puritani di Scozia*.[1] Early in February, he wrote to Romani: "I arrived here late, but better late than never. Bellini's success has been very great despite a mediocre libretto;[2] it keeps up constantly, for we already are at the fifth performance, and it will be this way until the end of the season. I tell you about it because I know that you [and he] have made peace. Today I begin my own rehearsals, and I hope to be able to give the first performance by the

[1] Bellini, neglected and almost deserted, died the following September 23 at Puteaux, outside Paris, under circumstances that never have been satisfactorily explained. He was not yet thirty-four.

[2] By Count Carlo Pepoli, Bellini having had a sharp disagreement with Romani, who had supplied him with the librettos of *Il Pirata, La Straniera, Zaira, I Capuletti ed i Montecchi, La Sonnambula, Norma,* and *Beatrice di Tenda.*

end of the month. I don't at all deserve the success of *I Puritani*, but I don't at all desire to displease."

Still not entirely satisfied with *Marin Faliero*, Donizetti persuaded Agostino Ruffini, the youngest surviving son of a family notable for its passing revolutionary activities and even more for its variety of talent, to make alterations in the libretto. On January 25, Ruffini wrote to his mother: "Donizetti has begged me to make some changes in a libretto of an opera to be played here, *Marino Faliero;* among others, a cavatina for Rubini. Afterwards, he begged me, too, to write a sort of scene that he wants to dedicate to Tamburini, and I have written it." Somewhat later, Donizetti discussed with Ruffini the possibility of a libretto based on Goethe's *Faust,* but nothing came of it; in 1838, Donizetti's friend Michele Accursi handed him another libretto, this one for an *opera buffa,* which Agostino Ruffini had derived from a comedy by his brother Giovanni, but nothing came of that either. But Giovanni Ruffini eventually was to prepare the libretto of *Don Pasquale,* again through the intervention of Michele Accursi.

The dress rehearsal of *Marin Faliero* was held on March 4, and the *première* took place on March 12, not quite seven weeks after that of *I Puritani.* The performance was applauded loudly and long by a glittering audience made up of French as well as Italian and other foreign Parisians, and including Adolphe Adam, Théophile Gautier, Jules Janin, and Giacomo Meyerbeer. Several numbers had to be repeated, and special enthusiasm was displayed for the duel scene and the gondolier's barcarolle.

Donizetti, writing to his Bergamo friend Antonio Dolci four days later, said: "I wanted to put you to expense only for the article from *Le Messager,*[3] but I think that I'll also send you two words about the second and third evenings, which were extremely brilliant; Rubini has sung as I've never heard him sing, and for that reason had to repeat the cavatina and the aria on both the second and third evenings. The success of Bellini with his *I Puritani* has made me tremble more than a little, but as we are different in character, therefore we both have obtained good success without displeasing the public."

The reactions of Bellini, who had attended rehearsals and performances of *Marin Faliero,* and who had come to believe and say that friendship between rival composers was impossible, were distorted and malicious. Writing to his uncle, Vincenzo Ferlito, the day after

[3] The addressee of a letter then was required to pay for the cost of its transportation and delivery.

the first performance, he said: "Donizetti's new opera staged last night, *Marino Faliero*, has had a semifiasco; perhaps the newspapers will not be unfavorable to him, but the public has been left discontented; and the proof will be the imminent [re-]appearance of *Puritani*." Obsessed by the idea that Donizetti, as Rossini's protégé, was being pushed to the detriment of other composers' operas, Bellini returned to the attack on April 1, writing Ferlito an extraordinary letter (it runs in excess of 3,750 words) of obsessive nature. In it he again and again denounced Donizetti, *Marin Faliero*, and Donizetti's *Ugo, conte di Parigi*, which in 1832 had followed *Norma* at La Scala by only a little more than two months.

"In fact," Bellini wrote to his uncle, "on hearing the announcement that Donizetti had been signed up, I had a fever for three days, understanding that a real conspiracy had been worked up; and, in fact, someone I know told me not to have much hope of success in Paris, that the success would be Donizetti's because he was brought here by Rossini." Stabbing at Donizetti over and over in terms that seem unbalanced, he referred to *Marin Faliero* as "the worst of all those operas which Donizetti thus far has composed, which number forty-eight"[4] and later adding: "The effect of *Marin Faliero* was mediocre. . . . At the second performance it seemed worse; at the third, everyone judged . . . that it was a real funeral . . . he left on the 25th [of March], I think, for Naples, convinced of his fiasco. . . . But what an opera it is which he has written! It is an incredible thing—he, who in *Anna Bolena* showed talent! This one for Paris lacks all novelty, is extremely common and vulgarly orchestrated—without concerted numbers: in a word, worthy of a young student."

Bellini's career as a composer was over when he wrote that astonishing summation of his competitive jealousy of Donizetti, and he already had begun to decline into the curious inertia that was to persist until his death five months later. His icy dislike of his leading competitor had led him to grasp some facts and then surround them with wish-fulfilling fancies, to exaggerate some of the flaws in *Marin Faliero* (many of them shared by *I Puritani*), to magnify out of proportion the extent to which *I Puritani* undoubtedly was more of an achievement and more popular than *Marin Faliero*—and to inflate those truths and partial truths into monsters puffed beyond recognition to coddle his own uncontrolled self-esteem. As his admiring but even-handed biographer

---

[4] In reality, counting three juvenile operas as having preceded *Enrico di Borgogna*, Donizetti had composed fifty operas in nineteen years. Bellini, who had composed ten operas in ten years, intended "which number forty-eight" to be especially damning.

Francesco Pastura wrote (*91*, 463): "For him it was not a matter of the unlimited success of his *Puritani*, but of that definitive success which, proclaiming him the victor in a contest between him and Donizetti, placed him 'in the position that was his due, that is, first after Rossini.' 'I say it that way,' he adds, 'because Rossini had made everyone believe that Donizetti was more talented than Bellini; but now Italy, Germany, and France accord me the position that I have acquired with so much assiduous preparation, and which I always shall know how to enlarge.' "

Comparisons and contrasts among Rossini, Bellini, and Donizetti always are interesting, and can be used as valuable tools of insight and criticism. It is clear, for example, that Donizetti to the end of his active life remained what Rossini had been until after the composition of *Semiramide* in 1822–23—an artisan whose métier was the provision of operas as fast as he could compose them and impresarios would stage them—whereas Bellini, almost from the beginning, had been something very different, a precursor of the Romantic composers of opera to whom each new work was to be a very carefully elaborated unique creative effort. But trying to decide which of the three composers was "greater" than the other two is bootless: Bellini would have been as incapable of the abounding wit of *Il Barbiere di Siviglia* or *Don Pasquale*, the massiveness of *Guillaume Tell*, or the Verdian passion of *Anna Bolena* as Rossini would have been of composing *Norma* or Donizetti *La Sonnambula*. But there can be no doubt that Rossini was the most versatile and roundly human of the three men, as Donizetti was the most kindly and humane.

During that brief first run of *Marin Faliero*—which seems to have been sung only five times, whereas *I Puritani* filled the Italien for either seventeen or eighteen performances and officially closed the season on March 31, 1835—Donizetti was summoned to the Tuileries for an audience with King Louis-Philippe and Queen Marie-Amélie. The King shook his hand and informed him that he was to be named a chevalier of the Legion of Honor. The Queen (a sister of the late King Francesco I of the Two Sicilies) joined her husband in honoring Donizetti, sending him a magnificent gold ring with his initials picked out in diamonds.[5]

---

[5] The decree officially nominating Donizetti a chevalier of the Royal Order of the Legion of Honor was not issued until February 2, 1836. The ring given him by Marie-Amélie was seen in Bergamo, in the hands of a jeweler who had purchased it from Donizetti's heirs, by Dr. Federico Alborghetti and Dr. Michelangelo Galli. On February 24, 1839, Donizetti also was named an Honorary Member of the Accademia filarmonica di Civitavecchia.

Donizetti seems to have left Paris for Naples by March 20 or 21,[6] not, as Bellini thought, on March 25. He was in Leghorn on April 10, for on that day he wrote from there to Innocenzo Giampieri, Keeper of the Royal Palatine Library at Florence: "I think that you will have read about the reception of *Marino*, discords and concords, in the musical papers, but . . . it was happy, even very happy; Paris is a great city in which artists are everywhere honored, respected, and well received. I saw *La Juive* at the Opéra[7]—and I say 'saw' because, as for popular music, it has none. The illusion is carried to the ultimate. You would swear that everything is real. Real silver and almost real cardinals. The king's weapons real, the armed men's costumes, doublets, lances, etc.— real; and those which were false—the doublets of the supernumeraries— were copied from real ones and cost fifteen hundred francs each! Too much reality—the final scene too horrifying, the more horrifying because of so much illusion. At Constance! A Jewess and her father thrown into a cauldron of boiling oil because she has had relations with a Christian!" Adding that he is en route to Naples, where his leave had expired at the end of February, and that he does not know what the King will say, Donizetti says: "I shall stop first at Rome for the half [Virginia, whom he had not seen since November] and then go right on."

The Donizettis were back in Naples by April 23, having been gone more than five months. They soon moved from their apartment at No. 6 Vico Nardones to No. 65 Via Corsèa, which Donizetti described to his Sicilian friend, Count Luigi Spadaro del Bosch, in a letter of October 19, 1836, as "third [i.e., fourth] floor, above the Inn of the Black Eagle, the entrance near the neighborhood police commisariat." He took up once more his duties as musical director of the Royal Theaters and as professor at the Conservatory. Writing to Giovanni Ricordi on April 23, he had enclosed messages for the soprano Luigia Boccabadati-Gazzuoli, asking her to leave immediately for Naples, to sing at the San Carlo and at the Fondo for a salary of six hundred ducati per month. He also promised Ricordi to compose a *sinfonia* for the mounting of *Maria Stuarda* scheduled for La Scala during the forthcoming season as a starring vehicle for Malibran. And,

---

[6] Donizetti therefore was not in Paris on July 28, 1835, when Fieschi's attempt to assassinate King Louis-Philippe resulted in the temporary closing of all theaters and other places of public meeting.

[7] The *première* of this most successful of Halévy's operas had taken place at the Opéra on February 23, 1835, with a cast headed by Julie Dorus-Gras, Cornélie Falcon, Adolphe Nourrit, and Nicholas Levasseur.

as so often, he sourly complained of the absence of good librettists. He was now considering the new opera for the San Carlo, for on May 18 he wrote Spadaro del Bosch that the subject of its libretto would be taken from Scott's *The Bride of Lammermoor*.[8] One week after that, and again on May 29, he addressed to the Society of the Royal Theaters urgent requests for approval of this subject, saying that if he received that approval at once, he thought to be able to promise completion of *Lucia di Lammermoor*—here so referred to—by August.

Donizetti's new librettist was Salvatore Cammarano,[9] a Neapolitan who had studied with Gabriele Rossetti and then had produced stage dramas before turning, in 1834, to the manufacture of librettos. He set to work on that for *Lucia di Lammermoor* as soon as the censors' approval of the story had been granted, turning the text over piecemeal to Donizetti, who composed and orchestrated the opera in less than six weeks, as the date of July 6 on the manuscript score shows. Writing to Gaetano Cobianchi ten days later, Donizetti said: "Our theaters go from bad to worse . . . the operas fail, the public hisses, the attendance is poor. . . . Now at the San Carlo we will have Persiani's old opera *Danao*, then my *Lucia di Lammermoor*, which now is finished. . . . The crisis is near, the public has indigestion, the Società teatrale is about to be dissolved, Vesuvius is smoking, and the eruption is near."

The entity running the Royal Theaters of Naples was indeed in difficulties because of too many recent failures. By the end of July, in fact, the Teatro San Carlo was bankrupt. King Ferdinando II intervened, retaining only some of the directors, and they under firm instructions to put their famous house in order. Because of the ensuing delays, rehearsals of *Lucia di Lammermoor* could not commence until mid-August. The head copyist of the Royal Theaters dated on August

---

[8] Both Salvatore Cammarano, the librettist, and Donizetti himself must have been aware (and not have cared) that *Le Nozze di Lammermoor*, an opera by Michele Carafa, had been sung at Paris in 1829—a failure, even though the role of Lucia had been entrusted to Henriette Sontag. They probably were unaware, however, that at Copenhagen on May 5, 1832, there had been staged a four-act "*romantisk Syngestykke*" entitled *Bruden fra Lammermoor*, its libretto an adaptation of Scott's novel by Hans Christian Andersen, its score by the Danish composer Ivar Frederik Bredal.

[9] Cammarano (1801–52) was to supply Donizetti with the librettos of *Lucia di Lammermoor*, *Belisario*, *L'Assedio di Calais*, *Pia de' Tolomei*, *Roberto Devereux*, *Maria di Rudenz*, *Poliuto*, and *Maria di Rohan*. He also wrote those of Giuseppe Persiani's *Inez di Castro*; Saverio Mercadante's *Elena da Feltre*, *La Vestale*, *Gli Orazi ed i Curiazi*, and *Virginia*; Giovanni Pacini's *Saffo*, *La Fidanzata corsa*, and *Bondelmonte*; Federico Ricci's *Luigi Rolla e Michelangelo*; and Verdi's *Alzira*, *La Battaglia di Legnano*, *Luisa Miller*, and *Il Trovatore*, this last libretto completed after his death by Leone Emmanuele Bardare.

20 a receipt stating that he had been handed the original score of the opera so that he could copy out the parts. Of this period at the end of August and beginning of September, 1835, Ciro Caversazzi wrote (*31*) that while creating *Lucia* "the Maestro . . . was attacked by a blinding pain in his head—by reliable testimony '*Tu che a Dio spiegasti l'ali*' was composed in that agony—which recurred in October, after the triumph. [A letter that Donizetti wrote to Giovanni Ricordi on October 17 (three weeks after the *première* of *Lucia*) begins: "From my bed, with the fiercest headache!"] Doubtless the hidden illness— weariness of the tissues having opened the way into the fortress of the mind—had assailed the cortex."

The rehearsals of *Lucia di Lammermoor* continued on through the first two weeks of September. The troubles of the Royal Neapolitan Theaters were not over. On September 5, Donizetti said in a letter to Giovanni Ricordi: "Here the Society is going to go bankrupt. La Persiani, not paid, doesn't want to rehearse, and tomorrow I'll protest." But the ways were smoothed, and on September 16 Donizetti wrote Jacopo Ferretti that the first performance would take place on the 28th. But what Guido Zavadini aptly called "its dazzling and triumphant baptism" actually occurred two days before that—at the Teatro San Carlo on September 26, 1835.

Lucia di Lammermoor very quickly became one of the most universally popular operas of the nineteenth century. It has retained some of that widespread affection to this day. Donizetti himself, writing to Ricordi three days after the *première*, was in a rare state of excited exaltation: "*Lucia di Lammermoor* went on, and allow me in a friendly way, to my shame, to tell you the truth. It pleased, and it pleased very much, if I am to believe in the applause and the compliments I received. I was called out many times, the singers even more often. His Majesty's brother Leopoldo, who was there, and who applauded, paid me the most flattering compliments; the second evening, I saw something extremely unusual for Naples, which was that in the finale, after great *vivas* in the adagio, Duprez was applauded vigorously in the malediction before the *stretta*. Every piece was listened to in religious silence and honored with spontaneous *vivas*. . . . La [Fanny] Tacchinardi [-Persiani], [Gilbert-Louis] Duprez, [Domenico] Cosselli, and [Carlo] Porto were very good, and the first two, especially, were prodigious."

The history of *Lucia di Lammermoor* could be made the far-ranging subject of a study in the morphology of taste. Its title role has

been impersonated by almost every soprano since 1835 who has supposed herself (or has been supposed by others) to have sufficient
agility and enough dependable very high tones; the role of Edgardo
has been favored by most of the non-Wagnerian tenors—for in how
many operas does the tenor hero have the final scene almost entirely
to himself, and without the intervention of the heroine? The opera's
second-act sextet,[10] "*Chi mi frena in tal momento*," achieved an almost
unique universal familiarity—both as composed by Donizetti and as
transcribed for solo piano and other instruments and instrumental
groupings by many composers.[11] The "Mad Scene" became the chosen
proving ground and applause-gatherer for an apparently unending succession of prima donnas.

With Rossini operatically inactive and Bellini dead, *Lucia di Lammermoor* went far toward establishing Donizetti as the most eagerly
sought-for of living Italian composers of opera—and therefore of all
Italian composers—for the rest of his active life. At the time of Donizetti's death in 1848, Verdi had not yet composed *Rigoletto, Il Trovatore, La Traviata, Simon Boccanegra, Un Ballo in maschera, La Forza del
destino, Don Carlos, Aïda, Otello*, or *Falstaff*. He had, it is true, composed twelve operas, but none of them—not *Nabucco* or *Ernani* or even
Macbeth—had raised him to a pinnacle of international renown and
success such as then was occupied, among Italian musicians, solely by
the man who had composed *Anna Bolena, L'Elisir d'amore, Lucrezia
Borgia, Lucia di Lammermoor, La Fille du régiment, La Favorite,
Linda di Chamounix*, and *Don Pasquale*.

The position occupied by *Lucia di Lammermoor* in the middle
decades of the nineteenth century is pointedly suggested by the fact
that it occupies a position of emotional crisis in two very different great
novels—*Madame Bovary* (1857) and *Anna Karenina* (1875–77). In
Flaubert's story, the scene is the opera house at Rouen. Emma Bovary
is there with Léon, and in the scene of the lovers' farewell she feels in
the music—not only of Lucia but also of Edgardo—the very revelation
of her own love, now being reborn. "The entire stretta was repeated,
the lovers talked of the flowers on their tombs, of an oath, of exile, of

[10] Many early accounts refer to this ensemble as a "quintet," perhaps thus
disposing of poor Alisa, who more often than not remains inaudible among her
five colleagues.

[11] Most enduringly popular of the *Lucia* transcriptions has been the piano
fantasia by Franz Liszt, but as a fixture of mid-nineteenth-century piano recitals,
Liszt's note-filled piece was rivaled by the *Grande Fantaisie* of Henri Herz. The
so-called "King of the Quadrille," Philippe Musard, also composed a greatly
admired *Lucia* piano quadrille.

fatality, of hopes, and when they bade their final adieu, Emma emitted a sharp cry that became mixed with the vibrations of the final chords." In *Anna Karenina*, Donizetti's opera appears more than once—when Anna, defying society, is looking for Vronsky and attends the opera to hear Adelina Patti—and the music of *Lucia* becomes part of the fabric of her sensibility and emotions—and when Levine, talking to a friend of Anna's, asks: "Were you at the Opera yesterday?" The friend replies that he was, and Levine says: "*Lucia* was splendid." The opera, then, had become a symbol of ill-starred love, of human relationships interfered with and destroyed by practical, social considerations.

Even the bitter and generally anti-Donizettian Berlioz put into his *Mémoires* this footnote to a remark that Italian music always is laughing: "A definite part of Bellini's music, and that of his successors, must, however, be excepted. Their style, on the contrary, is essentially dolorous, and the tone is either groaning or howling. These composers go back to the ridiculous style every once in a while so that the tradition of it may not become wholly lost. Nor should I be so unfair as to include among these false-sentimental works many sections of Donizetti's *Lucia di Lammermoor*. The second-act finale and the scene of Edgardo's death have an admirable pathos about them."

On September 23, 1835, during the frantic final preparations for the *première* of *Lucia* at Naples, Bellini had died alone in what amounted to friendly sequestration at Puteaux, outside Paris.[12] The date of Bellini's

[12] In May 1835, Bellini had gone to stay with his English friends, Mr. and Mrs. Samuel Levys, at their villa in Puteaux. On June 4, he wrote to his *fidus Achates*, Francesco Florimo, that he was bedridden with the diarrhea that he suffered from so often during the summer. On September 13, alarmed by reports of Bellini's continuing illness, Saverio Mercadante and Baron Augusto Aymé d'Aquino—the latter a nephew or grandson (*nipote*) of Michele Carafa—went to investigate for themselves the situation at Puteaux. They were refused admission, as D'Aquino alone had been the preceding day, though he was a functionary of the Paris embassy of the Kingdom of the Two Sicilies. On September 14, by agreement among Bellini's friends, Michele Carafa went to Puteaux and, by passing himself off as a physician, got past the keeper of the gate. D'Aquino's diary records that Carafa found Bellini in bed, but fails to state what his condition was. A doctor named Montallegri was taking care of him—but his host and hostess otherwise had left him alone in the villa, themselves staying in Paris. This seems to suggest that they feared he had contracted cholera, and certainly, as Francesco Pastura wrote (*91*, 522): "There can be no doubt that the manifestations of Bellini's illness had all the appearance of those which precede the onset of cholera: as a consequence, it must have seemed to the doctor necessary to communicate—with all the required secrecy—his suspicions to the Levys and to keep the sick man under observation in the most complete isolation, imposing absolute silence." On September 22, D'Aquino noted in his diary: "During these days, no one having been able to see Bellini, the discontent of his friends broke out this evening, at [Luigi] Lablache's. There was even talk of having the King's Procurator intervene." The next day, Dr. Montallegri sent a message to Édouard

death establishes the impossibility of a once widely believed story that after the first performance of *Lucia*, someone said to Donizetti: "This is a libretto that would have known how to inspire the poetic vein of poor Bellini," to which Donizetti was represented as replying: "Have I honored the memory of my poor friend? I invoked his beautiful spirit, and he inspired me for *Lucia*." Certainly untrue in detail, this hoary anecdote may well be a distortion of an actual conversation that occurred at a later date. Donizetti seems to have been unaware of the vindictive feelings that he and his operas had inspired in Bellini, and he was not a man to have refused to honor Bellini the composer if he had known of them. Indeed, he was to go to great lengths to participate in the honoring of Bellini's memory.

On July 25, 1835, the impresario Natale Fabrici (or Fabbrici) had offered Donizetti a contract to compose an opera for the Teatro La Fenice at Venice for the next Carnival season, suggesting a fee of seven thousand francs. Donizetti persuaded Fabrici to raise the proffered remuneration to eight thousand francs and then signed the contract, promising to reach Venice by January 1, 1836, with the completed score of an opera to a Cammarano text entitled *Belisario*. Although the excitement and weariness over the production of *Lucia di Lammermoor* had sent him to bed for several days with "nervous fever," he appears to have begun composing the Cammarano libretto by October. On the eighth of that month he wrote Fabrici: "I am very docile, and I'll write *Belisario* so as to please you. I recommend that the costumes of those times not be used in the preceding spectacles, and that for your good and mine. [Caroline] Ungher, [Antonietta]

Robert and Carlo Severini of the Théâtre-Italien, saying that Bellini's end was near: "A convulsion has rendered him unconscious, and he may not live until tomorrow." And in fact Bellini died at five o'clock that afternoon. D'Aquino's diary records that he arrived at the villa at 5:10, found the gate unbarred, and entered the deserted villa. He found Bellini dead on the bed. The gardener soon returned, telling him that Bellini had died at five o'clock and that, as Mr. and Mrs. Levys were in Paris, he had had to go out to inform people and get some tapers."

Gossip soon had it that Bellini had been poisoned, perhaps by Mrs. Levys, who was pictured—with what justice it cannot now be determined—as his jealous mistress. An autopsy was performed, and the report stated that Bellini had "succumbed to an acute inflammation of the rectum, complicated by an abscess of the liver." Many medical studies have been made of the symptoms and the autopsy, and it is at least possible that Bellini had cancer. Certainly Mrs. Levys did not poison him, but both she and her husband behaved irresponsibly in leaving him alone with a gardener and to be visited occasionally by a physician who seems to have been particularly inept. The autopsy stresses that the position of the liver abscess made it likely that it would sooner or later have caused Bellini's death in any case. But he could have had what he never received, the benefit of consulting physicians—and he need not have died absolutely alone.

Vial, [Celestino] Salvatori, and the tenor (whom I hope to know about soon) will be the principals. But it needs an excellent second bass, two other secondary parts, and a *seconda donna*. The rest is in the hands of Destiny."

On October 20, Donizetti wrote Giovanni Ricordi that he was planning to stop over in Milan on his way to Venice and mentioned his desire to "give the last proof of my friendship for the shade of poor Bellini, with whom I found myself composing four times,[13] and each time our relationship became that much closer. It was I myself who showed the Filarmonica why we should do something to attest to our common grief. The departure of an instigator left the thing in suspense. Now I should conduct a Mass at the Conservatory, and I have begun it, but the fact that the performance will occur in December will prevent me from conducting it, and that grieves me. Everything I was getting ready was canceled out by Destiny, which has set me for Milan—and, happy enough to do this, I am waiting for some good verses from the very distinguished [Andrea] Maffei, who will have a double cause for tears, the death of a friend and the combining of his verses with my music. I have lots to do, but an attestation of friendship for my Bellini precedes everything.[14]

On October 29, Donizetti wrote to his Bergamo friend Antonio Dolci: "In all confidence, my brother Francesco constantly torments me about two things; the first and most grievous is that *papà* is at the point of death and that he [Francesco] has to be up every night; the other thing is that he absolutely must have money, and on that he presses me terribly. If it is true that *papà* needs something, then he must have it; give him everything that *mamma* may ask for; but if it isn't true, write me so that I can be at ease. . . . I am composing [*Belisario*] for Venice, and I have no head for such sad news. Write me the truth." Donizetti almost certainly had good reasons for suspecting his brother's veracity—but the news of their father's condition was accurate.

---

[13] Donizetti and Bellini had composed operas for the same season at the same opera house on four occasions: at the Teatro Carlo Felice, Genoa, in 1828 (the revised *Bianca e Fernando* and *Alina, regina di Golconda*); at the Teatro Carcano, Milan, 1830-31 (*La Sonnambula* and *Anna Bolena*); at La Scala, Milan, in 1831-32 (*Norma* and *Ugo, conte di Parigi*); and at the Théâtre-Italien, Paris, in 1835 (*I Puritani* and *Marin Faliero*).

[14] The compositions here alluded to are a *Messa da Requiem* for soloists, four-voice chorus, and orchestra "composed expressly for the funeral of V. Bellini and dedicated to his memory," and a *Lamento per la morte di V. Bellini*. This latter, a setting of Maffei's verses beginning "*Venne sull'ale ai zeffiri*," is dedicated to Maria Malibran. Donizetti also composed a *Sinfonia per orchestra sopra motivi di V. Bellini* (1836).

On October 30, Donizetti wrote to ask the Minister of the Interior for permission to remain away from Naples during the coming December and January. He traveled north by sea,[15] reaching Genoa on November 30. He left there on December 2 and was in Milan the next day. His *Maria Stuarda*, with the new *sinfonia* that he had composed for this mounting, was to be the second opera of the Carnival season at La Scala. Visconti now invited him to provide an additional number, and Donizetti agreed, signing a contract that also obligated him to supervise the staging and conduct the rehearsals. This unforeseen development prevented him from carrying out his intention of visiting Bergamo.

On December 9, Donizetti's seventy-year-old father, Andrea, died of a tubercular ailment. A friend named Mariani evidently sent this news to Milan, for on an undetermined date Donizetti wrote from there to Dolci: "I have received a letter from Mariani. It tells me something that I cannot believe. . . . I turn to you so that you, so that Mayr, so that all, will carry out for me my duties as a son. Spend one hundred ducati, two hundred, but the ceremony shows the gratitude of only one son, seeing that one of us cannot because of distance, the other because it is impossible for him. I shall write you soon. Think of *mamma* so that she may have everything that she needs." The brother prevented from acting in time upon news of his father's death and funeral was, of course, Giuseppe, who was in Constantinople; the brother in no financial position to help was Francesco.

In another letter to Dolci, dated at Venice on January 13, 1836, Donizetti said: "I am wearying you, but for pity's sake, have patience. Here we start all over again. In November, Giuseppe sent two hundred francs. Before I left *mamma*, she said that she did not need anything, but now Francesco writes that he will have to sell the little presents that Giuseppe and I sent poor *papà* from time to time. How can that be? Either *mamma* needs something or she doesn't. It is impossible that two hundred francs, besides the rest, should have been used up. But if that is the case, go to *mamma* and ask her if it is true that she needs something, and then do me the usual favor of making a small loan. But Francesco must not take offense; tell him that I answered by writing to

---

[15] Donizetti apparently was somewhat nervous over reports of the spreading cholera epidemic, to which he referred several times. On October 24, for example, he had written to Natale Fabrici: "Here there is talk of many cases of cholera happening in Venice. Is that true?" And on October 29, in a letter to Spadaro del Bosch signed "Virginia and Gaetano": "I'll be leaving at the end of November if the cholera that has broken out in Venice too permits it."

you instead of to him. Recommend him to [Antonio] Bassi, I beg you, in my name, so that he may be favorable and *mamma* won't have the discomfort of finding herself driven out.[16] Answer me, put me at ease, and tell me if you received from Ricordi the one hundred bavare that I left for you."

Guido Zavadini (*138, 62*) commented thus on the death of Donizetti's father: "This sad loss, alas, opens the series of those misfortunes which soon, and repeatedly, were to seize, as we shall see, the bereaved Maestro, and which so embittered him as to alter his character profoundly and perhaps even to compromise his health." Donizetti no doubt grieved over his father's death, though in this regard Annibale Gabrielli—who was a grandson of Donizetti's brother-in-law Antonio Vasselli—made this interesting comment: "These letters—it cannot be denied—give one the impression of a sorrow that stays on the surface and does not penetrate *in imo corde*. Students of the psychopathy of Donizetti's genius can draw their own conclusions. To us it seems enough to ask if the minor intensity of his filial sorrow cannot be explained by the intellectual chasm that separated Sor Andrea from Gaetano."

Donizetti, in any case, soon was to have much more intimate causes for sorrow. But that these saddening deprivations causally led to the decay of his mental and physical powers seems, on the face of it, an oversentimental, romanticizing view. A much more believable explanation of his decay—overt symptoms of which still lay years in the future—is the strong probability that must be kept in mind if the events of Donizetti's life from this juncture onward are to be understood: it is that he was suffering from unchecked—and almost certainly undiagnosed—venereal infection. Only that hypothesis satisfactorily explains the nature of his final collapse and fatal illness (or, for that matter, the findings of the physicians who performed an autopsy on his body two days after his death).

The presence of that infection might also explain the fact that Virginia Donizetti gave birth to one deformed son and later suffered two other disastrous pregnancies, as well as the fact that she herself was to die—"of measles," it was said, or "of German measles," or "of scarlatina," or of taking an ill-timed bath—immediately after her third labor. Donizetti never indicated in any surviving document that he

[16] What Donizetti intended was that Antonio Bassi should assist Francesco in succeeding Andrea Donizetti as *portiere* of the Monte de' Pegni, especially so that Domenica Donizetti, who was then seventy, would not be required to vacate the living quarters that were perquisites of that job.

was aware of having contracted syphilis. He advanced no cause more cogent than work and weather and geography for the headaches and "fevers" that were to plague him. But strong inferential evidence, added to the reports written out by the physicians who examined him after the onset of the final stages of his illness—reports with all the stigmata of paresis—point so strongly toward his having suffered from syphilis for many years that very small room for doubt can be found.

Maria Stuarda, sung for the first time under its original title, was heard at La Scala on December 30, 1835. Maria Malibran, assigned its title role, had been vexed violently by the actions of the censors who had made cuts in the opera which she felt damaging to her role. Also, she had been very ill. She went onto the stage of La Scala to sing only because she could not face losing her fee of three thousand francs. Possibly her debilitated condition contributed to the indifferent reception accorded to the opera. Whether her irritation and physical weakness were important contributing causes or not, *Maria Stuarda* was not well received by the Milanese, and after a few performances was forbidden altogether, the year 1835 thus ending sadly and in disappointment for Donizetti.

Under date of January 27, 1847, Eugène Delacroix described in his *Journal* a meeting with Manuel Patricio García (1805–1906), a brother of Malibran and Pauline Viardot-García. The two men apparently discussed the relative merits of Malibran and Giuditta Pasta, the latter of whom Delacroix considered the greater singing actress. In the course of his report of this discussion, Delacroix wrote: "Mme Malibran, in *Maria Stuarda*, was brought before her rival, Elizabeth, by Leicester, who implored her to humiliate herself before her rival. She finally consented to do so and, falling to her knees, gave way to the most profound supplication. But, outraged by Elizabeth's inflexible hardness, she would rise up impetuously and fly into a rage that, he said, produced the greatest effect. She ripped her handkerchief, and even her gloves, to tatters. That, again, is one of those effects to which a great artist never will descend; they are of the sort that delights people in the loges and wins an ephemeral reputation for those willing to indulge themselves that way. . . . People whose minds do not rise very high, and who are not at all demanding in matters of taste—that is to say, unfortunately, the majority—always will prefer [to Pasta] talents of the sort possessed by La Malibran."

Writing to Dolci from Milan on January 4, 1836, Donizetti reported that he would leave for Venice by diligence that night. He asked

his friend to extend his efforts to help Francesco Donizetti to succeed
their father as *portiere* of the Monte de' Pegni. Also, cholera having
broken out at several places in Italy, Donizetti lectured Dolci on
methods for avoiding it. He reached Venice on January 7. To his
patent relief, he wrote Dolci on January 10: "Here there is not a
shadow of cholera, and they say that for your people too it has disappeared, and I have hope in God." He was less pleased with Antonietta
Vial, the soprano who was to sing the role of Antonina in *Belisario*.
He wrote Giovanni Ricordi on January 14 that a performance of
Rossini's *L'Assedio di Corinto* which he had heard had not pleased
the audience "or rather that La Vial did not please at all, at all,"
and called her "a bastard soprano, or contralto in disguise." The rehearsals at the Fenice of *Belisario*, the three-act *opera seria* that he had
composed to a text by Cammarano (who had derived it from Jean-
François Marmontel's *Bélisaire*),[17] began on January 17, and the opera
was sung for the first time on February 4, the night of a notably
violent wind-and-rain storm, when it initiated a run of eighteen performances. A letter that Donizetti wrote the next day to Giovanni
Ricordi and one that he sent Innocenzo Giampieri from Leghorn on
February 18 make clear that *Belisario* had been received with great
enthusiasm. But he did not overrate it. Writing to the Paris music
publisher Antonio Pacini more than two months later—the letter is
dated from Naples, "Today 19 April [1836] (it is raining)"—Donizetti
spoke first about *Lucia di Lammermoor*. Then he continued: "*Belisario*
is less thoroughly worked out, but I know that it makes its effect in the
theater, and a people is not deluded without some reason. . . . Yet I
myself place it below *Lucia* as a work." What he lacked was not the
poise and intelligence required for self-criticism, but only the time
for it and any overtopping need for perfection.

A particularly interesting revival of *Belisario* was that staged at
La Scala, Milan, on February 22, 1842, when the leading female role,
Antonina, was sung by Giuseppina Strepponi. Fifteen days later, in that
same theater, Strepponi was to sing in the *première* of *Nabucodonosor*,
the third opera of her future husband, Giuseppe Verdi. Eleven years
later, writing from Paris to Antonio Somma, the librettist of *Un Ballo
in maschera*, Verdi discussed the necessity of a librettist's adapting his

[17] Referring to Cammarano's libretto for *Belisario*, Théophile Gautier wrote
that in general a libretto is "the least important thing in the world, even in the
eyes of the poet, who writes it with no care other than to make well-scanned,
very rhythmic, very laconic verses, a sort of merit totally unknown to French
writers of texts."

lines to the composer's needs and vice versa. He said (November 19, 1853): "However, it will never be because of the demands of an artist, but rather because of some need of the art itself. Do you remember the aria 'Trema Bisanzio' from *Belisario?* Donizetti had no scruples about attaching 'sterminatrice' to 'Bisanzio,' thus producing a horrible misconstruction; but the musical rhythm absolutely demanded it. It would have been impossible to work out a motive to follow the direction of those verses. Then, wasn't it better to beg the poet to adjust that strophe?"

After the fourth singing of *Belisario* at the Fenice on February 8, Donizetti left Venice in a diligence so uncomfortable that he complained bitterly about it. He did not reach Milan until February 15, but that this delay was not caused by a stop en route at Bergamo is proved by the fact that he did not learn until March 4, in Rome, that his seventy-year-old mother, Domenica, had died at Bergamo on February 10. He embarked at Genoa, suffered during a storm en route to Leghorn—and there learned that Virginia had labored and brought forth a stillborn girl late in January and had herself been very weak and unwell since the premature delivery. Ahead of him, too, he still had the necessity of waiting out the days of quarantine imposed because of the spreading cholera. The understandably dark state of mind into which these successive blows, coming on top of his travel-weariness, had cast Donizetti is reflected in a letter that he wrote to Dolci from Rome on March 5:

Is everything over, then? If I did not have a constitution so strong that I myself am stupefied by it, I would be ready to join the others, and forever. Only three months absent, and in three months having lost father, mother, and a little girl, in addition to which my wife still is unwell because of the miscarriage at seven and a half months. I had a little strength left to give to the success of *Belisario,* to the Legion of Honor received, but having learned just yesterday of the loss of my mother too, I am in a state of such discouragement that only time will be able to get me out of it, if in any case I shall have enough to be able to live. I have seen Francesco's letter, sent me from Naples (because I am here in quarantine and leave the day after tomorrow). From it, I learned that you have thought of everything and for the second time I am ready to pay you, and I beg you to send me the accounting as quickly as possible. It will be for me to write to Giuseppe. . . . My friend, it will be very hard for me to revisit those places in which I have lost everything, but I hope to see you at Naples, and I tell you now and for always, remember that there you have a house, a bed, a fire, and a table. I find no way to thank you, and I beg you to give my greetings to our good Mayr.

Donizetti reached Naples on March 7 or 8, wondering how he would be received there, his leave having expired more than a month before. He found the cholera-threatened city in a state of suspended life, its usually thronging streets and narrow ways largely deserted. Also, as he wrote to Giovanni Ricordi on March 30, all the Neapolitan theaters were closed, "and yet nobody offers to take one away . . . therefore desolation . . . misery." To a man who seems never to have taken a true vacation after he became adult, idleness was unbearable. Donizetti at once entered into hopeful negotiations with Alessandro Lanari and Giovanni Rossi, hoping to receive a commission for another opera to be put on at La Fenice. At first these were fruitless, though Lanari finally agreed to what Donizetti considered reasonable payment—spelled out in his letter of May 21 as "ten thousand francs, paid in the necessary number of napoleone d'oro of twenty francs or their equivalent value"—for a two-act *opera seria* to be staged at the Fenice early the next year. This contract, for what was to be *Pia de' Tolomei*, finally was consummated on May 31. Also, the Conservatory had not been shut down because of the threatening cholera epidemic, and Donizetti's teaching there was a welcome occupation for part of his time. He also composed a string quartet in E minor—the first movement of which he later would orchestrate as the allegro section of the *sinfonia* for *Linda di Chamounix*—and an album of solo songs and duets which was published as *Notti d'estate a Posilippo* (1836), and later, in French translation, as *Nuits d'été à Pausilippe* (1840). The album became widely popular among amateur singers and recitalists.

The epidemic cholera, which had showed its face at Ancona in August, and which had caused the government of the Two Sicilies to take most elaborate precautions to prevent its entering the kingdom, erupted at Naples on October 2. It raged there through the late autumn, subsided somewhat during the winter—and by March 7, 1837, was said to have caused about 6,200 deaths in Naples and its environs. Bursting forth again on April 13, 1837, it then spread to Sicily, where it was accompanied by serious political disturbances. The official figures showed that about one tenth of the inhabitants of Sicily (or 65,256 people) had died of the disease by September 1837; the figure for Naples and its vicinity by then was 13,798. The disease raged terribly in Rome, as is shown by Antonio Vasselli's letters to Donizetti. On August 22, 1837, Donizetti received from him a letter in which he said: "The evil spreads and has been introduced into the monasteries and prisons. Two friends of mine died though in good circumstances and of regular habits. Thursday, 252 dead." In a letter dated August 26, Vasselli said: "The number of daily victims is larger than that at Naples if one takes into account the population and the tremendous numbers of people who have gone away. The Sanitary Bulletin for yesterday: 186 dead, but at least twice that many died." On August 29: "The infection is increasing. The Sanitary Bulletin for the 26th gave 184 dead, that of the 27th 186, that of the 28th 194, but many who are not reported are not included." On September 2: "You say that coffins are seen in Naples in the main street, but we have two cholera hospitals in the Corso, San Giacomo and Gesù Maria, and for that reason there is a flux and reflux of cadavers and sick people in the Corso enough to make one shudder at the stink."

Vasselli constantly referred to the deaths of prominent people and of his own and Donizetti's acquaintances and friends. And on August 31, he wrote: "The Sanitary Bulletin, which is not to be trusted, gives the figure of those attacked from July 28 to August 29 as 4,002, the dead at the number of 2,140." The disease also had been felt in southern France. Early in 1835, for example, Vincenzo Bellini, believing that delays in his receipt of letters from Italy were being caused by fumigation of all international mail, had remarked in a letter that the cholera "was wreaking havoc at Toulon."

This was also a time of political violence, and in March 1837, addlepated malcontents tried to set fire to the Teatro San Carlo. Perhaps in reaction against the otherwise constant dullness of life in the deathly city, perhaps springing back from the blackness of his own many recent sorrows—even perhaps, as a time-honored story has had it, to go to the assistance of unoccupied operatic performers or an impresario in straits—Donizetti wrote the libretto for a *farsa*, basing it on a vaudeville that he had seen in Paris: *La Sonnette de nuit*, by Léon-Lévy Brunswick, Mathieu-Barthélemy Troin, and Victor Lhérie. Then he swiftly set the little text, entitling the one-act opera *Il Campanello*.[18] When the Neapolitan theaters reopened, it was staged, June 6, 1836, at the Teatro Nuovo. It proved so welcome to the Neapolitans, who were much in need of light entertainment as distraction from disease, death, sorrow, and political strife, that Donizetti soon set another libretto of his own authorship. This one was derived from Scribe's *Le Chalet*, which he had heard as the libretto of Adolphe Adam's opera of that name, first sung at the Opéra-Comique, Paris, in 1834. Donizetti called it a one-act *opera giocosa* and brought it out as

[18] Sometimes billed as *Il Campanello di notte* or *Il Campanello dello speziale*.

Betly ossia La Capanna svizzera at the Teatro Nuovo on August 24, 1836, finding public reaction to it so encouraging that he prepared a two-act version of it which was staged at Palermo the next autumn.

In better spirits, Donizetti wrote on August 6 to Dolci:

That I am terribly slow in replying is something as old as the Testament; that you complain is something as wholly fair as Divine justice! That [you should say that] I now behave like a chevalier is a thing as unfair as ingratitude. Whether chevalier or teacher or member of various academies, I am always Donizetti, as I was in times when I counted for little. Not that I count for so much now, but I do live without lacking anything, and I am happy. I am about to buy the third floor of a house, which will cost me fifteen thousand francs, and then I'll be perfectly settled. . . . As for the cholera, you astonish me. Here the papers constantly announce improvement, and you on the other hand write me that it is raging. Poor teachers! Remember, if you ever get frightened and flee, come to Naples, where a room, food, a laundress, a box at the theater, walks, and some turns in a carriage await you. One flies by ship. A quarantine of eight days passes swiftly. And when the cholera reaches here too, we'll go out into the country or die together. . . . In a few days I go on with another opera at the Teatro Nuovo [*Betly*], poetry and music mine, as with *Il Campanello*, which turned out so well. In November, I'll go on at the San Carlo with the grand opera *L'Assedio di Calais*. And in Venice, *Pia* [*de' Tolomei*].

Early in September, he reported to Dolci that the Court had come to the Teatro Nuovo to hear *Betly*, "to which half of Naples is running."

Donizetti soon had in hand Cammarano's libretto for the three-act *opera seria* that he called *L'Assedio di Calais*, which he composed with all his accustomed rapidity. On October 3, he wrote to Agostino Perotti at Venice: "On the 15th I begin rehearsals of my *Assedio di Calais* for November 19. I have worked like a slave . . . three acts . . . ballets to suit . . . opera in the French style which will take up a whole evening. . . ." By the time of its *première*, with a cast that Donizetti had described to Mayr (letter of September 8) as "*cantanti minimi*," the epidemic was battering Naples. The first performance, at the San Carlo on November 19, though a gala honoring the birthday of Queen Mother Maria Isabella and with the Court present, was poorly attended. Three days later, Donizetti wrote to Dolci: "Greet our good Mayr and tell him that I have told you that my opera *L'Assedio di Calais* was given the nineteenth of this month and went very well, that I was called out six times, that His Majesty (whom I'm to see tomorrow) sent his chamberlain to me with the most flattering compliments. The third act, however, seems to me to make less than its effect because of the dances, which slow down the action, and which I may cut. It has cost me not a little weariness, but *perbacco* it makes its effect. . . . Farewell. I'll leave during the first days of December to go through the eighteen days of quarantine at Genoa. Oh, how boring! I'll spend the holidays in the *lazzaretto*." Despite his belief that *L'Assedio di Calais* was beginning its career effectively, it proved to be among the few of his mature operas which appear never to have been performed elsewhere after their first runs. Nonetheless, it is a carefully elaborated score, one of the Donizetti operas that almost certainly would repay worthy revival now.

Throughout October and November, Donizetti had been setting another Cammarano libretto, the *opera seria* text in two acts entitled *Pia de' Tolomei*. In the letter of October 11 to Perotti cited above, he wrote: "Do you think that, with all this, *Pia* is sleeping? Eh! I am at the second piece of the second act, and thus I still have time to revise and rethink it before orchestrating it." By contract he was bound to reach Venice by January 1, 1837, with the completed score in his luggage. Before leaving Naples, he signed—on his thirty-ninth birthday, November 29—a contract for the purchase of the apartment at No. 14 Vico Nardones, agreeing to pay for it five thousand six hundred ducati (about two thirds more than the amount of fifteen thousand francs which he had mentioned when writing in August to Dolci), an indication of the comfortable financial position in which he and Virginia now found themselves. In the deed of purchase from one Gennaro Riccioli, Donizetti is referred to as *"signor Cavaliere Gaetano Donizetti di Bergamo, Maestro di Cappella."*

Intending to stop off en route for a visit to Bergamo, Donizetti sailed from Naples on December 6. The next day, the vessel stopped in the roadstead at Leghorn, but he was unable to go ashore because of the sanitary regulations. He sent the Leghorn music publisher Vignozzi a note saying: "I'm here in the roads because of the cholera, which keeps us distant. I hope that all of you are as well as I am, and as we'll be leaving at five o'clock for Genoa, I beg you to post the enclosed to my wife in Naples, allowing me to wait until I return to repay you for any costs, because I hope that it will be accepted[19]—even though in Naples now it's almost over, about fifteen to twenty still die every day from Naples to Castellammare [di Stabia], the civil and military hospitals included." The manuscript of this letter is much

[19] Donizetti apparently doubted that the letter would get through to Naples because the sanitary authorities would fear its bringing new infection from the north.

blackened, almost certainly, as Guido Zavadini pointed out, as a result of having been fumigated.

Donizetti reached Genoa on December 8 and began the eighteen-day quarantine required there. While in the *lazzaretto,* he received the crushing news that during the night of December 12–13, fire had gutted the Teatro La Fenice. Thereupon, too, he received word from its directors that because the staging of *Pia de' Tolomei* there had been made impossible, they wanted him to accept a reduction of twenty-five hundred francs in his fee. They added that everyone else involved in the projected season had agreed to similar reductions. At first Donizetti felt that there was no reason for continuing his journey to Venice. But then, changing his mind because of a sensation that he must get to the scene as quickly as possible in order to protect his interests, he instead canceled his plan to visit Bergamo. Once out of quarantine, he set off by the most direct and rapid route to Venice.

Reaching Venice—where, on January 28, 1837, he was made an Honorary Member of the Società Filarmonica di Santa Cecilia di Venezia—Donizetti found it feasible to settle his problems with the Fenice management and Alessandro Lanari, the impresario. All agreed that *Pia de' Tolomei* should be played at the Teatro Apollo early in February. But the bass Celestino Salvatori, who had been scheduled to sing one of the leading roles, was taken ill, and this necessitated a further delay while Donizetti adjusted the part for the baritone Giorgio Ronconi and Ronconi learned it. *Pia de' Tolomei* at least reached the stage of the less desirable Apollo on February 18, 1837.

Two days after the first singing of *Pia de' Tolomei,* Donizetti signed an agreement with Lanari to compose another opera, this one to be ready to reopen the Teatro La Fenice the next year. Now the fee was ten thousand francs. On that day, Donizetti wrote Dolci that, his leave from Naples having expired two weeks before, he again would be unable to stop off at Bergamo and was departing for Naples by way of Ferrara the next day. "*Pia* pleased altogether except for the first act," he reported, not elaborating. Soon he was back in Naples at work in the theaters, teaching at the Conservatory, planning future operas. The internationally feted Maria Malibran had died at Manchester, England, on September 23, 1836, of complications resulting from a fall while riding horseback, and Donizetti now composed a *sinfonia* to be played as a prelude to a memorial cantata to be sung in her memory during an elaborate ceremony at La Scala, Milan, on March 17.

Virginia was pregnant again, and the Donizettis were deep into plans for moving from No. 65 Via Corsèa into their new home. He bought a carriage and horses. All was activity; much was bright hope, though the cholera epidemic hung on and Naples was not a happy place. On May 2, 1837, Donizetti told Antonio Vasselli in a letter: "On the 5th we move to No. 14 strada Nardones, third floor. Proprietors the Donzelletti couple,"[20] thus referring humorously to the misspelling of his name which had greeted him at Venice on his arrival there for the staging of *Enrico di Borgogna* in 1818. On the very day of the Donizettis' removal to their new home, Nicola Antonio Zingarelli died at the age of eighty-five. This Neapolitan musician had been director of the Naples Conservatory since 1813, and had taught, among others, Bellini, Federico and Luigi Ricci, and Rossini. His death meant that Donizetti would have to take up *pro tempore* the position of director, as was specified in his contract.[21] He also had to compose still another ceremonial piece, a Requiem Mass in memory of Zingarelli; this he completed in three days.

On June 13, Virginia labored and gave birth to a second son, who died almost immediately. In a distracted, not altogether comprehensible letter dated "Today, June 14 or 15 or 16, '37," Donizetti wrote his friend Agostino Perotti: "Donna Virginia gave birth the other day, but the male heir was dead, and 'oh my sweats in the air' (Paisiello's *Socrate*). . . . I shall do what the tightrope-walkers do when a foot slips and they cry out to regain their balance."[22] Virginia emerged from this third labor in very bad condition, and additionally may have contracted what has been referred to as *rosolia* (German measles), *morbillo* (measles), scarlatina, and meningitis. While these troubles rose around him, Donizetti managed to compose a required occasional hymn, *La Preghiera d'un popolo*, in honor of the birthday of King Ferdinand II's

[20] The ex-Via Corsèa ran about where the modern Via Armando Diaz now runs, northeast from the Via Roma for about four squares. The Vico Nardones (often referred to loosely as Via—and even Strada—Nardones) is a narrow street running west from the Piazza Trieste e Trento, one side of which is blocked by the Teatro San Carlo.

[21] The statement made by Francesco Florimo that Donizetti had been promised verbally by Nicola Santangelo, Minister of Internal Affairs, that he would succeed Zingarelli as permanent director of San Pietro a Maiella cannot be documented, but Donizetti undoubtedly believed that such a promise had been made, probably by the King. In a letter of May 21, 1837 (*43a*, 39), to Gilbert-Louis Duprez, he described his temporary position as that of "fellow and deputy in music at the Real Teatro San Carlo," but said nothing of his post at the Conservatory. "Oh, what a responsibility," he added. "But I have permission to go away, seeing that I have contracts elsewhere."

[22] *Carteggi verdiani*, ed. Alessandro Luzio, IV, 145.

second wife, Maria Teresa. He had been scheduled to conduct it, but on July 30, Virginia Donizetti, who was not to enjoy her splendid new apartment or ride through the streets of Naples behind her own horses,[23] died at the age of twenty-nine.

The suspicion that Virginia had died of cholera naturally has been entertained more than once, but no evidence supports it. Donizetti himself believed that she had died because, during postpuerperal weakness, she had contracted measles, German measles, or scarlatina and then had taken an untimely bath, thereafter passing into the delirium that ended with her death. In an undated letter written to Guglielmo Cottrau while she still was alive, he said: "The choleric monster is laying waste. Last night, eighty dead." Then, after some less serious remarks, he added: "I write jokingly, but my spirit is grave because Donna Virginia has been very sick, though now she is better. Diarrhea, her milk almost completely gone! She coughs. . . . Let us hope for the best." And to his Sicilian friend Count Luigi Spadaro del Bosch, late in August, evidently referring to Spadaro's wife being pregnant, he wrote: "Tell Donna Teresina not to fear the delivery, but certainly not to take baths when measles [morbillo] is abroad—that I lost everything that way."

For the time being, in truth, Donizetti seemed to have lost everything. In eight years he had suffered the loss of two sons, a daughter, his father, his mother—and now his wife.[24] Despite whatever he might in the future create or do or become, his feeling of ultimate loss over the death of Virginia never was to leave him entirely. Although he was to refer to her obliquely very often in letters, he never again wrote her name except to specify her epitaph. Six days after her death, he wrote a brief, agonized note to her brother Antonio, who from that time on became, with Antonio Dolci of Bergamo, the most intimate of his friends: "Oh! my Totò, let my grief find an echo in yours, for I need someone to understand me. I shall be unhappy forever. Don't drive me away, think that we are alone in this world. Oh, Totò, Totò, write me out of pity, for love of your Gaetano."

To Spadaro del Bosch on August 9, Donizetti wrote: "Friend! I

[23] On October 8, 1837, Donizetti would write to Antonio Vasselli: "I have sold the horses and lost nothing there. If I get the position [of permanent conductor of the Conservatory], I'll replace them; if not, good-bye. Now I have only the carriage."

[24] Verdi too lost his first wife, Margherita Barezzi, and his two children, Icilio and Virginia, all before his twenty-seventh birthday. But Verdi was blessed with a constitution much more robust, both physically and mentally, than Donizetti's —and had fifty-two years of active and productive life ahead of him after the last of the deaths that clouded his young manhood.

am a widower. . . . What more is there to be said? Forgive me if my grief does not bring me to give you long descriptions. . . . *I am a widower*, and you will understand what pain the writing of such words causes me to feel. . . . In replying, don't speak to me of my widower's state." But the sharpest outcry of pain was made in a letter to Antonio Vasselli on August 12: "Without a father, without a mother, without a wife, without children. . . . Why, then, do I labor on? Why? Oh, my Totò, come here, I beg you on my knees, come here in October. Perhaps you can be of some comfort to me . . . and I to you. . . . My Totò, write to me and forgive me if I importune you now more than ever. I shall be unhappy—you alone remain for me until she shall have interceded with God for my death and our eternal reunion." On August 31, in a letter dated "Naples, 31, today one month," he referred to Vasselli's having written him to ask that a lock of Virginia's hair be sent him: "If you wanted the hair, if it has pleased you, and if you have the courage to see it, to wear[25] it, that is a sign that you are more of a philosopher than I am; it is a sign that you are stronger than me. . . . Well, what does this mean? I want to say that I still cannot get used to believing in my disaster, that I still cannot indite a letter to you without my tears preventing me from going on with the writing." This letter crossed one from Totò (August 29) asking him to thank Teodoro Ghezzi for having sent the lock of hair.

Donizetti was curiously alone. The new apartment in the Vico Nardones was empty save for him. In Bergamo, whither he sometimes had spoken of returning with Virginia to live, no member of his immediate family now remained except his unsatisfactory brother Francesco.[26] Giuseppe, with whom he had much more in common, was established permanently in distant Constantinople and played no real part in his brother's life. In Naples, in Rome, in Bergamo, in Milan, and in Paris, Donizetti could count friends, admirers, even enthusiasts. But nowhere any longer had he close relatives available to whom he could turn for the warmth of personal intimacy. He was only thirty-nine. He shut the door to what had been Virginia's room but had become the scene of her death; he did not re-enter it for years—if, indeed, he ever re-entered it at all. His Neapolitan friends Teodoro Ghezzi and Aniello Benevento, justly worried by his physical state and depressed spirit,

---

[25] Or possibly to *carry* it, the Italian word *portargli* having several meanings.
[26] Donizetti's sister Maria Rosalinda, born on May 1, 1790, had died on February 8, 1811; his sister Maria Antonia, born September 20, 1795, and married to Giovanni Battista Tironi, had died on March 5, 1823; his parents' last child, a girl named Maria Rachele, born on March 21, 1800, had lived only fifteen days.

moved in with him, remaining for weeks to watch over him even at night, almost certainly fearing that he might either become gravely ill or perhaps even attempt to commit suicide.

Meanwhile, professionally embittered too, on August 5, Donizetti had written to the royal authorities to set forth his wish to be relieved of his duties as "deputy of music under the present management"—that is, as Director of Music of the Royal Theaters. The manuscript of this letter contains an annotation in his script: "Copy of the letter to free myself from the appointment as Deputy of Music, which went unanswered." In fact, Donizetti appears to have continued to hold this position some years longer: a letter that Prince di Ruffano, Royal Superintendent of Theaters and Performances, wrote him on May 30, 1838, for example, indicates clearly that he then still was Director of Music.

Once the first terrible upheaval had begun to spend its most violent force, Donizetti naturally turned to the work of composition for intermittent forgetfulness and consolation. He had promised a three-act *opera seria* to the San Carlo for September; he was under contract to compose another three-act *opera seria*, to a Cammarano libretto, for the reopening of the Teatro La Fenice at Venice early in 1838. And so, disregarding the fact that Saverio Mercadante, during the Carnival season of 1833, had had small fortune at La Scala, Milan, with an opera called *Il Conte d'Essex* (libretto by Felice Romani), he set to work composing for the San Carlo a libretto by Cammarano on the same subject,[27] calling the opera *Roberto Devereux*. He composed almost frantically, but found that this activity lightened his incessant grieving little. His letters continued to exhale the blackest despair. To Antonio Vasselli, on September 12, Donizetti wrote:

The start of my rehearsals [of *Roberto Devereux*] has been postponed; then, in the interim, whether with a good head or a bad one, I must think about the opera for Venice in January. The poet [Cammarano] must also think about the subject, and I must deliver the opera in December. I'll have to compose twelve *canzonette* in order, as usual, to take in twenty ducati for each, which I used to compose while the rice was cooking, whereas now the pen falls from my hand. I don't know how to do anything, but must do everything because everything is promised. Oh! my life, how you have saddened me, abandoning me alone on this earth. I try to laugh, to distract myself. I shall do everything for a little rest from this internal affliction. . . . I see the chasm into which I have fallen, and don't have the strength to lift myself up. The soul takes pleasure in sadness, but the spirit loses heart, and

[27] Cammarano, like Romani, seems to have derived its text from François Ancelot's tragedy *Elisabeth d'Angleterre*, and perhaps to have taken details for the story from Jacques Lescène Desmaison's *Histoire secrète des amours d'Elisabeth d'Angleterre et du comte d'Essex*.

for me, who must work and please, it is more painful to search for smiling images than to kill myself in the heat of happiness. Don't fear that we shall be alone when you come here, for I shall avoid every occasion on which we might fall into sadness because of our isolation. The two friends still sleep with me, and they won't leave then.

The next day, along with news that *Roberto Devereux* would be sung in October, and evidently replying to a letter in which Totò had compared his loss of Virginia to Petrarch's of Laura, Donizetti wrote: "I find your comparison with Petrarch just, with regard to the situation; but my sorrow, on the other hand, proves how far we are from feeling differently. There are moments when I would put myself in the hands of a hundred women if they could distract me for half an hour, and would pay as much as I could. . . . I try, I laugh, I hope, and I relapse again. No one would believe it, that I never tell anyone all of my sorrow, but you, you alone know me, and to you alone it is given to imagine it."

Totò evidently had suggested a possible subject for the Fenice opera, probably Bulwer Lytton's *The Last Days of Pompeii*. On September 19, writing once more to him, Donizetti said: "Your subject for the opera for Venice would be beautiful and good under other conditions. But do you find Ronconi adapted to it? Ungher? Moriani? I have selected *Un Duel sous le cardinal* [*de*] *Richelieu*.[28] It is an effective drama, and especially as I see it both *buffo* and *tragico*, a very important point for me, for Ronconi, and for Ungher." Things might have turned out better for Donizetti's immediate future if he had held to this plan, for the subject that, instead, he and Cammarano finally hit upon—that of *Maria di Rudenz*—was found too gloomy by audiences at the Fenice: the opera received only two performances when first staged. But Donizetti did not abandon altogether the notion of making an opera out of *Un Duel sous le cardinal de Richelieu*, not even when the play was taken up first by Giuseppe Lillo,[29] whose opera based on it, *Il Conte di Chalais*, was heard in 1839, and then by Federico Ricci, whose *Un Duello sotto Richelieu* was staged at La Scala, Milan, during that same year. The story held a

28 This was a drama by Joseph-Philippe Simon, called Lockroy (1803–91), a French comic actor and dramatist who later collaborated with Scribe and others on numerous librettos, perhaps the best-known of which, written with Eugène Cormon, was that for Louis-Aimé Maillart's *Les Dragons de Villars* (1856). It had been staged first in 1832.

29 Giuseppe Lillo was born at Galatina, Lecce, on February 26, 1814. After studies at the Naples Conservatory, where his teachers included Zingarelli, he became a professor there, successively of harmony and of counterpoint and composition. He wrote several operas, of which the most popular was *L'Osteria d'Andujar*, produced at the Teatro del Fondo in the summer of 1840. His mind having become disturbed, Lillo retired in 1861 and died at Naples in 1863.

notable fascination for composers: Bellini had been considering it before his death, after which the text remained in the hands of his friend Francesco Florimo. Florimo in turn gave it to Cammarano, who appears to have offered a libretto drawn from it first to Donizetti and then to Lillo. Four years after the Lillo and Ricci operas were staged—on June 5, 1843 —*Maria di Rohan*, the opera that Donizetti finally composed to Cammarano's libretto, would be heard at the Kärnthnertortheater in Vienna.[30]

At the San Carlo on October 9, rehearsals of *Roberto Devereux* at last got under way. At this time, Donizetti still held some hope of being named permanent Director of the Conservatorio di San Pietro a Maiella. But the royal authorities dallied, largely because he was not a native of the Kingdom of the Two Sicilies. In a letter of September 17, Donizetti had told Totò Vasselli that he had been with Ferdinando II and had attempted to discuss the matter, but had been put off with words of royal indecision. While this important question of his future remained unsettled, the first performance of *Roberto Devereux* was given at the San Carlo on October 29, 1837. Two days later, Donizetti wrote to the Ferrarese composer Angelo Lodi: "I composed the *Conte di Essex* [an alternative title for *Roberto Devereux*] and gave it two days ago at the San Carlo, and the results could not have been more flattering." At a repetition on November 15, attended by the Court, the box-office receipts were five hundred and fifty ducati.

On November 7, 1837, a Requiem Mass that Donizetti had composed for the funeral of a Neapolitan abbé named Fazzini was sung at the Church of San Fernando. On that day, he wrote Antonio Vasselli that *Maria di Rudenz*, the opera for the Fenice, which he was writing to a Cammarano text, was proceeding very slowly because he lacked all will to compose. On the next Tuesday, he was going to see King Ferdinando II to thank him for leave to go to Venice—and doubtless also

[30] In a letter of September 23 to Vasselli, after referring again to *Un Duello sotto Richelieu*, calling it "a sort of *Caterina di Guisa*," Donizetti said: "I certainly shall be glad to read *Rienzi*, which you say you are sending me. As for Bulwer in *The Last Days of Pompeii*, it bores me more than a little." A week later, he added: "*Rienzi* arrived yesterday, and today I am almost to the end of the second volume." It is interesting to speculate whether or not Donizetti ever became aware that in that same year Richard Wagner began to compose his *Rienzi*. He must, of course, have known that in 1825 (Teatro San Carlo, Naples), *L'Ultimo Giorno di Pompeii*, an opera by Giovanni Pacini to a text by Andrea Leone Tottola—written at least nine years before the appearance of Bulwer Lytton's novel—had been a considerable success. On October 5, he wrote Vasselli: "As for *Rienzi*, it doesn't seem to me to be the thing up to now (and I'm at the third volume); does it seem [right] to you? A man who tries to establish a free government?"

in the hope of extracting from His Majesty a final decision about the permanent directorship of San Pietro a Maiella. Nine days later, he wrote Totò that he would proceed to Leghorn by sea, then overland to Florence, Bologna, Ferrara, and so forth, if the weather turned out favorable, but otherwise would start out overland via Rome, where he would be able to stay no more than two days. "As for my returning, look, we'll see how that turns out. His Majesty said to me: 'Come back, and then everything will be decided.' " On November 21, he reported to Totò that the new opera was getting along, but four days after that his indecision about how to travel to Venice remained.

The tenor Giovanni Basadonna, it turned out, was leaving Naples by carriage on the night of December 3 for Rome and the north. On that day, Donizetti wrote Spadaro del Bosch that he would go with Basadonna to Rome, whence he would proceed to Florence and Ferrara, stopping off for a few hours in the latter city to visit with Angelo Lodi. And while he was traveling toward Venice,[31] *Lucia di Lammermoor* began its long, fantastically successful career in France. In that performance of the original Italian version at the Théâtre-Italien, the leading roles were sung by four of the brightest luminaries of the period: Fanny Tacchinardi-Persiani, Giovanni Battista Rubini, Antonio Tamburini, and Luigi Lablache. Paul Scudo (*118*), wrote of Rubini's performance as Edgardo: "As for the scene of the malediction which forms the dramatic nexus of the beautiful finale of *Lucia,* no other singer has been able to reproduce the sob of fury which Rubini there emitted from his trembling mouth." Ernest Legouvé said that in this scene, Rubini "suddenly was transformed into a tragedian, admirable by dint of being a sublime singer." And on December 18, Astolfo, Marquis de Custine, addressed to Donizetti from No. 6 rue de Rochefoucauld a long letter, part of which reads:

No performances at Paris ever have been as brilliant as the four evenings in which they have just given us *Lucia di Lammermoor.* The admirable coloring of that music has been felt from the first moment by the dull, cold Parisian public. You have electrified the dead; it is a miracle. Madame Persiani has a less even talent than Grisi, but a more original one; there is more of the unexpected in her manner, and the perfection of her method permits her to supply that which sometimes is lacking in her voice. In your music she has enraptured me; until then I had esteemed her more than I had admired her; but what is beyond everything is Rubini in the magnificent

---

[31] According to Eisner-Eisenhof (*48*, 10), Donizetti accompanied a violin recital by his friend Leo Herz at Bologna on December 3, 1837. But Donizetti dated a letter to Spadaro del Bosch at Naples on that day; the *accademia* at Bologna may have been on December 13.

finale of the second act. Tamburini also is very fine in the aria of Act I and in the duet of [Act] III—in fact, your friends are happy, and I, who count myself as among the first of them, have just written to the Duchesse de Canizzaro to tell her of your triumph.

Your music gives me a sickness for your country, which is not mine; and nonetheless I sense that it would suit me better than this one; I constantly hope to find the means of coming there to see you and to breathe your sweet Neapolitan air and listen to your songs, which are so well in harmony with the nature that surrounds you.

All unaware of what was taking place in Paris, Donizetti reached Venice on December 29, there to "extract the parts" of *Maria di Rudenz* and initiate its rehearsals. This was his fifth and last visit to Venice, where his *Enrico di Borgogna* had been mounted for the first time twenty-one years before, and it probably was now that (*48*, 11), passing some time with friends at the Albergo dell'Europa, he made—and lost—a wager that he could give from memory the titles of all the operas that he had composed. He was on intimate terms with Giovanni Agostino Perotti[32] and his wife and children, and was friendly with Count Karl Thaddäus Spaur und Thurn und Taxis and his wife, the Countess Philippine, and other members of the international and diplomatic colony. He was to remain in Venice until February 3, 1838; the first performance of his new opera on the stage of the splendidly rebuilt and redecorated Fenice[33] would not take place until January 30. In the watery city of cutting winds, then, Donizetti spent Christmas and New Year's Day far from his Bergamese and Neapolitan friends, as substantially alone as he had been since Virginia's death, while a tragic, debilitating year ended for him.

[32] Perotti, born at Vercelli on April 12, 1769, had studied with Padre Mattei at Bologna before Donizetti's studies there. Widely traveled, he appeared as an instrumentalist in Vienna and England late in the eighteenth century and composed some operas. His chief interest, however, was in sacred music; in time he succeeded Bonaventura Furlanetto as *maestro di cappella* at St. Mark's, Venice. His brother Giovanni Domenico was *maestro di cappella* at Vercelli Cathedral, and their names sometimes are confused. A group of warm, humorous, admiring letters that Donizetti wrote him was obtained for Verdi's autograph collection by Cesare Vigna. Their texts were published in Alessandro Luzio's *Carteggi verdiani*, IV (Accademia Nazionale dei Lincei, Rome, 1947), too late to be included in *138*.

[33] The beautiful Venetian theater did not achieve its present form until still another rebuilding in 1854.

CHAPTER VI

1838-1840

"... I want emotions on the stage and not battles."
—Donizetti, in a letter to
Count Gaetano Melzi,
June 26, 1838

WHEN Donizetti had written to Antonio Vasselli from Naples on November 21, 1837, to say that his new opera for Venice was getting ahead, he had added that it really did not please him at all and that he foresaw the audience at the Fenice slaughtering him for it. And when *Maria di Rudenz* finally reached its first performance on January 30, 1838, it was liked so little that only one repetition was called for. As quickly as possible, Donizetti's *Parisina* (1833) was rushed onto the boards at the Fenice to replace it, achieving a run of sixteen successive performances. The composer's friends and early biographers were almost unanimous in attributing the failure of *Maria di Rudenz* to its dour, gloomy libretto and to the condition of mind and spirit in which he had had to compose it. Edoardo Clemente Verzino, for example (*132*, 105) wrote: "That, after the death of his faithful companion, the Maestro's mind was shadowed strongly by sorrow would be proved by this . . . score alone. . . . It did not please, especially because of the lugubrious hue of the subject."

Donizetti's state of mind was not eased in Venice by the receipt of anonymous satirical letters making fun of him both before and after the failure of *Maria di Rudenz*. To his friend Count Ottavio Tasca of

Mantua,[1] on January 29, 1838, he remarked: "During my career, how many things have I not heard said to me? How many do they not say now? But, harder than porphyry, I try to do better and to put all that behind me."[2] And to Totò Vasselli on March 7 he was to write: "The letter from Bologna was a satire (anonymous) on me for the fiasco at Venice." How sharply he felt about *Maria di Rudenz* is demonstrated by a sentence in a letter that he wrote to Agostino Perotti on May 2, 1841: "I read now of the success of *Maria di Rudenz* at Ancona, so happy, and I still bleed for the severity with which it was held against me at Venice."

"I'm going back immediately to Naples, where I must do the opera for May 30 [*Poliuto?*]," he wrote Antonio Dolci in a letter dated January 18-19-20-21, 1838. His heart leaden despite the salving success of the revived *Parisina*, he was in Naples by February 24: on that day he wrote a letter to Michele Accursi in which he said that he had earned ten thousand francs at Venice and that he wanted that amount for an opera for Paris. He would pay the librettist; the roster of singers must be of his choice, as the selection of a subject would dictate his need for certain artists.

Ferdinand II received Donizetti amiably on March 6, but to all of Donizetti's proddings with regard to a final ruling on the permanent directorship of San Pietro a Maiella, His Majesty replied: *"Va bene, addio, cavaliere,"* an established formula for regally saying either nothing at all or a simultaneous yes and no. For some time, Donizetti had been toying with the notion of going to Paris. The possibility also existed that —Donizetti having decided to leave Naples—he might be appointed *censore* (that is, supervisor) of the Milan Conservatory, as his correspondence with Count Gaetano Melzi shows. What he certainly thought that he wanted was the kind of situation which Mayr had in Bergamo: a settled official position that would leave him free time for composing operas. However, he was to obtain neither the Naples directorship— which went to a native of the Kingdom of the Two Sicilies, Saverio Mercadante—nor that at Milan. Instead, he was to embark on a new

---

[1] Tasca had married Elisa Taccani, a soprano who had sung at the Teatro della Società in Bergamo in 1832.

[2] A paragraph in this letter gives an interesting sidelight on the economics of opera-giving in Italy in the late 1830s: "Let's talk about Naples. La Ronzi [de Begnis] gets one hundred ducati an evening in the winter and sings from eight to ten evenings each month. La Toldi gets four hundred and fifty ducati per months and sings five times a week. Barroilhet five hundred ducati, the same. (Well understood, San Carlo and Fondo.) La Ronzi they cannot afford to keep, she costs too much. The others—that is, Granchi, Barili, Bourgeois, Bonanni—are below two hundred [ducati] per month."

phase of his old career, turning out opera after opera for theater after theater.

When Charles Duponchel, Director of the Paris Opéra, wrote to ask Donizetti to compose two operas for Paris, he was all receptivity. On May 25, 1838, he replied that he would feel very flattered to compose for the Académie Royale de Musique, that he would await a formal contract, that Eugène Scribe must supply him with a libretto in five acts, which was then the standard format for serious opera in Paris, and that the dates on which his operas would be performed must be specified, particularly that of the first of them, for which he asked three months of rehearsals of three hours each day.[3] All this while, he was busily composing —to a three-act *opera seria* libretto that Cammarano had derived from Pierre Corneille's *Polyeucte*—an opera that he meant to call *Poliuto*. He was tailoring the title role for the special gifts of the great French tenor Adolphe Nourrit,[4] who then was in Naples, having abandoned the eminence of his position at the Paris Opéra, in part because he could not brook the increasing popularity and fame of his slightly younger rival, Gilbert-Louis Duprez.

Deeply disappointed and angered by Ferdinando II's failure to appoint him permanent Director of the Collegio di San Pietro a Maiella, Donizetti had decided to resign as both director pro tem and professor of counterpoint. On May 26, 1838, he wrote Dolci: "A few days ago I turned in my resignation at the Conservatory." On June 26, writing to

[3] Augustin-Eugène Scribe (1791-1861) was the most famous and by much the most successfully prolific writer of opera librettos in French. Working alone, in collaboration, or as a repair man summoned to smooth out flaws in existing librettos, he completed enough opera and operetta texts to fill twenty-six of the seventy-six volumes of his *Oeuvres dramatiques* (Paris, 1874-75). He wrote mostly for Daniel-François Auber—more than thirty light works and *La Muette de Portici* (*Masaniello*)—but of the more than seventy librettos that he turned out between 1823 and his death in 1861, others were used by Michele Carafa, Boieldieu, François-Joseph Fétis, Rossini (*Le Comte Ory*), Meyerbeer (*Robert le Diable, Le Prophète, L'Étoile du nord, Les Huguenots*), Cherubini, Adolphe Adam, Halévy (including *La Juive*), José Melchor Gomis, Alexandre Montfort, Marco Aurelio Marliani, Balfe, Xavier Boisselot, Victor Massé, Gounod (*La Nonne sanglante*), Verdi, (*Les Vêpres siciliennes*), Offenbach, and Donizetti (*Les Martyrs, Dom Sébastien, roi de Portugal, Le Duc d'Albe*). A potent concoction of ignorance, malice, and misjudgment of what an opera libretto is has led to the picturing of Scribe as the worst sort of hack, whereas in truth he was an extremely expert fabricator of exactly what his composers needed and wanted.

[4] Adolphe Nourrit (1802-39) had made his debut at the Opéra, Paris, as Pylade in Gluck's *Iphigénie en Tauride* in 1821. Five years later, he began to occupy the position of leading tenor at the Opéra, left vacant by his own father, Louis Nourrit (1780-1831). Outstanding tenor roles were composed with him in mind by Cherubini (*Ali Baba*), Meyerbeer (*Robert le Diable, Les Huguenots*), Halévy (*La Juive*), Auber (*La Muette de Portici*), and Rossini (*Moïse, Guillaume Tell*).

Count Gaetano Melzi, he said: "I went to see His Majesty: I handed in my resignation. I am fearful of the answer that I shall get—that it will not be accepted—and that will be hard on me if they send me from Paris a better poem than the first, which, despite its being by Scribe, contains only warlike things, whereas I want emotions on the stage and not battles. We'll wait to see what reply I'll get." And on July 15 he wrote Totò Vasselli that he had called upon the Minister of the Interior to insist that his resignation be accepted. But in fact he seems never to have been permitted formally to resign.

Francesco Florimo wrote (54, II, 46) that Ferdinando II's actual words to Donizetti in explanation of Mercadante's having been preferred to him for the position of permanent Director of San Pietro a Maiella were: "An admirer of your merit, I don't think that I am doing you any wrong, dear Donizetti, in refusing you the post of Director of the College of Music. If two posts of director were to be provided, perhaps I should confer the first upon you and the second upon Mercadante; but, having to provide only one, I think that I must give it to him, and that without wishing to enter into artistic reasons, but solely because he is Neapolitan." To this quotation, Florimo appended the following footnote: "From Donizetti himself I heard these words, which I report without entering into their merit or sharing the opinion of Ferdinando II. 'But,' Donizetti himself added to me, 'I who had gone there to complain did not know what to reply, as the King's answer had struck me dumb.' "

What was taking place with regard to the opera for Paris was made clear in a letter that Donizetti wrote to Gilbert-Louis Duprez on May 12, 1838:

I speak to you openly (with the understanding that you will not let anyone else see my letter). If Duponchel feels the desire to have me, I in turn ardently desire to write for you [i.e., for the Opéra]. I know that by the hand of an intimate friend of mine, M. Scribe now has sent Le Comte Julien. But I, without having read the poem, now have written that I do not want such a subject, that I rejected it to Romani. . . . A traitor to his country and love almost as an episode do not please me. You will see that I am speaking without having read the poem, for which reason I cannot offend M. Scribe. Well, then, I'd like to dry up the . . . like all the others, with an opera in five acts. I'd like them very short, as with Masaniello,[5] but five I want, and what's more I want a characteristic drama with two or three interesting and moving situations that will be outside the ordinary [things] done a thousand times in Italy. . . . They want me to write for a debutant, M. Candia, a young man for whom there are the highest hopes, but you know well that it's not good to risk one's own reputation with begin-

[5] Or Mas'Aniello, an alternative title for Auber's La Muette de Portici.

ners. They tell me that he's full of talent, and I believe it, and I'd not refuse to write the second part for him if the first part was with you, and all would be well.[6] I need to know the singers from close up, this because I don't want to risk ruining it or ruining me. I want you, then [Nicholas] Levasseur, then you, then Levasseur, then a very good *donna* and others. As for this last, I come now to speak to you about Mlle [Cornélie] Falcon. But first I beg you to get Duponchel to send the other libretto that he wants to send so that I can choose something more congenial to me without offending the writers, as in the end genius is capricious. . . . Oh! do it, or if you have doubts, call on that big friend [of mine] at rue Capron 3,[7] who has almost full powers [to act] for me. Mlle Falcon would be absolutely delighted (she says) to have me write an opera for her talents, but on that score it seems to me that we can't count much. I think that she needs a lot of rest because after she has sung a short time, her voice becomes veiled. Would to God that she was cured now. I know her and heard and appreciated her talent as the beautiful Jewess.[8] Who knows? She could be cured by this good weather. As for [Paolo] Barroilhet, he himself will write you. I warn you, however, that he has been with Barbaja for four years, and that it may be that he would have to be bought from him [Barbaja] if the price were not unreasonable. He is a good baritone. *Un peu exagéré.* Clear up this affair for me finally, and do it delicately so that Scribe may not take offense at the change that I want in the librettos. The libretto arrived four days ago, and still can't be brought from the steam-packet (incidentally, twenty-six francs duty from Marseille to Naples). I'll certainly read it, but in the meantime let me have others closer to my way of thinking. [Adolphe] Nourrit, it is true, is signed up for the San Carlo from September through Carnival. Write me or have them write me to close this deal, so that I mayn't find myself tied up elsewhere. I've handed in my resignation from the Conservatory in order to dedicate myself entirely to opera.

Donizetti, then, had had the courage to reject the first Scribe libretto sent him from Paris, though fearing that this action might prejudice his relations with the Opéra. Too, as he continued composing *Poliuto,* he sensibly was afraid that the Bourbon censorship would look askance at a libretto dealing with a Christian martyr and might well forbid performance of the opera. Writing to Totò Vasselli on July 11, he said: *"Poliuto* is almost done. The censorship makes dour faces, saying that it is too sacred." Four days later he added that celebrations were being prepared for the expected birth of a child to Queen Maria Teresa, for which royal event he had composed a cantata to lines of his own devising. This

[6] Thus did Donizetti perhaps reject the opportunity to supply the first role of one of the foremost tenors of the nineteenth century, the Marchese Giovanni di Candia di Cagliari—known as Mario—who, five years later, would create the role of Ernesto in *Don Pasquale.*

[7] Michele Accursi, who lived in Batignolles at this address.

[8] Falcon had created the role of Rachel in Halévy's *La Juive* at the Opéra on February 23, 1835. See p. 108.

Cantata per il fausto parto di Sua Maestà duly was sung at the San Carlo in August after the happy event.[9]

On August 12, Donizetti received the foreseen, dreaded word that the censorship, judging the text of *Poliuto* to belong to "too sacred a class," had ruled against performance of the opera. At once he complained to the Society of the Royal Theaters and the authorities at the San Carlo that the libretto had been approved in advance and that no negative criticism of the music had been advanced. When he realized that nothing would soften the decree of the censors, he proposed substitution of another of his operas: Barbaja, as impresario, had begun to insist that Donizetti had signed a contract to provide a new work for the coming season and must abide by it, but Donizetti had other contracts to fill. Also, the time remaining was too brief. Some sort of legal action resulted. In the end, Donizetti paid a penalty of three hundred scudi for cancellation of the contract and permission to leave Naples—and Barbaja staged *Pia de' Tolomei* at the San Carlo instead of the forbidden *Poliuto*, which was not to be staged in its original form until November 30, 1848, after Donizetti's death.[10]

Disgusted and desperate, Donizetti determined to abandon Naples. On August 18, he wrote Giovanni Ricordi that he would leave for Paris early in October. Unable to obtain formal separation from his official duties by resignation or any other means, he asked Ferdinando II for a three-month leave of absence. This was granted, and he sailed from Naples on the steamer *Leopoldo II* for Genoa and Marseille, reaching the French port on October 13. There he had to lay over for five days while awaiting departure of a mailcoach, which took him to Paris in what, in a letter of October 14 to Tommaso Persico, he had foreseen as "three days and three nights of rolling."

In the letter to Persico, Donizetti said: "Don't forget always to give me news of [Adolphe] Nourrit and whether, as I hope, he makes his debut [in Naples] quickly." The neurasthenic Nourrit, left without a suitable debut role by the censorship's decision to prohibit the staging of *Poliuto*, had sunk into a state of extreme mental depression. Donizetti's evident concern about him proved justified. On March 8, 1839, the tenor, then only thirty-seven, committed suicide by leaping from the roof of the building in which he had been living in Naples, thus cutting off one of the most splendid singing careers of his time.

[9] The child whose birth thus was being celebrated grew up to be Luigi, Count of Trani (1838–86) and almost, but not quite, the consort of Queen Isabella II of Spain.

[10] See Appendixes, pp. 355, 357, for a history of *Poliuto* and of its revision, in French, as *Les Martyrs*.

Reaching Paris on October 21, Donizetti took temporary lodgings at the house in rue Louvois No. 5 in which Adolphe Adam lived. In the second of Adam's two volumes (posthumous) of memoirs, the composer of *Le Chalet, Le Postillon de Longjumeau,* and *Giselle* wrote (*4,* 307–8):

Donizetti was tall, of frank and open countenance, and his physiognomy was an index to the excellence of his character; it was impossible to be near him without loving him, as he always offered some reason for appreciating one or another of his fine qualities. In 1838, we lived in the same house, rue de Louvois. We often visited one another there; he worked without a piano[11] and wrote without stopping, and one would have been unable to believe that he was composing except that the absence of any sort of rough copy made one certain. I noted with surprise a small white horn scraper carefully placed beside his papers, and I marveled to see that he needed to make such little use of that tool. "This scraper," he told me, "I received as a gift from my father when he forgave me and consented to my becoming a musician. I never have been without it, and though I use it little, I love to have it by me when I'm composing: it seems to me that it enriches me with my father's blessings."[12] This was said so simply and with so much sincerity that I at once understood what a heart Donizetti had. A few days after that meeting, I put on my opera *Le Brasseur de Preston*[13] at the Opéra-Comique. A spectator [seated] in the orchestra drew attention to himself by his enthusiasm and his frantic applause; it was Donizetti, and when I saw him on arriving home that evening, I found him happier over my success than I was, and I felt more honored by his friendship and approbation than by the happy outcome of my opera.

To Dolci, on November 13, Donizetti wrote:

I have been in Paris for more than three weeks. . . . I can tell you quickly what I am doing. . . . I am staging *Roberto d'Evreux* [*sic*] at the Italien. As for telling you what I'll do after that, here it is: I'll give the opera that was forbidden me at Naples [*Poliuto*] at the grand French theater of the Académie Royale de Musique [Opéra] in the French language. What I'll do after that I can't tell you, as nothing is settled yet, so forgive me. However, I

[11] That Donizetti had some sort of keyboard instrument in his rooms was indicated, however, by Charles de Boigne, who, in his *Petits Mémoires de l'Opéra* (*20*), mentioned that its keys were stained with ink. Also, the publisher Léon Escudier, in his book *Mes Souvenirs* (*50*) said: "From the earliest glimmerings of daylight, one found him at his piano seeking the inspiration that came to him with such ease that copyists had difficulty in keeping up with him." When writing a full score, Donizetti first put down the vocal parts and the accompanying bass; he filled in the rest of the orchestration later, as is proved by examination of several of his scores (see *138,* 251, n. 2), which sometimes show the vocal lines and those for cello and double bass in one ink, the other lines in a different ink. Such a manuscript in two colors of ink is reproduced in *138,* after page 368.

[12] The horn scraper described by Adam is now in the Museo Donizettiano at Bergamo.

[13] Adam's *Le Brasseur de Preston,* to a libretto by Adolphe de Leuven and Léon-Lévy Brunswick, was first heard at the Opéra-Comique on October 31, 1838.

can tell you that once *Poliuto* has been given to the French, I'll come back to Italy for a little breath, as after the courtesies, the suppers, the portraits, the busts in gesso, etc., that, though flattering in the matter of my self-esteem, nevertheless annoy a poor artist like me. I clearly see here that there are ways of earning a living in a thousand places, but I, used to little, to desiring little, cannot at all adapt myself to earning money. I am not Rossini and haven't his fortune, but when a man has enough to live on and to amuse himself enough, I think that he ought to retire and be satisfied. I live well, and after this French opera will be able to put aside three thousand scudi more. What do you want me to seek? . . . I don't want to act the fool like my brother the Bey [Giuseppe], who, after having earned perhaps more than I have, lingers on in old Byzantium to stroke his belly amid pestilences and the stake. I proposed to him that we should live together, and I don't know, but I think that his wife dissuaded him, being afraid that I wanted to live at their expense. I am alone . . . and it is sad to say that word . . . you will know how much grief is closed up in it, but as God wished it that way, my brother would have felt better. Then we would have taken Francesco with us . . . oh! vain illusions. He loves Constantinople, to which he owes everything. I love Italy because I owe to it, after my Mayr, my existence and my reputation. I turned in my resignation from the Conservatory to His Majesty the King of Naples, as I still want to work out a more peaceful life, if that is possible. His Majesty did not answer, and so I asked for three months. These expire in November, and now I've written for three more . . . either he accepts my resignation or I'll just act on it. Then, in March, I'll return to Italy for a short time and then come back to Paris for three months, and at that time *je quitte à jamais la France.* I don't want the theater to abandon me, but I want to abandon it.

For supervising the staging by the Théâtre-Italien of *Roberto Devereux* and *L'Elisir d'amore*—plus the composition for the former of a new *sinfonia, romanza,* and duet, and for the latter of a new rondo for Fanny Tacchinardi-Persiani and a new duet for her and Antonio Tamburini—Donizetti was paid twelve hundred francs. *L'Elisir d'amore* was sung at the Odéon. Of that performance, Théophile Gautier wrote: "*L'Elisir d'amore* is a triumph for Donizetti and for the troupe that performed it; all the numbers had to be repeated." He praised "the Italian, joyful, happy joviality of that gay, light, singing music, full of flowers and sunshine."

Donizetti secretly had contracted (the arrangement was to be canceled automatically if its existence was revealed) with Charles Duponchel of the Opéra to compose two operas to French texts, the first of them to be a four-act adaptation of *Poliuto* to a Scribe version of Corneille's *Polyeucte* and Cammarano's libretto—to be called *Les Martyrs.* This contract provided for the three thousand scudi that Donizetti had mentioned to Dolci. He also established contact with the music publisher Bernard Lafitte, turning over to him, for a fee of twenty-one hundred francs, six *ballate* that he had composed in Naples for voice and piano and adding a seventh to make a collection that was published as *Un Hiver à Paris ou Rêveries napolitaines.*

Roberto Devereux was presented by the Théâtre-Italien on December 27, 1838, with what Donizetti, in a letter of January 10, 1839, to Dolci, called "happy success." *L'Elisir d'amore* followed on January 17. One member of that first Paris audience for *L'Elisir* sat down that same night to write the following note to Donizetti:

Monsieur,

It is impossible for me to end this day without thanking you for the extreme pleasure that I just have experienced while listening to the ravishing music of *L'Elisir d'amore.* It is a beautiful comedy in music. It is animated, spiritual, tender, and at once melancholy and gay, and nothing better proves the fecundity of your talent. Despite our pretension in France of loving only the sad, I do not doubt that *L'Elisir* will have a big and enduring success. I hasten to be one of the first to pay you compliments: Do not disdain this homage from an elderly amateur who has been honored by the friendship of the greatest talents of her century.

Sophie Gay
née de Lavalette.

Thursday 17 at midnight.

The Donizetti-Scribe contract with Duponchel did not require delivery of the completed score of *Les Martyrs* until September 1, 1839, but librettist and composer were under pain of forfeiting thirty thousand francs if that deadline was not met. In January 1839, however, a suggestion was advanced that the opera be staged as early as May. On the fourteenth of January, Donizetti wrote to Fromental Halévy: "My dear Master and Honorable Colleague, For reasons that would be too lengthy to explain, not being able to put on my work immediately after that of M. Auber,[14] which is in rehearsal, I turn to you to ask you to be willing to take over my place with your opera *Le Drapier*.[15] In that way, the interests of the administration will be served and even improved, I am certain, and you will oblige your devoted Donizetti."[16]

[14] The proposal was that *Les Martyrs* should follow Auber's new opera *Le Lac des fées,* staged at the Opéra on May 1, 1839.

[15] Halévy's *Le Drapier* was sung at the Opéra for the first time on January 6, 1840.

[16] On January 15, 1839, Donizetti was made an Honorary Member of the Congregazione dei Maestri e Professori di Musica di Roma, under the protection of Saint Cecilia—that is, the Reale Accademia di Santa Cecilia. On the preceding day, Spontini had proposed twenty-four new members, all of whom were admitted: Adolphe Adam, Johann Caspar Aiblinger, Daniel-François Auber, Pierre-Marie-François de Sales Baillot, Luigi Cherubini, Carl Czerny, Charles de Bériot, Count

One reason for the unusual span of time which Donizetti required to get *Les Martyrs* ready for rehearsal appears to have been delay in his receiving the Scribe text in what he considered to be satisfactory form. In any case, both Halévy and the administration of the Opéra agreed to his request for later production, and he somewhat grudgingly settled down for a much longer stay in Paris than he had foreseen.

On April 8, 1839, Donizetti wrote to Mayr:

At the French Grand Opera I'll give my *Poliuto*, banned at Naples because of being too sacred, lengthened to four acts instead of three as it was, and translated and adjusted for the French theater by Scribe. For that reason, it comes to pass that I have had to make all the recitatives, write a new finale for Act I, add arias, trios, and such related ballets as they use here, so that the public may not complain that the *tessitura* is Italian, in which they make no mistake. French music and theatrical poetry have a cachet all their own, to which every composer must conform, whether in the recitatives or in the sung numbers. For example, a ban on crescendos, etc., etc., a ban on the usual cadenzas, joy, joy, joy; then, between one cabaletta and another they always have poetry that intensifies the action without the repetition of lines which our poets are accustomed to use. This *Poliuto*, changed into *Les Martyrs*, will be given within the year. Under penalty of thirty thousand francs, I am obliged to deliver the score on September 1. On January 1, 1840, I am obligated to present the finished score of the second grand opera, again in four acts, and concerning which I am bound under the same penalty[17] . . . I turned in my resignation from the Naples Conservatory; the King did not wish to accept it; then I asked for three months of leave, then for a year; they granted me six months, later they will grant me the rest and accept the resignation. By all this you will believe that I love, adore Paris. Well, you will be mistaken. I don't like it here, I burn with desires to return to Naples, there where I have my home, in which I have one room that I haven't entered for twenty months, but which is sorrowfully dear to me;[18] and there I hope to die.[19]

This elegiac mood continued: in another letter to Mayr, written on May 15, 1839, he said: "*Poliuto* is completed, and now I've begun *Le Duc d'Albe*. Oh, *maestro mio*, I'll bid the theater a bitter farewell as

---

Friedrich Wilhelm von Redern, Donizetti, Domenico Dragonetti, John Field, Giulia Grisi, Théodore Labarre, Luigi Lablache, Franz Liszt, Joseph Mayseder, Saverio Mercadante, Francesco Morlacchi, George Onslow, Johann Peter Pixis, Giovanni Battista Rubini, Louis Spohr, Antonio Tamburini, and Sigismond Thalberg.

[17] This opera would be *Le Duc d'Albe*, which Donizetti never finished, and which became the subject of prolonged litigation, arbitration, and discussion. See Appendixes, pp. 297-306.

[18] The room in which Virginia died.

[19] Guido Zavadini (*138*) pointed out that Donizetti mentioned his own future death in this letter of April 8, 1839, and again in a letter of April 8, 1844, to Dolci —and died on April 8, 1848.

soon as possible. I say 'bitter' even though it makes me rich, but I'll say it from the bottom of my heart because that will remove me from so many *souffrances*."

On July 5, having returned to Paris from somewhere in the country, Donizetti wrote to Giovanni Ricordi: "I have finished my grand opera, *Les Martyrs*, which will go into rehearsal during the coming October, and now I am composing another [*Le Duc d'Albe*], also for the Grand Opera, this libretto also by Scribe, and it will be staged after *Les Martyrs*." But when Halévy's *Le Drapier*, by then scheduled to be mounted before *Les Martyrs*, was delayed, Donizetti's reworked opera could not be put on as early as he had hoped and foreseen. To fill in the empty time until its rehearsals could be started, he agreed to compose still another opera, this one for the Opéra-Comique. So, to a two-act libretto in French by Jules-Henri Vernoy de Saint-Georges and Jean-François-Alfred Bayard,[20] he wrote *La Fille du régiment*.

In July, an episode of Donizetti's youth was recalled to him when Dolci notified him that the manuscripts of several pieces that he had composed in 1819 and 1820 for Marianna Pezzoli-Grattaroli had become available for purchase, she having died of cholera in 1836. In replying to Dolci, Donizetti referred to her having enabled both himself and Dolci to buy their way out of military service: "As for the music of which you spoke to me, I am not much tempted, seeing that after sixty-five theatrical works, few reasons for creation remain to me, and it is only out of curiosity that I might make the acquisition. But not when it enters their heads to make me pay for it as though it were something precious, which in the end would be an amount that not even that good lady paid me. I would have done a hundred times more for the favor that she did for you and me when you needed money in the conscription."[21] This letter again reflected Donizetti's depressed health and spirits: "La Signora Lucrezia,[22] the daughter, her husband, their son— are they well? I hope so. La Signora Basoni, her daughter[23]—all well, eh? Oh, how I'd like to see them again, but I fear that I never shall. . . . I cannot, I haven't the courage to come there where I had father and mother and not see any of them any more. I had a wife who took

---

[20] Vernoy de Saint-Georges and Bayard—the latter Scribe's brother-in-law— were among the most prolific French dramatist-librettists of their era. Bayard alone wrote some two hundred twenty-five comedies in a period of twenty years.

[21] The juvenilia referred to here are now in the Museo Donizettiano at Bergamo.

[22] Mayr's wife.

[23] Countess Rosa Rota-Basoni and Giovannina Rota-Basoni, in whose Bergamo villa Donizetti was to spend his final months and to die.

the place of everyone, and I have lost her! I am alone on this earth. The climate of Paris doesn't do well for me. I am getting thin."

The Théâtre de la Renaissance was in serious financial trouble, and when a subscription was taken for funds to assist it, Donizetti subscribed five thousand francs. Then, on August 6, 1839, its management staged the first performance of *Lucia di Lammermoor* in French and the explosion of popularity for the opera temporarily saved the theater. On August 9, writing to Tommaso Persico, Donizetti, though referring to the Renaissance troupe as *"juvenes et cani,"* remarked that his guiding star had watched over the successful outcome of that first performance. "It will suffice for you to know that I, being in bed with a headache, was forced to get up because the singers, choruses, and orchestra came with torches after the opera to repeat the choruses from *Lucia* under my windows, and I thanked them (in the royal manner) from above amid the shouting. Yesterday evening, the second performance, the theater crowded. For this theater, which was run badly, I subscribed for a loan of five thousand francs, and now the impresario has returned my subscription to me, saying that he no longer needs it, having located funds in various places for paying the past debts. This opera thus will make the rounds of France, and from time to time I'll have some francs from the provinces too. . . . Mme Nourrit succumbed to grief over her loss the other day, leaving several children orphaned[24] . . . *Les Martyrs* (or *Poliuto*) now has been arranged for piano and is being printed and will be given in January. Oh! it's an everlasting thing! I am terribly bored with Paris, the climate doesn't do very well for me, but I see that by staying here I can earn something. . . . Truly we have had a fine triumph with *Lucia*, and I wish only half of that for *Poliuto*, which now is called *Les Martyrs*."

When the French libretto—*Lucie de Lammermoor*—was issued for the first time, it carried as a preface the following open letter to Donizetti from the translators, Alphonse Royer and Gustave Vaëz:

Dear Maestro,
    Paris, like all the capitals of Europe, long has applauded your successes. The public in our provinces, lacking Italian singers, has waited impatiently for a French translation that could transmit to it some of your beautiful inspirations. We have selected *Lucia di Lammermoor* as the most poetic and impassioned work to which your musical genius has given birth, and we have tried to adapt it in a form and in words that would allow the theaters in our large cities to popularize it in France.
    The taste for music is well developed in the provinces. *Opéra-comique*

[24] The widow of the great tenor survived his suicide by less than five months.

does not in itself satisfy the progressive needs of this intelligent public; it now needs the lyric drama. Unhappily, this, which is the first necessity for their enterprises, too often becomes a cause of the directors' ruin. The Paris Opéra, into which gold is tossed with two hands—subvention and fashion— says to creators: "Dream, and I shall carry it out." The result is those splendid stagings, those sumptuous fairylands which make the provincial impresario wonder whether success is owing to that prodigious splendor or to the musical work; he himself cannot dress it up in so much silk and satin and gold in order to keep it shining for a long time if it is pale and puny; but he has too much to do to make sure that if the work fails, he himself does not fail at the same time.

Lucie de Lammermoor offers entirely different conditions. It is known that it is not the richness of the spectacle which brings success to the Théâtre-Italien of Paris; also we have simplified the production of the piece still further by avoiding in the middle of the acts those changes of scene which French dramatic form does not accept voluntarily; the new scenes that you have composed with us to render that imitation of the libretto appropriate to the demands of our theater constitute a veritable naturalization for your opera. As to our poem-libretto, it carries no literary pretension in itself: our sole aim is to offer to the theaters that will know how to appreciate your admirable *Lucia* score a success to be verified rather than a success to be made.

Your devoted servants,
Alphonse Royer, Gustave Vaëz.

Paris, January 12, 1839

Little more than a week after the very successful first performance of *Lucie de Lammermoor* at the Renaissance, Donizetti wrote (August 15) to an undetermined friend: "Does the brevity of my letters surprise you? Oh, fortunate you, whom the years do not sadden. With me, on the contrary, everything has turned to ennui. I am sad, melancholy, and feel my age strongly. Let's let art be. If you only knew! Imagine that [Robert] Schumann describes the triumphing *Lucrezia* as music for a marionette theater. Ah! I am gray and tired of working. The world believes me to be something that I am not, and I think that it will suffice for me to live discreetly." Donizetti in truth had worked too hard and too steadily for too many years. But there can be little doubt that his headaches and fevers, his state of pervasive depression, his prematurely graying hair (he was only forty-one), his reiterated wish to abandon the theater and retire on his earnings—that all this was in some part a result of increasing physical debilitation connected with the morbid condition of which he finally was to die.

Early in September 1839, Donizetti in Paris heard that La Scala was planning to stage his previously unperformed 1831 opera, *Gianni di*

Parigi. On September 6, he wrote to an unidentified Count to protest against this production, saying that he had sold it to no one and that it could be presented only "following a criminal abuse of confidence and a culpable theft." On September 10, however, the opera was sung at La Scala, the first world *première* of a Donizetti opera in which he himself played no staging or directing role. Sung on three evenings, it then was replaced with Rossini's *L'Italiana in Algeri*; given again on September 18, it was again retired some days later in favor of *Roberto Devereux*, and seems finally to have had a total of twelve singings. That season at La Scala was to close with the first production of Verdi's first opera, *Oberto, conte di San Bonifacio*, which was heard on November 17 and, though at first received as listlessly as *Gianni di Parigi* had been, was sung fourteen times.

Unaware of the shoals hidden immediately ahead, by October Donizetti was telling Persico by letter: "Next week I'll start the rehearsals of *Poliuto* at the Grand Opera. In the meantime, [I] having orchestrated and delivered a little opera [*La Fille du régiment*] to the Opéra-Comique, it will be presented in a month or, at most, forty days, and will be for the debut of La Bourgeois.[25] You will see by the manifesto that I sent you with Leopoldo [Tommaso Persico's brother] that I have promised two operas to the [Théâtre de la] Renaissance—that is, *La Fiancée du Tyrol*, which will be *Il Furioso* amplified, and *L'Ange de Nisida*,[26] which will be new, and thus I shall spend the winter in three theaters, these operas being in addition to the grand opera [*Le Duc d'Albe*] that I must deliver to the Grand Opera at the beginning of next year. You will understand that when one has too much to do, there is no time for playing the rooster with either old or young. Still, I do get bored and find diversion." Rumors were current, in fact, that Donizetti was playing the rooster with increasing excess and finding more diversion than was good for him. These gossiping charges naturally cannot be certified or contradicted by documentary evidence. What is known, however, is that the more advanced stages of his final illness were marked by intense eroticism.

Continuing the letter to Persico after reporting that a publisher

[25] Juliet-Euphrosine Bourgeois, also known as Giulietta Borghese, was to create the title role of Marie in *La Fille du régiment.*

[26] *L'Ange de Nisida* was the working title of the opera that later was recast as *La Favorite.* Donizetti appears never to have recast *Il Furioso all'isola di San Domingo* as *La Fiancée du Tyrol.* On May 9, 1840, he would tell Tommaso Persico in a letter: "The [Théâtre de la] Renaissance is closed, and I lose *L'Ange de Nisida*, an opera in three acts, good only for that theater. Auff! . . . The management was extremely silly, throwing money away on all sides."

had approached him with a suggestion that he compose three two-act operas per year (or six acts per year divided as he wished), for an annual fee of forty thousand francs, Donizetti turned to the problem of his apartment in Naples: "If the furniture is wearing out, sell it. God knows what will become of me. . . . Now that my heart is at rest about the Conservatory,[27] I'll take to vagabonding and will be all right. I'll come to Naples to sell the furniture perhaps, and then good-bye. Nothing of all this is certain yet, but that's how it will turn out. Malibran's sister [Pauline Viardot-García] made her debut at the Italien last night. A furor! In [Rossini's] *Otello*; Lablache (don't mention this to anyone) no longer seems to me to be in voice."

Reporting further to Persico on December 6, evidently in response to continued urgings that he sell his Naples apartment, Donizetti explained: "Wait about selling the house—I'll not remain forever in Paris. I am in rehearsal at the Grand Opera with *Les Martyrs* and at the Opéra-Comique with *Marie* [a working title of *La Fille du régiment*] this latter will go on first, and the other will go on in mid-February. Then the other [*L'Ange de Nisida*] at the Renaissance. . . . In the meantime, *Lucia* will be given at Havre, Nantes, and Liège, and it goes very well. The tale of what the musical director of the Grand Opera did to mix up the rehearsals had best not be told; but I coldly picked up my score, carried it home, and didn't return it until they had brought me an undertaking by which Messrs Scribe and Halévy assured me that [Halévy's] *Le Drapier* would be put on this month, thus leaving January for me so that I can put on my opera. I wrote a new aria for [Gilbert-Louis] Duprez, who is enthusiastic about it. May God protect us. . . . As for the house, we'll talk about that, as I don't have the courage to sell it because Paris is not my city."

Rehearsals of *La Fille du régiment* proceeded during January at the Salle des Nouveautés (Opéra-Comique), and this first-to-be-heard of Donizetti's operas composed to a French libretto was produced there on February 11, 1840. Sung only ten times, it was not at first a very popular attraction, its reception being much less warm than that accorded thirteen days later to the *première* of Ambroise Thomas's *Carline*. When several critics, including Berlioz, accused Donizetti of having warmed over for *La Fille du régiment* music that he had brought with him from Italy, he wrote to the editor of the *Moniteur universel* on February 16:

[27] Had the Bourbon authorities perhaps finally written their acceptance of Donizetti's resignation as professor of counterpoint at San Pietro a Maiella? No record of this survives.

An article published today in the columns of your esteemed paper, regarding the performance of *La Fille du régiment* at the theater of the Opéra-Comique, contains an error as serious as it is singular, and which it is my honor as well as my duty to correct. The writer of the column does not hesitate to assert that my score already has been heard in Italian, at least in great part, and that it is that of a small opera imitating, or translated from, M. Adam's *Le Chalet*. If M. Berlioz, who rightly places conscience among the first rank of the artist's duties, had taken the trouble to open the score of my *Betly*, the poem of which is in fact a translation of *Le Chalet*—a score that has been engraved and published in Paris by M. Launer—he would have been assured that the two operas that he mentions have no numbers in common between them; permit me, in turn, to affirm that the numbers that make up *La Fille du régiment* all were composed expressly for the theater of the Opéra-Comique, and that not one of them ever has figured in any other score whatever. I must limit myself, *monsieur le redacteur*, to clearing up that material error—on which, what is more, M. Berlioz's entire article rests—and I am confident that your high impartiality will not refuse to publish this rectification.   G. Donizetti.

Paris audiences did not hear ear to ear with the critics: *La Fille du régiment* soon caught on, becoming not only a favorite—fifty singings at the Comique by January 12, 1841—but also Paris's usual choice for the Bastille Day gala. Still, Donizetti was not done with Parisian procrastination or the strange ways of French journalists. On April 7, he wrote to Tommaso Persico: "You now believe that *Les Martyrs* has been give and regiven, eh? Not yet, and yesterday—for the fourth time—the dress rehearsal was scheduled and then postponed because of illnesses. Everyone, everyone except me—the singers have fallen ill, and even today one of them still is sick. Imagine that I am bursting apart and that I may die. You will know the agitation of a dress rehearsal. . . . Four times in that state, up to one hour from beginning, and then everything suspended. Imagine how I feel now, how horribly I suffer from nerves. Ah! if you knew how one suffers to put an opera on! You have no idea! it's enough to tell you that they drove Rossini to distraction . . . auff! But, by God, I'll see it through; now I am stubborn and want to give the opera only after Easter, as we're already into Lent. But such is my wish to leave here that I don't mean to be hard, and will have the part of Felice sung by the substitute. Felice now is a first bass; the part is important, but there are so many difficulties that I can no longer. . . . Why doesn't Barbaja give *La Fille du régiment* at the [Teatro] Nuovo? It's a subject that can be done: the Neapolitan *buffo* will fit it excellently; here they give it three or four times each week."

In that letter, Donizetti mentions Carolina Giusti, daughter of a well-to-do Neapolitan merchant who was ambitious to capture Donizetti as a son-in-law. Wearily, half in jest, but perhaps half in earnest despite himself, he tells Persico: "I'll be free at the end of October, perhaps. I'll come, marry Carolina, and return. All right? Yes! So then it's done . . . it will be done, that is. I'm horribly saddened by these delays. *Addio*." But no scrap of evidence survives to suggest that after Virginia's death in 1837, Donizetti ever seriously considered the prospect of a second marriage.

At last, on April 10, 1840, after Donizetti had been in Paris five and a half months, *Les Martyrs* was sung at the Opéra. Berlioz, while showering high praise on the orchestration, acerbly described the opera as "a credo in four acts," but its success nonetheless became extraordinary. After the first five singings, Duprez fell ill. But when he returned, it was revived and sung throughout June, after which Duprez had to be away from Paris. Then it was sung at the Opéra again as the opening attraction of the next season. Writing to Antonio Vasselli two days after the *première*, on April 12, Donizetti said: "I finally have given *Les Martyrs*. To tell you how I have suffered in order to give it, to tell you how many unpleasant mishaps turned up, would be something that would take forever; it is enough that you know that the dress rehearsal was announced five times—and five times someone fell ill; that the first performance was done with Duprez hoarse and the bass [Jean-Étienne Massol] with one arm in a sling! It's not up to me to tell you how it fared. I send you an article. When you have read it, send it, send it by common post to Persico so that he won't receive the first news from others. Today we're still having a small piano rehearsal because of certain little cuts. The article is from *Corsaire*, one of the journals that is harshest about everything. I'll send the *Courrier* and the *Commerce* to Naples and Milan. I'm not sending *France musicale* to Naples because others send it. Today I'm waiting for the [*Journal des*] *Débats*, a serious paper in which the writer is a very harsh enemy of everything that is not Beethoven or himself.[28] . . . Do you know that they wanted the third act repeated? The Devil! an act repeated! God free us from such boredom."

The stage investiture of *Les Martyrs*, produced by the leading Parisian specialists of the era,[29] won unusual and almost unanimous

[28] Here Donizetti meant either Berlioz or Étienne-Jean Délécluze.

[29] An *affiche* for the twelfth performance of *Les Martyrs* (April 13, 1840), reproduced in *78*, following page 148, reads: "*Opéra en quatre actes, paroles de M. Scribe, musique de M. Donizetti, divertissements de M.* [Jean] *Coralli* [the choreog-

praise. The second act, a large square at Mytilene, seemed to the on-lookers to be of rare beauty; the third act—in Pauline's quarters—was considered almost to equal it. Of the second-act setting, Théophile Gautier wrote: "All this disposition made one think of a beautiful picture by Eugène Delacroix: the *Justice de Trajan*." Unhappily, the opera as a whole did not delight the public quite so much as the scenery attracted them. Duprez himself later wrote (47): "Despite the very real beauties of that score, still much appreciated abroad, *Les Martyrs* won among us nothing but a *succès d'éstime*." Léon Escudier wrote in the same vein: "Despite one of the most remarkable of per-formances, the work of the Italian master could not withstand the public's indifference. After a very small number of performances, *Les Martyrs* vanished from the repertoire." Comments of that sort may well have led Alfred Loewenberg to say (77, I, column 807): "Not a great success in Paris." But in view of the statistics, which show twenty performances in two seasons, it is clear that Gautier and Escudier were contrasting the reaction to *Les Martyrs* with the colossal popularity of *Lucie de Lammermoor* and *L'Elisir d'amore*. In fact, *Les Martyrs* had by no measure been a failure, even at the beginning: on April 20, Donizetti had written to Innocenzo Giampieri: "My *Martiri* goes from good to better. Today the fourth performance. From three o'clock on, neither loges nor tickets. The spectacle is mounted in surprising guise. The performance is of the best."

A résumé of the critiques of the period shows that the portions of *Les Martyrs* which were appreciated most were the third-act sextet, the scene of Polyeucte's baptism, Pauline's entrance, the dungeon duet, the prayer of the Christians (with its imitation of faux-bourdon), and the final duet and cavatina for Pauline. In a characteristic sentence, Gautier said, however, that "the melody of the Hymn to Proserpine could have served just as well for a hymn to Venus . . . it totally lacked character and antique severity." What he clearly had enjoyed most was the overture, of which he said: "The sad, severe color of the andante, the chill, gloomy song of the four bassoons, the lugubrious rolling of the muted drums, the furious, implacable motion of the string instru-ments, the vocal prayer of the Christians behind the curtain—all this announces the immense drama of the point at which the old world is going to find itself in the presence of the new world."

---

rapher, with Jules Perrot, of Adam's *Giselle*]; *les décorations des 2ᵉ et 3ᵉ actes sont de Mʳˢ Despléchin, Séchan, Feuchère et Dieterle, celles des 1ᵉʳ et 4ᵉ actes de Mʳˢ Divoir et Pourchet*." This indicates the importance attached to the scenery.

During the performances of *Les Martyrs* at the Opéra, the *Panthéon charivarique*, a series of caricatures, published an unsigned caricature of Donizetti, showing him seated at a table with a plume pen in each hand, composing *opera seria* with his left hand, *opera buffa* with his right. He referred to this drawing in a letter of April 27, 1840, to Antonio Dolci, to whom he evidently sent a copy of it, writing: "You'll laugh, eh! to see me this way in this paper. I am writing with two hands, right and left, to show how fast I write; the lines are flattering. It's the paper that does caricatures of the celebrities . . . *acquavita!*" The lines under the caricature read:

Donizetti dont le brilliant génie	Donizetti, whose brilliant genius
Nous a donné cent chef d'oeuvres divers	Has given us a hundred different masterworks,
N'aura bientôt qu'une patrie	Soon will have only one homeland
Et ce sera tout l'univers	And that will be the entire universe

The ninth performance of *Les Martyrs* was attended by the entire Court except for King Louis-Philippe, who rarely went to opera. Donizetti wanted to dedicate *Les Martyrs* to Queen Marie-Amélie, who was an aunt of Ferdinando II of the Two Sicilies. When this wish became known at Court, the Queen received him at the Tuileries on May 5 and accepted the dedication. What was more important to him was that *Les Martyrs* continued to run at the Opéra, and that for each performance he was being paid two hundred and fifty francs. The contract specified payment to him of two hundred and fifty francs for each of the first forty performances, and of one hundred francs for every performance thereafter.

On May 29, writing to Persico, he included a clipping in French which reads: "The success of *Les Martyrs* does not weaken. The receipts for last Monday's performance were more than nine thousand francs. One must, furthermore, hurry to see this work, as Duprez begins his leave in June." Later in the accompanying letter, Donizetti wrote: "At this point I receive your letter of May 9. This cuts away my last illusions. What? Sgregli also stands in the way of an article?"[30]

Donizetti's fury over this rebuff gradually mounts almost to incoherence: "Oh, buffoons, buffoons! Well then, now that Maestro Giarrettelli and Maestro [Francesco] Florimo are the factotums of the Conservatory, I have no intention of being subject to anyone whatever.

[30] Sgregli evidently was a Bourbon functionary who had forbidden the publication in Naples of a translation of some Paris article in praise of *Les Martyrs*— in all likelihood because official Naples did not want the Neapolitans to know what had happened in Paris to an opera that they had not been allowed to hear.

With my name one does not serve under these *signori,* but one commands. Excuse this excess of *amour-propre* or French frenzy. Now, you see, I am more tempted than before to come, and more resolved to sell everything without even moving from here. Certainly it is not the Conservatory that attracts me, but when I see my name in the newspapers here and in Italy in some too sublime position, and in Neapolitan newspapers in one too despicable, then I laugh, I eat, I drink, and I'll do what my heart, what friendship, suggests to me. The two little articles attached hereto will demonstrate to you whether or not my opera merits the reprinting of an article. I . . . Bonjour. Thus I myself no longer know what I'll do! God, good . . . long live us, long live our friends, long live our families! My greetings to all the household. If you see me, you can see me, I'll be there, you'll see me. Anything that is broken in the house or wears out, sell it or burn it. Until next time. I'm hungry. Your Gaetano." What of course he did not know while writing this outburst was that on June 18 a royal decree would name Saverio Mercadante permanent director of the Naples Conservatory, thus finally quashing any remaining chance that he himself might return to Naples to stay.

Early in June, Donizetti received a letter from Vincenzo Jacovacci, then impresario for the Teatro Apollo at Rome, suggesting that he compose an opera for the coming Carnival. Donizetti's reply, dated at Paris on June 7, provides interesting insight into the conditions under which operas were composed at the time, as well as into his own thinking both as composer and as man of affairs:

By way of an unknown hand, I just have received a letter that you sent to my brother-in-law in Rome, and from it I learn that we may be able to reach an agreement about my composing an opera for the coming Carnival if small matters do not prevent it. What will the company be? Who will do the libretto? Will it be the first opera or the last? I ask all this so as to know that the artists will be worthy of Rome, as intermediaries sometimes praise to the skies those who do not merit it very much. As to the ownership of the score, I would not ask you for the entire property, but only for the transcription for pianoforte and voice, which would in no way diminish your right to have it performed and to sell it to be performed anywhere whatever. And if that does not please you, or you think that you might lose a great deal, I will cede half of the price that I would expect to receive in Italy—and then would myself supervise the translation, reserving to myself the proprietary right in France, where you, even if you wanted to, would be unable—once it had been published in Italy—to prevent its being republished by whoever wished to issue it.

This arrangement will be reached between you and me without detriment, believe me.

As to the libretto, I have been told that a good poem by Cammarano had but little success because of the music of Maestro [Giuseppe] Lillo.[31] If that is the case, you could send for the libretto, submit it to the censorship, say whether it pleases you and if you find it adapted to your company, and thus send it on to me afterwards. Thus, this would be a saving for you. And if you want a new libretto, surely writers are not lacking—you would know about them. If I ask when my opera would be staged, I ask it because of commitments that I already have here. For the rest, let us do it that way. I hope to leave here in a few days. Leave a definite answer for me in the post at Civitavecchia and send another here so that I can answer one of them in case I have not left by then. I hope that all this will be arranged.

I thank you for the good memory that you have of me, and, offering myself to your orders, am your faithful servant,

G. Donizetti.

N.B. It is clearly understood that I shall answer you quickly by post from Paris; if I stay here, I can know very soon when I must be in Rome.[32]

Donizetti left Paris some time after June 7. No documentary proof as to his whereabouts between then and the end of July has come to light, but he almost certainly spent some weeks in Switzerland. He was already in Milan, staying at the Albergo della Passerella, when he wrote to Dolci a letter dated "Milan, July 31 or August 1":

You believed me in Paris, whereas I was wandering over the dreadful and smiling mountains of Switzerland, and now perhaps you think that I am in Naples, whereas I'm writing to you from Milan. I would like very much to come to Bergamo to see our Mayr, my brother [Francesco], you, and our friends; but—as I don't know that you're aware—I have an action here against Ricordi[33] and cannot spend much time away from this city. Therefore I want to combine the useful with the delightful—that is, to come to

[31] Here again Donizetti refers to *Il Conte di Chalais*, libretto by Salvatore Cammarano, based on *Un Duel sous le cardinal Richelieu*, music by Lillo, produced in 1839. It was, of course, the story that he himself had considered earlier.

[32] Donizetti eventually was to set the Cammarano libretto that he alludes to in this letter (*Maria di Rohan*; Vienna, Kärnthnertortheater, 1843). But the opera for Jacovacci and the Teatro Apollo was to be *Adelia*, staged in February 1841.

[33] Exactly what Donizetti's disagreement with Ricordi was is not clear. After a mention of it in a letter that he wrote to Pietro Cominazzi in Milan on April 30, 1840, he continued to make further references to it—always incidentally and in passing—in letters written during the following ten months to Dolci and to the other prominent Milanese music publisher, Francesco Lucca. The difficulty eventually was settled satisfactorily, for Donizetti was to begin a letter of May 23, 1841, to Giovanni Ricordi by saying: "Now that I have been informed of the end of the dispute, I tell you not only that I am pleased that you have been reasonable. . . ." He ended it by saying: ". . . and we shall always be the same as if so disagreeable a thing had not happened."

Bergamo on the day of the first rehearsal of *L'Esule* [*di Roma*][34] and explain the movements and cut and adjust if there is any need. I put myself in your hands so as to be able to do this. You are (I hope) still the director of the operas, but if you no longer are because you have made too much money or because you have too fat a belly [*troppo trippa*], well, then, busy yourself with the idea and have them write me at least two days in advance so that I can do one act one time and one the next day (what I'm saying must remain between you and me). They tell me that [Ignazio] Marini is not good above C. If that's the case, have them spare him high notes when they're not in the principal motive, and so he'll be able to reach the end with enough voice. Mind that on the day selected there should be a military band, a harp, all the necessary instruments, or if not, I'm going with you and Mayr and [Giuseppe] Pontiroli, etc., to supper at the Dorotina.[35] I want to stay in Borgo so as not to disturb either you or my brother or myself with going and coming during the hot hours, it being well understood that none of you is to go to any trouble. And don't contradict me—if you do, I'll curse. In about ten days, I'll leave for Naples. I'll do the opera for Rome and then leave for Paris after the Carnival. Greet Mayr, Signora [Rosa] Basoni, Signora Lucrezia [Mayr], my brother [Francesco], and all our friends. Answer, answer, answer. Ask [Domenico] Donzelli if the aria needs any retouching[36] and write and write, general delivery. I am at the respectable Albergo della Passerella.

On or about August 10, Donizetti went to Bergamo, which he had not visited since November 1834. He was received like a returning victor. *L'Esule di Roma*, then more than twelve years old, was sung at the Teatro Riccardi on August 14 under the direction of Donizetti's boyhood friend Marco Bonesi. The cast, a distinguished one, included Eugenia Tadolini, Domenico Donzelli, and Ignazio Marini. A double line of military stood at the entrance to the Riccardi to hold the crowd. The performance was interrupted by cries of "*Evviva!*" which all but disrupted it. Donizetti sat in a box with Mayr, and when he embraced his seventy-seven-year-old teacher, the public broke out in near delirium. After the performance, Donizetti and Mayr went to the Albergo d'Italia through torchlighted streets. Flowers were tossed down from windows as they passed, and a local orchestra played *sinfonie* from *Ugo, conte di Parigi*, *Fausta*, and *L'Esule di Roma*. This native son had come home from remote regions of a faraway world. He was the con-

[34] Donizetti's 1828 opera was to be revived at the Teatro Riccardi on August 14.

[35] La Dorotina was a suburban villa belonging to Rosa Rota-Basoni. In a letter of 1844, Donizetti was to refer to it as the "Torototina." It evidently clung to his memory as a place of comfort, good food, and easy fellowship.

[36] Domenico Donzelli, the renowned Bergamasque tenor, was to sing in *L'Esule di Roma*, and Donizetti had provided him with a new aria especially for this production.

quering composer of *Anna Bolena, L'Elisir d'amore, Lucrezia Borgia,* and *Lucia di Lammermoor,* and the volatile emotions of his townspeople went out toward him in pride and in love. Verses honoring the occasion were penned by Antonio Colleoni, Temistocle Solera,[37] and Carlo Madonna.

Back in Milan after this eventful visit to Bergamo, Donizetti wrote to Dolci on August 15: "How tell you how much I am grateful for all that was done for me by my fellow citizens? How thank you? I know that it was you who gave birth to the thought of such demonstrations, and that then it spread like a spark among the others. . . . Finish your work, then, by making yourself the interpreter of my heart to my birthplace, the noble Signor Mayor, the Signori Councillors, Magistrates, patrons, and friends; tell them how sweet to me the memory of so many honors, of so much affection, will be for the rest of my life. To my colleagues the artists, many and many good things—to Donzelli, Tadolini, Marini, etc., etc. A thousand thanks to Mayr! To you, nothing —because you know me."

On that same day, Donizetti sent off a letter to Léon Pillet, director of the Paris Opéra, who had written to suggest that he return to Paris and compose a new opera there. The delays and infuriating interruptions that Donizetti had endured during the preparation of *Les Martyrs* had not made the large Paris theater any the less attractive to him. Answering Pillet, he said: "I have just this instant received your letter, and I hurry to answer. You know that I have a very fine arrangement [with Jacovacci] at Rome, despite which I have so [great] a desire to compose for France that I am going to try to break it. You no doubt recall the tribulations, all the irritations, all the injustices, all the delays through which I went for *Les Martyrs.* I hope that it will not be like that again, and that you will take into account the sacrifice that I am making by trying to break this engagement, in which I should not go through any of the irritations that I have suffered in Paris. I shall be in Paris very soon."

Some time after August 18, Donizetti left Milan and traveled back through Switzerland. Reaching Paris during the first week in September, if not slightly earlier, he temporarily stayed with his friend Michele Accursi in the rue Marivaux. What relationship, if any, Doni-

[37] Temistocle Solera (1815–78), a Ferrarese composer and writer, provided the librettos for Verdi's *I Lombardi alla prima crociata, Nabucco, Giovanna d'Arca,* and *Attila,* for Arrieta's *La Conquista de Granada,* as well as for his own *Ildegonda* —which libretto also was set by both Emilio Arrieta and the Mexican composer Melesio Morales.

zetti had to Accursi's supposed and Giovanni and Agostino Ruffini's genuine patriotic political activities is far from clear. In Volume III of the *Protocollo della Giovine Italia*, as Guido Zavadini pointed out, Donizetti's name appears several times (pp. 184ff.): "March 27, 1845. Use Donizetti's address sparingly."—"Don't use Donizetti's address any more. He is here. Send him together, to Spagni, bottles from our Cologne water factory, then I'll send him poetry by [Giuseppe] Giusti, [Ugo] Foscolo, and little works by [Attilio and Emilio] Bandiera." These jottings, which suggest plotters' code, indicate that Donizetti's address had been used for the handling of revolutionary communications, but do not implicate him certainly.

During September and October, having come to a definite agreement with Vincenzo Jacovacci that the opera he had promised to the Teatro Apollo could be delayed and would be composed to a libretto by Felice Romani entitled *Adelia*, Donizetti worked away at transmuting what he had composed of *L'Ange de Nisida* into *La Favorite*. As first conceived, this three-act opera to a libretto by Alphonse Royer and Gustave Vaëz, the translators of *Lucia di Lammermoor* into French, had been intended as a starring vehicle for the English singer Anna Thillon at the Théâtre de la Renaissance. But, as the result of a lawsuit brought against Antenor Joly, manager of the Renaissance, by the directors of the Opéra and the Opéra-Comique, that theater had been forced to close on May 23, 1841. Donizetti then undertook to transform the three-act plan of *L'Ange de Nisida* into a four-act opera, the leading role being designed for Cornélie Falcon, who had to be replaced before the *première* and who never sang in a Donizetti first performance.

Why Donizetti chose to rework *L'Ange de Nisida* rather than to complete *Le Duc d'Albe* is not clear.[38] He had expressed a wish to set a libretto involving monks and life in a cloister, and it may be, as Guido Zavadini guessed, that the subject of the Royer-Vaëz libretto irresistibly appealed to him. In any case, as the management of the Renaissance had collapsed, he no longer was bound to complete *L'Ange de Nisida* for that theater. Another point never entirely cleared up is whether Donizetti effected the expansion from the three-act division of *L'Ange de Nisida* to the four acts of *La Favorite* by dividing the first act of the original into two acts or by leaving the three acts intact and adding a new fourth act.

[38] From the incomplete score of *Le Duc d'Albe* he borrowed *"Ange si pur,"* remaking it into the most renowned single number in *La Favorite*, the aria now commonly referred to outside France by the opening words of its Italian translation, *"Spirto gentil."*

It has been said, apparently without reason, that the text for the "new fourth act" was supplied by Scribe. A statement by Alphonse Royer (*110*, II, 94) contradicts this assertion but does not settle the question of what use Donizetti made of the existing music of *L'Ange de Nisida:* "The music of the fourth act was composed in a single night. Vaëz and I had taken the words to the *maître* after dinner; the next day at the same time, he sang them to us at the piano, transfigured by his musical inspiration." Lacking both the autograph score of the partial first version and its libretto, we cannot know exactly how much existed of the projected opera or what Donizetti did to make use of it for *La Favorite.*

The Comtesse de Bassanville once told a circumstantial anecdote of the composition of that famous fourth act. According to her, on the very day on which Donizetti learned that his three-act opera must be extended to four acts, he dined with friends who had to go out after dinner. He asked to be left behind, for he had found the room warm and comfortable, and he was armed with music paper and writing materials. His hosts and friends left at ten o'clock. When they returned an hour after midnight, they found him dreaming by the fireplace, the act composed completely. This story must, of course, leave one wondering where Donizetti had obtained the text that he was setting. Also, it is known that the andante in the fourth-act duet was added during rehearsals of *La Favorite.*

What exactly can Edoardo Clemente Verzino have had in mind when he wrote (*132*, 112): "This opera [*La Favorite*] went through bizarre vicissitudes. Performed, Royer says, at the Théâtre de la Renaissance under the title *L'Ange de Nisida* by Anna Tillon [*sic*], it was played later at the Opéra by [Rosine] Stoltz. During that removal, one demi-character part was deleted and the first act was divided into two, so that the opera had four acts instead of three. A duet for soprano and baritone was taken from the score, then in preparation, of *Maria Padilla;*[39] an aria for the bass from another opera. The real composition —that is, of the third and fourth acts—remained exactly as at first except for the romance '*Ange si pur*,' ['*Spirto gentil*'] borrowed from the other manuscript, of '*Le Duc d'Albe*,' and another romance, '*Fernand, écoute le prier*,' which the Maestro had arranged during the several rehearsals at the instance of Stoltz." This merely compounds the puzzle.

The opera that Donizetti intended for eventual production at the

[39] Donizetti in fact began during the summer of 1841 to compose *Maria Padilla* to a three-act *opera seria* text by Gaetano Rossi.

Teatro Apollo, Rome, also underwent a series of vicissitudes before *La Favorite* went into rehearsal at the Opera. Romani's libretto, *La Figlia dell'arciere*, had been written six or seven years earlier and set (1834) as an opera by Carlo Coccia. When Jacovacci and the management of the Apollo read this text, they did not like the third act, and thereupon called in a writer named Girolamo Maria Marini to provide a new finale. When, in turn, Donizetti saw Marini's act, he found it unsatisfactory.[40] After some doubts, however, he accepted the revised libretto and set to work to compose the opera, *Adelia, o La Figlia dell'arciere*, probably starting to work at it before he had completed *La Favorite*.

Rehearsals of *La Favorite* began at the Opéra before October 1. On that day, Donizetti wrote to Totò Vasselli to acknowledge receipt of Marini's text for the final act of *Adelia*: "I am being killed by the rehearsals. At this moment I have finished my four acts, and rehearsing every day is something to die over. In recompense, I have the fact that all the singers are extremely well known except (as usual) for the secondary artists, but no one is missing, *et voilà tout*." The noted first conductor of the Opéra and founder of the Société des Concerts du Conservatoire, François-Antoine Habeneck, conducted the first performance of *La Favorite* at the Opéra on December 2, 1840.

The *première* of *La Favorite* marked a culminating date in the development of French romantic ballet. The choreographer of the incidental dances was Jules-Joseph Perrot (1810-92), the chief dancer his Neapolitan wife, Carlotta Grisi, a cousin of the great soprano Giulia Grisi and the less famous mezzo soprano Giuditta Grisi. Of Carlotta Grisi, Charles de Boigne wrote (20): "She made her debut in a *pas de deux* with Petipa in the second act of *La Favorite*, and the plaudits that she received produced upon Mme Stoltz the same effect that the laurels of Miltiades had produced upon Themistocles." On June 28, 1841, largely

[40] Coccia's *La Figlia dell'arciere*, produced at the Teatro San Carlo, Naples, in the winter of 1834, was a failure despite the fact that its cast included both Maria Malibran (Adelia) and Luigi Lablache (Arnoldo). In the confusing theatrical way of that era, the libretto had not been wholly the work of Romani. Romani had delivered a complete text in three acts, but the management had not liked his third act, which thereupon had been rewritten by the Marchese Domenico Andreotti, whose name, however, did not appear on the published libretto. The reason why the Romani-Andreotti libretto had to be tampered with still further by Marini for a Roman performance was that it included the heroine's suicide on stage as a result of false news that her fiancé had been decapitated: a suicide in view of the audience was frowned upon by the pontifical censorship. The final result was that the libretto should have been credited to Felice Romani, Marchese Domenico Andreotti, Girolamo Maria Marini, and Gaetano Donizetti.

as a result of the acclaim that Grisi had reaped in *La Favorite*, she would create the title role in Adolphe Adam's ballet *Giselle*, with choreography by Perrot and Jean Coralli. And *Giselle*, its story adapted by Théophile Gautier from a legend retold by Heinrich Heine and then adapted to ballet purposes by Vernoy de Saint-Georges, was to become and to remain the central work of ballet in its period of highest romanticism. Grisi's debut at the Opéra helped to define 1840 as one apogee of Paris's romantic age. That same romanticism, though tempered by holdovers of the eighteenth-century classicizing Italian *opera seria*, was evident in the score that Donizetti had composed for *La Favorite*.

Received with no show of disfavor, *La Favorite* was not an immediate success. Donizetti is said not to have attended that *première*, but to have strolled along the Champs-Élysées into the morning, not learning of the opera's mild reception until later that next day. Léon Escudier wrote: "At its inception *La Favorite* was judged to be one of the most mediocre works; at the first performances it had been condemned; the score did not even find a publisher." Scudo added: "That charming score, which today is one of the prettiest triumphs of our lyric theater, became accredited among us slowly." Charles de Boigne wrote that if the title role had been sung by another singer (he meant Cornélie Falcon), the success of the opera would have equaled, if it had not surpassed, that of Meyerbeer's *Robert le Diable*, which was first heard at the Opéra on November 21, 1831, and long was regarded, with Auber's *La Muette de Portici* and Rossini's *Guillaume Tell*, as one of the principal foundation stones of grand opera in the technical sense of that term.

After a few repetitions of *La Favorite*, however, the enthusiasm of its audiences began to increase rapidly. In the French provinces it quickly became an established favorite, Escudier asserting that "the provinces imposed *La Favorite* upon the Parisian public." It soon enough found a publisher, Léon Schlesinger, who paid Donizetti the then very large sum of twelve thousand francs for it. Soon it received the accolade of transcription: the German pianist Charles Voss composed a *Grande Fantaisie brillante* on melodies from it. It became an enduring integer of the Opéra's repertoire, and when it was revived in 1856, the role of Léonore provided a ringing personal triumph for Adelaide Borghi-Mamo; the role of Fernand was sung on that occasion by Gustave-Hippolyte Roger. In 1864, twenty-four years after the *première*, Rosine Stoltz reappeared in the role that she had created—and won Berlioz's unqualified approbation. She was then forty-nine.

By 1841, *La Favorite* had become so popular throughout France that Schlesinger paid a young German musician named Richard Wagner an advance of five hundred francs against a total promised fee of eleven hundred to make no less than six different transcriptions from its score. What the nearly starving Wagner had to do to *La Favorite* in this attempt to fend off complete indigence was to arrange it for voice and piano; for piano solo; for piano four hands; for flute quartet (with violin, viola, and cello); for two violins; and—incredibly—for cornet.[41] This extratheatrical popularity of *La Favorite* depended largely upon the familiarity not only of "*O mon Fernand*," but also of the cavatina "*Ange si pur que dans un songe*" ["*Spirto gentil*"] and of the aria "*Un ange, une femme inconnue*."

La Favorite reached Italy for the first time as *Leonora di Gusman* (or *Guzman*), in an Italian translation by Francesco Jannetti, at the Teatro Nuovo, Padua, in June 1842. The later, standard Italian translation, *La Favorita*, by Calisto Bassi, was sung at La Scala, Milan, on August 16, 1843. Again not greatly enjoyed at first hearing, it again caught on—and ran for twenty-five performances starring Marietta Alboni. Still another Italian translation, also called *La Favorita*, but with the characters' names altered (Alfonso of Castille becoming Louis VII of France, Leonora di Gusman a Greek girl named Elda), was sung at the Teatro La Fenice, Venice, during the Carnival of 1847. The opera suffered still other sea changes—into *Richard und Mathilde, Leonore, Riccardo e Matilde, Daila, Elda, Die Templer in Sidon*—and has retained a place in the repertoires of European opera houses since its first singing in 1840. Arturo Toscanini was to say of it: "The opera *La Favorita* is all beautiful; the last act—every note is a masterpiece."

Donizetti himself, in a letter of December 3, 1840, to Totò Vasselli, said simply: "The opera was given yesterday, the second." But he did send along clippings of reviews from the Paris press. Writing to the music publisher Francesco Lucca five days later, he said: "I have written now and have sent copies of two articles, from the *Courrier des théâtres* and the *Courrier français*, to Signor [Paolo] Branca. Nevertheless, I do not stop importuning all my friends to reaffirm its success, which every good Italian who loves his country and music should hear

---

[41] Wagner similarly made transcriptions from two of Fromental Halévy's operas, *Le Guitarréro* and *La Reine de Chypre*. In 1839, too, he had approached Luigi Lablache with an offer to compose for him a grand aria with chorus to be inserted as an added number for Oroveso when Lablache sang in *Norma*. One would like to believe that Lablache's refusal of the offer resulted from his sense of stylistic fitness.

about *volontieri*. The second performance was equally happy, and [Paolo] Barroilhet repeated the *terzettino* as at the first (an unheard-of thing at the Académie Royale)."

Some picture of the popularity to which Donizetti had attained in Paris at this time—or at least of that popularity as viewed by a great composer much less often performed—can be derived from an anecdote that Berlioz included in an article for the *Journal des débats* of May 14, 1863. A ship's captain who visits Paris periodically is represented as saying that each time he leaves the city, Donizetti's *La Favorite* is being announced, whereas each time that he returns, *Lucie de Lammermoor* is being promised. Another sailing man replies: "No, that's an exaggeration. . . . When *I* leave for India, it's true that I also see *La Favorite* [announced], but when I return, they don't always present *Lucie;* they often are giving *La Favorite* again."

With *La Favorite* excellently launched, Donizetti turned back to *Adelia.* By the end of November, he had sent the completed Act I and Act II to Jacovacci in Rome. Feeling that his third foray into the strange Parisian world of opera had been much happier than the preceding one, he sent a note to Gilbert-Louis Duprez on December 13: "In leaving I recommend to you my two children (*Les Martyrs* and *La Favorite*). I consider you as their second father. A thousand kind things to Madame. An embrace from your Donizetti." He left Paris that day, reaching Marseille a week later. There he embarked for Leghorn, expecting the trip to take the customary thirty-six hours. Five days later, having bucked a violent tempest all the way, the ship had got no farther than Toulon. Bruised and weary, Donizetti finally reached Rome on December 28, staying with the Vassellis. Before the Christmas-New Year period had passed, rehearsals of *Adelia* had begun at the Teatro Apollo and he had come to know the remarkable twenty-five-year-old soprano who was to sing its title role, Giuseppina Strepponi.

CHAPTER VII

1841–Autumn 1842

GIUSEPPINA STREPPONI already was well acquainted with Donizetti the composer: she had sung leading roles in thirteen of his operas, including *Anna Bolena* (of which she had been a leading attraction in many Italian theaters in 1835), *L'Elisir d'amore, Lucia di Lammermoor, Pia de' Tolomei, Belisario,* and *Maria di Rudenz.* Indeed, her success in *Lucia* and *Pia de' Tolomei* at the Teatro Argentina, Rome, in the spring of 1838 had provided important advancement to her burgeoning career. Now, very late in 1840 or early in 1841, she met Donizetti the man, who was to be so impressed that he would dedicate *Adelia* to her. And fifty-six years later, when a group of men at Bergamo were putting together a Donizetti memorial volume, the then eighty-two-year-old Giuseppina Strepponi Verdi, in the year of her death, would send them from Genoa on April 16, 1897, the following for inclusion in their publication (*18, 27*): "During my extremely brief theatrical career, I nearly always sang in the operas of the great composer of *Lucia* and *Lucrezia Borgia.* Later, Maestro Donizetti wrote *Adelia* for me, at the Apollo in Rome. It was then that I knew him personally and was able to admire—beyond his genius, familiar to all— his spirit, which joined his goodness and his vast culture to form the whole of a truly superior artist and gentleman."[1]

[1] Verdi himself was approached twice to contribute to the celebration of the Donizetti centenary. The President of the Committee for the Centenary Tribute to Donizetti asked him to compose a piece (Verdi referred to it as "a musical thought or an occasional cantata"), and the Mayor of Bergamo invited him to attend the celebrations. In letters of June 13 and September 14, 1897, he very politely declined

Clelia Maria Josepha Strepponi, known as Giuseppina, had been born at Lodi on September 8, 1815. She was young. She was attractive. And the corridors and *caffè* soon were pullulating with gossip about her, some of it connecting her name with that of Bartolomeo Merelli and that of the tenor Napoleone Moriani (who almost certainly was the father of her two illegitimate children, born in 1838 and 1841),[2] some of it about her and Donizetti. Franco Abbiati (*1*, 1, 368-70) wrote that these stories reached the ears of Strepponi's young admirer, Giuseppe Verdi, and jangled his nerves. Abbiati also reported some details of the Roman gossip of the period when *Adelia* was being staged:

It was said, for example, that Donizetti invariably came to grips with head-aches—and they allowed themselves to guess the unfortunate origin of these—every time that he had to compose a new opera. And they made it clear that the periodic sufferings of the Bergamo composer nonetheless resulted in some notable benefits, generating happy music if they seized him on the left side, serious music if they seized him on the right. But there was worse. For some time, according to the chattering voices, Donizetti's migraines had been turning into sudden shadowings of his still sovereign mind, darkenings all the more pernicious because not yet painful.

Was this true? Certainly it was true that Donizetti, a widower for four years [actually, three years and a half], trapped for more than twelve by an inexorable contagion,[3] gave frequent signs of disequilibrium. Among other things—these were the reports fresh from the theatrical corridors, reports that got on Verdi's nerves more than any others—the widowed Donizetti habitually became inflamed with abrupt amorous sympathies: as if out of a frenzy to search anxiously and indiscriminately for a companion who might serve to cool the illogical sultrinesses of his body and, at the same time, drive from him his sad and, alas, not unjustified forebodings of an approaching complete loss of mind. These no longer were migraines, the tongues of malice asserted, but baleful shadows from intermittent nights agitated by the senile specters of concupiscence.[4]

---

both invitations on the ground of his advanced age (he was then eighty-three). In the earlier letter, he said: "Donizetti knew how to create with his own hands such a monument that the composers who have succeeded him will not know how to raise a bigger one to him!"

[2] *137*, 86-88. In February 1839, too, she had had a miscarriage.

[3] This would set the date of Donizetti's contagion in 1828–29, almost exactly at the time of his marriage.

[4] Here, as in other passages in the pages cited, Abbiati appears to be stirring into the immediate situation materials belonging to the all-but-final stage of Donizetti's illness, when disordered lubricity and frequent masturbation were concomitants of his increasing lack of mental and physical control. Abbiati's book, in fact, though useful in many ways, is extremely unreliable in its handling of factual material; large sections of it amount to semifiction, principally because of his cavalier handling—or disregard—of source materials and the prolixity of his imagination.

Abbiati goes on to retail other gossip about Donizetti—rumors connecting him, for example, with Giuseppina Strigelli-Appiani; with one of the *marchesine* Sterlich[5]—to whom he felt attracted particularly because her physical appearance reminded him of his dead wife—with the wife of the baritone Magrini (" 'who went off pitch out of spite' "), and with the soprano Sophie Löwe, "destined to marry a Prince of Liechtenstein, [who] also would turn the head of the Bergamo musician during the Scala rehearsals of . . . [*Maria*] *Padilla*, composed for her as *Adelia* had been composed for Strepponi. That Milanese giddiness," Abbiati adds, "that too, was to be as fruitless as the Roman giddiness over Strepponi." What documentary basis exists for such specific assertions remains much less than clear.

If, in 1840-41 and later, as much smoke arose and swirled about as Abbiati believed that he could detect one hundred eighteen or nineteen years later, some fire undoubtedly burned. But in actuality it is impossible now to determine what Donizetti's feeling may have been for Strepponi or any of the other women and girls mentioned, whether in Rome, Naples, or Milan, whether before, during, or after the rehearsals and performances of *Adelia* and *Maria Padilla*. All that can be known is that Donizetti occasionally mentioned, always in jocular tones, the possibility of his marrying for a second time[6]—and that later, when his mind and body were weakening and darkening, he fell victim to lonely erotic excesses. Beyond these confirmable facts, everything written about Donizetti's amorous or erotic desires and adventures from 1840 to the day of his death is based on unsupported speculation.

During the rehearsals of *Adelia*, Donizetti was in contact with Paris, Milan, and Vienna about future operas. In the last-mentioned city, his former fellow student at Bergamo and first librettist, Bartolomeo Merelli, now was a powerful impresario, with one hand in the Kärnthnertortheater, the other in La Scala, Milan.[7] Merelli was to be

[5] The two *marchesine* Sterlich—Caterina and Giovanna—daughters of the Marchesa Adelaide Sterlich, often were mentioned affectionately in Donizetti's letters of 1843 and 1844 to Neapolitan friends. He was on intimate terms with their parents, and he felt drawn to one of the girls because she bore some resemblance in his eyes to his lost Virginia.

[6] On January 30, 1841, for example, twelve days before the *première* of *Adelia*, he told Antonio Dolci by letter: "Find me a wife, as I'm drying up alone. You'll make yourself still richer as a marriage broker—in Paris it's a career."

[7] Succeeding Duke Carlo Visconti di Modrone as chief impresario of La Scala in the fall of 1836, Merelli was to hold that important position until late in 1850 and again from the fall of 1861 until early in 1863. On April 1, 1836, he and Carlo Balochino became joint impresarios of the Kärnthnertortheater, establishing a re-

of decisive importance in turning Donizetti's thoughts and footsteps toward Vienna.

During the rehearsals of *Adelia*, Donizetti sat to the *bergamasco* sculptor Giovanni Maria Benzoni (1809-73) at his studio in the Piazza del Popolo for a bust portrait. The Ateneo di Scienze, Lettere ed Arti at Bergamo had commissioned the work. The sculptor's fee was raised by open subscription among the *bergamaschi*. Sixty-two of them bought and contributed enough certificates in Austrian lire to make up the 1,140 Austrian lire (about $515 in today's terms) paid Benzoni in May 1841. Donizetti considered the bust an excellent likeness, an opinion shared by his friends. Antonio Vasselli ordered a gesso copy of it, for which Donizetti sent him, by the hand of Felice Varesi, one of the laurel wreaths presented to him during the Vienna performances of *Linda di Chamounix,* advising him to cover the gesso bust with a green cloth to protect it from dust. The original marble remains at Bergamo in the Ateneo.

Rehearsals of *Adelia* at the Apollo had begun on January 16,[8] and the public's advance interest in the new Donizetti opera grew constantly. It was reported that just before the first performance, Donizetti himself thought it a stroke of good fortune to be able to acquire one ticket for the *première* at three times the published tariff. As it turned out, in fact, the theater sold more tickets than it had seats. The result was that on the night of February 11, 1841, the auditorium quickly was thrown into a condition of near riot by angry ticket holders demanding either seats or the immediate refunding of their money. The performance was started at last amid this hubbub, which lasted well into the sixth scene— at which point Strepponi abandoned the attempt to sing through it.[9] The others on stage, however, continued to sing, gradually losing their

gime that lasted until the revolution that overthrew Ferdinand I and Metternich in 1848. Merelli returned to the Viennese opera house in 1853, serving there for another two years, and his son Eugenio occupied the impresario's office there later. Merelli died in 1879, aged eighty-two.

[8] Annibale Gabrielli (*58*, *85*) wrote that while the *Adelia* rehearsals were proceeding at the Teatro Tordinona (popular orthography for the Tor di Nona or Torre di Nona, up to 1781 the name of the theater located where the Teatro Apollo was opened in 1796), *Maria Stuarda* was being sung at the Teatro Alibert (located on a very short street between the Via del Babuino and the Via Margutta). The Alibert was all but completely destroyed by fire in 1863; the Apollo was demolished in 1887.

[9] A short time earlier, Strepponi had suffered an attack of measles which had forced her to postpone to December 31 her appearance in the leading female role in a staging of Donizetti's *Marin Faliero,* and apparently she was not in proper health to sing at all on this evening—she may well have been pregnant—much less to sing against a turbulent and noisy audience.

places. Then the orchestra also fell silent. Poor Jacovacci, who seems to have been innocent of any deliberate wrongdoing, was arrested. The next day, Strepponi and others succeeded in extricating him from prison after the payment of a heavy fine. Understandably, the first reception of *Adelia* by both audience and press was unusually mixed. It nonetheless ran up nine performances before the Apollo closed its doors for the season.

Annibale Gabrielli, who received firsthand reports of Donizetti's stay in Rome from his grandmother, Antonio Vasselli's daughter Virginia, said (*58*) that the composer enjoyed spending his leisure hours at the then well-known Casino of the Arco de' Carbognani: "He was remembered there by that inexhaustible evoker of Roman anecdotal life, the Marchese Cesare Trevisani,[10] who died a year or two ago. He went to the Circolo of the Arco de' Carbognani every evening about Ave Maria time to play *oca* and billiards; there were talk and laughter and gossip about everything and everybody. And Donizetti found himself much more at ease there than in Parisian circles." A letter of April 12, 1840, which Donizetti wrote to Antonio Vasselli is addressed to him at the Arco de' Carbognani.

Before leaving Rome, Donizetti received from Constantinople an official communication signed Achmed-Fethy and dated January 22, 1841. It stated that Sultan Abdul Medjid had conferred upon him the Order of Nicham-Iftihar, an honor that he probably owed at least in part to the intervention of his brother Giuseppe. The diamond-set decoration itself reached him through diplomatic channels in Paris some months later, and the whole incident both amused and flattered him. On the day when he was to go to accept the decoration at the Ottoman Embassy in Paris, he signed a letter to Antonio Vasselli "*Il gran Kan de' Tartari, Gaetanusko.*" His bag of decorations and honorary memberships constantly grew larger; on November 23, 1841, he also was to be named a Knight of the Pontifical Order of San Silvestro, apparently a confirmation, under new rules, of the Order of the Golden Spur, which he had held since 1822.

Donizetti left Rome on February 19, 1841, traveling with friends as far as Civitavecchia. Out to welcome him as he approached that town came a committee including Pietro de Filippi, president of the local Filarmonica, the Marchesa Calabrini, and Maestro Tommaso Gori. They bore him off to a performance of his *L'Esule di Roma*. Describing the event to Totò Vasselli, Donizetti wrote: "Lucky you, not to have been

[10] Trevisani (1820–97) was a well-known patriot and writer.

at Civita [vecchia] for *L'Esule* or to have had supper at 11 o'clock at night, dying of hunger since one in the afternoon. Long live the Marchesa and the first tenor!" The next day, in the midst of shouts of *"Evviva!"* from a large throng, he boarded a ship bound for Marseille. Reaching Paris on March 2, he put up at the Hôtel Manchester, No. 1 rue Grammont, near the house being used by the Théâtre-Italien. The hotel, housed in a handsome eighteenth-century building, survives to this day. The Michelin *France* for 1963 listed it as a *"hôtel simple, assez confortable."*

Now Donizetti called on Scribe regarding a libretto for his new work for the Opéra. The famous librettist suggested a subject for which Donizetti felt no enthusiasm, so he went to see the authorities at the Opéra about it. When these negotiations came to nothing, he occupied himself with French translations of several of his early operas, including *Parisina* and *Belisario*. He still was receiving performance fees on *La Favorite*, which remained on the stage at the Opéra (twenty-second singing on March 15), and he therefore felt no immediate financial urgency. He composed a collection of piano-accompanied solo songs, duets, and quartets. These the Paris music publisher Meissonier purchased as an album for sixteen hundred francs. They were issued as *Matinées musicales*, with what now seems a peculiar dedication—to Queen Victoria. If Donizetti hoped thus to add an English decoration to his collection, his hope appears to have been frustrated.

On May 5, Donizetti was present at the ceremony memorializing Napoleon on the twentieth anniversary of his death. Writing to Antonio Vasselli on May 6, he said: "Yesterday (May 5) I went to the funeral service for the death of Napoleon. It was touching to see all those who served: some of them even had the uniforms of that period, moth-eaten, threadbare, frazzled; many had had them made new. They kissed the lid, the imperial crown; they wept, and Moncey,[11] the oldest marshal, who is almost a hundred years old [*sic*], was in dress uniform." In this letter he also said: *"Lucrezia [Borgia]* was given at Metz with great success, but here is the point: [Victor] Hugo brought suit against the publisher and the poet, as it is his property; stopped, then, after three evenings of the successful performances."

Aware that Mayr's seventy-eighth birthday was approaching, Donizetti also composed a celebratory cantata, *Il Genio*, to his own text beginning *"Dalla Francia un saluto t'invia."* Having scored it for voices and orchestra, he sent it off to Antonio Dolci on May 18 with a letter

[11] This was Bon-Adrien Jeannot de Moncey, Duc de Conegliano (1754–1842).

giving detailed instructions as to its performance. It was sung as the eleventh and final number on a program performed at Bergamo on Mayr's birthday, June 14. At about this time, too, Donizetti signed a contract with Merelli for an opera to be staged at La Scala, Milan, on Santo Stefano's Day, December 26. He asked Merelli for suggestions as to a libretto, but received no answer. Therefore he wrote Giovanni Ricordi on May 25, asking the publisher to stir up Merelli; he was planning to leave Paris, he wrote, and wanted to have the libretto in his bag. He told Ricordi of having rejected two librettos offered for the Opéra-Comique and said that the Marquis Alexandre-Marie Aguado wanted another four-act work for the Opéra—in addition to *Le Duc d'Albe*—but added that no agreement had been reached. Too, he had whiled away time by translating Cammarano's libretto of *Belisario* into French.

Still lacking a libretto to compose, Donizetti waited impatiently, arranging *Adelia* for a forthcoming performance at Naples, taking up a *Miserere* that he had sketched earlier for three male voices, chorus, and string orchestra with organ, and completing it. Then he sent it to Antonio Vasselli, asking him to see that it was presented to His Holiness Gregory XVI.[12] But these tasks could not fill his time or satisfy him. It was almost certainly at this juncture rather than, as Alborghetti and Galli first suggested and other biographers repeated, in 1840 that he conceived the idea of composing *Rita*.

Rita, ou Le Mari battu, an *opéra-comique* in one act to a text by Gustave Vaëz, never was staged during Donizetti's lifetime: it was first performed, posthumously, at the Opéra-Comique on May 7, 1860. At that time, Achille Denis published an article in the *Revue et gazette des théâtres* in which he said: "He [Donizetti] was strolling along the boulevard des Italiens one evening. He was melancholy—for eight days he had had nothing to set to music, and with Donizetti composition was a real necessity. Having run into Gustave Vaëz, his friend and collaborator on *La Favorite*, he said to him: 'Save my life by giving me right away one act of any sort, so that I can work.' They agreed on a comic subject, and Donizetti soon went home with the words of the first aria, the music of which was complete when, the next morning, Gustave Vaëz took him the words for the second piece. Thus the thing moved forward from that day, and at the end of a week it was all done—libretto, songs, and instrumentation."[13] Confirming Denis's

---

[12] It was in response to this presentation that Donizetti was made a Knight of the Pontifical Order of San Silvestro.

[13] Denis erred in placing this incident in 1848, the year of Donizetti's death—when he was not in Paris and composed nothing—rather than in 1841.

account, Gustave Vaëz himself wrote: "When I read the words of some of the pieces to Donizetti, it would occur that he would take my manuscript, sketch out five lines of a musical phrase, and note down the first draft of the motive sung in his brain during my reading. I have saved those singular autographs. For the rest, no one will marvel to hear that the score of *Rita* was composed in eight days."

With *Rita* finished, but without immediate prospects of staging it in Paris or of signing any new contracts there, Donizetti again began to long for Naples. Receiving from Gaetano Rossi part of the libretto for *Maria Padilla*, the opera promised to Merelli for La Scala, Donizetti began to compose that. In a letter of August 11 to Totò Vasselli, he spoke of leaving Paris and traveling by way of Strasbourg, Basel, and the St. Gotthard Pass, to arrive in Milan by the end of that month. "I am well advanced on the score for Milan, but I go along with my tail on the ground because [Erminia] Frezzolini is pregnant and will give birth in December or January. Imagine what a state I'm in . . . having composed half of the opera, I am being offered a Spanish [soprano] singer who is at Turin and of whom much is hoped, but . . . God knows.[14] But what can I do?" Both in this letter and in another written to Vasselli eleven days later, Donizetti twitted his brother-in-law for not yet having persuaded the Pope—despite the presentation of the *Miserere*—to confer the Order of San Silvestro upon him.

On August 18, Donizetti wrote from Baden to Merelli, expressing the hope of seeing him shortly in Milan. A gap in the surviving correspondence prevents our knowing further details of his movements until September 29,[15] when he wrote Vasselli from Milan to say that he was hard at work on *Maria Padilla* but still had no definite information to report on an opera projected for Vienna. He was staying at the home of his Milanese friends the Appianis, in Borgo Monforte, where he remained until March 9, 1842. He was delighted with Giuseppina Appiani, who, at about forty-five, remained a noted beauty and in whom (as in several other women) he continued to detect a resemblance to his lost Virginia.[16] At the Appianis, he completed *Maria Padilla*, which was ready except for the orchestration by November 2.

[14] The replacement of Frezzolini turned out to be not the "Spanish singer," but Sophie Löwe.

[15] Donizetti almost certainly was in Milan by September 11, when his 1828 opera *Alina, regina di Golconda* initiated a run of twenty-one nights at La Scala.

[16] Giuseppina Appiani was the daughter of a prominent politician, Antonio Strigelli. She had married a son of the well-known neoclassic fresco-painter, portraitist, and glorifier of Napoleon, Andrea Appiani. Raffaello Barbiera, in his *Il Salotto della contessa Maffei*, p. 109, remarked that, like Ninon de Lenclos, Giuseppina Appiani retained her beauty into her old age. See *137*, 101f., for her age.

During October, Donizetti was offered two concurrent positions at Bologna: that of Director of the Liceo and that of *maestro di cappella* at San Petronio. He wrote Dolci that he had refused them without knowing why, but Guido Zavadini shrewdly guessed that one of the causes for his refusal—which was repeated later, when Rossini urged him to accept—was his awareness that the positions had been declined first by Saverio Mercadante. Donizetti certainly would have felt some reluctance to accept posts that had been turned down by the very man who, instead of himself, had been appointed permanent Director of the Collegio di San Pietro a Maiella at Naples. Early in October (or possibly very late in September), Donizetti visited Bergamo with his friend the composer Placido Mandanici, both of them being guests of Rosa Basoni. But during November and December, with the orchestration of *Maria Padilla* progressing swiftly and his head buzzing with ideas for the opera meant for Vienna, he again worked away quietly at the Appiani home in Milan until rehearsals of *Maria Padilla* got under way at La Scala.

At midnight on Christmas Eve, Donizetti wrote Totò Vasselli that the dress rehearsal of *Maria Padilla* had been held. The opera opened the Carnival season at La Scala on December 26. Two days later, Donizetti thus detailed to Vasselli the way the second-night audience had reacted to the new opera:

Historic drama of the second performance of *Maria Padilla* at the I. R. Teatro della [*sic*] Scala, Milan, December 28, 1841.

Maestro on the stage.
Cavatina of Ines—the Maestro called out once.
Cavatina of Maria—the Maestro called out once.
Entrance of Don Pedro—applause; the Maestro called out once.
Duet of Don Pedro and Maria—much applause. The singers called out, the Maestro no.

Second Act

Chorus—applause.
Cavatina of Ruiz—[Domenico] Donzelli called out.
Duet of Maria and Ines—the Maestro called out twice.
Duet of Ruiz and Don Pedro—much applause.
Final *stretta*—little applause.

Third Act

Trio of the two ladies and the second tenor—applauded.
Duet of Ruiz and Maria—the Maestro called for after the adagio, everyone afterwards.

Chorus—nothing.

The romance of [Giorgio] Ronconi, or Don Pedro—the Maestro called out once.

Finale—the Maestro called out for the adagio. Everyone out at the end. The Maestro twice alone and twice with the singers.

And, in fact, *Maria Padilla* aroused enough enthusiasm at La Scala to hold the stage there for twenty-four performances. But when it was put on at La Fenice, Venice, in the Carnival season of 1843,[17] it was a fiasco, languishing through only two performances after its coldly received *première*. Donizetti tried revising it, but finally realized that nothing he could do would endear *Maria Padilla* to his audiences.

At the Appianis' in Milan late in 1841, however, Donizetti started to compose to a libretto by Gaetano Rossi, an *opera semiseria* that was to achieve international fame, to help him win the positions of court composer to the Austrian emperor and Master of the Imperial Chapel, and to go far toward making him as much a favorite in Vienna as he had been in Paris. This was the three-act *Linda di Chamounix*.[18] When Michele Accursi wrote and urged him to return to Paris, Donizetti replied that the trip seemed doubtful to him, largely because he had had no definite word from Léon Pillet of the Opéra. On January 2, 1842, he wrote Accursi that in March he was going to Vienna, but had not decided what he would do after that, though he was being besought to compose for both Venice and Naples. On January 18, he was in Bergamo, where he heard the *première* of *Lutaldo da Viclungo*, an opera by a fellow *bergamasco*, Girolamo Forini, with whom he had attended the Lezioni caritatevoli di musica under Mayr thirty-five years earlier and who had sung a role in his own *Piccioli Virtuosi ambulanti* at Bergamo in the summer of 1819. He remained in Bergamo only over a long weekend, but he was to spend another three days there in February on a visit to Mayr, who had had an operation for cataracts.

Gossip, which by 1842, was connecting Donizetti in hot intimacy with every young and middle-aged woman with whom he had relations of any sort, now had begun to feed on his Milan and Venice Maria

[17] The Fenice cast included Sophie Löwe, Almerinda Granchi, Cesare Badiali, and Fortunato Borioni.

[18] Maurice-Pierre Boyé (*22*) wrote that the libretto of *Linda di Chamounix* had been influenced by the melodrama *La Grâce de Dieu*, by Adolphe-Philippe d'Ennery, called Dennery, and Gustave Lemoine, who in turn had taken their inspiration from a *romance* of the same name by Loïsa Puget which had been sung by Mlle Clarisse at the Théâtre de la Gaieté, Paris. And in fact, Donizetti at first referred to the opera—as in a letter of December 31, 1841, to Michele Accursi (*43a*, *73*)— as *La Grâce de Dieu*. In that same letter, he mentioned two stormily successful concerts given at La Scala on December 7 and 28 by Sigismond Thalberg.

Padilla, Sophie Löwe. Writing from Milan to Michele Accursi on January 8, he said: "Did you read in a German paper that I will marry La Löwe? What damned fools! *Jamais, au grand jamais.* If there had been love between us at least, I'd say that they have made a mistake, but this way—they have made a joke." In view of those sentences, Guglielmo Barblan has written (*43a*, 8*): "Notable in the Correspondence is the particular fondness that linked Donizetti to the soprano Sophie Löwe after she was chosen as interpreter of the opera *Maria Padilla* (Scala, Santo Stefano, 1841). The more than forty-year-old composer resisted poorly the fascination of the twenty-six-year-old and rising German singer, destined later to become the Princess of Lichtenstein. That this fondness had remained platonic, or at least had been kept discreet and reserved, is difficult to believe now that from a letter of January 1842 addressed to Accursi we come to know that a 'German paper' had announced flatly a Donizetti-Löwe marriage." As with others of Maestro Barblan's readings of the runes, his reasoning here resembles wishful interpretation. Simply, no evidence whatever, one way or the other, links Donizetti to Sophie Löwe in more than the warm friendship of a composer for one of his important divas.

At about this time, Antonio Vasselli wrote in an astonished tone to say that one of Saverio Mercadante's operas had been a success in Rome. On January 18, Donizetti replied: "Why do you find it extraordinary that Mercadante should have pleased? I find that completely normal." He harbored no bitterness against the man who had succeeded, where he himself had not, in becoming *maestro di cappella* at Novara and permanent director of the Naples Conservatory and had been offered the Bologna positions before him. Indeed, writing two years later to the music publisher Guglielmo Cottrau, he was to say: "It is justice, finally, that Mercadante has been thought of for a decoration."

On February 16, 1842, Donizetti wrote Vasselli that *Linda di Chamounix,* the opera for Merelli's company at the Vienna Kärnthnertortheater, nearly was finished; he sent the completed score to Vienna on March 4. He intended to visit Bergamo again so as to spend more time with Mayr, but an invitation from Rossini intervened. To Antonio Dolci on March 2, Donizetti reported: "If you read the theatrical papers and perhaps also the *Gazzetta privilegiata* [*di Milano*], you will know on Sunday why my visit now has been made problematic. Rossini has written me to go to Bologna to conduct his *Stabat* [*Mater*],[19]

[19] This most renowned of Rossini's later compositions (a first incomplete version of which dated from 1832), was first heard incomplete on two occasions in October 1841, the first at the home of Pierre-Joseph-Guillaume Zimmerman, the

putting at my disposition his house, his future, and his life. Think well how honorific a matter this is. There will be a hundred singers and more. Then I'll go by diligence to Ferrara, Padua, and Vicenza, finding my companions for Vienna there. The *Stabat* will be on the 17th or 18th, and I'll leave from there on the 20th for Vienna."

Donizetti wanted to remain in Milan long enough to hear the first performance (La Scala, March 9) of Verdi's new opera, *Nabucodonosor. Nabucco,* as it soon came to be called, was sung by a cast that included Giuseppina Strepponi (Abigaille), Giovannina Bellinzaghi (Fenena), Teresa Ruggeri (Anna), Giorgio Ronconi (Nabucodonosor), Corrado Miraglia (Ismaele), Prosper Dérivis (Zaccaria), Gaetano Rossi (High Priest of Baal), and Napoleone Marconi (Abdallo). Up to December 4 of that year, it had been sung at La Scala sixty-seven times. Verdi's biographers, to whom Giuseppina Strepponi became a sort of lay saint, have written of her triumph in *Nabucco.* But Donizetti, who was there, knew the truth, which was that she sang badly at the time. On March 4, writing to Antonio Vasselli, he had said that she was "the only one who has had no applause, that her Verdi doesn't want her in his opera [*Nabucco*], and that the impresario [Merelli] has forced him to have her." The late Frank Walker, in his monumentally patient collection of Verdi detective-work essays (*137*), wrote: "The truth is that the strain of years of continuous overwork, interrupted only by pregnancies [she had had a child in 1838 and a miscarriage in 1839 as a result of her liaison with Napoleone Moriani—and was to have a second child by him in 1841], had now begun to tell and was to lead, during the production of Verdi's opera, to loss of voice and almost complete collapse." Walker showed that pious Verdians have gone so far as to falsify quotations from criticisms of Strepponi's performance in *Nabucco* —and that in fact its first critics largely overlooked her while praising her colleagues. When *Nabucco* was revived at La Scala for fifty-seven added performances in the fall of 1842, the Abigaille was not Strepponi, as has been broadly hinted, but Teresa de Giuli. Donizetti, then, had been reporting the truth, as he usually did.

At that historic performance of *Nabucco*, Donizetti sat in a box

---

second—a few days later (six sections)—at the home of Henri Herz, this time with Pauline Viardot-García as one of the soloists. It had been performed complete for the first time at the Salle Ventadour, Paris, on January 7, 1842, when the singers had been Giulia Grisi, Emma (Howson) Albertazzi, Mario, and Antonio Tamburini. Donizetti was to conduct it at the Archiginnasio, Bologna, only five months after its first, partial performances and only a little more than two months after it had been sung complete for the first time.

with Giuseppina Appiani. A group of his Bergamo friends, including Antonio Dolci and Countess Rosa Basoni, occupied another box. The day after that *première*, Donizetti left Milan, having been there for more than five months. On March 12, he was in Bologna, where the rehearsals of Rossini's *Stabat Mater* already were well advanced—he was required only to put the final touches on it at the last rehearsals. Annibale Gabrielli wrote (*58*, 88) that on the day of the final rehearsal, Rossini appeared, grasped Donizetti's hand, and said in a high, emotional voice: "*Signori*, I present to you Gaetano Donizetti: I confide the performance of the *Stabat* to him as the only person capable of conducting and interpreting it as I created it." It was sung under Donizetti's direction on March 19, 20, and 21, and aroused vibrating enthusiasm.[20] Rossini, suffering from a bladder complaint and exacerbated nerves, did not wish to attend, fearing that he might become overexcited. But Donizetti persuaded him to be present at the third singing. Acclaimed enthusiastically, he embraced and kissed Donizetti to the delight of the audience, which thereupon applauded the two men frantically. In memory of the occasion, Rossini gave Donizetti four diamond studs. Padre Stanislao Mattei, who had taught both of them at the Liceo there in Bologna, was not present to witness this triumph: he had died in 1825, aged seventy-five.

Antonio Vasselli must have predicted that Donizetti would earn very small pay by his conductorial labors, for on April 4 Donizetti wrote him from Vienna: "Do you know that Rossini gave me four studs for having conducted the *Stabat?* If one considers their value, you have won; but if one thinks of their donor, I am right. Do you understand? If you could see how he *really* wept on leaving me!" Rossini later referred to Donizetti as "the only *maestro* in Italy who knows how to conduct my '*Stabat*' as I wish it," also writing (April 24, 1842), to Lambertini, director of the *Gazzetta privilegiata di Milano* that he was very grateful to the "excellent performers, and in particular to Donizetti, who has done me an immense service with his vigor and his intelligence. The condition of my health did not allow me to conduct the *Stabat*: who better than he in that case?"

---

[20] The leading singers were Clara Novello—the young English soprano had made her operatic debut at Padua the preceding year—Nicholas Ivanoff, Count Pompeo Belgiojoso, and Clementina degli Antoni. Some members of the chorus were well-known singers of the time, including Rosa Bottrigari-Bonetti and the bass Zucchelli (whom Rossini called "my fine Don Magnifico," referring to the character in *Cenerentola*), and one of them was to become very famous indeed: Marietta Alboni. The best instrumentalists were recruited for the orchestra, including the trombonist Gaetano Brizzi, of whom Donizetti said that on the Day of Judgment the Eternal Father would call upon him to wake the dead.

On March 20, Donizetti wrote to "Tommasiello"—his Neapolitan friend Tommaso Persico: "We are at the third and final performance [of the *Stabat Mater*] today. The enthusiasm is impossible to describe to you. After the final rehearsal, which Rossini attended in full daylight, he was accompanied to his house amid the shouting of more than five hundred people. The same thing the first night under his windows, though he was not in the room. And yesterday the same. And La Novello and Ivanoff and the dilettante Degli Antonj and Count Pompeo Belgiojoso of Milan and I have been *écrasés* by the applause and shouting, poems, etc." Later in this letter, he said: "Rossini besieges and seduces me to accept the direction of the Liceo and the *cappella* here.[21] If it does not prove to my liking, I can leave whenever I wish. Leaves: twice yearly. What shall I say?" Donizetti appears to have made his demands excessive partly in the hope of postponing a decision until he could learn how matters would turn out for him in Vienna and partly out of consideration for the composer Giovanni Tadolini, who was known to yearn for this appointment. But he considered the prospect carefully, dreaming of a somewhat settled life as preferable to the "Bohemian" existence of which, he told Totò Vasselli—who kept urging him to accept the Bologna positions—he was so weary (letter of April 8, 1842).

On March 21, Donizetti left Bologna for Vienna armed with a letter of introduction from Rossini to Prince Clemens von Metternich, then in the thirty-third of his thirty-nine years as Austrian Minister of Foreign Affairs. At Vicenza on March 23, he met the singers signed up by Merelli for the Vienna season. They all reached the Austrian capital four days later. On March 30, Donizetti wrote Tommaso Persico: "Vienna is beautiful, beautiful, beautiful." Rehearsals of *Linda di Chamounix* began immediately at the "Teatro di Porta Carinzia"—that is, the Imperial Opera House, or Kärnthnertortheater. While these were proceeding, Michele Accursi was continuing to plead with Donizetti to come to Paris and Rossini was still urging him to accept the two positions in Bologna, notably in a letter dated April 12:

My well-loved Donizetti,
    I send you some emendations made in your proposition as it was left with me by the Marchese Bevilacqua, and I pray you to consider them, but without regarding this as an ultimatum. Because you indicated that you

[21] That is, of the Liceo that both he and Rossini had attended, as well as of the chapel of San Petronio. Saverio Mercadante had accepted Rossini's offer of these positions—and then had withdrawn just a few days before he was supposed to take them up. Giovanni Pacini then had been approached but had asserted that he did not think himself "capable of so much." Donizetti, then, was Rossini's third choice in this part of his attempt to rejuvenate the truly decadent Liceo.

would give the harmony lessons, it occurred to the above-mentioned Count that you would want to give the lessons in counterpoint, high dramatic composition, ecclesiastics, etc. But I clearly recall that you do not wish to have the boredom of the scholastic part, but want to occupy yourself only with the most interesting part, and in that we are perfectly in accord. If the Comune must take on the expense of a *maestro* for harmony and counterpoint, it will be necessary for you to be satisfied with fifty zecchini per month; I would like you to reflect that during your leaves, your remuneration, however small, will not be suspended or diminished, which means that for your months of service you will have about seventy-seven zecchini monthly. This is a misery, it's true, but we are at Bologna! Six months of leave as a condition in a contract are too many; it seems to me that four and a half months would suffice. Your presence at Bologna is indispensable in mid-September, the period during which admissions to the Liceo are made and they get ready for the opening of the school, which takes place at the beginning of October; the time at which they prepare the *festa* for the patron saint at San Petronio; and the period, finally, of the big performance of the autumn. Once you are established here, I guarantee you all the leaves you want. I will take this up verbally with the Senator, and in that, as in anything else, I will be the intermediary, sure to succeed in contenting you. Don't abandon me, Donizetti! The feelings of gratitude and of affection which I hold for you merit some sacrifice on your part. If you wish to bring capital to Bologna, I will make good, secure investments for you; doing that, you will find yourself well compensated for your current sacrifices. The Marchese Pizzardi will pay you six hundred Austrian lire, with which you can acquire, if you like, a scarfpin that [Nicholas] Ivanoff offers you as a reminder of the beautiful gift that you gave him. I await your decision like an inamorata. Remember that you are idolized at Bologna. Think that here one lives handsomely for a few scudi; reflect, decide, and console him who is blessed to call himself your affectionate friend,   Gioacchino Rossini.

Donizetti's reply to that letter appears not to have survived. On May 10, however, he wrote Giuseppina Appiani that it, in turn, had elicited no reply from Rossini, whom he therefore thought might be "*vexé, contrarié.*" Four days before that, he had written Totò Vasselli that he had hopes that the Bologna question might be settled in a few days: "I am still waiting for his [Rossini's] letters. Bologna is sad, I will be bored, but at least I'll have some place to rest myself. The distraction and satisfaction of shaping pupils will serve to prepare me for a less sorrowful decrepitude, if I ever reach it. By every courier I expect news of the yes or the no." By that time, however, he very apparently had decided that, for him, Vienna was preferable to Bologna.

Vasselli and others of Donizetti's friends were not only disappointed, but also slightly affronted, at his preferring what they thought of as an uncertain position at the Vienna court—the center of the despotism that still held much of northern Italy in its iron fist—to very honorable, settled positions in Bologna. As late as July 25, Donizetti was writing to Vasselli: "Your scolding me about the Vienna situation rather than the Bolognese is as comic as Gaetano. To let pass by a thousand Austrian lire per month for doing nothing and many months of freedom in order to earn fifty scudi, give lessons at a conservatory, direct it and conduct, and make pieces for the chapel, with two or three months of leave! That's how one lives at court, and I prefer . . . the courtly! What difference does it make to you if I'm not at Bologna? Can I then live in Rome at the expense of others, be with you all the time, and entertain myself? Well, I hope that you will see Vienna, *per bacco!* You ought to, in the end, with the sight of your brother-in-law in sword and gold embroidery in the ranks of the Aulic councillors!"

Donizetti meanwhile had made his Vienna debut on May 4, conducting Rossini's *Stabat Mater* in the presence of the Emperor Ferdinand I, his wife the Empress Maria Anna, and his widowed mother the Empress Maria Theresa. On May 6, he wrote Vasselli: "Two days ago at court to perform the '*Stabat*' with two pianofortes, sixteen choristers, La Tadolini, La Brambilla, Moriani, Donzelli, Badiali, and Dérivis. It went very well, and His Imperial Highness the Emperor and the two empresses (the widow and the reigning), all the brothers and their wives, besides the Prince of Salerno, came to me over and over again to testify to their pleasure in so perfected a performance and to the sensations that they had experienced. . . . I was surrounded by the entire Imperial family as if I belonged to them. *De hoc satis.*" Shortly later, he received a diamond-studded scarfpin as a signal of their satisfaction with him. To this further show of imperial favor he responded by sending the Emperor an *Offertorio* in five voices (a soprano representing the Angel, a four-voice chorus representing the Church), the text being the Ave Maria, the accompaniment for two violins, two violas, cello, and contrabass. The piece bears this inscription: "Composed for the Imperial Royal Chapel, dedicated to His Majesty Ferdinand I, Emperor of Austria, by Gaetano Donizetti of Bergamo, 1842, Vienna."

On April 11, writing to Dolci, Donizetti reported: "I just have come from the famous painter who makes such good portraits, and my own is completed too." The painter was Joseph Kriehuber (1800–76). Late in May, Donizetti told Giuseppina Appiani: "And my portrait? Do you know that even the famous Kriehuber, who has done so well in making likenesses of all the artists, went wrong with me? . . . To me it seems that he has made an enormous forehead, then, a head much larger than mine. . . . Certainly, if the original be not present, you will say that this is D . . . but in my presence, no, and everyone says so."

Donizetti by no means had been unknown to the Viennese public before 1842. Beginning with *L'Ajo nell'imbarazzo*, which had had seven performances at the Kärnthnertortheater between March 28 and May 20, 1827, stagings of seventeen of his operas had made his name and works familiar to them.[22] His presence therefore created a considerable commotion among the city's musical people; the *première* of the opera that he had composed especially for them was awaited somewhat breathlessly. As the piano rehearsals of *Linda di Chamounix* ended and the orchestral rehearsals began, however, Donizetti still was planning to leave Vienna before the end of May. In a letter to Dolci on May 15, he said: "By the end of this month I'll no longer be in Vienna, and I've let my house for the 29th. Where I'll go then I myself don't know, whether to Naples or to Paris or to Milan. All of that can be decided between one day and the next by letters that may arrive. Most of all I'd love to come to Milan, but I haven't seen Naples for four years and more,[23] and I want to clean up my affairs at last and then, if it's possible, to be a little more peaceful." That his thoughts repeatedly turned to Italy also was proved when, in the same letter, he told Dolci: "Tomorrow I sup with his Highness [Prince] Metternich, and I want to speak about our poor Bergamo, despondent because of the railway that hasn't been conceded."

In one of the most staccato and high-spirited of all his letters, Donizetti informed his friend Gaetano Cobianchi of Paris about the opening of the Italian season at the Kärnthnertortheater:

[22] The tally of Donizetti operas performed in Vienna between 1827 and 1893 —at the Kärnthnertortheater and the new Opernhaus—is an impressive testimonial to his popularity. Of the twenty-five Donizetti operas sung at the two theaters during those sixty-six years, the largest numbers of performances were run up by *Lucia di Lammermoor* (286), *Lucrezia Borgia* (237), *L'Elisir d'amore* (193), *Don Sebastiano* (162), *La Figlia del reggimento* (139), *Linda di Chamounix* (129), *Don Pasquale* (82), *Maria di Rohan* (71), *La Favorita* (68), and *Anna Bolena* (43). The others were *L'Ajo nell'imbarazzo*, *Alina, regina di Golconda*, *Le Convenienze ed inconvenienze teatrali*, *Il Furioso all'isola di San Domingo*, *Gemma di Vergy*, *Maria Padilla*, *Marin Faliero*, *Olivo e Pasquale*, *Otto Mesi in due ore*, *Parisina*, *Poliuto*, *Roberto Devereux*, *Torquato Tasso*, and *Ugo, conte di Parigi*. In those sixty-six years, a grand total of 1,694 complete singings of Donizetti operas was heard at Vienna's leading operatic theater.

[23] Donizetti actually had been away from Naples three years and about eight months, having left there last in September 1838.

The opening of the Italians was made with Mercadante's *La Vestale*;[24] the fiasco was so strong, especially for the poor Marini, that from the first of April on she did not appear on the stage. There was an attempt to relieve the situation a little with *Anna [Bolena]*, but the public does not want La Tadolini except as a *buffa*, besides which Moriani was taken sick after two performances. They had recourse to *Belisario*, but after five hundred and some performances in Italian and in the German language, it no longer could. . . . Then *L'Elisir [d'amore]*, ah! at last La Tadolini well placed, but the theater still badly filled. . . . Then they did Ricci's *Corrado d'Altamura*[25] . . . said and done . . . in fact, it was a success in several numbers . . . let's give *Il Bravo*[26] . . . instead of La Marini let's have La Schrikel, who is here. Yes! . . . It is done . . . On with it. Stop! The Bravo [Domenico Donzelli, scheduled to play the title role] has the gout. . . . Oh, *cazzo*! what to do while waiting? Let's give the ballet that Mlle Blangy herself is going to stage . . . get on with it, quick, quick . . . *Giselle*. Alas, a pitiful mounting. Blangy and Giselle, you take a walk. . . . Let Donizetti start rehearsing. There you are, by the grace of God. But what to do while waiting? Wait, Donzelli is better. . . . *Bravo*, and then? Yes! . . . There we are. First performance with Tadolini, Schrikel, Donzelli, etc., all arranged; until tomorrow. . . . The next day, a doctor's certificate . . . Donzelli's gout. Hurry up, then, Herr Donizetti. Here I am, get on, get on . . . stop, for two days we must rehearse [Rossini's] *Otello* for Donzelli's benefit! That's fine. Begin again, Herr Donizetti. Here I am. And here we are! Within twelve days, then, *Linda [di Chamounix]* will be given (by the grace of God), and after that where will Donizetti go? I don't know. How? . . . To you, a thousand embraces from your debtor for five francs for a collect letter.

Writing on April 30 to Michele Accursi (*43a*, 81), Donizetti thought that *Linda* would be sung before May 15. "In *Linda* I think that there's a duet that must make as much of an effect as 'Suoni la tromba' in *Puritani*, between Dérivis and Varese [*sic*]." This very probably referred to the first-act *scena e duetto* "Quella pietà si provvida." Actually,

[24] More than thirty-two years after the *première* of Gaspare Spontini's renowned setting of Victor-Joseph Étienne de Jouy's *La Vestale* (Opéra, Paris, December 16, 1807), Mercadante's setting of a libretto by the same name, the work of Salvatore Cammarano, was heard at the Teatro San Carlo, Naples (March 10, 1840). Although, unlike Spontini's opera, it had a tragic ending, it won a very considerable and long-lasting success.

[25] Federico Ricci's *Corrado d'Altamura*, with text by Giacomo Sacchèro, had first been heard at the Teatro alla Scala, Milan, on November 16, 1841, and later was widely performed.

[26] This could have been either Marco Aurelio Marliani's *Il Bravo* (Théâtre-Italien, Paris, February 1, 1834), with a text based on James Fenimore Cooper by Arcangelo Berrettoni, or the opera of the same name by Mercadante, text by Gaetano Rossi and Marco Marcelliano Marcello, first heard at the Teatro alla Scala, Milan, on March 9, 1839, when it began a run of forty performances. Mercadante's highly successful opera was heard all over Europe and was being revived in Italian opera houses just before 1900.

the first performance of the opera[27] was sung at the Kärnthnertortheater on May 19, 1842. Donizetti reported that *première* to Vasselli thus two days later: *"Linda di Chamounix*, opera in three acts; singers: Tadolini, Brambilla, Moriani, Varese [*sic*], Dérivis, Rovere. The Maestro called out seventeen times, alone and with the singers. The theater packed. Second performance: an enormous wreath of flowers tossed at the Maestro. Monday, third performance (and Moriani now not very good), Moriani's [benefit] evening. The composer directed his music in person. The papers speak with much enthusiasm, but as they are in German and his Roman brother-in-law, like the writer, doesn't understand . . . therefore I've sent them instead to Paris and Milan, where they will be translated and sent to the Italian papers. . . ."

Writing to Giovanni Ricordi on May 24, Donizetti said: "You will have learned of the success of your *Linda*, at least of that of the first and second evenings; now I can tell you about the third. Moriani's [benefit] evening, two thousand two hundred florins. I think this the finest eulogy that can be made of my poor music. The entire Imperial Family was there yesterday evening, and did not depart until having seen me come out twice, uniting their applause to the public's. After the second act on the second evening, a huge wreath of exquisite flowers was thrown to me, and the next day another, of laurel, from an unknown hand, was sent to me at my house. Yesterday evening after the second act another huge wreath, which in view of the public I instantly gave to the distinguished Tadolini. All the artists contended with each other in zeal, all have the right to applause. But La Tadolini has awakened in a surprising way . . . She is a singer, she is an actress, she is everything—and, imagine, she was applauded when she merely walked on in the third act! If you will see *Linda* with Tadolini, you will truly see a madwoman of a new kind. She was so obedient to me in weeping, laughing, remaining stunned when she should, that I myself say that this scene is on a higher plane (performed thus) than any of the other scenes I have written for madwomen."

Crowds were turned away from the Kärnthnertortheater each evening, and it was said that no such success ever had been recorded in Vienna. Small wonder, then, that Donizetti decided to dedicate the

---

[27] The opera did not then include what was later to become its most popular single number, Linda's *"O luce di quest'anima,"* which Donizetti composed to his own text especially for Fanny Tacchinardi-Persiani when she was going to sing the title role in Paris in November 1842, and which was heard in Italy for the first time when Eugenia Tadolini sang it in performances of *Linda* at the Teatro San Carlo, Naples, during the Carnival of 1843.

opera "to Her Majesty the Empress Maria Anna Carolina." On May 28, too, he was made a member of the venerable Musikfreunde, his diploma being signed by the organization's vice-president, the notable musical scholar and writer Raphael Kiesewetter, Edler von Weissenbrunn. Donizetti was feted everywhere. Metternich tendered a supper in his honor and arranged a special musical matinee so that he could hear Henriette Sontag sing. "She sings marvelously well," Donizetti wrote Michele Accursi on May 22. To Dolci on May 30, he said: "I found the Princess Metternich[28] the most amiable woman you can imagine with me, whereas many others say the opposite. She said that she [did not] like me, but only because I made her cry too much at *Linda*—but that too is a compliment."

In a letter of May 24 to Vasselli, Donizetti mentioned that on that very day he had completed "a little musical album (to pay for the trip). . . ." This was to be published both as *Ispirazioni viennesi* and as *Inspirations viennoises*. It is made up of five solo songs and two duets. Most of them are to texts by Carlo Guaita, and several of them were to become sentimental favorites both in concerts and recitals and in salons whenever there was private music making.

On June 4, in the highest good spirits, Donizetti wrote to Giuseppina Appiani:

This evening (Saturday) is Tadolini's [benefit] evening, and I myself will conduct, because that thing on the announcement brings in some hundreds of florins more . . . . I don't know if you're familiar with Figaro's aria in Rossini's *Barbiere*—*tutti mi chiedono, tutti mi vogliono*, etc. . . . That's the way it is. . . . Paris [says]: come at once. No! Naples: come running. No! Bologna: settle down here, here are the terms. No! Would you like to accept—(now comes the *adagio*)—the position in V . . . i . . . e . . . n . . . n . . . a of *maestro di corte*? Say so, for then you'll be made a proposition. . . . But what ought I to do? *Maestro di corte* is all right, it seems to me . . . if the pay is reasonable. The title is decorous . . . the work can't be very hard.

The Théâtre-Italien wants some operas, therefore one each year! Leaves, etc. But—my Milan? Oh, I'd leave everything [else] for that ungrateful Milan, which makes a bad face at the birth of *Anna, Elisir, Lucrezia, Gemma, Padilla*—and yet, if I have worked with gusto, it has been for Milan. And still I desire Milan—and still Milan doesn't want me! . . .

---

[28] Princess Metternich (not to be confused with her daughter-in-law, the famous hostess of Second Empire Paris) belonged to a very distinguished Austrian family. Both her social position and her great wealth had been influential in launching her husband's career. She was a granddaughter of Prince Wenzel von Kaunitz-Rietberg, who had been important in determining Austrian domestic policies from about 1753 to his death in 1794.

Metternich introduced me here the other night to the Count and Countess Borromeo. I had the most flattering recognition from His Highness Metternich on the occasion of the party given at his villa on His Majesty's birthday. Everything was diplomacy, luxury, and yet he and several Royal Princes did not disdain my arm: *celà soit dit en passant*. It was the first time that I had the calvary on me[29]—I shone like a comet with a tail.

Rossini's *Stabat Mater* now having become a Donizetti specialty, he conducted two enthusiastically applauded public performances of it at the Redoutensaal on May 30 and June 8, this time with full orchestra, earning a thousand Austrian lire. In late June, too, he learned that he was to be appointed *Maestro di Cappella e di Camera e Compositore di Corte*.[30] In an undated letter to Dolci, he said: "Tomorrow, by the railroad, which saves one [the time required by] five posts, we leave Vienna and come to Italy after a thousand plaudits, shouts, dinners, and suppers. I have taken my leave of His Majesty and of all the Royal Imperial Family. The Imperial Royal Maestro (for I am *Maestro Direttore de' Concerti Privati di S. M. I. R. A.*,[31] with twelve thousand Austrian lire per year and many months of leave) wants to see you and to embrace our good Mayr. I think that this title and this position, occupied by Mozart, by [Leopold Anton] Koželuch, and then by [Franz] Krommer, is very flattering for a composer. Henceforth I hope that I shan't cut a ridiculous figure; otherwise, with the right [to wear] a gilded habit and sword, I shall challenge you to settle all accounts. His Majesty, not to mention all the Royal Princes, shows me the greatest favor. . . . There have been those to say that I am signed up to do nothing for six months and to relax for another six months. Every piece ordered will be paid for by the Court."[32]

Donizetti left Vienna on July 1, going directly to Milan, where he planned to stay with the Appianis for two weeks before proceeding to the coast to embark for Naples. Writing from Milan to Totò Vasselli on July 13, he again mentioned that the court position to which he had been appointed in Vienna once had been occupied by Mozart: "You wanted me placed, and behold me as Imperial Royal Chamber Composer and Director of the Private Concerts of His Imperial Royal Austrian Majesty, with a thousand Austrian lire per month, staying six months in Vienna and six at liberty; a position that Mozart had. Behold me, no longer a gypsy, but with sword and cape. . . . I don't know

[29] Donizetti evidently is referring to the weight of his court dress.

[30] The official patent of appointment, signed by the "Imperial Royal Councillor Baron Joseph von Sacken," was dated July 3, 1842.

[31] His Imperial Royal Austrian Majesty.

[32] Jokingly, Donizetti signed a letter of June 6, to Tommaso Persico, "The Pillar of Italian *bel canto*, etc., etc., etc."

when I'll be coming from Civitavecchia, but soon. . . ." And on Bastille Day, he wrote to Vernoy de Saint-Georges, the prolific Parisian librettist who (with Bayard) had provided him with the text of *La Fille du régiment*, agreeing to work with him on a comic opera, the prima donna's role to be written for Elisa Rossi. He added that he expected to be in Paris toward the end of August:

"The poem [should be] interesting—that is to say, the heart should speak in it. I have faith in your ability, in your experience of the stage— few characters. It is well agreed that we should have the best artists. La Rossi without doubt. I suggest to you above everything else not to write [for] too many pieces of music, so that none will have to be deleted as [happened] in *La Fille du régiment*. I asked you[33] to send me to Naples the choruses, Rossi's cavatina—in sum, the pieces that cannot stand in the way of our working out the canvas later on between us. . . . I should like the opera to be staged in December, not later, as it is necessary for me to be in Vienna during the first days in January. I will be ready to start rehearsing in October. I am very unhappy at not being able to come to Paris sooner, but you know that I work rapidly. Your verses will make my work easy. I am going to disentangle myself from my Rome commitment. You can count on me, so arrange our turn for beginning the rehearsals. I have only one final thing to ask of you—silence for a while, as I do not wish the director at Rome to learn that after a project [was] started, I accepted another later on."

The opera foreseen in this letter never was completed. Almost certainly, it was to have been a three-act *opéra-comique* to be entitled *Ne m'oubliez pas*, which Donizetti actually began to compose later in 1842 and to which he made an apparent reference in a letter from Vienna to Dolci on April 21, 1844: ". . . an opera that I have in my portfolio (French) (translating it) . . ." Why Donizetti abandoned this project, to compose *Don Pasquale* as his next opera instead, cannot now be determined. The Library of the Paris Conservatory has seven completely orchestrated numbers for *Ne m'oubliez pas*, one or more for each of its proposed three acts.

Donizetti was at Bergamo again for several days from July 18 on. The weather had the sultriness of summer in the Lombard plain, and he was unwell. His friends at Bergamo evidently displayed their concern about the state of his health—which by this time had begun to tell upon his formerly erect posture, notably clear eyes, and animated ex-

---

[33] Donizetti had written about the projected libretto to Vernoy de Saint-Georges earlier, and now merely was adding finality and details.

pression. On July 29, back in Milan, he wrote to Dolci: "I was not exactly in a bad mood in Bergamo except for a little headache when I was at Signora Basoni's home; I renew my apologies to her." Of this visit to Bergamo, Dr. Federico Alborghetti and Dr. Michelangelo Galli wrote (5): "His old friends observed with stupefaction that in little more than two months, he visibly had grown older. The tall figure, which he usually [had] carried erect and majestic, had begun to sag at the shoulders. His face and forehead were furrowed with deep lines; his eyes, still glowing and full of expression, appeared sunk deeper in their large sockets. His hair and beard were speckled with white." Donizetti was not yet forty-five at the time. He was not to visit Bergamo again for two years, and then, in July 1844, his friends were to find this physical deterioration justifiably alarming.

In reply to a rebuke from Totò Vasselli for having chosen Vienna rather than Bologna, Donizetti wrote him on July 25 from Milan the letter quoted above.[34] It is a very curious document, begun in macaronic Latin, continued in French, lapsing briefly into Italian, ending in Latin. Of Donizetti's jerkily phrased, exclamation-spotted, alternately frenetic and passive-melancholy letters of this period, Annibale Gabrielli wrote (58): "After the clamorous celebrations fallen to his lot because of *Linda*, after this nomination as maestro director of the private concerts of his imperial and royal majesty, after he was assured of his twelve thousand Austrian lire per annum, Donizetti appeared more overexcited than ever. Certain letters to Dolci from this period, by their uneven style, their jerky form, with expressions in dialect strewed here and there, now reveal an aggravated psychic state in the Maestro; and in his correspondence with Vasselli, these things are met with again in curious letters written in macaronic Latin."

Donizetti's epistolary style always had been alternately jocular and serious, particularly when he was writing to his closest friends, and excessive emphasis surely should not be placed upon the mere fact that he now employed many ellipses, dropped into *bergamasco*, joked in macaronic Latin, sprinkled his paragraphs with French, left many sentences in mid-career, unfinished, and repeated obscenities automatically. But it is impossible not to agree with Gabrielli that Donizetti's letters of the second half of 1842 give off a peculiarly frantic, sometimes almost unbalanced, feeling, difficult not to speculate that his disease had begun to exact its toll from his thinking processes.

[34] See p. 177.

On July 30 or 31, Donizetti quit Milan, proceeding to Genoa to embark. He was in Civitavecchia on August 3. From there he wrote to Vasselli, beginning the letter:

I still am under the impress of a very sad day for me [July 31, the fifth anniversary of Virginia's death], and your last letter increases my sadness. It doesn't matter! I'll try to divert myself if I can. [Later in the letter, he returned to defending himself]: Your censure of my having accepted the extremely honorific position is unjust. Six free months are a beautiful thing; a thousand lire per month in Vienna and away from it are not to be despised. Do you know that in Bologna they did not want to grant me three months together? Do you know that I should have had to be in Bologna without fail on St. Petronius' day [October 4]? That it would not have been enough to compose new music, that they wanted me there in person? Do you know that what was asked was fifty, and not sixty [zecchini], and that I should have had, in case of any shortage, to pay another [man to take my place], in addition to a thousand other trifles? Do you know, on the other hand, that my position was Mozart's? That [with] His Majesty, when there are two concerts per year, it is many, and that if I must write to order, I am paid for it there? Think it over more clearly and give me courage, as my heart is being broken over leaving Naples, and that not for Naples, but for myself. . . . What is this that you speak to me about, concerning other women? Oh, really, laugh, and believe me that I still weep as on the first day. . . . Oh, if I could find distraction! Believe it . . . I am trying to numb myself . . . Enough! As to the contract with Rome, it was an infamous stinginess. [Napoleone?] Moriani wanted to give me ten thousand Austrian lire, not even francs! And I was to pay the poet, and he chose Cammarano. See clearly that I don't care about that, and am composing for Paris instead. . . . I leave at once for Naples; the weather is magnificent. Have no fear, I'll write you from there. Write me happily, as I have need of that these days. . . . Do you want the piano?

So, early in August, Donizetti returned to Naples, which he had not seen since October 1838. He had been under contract since April 22, for a fee specified at twenty-four hundred ducati, with the Royal Theaters there to compose an opera for performance at the San Carlo in June or October. At once he discussed matters with Edoardo Guillaume, an agent of the management. As late as August 18, however, he still had no agreed-upon subject for the libretto. Now he was increasingly unwell. On August 27, he wrote to Vasselli: "I have been at home for three days, with a great fever, and it is the second in twenty-five days." To Dolci he wrote two days later: "Here, in twenty-five days I have been in bed with fever. . . . How much pleasure I have taken in seeing Naples and finding all my friends still unchanged, and seeing a large audience that gathered somewhat unexpectedly at the theater to see me again![35] Condemned to bed with fever, I had to get up and go and display myself, almost forced by police."

One of Donizetti's reasons for this visit to Naples, apart from the desire to see his friends and the hope of settling the question of a new opera for the San Carlo, undoubtedly was the intention to sell his apartment in the Vico Nardones and wind up his personal affairs. But from Genoa on September 15 he was to write to Dolci: "I have left my Naples with displeasure, as there I found truly constant friends. It will suffice for you to know that this year I wanted to sell everything, but lacked the heart to do it, thinking that next year I should no longer have a home of my own to work in. . . . So it all remains the same, all of it taken care of, and I'll find all of it (if I don't die) there in 1843."

Donizetti embarked at Naples on September 6. The ship ran into a violent storm that stretched the voyage to Genoa to eight days, including a whole day of lying-to off Leghorn. From Genoa on September 15, in the letter to Dolci already quoted from, he said that he was leaving there that day, and added: "After a three-month stay in Paris, I'll go to Vienna to carry out my duties. . . . That's proper. I am sad enough, though covered with honors, with applause, feted everywhere. It doesn't count! Nothing fills the void. . . . I am going to Paris for the translations of *Padilla* and *Linda;* God knows what else I'll do." In a postscript to a letter to Giovanni Ricordi which he wrote that same day, he said: "Keep an eye on our friend Sacchèro." This referred to the Milanese writer Giacomo Sacchèro, who was to provide him with a libretto, at first called *La Regina di Cipro* but later renamed *Caterina Cornaro,* which he would be composing in Paris later that year, intending it to be his next opera for Vienna.

During the final days of September or the first days of October, Donizetti was back at the Hôtel Manchester in the rue Grammont, Paris. The amount of feverish activity and hard work which he was to find it possible to crowd into the next three months suggests simultaneously that his physical and mental faculties were not yet seriously impaired and that he felt driven by some dread of the pressure of time. During that period, in addition to many relatively small tasks, he would translate *Linda di Chamounix* into French and add several numbers, including "*O luce di quest'anima,*" to it; he would begin the composition of a two-act *opera seria,* and he would compose a three-act *opera buffa* that remains his comic masterpiece, if not his masterpiece *tout court—Don Pasquale.*

[35] *Maria Padilla* was being sung at the San Carlo.

CHAPTER VIII

Autumn 1842-1843

IN Paris in the fall of 1842, Donizetti began to compose, to Giacomo Sacchèro's libretto, an opera meant to be called *La Regina di Cipro*. When he had completed the first act, he learned that an opera on the same pseudohistoric subject was to be staged in Vienna. This was Franz Lachner's[1] *Catharina Cornaro*, which had received its first performance at Munich on December 3, 1841. The vicissitudes of this story about Caterina Cornaro, Queen of Cyprus, who was painted by both Veronese and Titian and whose cousin, Cardinal Pietro Bembo, wrote about her, make an interesting picture of some operatic usages of the period, when the earlier attitude of composers toward librettos—that they were exemplary texts suitable to set over and over—had not vanished altogether.

Alois Joseph Büssel's German text for Lachner's opera was a translated version of a French text by Jules-Henri Vernoy de Saint-Georges, who had sold it almost simultaneously to Lachner and to Fromental Halévy. Nineteen days after the *première* of Lachner's *Catharina Cornaro* at Munich, Halévy's opera, *La Reine de Chypre*—composed to the text in its original French form—was staged in Paris at the Opéra.[2] Doni-

---

[1] Franz Lachner (1803-90), a German composer-conductor who studied in Vienna and was on very friendly terms with Franz Schubert, conducted at the Kärnthnertortheater from 1827 to 1834. His oratorios, operas, symphonies, and other pieces are now neglected; he is remembered chiefly because Cherubini's *Médée* almost invariably is played today with the recitatives that he composed to replace its original spoken dialogue.

[2] Irrelevant to this account, interesting per se, is the fact that an English version of Vernoy de Saint-Georges's libretto, this by Alfred Bunn, was used by the

zetti must have been aware of Halévy's opera, but knowledge of its impending production would not have kept him from proceeding with *La Regina di Cipro* any more than the existence of Auber's *Le Chalet* had kept him from composing *Betly* in 1836. But news that Lachner's opera was going to be staged in Vienna that very November drove him to suspend work on *La Regina di Cipro*: even then, two new operas on the same subject could not be staged in the same city that close together. He now had no choice but to look for another subject for his Vienna opera, which turned out to be *Maria di Rohan*.

Shortly after Donizetti had reached Paris, he had received from Jules Janin a verbal suggestion that he compose a new opera for the Théâtre-Italien, of which Janin had become director. This proposal was repeated in writing on September 27, the suggestion being a contract for a new *opera buffa* to be tailored to the remarkable talents of Giulia Grisi, Mario, Antonio Tamburini, and Luigi Lablache. No mention was made at first of the name of the proposed opera or of its subject, which perhaps had not been agreed upon then. But on October 8, writing to his Viennese friend and translator Leo Herz, Donizetti said: "My *opera buffa* will go into rehearsal after the giving of *Linda*. Title, *Don Pasquale*."

Donizetti's Paris factotum, the Italian exile and politically treacherous double agent Michele Accursi, drove another Italian exile in Paris, Giovanni Ruffini,[3] into fashioning a libretto for the new opera from a two-act libretto by Angelo Anelli which had been composed by Stefano Pavesi as *Ser Marc'Antonio*, an opera that had evoked considerable acclaim at La Scala, Milan, in 1810. On September 29, Ruffini wrote his mother that Accursi, in a great rush, was after him for something. Six days later, he told her what Accursi had wanted: "Maestro Donizetti, being in Paris and writing an *opera buffa* on a story that already has been used, has found need for a working stonemason of verses to remake the old libretto, to cut, change, add, plaster, and I don't know what. And that mason, by suggestion of Michele [Accursi], is I, your servant Brighella. You know what a long and boring thing it is to rebake old loaves, the more so when one has a two-edged sword at one's back: Michele, who gives me no peace, and Donizetti, who would like me to bring him pieces to set to music not every day, as I do,

---

composer of *The Bohemian Girl*, Michael William Balfe, for his opera *The Daughter of St. Mark*, which received its first singing at Drury Lane Theatre, London, on November 27, 1844.

[3] Giovanni Ruffini was an older brother of Agostino Ruffini, who had helped Donizetti with final changes in the libretto of *Marin Faliero* in 1835.

but every hour. His facility and fecundity are prodigious. He'll toss you off a long duet in an hour; it will be beautiful, what's more. For the rest, I—a poet, you understand—am on a great footing of intimacy with the Maestro, with whom I hold consultations each day. He's a good and able fellow, without pretenses, simple in manner, and today we talked about a certain brother of his, at one time bandmaster at Genoa in the *reggimento di Casale*, and whom I knew; he too has the musical protuberance. At present he's in Constantinople, leader of some of the Sultan's music; he's very well and happily making money."

On October 11, Ruffini wrote his mother: "I've been eating up the paper, as they say. It's not a question of doing it well or doing it badly, but of doing it fast." On October 18: "The versifying machine continues to grind out a given quantity every day." By October 23, he was able to say: "My *opus magnum* is reaching its conclusion." Not very happy with the results of this rushed labor, Ruffini became unhappier still as Donizetti began cutting verses here and there, making incessant new requests, dropping new suggestions. Finally, he seemed to Ruffini to have destroyed "that little bit of logical connection which I had studied to put into my pieces." For the final rondo, for example, Ruffini submitted several versions of the text—and thought that the one finally used was the poorest of them. Then Tamburini made trouble, asserting that Lablache's role was juicier than his and threatening to leave the cast if that imbalance was not corrected. The effort to please him involved additional work for both Ruffini and Donizetti. So far was the final text of *Don Pasquale* from what Ruffini had wanted it to be that he asked that his name not be connected with it, as he explained in another letter to his mother: "I have not put my name to it, be it understood, because, it having been written in such haste and my freedom of action having in a certain sense been paralyzed by the maestro, I don't, so to say, recognize it as mine."

Donizetti nevertheless paid Ruffini five hundred francs for the libretto, about the going price at the time for a text of that genre and length. It was issued as the work of "M.A." for a reason made clear by the contract letter that Michele Accursi wrote to Giovanni Ricordi on November 30, 1842, from Paris: "I, the undersigned, author of the poem *Don Pasquale*, set to music by the Signor Gaetano Donizetti, do cede in favor of Signor Ricordi of Milan the rights in that libretto for all of Italy and Germany on the condition that the true name never be printed on the poem." It is notable that Accursi did not write "*il mio nome*," but "*il vero nome*." In addition to Ruffini's dislike of the finished text—a dislike justifiable on purely literary grounds, but unjustifiable if the lines be judged as arranged for musical setting—the possibility exists that he did not wish the Italian authorities to know his whereabouts. In any case, the initials "M.A." led to the incorrect statement, which has appeared in hundreds of books, that the libretto was the work of " 'Michele Accursi,' pseudonym of Giovanni [sometimes even Giacomo] Ruffini." To add to this confusion, the libretto also has been attributed at times to Salvatore Cammarano: a text distributed at the Metropolitan Opera House, New York, at one time went even farther astray, assigning it to "Camerano." It should be attributed to Angelo Anelli-Giovanni Ruffini-Donizetti.[4]

Almost tearing the incomplete, unrevised lines from Ruffini's hands, Donizetti rearranged them as he composed. Although he jokingly wrote Antonio Vasselli on November 12 that *Don Pasquale* had cost him "ten days of effort" and on January 4, 1843, was to amend this in another letter to Vasselli to "an immense effort (eleven days)," he actually worked on it intermittently from about October 1 to past the middle of December. Despite numerous hoary assertions about the rapidity with which he composed and orchestrated this opera, the truth is that on December 8 he had not yet composed its final rondo and on December 15 he still needed to compose a *cabaletta brillante* for Tamburini's role (Dottore Malatesta). He had, however, orchestrated much of it by November 12 and was telling the precise truth when, on July 15, 1845, he was to write to Mayr: "In my usual manner, I work from seven o'clock in the morning to four in the afternoon." The supposedly occult formula for his "terrible facility" was in large part his habit of work.

The first Paris performance of *Linda di Chamounix* was heard at the Théâtre-Italien on November 17. Its reception by that Paris audience in no way suggested its future popularity. Six days after that performance, Giovanni Ruffini wrote to his mother: "I'm in a rage, but in a proper rage with the unintelligent and blasé public of the Théâtre-Italien. . . . *Linda di Chamounix*, a fine opera by Donizetti, which by itself would be enough to establish a maestro's fame, has been received very coldly. I don't dissimulate the many causes that, independently of the intrinsic merit, have contributed to this failure, which, among others, would be the bad libretto and the *bon ton* of not showing enthusiasm for anything which reigns in the auditorium of the Théâtre-Italien, all made up of *fashionable*[5] society. But despite these and other

---

[4] See also pp. x–xii, 362.
[5] The italicized word is in English in the original letter.

reasons, a good part of the responsibility still falls on the small intelligence of this Parisian public. Pieces of music that ought to destroy the
theater with applause, pieces received at the rehearsals with indescribable enthusiasm by the orchestra and the singers, left the public inert,
cold, and silent." On that same day, Michele Accursi wrote: "I believe
that I have more than once made the wish of Caligula or Nero—which
is that the Roman people had only one head."

But *Linda di Chamounix*—which, after all, enjoyed a cast including Fanny Tacchinardi-Persiani, for whom on this occasion Donizetti
had added *"O luce di quest'anima"* to the opera, Marietta Brambilla,
Mario Antonio Tamburini, and Luigi Lablache—was to survive that
first-night indifference and establish its position in Paris. Demands for a
French version of it began to arrive from the provinces almost at once.
So, in the midst of all the other things that he was doing, Donizetti
himself translated Rossi's libretto, at the same time composing some
additional numbers as required by French taste. But even that added
labor could not fill his days, and he still had to compose the new opera
for Vienna, for which he had not hit upon a subject. Word that he
was in need of a libretto appears to have been spread about, for it
was almost certainly at this time that Alexandre Dumas *père* wrote him
a note saying: "If you are seeking a drama, extinguish your lantern.
Your man is found. I have three acts at your service."[6]

But now Donizetti recalled *Un Duel sous le cardinal de Richelieu*,
the play by Lockroy which he had considered in 1837 and which
Giuseppe Lillo, using a libretto by Salvatore Cammarano which originally
had been meant for Bellini, had set as *Il Conte di Chalais*, staged unsuccessfully at Naples in 1839. He snatched up the Cammarano text
and started to compose it. On November 27, he wrote to Antonio Dolci
to say that he had composed two acts of this new opera, *Maria di Rohan*,
in twenty-four hours. "When the subject pleases," he explained, "the
heart speaks, the head flies, the hand writes." He would orchestrate
this three-act *opera seria* at Vienna early in 1843.

Twelve days before the first Paris performance of *Linda di
Chamounix*, that opera had been given an unsuccessful Roman *première*.
Alberto Cametti wrote (27, 213–14) that not only had its score been
mutilated, but also the busy censors had done particularly disfiguring
work on its libretto:

[6] This undated note is quoted in *114*, 50, and in all likelihood is nearly contemporary with another note, in which Dumas asks Donizetti to inscribe a few
lines of *Linda di Chamounix* in his autograph album, which he will pass by the next
day to pick up.

The censorship, for its part, found plenty of work to do in the *melodramma*, for in addition to the usual words inadmissible in the theater (the first two verses of the introductory chorus, for example, were changed because their reference to the church was irreverent), it wanted to make the role of the Marchese more proper, cutting out everything that would make him seem a libertine and changing him into an old fool wanting nothing but to take a wife! From that arose, beyond the natural absurdities, constant changes of the text, and especially in the duet between Antonio and the Prefect in the first act and that between Linda and the Marchese in the second.

Thus, in the first number, the lines *"Arde per Linda il perfido/D'un esecrato amor"* [The perfidious one burns for Linda with an execrated love] were changed to *"La man di sposo ei porgerle/ Osa sperare ancor"* [He still dares hope to extend a husband's hand to her]; and Antonio's invective: *"Perchè siam noti poveri/ Ci credon senza onor!"* [Because we are born poor, they think us without honor!] prudently was varied as *"Io, benchè abbietto e povero/ Saprò spregiarlo ancor"* [I, though miserable and poor, yet will know how to despise him].

From another duet I shall cite only these verses among the numerous alterations: *"Amo le belle, sì questo è vero,/ Ma la mia pelle voglio salvar"* [I love the pretty girls, yes, that's true, but I want to save my skin], which became: *"Vorrei sposarmi, sì questo è vero,/ Ma la mia pelle voglio salvar"* [I'd like to get married, yes, that's true, but I want to save my skin] . . . just as the embrace that Carlo begs Linda for in the succeeding duet was changed into a vow of fidelity!

Antonio Vasselli must have tried by letter to convince Donizetti that *Linda di Chamounix* had won approval at the Valle. But on November 27, Donizetti wrote him: "You wanted to deceive me with the success of *Linda* in Rome, but my friend Varese [Felice Varesi] (whom you will greet) has written me the genuine truth. You will tell Varese that he should save a little of his voice for us at Vienna too: and I hope that you'll give him the letter when you see him, eh? Write to me more often, and specially now that [your] *mamma* isn't very well; greet her, and greet for me all the wives and the marriageable girls, to whom I hope to make love next year."

Almost as though with his left hand alone, Donizetti at this juncture began to prepare what he referred to as "the little *Miserere* for his Majesty the Emperor, to whom I promised it."[7] This was for several

---

[7] This *Miserere* was, in fact, a slightly reworked version of the one that Donizetti had sent to Rome for presentation to Pope Gregory XVI in the justified hope of eliciting a papal decoration in return (see p. 168). In its "Roman" form, it was sung for the first time on March 4, 1842, in the Marchesa Marianna Muti Costaguti's Palazzo all'Aracoeli, with Commendatore Vincenzo Costaguti conducting, the tenor Count Matteucci, the soprano Barbara De Sanctis (taking the lines of the second tenor), and the basses Sottovia and Canestrini. Both the mixed chorus—in which the women sustained the lines of the second tenors—and the orchestra were composed of amateurs.

voices and orchestra. It was sung in its "Viennese" form for the first time at Vienna on Holy Saturday, April 14, 1843. If, as seems almost certain, a letter of Donizetti's written at Paris on December 2, 1842, was addressed to Scribe, then the sentence "You will understand that it will be very difficult for me to work without having fixed the subject with you" shows that he also had begun at this time to think about still another opera. To be composed during 1843 and staged at the Opéra on November 13 of that year, this was *Dom Sébastien, roi de Portugal*,[8] a full-fledged grand opera.

Rehearsals of *Don Pasquale* continued at the Théâtre-Italien through December. On December 24, Désiré Raoul-Rochette, Perpetual Secretary of the Académie Royale des Beaux-Arts, wrote Donizetti an official letter to say that the Académie had decided to nominate a composer to one of its three vacant *fauteuils* and that he had been selected to stand for the honor. The election was to be held one week later, and, as Raoul-Rochette wrote, there was every reason to suppose that it would confirm Donizetti's nomination. The letter contains this notation in Donizetti's script: "Elected corresponding member on the first ballot unanimously yesterday 31 December." Election to the Académie was only the highest of several honors awarded to Donizetti in 1842, the first having been his appointment as an honorary member of the Vienna Musikfreunde on May 28, the second his official appointments to the court positions in Vienna. In 1842, 1843, or 1844, too, he was decorated by the Emperor of Austria with the Order of the Iron Crown.

While *Don Pasquale* was being readied at the Italien, nobody but Donizetti appeared to have any confidence in it. Neither Dormoy, the company manager, nor his assistant and future successor, Vatel, nor the participating artists themselves seem to have detected anything extraordinary in the score. The atmosphere of the rehearsals was frigid. Members of the orchestra were given to expressing their low opinion of the music in loud tones—and to making rude drawings on the margins of their parts.[9] Charles de Boigne wrote: "At the final rehearsal, the only people in the auditorium were Vatel, Dormoy, Donizetti, and his publisher. The orchestral musicians gave no sign of approval: the silence

[8] Scribe derived this libretto from a verse drama, staged at the Théâtre Porte Saint-Martin on November 13, 1838, by Victor Hugo's brother-in-law, Paul Foucher, who seems in turn to have been influenced by Dryden's tragicomedy, *Don Sebastian* (1691).

[9] Léon Escudier (50, 33) wrote that one of these drawings showed Donizetti being given a clyster. How much, if at all, this animosity reflected French composers' jealousy of Donizetti's success has been a subject of extended speculation.

of death. The work had been condemned, judged. Donizetti took his publisher to his apartment and pulled out of one of his cartons a piece that he asked his publisher to deliver to Mario so that he could work at it immediately. Donizetti intended to rehearse him in it that same evening. This piece [*"Com'è gentil"*], which *Don Pasquale* had been lacking, was the delicious serenade that Mario sighed so tenderly at the end of the third act." Léon Escudier (*50*) wrote that at the final rehearsal he had heard Vatel say to Dormoy: "That text and that music would be good, at best, for tumblers." Donizetti, who had composed the opera in a very fever of delight, was sure. "Have no fear for me," he told Escudier. "My work will be a success." And Michele Accursi, writing a business letter to Giovanni Ricordi, said that he thought *Don Pasquale* to be Donizetti's *Il Barbiere di Siviglia*.

The *première* of *Don Pasquale* at the Théâtre-Italien on January 3, 1843 (which happened to be one day after the first performance at Dresden of Richard Wagner's *Der fliegende Holländer*), marked the climax of Donizetti's life as a composer. Giuseppe Verdi's brilliant star now was climbing rapidly over the Italian peninsula, but Donizetti remained the most famous of active living operatic composers there, as he certainly was in Vienna and several other European centers—and perhaps even in Paris. He was becoming increasingly popular in both North America and South America. His financial condition and prospects were excellent. Although his health intermittently was bothersome, he still had available his huge resources of energy and, except at infrequent intervals, all of his mental acuity. He had traveled a very long road indeed from his subterranean birthplace in Borgo Canale little more than forty-five years before. And now the latest of his nearly seventy operas had become an established success in Paris.

In the *Journal des débats* of January 6, 1843, Étienne-Jean Délécluze wrote: "From Bellini's *I Puritani* on, no opera composed expressly for the Théâtre-Italien has had a more clamorous success. Four or five numbers repeated, callings-out of the singers, callings-out of the Maestro—in sum, one of those ovations which are given prodigiously by the dozen in Italy to even the most mediocre little composers, but which in Paris are reserved for the truly great."

Lablache's creation of the role of Don Pasquale was to become legendary; his costume—a white bombazine *robe de chambre*, nankeen pantaloons, and black silk nightcap—established a tradition. Léon Escudier wrote of him: "When he came on, with his bright face, advancing timidly with a svelte air, and weighed down despite himself

by his gigantic corpulence, laughter broke out throughout the hall."
Each day, the gardener in charge of the Marquis Alexandre-Marie
Aguado's famous greenhouses arrived at the theater with a camellia
for Lablache to wear in his buttonhole. Grisi enchanted everyone as
Norina. Mario triumphed too, especially in *"Com'è gentil,"* with its
tambourine accompaniment offstage. Scattered praise for Tamburini's
impersonation of Doctor Malatesta was all but buried in praise of his
three chief colleagues. The popularity of *Don Pasquale* soon spawned
the usual tribute of transcriptions and arrangements: Adolphe Adam
made a piano version of *"Com'è gentil"* and Johann Baptist Cramer
composed a *Valse brillante* on assorted melodies from the opera. Only
Heinrich Heine, in a Paris report to the Augsburg *Gazette,* was acerb
about *Don Pasquale:* "In the so-called lyric theater," he wrote, "novel-
ties have not been lacking this winter. The *Bouffes* have given us *Don
Pasquale,* a new work by Signor Donizetti. This Italian does not go
without success. His talent is great, but even greater is his fecundity,
in which he is exceeded only by rabbits."

No more than at any other time did Donizetti preen himself on
his success. Writing to his pupil and friend Matteo Salvi on the day
after the *première* of *Don Pasquale,* he said: "Yesterday evening I gave
Don Pasquale. The result was of the happiest. Repeated the adagio of
the second-act finale. Repeated the *stretta* of the duet between Lablache
and Grisi. I was called out at the ends of the second and third acts.
Not a piece, from the *sinfonia* on, but was applauded more or less. I
am content." To Tommaso Persico, from Vienna on January 2, he reported: "Even today I received eight papers from Paris talking about
Don Pasquale. I myself am stupefied, but that's the way it is: nineteen
thousand francs in eleven days! A stroke of fortune. *Voilà tout. Un
imprudence . . .*"

With amusing appropriateness, *Don Pasquale* is dedicated to the
wife of Donizetti's Paris banker, Mme Zélie de Coussy. The first edition,
carrying the dedication to her from *"Gaetano Donizetti, Maestro di Cappella e Compositore di Corte di S. M. l'Imperatore d'Austria,"* includes
the following annotated list of characters:

Don Pasquale, elderly bachelor, cut out along antique lines, economical,
credulous, obstinate, a good fellow at bottom   Sig.r Lablache
Dottor Malatesta, a man of expedients, jocular, resourceful, doctor and friend
of Don Pasquale and very close friend of   Sig.r Tamburini
Ernesto, nephew of Don Pasquale, youthful, enthusiastic, requited lover of
Sig.r Mario

Norina, young widow, impulsive nature, impatient of contradictions, but genuine and affectionate   Sig.a Grisi

Sharing in the triumph of *Don Pasquale,* Giovanni Ruffini had written his mother the day after the *première* of *Don Pasquale:* "My dear, we—see how much vanity there is in that *we*—have had a *succès fou.* Beginning with the overture, each and every one of the pieces applauded, some of them fanatically; one finale and two duets repeated; Donizetti brought out at least twice in the face of the opposition, the members of which, flattened by the general applause, didn't even dare to give a sign of disapproval, but contented themselves with chafing in silence." And when, on January 7, Donizetti left Paris, he charged Ruffini with the task of writing new lines to the Pasquale-Malatesta duet and adding some verses to the final rondo. For by then it was clear that *Don Pasquale* was going to run out the season at the Italien. Actually, at the closing performance on the last Sunday in March, the box office was to take in twelve thousand francs.

Leaving Paris on January 7, going by way of Strasbourg, Munich,[10] and Linz, Donizetti reached Vienna on January 16. Two weeks later, he outlined his plans for 1843 in a letter to Antonio Vasselli: "At Vienna I'm doing a *Duel under Richelieu* (French drama); at Naples, *Ruy-Blas,*[11] given a new locale; at Paris, for the Opéra-Comique, a Flemish subject [*Ne m'oubliez pas?*]. For the Grand Opera, where I am to go on instead of Meyerbeer,[12] I am using a Portuguese subject in five acts. And all this during the course of this year. And first I am remounting *Les Martyrs,* which is creating a furor in the provinces. And next spring I'll give the other, that is, *Le Duc d'Albe,* in four acts." A joking sentence with an ominous, or perhaps scabrous, overtone follows: "And all of this without [prepaid] postage and with a new illness contracted in Paris, which still has not passed and for which I am awaiting your prescription."

On February 4, writing to Tommaso Persico and enclosing a letter for Vincenzo Flauto, then impresario at the Teatro San Carlo—clearly a

[10] At Munich on January 14, Donizetti composed a setting of Victor Hugo's "*La Fiancée du timballier,*" inscribing the autograph "To the Gayard couple, January 14, 1843, Munich."

[11] Donizetti never composed this projected opera. The subject was used by, among other composers, William Howard Glover (*Ruy Blas,* Covent Garden, 1861), and—more successfully—Filippo Marchetti (*Ruy Blas,* La Scala, 1869). Both were to librettos derived from Victor Hugo's drama.

[12] No new opera by Meyerbeer was produced in Paris between *Les Huguenots* (1836) and *Le Prophète* (1849).

plea to be freed from his promise to compose an opera for the Neapolitan theater—Donizetti said:

On reading the page to be given to Signor Flauti [*sic*], you'll turn your nose aside, but that's the way it is. I recommend that the thing be accomplished without a lot of noise, and I swear to you that only the journey [to Naples] stops me, as three days after my arrival here, I spent three days in bed with fever. If they want to free me, I'm ready; if they want the score without me, I'm also ready; but if they try to reduce me to two thousand ducati after the first evening, effective, and without release, as in the contract, then advise them not to write to me, that it all is useless, that on the contrary I'll not accept any proposal whatever. If I earn nineteen thousand with *Pasquale* and sixteen here, it seems to me that they can be content to pay such a sum for an *opera seria*. Read carefully the objections that I've made to the libretto, to the company, etc., then mark well the day on which you give them my letter, make them give you a receipt and the answer within a proper period. Here I'll complete my obligation at the end of June; therefore I can be in Naples in July, but if I fall ill because of the fatigue, of the discomforts, as you know that I fell ill last year? Therefore persuade them either to break [the contract] or to fine me five hundred ducati; but the answer should be communicated to you within six days; this should not under any condition slow down Cammarano's work, which I deem advanced according to the contract, even if my suggestions should be rejected. I shall be awaiting their reply and yours so that I can put my mind at ease about my future and my health. A categorical reply, clear and without cavil, and then I'll be quiet. If not, you well know that with the clause of article 5 (if caprice seizes me) I can have my opera sung by whomever I wish to sign up. As a very great favor, you will have to obtain one of these two things, but to obtain it within the required time and in a regular way and without bad tempers; because if my fevers should not be believed in, I have doctors [Giovanni Antonio Lorenzo] Fossati and Maroncelli at Paris, and a doctor here as well, all ready to give me a thousand attestations that the heat now excites nervous fever in me and that my head now often suffers such an illness.

Too, in a letter of February 14 to Antonio Dolci, after telling of his many activities, social and musical, Donizetti said: "In the midst of these tiring things, I am well. The trips don't kill me. From time to time I have my usual fever, which pays me a visit, but it doesn't last more than twenty-four hours. The force of it leaves me prostrated for some time. Then, back to work again, and with greater ardor."

Donizetti, then, had been forced to take his uncertain health seriously enough so that to be freed of the necessity of going to Naples in midsummer he was prepared to forfeit five hundred ducati. In the event, however, he was to fish from his luggage the incomplete opera to Sacchèro's libretto *La Regina di Cipro* and recast it as *Caterina*

Cornaro, an *opera seria* in a prologue and two acts. This he would complete at Vienna in June 1843; it would be produced—but without his personal supervision or intervention—at the Teatro San Carlo in January 1844. Persico and the letter that Donizetti had sent him for Vincenzo Flauto must have been persuasive emissaries.

The new Italian season at the Kärnthnertortheater was to include *Nabucco,* a Verdi opera still unknown to the Viennese. On February 6, Donizetti wrote to Giovanni Ricordi: "Send ahead the choruses from *Nabucco* so that I can study them well." Fully appreciating Verdi's talent and value, Donizetti was to offer to take a hand the next year in the Kärnthnertortheater staging of *Ernani,* thus winning Verdi's astonished gratitude. By February 21, 1843, he had put the final retouchings on the "little *Miserere*" for the Emperor. The next day, he wrote, as from Wipplingerstrasse 394, a letter to a court official, probably the Grand Chamberlain Count Moritz Dietrichstein, to express the desire that he be received by the Empress so as to present the *Miserere* to her in person. He himself conducted the piece in its first singing, probably at the Convent of St. Elisabeth, on Good Friday, April 14.

Donizetti also had been scheduled to conduct at a *concert spirituel* of the Musikfreunde the *Offertorio* that he had composed in Paris the preceding May. But in a distressing letter of March 2 to Dolci, which is full of exclamations, broken phrases, passages in *bergamasco,* and nonsequiturs, he said: "Since the last Friday before Lent, I again have had to be in bed with the fever, and I am at home again today, the first of Lent. But tomorrow I go out to go to the Musikfreunde to conduct at the *concert spirituel* my *Offertorio,* without having rehearsed it. God knows what tempos they have taken! I'll be the one to follow them—and *sciao!* I feel well now, only weak. Auff! *A polenta and little birds would cure me right away, but one of the little ones, however.*"[13]

Having completed the orchestration of *Maria di Rohan* in April, Donizetti turned to the task of finishing and orchestrating *Caterina Cornaro.* This work was interrupted by the onset of rehearsals of *Maria di Rohan* and by productions of his 1828 opera *Alina, regina di Golconda* and of *Don Pasquale.* Of *Alina,* Donizetti wrote to Giacomo Pedroni on May 25: "I hasten to announce to you the fiasco of *Alina* with Mme [Pauline Viardot-]García, [Agostino] Rovere, Felice Varesi, and Severi. The protagonist put at the end of the opera a

---

[13] The italicized sentence is in *bergamasco* in the letter: "*Una polenta e osei l'am guariraff seubet; ma de quei pissinì pero.*"

rondeau by Bériot[14] (one knows it from *L'Elisir*). The opera fell flat nevertheless. . . . This evening, *Pasquale*, of which they always repeat the two duets in the second act. The day after tomorrow, the first orchestra rehearsal for *Maria di Rohan*. . . . I have sent to Naples the second and third acts of *Caterina [Cornaro]*. In a few days the first act will go forward also. After that, I'll give myself wholly to *Le Duc de Bragance* [working title of *Dom Sébastien, roi de Portugal*], the dedication of which the Queen of Portugal [Maria II] now has accepted."[15]

A surviving memorandum in Donizetti's handwriting gives some instructions as to costuming for the new Vienna productions:

Richard, Count of Chalais—Tenor, very rich, first minister of Louis XIII— [Carlo] Guasco.
Henry, Duke of Chevreuse—[Giorgio] Ronconi—rich, first act less rich.
[Eugenia] Tadolini—Maria, Countess of Rohan—first act, rich costume (lady of the court), very simple afterwards.
Viscount of Suze, cavalier.
[Michele] Novaro—Armand de Gondì—black and red without embroidery.
[Gustav] Hölzel—Di Fiesque—quasi-military costume.
2, group (Aubry, Chalais's servant
     (A servant of Chevreuse's
Ladies and cavaliers at the King's fête, very rich—soldiers.
Mad. Tadolini 3 costumes: 1 rich, for the fête, black domino afterwards— robe of deep-colored satin.
Chevreuse 2 costumes.
Chalais 2 costumes.
Tadolini 3 costumes.
Fiesque 2 costumes.

D. Pasquale:

Nearly all the choristers in livery—maître d'hôtel in black—sub-maître d'hôtel, lackeys, footmen, coiffeurs, modistes.
Don Pasquale—first act—dressing gown—white quilted redingote—pantaloons in white shoes—slippers—2nd act—as an old modern dandy.

Donizetti

[14] The Belgian composer-violinist Charles-Auguste de Bériot (1802–70), who had married Mme Viardot's sister, Maria Malibran, not long before her death.

[15] In this letter to Pedroni, Donizetti mentions for the first time a woman named Christine, or Cristina, Appiani, a close friend (and clearly at one time the mistress) of Pedroni. Apparently she had fallen upon financially poor days and was going to Rome (we learn later, from Donizetti's letter of July 3, 1843, to Totò Vasselli, that she had become governess to the children of the Principe di Compagnano). Her husband had committed suicide, leaving her with enormous debts and two young children to support. Donizetti referred to her in two other letters to Vasselli (January 6, 1844, and August 14, 1844), and it is possible, as Frank Walker suggested (*137*, 100–101) that an intimacy between her and Donizetti helped give rise to the unlikely stories spread through many books that he had a love affair with Countess Giuseppina Strigelli Appiani, an entirely different woman with whom she has been confused persistently.

For the original Paris production of *Don Pasquale,* Donizetti had wanted the principal characters costumed as 1843 bourgeois. All the singers but Lablache had rebelled against this idea, and Giovanni Ruffini had shared their point of view, remarking that the nature of the story called rather for "perukes and velvet habits." Donizetti's answer—according to a letter that Ruffini wrote to his mother on December 15, 1842—was that the music did not permit the period costumes. In the event, however, he had bowed to the singers and Ruffini.

Donizetti conducted the first performance of *Maria di Rohan,* at the Kärnthnertortheater, on June 5, 1843. The next day he reported to Antonio Vasselli, to whom the opera is dedicated: "I must announce to you with the greatest sorrow that last night, June 5, I gave *Maria di Rohan,* with Tadolini, Ronconi, and [Carlo] Guasco. All the talent was not enough to save me from a sea of . . . applause. Calls in every act . . . In short, a complete fiasco, with hissing. Everything good, everything, everything! Write this to Naples; write it to your wife and daughter, to the entire household and friends. The whole imperial family came from the country expressly, stayed until after the end of the opera to . . . hiss. And you'll see how it will go this evening . . . what a *sinfonia, sor* Totò. *Bergamus et non plus ultra!*"

On June 7, Donizetti wrote to Tommaso Persico to inform him that Act I of *Caterina Cornaro* was being sent to him. Evidently in view of earlier correspondence concerning Donizetti's divesting himself of his Naples apartment and Persico's dispersing its contents, he added: "Give the pianoforte[16] to Totò and tell him that I would not have given it to anyone [else] for all the gold in the world because it was . . . hers;[17] also because I owe my reputation to it. The removable bells[18] are in a drawer in the library. Send him all the published scores."

[16] This piano had been manufactured in Vienna by Carl Strobel, who was active in the business from about 1816 to 1821. It was to remain in the Vasselli family until 1875, five years after Antonio's death. Then his daughter, Virginia Vasselli Gabrielli (mother of the Donizetti biographer Annibale Gabrielli), gave it to the city of Bergamo, where it now is in the Museo Donizettiano.

[17] Nearly six years after Virginia's death, Donizetti still could not bring himself to refer to her by her name.

[18] These *"campanelli levati"*—as well as cymbals—were for a time added to pianos with the aim of varying and greatly increasing the volume of sound. Placed in the part of the piano's tail farthest from the player, they were often removable at will, and were operated by foot, one or two extra pedals being supplied. Under date of July 30, 1962, Professora Dina Zanetti reported to me from Rome that she had talked to a piano tuner who only recently had been called in to tune a piano that once had included such removable bells; it belongs to a convent.

Annibale Gabrielli (*58*, 105–6), relying on family documents and memories, wrote:

And their friend Tommasino told Vasselli about Donizetti's gift: "The Maestro wants me to send you the pianoforte and all the published scores that are in his apartment. I have real pleasure in doing so because you deserve this; and also because this instrument will recall that angel of goodness [Virginia] to your memory." Donizetti himself wrote to Vasselli from Vienna about the pianoforte in that section of a letter (July 3, 1843) now very well known, which, as incised into a metal plaque affixed to the piano, was read with sincere emotion by all those who saw the pianoforte at the Musical Exposition at Bologna first, and then at the Donizettian Exposition at Bergamo [1897]. "Don't sell that pianoforte at any price, for it holds my whole artistic life inside it. I have had it in my ears since 1822: there were murmured the *Anna*s, the *Marie*s, the *Fausta*s, the *Lucia*s, the *Roberto*s, the *Belisario*s, the *Marino*s, the *Martyr*s, the *Olivo*s, *Ajo, Furioso, Paria, Castello di Kenilworth, Ugo, Pazzi, Pia, Rudenz.* . . . Oh, let it live as long as I live! I lived with it in my age of hope, my married life, my loneliness. It heard my joys, my tears, my deluded hopes, my honors . . . it divided with me the sweat and the weariness . . . with it I lived my genius, in it lives every epoch of my career, of yours, or [rather] of your careers. Your father, your brother, all of us have seen it, known it, tormented it; it was a companion to all, and may it be one always to your daughter[19] as a gift of a thousand sad and gay thoughts."[20]

Thus ended the beloved apartment, which at one time had been Donizetti's major ambition for his Virginia. The furniture and the clothes were sold—sold, it seems, the apartment itself. No one later thought of putting up even a modest stone to indicate that home, where at least four of the most vital Donizettian operas were created.[21]

And yet, Naples was the Italian city in which the eternal wanderer, poor Donizetti, remained established the longest. Someone who noted this forgetfulness once received this as an answer: Nothing is known about that house. In 1893, however, I myself was able to disperse all uncertainty as to the identification of Donizetti's house, establishing by means of one of Vasselli's unpublished letters that it was in Via [Vico] Nardones, number 14.

Once Donizetti had reached the difficult decision to dispose of his well-loved piano, he began to worry about the fate of *Caterina Cornaro*,

[19] Significantly, Vasselli's daughter was named Virginia.

[20] In the last, brief, unhappy paragraph of this same letter, Donizetti wrote: "I had the fever last night. Today, an onion, and out for a walk."

[21] Gabrielli's chronology is unclear at this point: when Donizetti visited Naples for the last time in 1844, he certainly stayed at his apartment in the Vico Nardones. When the apartment and its contents were disposed of remains undetermined. Also, the fact that Donizetti had lived there was commemorated in 1904 by a plaque placed on the street-front wall: "In memory of Gaetano Donizetti who, in the year 1837, lived in this house, the Royal Conservatory of Music placed (this plaque) 1904." Dr. Carlo Betha of Naples kindly sent me photographs of the plaque and the central areaway of the house taken in June 1962.

which was to be given a *première* without his personal supervision or presence. Toward the end of June, he wrote to his friend the Neapolitan painter Teodoro Ghezzi:

So that, as you say, articles and news regarding me should not pass into oblivion without your knowing about them, behold what I tell you that *Maria di Rohan* (*Il Conte di Chalais*) continues triumphantly on its way. This evening, *Lucrezia Borgia* will be given with the prima donna [Teresa] De Giuli[-Borsi], and as this letter will be posted tomorrow, you will have news about that too, at the end. In the meantime, know that my health has not improved more than a trifle. The other evening, I met Gabriele Quattrini and Emo de' Marchesi Tamburri, and they came to the house with me, and the former, who took my pulse, was a witness to my not very good condition. It doesn't matter. I feel worse than you do about not being able to attend the rehearsals and staging of *Caterina* in person, but what can I do? How could I, in one month, come to Naples, rehearse, and get back to Paris for my very old contract, which is going to be performed at the Académie Royale? I would have to fly. At least, this way I'll leave in my carriage when I feel better, I'll sleep when I wish, I'll stop when I'm ill, and the hours won't be counted against me as they would be if I were to make the trip to Naples. I wrote Signor Flauto, and I also have surrendered five hundred ducati; I think that when a Maestro sends certificates of a real illness, gives up money, and renounces staging his new score himself—I think that these are reasons that should be believed in by all if the Maestro is considered a man of honor.

Donizetti went on to discuss the casting of *Caterina Cornaro*. Referring to possible difficulties with the censorship, he added:

I mention and pray for the libretto, as I'm ready to take back my opera if I must see it sacrificed like *Padilla*, in which, wherever it originally had said "What horror," the words were replaced with "Oh, greatest joy"—and with the music unchanged. I have worked hard and conscientiously on this opera and wouldn't wish to see an interesting subject rendered ridiculous because of the whims of a few or because of perfidy. This bears on the management's interests, and I hope that you will take an active part in it. . . .

Do you know about the gift (in diamonds) given me by Her Majesty the Empress? Do you know about the very happy success of *Don Pasquale?* Of *Maria di Rohan*—that now this opera is to be presented in Paris with Ronconi himself, Grisi, and Mario?[22]—that the *Miserere* was sold and is being printed everywhere?—that *Linda* is earning large sums of money in London?—that the new opera for Paris now is dedicated to and accepted by Her Majesty Donna Maria of Portugal as a patriotic thing? That here I am well looked upon, well treated, respected, honored—that in six months I have given two concerts occupying three hours at court, and that I am

[22] For this production of *Maria di Rohan*, Donizetti recast the second tenor role, Armando di Gondì, to be sung by the contralto Marietta Brambilla and added an extra number for her.

paid a thousand lire in advance each month even when I am absent on leave?—that I find them on my return? . . .

P.S. Last night *Lucrezia* gave much pleasure, though it had been seen many times before with both [Caroline] Ungher and [Erminia] Frezzolini! This De Giuli has a magnificent voice, is not a great actress because she is new, but for the large theaters, in which it can't be seen whether she is beautiful or ugly, she fills the hall like Tadolini. The tenor Guasco is a bit tired out; Ronconi does very well. Tomorrow the *Barbiere* [*di Siviglia*], with [Pauline] Viardot[-Garcia]; then *Pasquale*, then *Rohan*, then the *Templari*,[23] then *Linda*, and that way we'll run out the month and the season together.

On June 30, Donizetti reported to Dolci: "Behold, here we are at the end of the Italian season in Vienna. Tomorrow the company breaks up. And I leave for Paris within ten days. I got my leave twenty-four hours after I requested it. . . . Now I'll leave in my own carriage and make my trip like a prince. I have had made a sort of little table on which I can scribble *s'il le faut*. I go back to Munich and hope to see our Aiblinger.[24] The opera for Paris moves forward little by little. [Matteo] Salvi is working on his [opera]. So, behold yourself informed about everything."[25]

On July 9, Donizetti wrote Dolci that Salvi and he would be leaving Vienna for Paris two days later by way of Linz, Munich, Stuttgart, Karlsruhe, and Strasbourg, traveling in the newly purchased carriage, "which we now have tried out." He explained that he would not have time to stop at either Genoa or Milan because he must go into rehearsal at Paris as quickly as possible. He referred again to his inability to get to Naples for the staging of *Caterina Cornaro:* "At Naples I'll lose twenty-five hundred francs and not go." From Munich

[23] Otto von Nicolai's *Il Templario?* This opera, to a libretto derived from Scott's *Ivanhoe* by Girolamo Maria Marini, and first heard at the Teatro Regio, Turin, in 1840, had been staged in Vienna for the first time on May 31, 1841; it was widely performed for many years.

[24] Johann Caspar Aiblinger (1779–1867), the Bavarian composer of sacred music who had studied with Mayr at Bergamo.

[25] At the bottom of this letter, in another script, this appears: "Will you know that I am going to Paris? And with whom? How? Can you guess?—His pupil, Salvi." Matteo Salvi of Bergamo, who had been studying with Donizetti, was on the road toward a briefly successful career as a composer of operas. His one-act opera *La Prima Donna*, to a libretto by Carlo Guaita, had been sung in Vienna on April 29, 1843, with a cast including Eugenia Tadolini, Lorenzo Salvi, and Agostino Rovere; his later operas were *Lara* (La Scala, Milan, November 4, 1843), *I Burgravi* (La Scala, Milan, March 8, 1845), and *Caterina Howard* (Kärnthnertortheater, Vienna, June 10, 1847). Spending most of his later life in Vienna, Salvi died at Rieti on October 18, 1887. He was to complete Donizetti's *Le Duc d'Albe* for its *première*, in an Italian translation by Angelo Zanardini, at the Teatro Apollo, Rome, on March 22, 1882. See p. 394.

on July 15, he wrote to Mayr to say that he had seen Aiblinger, that he and Salvi were leaving by train for Augsburg within two hours. This is the renowned letter in which he mentioned having seen a painting of Mayr's birthplace at Aiblinger's and went on to say: "My birth was more secret, however, as I was born underground in Borgo Canale—you went down by a cellar stairs to which no suspicion of light ever penetrated." The passage continues: "And it was like an owl that I took my flight, carrying in myself both sad and happy omens, not encouraged by my poor father, who always repeated to me, It is impossible that you should compose, that you should go to Naples, that you should go to Vienna. . . . I had only my moral strength as a shield against such humiliations. I say to you, and I do not brag, that I have had many unhappy experiences. . . . I am happy, loved, esteemed . . . what more? I have someone in Heaven who prays for me, for you, for us all."

Reaching Paris about July 20, Donizetti briefly stayed with Michele Accursi at No. 19 rue d'Antin before moving into his usual Paris home, the Hôtel Manchester in the rue Grammont.[26] There he began to work on *Dom Sébastien*. Middle age and the inroads of disease had not attenuated his capacity to labor up to ten hours a day during the rest of July and all of August. On September 2, he wrote Mayr that the five acts of *Dom Sébastien* were almost finished. Fifteen days later, he wrote Totò Vasselli that four of them had been orchestrated. And on October 5, in a letter to Teodoro Ghezzi, he said: "My opera in five acts will be given a month from now, and I'll know whether its reception is good or bad. You can imagine what a staggering spectacle— Portuguese, Arabs, a procession of the Inquisition (auto-da-fé), a royal procession with a catafalque—the underground dungeons of the Inquisition. The poor King of Portugal is dragged everywhere until they kill him and Philip II takes possession of Lisbon. . . . I am terribly wearied by this enormous opera in five acts which carries bags full of music for singing and dancing. A few notes yet, and then it is all done. If I can break [my contract] with the Opéra-Comique next summer, I'll come to Naples."

During this period, newspapers in either Vienna or Milan, or both, were carrying on an extended polemic on the subject of composers of

---

[26] From Paris on August 10, Donizetti wrote a long letter to his friend and banker in Vienna, August Thomas, of the banking firm of Arnstein and Heskeles, largely to complain in detail about defects in the new carriage, which he had had built for him by Luigi Laurenzi, to whom—evidently through Thomas—he had paid eight hundred florins of the price agreed to.

opera who rearranged (or allowed such impresarios as Merelli to re-arrange) their operas, transposing numbers, introducing numbers from other operas by themselves or others, rearranging vocal lines to suit the capabilities of special singers. Apparently much of the adverse criticism was aimed at Donizetti, who was caricatured again as *Maestro Orgasmo* because the speed with which he worked led him to all these "abuses." Writing to his Viennese friend Leo Herz on October 18, he said: "In the midst of all this chatter being carried on in the newspapers, I sent you four lines that you will place or not place as you think [best]." And on October 31, writing to Count Gaetano Melzi, he said: "As to Orgasmo and Merelli, put your spirit at rest. I thought with the letter that I published that I would open the eyes of the Direction of Theaters, I thought that I would help my confreres, I thought that I could remove from our shoulders the whirlwind of hissing that weighs us down whenever a composer introduces pieces from one opera into another, or transposes, or points,[27] things all extremely damaging to the poor composer, who cannot appear on the stage to say 'This is not mine, this was not fabricated this way, this does not go so adagio or so presto; this does not fit the voice of A., of B.' The public and the journalists, led into error, disapprove and hiss without examining the question. My letter was no more than a *vox in deserto; fiat.* Last Sunday, *La France musicale* published a small article about these assassins, but it will have effect only in France and not where the plague exists. Furthermore, Merelli is accustomed to doing this, the proof being my *Fausta* at Bergamo. He said then that I had revised it, and to make it seem as though I had, added a cavatina by Maestro [Luigi] Savj[28] and the finale of *Les Martyrs.*"

At about this time, the *Panthéon musical,* one of the most famous and widely reproduced of musical caricatures, the work of C.-J. Travies, was published in Paris. Donizetti wrote a (see Plate 15) description of it to August Thomas on November 2: "The *Panthéon musical* has come out. I am [standing] on a locomotive, dressed in court habit, with a camellia, like Don Pasquale, and I am tossing scores in all directions. Auber on a bronze horse (the pedestal [of which] reads 'Auber Foundry'), Carafa on a wooden horse, Meyerbeer, dressed as Robert le Diable, is holding a framed picture on which his two 'invisible' scores are [represented by] two figures, the Prophet and the African.

[27] The Italian verb *puntare*, having no exact English equivalent in this sense, is used to mean adapting existing music to the particular needs or capabilities of performing artists.

[28] Luigi Savj (1803–42), a Parmesan composer.

Halévy is below him and seems to be stealing a piece of his clothing. Spontini is gazing at the dawn that is breaking, turning his ass toward everyone and everything as if because he can find nothing to do. Berlioz, in a carriage with coronets and flowers, is writing his impressions so that they can be published in the [*Journal des*] *Débats.* Clapisson is dressed all in black, with black tails. Thomas is [sitting] on top of a double ladder [marked] *Mina,* the most recent of his operas to please. Adam is riding a donkey and is dressed as a postillion (*de Longjumeau*). Rossini, in a corner of his own, is naked on clouds, like a river [god], leaning on a vase from which a stream of water issues; underneath [him], in the lake [thus] formed, are other, little composers who are looking for inspiration in the water mentioned; the beautiful [part] is that Rossini is showing his back and not his face. Labarre (harpist), with a guitar and dressed as a troubadour, etc. I'll bring the print, and if it hasn't reached there already, you'll laugh when you see it." The caricature has this verse beneath the figure of Donizetti:

Fabriquant à la vapeur	(Making, under full steam,
Une multitude de partitions	A multitude of scores
Populaires dans tout l'univers	Popular everywhere in the uni-
Et mille autres lieux.	verse
	And a thousand other places.)

Rehearsals of *Maria di Rohan*—to which, in addition to transposing the second tenor role of Armando di Gondì so that it could be sung by Marietta Brambilla, a contralto, Donizetti had added three new numbers—were announced to Leo Herz in a letter of October 30: "Today I begin my rehearsals of *Rohan: deux batterie.*"[29] At the Théâtre-Italien on the day Donizetti was writing, *Belisario* was sung by a stellar cast including Giulia Grisi, Giorgio Ronconi, and Lorenzo Salvi. Almost at the same time, at the Opéra, rehearsals of *Dom Sébastien* were begun. And in fact, Donizetti was to live through the rigors and strain of what amounted to two Paris *premières* within twenty-four hours. *Dom Sébastien,* sumptuously and extravagantly staged, was heard first, at the Opéra, on November 13.[30] The reaction of its first audience was predominantly enthusiastic, and the opera was set for thirty-three performances. The first eight of these brought to the box office, subscriptions aside, the notable sum of sixty thousand francs; at the end of nineteen performances, this amount had risen to one hundred and thirty thousand francs. But the critical appraisal of *Dom Sébastien*

[29] That is, two operas in preparation at once.
[30] Donizetti wrote to August Thomas the next day, saying that in the third-act climax about five hundred people had been on the stage.

was icily reserved when not denigrating.[31] Before Donizetti had had time to discover what the fate of *Dom Sébastien* was to be, however, the first Paris performance of *Maria di Rohan* took place at the Théâtre-Italien on November 14, the evening after the *première* of *Dom Sébastien*. The older opera was an immediate, unquestioned success with both audience and critics.

On November 20, Giovanni Ruffini, who had been called in again by Michele Accursi to help Donizetti—this time to supply additional verses to the libretto of *Maria di Rohan*—wrote his mother: "The past week has been, if I may say so, a week of terrible theatrical fatigue. On Monday *Dom Sébastien*, on Tuesday *Maria di Rohan*, and thus throughout the week with only one lacuna. There is a lot of beautiful music in these two operas, a lot of beautiful pieces! *Dom Sébastien*, a colossal score, has twenty-four. The success of the two operas has been all that could be desired; that of *Dom Sébastien* greater than that of *Maria*. These successes are the more strange when one reflects that Donizetti has as obligatory enemies all the composers and writers of music, then the journalists and music critics, all the publishers of music except the one to whom he sells the score, which he can't sell to more than one—isn't it so?—and with the mass of the not very intelligent public Donizetti is a little in the situation of Aristides, of whom that citizen, asked why he should be ostracized, answered: 'Because I'm tired of hearing Aristides constantly spoken about.' Despite all these obstacles, I tell you, things have gone marvelously, and the journals systematically hostile to him begin to be persuaded. Success, then, in honor and in money, as he has sold the score of *Dom Sébastien* for thirty thousand francs." Three weeks later (December 11) he added: "*Dom Sébastien* makes a profit at each performance and wins fame and money for the composer."

Because the audiences' enthusiastic reactions to *Dom Sébastien* had been called into question by the reviewers' caveats, Donizetti—who believed this opera to be his masterpiece—came to feel bitterly disappointed about it, a state of depression that was not to be lightened until it was mounted in German at the Kärnthnertortheater, Vienna, on February 6, 1845, winning the almost unqualified praise that he felt to be its due. From the time of his first visit to Paris in 1835 and the production of *Marin Faliero* at the Théâtre-Italien on March 2 of that year, Parisian audiences had lived under the spell of his music, seldom failing to support performance after performance of any Donizetti

[31] But see p. 365. Several of the critics noted that so lugubrious a libretto was particularly unfortunate at the moment because Louis-Philippe's eldest son, Ferdinand-Philippe, Duc d'Orleans, recently had sustained a mortal accident.

opera they were permitted to hear. But always he had had difficulties with Parisian managers, impresarios, and, above all, reviewers and critics, from Délécluze to Berlioz.

The tenor Gilbert-Louis Duprez wrote (47, 95): "He [Donizetti] often told me how his pride as a composer had suffered in Paris. There he never was treated according to his merits. I myself saw at the Opéra-Comique how many times *La Favorite* had to be given before it became established. When he gave *Dom Sébastien*, no annoyance, no vexation was spared him." Verdi, writing in 1855 to the Marchese Caracciolo after the Opéra's staging of *Les Vêpres siciliennes*, said: "Poor Donizetti was treated much worse than I have been, and the great Maestro fled from Paris, smiling to himself and wrapped in that mantle of glory which all the Délécluzes of his time had not been able to drag from his shoulders."

Because such writers as Alborghetti and Galli (1875), Verzino (1896), and, particularly, Annibale Gabrielli (1904) had access to oral testimony now lost except as reflected in their writings, it is worth while to quote their remarks about the exacerbated condition of Donizetti's nerves and mind at the time of the first performance of *Dom Sébastien*. Alborghetti and Galli said (5, 183): "When *Dom Sébastien* was given for the first time—that is, on November 13, 1843—the Maestro carried on all his person the evident traces of a deep alteration, both physical and moral. It seemed that in the brief span of a few months he had fallen from the fullness of virility into advanced old age: bent, turned white,[32] with his eyes languid and sunken, his movements flaccid and abandoned, he managed his body with difficulty: impatient, irascible, gruff, his character as much altered as his physiognomy, he provoked about him a curious reaction of envious rancor and base malice because that which was nothing but the unconscious expression of his infirm mind was thought to be the deliberate intention of a new haughtiness."

Verzino wrote (*132*, 125–26): "The directing management [of the Opéra], during the period of the rehearsals, employed many tergiversations, placed many obstacles in the [way of] the Maestro, so that Donizetti is said to have exclaimed: '*Dom Sébastien* is killing me.' Royer recounts that Donizetti began to feel the first symptoms of his illness while he was composing this score.[33] The Maestro was then

[32] Donizetti closed a letter of January 8 or 9, 1843, to Dolci with the phrase "Your friend Griselda," referring to the virtuous gray-haired woman in the *Decameron*.

[33] Verzino, who was fully aware that Donizetti had been ill often before

very irritable, he who always had been so even-tempered and calm. In his letters he complains of the alterations imposed by the director of the theater and accuses his librettist, Scribe, of not defending him sufficiently."

Gabrielli, against the background of his family store of memories and documents, said (*58*, 109): "The earlier biographer [Filippo] Cicconnetti [*33*] attributed Donizetti's increased irritability and misanthropy to the annoyances that he suffered in Paris over the rehearsals and performance of this favorite opera. But looking with a more modern eye at the psychic and physical condition of Donizetti during those months, it is easy to see that the impresario's small impositions, the frequent changes desired by the direction, the idle chattering, the stage envies, found the Maestro's spirit already predisposed to the more desperate melancholy. So, whereas Parisian theatrical circles believed and proclaimed him invaded by a new, antipathetic vanity, in fact poor Donizetti by then was nothing but a sick man."

The climax of the difficulties during the rehearsals of *Dom Sébastien* had come when Rosine Stoltz had refused to remain on stage while Paolo Barroilhet, in the role of Camoës, sang a barcarolle. When Donizetti strongly objected to her absence during that part of the scene, Stoltz consented to remain—if the second verse of the barcarolle was deleted. That compromise was agreed to by the direction, and at that point Donizetti's anger got the better of him. He threw down his score, denounced Stoltz for having wounded his artistic dignity, and walked out of the theater. "Three friends," Léon Escudier wrote, "and we among them, followed him home. He said nothing more. He gave vent to rattling sounds of rage. His mind was confused."

Reporting the same incident, Charles de Boigne (*20*) wrote: "Donizetti left the rehearsal furious, inflamed. His head was whirling. His legs were unsteady. If his *fidus Achates*, Accursi, had not supported him, almost carrying him to his carriage, he would have fallen." Escudier and Boigne agreed in dating the decline of Donizetti's mental clarity from that event, Escudier writing: "From that day forward, Donizetti was stricken in the brain. From that day dated the frightful sickness that undermined his faculties little by little and ended by carrying him off." Boigne, taking into account that some of Donizetti's friends blamed Stoltz for his mental decline, said: "Doubtless it would be

---

November 1843, here almost certainly meant that at the time of the composition of *Dom Sébastien*, Donizetti began to realize for the first time the terrible message brought by his symptoms.

ridiculous to accuse Mme Stoltz of having hastened the denouement of that deplorable crisis, but what is certain is that the first symptoms of the disease broke out after that scene during which the second verse of the barcarolle was taken from Barroilhet by the authorities."

Still, Donizetti was in command of most of his mental powers, and he could not remain excessively bitter even at the judgments of the reviewers—they had not prevented audiences from continuing to flock to the Opéra to hear *Dom Sébastien*. On December 2, for example, he wrote to Leo Herz: "Yesterday evening, I attended another *Camoëns*,[34] in one act, at the Opéra-Comique—St.-Georges and Flotow, and it includes some well-done things."[35] Too, *Maria di Rohan* continued to run along at the Théâtre-Italien. He had been paid sixteen thousand francs for *Dom Sébastien;* his dedication of it to Queen Maria II of Portugal was shortly (January 19, 1844) to bring him the Cross of the Military Order of the Conception. What worried him most was the fate in store for his *Caterina Cornaro* at Naples. Writing to Teodoro Ghezzi on November 18, 1843, he remarked: "In the meantime, to find strength inside myself to support the surgical operations that will be performed on *Catterina* [*sic*] in Naples either because of insufficiencies or because of impotence, I am comforting myself with Paris successes—in twenty-four hours, two operas new to Paris—*Dom Sébastien* in five acts and *Maria di Rohan* at the Italien in three acts. I wouldn't know how to tell you which of the two pleased the more. I do know that at the Opéra they took in eight thousand francs beyond the subscription on the opening night, and that at the Italien they repeat arias, duets, etc. to dreadful full houses.[36] Now I'll leave for Vienna on the fifteenth of the coming December, and then I'll know about the outcome of *Catterina* (if it will be given)."

Writing to August Thomas on November 19, Donizetti said that he was leaving "amid the maledictions of composers living in Paris," and there is reason to suppose that the continuing public success of his operas indeed was irritating, not only to native French composers, but also to foreign musicians living in Paris, because they hoped to climb the gleaming ladder to the stage of the Académie Royale de Musique. He did not leave for Vienna as early as he had planned, but remained

---

[34] The great Portuguese poet Camoës is a principal character (originally sung by Paolo Barroilhet) in *Dom Sébastien*.

[35] Friedrich von Flotow's *L'Esclave de Camoëns*, with a libretto by Jules-Henri Vernoy de Saint-Georges, was given its *première*, in one act, at the Opéra-Comique on December 1, 1843. In various enlargements and translations, it was to have a very long career, sometimes as *Indra das Schlangenmädchen*, sometimes as *Alma l'incantatrice*.

[36] "*a pieni orribili*," very probably also a pun on *pene orribili*, "horrible pains."

in Paris until December 20. The delay was necessitated in part by need for time to formalize a contract, in part by his becoming seriously ill. His migraines returned fiercer than ever, now allied to spells of giddiness. The doctors whom he consulted prescribed medications and recommended complete rest, abstention from all work. Late in November, Donizetti sent Vasselli a letter in macaronic Latin, saying that he had fallen ill and that his head whirled, making him move like a drunkard. The physicians, he wrote, had told him not to work at all and had given him purgatives that had brought on the evacuation of much feces and bile. The tone of this exceedingly strange letter is jocular, but it again forcefully suggests mild mental disturbance.

During this delay, illness, and convalescence, Donizetti remembered that he had promised to prepare, as the composition that his court position in Vienna required him to present formally each year, a piece for the Imperial Chapel. Therefore he refashioned a *Parafrasi del "Christus"* that he had composed, to a text by Serafino Gatti, in Naples in 1829, for soprano, contralto, and string orchestra. Then, nine days before leaving Paris, he wrote Vasselli a letter that begins in prose but passes into fifty lines of rhyme recounting his illness—here he says that only digitalis had helped—and outlining the plan of his trip to Vienna. Half in jest, he reports that he is losing his teeth, that his hair is turning gray, and that "everything tells me that we are nearing the end." He could not have known that in fact this was the sober truth.

On December 18, at the Odéon, the popular Parisian comedian Rouvière appeared in an adaptation by Hippolyte Lucas of Calderón's *El Médico de su honra*, for which Donizetti had composed a song, the *"Chanson de l'abeille,"* which was greeted enthusiastically and was to become very popular. Whether Donizetti was present at its first singing is not known. But two days later he left Paris alone for the ten-day carriage trip via Stuttgart and Munich, reaching Vienna on December 30 after what he described, in a letter of January 6, 1844, to Totò Vasselli, as "a rather boring journey, alone in the carriage, running along for fifteen or sixteen hours each day over the worst roads, and fairly cold." Later in the letter, he wrote: "I need rest. After the two operas at Paris, I was put on syrup of digitalis, four spoonsful per day; it did me good, but now, however, I have stopped it because I am better. What a difference between Paris and Vienna: there everything is agitation; here everything is calm. I grant you that after such strong emotions, the German quiet is a restorative for me. If it were to become permanent, it would upset me, but right now I find it a balm."

CHAPTER IX

1844-July 1845

O N January 28, 1844, from Vienna, in a half-French, half-Italian
letter to Giuseppina Appiani—who by then had begun to
patronize and befriend Verdi as earlier she had befriended
Bellini and himself—Donizetti said. "They tell me . . . that you
breathe and palpitate only for Verdi, and your letter itself betrays
you . . . but I approve of your passions; as long as you love artists of
great talent, so long shall I esteem you; I cannot become irritated—
my period for [your] sympathy is past; it is high time for another to
occupy the place. The world wants novelty; others certainly gave way
to us, we must cede our place to others. . . . Very happy, then, to cede
it to people of talent, like Verdi. Friendship always has fears, but be
very tranquil about the success of this young man. The Venetians
appreciate him as much as the Milanese, for the heart is the same everywhere. Talent wins appreciation everywhere, etc. In any case, if his
success doesn't fulfill the hopes of his friends, that will not prevent the
good Verdi from occupying in a short time one of the most honorable
positions in the cohort of composers." Later in the letter came the now
almost invariable warning: "I arrived here at the end of the year—six
days later, I was taken by the fever (twelve days) and was obliged to
rest at home. Only today do I present myself for the first time to Her
Majesty the Empress."

From a childhood friend at Bergamo, Adelson Piacezzi, meanwhile,
Donizetti had received a sumptuous gift: a copy of the 1497 edition
of the *Divina Commedia* with the commentary of Cristoforo Landino,
illustrated with woodcuts. "Of what a gem you have made me the

possessor!" he had written Piacezzi on January 9. "I always have loved (if not understood) Dante, but by your gift you have doubled that affection and veneration. I should have accused you of cruelty if it had fallen into other hands. The friendship that has united us since the first years of our youth spoke to you on my behalf, and may you also be blessed a thousand times." This gift was to bear incidental fruits very rapidly.

At the Teatro San Carlo, Naples, on January 12, 1844, occurred the second *première* of a Donizetti opera which he himself did not supervise or attend: that of *Caterina Cornaro*, the last of his operas which he completed. The time that it required for letters to travel from Naples to Vienna meant that Donizetti would have no news of its reception until the end of the month. He had justified forebodings. In the letter of January 6 to Vasselli already cited, he had said: "I am awaiting with anxiety the news of the fiasco of *Caterina Cornaro* at Naples. La [Fanny] Goldberg as the prima donna is, without being aware of it, my first ruination. I wrote for a soprano—they give me a mezzo! God knows whether [Filippo] Coletti, whether [Gaetano] Fraschini, understands the roles as I intended them; God knows what a slaughterhouse the censorship has created. And while I pass from doubt to doubt, from fear to fear, I believe that the opera already is sentenced. . . . *Sic transit gloria mundi*. I foresee great fiascos in Italy: Turin, Milan, Venice, Trieste. God knows how many others will bedeck the tresses of the white Carnival!"

A letter to Dolci which Donizetti wrote on January 29 makes it clear that he still is awaiting word about the fortune encountered by *Caterina Cornaro*. This was seventeen days after the *première;* he received the feared, foreseen bad news a day or two after that. In letters of January 31—or, at the latest, February 1—to Dolci and Ghezzi, he laments and fulminates over news that *Caterina Cornaro* had been a failure and, worse, that rumors had been spread that the opera actually was not his own work, that he had palmed off a hoax on the Neapolitans. He exploded to Ghezzi: "Fiasco? So be it, a fiasco! But that it should be said that this music is not mine, or that I composed it while asleep or in revenge against the management, no. I assume all responsibility, blame, and punishment. Why would I have had it composed by others? Did I perhaps not have the time? Why asleep? Don't I, perhaps, work with ease? Why for revenge? Could I be thus ungrateful toward a public that has suffered me for so many years? No! It could be that genius, practice, taste have deceived me, that I lack them all, but that I should descend to vile things, to hidden deceptions, never! As for the reminiscences? *Eh, mon Dieu!* and who doesn't make them? As for stealing (and, what is worse, without meaning to), and who does not steal? Note well that I do not mean at all to justify myself; I repeat that I assume all responsibility. I should have thought that several pieces did not merit all the fuming censure, that the duets, the quartet, etc.—but what's the use of discussing it now? That would be only to draw new blood from the wound. If a copy of this score comes back into my hands, I'll give proof to the Neapolitans that I obey their advice; the mistake, then, has been my believing that this music perhaps was not unworthy of their indulgence." To Dolci he wrote merely: "I have read about the fiasco of my *Caterina Cornaro* at Naples. . . . It hurts me a lot because I even thought that I had composed something good. . . . It is painful to lose some months' work, but that is the law for everyone, and my head is bowed, and I humble myself."

Most interesting of these letters is an undated one (probably written about February 1) to Ghezzi: it shows Donizetti in revived spirits, in the mood to try putting things right:

I understand perfectly the amount of displeasure that you must have felt as a victim of the downfall of *Caterina Cornaro*! I have a thousand proofs of your goodness of heart, and your displeasure has found a very deep echo in my heart. An opera very well may not prove popular, but that it should be said that I—either for money or only for a low vendetta—should have composed a score just in order to have it condemned, that never! . . . Do you think that I'm going to abandon the score? No! The *stretta* of the introduction doesn't please? I'll do it over. Give me, and as quickly as possible, an exact report on the numbers that were disapproved of, as well as of those which La Goldberg found most uncomfortable. Perhaps you'll say that it all was bad, but even amid the bad there is the worse. Don't be delicate about it. The fiasco gives you the right, as friendship does even more so. I'll see if I can recast the thing, for I confess to you that I had not thought it so infamous. Tell me, further, where it lacks effect, where it is short, long, where there are reminiscences, the defects of the libretto, etc. I want to know everything, everything, and as soon as possible. . . . The priests of the fine arts ought not to have those who feel and who share their pleasure and their pains. Not wanting to, they create unhappy people. What can I say? What can be said by a heart like mine, which feels its own pain and still finds tears and recognition for those who share its torture with it? Oh! may you have some balm to make you forget what happened, to transfer to me all your suffering. . . . If fortune doesn't smile on me, that is Heaven's desire. It did not wish me to have it for this. . . . Greet whoever is not angry at me, whoever doesn't dislike me, and also believe that my sorrow exceeds that of all my friends.

Speculating on the stunning failure of *Caterina Cornaro*, Guido Zavadini (*138*) wrote: "His [Donizetti's] vein surely was weary; the singers (Goldberg, Fraschini, Coletti, Beneventano), having to do without the presence of the Maestro, perhaps did not know how to find the right interpretative color and warmth; the libretto, crippled by the censorship, rendered almost ridiculous and unrecognizable; probably all these causes together must have brought on the failure." Lacking any present possibility of hearing a first-rate performance of this last of Donizetti's completed operas, no one can judge it appositely by merely studying the score: Donizetti was first and always a man of the opera stage, and his operas require now what he himself required to bring them to full life. Zavadini's speculations can stand, then, and certainly it is not unlikely that a man already as fatally ill as Donizetti was by 1843 would have composed at less than his best. Perhaps more than any cause of the disaster of *Caterina Cornaro*, however—more than the stupidities of the censors or any insufficiencies on the part of the singers—what contributed most to that fiasco was the fact that the opera had not been staged, supervised down to the moment of the first curtain, and therefore cut, expanded, and adjusted to stage realities and the singers' capabilities by Donizetti himself. What, for example, Verdi, an even greater man of the theater, thought of Donizetti's abilities as a stage director was to become clear shortly.

Before leaving Paris in December 1843, Donizetti had contracted with Léon Pillet, director of the Opéra, to provide an opera for the coming year. Now, in Vienna, he began searching for a suitable subject, though his real wish was that he had not entered into the contract or might find a way to cancel it. He rejected the story of Joanna the Mad, the unhappy daughter of Ferdinand and Isabella, which Scribe had suggested to Pillet, who seems not to have liked it. So, on January 23, 1844, Donizetti wrote to Pillet suggesting that another composer take his place during the coming season, adding that, as a result, Scribe would not have to elaborate a *Jeanne la folle*,[1] seen in advance as unsuitable for the Opéra. On February 22, Donizetti told Vasselli: "If the rupture of the contract occurs, imagine my happiness. Bergamo, Rome, Naples, *en avant, marche!*" He was to have his wish, though not by the means that he would have chosen. Not bound to do more for Paris than tinker further with the incomplete score of *Le Duc d'Albe*, he could devote his remaining energy and time, when he felt well enough,

[1] Scribe finally wrote a *Jeanne la folle*, which was set as an opera by Antoine-Louis Clapisson and produced on November 6, 1848, after Donizetti's death.

to lighter tasks required by his concerts at court and by the composition of an offertory *Ave Maria*, to a text from Dante, for soprano, contralto, and string orchestra. This was sung at the first Lenten *concert spirituel.*

Still awaiting word as to whether or not Meyerbeer would allow *Le Prophète* to be staged at the Opéra in 1845—and thus free him from having to provide the Paris theater with another big work so soon—Donizetti told Teodoro Ghezzi in a letter of February 21, 1844: "In any case, tell Tommaso [Persico] that I have half done the decisive letter that will indicate to him what he should do with my furniture, but that I'm waiting a few days to send it so as to know from Paris whether or not they'll be giving my opera." But no 1844 letter to Persico survives before one dated August 9—and that is to ask him to welcome Giuseppe Donizetti on his arrival at Naples and take him to the apartment. Donizetti, then, still could not make up his mind entirely to dispose of his only home or its contents.

Now Donizetti was to be depressed even more: word arrived from Bergamo that his brother Francesco was seriously unwell. Writing on February 20 to Vasselli, Donizetti said: "You will know that my brother in Bergamo has been in bed for a month. . . . Now that I could enjoy myself in peace for a few days, behold this illness, which disturbs me terribly. Also, because I don't want to go to Constantinople, Giuseppe writes me a very troublesome letter. I have answered, and I see myself as constantly more isolated on the earth. Patience! All this saddens me, and I don't enjoy that quiet toward which I have been hurrying for years and which I'll never find."

On March 29, writing to Vasselli, Donizetti referred to the fact that Giuseppe was soon to arrive on a visit from Constantinople: "As to my Turkish brother, I have balled you up by saying April; he will be in Vienna toward the end of May. He will go to Genoa to see that handsome figure of an ass, his son [Andrea], who doesn't know as much about [the laws of] Justinian as I do about the Sultan's beauties. . . . You will know, *Sor Patronus Palatii*,[2] that I have canceled my double contract with Paris for an *opera seria* and a *buffa*, and that (permission obtained) I will spend the entire summer in Italy. Where I'll go after that will develop. If he wants to push on to Naples, we'll come by there [Rome] at your expense, passing through Canneto, Civita Castellana, etc. If not, he'll stay on at Bergamo, and in unhappiness I'll go to bore myself in Naples without passing through

[2] Antonio Vasselli recently had been given an appointment as Advocate of the Sacred Rota, and Donizetti made great play with his high-sounding Latin title.

Rome, because the weather, the circumstances, the hours, the roads, what's to be done, etc., don't permit it. I worked desperately until November with *Dom Sébastien;* since then I haven't written a note, and for the time being I won't write one. I'll die of hunger and thirst if I don't work, it's true, but at least I'll leave you the liberty to support me."

During April he received word that Lucrezia Mayr, the wife of his now octogenarian teacher and friend, had died. In a lugubrious, almost funereal mood, Donizetti conveyed his reactions to this latest sad news to Dolci in a sincere—if, for him, banal—letter dated April 8. On the day on which he wrote this letter, Donizetti had exactly four more years to live. Writing a letter of condolence to Mayr on April 10, Donizetti told of expecting his "Turkish brother" in Vienna in May. "Then we'll decide what we're going to do." Clearly, Giuseppe Donizetti realistically was worried over the future of both of his brothers and felt—particularly as Gaetano would not, and Francesco probably could not, come to Constantinople—that he must visit Gaetano in Vienna and Francesco in Bergamo and work out future arrangements for them. On April 10, too, Léon Pillet wrote to Donizetti from Paris to suggest new conditions for the composition of a work for the Opéra. Donizetti replied on April 17, accepting November 1845 as a date for which the new opera could be scheduled.[3] Four days later, writing to Dolci, he said: "As you know, I freed myself from the grand opera in five acts for Paris for this winter. It will be next year instead. In the meantime, up comes the impresario of the Italien, who wants . . . an opera that I have in my portfolio (French) (in translation) [*Ne m'oubliez pas?*]. The publisher offers me seventeen thousand francs, the impresario three thousand to stage it. Altogether, that would be twenty thousand francs. We'll see if the thing can be worked out. Nothing [no contract] is in writing up to now."

Writing Donizetti about singers who might be signed up for the projected new work at the Opéra, Pillet also told him that by the death of Henri Berton on April 22, 1844, a regular seat in the Institut de France (i.e., in the Académie des Beaux-Arts) had fallen vacant. Pillet thought that Donizetti (already a corresponding foreign member of the Académie des Beaux-Arts) could be elected to it if he would renounce his nationality. Replying on May 14, Donizetti rejected the suggestion:

---

[3] Toward the end of this letter, Donizetti reported: "La [Pauline] Viardot-García made her [Vienna] debut in *Il Barbiere* [*di Siviglia*] with Ronconi, both of them very good. La [Fanny] Elssler a great success in *Giselle*, too. The Direction [of the Italian opera] here withdrew for the coming year, but now is sorry and wants to continue. [Bartolomeo] Merelli is working toward that end."

"I owe everything to my country, and my making myself French would be black ingratitude." Two days later, he conducted at a large court concert in which the leading singers of that Italian season at the Kärnthnertortheater took part.

As a member of the Académie des Beaux-Arts, Donizetti was required to send to the perpetual secretary at stated intervals papers on some artistic matter. In 1842, he had considered writing on *bergamaschi* of the past who had excelled in music. Whether that *mémoire* was sent in is not known, but Donizetti did send one in on May 26, 1844: The Bergamo Civic Library has a seven-page sketch of this paper in Donizetti's autograph. It was read at a sitting of the Académie on June 8, after which the perpetual secretary, Désiré Raoul-Rochette, wrote to Donizetti:

The receipt of your letter of May 26 . . . gave me great pleasure, and I hastened to read it to the Académie at the sitting of last Saturday, the 8th instant. To tell you with what satisfaction that reading was received by the entire Académie would truly be impossible for me.[4] Not a single one of your ideas but was enjoyed as it merited being, not a single one of your observations but has been judged as much full of essence and taste as expressed with elegance and spirit. Those of our musicians who were present —Spontini, Carafa, and Halévy—the last two above all,[5] applauded vigorously and openly everything that your letter included of the well thought out and the well written about the two systems that divide the musical world; and everyone found that what you say about the conciliation attempted by the French school in taking up what is best in the two rival schools is as judicious on your part as it is honorable for your nation and worthy of a man who himself belongs to it [the French school] in a certain sense because of the success that he has won and by the nationality that he has acquired through his works. In short, my dear and illustrious confrere, that sitting, which was taken up entirely by the reading of your letter and with the comments—all flattering for you—which it occasioned, left in all spirits the best impression that I could desire for you, and never was it sweeter

[4] Under date of July 18, 1962, J. Bourcier, Secretary-Archivist of the Académie des Beaux-Arts, wrote me in reply to my inquiry as to whether Donizetti's *mémoire* survived in the archives: "The *mémoire* in which you are interested also is mentioned in the official report of the sitting of the Académie Royale des Beaux-Arts of Saturday, June 8, 1844: 'The perpetual secretary reads a letter that he has received from Monsieur Donizetti, correspondent of the Académie, which contains observations full of good sense and taste on the Vienna Conservatory of Music and on the present direction of German music. That letter arouses the highest degree of interest in the Académie.' Unhappily, Donizetti's letter to Raoul-Rochette is not found in the archives of the Académie Royale des Beaux-Arts."

[5] It is amusing to see reflected here the unbending pride for which the stiff Spontini was known. Sixty-nine years old, somewhat *démodé* as a composer, he recently had been experiencing the hostility of Léon Pillet at the Opéra and appears to have been in no mood to applaud the ideas, however sensible, of the much more popular Donizetti.

for me to serve as interpreter of the feelings of the Académie. Our mutual friend, Monsieur D. Dietrichstein, speaks to me of the success that you have had this year in Vienna, where you have been the presiding deity. I hope that Paris, which loves you no less, will not be less obligated to you; and I am not the last of those who await your return with the greatest impatience, in the expectation of the new pleasures that you are preparing for them, and that new successes will crown them. You will have learned of the death of our poor old [Henri] Berton. [Adolphe] Adam will have the field free, and the election will not be disputed.

On March 9, 1844, Verdi's *Ernani* had been given its successful *première* at the Teatro La Fenice, Venice.[6] The first non-Italian city to hear the new opera was to be Vienna, where it was scheduled for May 30. Perhaps still smarting from his own crushing experience with *Caterina Cornaro* at Naples, Donizetti wrote to Giacomo Pedroni of Ricordi's to suggest that he would be happy to take a helping hand in staging Verdi's opera at the Kärnthnertortheater, knowing that Verdi himself would not travel to Vienna. Pedroni at once informed Verdi, who replied to him: "I received your note of yesterday late and couldn't answer you. You can imagine my pleasure on hearing that Donizetti is assuming the direction of my *Ernani*. That way, I'm sure that it will be interpreted in the musical spirit of the composition. When you see him again, assure him in my name of my gratitude for this very great favor."

To Donizetti himself, Verdi—particularly grateful because he sensed that the Italian company at the Kärnthnertortheater that season was ill suited to performing *Ernani*—wrote: "It was a pleasant surprise for me to read the letter that you wrote to Pedroni, in which you kindly offered to tend to the rehearsals of my *Ernani*. I do not hesitate at all to accept your courteous offer with the greatest gratitude, certain that my notes can only derive great profit from the moment when Donizetti deigns to think about them. Thus, I can hope that the musical spirit of that composition will be judged properly. I beg you to be willing to occupy yourself with the general direction as well as with the editing that may be required, especially in the part for [Paolo] Ferretti.[7] To you, Signor Cavaliere, I will not pay compliments. You are among the small number of men who have supreme talent and do

[6] The first cast of *Ernani* included Sophie Löwe, Carlo Guasco, Antonio Superchi, and Antonio Selva.

[7] In view of Verdi's well-known insistence that his music be performed as written, his willingness to allow Donizetti to edit *Ernani* to fit the abilities of the singers is particularly interesting and indicative of his opinion of his fellow composer.

not need individual praise. The favor that you are doing me is too distinguished for you to be able to doubt my gratitude. With the most profound esteem, your most devoted servant, G. Verdi."

On May 3, Donizetti had written to Adelson Piacezzi concerning the early part of the Italian opera season at the Kärnthnertortheater: "*Veritas ante omnia.* The opening, with *Norma,* was worse than unhappy. In it, the much-praised [Antonietta] Montenegro, a victim of the lavish eulogies in every letter coming from Milan, was not found worthy of the reputation with which she came honored. Once the cavatina [*"Casta diva"*] had been sung and the opposition to what was happening had been felt, she felt mortified, and good-bye. [Ignazio] Marini is a townsman [of mine], and I should keep silent . . . but . . . he did not sing on pitch, he aroused hilarity. [Paolo] Ferretti defended himself. . . . Adalgisa vanished after two performances. *Norma* was succeeded by *Linda* [*di Chamounix*], and it was shown a good face, as to an old acquaintance well accepted. In it, La Tadolini, [Felice] Varesi, [Michele] Novaro, and even the German Prefect were prodigiously applauded. La [Fanny] Elssler came on then in *Giselle* and won the public vote with her beautiful talent. And her success still continues, and we are at her eighth performance, she having done four of *Giselle* and four of *A Painter's Dream.* Between these ballets *Maria di Rohan,* which I did last year, has been alternated. In it, [Nicholas] Ivanoff made his first appearance and was well received and well applauded. Ronconi is immense in it. Now [*La*] *Gazza* [*ladra*] is being rehearsed; it will be given soon. Then *Ernani,* then *Don Pasquale.* The theater is getting along well. La Montenegro only needs another opera to re-establish herself, and she deserves it, and we hope that she will have it."

His hopes for poor Antonietta Montenegro were to be dashed. Writing to Giacomo Pedroni on June 23, Donizetti reported: "I communicate to you the enormous [*piramidale*] fiasco of *Roberto D'Evereux* [*sic*].[8] La Montenegro had every sort of [bad] luck, even to beginning a phrase a third low, stopping in the middle, then beginning it again a third above. The false notes produced yesterday evening by her, by Ronconi, by Varesi from time to time, are indescribable. Ivanoff, who naturally has a reasonably accurate voice, was so caught up that he managed to pay court to the others. He was poorly applauded after his cabaletta in the second act, and after his aria was called out twice. The others too, from time to time, had some bravos, *mais fort contrarié.* I had attended two acts of the final rehearsal, in a

[8] Sung at the Kärnthnertortheater on June 22, 1844.

box, but the third [act] was impossible for me—there were too many, too many false notes, not knowing parts, not acting, etc. They tell me that yesterday evening was even worse. . . . I don't think that it will be given this evening, though it was announced. . . . Day after tomorrow, they say, *I Normanni a Parigi*,[9] about which I can't tell you anything, as you know I don't go. . . . And with it will end the lovely Italian season, which could have been one of the most brilliant and was the most disastrous."

Giuseppe Donizetti reached Vienna from Constantinople early in June and stayed there until June 22. The two brothers agreed to meet again later on at Bergamo—whither Giuseppe was bound, to see his brother Francesco and his son Andrea, the latter about to be graduated. They also decided to travel together later from Bergamo via Genoa to Naples. As it turned out, however, Donizetti was taken ill with what he believed to be a return of the intestinal inflammation that first had come upon him in Naples in 1829, and Giuseppe therefore lingered on in Vienna, going to Bergamo only when his brother appeared to have recovered. On July 2, Donizetti wrote Antonio Vasselli in jocular tone: "If I was sick, that should make no difference to you! Oh, lovely, am I not perhaps the boss of my own bowels? Yes sir, I've taken two enemas, two doses of castor oil, purgatives, powders, hot applications—and for this? I am still a handsome young fellow, and I don't give a. . . ."

Donizetti, who had been planning to leave Vienna about July 5 or 6, actually left about July 12 or 13, proceeding by very easy stages so as not to become too tired. From Brescia he went on to Bergamo, where he wanted to be on hand for the arrival of a Bösendorfer piano that he had ordered in Vienna for Rosa Basoni. On July 21 from Bergamo, he wrote to her at nearby Lovere to say that the piano was about to appear, and that he therefore would come to see her on the following Sunday, July 28. On Saturday, July 27, with Dolci and some other friends,[10] he went to Lovere, about twenty-six miles from Bergamo, where they all were guests of Countess Basoni. The next day, a students' concert in Donizetti's honor was held at the local Istituto Tadini. The unpublished memoirs of Rosa Basoni's daughter Giovanna, later the Baronessa Scotti,[11] record that during this performance, Donizetti began to drowse and then, apparently exhausted by his recent traveling, fell sound asleep.

Back in Bergamo, Donizetti wrote to August Thomas on July 30:

[9] An opera by Mercadante, with libretto by Felice Romani, first sung at the Teatro Regio, Turin, on February 7, 1832.

[10] Giuseppe and Andrea Donizetti apparently already had left on their way to Naples, where they planned to embark for Constantinople.

[11] The manuscript of these memoirs is in the Museo Donizettiano at Bergamo.

"I am well, but during the first three days after I left Vienna, I had the fever and took only four steps each day. My native air has done me good." Leaving his carriage to be picked up on his return from Naples, Donizetti went to Milan on July 31. There he waited for Antonio Dolci, who was to go the rest of the way with him. On August 1, from Milan, he wrote Vasselli: "So that our journey may fill the populace with greater stupor, we have resolved to take with us, not the servant, but, instead, a *bergamasco* friend who had the good luck to be our companion in musical studies (*temporibus illis*), the great Dolci, who [takes care of] paying the pension to my monkey brother [Francesco], etc." The two men left Milan on August 3, reaching Genoa the next day. There both of them fell ill, Donizetti with a fierce migraine, Dolci with digestive trouble; this misfortune caused them to linger on in the port until August 10, when they finally embarked on the steamer *Antonietta* for Naples via Leghorn and Civitavecchia. They found a particularly distinguished group of passengers aboard: it included Alphonse de Lamartine and his family, Jérôme Bonaparte's son Prince Napoléon, and the Prince of Orange and his wife.

Donizetti had intended to stop over briefly at Rome to visit the Vassellis and his friends there. But he had received word that his brother Giuseppe was preparing to sail from Naples for Constantinople on August 25. He therefore wrote Totò Vasselli from Naples on August 14 to apologize for not having stopped to see him in Rome, remarking that he had felt it essential to be with Giuseppe, especially "because it will perhaps be for the last time." In Naples, he took some part in a staging at the Teatro Nuovo of *Betly*, which had been sung there eight years before, adding a new duet to it. Giuseppe tarried in Naples, but not quite long enough to attend the performance of *Betly* on September 7, when the audience gave Donizetti an extremely warm welcome: ". . . therefore applause, calls, and a handsome gift (a lesson for the Kärnthnertortheater)," he wrote August Thomas on September 23. The direction of the San Carlo had decided to take advantage of his presence in Naples to stage *Maria di Rohan*, but when this production began to run into the traditional delays, Giuseppe decided not to wait for it. He and Andrea sailed on September 5. The two brothers were not to meet again.

Donizetti himself, having stayed in Naples more than a month, also decided not to wait for the performance of *Maria di Rohan*: he and Dolci left the city by post chaise on September 14, reaching Rome at noon the next day. From there, on September 19, Donizetti wrote a sad letter to his Neapolitan friend the lawyer Aniello Benevento: "I attended the first performance of [*Anna*] *Bolena*.[12] *Libera me, Domine*. Some of them had merit, but it passed unnoticed. Dolci, who presents his greetings, runs about astounded among the antique epochs, those of the Middle Ages, and those of the present. Now the antique ruins halt him, now the Raphaels surprise him, now the palaces of the princes enchant him, and by dint of Oh! Ah! Ih! he runs around, sweats, pretends to understand and enjoy. . . . I have left my own gaiety behind, I have turned sad. . . . I come back to rest at the house all day. . . . Tell me that all are well and that you love the sad G." He and Dolci had been in Rome about two weeks, and were on the verge of starting for Bergamo when the direction of the San Carlo sent Donizetti an urgent invitation to return to Naples to attend the first San Carlo performance of *Maria di Rohan*. Although very weary and unwell, he agreed to go. Thereupon, Dolci set out alone for the north. Planning to take Totò Vasselli and four of the ladies of his family to Naples with him, Donizetti wrote on September 26 to Teodoro Ghezzi: "Remember that the house [the apartment in Vico Nardones] is to be in order. I know that Totò has written you about the Inn, [but] remember that we'll eat at the house."

On October 2, Donizetti, Antonio Vasselli, his wife, and the three other women went to Naples, expecting to attend the first San Carlo performance of *Maria di Rohan* within a few days. But the rehearsals dragged on through October and the first week of November, and Vasselli and his party had to return to Rome. Vasselli wrote to thank him for his hospitality, and on October 22, Donizetti replied: "Get along with you, what's all this nonsense about thanks? . . . The house is for everyone, and if I had had beds, you'd not have stayed downstairs [i.e., at an inn]." Writing to August Thomas on that same day, Donizetti reported: "For two days we have been rehearsing. There is Coletti with Fraschini, there is the fat Tadolini, and a dog of a Gondì [Luciani]." To Thomas, on November 6, he wrote: "Today we should give *Rohan*, the tenor [Fraschini] is sick, I hope that the illness won't last long, but in the meantime it's a delay." The first singing of the opera did not take place at the San Carlo until November 11. Then Donizetti was acclaimed wildly by a capacity audience; the opera unquestionably was a major success. He wanted to leave Naples the next morning, but was persuaded to remain for the second performance, at which he again was greeted by a great outpouring of recognition, enthusiasm, and affection.

Donizetti sailed from Naples on November 14 and was in Civitavec-

[12] At the Teatro Argentina, with a cast headed by Marianna Barbieri-Nini and Francesco Ciaffei.

chia the next day, Leghorn the day after that, and Genoa on November 19. After a two-day stopover in Milan, he was back in Bergamo on November 23. He had thought of staying there only a day or two before setting out in his carriage for Vienna, which he hoped to reach by November 28. But he found Mayr seriously ill, and so delayed his departure. From Vienna on December 6, he was to write to Cottrau: "I left Bergamo sadly. Two days after my arrival, Mayr had to take to his bed, and I fear never to see him again; I therefore remained a little longer in order to distract him, but then I had to leave." Not only was Donizetti never to see his teacher and friend again, but also he himself was to be in no mental state to be made aware when Mayr died at Bergamo on December 2, 1845, at the age of eighty-two.

Heading a letter "Vienna—what date have we? 6, 7, 8 December" in joking reference to Dolci's having chided him for laxness about datings, Donizetti told his friend: "The snow falls, the cold is intense, it accompanied me throughout the whole trip, the snow already was lying on the roads, the fields, and the mountains. Now it is visiting the city. Now a Sunday is ending . . . and where to go? Stay alone in the house? What joy!"

Some reason exists for supposing that Donizetti abandoned himself to erotic excesses during this final visit to Vienna. But the exactness of two notable references to those probable excesses is doubtful. The prolix and notoriously inexact Raffaelo Barbiera wrote (9, 165f.): "But an applauded performer of *Linda*, the celebrated Felice Varesi, who died at Milan in 1898, confessed to me during his last years the actually painful stupefaction that he felt on seeing the idol of Vienna shun the delightful precincts of the Royal Palace in order to wander late at night through the dark paths of the Prater, trailing dreadful phantoms. The fascination of the dreadful for the man who created *Lucia* and who at heart was noble and very religious! . . . We are in the obscure labyrinths of the human psyche."

We are indeed, for though Donizetti was admirable in most ways, likeable—lovable even—"noble" is not a word needed to describe him. And no proof of any sort exists that he was more than conventionally religious. The story of his pursuing *"orride larve"* (prostitutes?) along dark Prater paths is by no measure incredible. But the date of the supposed incident would have to be either 1842, when Varesi sang in the *première* of *Linda di Chamounix*, or 1844–45, when he sang in it again at the Kärnthnertortheater. And if Varesi lived until 1898 (he seems actually to have died at Milan in 1889), he would have been over eighty "during his last years," having been born at Calais in 1813. The story as told by Barbiera becomes suspect in detail as reported on the basis of an anecdote told him by an octogenarian more than half a century after the supposed encounter. And if Varesi died in 1889, the anecdote becomes more suspect still: in that case, Barbiera was reporting it more than forty years after a septuagenarian Varesi retailed it to him. This is not, of course, to assert that Donizetti did not consort with purchasable beauties.

More interesting—and more considerable as coming from a much more reliable writer—is a tantalizing passage in Alessandro Luzio's *Carteggi verdiani*, iv (Rome, 1947):

In the *Lettere inedite*[13] and despite the many clumsy surgical cuts and the frequent "dots made necessary by the usual considerations of decency" (as the editors assert), the reader is struck disagreeably precisely by the continuous vulgarity of the excessively free language, which skims the pornographic: nor is it to be marveled at that the inevitable result of the frenzy to "distract himself," to dedicate "eight hours each day to toil and the rest to pleasure [*cuccagna*]" (page 78), with the pernicious use and abuse of "digitalis" thrown in, should have been progressive paralysis.

In Vienna above all Donizetti found the Circe who little by little bestialized him, brought about his downfall, as I came to know from indisputable proofs that I saw when the first centenary of Donizetti's birth was celebrated in 1897.

I was living, a fairly fortunate exile, in an oasis of studies in the Austrian capital; and I was invited by the very Italian national colony of Vienna to hold a Donizettian commemoration, which did not turn out too badly and was given a cordial welcome on the first page of the Casa Ricordi's "Gazzetta Musicale" on October 21, 1897.

In the exposition of autographs then held in Vienna, I was able—through the courtesy of Eisner-Eisenhof[14]—to examine an extraordinary document kept from the eyes of the public and reserved solely for a very few "discreet" visitors. It was a long letter in verse (to his Vienna publisher) such as Donizetti had the habit of writing, one could say daily, and setting forth a lot of rhymed octosyllables in the doggerel libretto jargon of his epoch. Well, the letter, which overflowed with admiration of and desire for the florid and accessible Viennese beauties, revealed in semi-Aretinian jargon that the composer of *L'Elisir* [*d'amore*] was not satisfied to celebrate his aphrodisiac rites with one girl alone, but hankered—we'll say it this way—to drive a tandem. Because of that insane, disastrous squandering of his forces, it was precisely at Vienna that Donizetti's brain suffered a first blinding shock, from which no cure succeeded later in saving him.

[13] *Lettere inedite di G. Donizetti*, ed. Filippo Marchetti and Alessandro Parisotti (Rome, 1892), *80*.
[14] Angelo von Eisner-Eisenhof was a Viennese music lover who greatly admired Donizetti. His *Lettere inedite di Gaetano Donizetti* was issued at Bergamo in 1897 (*48*).

That Donizetti's letters increasingly had become starred with repetitive obscenities is true, and no doubt whatever is possible that Luzio saw the rhymed letter he describes. Nor is it less than likely that the pathological lubricity that Donizetti was to suffer from after his breakdown in Paris in 1845 had begun to drive him in Vienna earlier. But it is not possible to escape the feeling that Luzio, not so well acquainted with Donizetti and his jocular style of letterwriting as he was with Verdi, took much too literally and solemnly some of Donizetti's customary joking and badinage. A wish for two girls at a time rather than merely one sounds like exactly the kind of half serious, half comically intended desire that Donizetti expressed so often. That the "Circe" charms of the girls of Vienna were the basic or original cause of Donizetti's physical and mental collapse is an untenable hypothesis in view of his long history of illness; that overindulgence in those charms hastened his collapse is very probable. But aside from Luzio's assertion that Donizetti suffered his first serious mental breakdown in Vienna, no proof of any such attack before 1845 in Paris survives. He seems, therefore, to have telescoped causes, results, and events in a technique of double exposure which leaves matters much less than clear.

Continuing his letter of "6, 7, 8 December," cited in part above, Donizetti wrote: "I arrived Friday [December 5] at nine in the evening. You see that I made it fast enough even though I lost half a day at Udine. I haven't seen Their Majesties yet, but I'll see them before Thursday, when there will be a small concert at His Majesty's. I left Bergamo saddened by various things. and above all because of our Mayr, who spoke to me of our not seeing each other again—philosophically, but that upset me all the more! I hope that you won't forget to send me word about him. I notice that each time I go home, somebody vanishes—the other time [Girolamo] Forini, this time [Giuseppe] Pontiroli[15]. . . . I don't understand such a mysterious thing; I don't believe that I've dishonored them. I don't think them envious . . . what is it, then? Their disappearance has wounded me to the heart, but I'm certain, in any event, that I did nothing wrong to them. . . . I am sad with this weather, but what can be done about it? One hears no carriages, no people shouting . . . everyone, everyone, *renfermés* . . . what a beautiful winter! I would like to be at the Torototina;[16] that's my wish, and not here! There

---

[15] Girolamo Forini—who had sung a role in Donizetti's *Piccioli virtuosi ambulanti* at Bergamo more than twenty-five years before—and Giuseppe Pontiroli had been schoolmates of Donizetti. Both had become instructors in the music school that they all had attended. Donizetti either had lost their friendship or had suffered some imagined coolness on their part, as neither of them had died when he wrote this letter to Dolci.

[16] La Dorotina, Countess Rosa Basoni's villa outside Bergamo.

in the hot salt baths . . . auff! God wishes it otherwise, I must die alone and here. Live, I beg you . . . you can live, be hard. I am half destroyed, it's a miracle that I'm still on my feet. Live, live blessed, and think of me now and then. I embrace you with all my heart."

And thus 1844 sank to a melancholy, inactive close for Donizetti and it was 1845, the last year during which he was to be capable of even such sad, diminished participation in active life. Now all the signs were alarming. On the last day of 1844, he wrote to Carlo Balochino, co-impresario for the Kärnthnertortheater: "I have been in Vienna for a month and have not had from the management any notice that one of my operas is being put on. Now I am told about rehearsals, advice . . . what rehearsals, what advice? If I can be useful to you, I'll do it when the orchestra rehearsals are on, but now the *maestro concertatore*[17] must do the rehearsals." And on January 12, 1845, he wrote to Guglielmo Cottrau: "I have given up doing an opera for London for June, twenty-two thousand francs. Before that, I refused another here. I am not well. I am in the hands of a doctor . . . rheum in the head, producing a kind of hammer that beats on my brain constantly and bewilders me." On February 11, he wrote Cottrau: "My health has improved, the cough diminished, and I don't suffer any longer those terrible pains which for almost a month tormented me day and night." And on February 15, to Antonio Dolci: "The cold is killing me . . . my nerves suffer. The sick lung oppresses me . . . let's go forward. Farewell."

Donizetti nonetheless was working to the edge of his ability on the performance of his favorite child, *Dom Sébastien*, at the Kärnthnertortheater. Although it was to be sung in Leo Herz's German translation and Donizetti's knowledge of German was very limited, he supervised the final preparation of the performance, rehearsed it, and conducted the *première* on February 6. "How I sweated, dear Pedroni," he wrote to Ricordi's lieutenant on February 7, "while chasing after the notes of the recitatives without knowing what they were saying." Because Viennese audiences, very unlike those in Paris, wanted an opera to be over by ten o'clock, he had had to cut the score drastically. Also, he had removed from it the funeral scene that had been received so badly by the critics in Paris, and in general had lightened the opera's pervading gloom a little. It at once became a success, as Donizetti himself was to witness when he also conducted the second and third performances before handing the baton back to the theater's regular conductor. Every number was applauded, many numbers had to be repeated, and the third-act

[17] That is, the conductor in charge of general musical preparation of the opera during rehearsals.

septet had to be sung three times, a thing previously unheard of at the Kärnthnertortheater, where it was to be heard 122 times before passing to the new Opernhaus (forty more performances up to April 22, 1884).

Writing to unnamed Paris friends on February 8, Donizetti said: "I still cannot give you extended details of the performance of *Dom Sébastien*, which took place the other evening, but I can announce to you a warmer reception than his opera was awarded in Paris. Three numbers were repeated, the applause still resounds in my head. I was pulled out onto the stage and obliged to show myself I don't know how many times, which didn't please me. Believe it, my dear friends, at Paris they will change their minds about *Dom Sébastien*, an opera with which I took great pains and which I think a capital work. I don't like to talk about myself, but I assure you that I was much hurt by the way your papers treated my opera, a manner that caused me to spend more than one sleepless night. I am not at all satisfied with the director, who forced unfortunate changes on me, and Monsieur Scribe could have helped me more than he did. But no more recriminations; in time, justice will be rendered regarding all that and *Dom Sébastien* will be found bearable. The Viennese climate is not favorable to me: my head is no better, and if this continues, I'll find myself forced to go to spend some months resting in Bergamo. Farewell, my good friends, don't despair of *Dom Sébastien*. You would be enchanted if you were here: time will avenge all the injustices. I clasp you both by the hand." It is at least likely that this letter was written to Auguste and Zélie de Coussy, she the dedicatee of *Don Pasquale*, he Donizetti's Paris banker.

The operas that Donizetti had been forced to refuse to undertake were an *opera seria* for Paris and an *opera buffa* for London. To his brother Giuseppe, in a letter postmarked at Vienna on February 7, he had written: "I had the outline of the libretto for Paris, and I rejected it at first glance. It resembles lots of others, seems like a great drama in prose, for wars, fires, omens, conspiracies rain down from all sides, and all this over a small boy who appears in all the acts and never speaks . . . you know that small boys should be in bed at nine, whereas this one would yawn in the public's face or cry or wouldn't give a damn about the racket the others were making and would eat bonbons *pendant que la mère pleure. Nein; nein*. I have given up an *opera buffa* for London, for twenty-one thousand francs, because they wanted me to have it by June 1, and that's not possible for me. But then, Mr. Lumley[18] is a Hebrew, a lawyer, and an impresario. Therefore, disputes for certain."

[18] Benjamin Lumley was manager of Her Majesty's Theatre at this time. From Turin, on November 12, 1841, Felice Romani had sent Donizetti a letter in-

For Donizetti to reject a handsome contract because the desired opera would have to be composed in a little less than four months was for him to confess that weariness and sickness had deprived him of his former creative facility and speed. Everything points to his having come to understand during 1845 how very unwell he really was. He may even have experienced some terror over his continued difficulty with control of his state of mind, mental activity, and physical motions. On October 15, 1844, he had affixed to a miniature portrait of himself painted by M. Albanesi in Naples these words: "Ah! it is not true, they lie.[19] So young I am not. The days of rejoicing are past for my poor heart. In the future I see only a tomb closing over me. (The portrayed one, Donizetti)."[20] Moods of such realistic pessimism now surged and ebbed with increasing regularity. On February 21, he wrote to Totò Vasselli: "Yessir, [the report of] my illness is much more than correct (but it's over now). Today I have a callus that makes me limp with great pleasure. I, miserable *pendant ma maladie*, great boiling mustard on my neck, and I took great baths. Everything may be, but in any case it is certain that this climate is murderous."

On February 25, Donizetti was feeling well enough to conduct a concert at Prince Metternich's palace. He himself had organized and trained the group of titled amateurs for this occasion. On March 8, too, he conducted a court concert "*en grande tenue*, as they say—that is, with my gala uniform of scarlet cloth embroidered in gold."[21] The season of

troducing "this young English gentleman" (who was to deliver it in person), adding "he is dear to me because of his personal qualities." In reply, from Milan on November 18, Donizetti reported that he had spoken with "Lummlay," and the context makes it clear that they discussed the possibility of a Romani-Donizetti opera for London. On February 16, 1842, Donizetti wrote Antonio Vasselli that because of Romani's failure to deliver, as promised, the first act of "a poem for London," he was missing the opportunity to earn twelve thousand francs in two months in that city. That Romani had indeed made a promise to Lumley is proved by a letter that he wrote from Turin on November 23, 1841, to Donizetti. In it he said: "It is true that I have promised Mister Lumley to write a *dramma* for London, and I'll write it with the greatest pleasure if you will clothe it in the beauty of your notes." This projected Romani-Donizetti opera never came to fruition.

[19] A line from the closing scene of Act II of *Linda di Chamounix*.

[20] This miniature, with the inscription, now is in the Museo Donizettiano at Bergamo. Against a dimly sketched-in background of the Bay of Naples, a steamship, and the smoking Vesuvius, it shows Donizetti blue-eyed, very pink-cheeked, with a moustache, copious dark hair, and profile chin whiskers. Over a white shirt and what appears to be blue pants, he is wearing a collarless gold-brocaded coat lined in red and tied around the waist with a rope. He is seated in an armchair. In the lower lefthand corner of the miniature, in yellow, are a harp and a syrinx surrounded by leaves; in the lower righthand corner are a purple pansy and this legend: "M. Albanesi. As a sign of the great admiration and respect for him." See Plate 16.

[21] During March 1845, the baritone Paolo Barroilhet, on the occasion of his benefit night at the Paris Opéra, sang the solo part in *Cristoforo Colombo*, a can-

Italian opera at the Kärnthnertortheater was scheduled to open on April 2 with Verdi's *I Due Foscari*. On February 26, Donizetti had written to Cottrau: "You'll see if I was right to say that Verdi has talent! and yet, *I Due Foscari* doesn't show him at his best except in flashes. I'll listen to the rest. Envy apart, which I don't know, he is the man who will shine, and you'll see." On April 4, again to Cottrau: "Last evening, the first performance by the Italians: *I Due Foscari*. By a hateful chance, the waltz in the trio made them laugh; they called it a Strauss waltz . . . it is or it isn't. . . . I wasn't there, but today they have filled my head with it. See what four measures can mean!"

Donizetti appears to have spent the rest of April in very intermittent activity. In the letter of April 4 to Cottrau already cited, he said: "I am completely occupied with a grand concert under the protection of His Imperial Highness the Archduke Franz Karl, for the 11th. Then there will be another, for the orphans, under the protection of Her Majesty the Empress; later a court *en petit comité*." But he was not composing. He had no definite plans for the future. It is impossible not to suppose that he spent much of his time in bed, or at least under constant medical care; otherwise, he almost certainly would have been at the first singing of *I Due Foscari*, for example. On April 16, in a letter to his brother Giuseppe addressed "*À Monsieur Le Chev. Joseph Donizetti, Colonel de la Garde Imp. de S. M. le Grand Sultan, Pera de Constantinoples*," he wrote: "I hope that you are well. For some time I had a strong congestion of the head. *Tout passe*."

On April 27, writing to the editor of a musical paper, one "Sig. Smith," Donizetti said: "I read in the Leipzig journal *Das Signal*, No. 6 under date of the 26th instant, an article about me, with the result that this estimable journal has fallen into a double error. It says that I am going to the Prussian capital to fill an honorable position in my art. And it adds that I have been invited to stage my *Dom Sébastien* [there]. I have had no invitation with regard to this last work, and as to the first [statement], there never has been any possibility of this question, given the fact that the position I have the honor to occupy with His Majesty the Emperor and King would not allow me to assume other duties of such a nature. Furthermore, in a country [Prussia] where are to be found together Spontini, Meyerbeer, Mendelssohn, they are too abundantly supplied [with composers] to need another."

Reports that Donizetti had been invited to Russia evidently were

---

tata for solo voice and orchestra, which Donizetti had composed for him. The library of the Conservatorio di Santa Cecilia at Rome has a *scena* and a *cavatina* from this cantata in autograph.

Donizetti at eighteen, as a student at Bologna (1815). The inscription to his right reads: "Or sì farò portenti—dall'armoniosa penna—mi pioveranno incantatori accenti—Al maestro S. Mayr riconoscente offre G.no Donizetti d'anni 18—5 nov.bre 1815" (*Now, yes, I shall create wonders—from* [my] *harmonious pen— let enchanting accents pour—To Maestro S. Mayr, in gratitude, this is offered by Gaetano Donizetti, eighteen years old—November 5, 1815*).

Giovanni Simone Mayr in 1827. His right hand rests on his opera Medea in Corinto *(1813); on the shelves to his left, copies of his* Ginevra di Scozia *(1801),* La Rosa bianca e la rosa rossa *(1813).*

Antonio Dolci in 1833

*Domenico Barbaja, apparently in
the anteroom of a rehearsal hall*

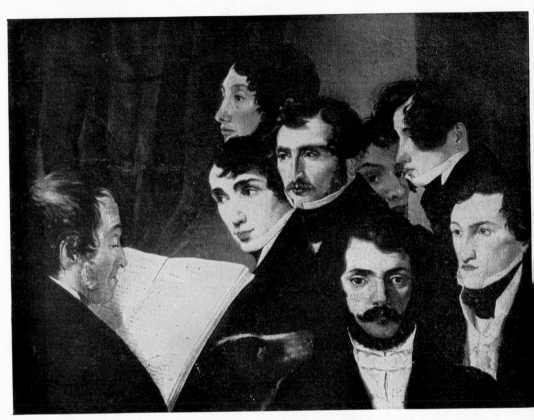

"*Giovanni Simone Mayr and His School*," *with Mayr reading from a manuscript book at the left, Donizetti in the center of the group. Identification of the other young men remains uncertain; the statement that one of them was Giovanni Pacini is dubious, as he never studied with Mayr.*

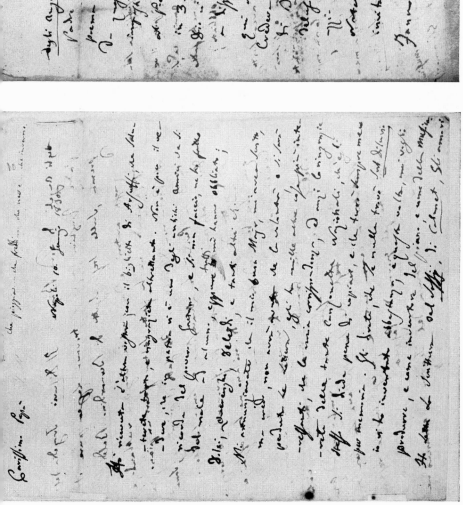

Pages 1 and 2 of Donizetti's letter of January 10, 1830, to his father. See p. 68, n. 20, for discussion of the passage beginning in last line of page 1 and continuing through the first three lines of page 2.

(UPPER LEFT) *Jacopo Ferretti, librettist of* L'Ajo nell'imbarazzo, Olivo e
Pasquale, Il Furioso all'isola di San Domingo, Torquato Tasso; (BOTTOM LEFT)
Felice Romani, librettist of, among other Donizetti operas, Anna Bolena,
L'Elisir d'amore, *and* Lucrezia Borgia; (RIGHT) *Giovanni Ricordi,
founder of G. Ricordi & C., Milan*

*Virginia Vasselli Donizetti at twenty (1829), painting formerly belonging to the
Gabrielli-Vasselli family, Rome*

(ABOVE) *Lithograph after design by Alessandro Sanquirico (1777–1849) for antechamber to the Queen's quarters in* Anna Bolena; (BELOW) *Lithograph after Sanquirico's design for courtyard scene in* Ugo, conte di Parigi, *probably for 1832* première *at La Scala, Milan*

Donizetti in the middle or late 1830s at Naples, from a drawing attributed to Giuseppe Cammarano

(UPPER LEFT) *Domenico Donzelli, tenor from Bergamo, who created roles in* Zoraide di Granata, Ugo, conte di Parigi, *and* Maria Padilla, *as well as that of* Pollione *in Bellini's* Norma; (UPPER RIGHT) *Luigia Boccabadati-Gazzuoli, soprano and contralto from Modena, who created roles in* Elisabetta al castello di Kenilworth, I Pazzi per progetto, Il Diluvio universale, Francesca di Foix, *and* La Romanziera e l'uomo nero; (LOWER LEFT) *Fanny Tacchinardi-Persiani, soprano from Rome, who created the title roles of* Rosmonda d'Inghilterra, Lucia di Lammermoor, *and* Pia de' Tolomei; (LOWER RIGHT) *Ignazio Marini, basso profondo from Taliuno, near Bergamo, who created roles in* Gianni di Parigi, Gemma di Vergy, Adelia, *and the first integral* Maria Stuarda, *as well as the title role in Verdi's* Attila

Donizetti, lithographed top of an olivewood table given him about 1837 by Neapolitan admirers. The three outside bands contain the names of his operas and cantatas; between the portrait and the vertical panels of conventionalized operatic scenes, a biographical sketch appears.

Donizetti, marble bust made from life at Rome in 1840–1841 by Giovanni Maria Benzoni of Bergamo for the Ateneo di Scienze, Lettere ed Arti di Bergamo, where it remains. "The bust seems to me an extremely good likeness, and everyone says what I say . . ."—Donizetti, in a letter of February 18, 1841, to Antonio Dolci

Terrace scene at Bergamo about 1840, painted by Luigi Deleidi, called Il Nebbia.
Left to right: the host, Michele Bettinelli; Donizetti; Antonio Dolci;
Giovanni Simone Mayr; Deleidi, shown sketching

Caricature of Donizetti in an unsigned lithograph from
Le Charivari, Paris (series Compositeurs of the

Self-caricature by Donizetti:
"Mon portrait fait par moi même"

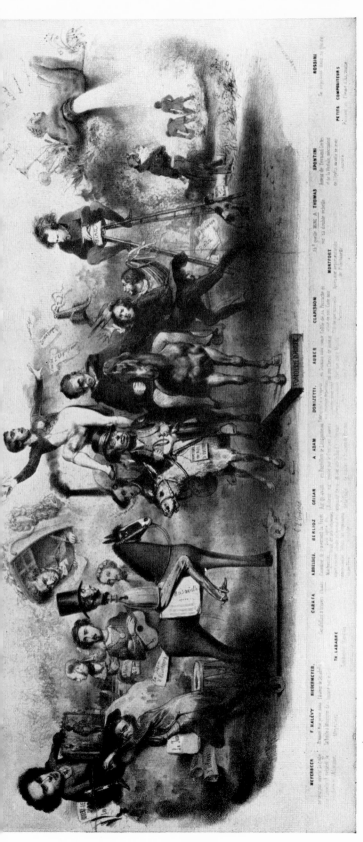

Panthéon Musical, multiple caricature of 1843, after a drawing by C.-J. Travies. From left to right: Meyerbeer, who "does not wish to open the cage in which he keeps Le Prophète and L'Africaine"; Fromental Halévy "taking a hold on Meyerbeer's music box"; Louis Niedermeyer, "the composer of Stradella inspired by Le Lac [his best-known romance]"; Théodore Labarre [with guitar], "French troubadour improvising songs"; Michele Enrico Carafa [with carafe body, on a hobbyhorse] "caraf-ing à travers Chants"; Adrien-Louis-Victor Boieldieu "crowned with Marguerites and aspiring to his father's laurel wreath"; Berlioz, who "traversing the forest that he disturbs with the noises of his symphonies, addresses his travel impressions to the Journal des Débats"; Albert Grisar: "The Air that the composer has while composing that of La Folle"; Adolphe Adam, "as the Postillon de Longjumeau, riding the Favored Courser [Coursier Favori] of his friend the King of Yvetot, about to visit the Brasseur de Preston"; Donizetti, "making under steam a multitude of popular scores throughout the universe and a thousand other places"; Daniel-François-Esprit Auber "in a Black Domino riding his Bronze Horse, dreams of another Dumb Girl of Portici"; Antoine-Louis Clapisson, "coiffed with his Parrot [Perruche] and armed with his Code noir, looks for a new score"; Alexandre Montfort "after a performance of Polichinelle"; Ambroise Thomas: "Ah! that grimace by Thomas [mine à Thomas, a pun on the title of his opera Mina] on The Double Staircase"; Gaspare Spontini, "composer of Fernand Cortez and La Vestale, unhappy with the Opéra, goes out to see the dawn [L'Aurore] rise"; Minor Composers "drawing water from the river of harmony", which is flowing from an urn held by Rossini, "resting on his glory" against a halo formed by the names of some of his operas. See pp. 205-6 for description of this caricature and Donizetti's comment on it.

Donizetti, miniature painted at Naples in 1844 by Albanesi. See p. 229 for description of it and Donizetti's comment on it.

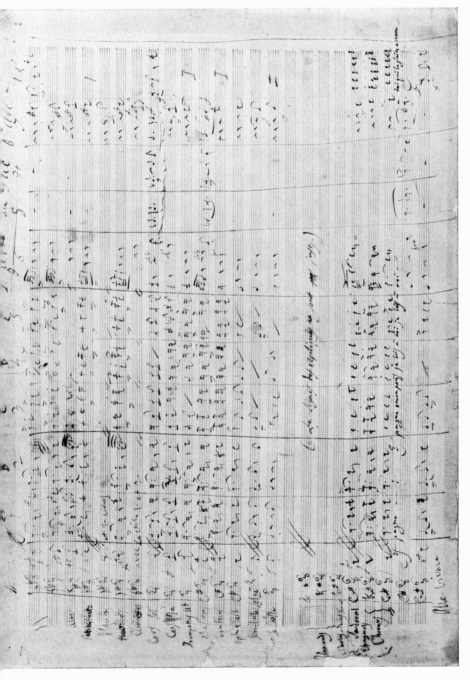

Autograph of page 1 of Act 1 of Le Duc d'Albe (Carlo, Sandoval, and chorus: "Espagne! Espagne! O mon pays, je bois à toi!")

Scrawl by Donizetti on May 20(?), 1846, at Ivry, apparently addressed to his brother Giuseppe to say that his condition had improved. Giuseppe's son, Andrea, is mentioned. Identification of the music appears impossible.

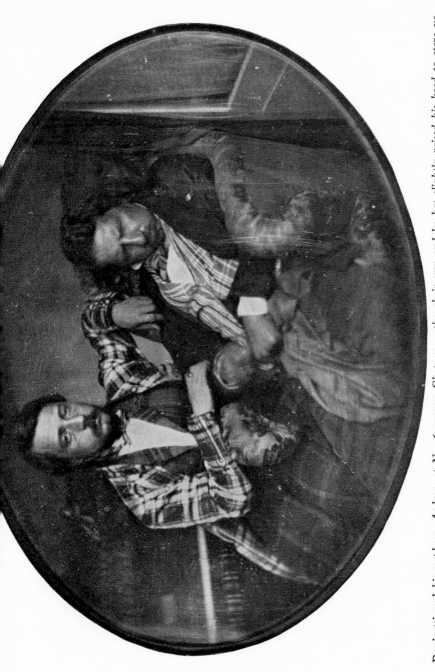

Donizetti and his nephew, Andrea, at No. 6 avenue Chateau-briand, Paris, between June 6 and August 3, 1847. The reverse of the copy of his daguerreotype in the Museo Donizettiano at Bergamo is inscribed "To the gentilissima Signora Rosa Basoni, Andrea Donizetti offers this sad souvenir as a testimony of his esteem. Paris, August 3, 1847." The Museo Donizettiano also has a badly deteriorated copy of another daguerreotype taken at the same time: in it, Donizetti's right hand rests on the chair-arm and he has slightly raised his head to stare vacantly toward the camera. That copy has this inscription on the reverse: "Paris, August 3—avenue Chateaubriand 6—Andrea Donizetti sends this sad souvenir to his friend Signor Antonio Dolci of Bergamo!!" A daguerreotype reproduced in the catalogue of the centenary exposition held at Bergamo in August-September 1897 may be this second picture, but also may be a third daguerreotype made at the same time.

19

Giuseppe Donizetti as a pasha in an anonymous painting made at Constantinople in 1852

spreading about at this time too. In a letter of May 20 to Tommaso Persico,[22] he said: "And you too have heard one of those [rumors] about Russia? But it's not true, no, no. And even if it had been true, I'd have said 'no' the same way. I am extremely nervous; the cold is killing me. At Berlin, too, a journal said: M.r. Donizetti is coming here to occupy the most luminous position in music, and will stage his *Dom Sébastien*, etc. I hastened to reply to the journals here that nobody has written to me and that, too, here I occupy the most honorable position. That concerning *Dom Sébastien*, if it is to be given, I know nothing about it, and that in a capital where there are a Spontini, a Meyerbeer, a Mendelssohn, they have such riches as not to have time to wish for other composers. Outside of that (between you and me), if I can't bear this cold, imagine the Prussian cold, then! Worse still in Russia."

Early in May, Vatel, now impresario of the Théâtre-Italien, traveled from Paris to Vienna expressly to call upon Donizetti. His hope was to elicit a new opera. Léon Pillet also wrote to him from the Opéra, all but begging him for an opera—Meyerbeer still was fussing over *Le Prophète*, and something to take its place in the forthcoming season had to be found. Nothing is known about Donizetti's reactions to these pleadings, but he did take earnestly the possibility of composing another opera for the Italien. On May 27, he wrote to Giovanni Ruffini: "It is true that Monsieur Vatel has been here: it is true that he wants an opera; and it also is true that I said: Ruffini will write the poem. You know that I never have mixed in others' affairs; he told me that at the most he could pay you a thousand francs. I answered: you agree about the price between you. . . . As to the subject, I'd like to compose (because I have seen it, and it appears to me to be adaptable) *Onore vince amore*, by (I think) the Barone di Cosenza. It was played at Naples by De Marini, Vestris, Lombardi, and La Tessari. We'll make De Marini into Lablache, Vestris into Ronconi, Lombardi into Mario, La Tessari into La Persiani. Who will be in the secondary and tertiary parts I don't know, but they must be kept few." Nothing whatever was to materialize of these preliminary musings.

As May drew to its close, in fact, Donizetti had not decided what to do next or where to go from Vienna. He expressed unhappiness over a lack of glitter in the Kärnthnertortheater season of Italian opera, which he felt had been brought about by a poor collection of singers. Should

---

[22] This letter begins "All of you have understood me badly in believing that I'm sorry about having rented part of my apartment: that was a sad memory, a fleeting sigh from the bottom of my heart. And how many things one does unwillingly; who can silence the past?" This appears to prove that as late as 1845 Donizetti had not sold the apartment at No. 14 Vico Nardones.

he go to Paris? To Naples? Well into June, he was occupied with giving
instructions about a monument to be erected in the Cemetery of Poggioreale at Naples for the permanent burial of Virginia's remains. He had
his Naples friend Aniello Benevento supervise its design and erection, and
then ordered inscribed on it: "To Virginia Vasselli *Romana*—taken in
the flower of her years—to the domestic affections—Gaetano Donizetti
husband—p.—Perishable memorial to eternal sorrow—the year of Our
Lord—1845."[23]

During June, after having decided to institute suit against Léon Pillet
for fifteen thousand francs for the nonproduction of *Le Duc d'Albe*,
Donizetti finally chose Paris as his next goal. The contract for that opera
had specified that if it should not be produced, the management would
pay a penalty of fifteen thousand francs each to the composer and to the
librettists, and it appears that Pillet had rejected the idea of staging the
(then incomplete) opera and had refused to pay the stipulated forfeit.[24]
There can be little doubt that if Pillet had agreed to carry out his part
of the agreement, Donizetti still would have been able to complete the
opera.

On June 18, Donizetti wrote to Giuseppina Appiani: "I have spent a
horrible winter. Under the influence of this climate, my nerves
have become so sensitive that a stay of one year would kill me. I'll leave
for Paris about July 10." And on that date he left Vienna for the
last time.[25]

[23] Donizetti himself was not to be buried beside Virginia in Naples; but in
1864, the chief companion of his final illness, his brother Giuseppe's son Andrea,
dying in a madhouse at Aversa near Naples at the age of forty-five, was to share
the cemetery plot.

[24] This suit dragged on until April 1846, when the plaintiff was awarded a
judgment that required Pillet to pay the penalty and leave ownership of the score
to Donizetti. But that was by no means the end of the complicated prehistory of
Le Duc d'Albe. See Appendixes, pp. 297-306, for additional details of its history.

[25] On July 1, 1926, the *Revue musicale*, Paris, published twenty-six letters
from Donizetti to the Countess Amelie von Taaffe, the wife of Ludwig Patrick
von Taaffe, the Irish-Austrian president of the Imperial Supreme Court. Internal
evidence suggests that all the letters were written over the period from 1843 to
1845. They are friendly, not to say intimate, in tone, and a large part of their contents deals with the Bohemian child prodigy Julius Benoni (1833-?), whom the
Countess evidently was sponsoring. While very young, Benoni had showed
extraordinary talent at improvising music, and Donizetti had been teaching him
composition. Benoni's compositions included operas, a Mass, a large piece for
orchestra and chorus, and songs. In about 1855, however, he abandoned music
and became a farmer, his talent not having matured enough for him to find adult
satisfaction in it. Donizetti's letters to the Countess von Taaffe are to be found in
138, 663, 665, 674, 849-56; they consist mostly of a few lines each. The letters are
now in the Moldenhauer Archive, Seattle, Washington.

CHAPTER X

August 1845—September 1846

"Voilà le secret de ces facilités
prodigieuses; une fatigue immense
et pour résultat la folie."
—THÉOPHILE GAUTIER

No letters from Donizetti are available with dates between June 30, 1845, at Vienna, and August 5 of that year, at Paris. What is known about him during those five intervening weeks is that his Parisian friends were shocked and saddened by his appearance and his condition. Léon Escudier described him at this time as having his "head full of new sicknesses," his expression dull, his eyes feverish, his hands trembling. When he went out in the evening, Charles de Boigne reported, he stopped in at seven or eight cafés to drink *riz-au-lait*. One evening, he searched the cafés for one of his "companions in *riz-au-lait*," a friend with whom he had been only a few minutes earlier and with whom he had made an appointment for the next day. Feeling some irrational, overmastering need to see the man again immediately, Donizetti wandered from café to café muttering: "Wait until tomorrow? That is impossible. It must be this evening, this very evening." When he noticed the astonished looks on the faces of strangers in the cafés, he found it impossible to finish the sentence, Boigne said, but at last added: "This very evening I must write on his back: On such and such a day at such and such an hour, I outwitted M. de X . . . for the first time." His physical and mental debilities soon became so pronounced that it no longer was possible for him to go out unaccompanied. Paul Scudo (*118*) wrote: "We then had the sorrow of running into him many times accompanied by a domestic," adding that Donizetti's formerly flashing eyes seemed "extinct," his forehead covered with a "sinister veil."

On August 5, Donizetti wrote a note to Auber: "I am obliged to give up for tomorrow the pleasure of attending the meeting at the Conservatory because of an indisposition that I wish to take care of. I have the honor to inform you of this so that you may be able to take your steps in consequence. I hope that you are proceeding from well to better and that I soon shall congratulate myself on your complete cure." Six days later, he wrote a disjunct, horrifying letter to Antonio Vasselli, the last that has survived of the many he wrote to his beloved brother-in-law:

I thank you for the happy days that you wished me. I didn't leave Vienna on the tenth of June, but of July. This morning I had a consultation of three leading doctors—[Gabriel] Andral, [Philip] Ricord, and . . . and . . . and . . .[1] They agreed among themselves, after asking me a thousand questions, that I should leave . . . that I should travel . . . that I should change climate. I at once chose either Rome or Naples, because [there] I am in my own home. Rome (they said) is too far from the sea. Sooner Naples: There I could take sea baths, which would have to be at Castellammare [di Stabia]. Imagine whether I accepted! I leave everything. I must not compose for two years—already I haven't composed for two years because of having no desire to. Now that I'm wanting to, the doctors don't want me to. You know, dear Totò, whether I always had trouble with my lungs, you know whether I told you that; now it is a dismal ailment. Twelve leeches at the place of defecation. Decoction four times a day (boiled arnica). My head (to tell the truth) was very heavy, and I didn't say no except in words. Now I move it, and it's a result of the climate, as I did then, before the medicines.

A footbath of hot water takes place every two days. . . . I am *nervous*, and you know it, and you always have known me . . . and you always

---

[1] A long, interesting examination of Donizetti's illness, with data on the numerous physicians who attended him, appeared in the *Minerva Medica*, Turin, in 1938 (Vol. XXXIX): *"La Malattia e i medici di Gaetano Donizetti,"* by T. Ogliaro. The name that Donizetti could not recall was that of Dr. Jean-Nicolas Marjolin (1780–1850). Gabriel Andral (1797–1876) was a professor of general pathology who pioneered in studying the chemical constituents of the blood in diseases; his *Essais d'hématologie pathologique* (1843) was a pathsetting work. Philip (or Philippe) Ricord (1799 or 1800–89), the foremost specialist in venereal diseases of his time, proved that John Hunter's belief that gonorrhea and syphilis were the same disease was incorrect. He also was known as an orator and a wit. His *Traité pratique des maladies vénériennes* had been issued at Paris in 1838, and that he should have been one of the physicians called upon to examine Donizetti probably indicates that Donizetti himself or some of his friends suspected that his condition resulted from a venereal infection.

can tell me anything when I shall be in Naples. Don't answer me just now! Five operas!!!—A single one would be the end of me; one must expect this when one is a Christian. What were you going to tell me? How? You don't have the strength to compose an opera? . . . You? Yes! I have it! My head? It is free! My imagination? It is free! My writing? It does me no harm. But an imperceptible secret of the doctors tells me that I have nothing, unless it be that I might fall back into the same blood sickness in the head, which then would congeal. Do I have an appetite? I digest! The foods prescribed are light. I continue with the potions. I avoid wines. I drink Bordeaux and Vichy mineral water. I go out; I take a walk; but only this morning Andral felt my chest; he pounded on all my ribs (right side) and said to me: You must take those remedies so that during the coming winter they will not react on your nerves as they do now. Therefore we order you to travel a little; and when you become inured to all the rigors of the winter, you'll be able to compose as much as you wish. Avoid the strong sensations of popular plays. Your spirit is too tender . . . your head is too fatigued. . . . Choose Naples because . . . I hope to see you . . . we'll be neighbors! . . . I have my home. I write to you and beg you to copy this for Aniello [Benevento]. Tell him that if I don't improve constantly, I'll leave within four or five days! Marseille, etc., but don't let all this reach anyone's ears, as I must avoid sorrows and sensations. I'll write to you, to Naples, etc., etc. Now I dress and go out. Democritus, now I write to you ! ! ! Imagine, two years of idleness; Michele [Accursi] without notes. The journalists without the donated *romanza*? . . . "My ship passes, covered with forgetfulness!" . . . I must ask His Majesty the Emperor for permission . . . he is so reasonable that I don't even go to Vienna: he will accept the [doctors'] certificate. [illegible word[2]] the fur? Honored baron! Farewell. Greet Rosona [Donizetti's mother-in-law, Vasselli's mother], your wife, your sisters, Irene [Vasselli's niece], Virginia [Vasselli's daughter], Gaetano [Vasselli's brother]. Our friends. Sterlich. Cavalcanti. Gaëtan.

As a postscript, Donizetti added: "I'll stay at Castell'a mare [*sic*] for a month for the baths, but no one must look for a house for me."

At some time during this period, Donizetti seems to have thought of composing an opera to an adaptation of Molière's *Sganarelle* by Count Giovanni Giraud. This idea appealed greatly to the impresario Vatel, and when it proved impossible for Donizetti to compose the opera, he urged that Donizetti make a *pasticcio* of numbers from such of his earlier works as no longer were being performed. This offended Donizetti, who dismissed him abruptly. Then, thinking better of it, he wrote to Vatel: "You made such a woeful grimace when leaving me that I have reconsidered my refusal. I have considered *L'Ajo nell'imbarazzo* (given at Rome in 1824). Seek out that score, send it to me. There are changes

[2] Throughout this letter, Donizetti's script suggests either a hand quivering from physical weakness or a state of mental uncertainty. A facsimile of this letter appears in *58*, 121–23.

to be made, pieces to be deleted, others to be inserted. It is a matter of one week." With the old score in hand, he set to work, but it seems to have been after he had been at this labor for about a week and had showed increased signs of overexcitation that the doctors ordered him to drop it and do no work of any sort.

As Guido Zavadini noted, it now was almost as though with the intention of bidding a final farewell to his friends one by one that Donizetti wrote letters to Dolci (August 21 and September 26), Ghezzi (October 2), and Persico (October 7). The August 21 letter to Dolci repeated much of what he had told Vasselli ten days earlier, but added a few significant details: "Broth only, and a little jam, with a glass of Bordeaux (even that ruined with Vichy water). . . . No mushrooms, no pepper, no ordinary wine, but only Bordeaux. See no tragedies, supper not later than six o'clock. That dog of an Andral (he has the face of a very handsome man) constantly stares at me because he never has known me. Then he attacks my pulse . . . and I have no fever. He taps with great force on my right ribs, and I say: you're not doing any harm whatever, and he smiles. . . . My head is cured, and that's enough for me. My nerves become irritated every time I write, therefore? . . . Patience! The tomb! It is finished."

At about this time, learning that Berlioz was going to Vienna, Donizetti gave him a letter of introduction to his friend and translator Leo Herz, writing in French: "I think that I am giving you a real gift in introducing you to M. Berlioz, who much wishes to visit Vienna and make known some of his brilliant compositions there. His name requires no recommendations; therefore I write only to put you in touch with one another, persuaded as I am that you will do everything in your power so that he may have in you a counsellor, a guide, a friend. My health seems to be improving rather slowly, a lot is expected of the climate and of rest. Thousands of friendly greetings. Donizetti." A postscript in three languages follows: [in Italian] "I have made you write— I am fluent in effects; I am better. *Guten tag auf Wiedersehen. J'embrasse Madame.*"

On August 30, two doctors—Andral and Rostan—signed a diagnosis of Donizetti's case including their recommendations for treatment:

The undersigned physicians, consulted by M. Gaetan Donizetti, composer of music, etc., living at rue Grammont N. 1, have ascertained in him an unhealthy condition of the nervous centers, a consequence of the excess of labors in which he has been indulging. They have decided that it is important for M. Donizetti to abstain from all intellectual fatigue and that for the

time being he should abandon all varieties of work. Here is the treatment to which he should conform:
1. Light counterirritants for the intestinal canal;
2. Footbaths;
3. From time to time, application of some leeches to the anus;
4. Dry cuppings of the nape of the neck and on the dorsal region;
5. Vesicatory on the neck, later moved to one arm;
6. Light feeding.
Later, trips and sea baths may be very favorable for him.
Paris, August 30, 1845   Rostan, Andral

Ten days after that prescription, Donizetti wrote to Cottrau: "What can I tell you? That I have been at the edge of death? Hear it said— that I fell out of bed during the night . . . that I was found on the floor in my shirt in the morning . . . that I didn't come to for twelve hours. . . . You wouldn't believe how much weight I've lost. All feeling is forbidden me. I had four operas to compose, I have had to give up all of them. I told them that I want to die in Italy! I wanted our mineral waters for my lungs. Donizetti." Nine days later, he wrote again to Cottrau: "Today my health is much better, but I still am in bed— leeches, mustard plasters, etc. I am revising *Gemma di Vergy,* which will be given at the Théâtre-Italien, its orchestra expanded, with [Giulia] Grisi, Mario, Liprandi, [Giorgio] Ronconi."[3]

A letter that Donizetti wrote to Teodoro Ghezzi on October 2 testifies to the worsening of his condition:

I write you three hours after a surgical operation done on the back of my neck (a vesicant). Then twenty-five leeches behind the ears, and another twenty. Where? Where nature obstructs me: we shall see. Now the poor back of my neck has made me suffer since yesterday . . . I suffer! the surgeon exposed it this morning, pulled it, cut . . . now . . . with a certain thing on top, they are keeping my head up. What pain—and why. Persico Leopoldo[4] will be leaving on the trip to Naples. How much it pains me not to be there. And how much more, perhaps, it would pain me if I were there and should have the mortification of either nothing or a No. Ah! the compensation has been barbarous. *Pas même son nom!* Melancholy seizes me. My oversensitive nervous system resents my weeping. With tears in my heart I pretend happiness. I have changed entirely. Everyone here and in Vienna reproves me. What to do? What to say? Six months! I write, no answer . . . a greeting by way of others, always, always! Her silent manner has left

---

[3] The first Paris performance of Donizetti's 1834 opera *Gemma di Vergy* occurred at the Théâtre-Italien on December 16, 1845, with Grisi in the title role. He was not able to attend.

[4] Reversing the first and last names, as Italians often do, Donizetti here referred to Tommaso Persico's brother Leopoldo, who had been visiting in Paris.

me beside myself. I let go four operas in Paris alone. Now I let go of Madrid and London.

In a postscript, he added: "My nerves are so aroused that I fall from bed at night, and it seems to me that the bed rolls over on me. I don't know whether I'm still alive, as I fall head down, without helping myself with my hand, as if strangled. I have a manservant in the room now while I sleep. But *a night light*, and I won't fall out any more? No! Silence! I commend the *tombeau* to you!"

Parts of this letter, and notably those passages referring to someone's silence and failure to answer letters, now are indecipherable (and that Donizetti was referring to a woman is in itself guesswork, as neither "*son nom*" nor "*il suo modo silenzioso*" makes it certain). It is unlikely to have been Zélie de Coussy, who was right there in Paris. Giuseppina Appiani? Sophie Löwe? Another woman, one whose name does not even occur in all the writing that has been devoted to Donizetti over a period of more than a century? We very simply do not know. What we do know—this letter itself is part of the proof—is that he was in a state of partial mental confusion which was worsening day by day.

On October 7, Donizetti wrote to Tommaso Persico:

I still am sick; I have a vesicant; soon I'll be dry. The poor *Madama* [Signora Marotta, caretaker of Donizetti's Naples apartment?] has written to me from her bed in my house, wanting to know how I am, what I am doing, whether or not it is true that I am in such danger, etc., etc. . . . The geographical location of Paris is not such as to damage physical conditions like mine. I always have been well here, but this time things have become bad. Also realize that as soon as I reached here, I became a thousand times better, and that within a few days of my arrival. . . . The beginning of my illness began to blow up in Naples last year: the difficulties encountered, the likeness . . . the silence! Would you know that the blood in my head didn't make me die because God did not wish it? I fell out of bed during the night and pounded my head on the floor so as to drive it out. Well, then, you can guess. I wanted to stay with the light lighted, and behold that in those hours when I fell (two or three hours after midnight), I felt my heart pounding and woke up. I saw the light . . . everything was silent. . . . I became peaceful again, and from that time forward I've had the manservant sleep in the room. I tell the doctors that because of the blood in my head and because of my sensitive nerves, the night is the saddest thing, worse than the privations of food, of drink, of hours measured out for living and sleeping. Light, light! Either that of God or that of oil and wax! Twelve hours of convulsions—twenty-four leeches, washing, remedies for vomiting. Fiery mustard plasters on my thighs. Nothing. Nothing.

To Count Gaetano Melzi, Donizetti reported on October 14: "I am tolerably well now because fifty leeches, besides some other things (and now a vesicant) have taken so much blood from my head, etc., etc. In short, it seems to me as though the thing will move along." And a week later, in a letter for Giuseppe Donizetti, which he handed to someone leaving for Constantinople: "I still have *la fièvre nerveuse*. This gentleman will tell you that I still am weak, but not so much as before, however. Don't answer me here, as one of these days I'll be leaving. Greet Angela and Andrea.[5] I embrace you and will write you from Vienna, where I perhaps will find myself. The climate of Vienna is not the most beautiful; and I will lose the twelve thousand *Swantziger*. Have a good time—father, wife, and son. Your Gaetano."

Donizetti had not been answering worried letters from Vasselli, Aniello Benevento, Dolci, and others of his friends. On October 9, Marco Bordogni[6] wrote to Antonio Dolci from Paris: "I have received your dear letter, sent me from Bergamo, and have delivered to our mutual friend Donizetti the one that you sent me for him. I went to see him as soon as I reached Paris. His health is a little worse, but the doctors hope that rest and a change of climate may be able to re-establish it. I think that his friends should persuade him to leave Paris and to give up his relations with a woman who is in large part the cause of his illness!"

Identification of the woman thus referred to—she or another woman is assigned the same destructive role in Lorenzo Monterasi's letter of October 28 to Dolci and in Andrea Donizetti's of November 7 to Antonio Vasselli—seems impossible. Guido Zavadini suggested (*138*, 929) that it might be the Countess Sophie von Löwenstein. After Donizetti's death, this woman wrote long, rambling, infatuated letters to Dolci (from Montpellier, May 7, 1848) and Rosa Rota-Basoni (from Geneva, October 10, 1848)—the latter running to some twenty-five hundred words—and to Rosa and Giovanna Rota-Basoni jointly (from Geneva, January 4, 1849). These outpourings reveal a very powerful psychosexual attachment to Donizetti—strong enough to have induced the Countess to assert that she had traveled three times from Leghorn to Paris in the hope of extracting him from the sanatorium at Ivry, strong enough to lead her into vague accusations, with all the stigmata of jealousy, against others of Donizetti's friends and some of his relatives. Countess von Löwenstein unquestionably had had Donizetti's well-being at heart. But she appears to have been convinced that it depended en-

[5] Angela Tondi Donizetti, Giuseppe's wife, and his son.
[6] Giulio Marco Bordogni (1788–1856), a former pupil of Mayr, had sung in opera at Trieste from 1803 to 1813 and at La Scala, Milan, for two years or more thereafter. Later he had become a professor of singing at the Paris Conservatory. He had known Donizetti since early in Donizetti's life.

tirely upon his being with her in her villa at Nice. She is a possible candidate for the role of *femme fatale*, whether real or as imagined by Donizetti's friends. But she is much less likely for the role than another woman, as Andrea Donizetti referred to "a French woman who is bent on his ruin," and the Countess von Löwenstein was not French, but German.[7]

A much more likely candidate for this shadowy role is Zélie de Coussy, the wife of Donizetti's Paris banker. That there was animated gossip about her at the time is proved by a letter that Antonio Vasselli wrote to Andrea Donizetti on February 2, 1846, in which the following appears: ". . . the stories that were making the rounds referred to the De Coussy firm, and it was said that the twenty thousands ducats that Gaetano had withdrawn from the Banchi di Napoli had been entrusted to Signor De Coussy, who paid the interest but had not guaranteed the principal. It was said that *Madama* [Zélie de Coussy] had enchained Gaetano with incredible art." Also, Andrea Donizetti and perhaps some others appear to have had an undocumented suspicion that Mme de Coussy was involved in the inexplicable actions of Gabriel Delessert, the Paris Prefect of Police, who was to make Donizetti's departure from Paris after his breakdown so exceedingly difficult. Her motive, the implication seems to have been—as hinted in Vasselli's letter quoted from above—a double one: she could have been Donizetti's artfully sinister mistress; she and her husband could have had a sizable financial interest in not allowing the paralyzed Donizetti to be removed from their control and returned to Bergamo. Certainly, some of Donizetti's pitiful final notes, written from the mental sanatorium at Ivry, were addressed to or intended for her. She was to make seemingly frantic efforts to visit him after his temporary removal from Ivry to an apartment in Paris—and was to find her way barred at Andrea Donizetti's orders. But those facts do not in themselves constitute proof that she was, or could have been, the basic cause of Donizetti's collapse.

For even supposing that Donizetti had been having sexual relations, excessive and harmful to a man in his condition, the woman involved could not have been "in large part the cause of his illness," however much she might have hastened its evolution. As his medical history, derived from statements in his own letters, proves, the symptoms of his morbid condition long antedated his acquaintance with either the

---

[7] Charlotte Sophie, Gräfin von Ysenburg (1803–74), in 1827 had married, as his second wife, Georg Wilhelm Ludwig, Fürst zu Löwenstein-Werthheim-Freudenberg (1775–1855).

Countess von Löwenstein or Zélie de Coussy. But that by the autumn of 1845 Donizetti realized that his friends considered his condition desperate is demonstrated in his answer to the letter from Dolci which Marco Bordogni had delivered to him, part of which reads: "Why are my friends upset? I have told you a thousand times that if I am sick, then someone else will write for me; if I die, the newspapers will say so, but when there is silence (though I did write to you), if I am silent, that is a sign that things are better than that. I thank you for your solicitude."

Dolci had written of his worries to Lorenzo Monterasi at about the time when he had sent the double letter to Bordogni. For on October 28, Monterasi answered him from Paris:

My very dear Dolci:

You can't imagine the pleasure it has given me to receive your dear letter of the 20th instant, which arrived the evening of the 25th. Day before yesterday, I went to see Donizetti, but he had gone out early and did not return all day. Yesterday I went back and found him in a bad temper because he was giving a lesson and his servant had gone out without his knowing it, and he himself therefore had to go to open the door. Then I told him that I had received your letter, and I told him, too, about your anxieties, caused by his long silence, in answer to which he told me that he had received your letters and had written a few days ago, a somewhat sad letter. (His words) "With my friends I ought to say what I feel in my heart, but now I'm almost sorry that I did so." I could not talk with him long, seeing that (as I said above) he was busy. Then I went to see Signor Acursio [Accursi], his intimate factotum and secretary, who told me that the Maestro constantly receives letters from Rome and Naples begging him to come to spend the winter there in tranquillity. To these entreaties, it seems, he doesn't wish to give in; also, he seems instead to have decided to leave for Vienna. As they cannot make him leave for Italy, they will do everything possible to keep him in Paris, and it seems to me certain that he won't leave.

A report on his physical and moral state. I'll tell you: I was in London when I heard it said that Donizetti had lost his mind. Even though I didn't believe that, nevertheless it made a tremendous impression on me. I reached Paris on September 21, and the next day I went to see him, and to my great pleasure discovered that he was eating in a way not to leave me any doubt that he was perfectly all right in the head and in the stomach. From then on, I have seen him almost every day, and never have seen in him any symptoms of mental derangement. Some people tell me that in pronouncing rather long sentences he sometimes has hesitated in replying, but very seldom. They have put bloodsuckers, cataplasms, and vesicants on the nape of his neck, for which reason some have supposed him stupefied because he could not move his neck freely. The vesicants seem to have done him good. A week ago they took the vesicant off, and it seems that there was a slight relapse.

Report on the oldtime relation that he has in Paris with *Madama* [Countess Sophie von Löwenstein? Zélie de Coussy?]: I am convinced that it is salutary rather than noxious; and that this person has the Maestro's health more at heart than anyone else has. Now she is intent only on obtaining every means of help for him that is possible, and every means of distraction; but not in the way that many misinformed people are disposed to believe. I repeat that it would be better for him to have an old liaison, even if it were pernicious, as the misinformed believe; I say that an old relationship does not lead him to abandon himself in such transports as he might indulge with a new one.

The single reason why it would be good for Donizetti to be far from Paris, other than the nonbeneficial climate, is the continuous drain of visits, musical consultations, newspapers, theatrical emotions, while his operas are restaged here and there, etc., etc. On the other hand, if he were removed, perhaps that would be worse; then melancholy might be added to solitude, whereas he always had been used to living amid people and affairs.

In the event, however, not Dolci, but Antonio Vasselli, took the step that assured the necessary help for Donizetti. The day after Donizetti had dated his letter of October 21 to his brother Giuseppe, Vasselli— deeply disturbed at having received no direct word from his friend since the letter of August 11 and no indirect replies to requests for information about the sick man which he had sent to others—also wrote to Giuseppe in Constantinople: "I have waited until now to warn you that Gaetano needs to be removed from Paris, having hoped that he would yield to my advice. I have written him five extremely urgent letters, but I cannot go there. You go, and save him." This cry for help reached Constantinople in only fourteen days. On November 7, two days after its arrival, Andrea Donizetti wrote Vasselli:

On the 5th of the current month we received your letter of October 22, in which you tell us that Gaetano is seriously ill and needs someone of his family to help him, not having a single true friend in Paris and, furthermore, being guarded by a French woman who is bent on his ruin.[8]

I leave it to you to consider to what an afflicted state your above-mentioned letter has reduced us. Poor Gaetano! Then our presentiments have been verified! You complain of his silence; know then, that we too, with Ghezzi, Dolci, and all his friends, have been without letters from him for a long time. I will tell you, too, that we have been on the verge of believing that our letters were not being delivered to him. In this state of affairs, my father has thought of having me leave for Paris in spite of the bad weather at this time of the year and of the recent illness of my mother, from which,

[8] This may indicate Zélie de Coussy. But either the wife of Count Rudolf Appony or the Countess Sophie von Löwenstein (who, though German by birth, evidently spent considerable time in France—she had a villa on the Riviera) might have struck Andrea Donizetti as a Frenchwoman.

however, thank Heaven, she is happily cured. The trip is too long and fatiguing for my father himself to be able to undertake it, not to mention the bad weather at present or his position, which he would not be able to leave without advance permission, permission that certainly would be granted him, but after a loss of precious time.

The young man sailed from Constantinople on November 13. On October 25, meanwhile, Donizetti had written to Dolci: "Didn't I perhaps answer you a short time ago? I have no fever, more vesicants, more leeches. I don't fall from the bed at night any more. The twelve hours and a half of unconsciousness on the floor and out of the bed have never recurred. . . . I won't even be in Vienna; I am weak, I cannot turn my head very much." And on November 10, to Leo Herz: "I am in danger of dying. At Vienna the climate kills me, and thus it's well that I shall suffer less. . . . You see that as I'm not in a good state I must delay my arrival. Tell [Pietro] Mecchetti [a co-impresario at the Kärnthnertortheater] and Count Moritz Dietrichstein that if the poor Donizetti should be taken ill on the way, they should pay his respects to His Majesty for him."

When Andrea Donizetti reached Milan, he received a letter from Antonio Vasselli, who sadly said: "I am extremely grieved at having lost that influence over your uncle which proved to be my consolation. He does not deign even to answer me, and I have had to obtain word of his health indirectly." Regarding the stories about Donizetti's mental disturbances as a calumny, Totò urged upon Andrea the need to persuade his famous uncle to return to Italy—he suggested Milan, Naples, Rome, Bergamo, even Bologna—rather than remaining in Paris or going to Vienna. Andrea also received a letter from his uncle Francesco, who advised him not to start for Paris without ascertaining first that Gaetano was still there: Antonio Dolci had received the letter in which Donizetti had said that he shortly would be leaving for Vienna. This warning may perhaps in part explain why Andrea's journey from Constantinople to Paris occupied six full weeks. He reached Paris only on Christmas Day, when he put up with his sadly ailing uncle at the Hôtel Manchester.

Three days before Andrea's arrival—but certainly aware that his nephew was en route and would arrive shortly—Donizetti wrote him a particularly curious and irresponsible letter: "I leave tomorrow or the day after tomorrow. And it will be tomorrow, but I'll leave such information that from this friend you'll receive everything. Don't lose this letter, and give it to him. He will find [you] economical lodgings. Vatel, further, is the impresario of the Italien and a very fine man; but go in my name. If there is extra work, offer yourself without pay. Giuseppe, Angela—are they all well? I hope so. Day after tomorrow I leave for Vienna. Greet and embrace everyone. For anything that you must buy here, it's better to have a friend's help; in everything and for everything. Greet my friends, as [your] *papà* and *mamma* are in the Orient. I embrace you. Gaetano. I suffer over not being able to clasp your hand."

In fact, no possibility can have existed that Donizetti could leave Paris alone or that the doctors in charge of his case would have countenanced so rash an enterprise. On the spot, Andrea Donizetti saw that his uncle's condition was desperate. He considered the idea of moving the patient elsewhere. Countess Sophie von Löwenstein offered her villa at Nice, but when Andrea explained this to Donizetti, he discovered that his uncle's wish now was to go to Italy. Dr. Philip Ricord, however, said that such a journey was impossible during the winter because of the patient's advanced state of physical and mental decay. Andrea rightly insisted that Ricord put this opinion in writing. On January 16, 1846, Ricord gave him this document: "I still am of the opinion that it is necessary that your uncle, M. Gaetan Donizetti, should make a trip to Italy for his health; [but] the bad season in which we now are does not permit his leaving immediately. It will be much better from every point of view that he wait for the first good spring days."

Not satisfied with that, and no doubt feeling his lonely responsibility very sharply, Andrea then called in for consultation two other highly respected Paris specialists in mental diseases, Dr. Juste-Louis-Florent Calmeil (1798–1895) and Dr. Jean Mitivié (1796–1871). With Dr. Ricord on hand as attending physician,[9] they examined Donizetti exhaustively on January 28, giving Andrea this written opinion:

The undersigned physicians, Mitivié, physician of the Salpêtrière, Ricord, surgeon of the Hôpital du Midi, Calmeil, physician of the Maison Royale de Charenton, met at Paris, in the rue de la Michodière, No. 8, on January 28, 1846, to deliberate on the condition of Monsieur Gaetan Donizetti and to examine the course that they should take with regard to him at this time in view of the point reached by the malady of which he is ailing.

The undersigned have been able to assure themselves that M. Donizetti's malady has followed a slow, insidious march; the excess and frequency of the emotions to which he has been exposed[10] must have contributed to the birth of the derangement at present existing in his brain. At all times, further, something peculiar has taken place in the head of this celebrated artist; each

[9] Calmeil and Mitivié would now be referred to as psychiatrists, but of course were medical men as well.
[10] This phrase may have referred equally well to the emotions that the doctors supposed involved in his career as a composer and to his increasing sexual urgency.

time that he has devoted himself to composition, it has seemed to him that only one hemisphere has taken part in the conception and that a sort of partition has separated the two halves of his brain.

One evening in 1843, M. Donizetti complained of feeling an extraordinary sensation in his head, and he attempted to give an idea of it by saying that it seemed to him that lightning had just crossed his brain.[11] Later on, in Italy, it was thought that a sort of turgescence could be remarked in his face, accompanied by sottishness of the physiognomy. Still later, he began to show himself distracted on one occasion when he was interested in sustaining his usual superiority and an able female singer had occasion to complain of his accompaniment.[12]

Finally, in mid-1845, the signs of a morbidity at work in his brain became more numerous and less equivocal each day. M. Donizetti was no longer able to compose and produce as in the past; his ideas seemed less numerous than before; he easily succumbed to the heaviness of a frequent sleepiness, his walk appeared heavy, his body tended to stoop; his whole physique took on an unfavorable appearance, a multitude of nuances that allowed there to be seen in his betraying manners a relative weakening of the faculties of understanding and imagination.

In the month of August 1845, the weakening of his legs became at times so evident that M. Donizetti was subject to falls; for moments at a time, his memory left him, being totally absent; a more and more marked change came over M. Donizetti's habits, his tastes, his manner of life. Wise professors, summoned to him, announced the existence of a malady of the great nervous centers and prescribed the application of a treatment that has been followed religiously under the direction of Monsieur Doctor Ricord.

The autumn of 1845 was marked by several recurrences of intervals that

[11] On May 23, 1910, *L'Eco di Bergamo* published the following undated letter (present whereabouts of the autograph unknown) from Donizetti to an unidentified friend: "*Caro Amico.* Yes, yes, reproach me, but you will be doing something, if not unjust, certainly painful. I am passing through a strange period. It seems to me, when I'm composing, that ideas come to me only from one half of my brain, and that even that is divided into two parts. From time to time, then, I have a terrifying sensation: it seems to me that a bolt of lightning strikes my brain, breaks it open, and reduces it to pulp. This is not the first time that such a thing has happened to me, but I believe and hope that in time and with rest, it will pass. And I need rest; I work too much. But among the strange phenomena that I have noticed for some time there is also this. When I'm composing happy music, I feel a painful pulsation on the left side of my forehead, whereas if I'm writing serious music, I feel the same pain on the right side; and in one situation and the other the pain is accompanied by a sensation of heat that disappears once the composition is finished. Add to this my usual migraines and you'll see what diversion is being enjoyed by your Donizetti." This letter emits a false tone, and unless proof of its authenticity materializes, I shall consider it a forgery. It is exactly the sort of document that a knowing forger would create.

[12] Where had the physicians obtained information and stories of this nature? Perhaps in part from Andrea, who would have had them secondhand. Also, it is difficult not to suppose that they can have misinterpreted answers that the befuddled Donizetti made to questions they shot at him. The anecdote about the "female singer" has been mentioned elsewhere: it involved Donizetti's forgetting the piano accompaniment that he was supposed to be playing.

allowed M. Donizetti's friends to have hope again of seeing him cured, but also was marked by phenomena of incontestable gravity. Often during the night when M. Donizetti abandoned the horizontal position to make some movement of his arms, a sort of commotion operating in the interior of the cranial box caused him painful terror; it seemed to him that the floor sank beneath him, that something traversed his brain from front to back, and that the house had fallen into ruins. On the morning after one such shock, M. Donizetti was found stretched out on the floor, and it was only after being suitably relieved that he was able to return to full consciousness.

Today, finally, M. Donizetti's malady tends to disclose itself under its true likeness. The heaviness of his motions is evident; this sick man avoids the obstacles and dangers of the street only with difficulty; at times his pronunciation is clogged; his postures, the positions of his head and body, indicate lack of energy in his muscular system.

Not only are his memory and other intellectual faculties marked by lack of capacity and understanding, but also, false, unreasonable ideas have become mixed into the sick man's reasoning, so that he imagines that he is being robbed, that he is being deprived of sums of money that really are not at his disposition.

His character has become either irritable or taciturn; the excitement of his genital organs no longer allows M. Donizetti to resist the impulse of his desires, and he more and more compromises his health in giving reign to partly unhealthy needs.

After all that has been set forth, the undersigned are brought to think that M. Donizetti is the victim of a chronic infection of the great nervous centers, that this infection occupies principally some points in the pia mater[13] and the surface matter of the brain, that it has been complicated by moments of congestion of the blood capillaries, complicated by serous infiltration of the cellular plexus of the meninges, and that, finally, it tends to diminish the stability of the nervous pulp.[14]

They believe that at the present time there has been a *recrudescence* in some of the affected nuclei, and that the aggravation of the symptoms should in part be attributed to the activity of this cause.

They believe that M. Donizetti no longer is capable of calculating sanely the significance of his decisions, and that if he is left free to carry out his impulses, he can only excite the progress of the disease.

They cannot advise a prompt removal from Paris, as they had at first intended; they fear that a trip would be liable to complications by acts of madness and that, on reaching their destination, they would find it difficult to locate a suitable clinic.

Summing up, they believe that M. Donizetti should be placed for the

[13] "The delicate and highly vascular membrane of connective tissue investing the brain and spinal cord, internal to the arachnoid and dura mater. . . . It dips down between the convolutions of the brain and sends an ingrowth into the anterior fissure of the cord."—*Webster's New International Dictionary*, Second Edition

[14] That this was a remarkably correct diagnosis was to be proved by the findings of the autopsy performed on Donizetti's body. See Appendixes, pp. 288-90.

present in an establishment designed for the treatment of mental alienations, and that it always will be possible for them to have recourse to a trip if it is judged necessary.

Paris, January 28, 1846   Calmeil, Mitivié, Ricord.

Andrea Donizetti appears to have been very reluctant to consent to the drastic action of placing his uncle in a mental clinic. But by January 31 he had little choice: on that day, two of the consulting physicians—Calmeil and Ricord—signed another, shorter statement intended either for police or sanitary records or for Andrea's peace of mind:

We the undersigned doctors of medicine of the Faculty of Paris certify that M. Gaetan Donizetti is the victim of a mental disease that brings disorder into his actions and his decisions; that it is to be desired in the interest of his preservation and his treatment that he be isolated in an establishment devoted to cerebral and intellectual maladies.

Calmeil, Ricord.

Dr. Mitivié did not participate in this certification because the clinic chosen was his property, though it was administered by Dr. Jacques-Joseph Moreau de Tours.[15] People were to be told that Donizetti had been taken to the Riviera to recuperate; not even his manservant was told the truth. Andrea gave his consent. On the day of the certification, or possibly on February 1—the documentary evidence on this point is not entirely clear—Donizetti's carriage drew up outside the Hôtel Manchester to pick up Donizetti, Andrea, Dr. Ricord, and the servant (who already had been dismissed, having been told that as his master was being taken to Nice, he could return at once to Vienna; he was let out of the carriage along the way). This somber group reached Dr. Mitivié's clinic at Ivry at noon. Donizetti was made to believe that the carriage had broken down, that they had to put up in a hotel during the time required for the repairs. But he was assured that they would reach Vienna by February 12, the day when he was supposed to report there at court. Then, in the rain, he was led into the asylum. On that day began perhaps the most extraordinary two years that a famous man ever has been subjected to as an approach to the desirable release of death.

When Andrea had become convinced that his uncle could not go to Vienna, he had approached Count Antony Rudolf Appony, the Austrian ambassador at Paris, with the request that the sick man be granted a leave. On February 24, Appony wrote him and attached a letter

---

[15] Jacques-Joseph Moreau de Tours (1804–84) was a noted alienist and a leading propagandist for the reform of the treatment of insane patients in asylums. He is treated historically as a precursor of the more famous Jean-Martin Charcot.

for Donizetti as an official extension of his leave: "I have the honor to inform you that His Majesty the Emperor has deigned to accede to your request for the granting of a leave for the term of one year so that you may give your health the care that it requires. I must, at the same time, invite you, Monsieur, not to let your leave expire without informing M. the Grand Chamberlain, Count [Moritz] von Dietrichstein, if, and at what point, it will be possible for you to take up again the functions in your charge." Shortly later, Metternich sent to Paris an emissary whose duty it was to send almost daily reports to Vienna on the condition of the sick man at Ivry.

Guido Zavadini and others have argued that Donizetti should have been allowed to remain in his Paris hotel apartment rather than being closed up in a clinic. They point out that he was not violent, but was suffering from a creeping paralysis. But no grounds exist for suspecting the good faith of Andrea or the very eminent medical men involved, and trying to treat Donizetti at home, even with the care that he might have had from nephew and manservant, undoubtedly seemed—as in fact it was—impractical, given the state in which treatment of physico-mental afflictions then stood. Donizetti did not improve in the clinic at Ivry; in fact, he deteriorated still more there. But it is unreasonable to assert, as some commentators and biographers have asserted, that he would have been better off from the beginning if he never had been taken to Ivry. The fact that it proved possible, nearly seventeen months later, to maintain him outside that institution is beside the point: during those months he had become all but totally paralyzed and therefore no longer was able to harm himself by excessive sexual activity or otherwise. Too many intangibles and unknown factors make ethical judgments about his incarceration at Ivry as slippery now as medical judgments were then.

When Donizetti could no longer be kept believing that his carriage had been detained for repairs, Dr. Moreau de Tours tried to convince him that there had been a robbery in which his manservant had been involved and which the police were investigating with great care. Donizetti seems to have grasped in confusion at the notion of robbery and then to have come to believe that he himself was under arrest—which, in effect, was not far from the truth. A number of letters in his quavering script, some dated and some undated, survive from the first weeks of his incarceration at Ivry. These often are incoherent, but all of them reveal complete misconception of his true situation and a belief that he has been made the victim of a terrible and horrifying mistake. They were not sent, but were preserved by Andrea Donizetti.

A letter dated "Ivry 5"—that is, February 5, 1846—to the Countess Appony, wife of the Austrian ambassador at Paris, begins: "Pity; pity! They have arrested me; why? My servant, it seems that he was a thief. Keep the carriage there; but arrest me, me too? in my carriage? Steal! Dishonor me! It's a mistake! Meanwhile, I await your pity. Donizetti." After the signature, the letter surges on as if in fresh, muddled grief and anxiety: "I ought to be in Vienna before the middle of this month. Pity, pity, I am innocent! the carriage is mine. I must find myself in Vienna by the 12th. Oh! Only you, Countess, know that I must compose a Mass for the Royal Imperial Chapel of the court at Vienna. Speak to his Excellency, your Excellent husband. This will be my last letter. I, rob . . . the robbery mine? Oh! Mistake!—I will return if you want me to. Rob myself? I ask you this favor because I am obliged to serve His Majesty in the Imperial Royal Chapel . . . they say that the servant has robbed me. And what did I have to do with that? Your servant, Gaetano Donizetti."

Then, already having ended and signed the letter twice, Donizetti rushed on: "Make my tears stop flowing immediately: the carriage is mine; but get me out. I will leave here—I will do everything [illegible] been the servant . . . certainly the Virgin Mary will touch your heart. A theft, which was made against me at Paris [illegible] week has made a mistake [cancellation] my name [cancellation] has had no effect. Oh! Countess! I seem near death. Come back sooner than make me come back.[16] I beg you in the name of God and His Son, may the prayer take effect! Oh! Get me out of here: I go to Vienna, where I have had the permission! . . . I am arrested on French soil? and on the return, at Yvry [*sic*]?

"I do not understand! . . . I eat little and have come to the end even of that . . . I explain myself: I have had, but now am over, that small sore on my arm. Tuesday they arrested me, and the police prevented my continuing on. Is it possible? Oh! Excellency: I write to both of Their Majesties. Oh! the tears . . . [words struck through]. How will I explain this now? Majesty? Enough! Enough. His Majesty is so good that I shall return to my senses and know that I have been pardoned, that they will not take the bread from the mouths of innocents. A certificate that Signor Ricord will make out will be help enough. With what a heart, if I had no faith in Ricord and in the insignificance in the insignificance [*sic*] of the little sore that goes away with butter: During this week. It is not important: . . . ."

---

[16] This sentence, though struck through, remains legible.

On February 6, Donizetti wrote somewhat similar, equally dis-
traught letters to Count Appony, to a woman—very probably Zélie de
Coussy—and to Countess Appony. The next day, he wrote to Antonio
Dolci at Bergamo:

                                                    Ivry – 7 – February 1846

Eight days shut up in an institution, without [being able] to help myself; no
letters from Bergamo; from anywhere . . . Andrea will have left (I believe;)
His Majesty has been content that I should have chosen this little lodging,
where fortune persecutes me . . . (after the thieves.) I am without a manservant!

A letter in reply, for having done well. . . . The place that His Majesty
has seen that I have chosen, and he says to me: Extend my compliments,
and Appony! . . . eat . . . drink . . . sometimes permit yourself some diversion, for which I pay. Give yourself the most beautiful things; for which
I pay; [he has] me [?] seen, I have selected it . . . Bravo ! ! ! The wines,
ah: the best; the pension; pension; I pay for it . . . I take care of it myself;
I always have paid it.—He will have the answer that I pay for everything:
without getting out of it: I accord to you a pension for life, whether here,
whether there; Only bring some piece for the Imperial Royal Chapel (a fat
thing). Your grateful, most humble servant

                                                                Donizetti

He continued pouring out these disjunct screeds: to Countess
Appony on February 7; again to her without date; to Zélie de Coussy
without date; to August Thomas ("Ivry: 8 or 0.–The thieves"), in this
last still pitifully asserting: "I leave within six days; Vienna . . ." Thereafter, no other letters from Donizetti appear to survive until May, and
a great silence descends upon him. Almost no one seems to have been
permitted to visit him at first, so that he saw few people except the doctors and a male nurse, Antoine Pourcelot, who became devoted to him
and stayed with him until his death. Andrea and a few other people
were allowed to call. And after the terrible agitation of the beginning
of his incarceration at Ivry, Donizetti settled down into blank, unchang-
ing days of torpor. A billiard table may have offered him some diversion
at first, but the swift advance of his disease gradually crushed him to a
partial immobility that in time became all but total. A written report on
his condition, dated April 7, reads in part:

The undersigned[17] have tried to converse with M. Gaetan Donizetti and
they very quickly have recognized that the obliteration of M. Gaetan Donizetti's intellectual faculties does not permit him to sustain the simplest conversation properly.

[17] Dr. Félice Voisin (1794–1872), Chief Physician of the Insane at Bicetre, and
Dr. Achille-Louis Foville (1799–1876), Chief Physician of the Maison Royale at
Charenton, a predecessor of Charcot and author of a then well-known treatise on
the nervous system.

They desired to see him walk, and have recognized that the strength directing voluntary movements is curtailed scarcely less than that manifested by his intelligence.

Finally, they watched M. Gaetan Donizetti led to the billiard room, and the suggestion made him that he play a game. In this light exercise, M. Gaetan Donizetti simultaneously manifested his intellectual decadence and the enfeeblement, the lack of sureness, in his voluntary movements.

After these various observations, the undersigned physicians have been left with the profound conviction that M. Gaetan Donizetti has been struck by a double affection of the cerebro-spinal nervous system; that with regard to his intelligence he is in a state of insanity, and with regard to his voluntary movements in a state of general paralysis.

This double malady of the nervous system is so evident with M. Donizetti that the practicing physicians who have observed him only once cannot have the slightest doubt of it.

In view of the fact that this deplorable condition of mental and muscular sickness will last, M. Donizetti, completely unable to understand and carry out what is necessary for his preservation, has need of intelligent help, the devoted vigilance of men habituated to the treatment of maladies of the cerebro-spinal nervous system.

Teodoro Ghezzi visited Donizetti at Ivry at about the time of the examination by Foville and Voisin. The visit was a most unhappy one. In a letter that Antonio Vasselli wrote to Andrea Donizetti on April 20, he said: "I cannot conceal from you that this [the Foville-Voisin report], together with the result of the first encounter that Teodoro had with Donizetti, has deprived me of all hope of saving [him]. I had not thought it possible that Gaetano would not be moved by the name of his *Virginia* or that the sight of Teodoro—of this rare and affectionate friend of his —would have been able to bring on a crisis. Now everything is finished. . . . As for me, I don't know how to deceive myself after the tragic scene of the meeting with Teodoro which you described to me" And on May 8, Vasselli wrote Andrea a letter of which one passage casts retroactive light on one of the factors that had led the physicians to insist on Donizetti's isolation: "I want to propose to you that you remove him from that place, because now that the stimulation for women has stopped in the sick man, he could be better off in Paris than in the sanitarium."

And toward the end of May, Andrea, by then convinced finally that any real improvement in his uncle's state had become impossible, decided that the sick man should be removed to Italy. At about that same time, perhaps dimly aware of Andrea's thoughts, Donizetti wrote an almost totally illegible note to his brother Giuseppe, beginning "My very dear brother" (see Plate 18). Early in June, Andrea called in three outside physicians to give Donizetti another thorough examination for the purpose of determining whether or not he could be transported to Bergamo. This report[18] was dated June 12; in part it read:

The undersigned physicians . . . after having listened to the able physicians to whose care he [Donizetti] has been confided for several months; after having been made *au courant* by them with all the details of the malady from its origin up to this date; after having seen, examined, attentively interrogated the sick man; declare unanimously,

That if the trip is directed by a physician who will regulate the sick man's regimen each day, the distance to be traveled, the hours during which the transport from one place to another can be effected or should be forbidden, and the times of rest or of momentary interruption that might become necessary . . . they see no serious inconvenience to undertaking the trip at once;

Considering, on the other hand,

That if the malady of M. Donizetti has reached such a degree of development and gravity—as it appears to the physicians who have been treating it—as to be absolutely beyond the resources of their art, nature nevertheless sometimes has mysterious resources that operate by miracles, and that the air, the appearance, of the places that saw M. Donizetti's birth, the seeing of his childhood friends, the return to the bosom of his family, can favor a happy change in him, the consultants think:

That this trip can be useful to the sick man; in consequence and for these reasons, the consultants advise that M. Donizetti leave for Italy without delay.

Having been handed this reasonable report, Andrea wrote to Bergamo to find out where Donizetti could be housed and cared for there. He received word that Countess Rosa Basoni wished to put at Donizetti's disposition her city palace or either of her two country villas. Although Donizetti himself almost certainly was too disturbed mentally to be aware that his liberation from the "arrest" at Ivry appeared to be imminent, Andrea thereupon began to make plans for the journey.

But at this juncture forces were brought into action which were to succeed in preventing Donizetti's departure from France for more than a year. On July 3, an order from Gabriel Delessert, the Paris prefect of police, forbade the authorities at Ivry to allow Donizetti's release until he had been examined further, this time by Dr. Louis-Jules Béhier, who was attached to the prefecture. When Andrea Donizetti requested that Dr. Béhier be accompanied in the examination by other physicians, that

---

[18] It is signed "C. Cabarrus, Chevalier of the Legion of Honor; Pierre-Eloi Fouquier [1776–1850], Physician to the King, Professor of the Faculty of Medicine of Paris, Physician of the Hôpital de la Charité, Officer of the Legion of Honor; Louis-Charles Roche [1790–1875], President of the Royal Academy of Medicine."

was arranged. Three doctors[19] saw Donizetti on July 9 and signed their report to the prefect the next day. In part it reads:

We found the sick man in a garden, and we realized at once that Signor Donizetti walks with very great effort. His legs, half bent under the weight of his body, do not allow him more than the very small steps made by dragging his feet, which he lifts up with difficulty. Examined more directly, Signor Donizetti presented to us all the signs of the third degree of general paralysis. The tongue is impeded, and this trouble is noticeable even when he replies in monosyllables, which he always does. His responses are either negatives or affirmatives, and for the rest, they fall reasonably enough; nevertheless, his memory is completely lost, his intellectual faculties are almost completely destroyed; in a word, his intelligence seems absolutely worn out and overthrown. The difficulties with urine and fecal matters which the sick man presented a short time back now are more remote, and even have been suspended entirely for the past fifteen days or so, but what continues and renders the sick man's situation still more grave, if that be possible, is very frequent congestions toward the head, congestions that could have the deadliest consequences, and which require constant, very active surveillance.

In this situation, after having weighed deeply all the circumstances, after having understood in detail the precautions that Signor André Donizetti would take for his uncle's trip, we do not hesitate to declare from the very first that this removal would not procure any advantage; that in the sick man's condition, no salutary effect could be hoped for from the air of his country, from the seeing of places in which Signor Donizetti was born, from seeing his childhood friends, circumstances absolutely inefficacious in so advanced a malady. Finally, in the presence of this situation, and above all of the repeated congestions that the sick man undergoes, we formally believe that the trip that it has been desired to have him make not only would be inefficacious, but would also be very dangerous; that even with all the precautions taken in advance, an accident could follow, and that if Signor Donizetti could reach Bergamo without succumbing (which would not be impossible), his end certainly would be hastened by this removal.

While rendering full justice to the noble feelings that guide the nephew of Signor Donizetti, then, we are of the opinion that the trip should be forbidden formally as offering very real dangers and being far from allowing hope of any useful result.

On July 16, Gabriel Delessert, the prefect of police, notified Andrea that Donizetti could not be moved. The incarceration at Ivry thereby, for the time being at least, had been placed beyond the reach of appeal. Now Andrea, further disturbed by word from Constantinople that his mother was in poor health, decided that he must go home. In August, therefore, he sought a final opinion, this time from the physicians prac-

[19] The report is signed "Bonneau, [Louis-Jules] Béhier, [Ulisse] Trelat."

ticing at or connected with the Ivry clinic. On August 30, Calmeil, Moreau, and Ricord signed a lengthy document, in which they said in part:

They were astounded by the state of enfeeblement to which the paralysis has reduced all the muscular system.

M. Donizetti still can hold himself upright and walk on a flat surface leaning on the arm of a domestic, but his steps are very unassured, his motion is wavering; the body, strongly leaning to the right, also tends, because of its weight, to lean backwards, so that falls are imminent and progress would become impossible if the domestic did not take great care to maintain his master's equilibrium.

For some days, the head has been greatly bent onto the chest, where it is fixed by stiffness of the flexor muscles.

The attempts that were made to move the head back provoked a painful sensation: neither redness nor warmth nor any appearance of tumefaction exists at the neck.

The stools are expelled at very long intervals; the urine runs drop by drop beyond the sick man's control.

Articulation is almost impossible, and words are rare and isolated.

The pulse preserves little strength. M. Donizetti does not seem to be conscious of his condition, so great has been the progress of his cruel malady as acting on his fine faculties. . . .

Definitively, the undersigned, taking into account the group of morbid phenomena that struck them, judged that the alterations that have developed in M. Donizetti's brain have all but reached their highest degree of intensity. They are inclined to think that at this time there also exists in the cerebral cavities a certain amount of serosity, and that the accumulation of this liquid contributes to the enfeeblement of the moral and intellectual forces.

They consider that a termination as unfortunate as it is inevitable must be foreseen in a very short time.

If they be required to pronounce on the possibility or impossibility of having M. Donizetti travel, they reply with the assurance of perfect conviction:

that for the present no experienced man gifted with the smallest prudence would dare to take upon himself the responsibility of displacing a sick man fallen into the condition in which M. Donizetti is found;

that the motion of the gentlest and best-balanced carriage would expose the head and the neck to dangerous rocking;

that the loosening of the bladder could be replaced suddenly by a constriction necessitating the employment of catheterism, an operation painful and often delicate;

that the erosions which, under the influence of fatigue, are digging into the circumvolutions of the brain could be exposed to a sudden afflux of blood capable of bringing on immediately violent convulsive attacks;

that invasion of the incidents that have come to be very numerous will be more to be feared within eight days, or in a few weeks, that at present, transporting him to his country should be renounced definitely.

Considerations of another sort, though more than very secondary, could be added to these as opposing any removal: M. Donizetti's celebrity requires the greatest possible dissimulation of the impressions that his present condition would give birth to in the souls of those who would see him; out of respect for him, he in his last moments should be kept from the eyes of strangers.

Finally, devotion itself is obliged up to a certain point to submit to the yoke of opinion: M. Donizetti's career has attracted to him the regard and protection of the great; what must be avoided is giving an appearance of injury where there are nothing but praiseworthy feelings and proper, elevated intentions, as with the family of M. Gaetan.

One member of the Donizetti family by this time had grown very impatient: in Constantinople, Giuseppe, evidently feeling that Andrea had failed to carry out his mission satisfactorily, had decided to order him to leave Paris and return home. Too, Andrea must have thought that any reason for his remaining in France now had been removed. Preparing to leave, on September 7, he evidently asked his uncle to write out a greeting, probably intending to give it to Francesco Donizetti in Bergamo. The resulting almost illegible scrawl includes these words: "Gaetano Donizetti makes greeting. Andrea leaves today. 8 September 1846."

Then Andrea was gone, and Donizetti was alone in France.

CHAPTER XI

September 1846–April 1848

ANDREA DONIZETTI carried with him to Bergamo a box containing his uncle's jewelry and decorations and a bundle of musical autographs. He left the scores there with Antonio Dolci and with his uncle, Francesco Donizetti, first sealing and signing the package; he also left the jewelry there. Among the music contained in the bundle were to be found later the unperformed one-act opera *Rita* and the unfinished *Le Duc d'Albe*.[1] Andrea asked Francesco for a "*procura assoluta (generale)*"—that is, a total power of attorney—so that he could be in a position to take care of all of Donizetti's affairs. Francesco refused to give this to him, fearing that Donizetti, in a possible period of sanity, might realize what had happened, fly into a rage about it, and then cut off the allowance (Francesco referred to it as "that little which comes to me daily") with which he had been eking out a living. Francesco's decision was to have long-lasting effects and to influence the future possibilities of staging both *Rita* and *Le Duc d'Albe*.

While in Bergamo, too, Andrea called upon Rosa Basoni and her twenty-year-old daughter, Giovanna (Giovannina), later the Baroness Scotti. Giovanna Basoni left behind her at her death an unpublished manuscript of memoirs which now is preserved in the Museo Donizettiano at Bergamo. In them it becomes clear that she did not like

---

[1] *Rita* was to be sung for the first time in Paris at the Opéra-Comique on May 7, 1860, *Le Duc d'Albe* not until March 22, 1882, at Rome, and then only in a much-tampered-with version in Italian translation, as *Il Duca d'Alba*.

Andrea Donizetti and was to be trusted more in describing events and scenes that she herself had witnessed than in judging—or imagining— events in which she had personally taken no part. She wrote:

During the month of September [1846], Signor Andrea left for Constantinople, abandoning his uncle and ordering that nobody dare to remove him from Ivry, and leaving the dispositions for his embalming and funeral! . . . As if the poor sick man had been at the edge of death; such was what his nephew was pleased to say, passing through Bergamo on his way to Constantinople: My uncle is at the end, they are forced to make him eat with a machine, he does not speak, and he no longer knows anyone.

And he begged Signor Dolci that when the sad news should become known, he take himself to Paris to have the body of his friend embalmed and transported to Italy. For all reply, Dolci turned his back on him and began to weep. . . . What is certain is that at this time the illustrious Maestro spoke, walked, played at billiards, and they never had him eat by means of the machine, nor was he as mad as his nephew said.

A letter that Francesco Donizetti wrote his brother Giuseppe on September 22 tells us that Andrea had left that day for Milan, en route to Constantinople. After his departure, news of Donizetti's condition reached Bergamo in frequent letters from Michele Accursi. And meanwhile, in the corridors, salons, and cafés of Paris, discussions about Donizetti's whereabouts and condition continued. Some of his friends and well-wishers who were in on the "secret" of his place of incarceration managed to visit him—among them Countess Sophie von Löwenstein, Michele Accursi, Francesco Florimo, Gilbert-Louis Duprez, Lorenzo Monterasi, Teodoro Ghezzi, and Baron Eduard von Lannoy.[2] This last-mentioned man, who had been a member of the executive board of the Vienna Conservatory, saw Donizetti several times and came to harbor a feeling of special warmth toward him. Realizing the senselessness now of keeping this helpless, hopeless invalid imprisoned in the clinic at Ivry, Lannoy, on January 22, 1847, wrote to Giuseppe Donizetti in Constantinople a letter that was to result, after still further delays, in extricating Donizetti from Ivry:

Signor Giuseppe Donizetti,
Beyond doubt you know, o Signor, that I have dedicated to your brother Gaetano a sincere and disinterested friendship; you know the lively interest that I take in this unhappy man, and it is that which bids me to write

---

[2] Lannoy, who had been born in Brussels on December 4, 1787, had spent his childhood in Austria, where he studied music. After more advanced studies in Paris, he went to Vienna in 1813, where he became active in the Gesellschaft der Musikfreunde and at the Conservatory. He also composed, his works including several operas.

you this letter of mine. I have been in Paris for many weeks, and have seen your unhappy brother several times at Ivry. I am informed about everything. He, then, fully understands the matters of which I speak to you—not in order to criticize you or wishing to offend you, but to fulfill my duties toward my friend and to present the matter to you from the true point of view.

A year ago, the confinement was necessary. Now it no longer is. Gaetano no longer can walk without being held up by his two custodians, and cannot even rise from a chair without their assistance; as a result of that, it no longer is possible for him to abuse his liberty. He is being extinguished little by little. The paralysis makes slow progress, to be sure, but it is continuous. It no longer is possible to hope to save him, but what can be—what should be—done is to render the last months of his existence less lugubrious, less melancholy.[3]

He still is aware of the presence of his friends. His expression becomes animated, he tries to speak, he smiles and weeps. Dr. Moreau says that the visits he receives produce more good results than bad; but to go to Ivry to spend one hour with the poor sick man, it takes five hours, carriages are costly, and the unhappy Gaetano spends too much time abandoned to his custodians alone.

If he were to be transported into Paris, he could be taken care of by the same physicians, have the same custodians and the same treatments. So that if on the physical side he could be as well off as at Ivry, on the moral side he would be a thousand times better off because his friends would see him every day and at any hour. The last days of his life would be gladdened, and the celebrated Maestro would not die in an asylum, but in his own apartment.

His upkeep now costs five hundred francs per month. At Paris it would cost one thousand, perhaps even fifteen hundred. Gaetano has about twenty thousand francs of income. Now, is it better that he should save fourteen thousand francs per year and die sadly in dismal desperation, or that he should save little or nothing and live for some months in as happy a state as still is possible for him?

I beg you, o Signor, to consider these alternatives carefully and then be willing to answer me. His friends are disinterested, do not wish to profit from Gaetano's misfortune or to live at his expense; the accounts would be perfectly in order and confirmed by all the justifying items.

In the case that neither fraternal feeling nor all the other considerations should decide you to agree to Gaetano's leaving Ivry to be placed and helped in his Paris home, which I beg you to write to the Signor Conte di Lesser, the other relatives[4] will be forced to have recourse to the law. The French Civil Code expressly states: An adult who is in a steady condition of im-

---

[3] This paragraph of Lannoy's letter exculpates Andrea Donizetti from the charges against him made and implied in Giovanna Basoni's memoirs. But at the same time it strongly suggests that he lacked the forcefulness that was to prove able, when brought into play, to free Donizetti from his by then needless confinement.

[4] It is difficult to imagine what Lannoy can have meant by "other relatives." Not Andrea, certainly, or Francesco. Could the Vassellis have been involved?

becility, dementia, or frenzy, *must* be disqualified even though lucid intervals be present.

It would be essential, then, in that situation, to approach the courts, which would not fail to pronounce the disqualification, to name a guardian, and to obtain from him that which you, o Signor, would have refused.

You have too noble a heart, o Signor, to permit us to go to that extreme; then agree to the just demand of the unfortunate Gaetano's friends and, thus fulfilling your duty as a brother and a good relative, spare yourself the regrets that undoubtedly would torment you later, and from which some thousands of francs surely would not free you.[5]

Excuse my frankness, but I have thought it my duty to tell you everything that I feel in my heart and to scant nothing to improve as much as possible the last days of the life of my sick, unhappy friend.

Baron Eduard von Lannoy.

Now, and especially because newspapers and other periodicals had learned of Donizetti's incarceration at Ivry and had begun to raise their voices in favor of freeing him, Giuseppe Donizetti decided to send the hapless Andrea back to Paris to find out what might and must be done for Gaetano. Andrea sailed from Constantinople on March 4, 1847, stopped briefly en route at Bergamo, and reached Paris on the evening of April 23. When he went to Ivry the next day, he found Donizetti much worsened since he had seen him for the last time seven and a half months earlier. His uncle, however, recognized him—and smiled. Andrea handed him a portrait of Giuseppe that he had brought with him, and the sick man appeared to recognize its subject, holding the picture in his hands for some time before letting it fall to the floor. When Andrea then picked it up and handed it to him backwards, Donizetti realized what was wrong and turned it around so that he could look again at his brother's likeness.

The next day, Andrea wrote Antonio Dolci a description of the state in which he now found Donizetti: "Seated in the armchair with eyes closed and a sweet expression on his physiognomy, he could, for a moment, deceive someone who was seeing him for the first time and convince him that he was resting; but the thing is very different from that! He is seated constantly because he cannot stand on his feet! . . . He still moves some steps in the garden, but held up by the two servants. . . . His life, in short, is worse than death."

On March 20, 1847, Lorenzo Monterasi, who, in October 1845, had

---

[5] Lannoy here strongly suggests that he, and perhaps Donizetti's other friends in Paris, thought that Giuseppe Donizetti had been—or was—opposing the removal of Donizetti from Ivry because keeping him there cost comparatively little and he was hoping to inherit the money thus saved. No documentation—and nothing known about Giuseppe—suggests that this implied accusation had the smallest foundation in reality.

visited Donizetti often and found himself unable to believe in the seri-
ousness of Donizetti's illness, wrote to his sister Giuditta Monterasi
Varisco:

Paris, March 20, 1847.

Some days ago, I went to see Donizetti, who now for thirteen months has
been living in a house, called a sanitarium, at Ivry, a village three miles from
Paris. You can't imagine how my heart pounded when I was merely approaching that house. Arriving at the gate, I handed a letter to the porter
(for no one can enter without permission), who introduced me to Monsieur
Moreau [de Tours], Directing Physician of the Establishment. While I was
crossing with him the beautiful garden onto which opens the room in which
the Maestro lives, he told me that he had lost all hope of a cure, seeing
that for two months he no longer has spoken and almost always has had his
eyes closed and has not said a word. He told me that [Donizetti] eats everything put before him, without realizing what it is, that his two legs are
paralyzed, for which reason, when they have him walk in the garden, he
must be held up by the two men who are exclusively at the Maestro's service;
his hands too have been affected, and now it is necessary to feed him as they
feed children. He told me, too, that [Donizetti] has entirely lost all sensation,
as even if they pinch him strongly, he shows no sign of discomfort. As we
were talking, we entered a very clean room on the ground floor, and there I
saw the Maestro seated in an easy chair near the fire. Less than half an
hour earlier, they had shaved him and made his toilette, so that he had a good
complexion; and though his eyes constantly stayed closed, he resembled someone peacefully asleep. I pressed a kiss on his revered forehead and then called
him several times by name. He opened his eyes finally, closed them again,
and reopened them several times, and then gave me a light smile—a thing
that he does only to those (as the Doctor told me) whom he finds very
sympathetic. I began to talk in *bergamasco* and to mention the names of his
most intimate friends, and then he reopened his eyes and looked at me, now
with the air of someone trying to recall something once known. Then, not
finding it, he reclosed his eyelids and turned his head to one side, for I ought
also to tell you that the paralysis also attacked his neck and that the poor
Maestro always is bent toward the left side.

In addition to being dressed very properly, he has a coat of very fine
wool lined with fur, two pairs of woollen hose, and a muff hung around his
neck to keep his hands warm. During the hour and a half that I was there, I
got him to answer "Yes" twice, but he did not say another word. He gave me
his hand three times, and the Doctor told me afterwards that he had not
lavished such signs of sympathy on anyone else.

His stomach is the only thing that is in good order. For the rest, he is
not too thin and has good color, for which reason, if one did not know his
sad state, one would say: clearly he is sleeping. Too, he is receiving the
greatest attention, and it is for that reason alone that he will be able to carry
on until the Supreme Goodness may be pleased to summon him to the blessed

repose of the Great Men. Oh! mortal fragility, the man of Melody, the Genius of the century . . . now he sleeps ! ! !

At about this time in 1847, the usually acidulous Heinrich Heine, touched by a description of Donizetti's condition, wrote: "The news about the sick condition of Donizetti becomes more saddening from day to day. While his melodies ravish the world with their happy accents and are sung and trilled everywhere, he himself sits, a frightening image of insanity, in a sanatorium not far from Paris. Only in the matter of his dress did he maintain up until a short time ago a puerile ray of reason, and therefore had himself dressed carefully every morning in complete court gala, the habit adorned with all of his decorations. Thus he sat, immobile, his hat in his hand, from early in the morning until late in the evening. But that too has stopped. He recognizes no one. Such is the fortune of poor mankind."

Removal of Donizetti to Italy still was forbidden, but on May 26, in response to Andrea's continuing appeals and demands, the prefect of police issued an order permitting his being taken from Ivry to Paris on the condition that his custodian or male nurse remain with him and continue to assist him. Probably with the help of Michele Accursi, Baron Lannoy, and others of Donizetti's friends, a house suited to his needs was located just off the Champs-Elysées, at No. 6 avenue Chateaubriand. In the company of Andrea, Giacomo Fuddini, Dr. Mitivié, and the nurse-guardian Antoine Pourcelot, the dying man was taken from his imprisonment of sixteen months and twenty-three days at Ivry.

On the beautiful summer morning of June 23, 1847, Donizetti entered his temporary Paris home. There, though his physical state was beyond any possibility of amelioration,[6] his daily life became much less sordid and oppressive. Many people called upon him. Almost every other day, he was taken for a drive of three or four hours in his carriage. Those with him during these excursions noted that sometimes he seemed interested in what he saw: his facial expression intermittently showed intelligence, even curiosity about the life going on in the streets of Paris and Saint-Cloud. Giovanni Ricordi went with Donizetti on one of these carriage rides and described the experience as at once disturbing and moving.

"His insanity," Charles de Boigne wrote, "was gentle, silent. Stretched out in a large armchair in the middle of the garden, covered

---

[6] A physician in residence named Rendu appears to have been with Donizetti much of the time in the avenue Chateaubriand; he later accompanied Donizetti on the difficult trip to Bergamo.

with flowers—above him, around him, at his feet—his head sunk on his chest, he spent his days without pronouncing a single word. He did not recognize anyone, not even his friend and brother Accursi, who never left him, who cared for him with unlimited devotion. They tried some musical experiences on him, but they were unsuccessful; a single piece, the cavatina of the Mad Scene in *Lucia,* produced some impression upon him. At the first chords, he raised his head, opened his eyes, and beat time; then, when the cavatina was over, his eyes closed, his head sank down again onto his chest, and all glimmer of intelligence went out."

Giuseppe Verdi, after the disappointing *première* of his *I Masnadieri* in London,[7] was in Paris, and on August 22, in reply to a request from Giuseppina Appiani, he wrote: "You ask me for news of Donizetti. Up to now I haven't seen him because I have been advised not to, but I assure you that I have a very great wish to, and that if the occasion to see him without anyone's knowing it turns up, I'll undoubtedly do it. His physical appearance is good except that his head constantly is bowed on his chest and his eyes are closed. He eats and sleeps well and says not a word, or some very indistinct words. If someone is announced to him, he opens his eyes for a moment. If someone says to him 'Give me your hand,' he extends it, etc. This seems to be an indication that his intelligence has not been entirely put out. But for all that, a doctor who is one of his most affectionate friends told me that these signs are rather of habit, and that it would be better if he were animated, even if he were a raging maniac. For then there could be hope, whereas this way all that can be hoped for is a miracle. For the rest, he is as he was found six months, a year, ago: no improvement, no worsening. There you have Donizetti's true present condition! It is desolating, it is too desolating. If something happier occurs, I'll write you at once."

On August 15, 1847, Andrea Donizetti wrote a letter to a General Pepe.[8] Saying that his uncle's condition was hopeless, he added that he again was projecting the transfer to Bergamo, which had been stopped by the police in 1846. The doctors still had fears that the jolting of the carriage would harm Donizetti, but the many rides—fourteen of them —which he already had taken, far from harming him, appeared to have

[7] *I Masnadieri* had its *première* at Her Majesty's Theatre on July 22, 1847, when the cast included Jenny Lind and Luigi Lablache. It achieved only three performances, the last one conducted by Michael William Balfe, composer of *The Bohemian Girl.*

[8] This probably was Gabriele Pepe (1778–1851), a well-known patriot from Città Campomarano in the Molise. His nephew, Marcello Pepe, at some time had studied with Donizetti.

done him good, as a statement left behind by Dr. Mitivié after his visits would prove.[9] But Andrea still felt that he could not undertake to remove his uncle to Bergamo without the approval of competent medical judges. He therefore had summoned for a consultation at two-thirty on the afternoon of Tuesday, August 15, no less than six physicians: Andral, Calmeil, Chomel, Fossati, Mitivié, and Rostan. Referring again to the possibility of the journey, Andrea told General Pepe: "If this cannot be brought about, the man who worked so much for his own glory and for that of the nation to which we have the honor to belong will have to end his days far from the place where he was born, far from his friends! But I have hope."

And on August 17, the sextet of physicians signed the following statement:

The undersigned physicians are of the opinion, to the number of four against two, that despite the mishaps that the journey can bring about, M. Donizetti can be transported to Milan if all proper precautions be taken;

The minority, composed of Messieurs the Doctors Andral and Calmeil, fearing that the journey can be detrimental, think that it will be preferable that M. Donizetti remain in Paris.

Paris, August 17, 1847   Fossati, Chomel, Rostan,
                                          Mitivié, Andral, Calmeil.

In the very long letter (September 8, 1847) recounting the events from August 17 through the first week of September which Andrea Donizetti wrote to Leo Herz, he said: "Monsieur Doctor Béhier, police physician, at once came to me to declare, in impassioned language and with despotic manners, that he is opposed to my uncle's departure! . . . Not recognizing his right to meddle in my family's affairs, even though he came to my place representing Monsieur the Prefect, I paid no attention whatever to what he said, doubtless in the interests of the sick man. While rendering justice to his talent, it is nevertheless permissible for me to think that he could very well be mistaken both as a man and as a physician." Further—and it is impossible not to wonder what motive the police can have had for wanting to keep Donizetti in Paris—Béhier appears to have submitted a stronger version of the minority report to Andrea. This document, signed by Dr. Calmeil, reads:

M. Gaetan Donizetti has now reached the final period of general paralysis. Thanks to his robust constitution, to the intelligent care, to the detailed attention with which he has not for an instant failed to be surrounded, his

9 See Appendixes, p. 279, for the declaration on Donizetti's condition and the advisability of moving him made on August 4, 1847, by the Milanese physician Giovanni Antonio Lorenzo Fossati.

264)

physical health has held up while his intelligence and his mental powers have been eclipsed and the principal movements of his body and his members have been made almost impossible.

His family, in its solicitude, has selected for him in a beautiful and agreeable quarter, a well-aired habitation at the gate of promenades and of the country, communicating with a garden on the same level. It is there, in my view, that what is most reasonable can be done for a poor invalid placed in the conditions in which M. Donizetti is found, and it is precisely because it seems to me that there almost all that which, humanly speaking, one could desire for the preservation and well-being of M. Gaetan has been assembled, that I have thought it my duty to insist for more than a month to M. André Donizetti that he should resign himself to letting his uncle end his existence in a place in which his days flow away, in a place free of all shock, of all commotion.

I understand that M. Donizetti's family must have the desire to have him see again his country, his natal town; I feel that it is painful for them to see M. Gaetan being extinguished far from his haunts, I feel how much it must cost the devotion of a brother,[10] of a nephew, to establish themselves permanently with an invalid when other affections impose other more or less imperious duties upon them. But these considerations, these inconveniences, which one must deplore, are not the work of men. And they are at least attenuated in my eyes when I think that, in order to remedy them, it would be necessary to expose M. Gaetan to all the eventualities of a journey as long as it would be painful.

I swear it, I would not find enough daring to advise the removal of M. Donizetti at the hour he has reached; I picture his brain as channeled by many centers of destruction. I believe that the membranes and the cerebral cavities are either infiltrated or distended by surges of serosity.[11]

The medulla oblongata itself seems to me to be injured; well, all that is needed to bring on a fatal result in such cases is a shock.

Each day, paralytics entirely as robust as Donizetti pass from life to death in the batting of an eye, and one scarcely has left them in appearance full of resistance when one learns that they have died. How regrettable it will be for his family if this happens to Donizetti in the middle of a public highway!

I well know that everything that is to be feared may not happen, that in a strict sense M. Donizetti can be struck down equally in his bed, in his chair, but from the moment at which Donizetti is removed from his habits of calm, from a regularity that leaves nothing for which to envy opulence, opinion will be found to reprove and to blame.

Paris, August 23, 1847   Calmeil.

This report was precisely what the prefect of police had been wanting to read: he now at once notified Andrea by letter that Doni-

[10] Francesco Donizetti, who had reached Paris on July 12.
[11] The findings of the autopsy performed upon Donizetti's body more than tended to confirm Dr. Calmeil's belief. See Appendixes, pp. 288–90.

zetti must not be removed from Paris. The situation thus became exactly what it had been at Ivry. The police, believing that Andrea Donizetti was capable of trying to remove his uncle from Paris by stealth, on August 26 posted agents in the concierge's quarters of the house at No. 6 avenue Chateaubriand. The next day, when an attempt was made to take Donizetti out for his accustomed carriage ride, these men prevented his leaving the house.

The background and significance of these police actions—perhaps well-intentioned, but certainly highhanded and arbitrary—cannot now be determined. Possibly the prefect and his assistants were acting in all good faith, convinced that to take Donizetti on the long journey to Italy would be equivalent to signing his death warrant. But not to speculate that the police were acting under some sort of pressure is humanly impossible. Who, then, would have had powerful reasons for wishing to keep Donizetti in Paris—even to make certain that he would die there rather than in Bergamo? Auguste and Zélie de Coussy—he, as Donizetti's banker, with some dishonest intention of manipulating the funds on deposit and accruing with him, she for amorous or sexual reasons? No shred of evidence answers this speculation affirmatively. Léon Pillet or others connected directly or indirectly with the Opéra, in some frantic eagerness not to let go of the unfinished opera, *Le Duc d'Albe*? This equally seems unlikely, particularly in view of what can be discovered and surmised of the character of Pillet, who, in any case, is likely to have known that the autograph of the incomplete opera was no longer in Paris, but had been taken to Bergamo. Countess Sophie von Löwenstein, wanting to keep Donizetti out of the immediate control and surveillance of his family because of its unfriendliness to her? This is sheer fictionizing. And, in any case, what basis would there be for supposing that the Countess would have been able to suborn the prefect of the Paris police even if she had wanted to? That the actions of the police now appear peculiar is true. Everything else is completely unsupported speculation.

Now really desperate, Andrea Donizetti decided that he must have recourse to the law. He consulted three eminent advocates—Marié, Adolphe Crémieux, and Antoine Berryer—as to what rights he, as the designated representative of Donizetti's family, had in the matter. They confirmed his belief that he should take the matter to court and stiffened his resistance to the actions of the police. In a letter of September 8 to Leo Herz in Vienna, Andrea wrote: "I have had the honor more recently to write several letters to Monsieur the Prefect of Police and to tell him that it was impossible for me to admit Monsieur Doctor Béhier to my house; but at the same time I did not refuse a final consultation held by the official physicians at his wish, it being foreseen that M. Mitivié would take part. . . . Despite that, Monsieur Béhier came again, the sixth of this month, to visit my uncle—on the part of Monsieur the Prefect, he said. I was within my right in opposing the visit, and that is what I did."

In the meantime, Andrea had been writing accounts of these events to his father in Constantinople. And on August 16, Giuseppe Donizetti had forwarded a detailed memorandum of the situation to Count Sturmer, the Austrian Minister Plenipotentiary at Constantinople, begging him to use his good offices to persuade the Imperial government at Vienna to take steps to effect Donizetti's release from France.[12]

Count Sturmer's intervention finally produced the desired result. Precise instructions soon were dispatched from Vienna to the Austrian embassy in Paris. It quickly became evident that sufficient pressure from above could brush aside the police officials who virtually had been keeping Donizetti a prisoner in a foreign country. As Guido Zavadini wrote (138, 156): "It is impossible in fact to understand the arbitrary motives for which they did not wish to let Donizetti return to his own country, or what recondite purposes were hidden under those hateful restrictions. Donizetti was an Austrian subject. He belonged to the Imperial Household as *maestro compositore di corte*, as which he was looked upon as belonging to the ranks of the Aulic councillors. The government to which he was subject, then, had every right to intervene and to make its will prevail. Diplomatic practices at once produced the desired effect, and a few days sufficed to free Donizetti from this new species of imprisonment, after that of Ivry, and thus finally to make it possible for him to see the sky of his own country again."

Giuseppe Donizetti was unable to leave Constantinople at this time, perhaps because of his wife's illness, perhaps for official reasons. He may, additionally, have had by then what appears to have been justified faith in his son's ability to represent the family's interests in Paris. On July 12, however, Donizetti's other brother, Francesco—who never before had been more than a few miles from Bergamo except perhaps when in military service—had reached Paris, perhaps by Giuseppe's orders, perhaps sent for by Andrea, but in any case there to assist in the complex enterprise of transporting Gaetano to Bergamo by carriage.

[12] For the text of this letter, see Appendixes, pp. 282–84.

At noon on September 19, 1847, Donizetti set out from Paris on what was to prove a seventeen-day trip to Bergamo. With him traveled his brother Francesco, his nephew Andrea, Dr. Rendu, and his nurse-custodian Antoine Pourcelot. The party went by train to Amiens, reaching there at four-thirty that afternoon. Thence they proceeded to Brussels, reaching there at nine o'clock that night.[13] On September 21, from Brussels, Andrea Donizetti wrote to Giovanni Ricordi:

Dear Ricordi,
    Undoubtedly you will be pleased to receive news of my unhappy uncle Gaetano. Here it is, and official.
    "Donizetti made the first part of the trip well enough. We left Paris at noon to reach Amiens at four-thirty. Donizetti was not at all tired; he took a little bit of exercise in his room and dined with a good appetite. We left Paris on the Chemin de Fer du Nord." Doctor Rendu.
    "September 19, 1847, Brussels, evening. The trip from Amiens to Brussels went off without incidents. Donizetti dined with good appetite and passed a good night." Doctor Rendu.
    If this letter of mine is published in your paper, I authorize you to say that you received the above news from me. Your most affectionate
                                                            Andrea Donizetti.

From Brussels, in two carriages—Dr. Rendu riding with Donizetti —the party moved on across Belgium and Germany to Switzerland, where they crossed the St. Gotthard Pass. At some stop along the way, a carriage going in the opposite direction met them. From it, Alfredo Piatti, the noted cellist, whose father, Antonio, had gone to school with Donizetti in Bergamo, stared into the interior of the carriage in which Donizetti was riding. He saw the sick man enveloped in a mantle, his head sunk onto his chest. Around him were other men, their faces showing affectionate anxiety, a concentration of melancholy thoughts.

The two carriages reached Bellinzona on October 4, Como the next day. As originally laid out, the itinerary had called for them to continue on to Bergamo by way of Milan. But Dr. Rendu now suggested that, instead, they take the shorter road from Como by way of Lecco. This they did, reaching Bergamo on the evening of October 6, when they drew up outside the Countess Rosa Rota-Basoni's palace in the Contrada San Cassiano (since renamed Via Donizetti) in the upper town. There they were welcomed by the mayor and, more personally, by Rosa and Giovanna Rota-Basoni, Marco Bonesi, and Antonio Dolci.

[13] Donizetti's carriage apparently had been sent ahead to await them in Brussels. Maurice-Pierre Boyé (22) wrote: *"Le plus terrible [incident] fut la second attaque qui foudroya Donizetti à Bruxelles, la première remontant au 17 août 1843."* I have found no other reference to this incident or to an attack on August 17, 1843.

The next day, Dr. Rendu, who had made careful notations of Donizetti's reactions along the way, wrote out a summary report: "Donizetti passed a good enough night. This morning his physiognomy is good, and he seems to have felt no fatigue from the trip. It would be difficult to detect a change in Donizetti's state of health. That state seems to be the same in every way as that in which the patient was found before leaving Paris, and I remain convinced that the journey was in no way prejudicial to Donizetti. Bergamo, morning of October 7, 1847."[14] Very soon after Donizetti had reached Bergamo, he was visited by Michele Novaro, who had sung in the *première* of *Maria di Rohan* at Vienna in June 1843. Novaro (quoted in *115*, 34) wrote that he saw before him "the ruins of a pallid, thin man, weak in all his members, held up under the arm by two attendants who tried to move a few steps someone who was no more than the shadow of a living man."

Soon, his second mission accomplished, Andrea Donizetti left on the return trip to Constantinople,[15] leaving his uncle in the lavish, affectionate care of the two devoted Basoni women. Day after day thereafter, Donizetti sat in a wing-backed chair, his body leaning to the left,[16] his chin sunk slackly onto his chest, his hands firmly clenched, one of them at first always clutching a handkerchief, both of them in constant danger of being torn by his fingernails. He spoke very rarely, uttering only occasional monosyllables, and mostly he appeared to be quite unaware of what was occurring around him. On a few occasions, Giovannina Basoni seated herself at the Bösendorfer piano that he had ordered in Vienna and, to her own accompaniment, sang one or another aria from one of his operas. On some of these occasions, those watching him, including Dr. Cassis, were delighted to notice that he seemed to be listening to her singing and enjoying it. But Antonio Vasselli wrote Andrea Donizetti that Giovanni Battista Rubini had

[14] See Appendixes, pp. 284–88, for (1) the declaration made to the Bergamo Tribunal on October 10, 1847, by Rosa and Giovannina Basoni and two officials; (2) a summary report and consultation on Donizetti's condition signed at Bergamo on October 11 by Dr. Rendu and the two local physicians in attendance, G. Cassis and L. Calvetti; (3) a report on Donizetti's mental condition signed at Bergamo on October 14, 1847, by Doctors Calvetti, Zendrini, and Longaretti; (4) Andrea Donizetti's declaration of October 15 to the Bergamo Tribunal.

[15] In 1858, Andrea Donizetti married Giuseppina Gabuzzi, by whom he had two sons, Giuseppe (1859–1942) and Gaetano (1861–194?). He himself died in the insane asylum at Aversa, near Naples, on February 11, 1864, at the age of only forty-five and was buried in the plot of the Neapolitan cemetery of Poggioreale which contains the tomb of Virginia Donizetti.

[16] Because Donizetti leaned forward and to the left, an extension was built out from the right wing of the chair to afford a resting place for his head. Discrepancies in published reports, some of which have him leaning to the left, some to the right, result from some writers referring to Donizetti's right and left side, others to the right and left sides as one looked at him face on.

visited Bergamo and had joined Giovannina Basoni in the duet from *Lucia di Lammermoor* and that Donizetti had given no sign of recognition whatever. Still, fleeting intimations that his consciousness had not been obliterated totally and finally appear to have misled some of those near him into believing in a slight improvement in his mental condition. Thus he passed his fiftieth birthday, November 29, 1847.

In February 1848, Donizetti suffered an attack of "fever," but appeared to recover from it. Both Dr. Cassis and Antonio Dolci (who held no grudge against Andrea Donizetti, despite Giovannina Basoni's aspersions) sent regular, almost daily reports on the dying man's condition to both Giuseppe and Andrea Donizetti in Constantinople. Now he was scarcely more than a peaceable, inert, wasted body. On March 31, Dolci went to Milan to make arrangements with two doctors named De Filippi and Piantanida to come to Bergamo to examine the invalid. Reporting this on April 3 to Giuseppe Donizetti, Dolci continued: "Scarcely had I returned on April 1 when I was summoned to see him in a hurry, and found him seized by an extraordinary contraction of the eyes, with swallowing rendered almost entirely impossible, with a contraction of the right angle of his mouth, with cessation of all motion in the right arm and leg—in short, with the symptoms of serous apoplexy, which, with grave danger to his life, still have not abated. Today this morbid condition is associated with a very burning fever and profuse sweats. Twice leeches were applied to his head, and a good five or six times it was irritated externally by means of the application of repeated mustard plasters and of a full vesicant. Nothing, or almost nothing, can be introduced into his stomach because of the impediment to swallowing and because of the contraction of his muscles, which keeps his teeth clenched. You will see, then, that the unhappy Maestro is reduced to a much worse state by an unforeseen increase of his malady."

Now Dolci wrote to Giuseppe Donizetti every day.[17] One day Gaetano was a trifle better; another day he suffered from a torrid fever that no treatment would diminish. One day he would take a spoonful of broth; another day they would be unable to pry apart his jaws. On April 4, his condition seemed so desperate that a priest remained with him throughout the night. The Basoni women, the servant Antoine Pourcelot, and the unwearying Dolci scarcely left his side. On April 6, it was necessary to "practice indirect feeding on him." Frequently he had convulsions.

The ultimate death struggle began on the evening of April 7, and

[17] See Appendixes, pp. 291–93; for Giovanna Basoni's letter to Margherita Tizzoni delle Sedie, describing Donizetti's last days.

at five-thirty in the afternoon on April 8, Donizetti died—held, it was said, in the arms of Antonio Dolci.

"The announcement of his death spread rapidly through Bergamo," Annibale Gabrielli wrote (*58*, 139), "but exactly during those days, the army of Carlo Alberto had entered Lombardy! And at Paris, Louis-Philippe had ceased to reign, and at Vienna rioting in the streets continued after the uprising of March 13. Thus the death of Gaetano Donizetti passed almost unnoticed outside the circle of his most affectionate townsfolk."

Donizetti was buried, not in the Neapolitan cemetery of Poggioreale, where Virginia's tomb stood, but in Bergamo, in the chapel of the noble Pezzoli family in the Cemetery of Valtesse. In *Derniers Souvenirs d'un musicien*, Adolphe Adam quoted this letter, sent to him by the nurse-custodian Antoine Pourcelot: "The excellent M. Dolci organized everything and neglected nothing to render the funeral worthy of the great man. More than four thousand people attended. The procession was made up of many of the Bergamo clergy, of the most important personages of the town and the suburbs, and of the entire civil guard of the town and the outlying areas. The muskets, blended with the lights of three or four hundred torches, gave it an imposing aspect. It was all animated by three bodies of military music and favored by the most beautiful weather in the world. The service began at ten o'clock in the morning, and the ceremony ended at two-thirty. By the statements of the inhabitants of Bergamo, no such honors ever have been rendered to any personage of that town."[18]

Twenty-seven years later, in September 1875, Donizetti's remains were exhumed at Valtesse and, with those of Mayr, deposited in the church of Santa Maria Maggiore, under monuments already erected there.[19] At the exhumation, the discovery was made that the cap of his skull was missing. An investigation was started immediately and quickly resulted in its recovery. A Dr. Gerolamo Carchen, who had been attached to the insane asylum at nearby Astino, it was discovered,

---

[18] For the text of the report on the autopsy performed upon Donizetti's body on April 11, see Appendixes, pp. 288–90.

[19] The Donizetti monument, by the sculptor Vincenzo Velz, had been erected at the orders of Francesco and Giuseppe Donizetti. It had been inaugurated while Giuseppe still lived, on June 16, 1855, in the presence of Andrea Donizetti. The inscription on it now reads: "To Gaetano Donizetti/fecund troubadour of sacred and profane melodies/His brothers Giuseppe and Francesco/With affection place/this monument/1875." By 1875, the only surviving Donizettis of Gaetano's branch of the family were two grandnephews, Andrea's sons, Giuseppe and Gaetano.

had made away with this piece of bone.[20] Now his heirs were approached. They willingly gave up the memento, of which they had known only that it was part of the skull of a well-known man. The cap was brought together with the rest of Donizetti's remains and found to fit the skull, but was not reburied with them. Instead, it was placed in an urn, where it remained another seventy-five years, one of the most astonishing of the memorabilia, souvenirs, manuscripts, and other objects housed in the Museo Donizettiano at Bergamo. Perhaps the most astonishing of them still is there: the long-tailed black wool coat in which Donizetti was buried in 1848, and which was (to quote Guido Zavadini in *140*) "recovered almost intact, at the time of the exhumation of the remains in the Cemetery of Valtesse (1875)."

The fascination with Donizetti's remains was not exhausted by the autopsy or that first exhumation. In July 1951, the Municipal Council of Bergamo decided that the cap of their fellow townsman's skull ought to be inserted into the coffin containing his other remains. On the afternoon of July 26, in the solemn presence of a small group of officials and Church authorities, the tomb in Santa Maria Maggiore was unsealed, the outer casket of copper opened, and the cover of the inner, wooden coffin removed. The cap of Donizetti's skull had been brought from the Museo Donizettiano. The members of the official committee noted, as reported by one of its members, Camillo Fumagalli (*56a*), that the piece of bone still fitted into the rest of the skull perfectly. Resisting the expressed wish of one of its members that a photograph be taken of the remains and that of another member that the glass tube in the coffin be opened so that the parchment it contained might be read, the committee merely watched while the eighty-three-year-old Guido Zavadini—who had devoted much of a lifetime to Donizetti research, and whose sensations and thoughts on this occasion must have been strange and intense—attached the cap to the rest of the skull with three pieces of transparent adhesive tape. The remains then were covered with a fresh piece of hand-washed linen. The coffin and then the copper casket were closed and resealed, and the much-disturbed physical remains of Gaetano Donizetti were restored to the quiet of their tomb.

[20] Souvenir hunters had been busy even at the original autopsy. When Cesare Vigna obtained for Verdi's autograph collection some letters that Donizetti had written to Agostino Perotti, he sent with them, in his words, "a little lock of Donizetti's hair which was cut from his hair at the autopsy performed by several of my physician friends."

APPENDIXES

Personal Documents

Genealogical Tables

THE DONIZETTI AND VASSELLI FAMILIES

THE following genealogical tables do not pretend to completeness, but only to the presentation of as much information as could be derived from published sources and from documented inferences. Thus, the statement that an individual married and had four children should not be taken to mean that the couple had only four children: it means that references to only four children were encountered. The invaluable basic source of the data in *The Donizetti Family* below was the genealogical table in Ciro Caversazzi's *Gaetano Donizetti: La Casa dove nacque, La Famiglia, L'Inizio della malattia* (Bergamo, 1924), for my copy of which I wish to thank Maestro Giuseppe Cesati, Curator of the Museo Donizettiano, Bergamo, who kindly sent it to me as a gift.

HERBERT WEINSTOCK

The Donizetti Family

IN the following genealogical table, each name is *preceded* by a parenthetic Arabic numeral in italic; this numeral is repeated at each reference to that individual. Each name is *followed* by a Roman numeral giving the number of generations in descent from the earliest-known ancestor, Francesco Donizetti.

(*1*) Francesco Donizetti had a grandson,
(*2*) Ambrogio Donizetti (III, 1732?–97), who married:

first, (*3*) Rosalinda Cereda (?-1767), by whom he had four children—
   (*4*) Francesco Andrea (IV, 1759-61)
   (*5*) Giovanni (IV, 1761-1832)
   (*6*) Maddalena (IV, 1763-?)
   (*7*) Andrea (IV, 1765-1835)
second, (*8*) Maria Gregis (?-1784), by whom he had nine children—
   (*9*) Giacomo Antonio (IV, 1769-84)
   (*10*) and (*11*) the twins (*10*) Domenico (IV, 1771-?) and (*11*) Maddalena (IV, 1771-?)
   (*12*) Maria Margherita (IV, b. & d. 1773)
   (*13*) Antonio Giuseppe (IV, b & d. 1774)
   (*14*) Angela (IV, 1776-1816)
   (*15*) and (*16*) the twins (*15*) Giuseppe Giovanni (IV, 1779-?) and (*16*) Maria Annunciata (IV, 1779-?)
   (*17*) Giuseppe Antonio (IV, 1781-1825)
(*5*) Giovanni Donizetti (IV) married (*18*) Angela Piazzoli, by whom he had three children—
   (*19*) Ambrogio (V, 1803-60)
   (*20*) unnamed (V, b. & d. 1805)
   (*21*) Maria Rosalinda (V, 1807-?)
(*7*) Andrea Donizetti (IV) married (*22*) Domenica Nava (1765?-1836), by whom he had six children—
   (*23*) Giuseppe (V, 1788-1856)
   (*24*) Maria Rosalinda (V, 1790-1811)
   (*25*) Francesco (V, 1792-1848)
   (*26*) Maria Antonia (V, 1795-1823)
   (*27*) DOMENICO GAETANO MARIA (V, 1797-1848)
   (*28*) Maria Rachele (V, b. & d. 1800)
(*6*) Maddalena Donizetti (IV) married (*29*) Giacomo Carminati
(*14*) Angela Donizetti (IV) married (*30*) Giacomo Corini
(*19*) Ambrogio Donizetti (V) married (*31*) Giovanna Sonzogni, by whom he had three children—
   (*32*) Angela (VI, 1838-?)
   (*33*) Anna Maria Adelaide (VI, 1840-49)
   (*34*) Giovanni (VI, 1844-87)
(*34*) Giovanni Donizetti (VI) married (*35*) Maria Rota, by whom he had two children—
   (*36*) Annetta (VII, 1873-?)
   (*37*) Cesare (VII, 1879-?)
(*23*) Giuseppe Donizetti (V) married (*38*) Angela Tondi (who after his death took as her second husband Giuseppe Salvadori), by whom he had one child—[1]
   (*39*) Andrea (VI, 1818-64)
(*39*) Andrea Donizetti (VI) married (*40*) Giuseppina Gabuzzi, by whom he had two children—
   (*41*) Giuseppe (VII, 1859-1942)
   (*42*) Gaetano (VII, 1861-before 1942)

[1] See the Foreword, p. xii, for the possible existence of a second child, Marianna.

(*41*) Giuseppe Donizetti (vii) married first (*43*) Maria Ferro, second (*44*) Eugenia Micci Labruna

(*42*) Gaetano Donizetti (vii) married (*45*) Ortensia Huroch

(*26*) Maria Antonia Donizetti (v) married (*46*) Giovanni Battista Tironi

(*27*) DOMENICO GAETANO MARIA DONIZETTI (v) married (*47*) Anna Virginia Vasselli (1808-37), by whom he had three children—

    (*48*) Filippo Francesco (vi, b. & d. 1829)

    (*49*) unnamed girl (vi, b. & d. 1836)

    (*50*) unnamed boy (vi, b. & d. 1837)

The Vasselli Family

IN this sketch for a genealogical table, each name is preceded by a parenthetic Arabic numeral in italic; this numeral is repeated at each reference to that individual. Each name is followed by a Roman numeral giving the number of generations in descent from the earliest-known ancestor, Luigi Vasselli.

(*1*) Luigi Vasselli (1768 or 1770-1832) married (*2*) Rosa Costanti (1768?-), by whom he had one child

    (*3*) Antonio (ii, 1795-1870), known as Totò

    (*4*) Francesco (ii, 1800-?)

    (*5*) Gaetano (ii, 1806-?)

    (*6*) Anna Virginia (ii, 1808-37)

(*3*) Antonio Vasselli (ii) married (*7*) Isabella Marchetti[1] (1818?-1903?), by whom he had one child—

    (*8*) Virginia (iii)

(*8*) Virginia Vasselli (iii) married a Gabrielli, by whom she had one child—

    (*9*) Annibale[2] (iv)

(*4*) Francesco Vasselli (ii) married (*10*) Serafina Smaghi (1803?-   )

(*5*) Gaetano Vasselli (ii) married and had one child—

    (*11*) Irene (iii)

(*6*) Anna Virginia Vasselli (ii) married DOMENICO GAETANO MARIA DONIZETTI (see *27* above, in *The Donizetti Family*)

The Record of Donizetti's Baptism

THE entry regarding Donizetti's baptism in the parish records at the Church of Santa Grata in Vites, Bergamo, reads:

---

[1] Isabella Marchetti was the daughter of a woman named Rosa Marchetti, who also had a daughter named Rosa.

[2] Annibale Gabrielli was the author of *Gaetano Donizetti: Biografia* (see Bibliography, *57*, *58*).

Parocia Sanctae Gratae inter Vites.

Bergomi 3 Xmbris 1797.

Dominicus Cajetanus Maria filius Andreae Donizetti ed Dominicae Nava Legitimum Iugalium natus die 29 9bris in hoc suburbio, hodie baptizzatus a me Antonio Mauro Bonzi Praeposito. — Patrino Dominico Iraina ex Zanica.

(Parish of Santa Grata in Vites.

Bergamo, December 3, 1797.

Domenico Gaetano Maria, son of Andrea Donizetti and Domenica Nava, legitimate spouses, born the day November 29 in this suburb, today baptized by me, Antonio Mauro Bonzi, rector. — Godfather, Domenico Iraina ex Zanica.)

The Record of Donizetti's Marriage to Anna Virginia Vasselli

THE registration of Donizetti's marriage long was searched for in vain in the churches of Rome. It finally was found accidentally in the *Libro dei matrimonii* of the Parish of Santa Maria in Via—listed under the letter B because the composer's name had been miswritten as Bonizetti. On the back of folio 16 in the *Libro dei matrimonii* for the years 1825 to 1830 at Santa Maria in Vita, the following appears:

Die prima junii anno millesimo octigentesimo vigesimo octavo dispensatis denunciationibus, nulloque detecto impedimento de licentia Ill.mi et R.mi D. D. Josephi Della Porta Patriarchae Constantinopolis et Vicesgerentis in urbe, habita per acta D. Francisci Gaudenzi not. sub die 31 maji proxime elapsi quam apud me servo, ego infrascriptus parochus de mane in hac ecclesia parochialis ad altare SS. Annuntiatae interrogavi Ill.mum D. Dominicum Cajetanum Bonizetti filium D. Andreae e civitate Bergomi a paucis diebus Romae commorantem, et honestum puellam Ill.mam D. Annam Virginiam Vasselli filiam D. Aloysii romanam ex hac paroecia, et habito eorum muto consensu per verba de praesenti eos in matrimonium conjunxi juxta ritum etc. et Trid. Conc. praesentibus notis testibus Joanne Baptista Zampi ab urbe veteri filio q. Philippi ex paroeciae S. Mariae in Aquiro, et D. Antonio Vasselli romano filio D. Aloysio, et fratre sponsae hujus paroeciae solemnia completa fuere.

Ita est Fr. Francis. Ant. Philippi, parochus S. Mariae in Viam.

(On the first day of June 1828, dispensed from banns and with no impediment discovered, with permission of the Illustrious and Most Reverend Doctor of Divinity Giuseppe della Porta, Patriarch of Constantinople and Vice-regent in this city, under the seal of Don Francesco Gaudenzi, notarized on the 31st of May just past, which record I hold, I, the undersigned parish priest, this morning in this parish church, at the altar of the Most Holy

Annunciation, questioned the Most Illustrious Don Domenico Gaetano Bonizetti, son of Don Andrea of the city of Bergamo, who was staying a few days in Rome, and the virtuous Donna Anna Virginia Vasselli, daughter of Don Luigi of Rome and of this parish, and, having obtained their mutual consent by word of mouth, at that very time joined them in marriage according to the rites, etc., of the Council of Trent, in the presence of the known witnesses, Giovanni Battista Zampi of the Old City and son of Filippo of the Parish of Santa Maria in Aquiro, and Don Antonio Vasselli of Rome, son of Don Luigi and brother of the bride, of this parish, the solemnities were completed.

So be it. Father Francesco Antonio Filippi, parish priest of
Santa Maria in Via.)

Declaration Made by
Dr. Giovanni Antonio Lorenzo Fossati, August 4, 1847

I just have visited my very old friend M. Gaetan Donizetti, who is now to be found on the ground floor of a handsome house situated in one of the most beautiful quarters of Paris, No. 6 avenue Chateaubriand, a healthful and well-aired house with a very agreeable garden.

The condition of the ailing man is that which has been recognized and diagnosed by all the physicians who have visited him up to now: he is in a state of complete insanity, with general paralysis. Nevertheless, the functions of the vegetative life are preserved in good state; he eats, he digests well, and the nutrition operates sufficiently, for he is not noticeably thin, given the duration of the illness.

I have been asked the question if, knowing his present state, it will be possible to transport him to Italy. If all possible precautions are taken to avoid violent shocks, the heat, etc., which could be damaging to him, I think that the invalid could stand the journey, as he is able to promenade in a carriage for three or four hours each day; but nobody can guarantee that an accident will not take place during the journey, for he must look forward to a sad end, unhappily inevitable, sooner or later. Despite that, if he were my brother,[1] I should not hesitate to take him with me, and my conscience would not reproach me even if the sorrow of losing him should come upon me a short time after my arrival.

Paris, August 4, 1847   Dr. Fossati.

---

[1] Had this written declaration been requested by Francesco Donizetti? Or was it, perhaps, intended for forwarding to Giuseppe Donizetti in Constantinople?

Declaration of Maestro Antonio Dolci
to the Tribunale di Bergamo, August 15, 1847

IN my infancy, I came to know Gaetano Donizetti, with whom I was a fellow student while learning my first musical lessons. He was born in this city of parents of low condition. From the age of sixteen or seventeen, already very deep in his art, he began to move about the various provinces of the Lombardo-Veneto Kingdom, and first at Mantua and Venice. And it can be said that he had no fixed home from that epoch forward, for in case of necessity he carried his home with him, to one city in order to write musical works, to another to attend to the staged productions of his operas. His truly extraordinary genius quickly made him famous throughout Europe and at the courts of kings; he came to be summoned to the most important capital cities, and his compositions—which besides rendering him famous, earned him a considerable fortune—were appreciated with much pleasure everywhere. At times I was made aware of this prosperous state of his fortunes through letters, sometimes verbally during his visits to his homeland—but, however, without taking any special part in his activities.

A great man because of his extraordinary talent, he was not, as I see it, very careful about his interests. And even when far from home, he did not forget his parents, to whom he intermittently made visits and contributions, and to whom I myself often made advances for him, amounts that I always was repaid in full. They being in bad financial straits while he was, I think, in Naples, I remember his having written me that his parents had no means, and I can testify that nothing more was to be claimed from their estate than a gold box that he had given his father.

From about the age of thirty on, he did not return to Bergamo except for short stays, one could say to visit his friends, and for the most part he made long stays in Paris, in Naples—where he also had a residence of his own—in Rome, and elsewhere, and always with the object of his productions, of which very many of great prestige could be enumerated. Between the years 1840 and 1842, Donizetti was summoned to Vienna, and there was appointed *maestro di camera e di corte* to His Majesty the Emperor, with an annual stipend of twelve thousand Austrian lire, and with the obligation to remain there only six months of each year and to compose some music, whereas during the other six months he was free to go wherever he pleased, and thus could always occupy himself with composing music. During some meetings in which we talked, he told me that besides the stipend mentioned, he could count on receiving from eight hundred to a thousand francs per month from Paris theaters, for which reason—if these emoluments be considered together with others that he received from other theaters of Europe—he must have formed a considerable fortune. But I do not find myself in any position to indicate, even approximately, the size of it. I do, however, know that, though not very watchful of his own interests—so that I believe that he would entrust his capital on faith and without guarantee—he was not a great spender, and I therefore hold that he must have saved not inconsiderable amounts.

In this city he has a brother named Francesco, who now is in Paris to assist the unfortunate man and to arrange his transportation to his native soil; he has another brother, named Giuseppe, in Constantinople, and that one has sent his son, named Andrea, to Paris, also to interest himself in his uncle's removal.

Once before, and that shortly after he learned about the misfortune of the sickness and about the passive state of his [uncle's] faculties, Andrea Donizetti of Constantinople went to Paris to visit him and to find out about his affairs. During that meeting, he was able to determine that the unhappy man's wish was to return to Italy, but whenever he tried to take steps to transport him here, he always encountered obstacles set up by the prefecture of police, which, for reasons that I do not know, opposed the departure.

In September 1846, Andrea Donizetti, having left Paris, came to Bergamo. He informed me of his uncle's sad state and what had been done for him. On that occasion, he, in company with his uncle Francesco, interested me in taking on deposit two packages, one of which they told me contained music, whereas the other consisted of a small box, very familiar to me, in which Donizetti Gaetano kept his decorations, gifts, and medals of honor, objects that Andrea said he had brought from Paris, having decided on this confidential consignment because of his feeling that maybe the maestro, recovering the use of his intellectual faculties, might ask for an accounting of these effects and of their having been removed to a place where they might not get lost. Given the bonds of friendship by which we have been joined, I almost felt that by receiving that deposit I was doing a work that would please the unhappy man. And in fact, on September 27, 1846, I accepted from Andrea and Francesco Donizetti two sealed packages consisting of one small box and one bundle, but without effectively knowing what they contained, having received everything under seal and without any other responsibility whatever.

On April 2 of this year, having come to Bergamo again, Andrea Donizetti, in accord with his uncle Francesco, came to me and opened the larger package, extracting from it a book containing the poetry of the *dramma Le Duc d'Albe*. Under that circumstance, I saw that the package itself contained music composed by Gaetano Donizetti for that same *dramma*, and they, after having sealed everything again, again left the bundle and the small box on deposit with me.

On August 24[1] of this year, I received a letter from Paris, from the above named Andrea and Francesco Donizetti, who charged me to forward the package of music in a careful way. And as the letter was signed by both of them, and I had instructions not to consign anything to anyone aside from those two, I immediately sent them the package because they had asked for its prompt transmission, and in the letter had informed me that

---

[1] An error, probably for July 24 (Francesco Donizetti was in Paris before that date). Dolci, it must be remembered, was making the present deposition on August 15.

this musical production already was sold to a publisher [Schönenberger].

At present I find myself in possession only of the small box, the contents of which I do not know, but which I believe to be the decorations, and I shall be prompt to submit it when it is asked of me by the Tribunal.

I can report these details out of my own direct knowledge, and it may be that I shall be able to describe other circumstances when I am asked to.

In later letters received from Paris, it has been indicated to me that new plans for the transportation of the unhappy man to this city are being put into action. I know that not many days ago a consultation of six leading Paris physicians was held on the condition of the sick man.[2] But very little hope was furnished me, and I also was told that if nature does not work, the remedies of science can do nothing favorable.

As for me, I am disposed, if it be required, to assume the duty of trustee for the unhappy Gaetano, it being clearly understood that I shall be free to seek consultation with persons who can advise me in the carrying out of such a duty; and as soon as this Tribunal thinks to ask such a duty of me, so quickly will I make the application, so that I may help in trying to obtain the removal of the person, in the hope that the air of this, his country, can assist in the recovery of his health, or at least in the improvement of it, and that his custody and upkeep—should the malady come to be prolonged—thus can be reduced greatly, knowing that up to now, according to letters received from Paris, excessive expenses have been contracted for him.

As the last thing, I shall add that Gaetano Donizetti is a Knight of the Order of the Iron Crown, conferred upon him by His Majesty the Emperor of Austria, and that he also was honored with other distinguished orders by other states.

Bergamo, August 15, 1847   Antonio Dolci.

Petition of Giuseppe Donizetti to the Austrian Ambassador at Constantinople, August 16, 1847

To His Excellency *il Signor* Count von Sturmer, Knight Grand Cross of Various Orders, Internunzio and Minister Plenipotentiary of His Imperial and Royal Austrian Majesty to the Ottoman Porte. Excellency:

About two years have passed since my family was stricken by a cruel disaster in that the person of my unhappy brother, Gaetano Donizetti, was afflicted by a grave infirmity that has no name.

Further, all the remedies administered to the illustrious invalid in Paris were useless; useless the attempts of every sort made in that capital, not only to give him back his whole health, but even, at least, to bring him some alleviation.

Now only a single hope remains of perhaps being able to give a more than slight comfort to the invalid, that of bringing him back to

[2] See p. 263 for report of this consultation by Andral, Calmeil, Chomel, Fossati, Mitivié, and Rostan.

his birthplace, to breathe the air of his country, to see his relatives and friends in Bergamo again.

[This would be arranged] were it not that the Paris prefecture of police, which appears to take the greatest interest in Gaetano Donizetti's sad situation, persists in making difficulties over consenting to his leaving Paris, as it already was opposed to the same journey last year.

Today, however, the concordant opinion of many physicians who are among the first in Paris is that such a journey can be undertaken without a shadow of danger.

To this end, the consulting physicians have taken all the reports into careful consideration, the conditions and precautions that should accompany the above-mentioned journey, the details of which, as sent me from Paris, I sum up.

[He would have] a commodious carriage, in the company of, and with the presence of, a physician and of his nephew Andrea Donizetti (my son), not to mention those of his faithful domestic, who has assisted the invalid during his stay at Ivry, and who still assists him.

The trip from Paris to Basel will be made partly by railroad and partly by steamer on the Rhine. From Basel to Bergamo, overland in short daily stretches.

The hours of travel, the rests, the stopovers of one or more days will be regulated by the physician according to the needs and comfort of the invalid.

Arrived at Bergamo, now that a house convenient in all details has been chosen, he will remain surrounded by the loving care of a brother [Francesco], by the friendly surveillance spontaneously offered him with his personal guarantee by *il Signor* Count G. Lochis, mayor of Bergamo, by the continuous assistance of the same domestic, and by the company of numerous friends whom the invalid has in that city.

And even though his malady has reached a period in which, so the doctors say, hygienic methods alone are required, those of science now being useless, still the best of the Bergamo doctors and, if needed, also the first doctors of Milan, will go to visit him periodically.

Above all, I dare to hope that the High Government of His Imperial Royal Austrian Majesty will deign to give his Excellency the *signor* Ambassador of Austria at Paris the instructions needed to obtain from the competent authorities permission for my unhappy brother's departure.

This hope of mine is founded on the many proofs of solicitude with which the revered government has been pleased to honor the invalid, Gaetano Donizetti, and so that it will deign to take into consideration the reasons that his family has, because the last days of the life of this great artist should come to an end in the place where they had their inception, among his own people, and not among strangers, given that today his journey can be undertaken without any danger.

To that end, I make my most humble prayers to Your Excellency, that you will interpose your good offices before the High Government of His Revered Majesty, with special recommendations that the begged-for instructions to be given to the Ambassador at Paris be sent off at the earliest moment, so that the good weather may permit the undertaking of the journey spoken of, remembering that the shortest delay will cause the loss, perhaps for always, of that thread of hope which persists regarding the removal of the invalid from the cloudy sky of Paris to the smiling city of Bergamo.

Full of faith in the benevolent and powerful intercession of Your Excellency, I have the honor to be, with the most profound respect,

Your Excellency's   Humble and devoted servant,

Constantinople, August 16, 1847   G. Donizetti.

Declaration of the signore *Rosa and Giovannina Rota-Basoni* to the *Tribunale di Bergamo, October 10, 1847*

THE friendship that linked me for so long to the unhappy Maestro Cav. Gaetano Donizetti decided me even earlier to make application so that, brought home, he should be taken to my house, and this always was the liveliest desire also of my daughter Giovannina. It also was seen that my said house, both because of the happy and salubrious location in which it stands and because of the comforts that it could furnish to the illustrious Maestro, could in some way help in his recuperation. With the liveliest pleasure and satisfaction, he was brought from Paris on the sixth of the current month, and it gives me pleasure to be able to say that whereas during the first days he did not show any sign whatever of consciousness, at present there are intervals during which he absolutely induces the conviction that he recognizes being near us and surrounded by the sincere solicitude of friendship.

From time to time my daughter attempts to entertain him on the clavicembalo and with singing, and during these interpellations, he appears to be making an effort to display gratitude. As much for myself as for my daughter, his stay remains highly consoling, and I will say with the maximum truth that we should experience the greatest sorrow if he were to be removed, whether out of persuasion that he probably could not be placed in a more suitable house or situation or because of the conviction that the proximity of the members of our family and of ourselves can only surround him with the greatest moral comfort while his health improves well. I observe to the court that each time that he stayed in Bergamo, he was a guest in this house; that even the servants know him, so that surely nothing seems to him new or displeasing, the more so because the *signor* Maestro Dolci also being very close to us, as to him, in friendship, each day he finds another opportunity to lend his presence with no less friendly zeal. I therefore repeat to the Tribunale not only that I am disposed to have the celebrated Maestro and fine friend as my guest, so that I do not find myself desiring any other arrangement (as I should not dare to consider), but also that it would be the greatest sorrow to me as to my daughter, and we scarcely can yield to the idea that it might be desired to move him, especially in these first moments, seeing that from his residing with our family there is good reason to hope for some absolute improvement.

Bergamo, October 10, 1847

        Rosa Rota-Basoni
        Giovannina   Rota-Basoni
        Casella, counsellor
        Marieni, practitioner.

Report on the State of Donizetti's Health by Doctors Cassis, Calvetti, and Rendu, Bergamo, October 11, 1847

THE undersigned physicians, invited by the family of the illustrious invalid, after having heard the description of the beginnings, the evolution and progress, of the malady, given to them clearly and exactly by *il signor* Dr. Rendu, who accompanied the *signor* Gaetano from Paris all the way to Bergamo; having read and attentively examined the following documents, presented to them by the *signor* Andrea Donizetti, nephew of the invalid:

    1. consultation dated January 28, 1846, signed Calmeil, Mitivié, Ricord;

    2. consultation dated April 7, 1846, signed Foville, Voisin;

    3. consultation dated June 12, 1846, signed Cabarrus, Roche, Fouquier;

    4. report to *il signor* Prefect of Police by the doctors Bonneau, Béhier, Trelat;

    5. consultation dated August 30, 1846, signed Calmeil, Moreau, Ricord;

    6. consultation dated August 17, 1847, signed Andral, Chomel, Rostan, Fossati, Calmeil, Mitivié;

    7. consultation, dated August 13, 1847, signed Calmeil;

having, further, examined attentively the daily bulletins of the journey, presented to them by *il signor* Dr. Rendu;

having diligently observed the invalid both with regard to his moral life and with regard to his involuntary organic functions,

DECLARE

That *signor* Gaetano Donizetti is at present affected by universal paralysis, with abolition of the will and the intelligence, resulting from organic alterations, and probably from serous effusion into the substance and coverings of the large nervous centers, alterations and effusions that, taken all together, lead to the belief that they are the results of a phlogistic condition of the parts attacked.

The undersigned therefore are of the opinion that at the present it is necessary that the invalid be watched attentively and assisted for possible contingencies of an increase of the malady or the recurring incidental congestions, yet at the present time should not be subjected to any medical cure directed to the end of carrying out experiments in the useless hope of improvement, but that they should be limited solely to attentive regulation of the hygienic system of life to which the invalid indispensably, and with all solicitude, should be subjected.

Done at Bergamo this day, October 11, 1847

Dr. G[iovanni] Cassis
Dr. L[uigi] Calvetti
Rendu.

Report on Donizetti's Mental Condition by Doctors Calvetti, Zendrini, and Longaretti, Bergamo, October 14, 1847

COMPLYING with the order of October 11 current N. 16156, calling for a mental investigation today of the *maestro di musica* Cav. Gaetano Donizetti; the assumption of the examinations by the French physician D. A. Rendu, and the exhausting by his [Donizetti's] brother and nephew of the steps necessary to take in order to discover the condition of the invalid's estate, the Porri committee—composed of the Imperial Counsellor Porri and the Practitioner Marieni—went to the habitation of the above-mentioned *signora* Rosa Basoni, found the invalid upstairs in the upper rooms seated on a *dormeuse*, and the medical experts Calvetti, Zendrini, and Longaretti, named in the same order, and they having taken the required oath, passed to examining the invalid and found first

1	1
Interrogated on general matters	Answered nothing
2	**2**
Questioned again	Nothing
3	**3**
At interrogations m a d e by the nephew Andrea Donizetti and the brother Francesco Donizetti and by the medical experts, who grasped his hands and touched his head	Opening his eyes and fixing them on one or another of the people present, he again closed them without having answered anything and without giving any sign of having understood the questions addressed to him.

After which the invited persons and the *signori* Calvetti, Zendrini, and Longaretti pronounced the following

JUDGMENT

The undersigned experts, having examined *il signor* Cav. Gaetano Donizetti with the aim of verifying the present state of his mind, have remarked as follows:

As can be gathered from Donizetti's relatives and the public notices, he has been found for two years invaded by a gradual phlogistic infection of the cerebrospinal apparatus, with the progress of which were associated symptoms that went on increasing gradually until, in November, 1846, he was taken by paralysis and intellectual disturbances, and therefore by abolition of the sensory, intellectual, and moral faculties, a period in which the state of his illness became stationary.

In fact, during the entire time when the patient was subjected to examination he gave no sign of understanding the interrogations directed at him or of recognizing the people or the objects around him; he did not proffer a single word, nor was he able to perform any movement; that also he always gave the impression of a man seized by indifference and apathy toward every manner of thing, except that when called by name or excited in some other way, he opened his eyes and fixed them on the person's face.

For the rest, the functions of his organic life are maintained with enough regularity. He eats properly, sleeps peacefully, is well nourished. But his excretions occur without the aid of his will.

After which the experts agreed in declaring that the aforesaid *signor* Donizetti is found with his intellectual faculties so disturbed and abolished as to render him completely incapable of understanding and administering his own interests.

Read, this was confirmed and signed by the participants.

> Dr. L[uigi] Calvetti
> Dr. A[ndrea] Zendini
> Dr. G. Longaretti
> Francesco Donizetti
> Andrea Donizetti
> Porri, counsellor

Bergamo, October 14, 1847   Marieni, practitioner.

Declaration Made by Andrea Donizetti to the Tribunale di Bergamo on October 15, 1847

ON November 5, 1845, my father received at Constantinople a letter addressed to him by a certain Vasselli of Rome, to whose attention it had come that my uncle, Cav. Gaetano, was in a very deplorable state of health. He at once ordered me to go to Paris, and in fact I reached there on December 25 of that same year and found my uncle in the house at No. 1 rue Grammont, in which he remained until February 1 [1846], on which day he entered the establishment of Doctor Mittivié [*sic*], located at Ivry (Seine), where he stayed until June 23, 1847, and whence he departed to enter a house located at No. 6 avenue Chateaubriand, which he later left on the past September 19 to come to Bergamo.

But I did not remain with my uncle all of that time, as on September 7, 1846, I betook myself to Constantinople, whence I departed again for

Paris on the past March 4 and arrived there on April 23, after which date I was near him constantly.

When I visited my uncle for the first time, I did not find him in so deplorable a state as that he now is in, and though even then he did not always talk sensibly, he nonetheless preserved his will, a will that was constantly lessening and which did not return to him when I went back to him for the second time, when I found him in the condition in which he was seen and inspected yesterday by the Imperial Royal Tribunal.

Autopsy on the Cadaver of Donizetti in the Cemetery of Valtesse

Bergamo, on April 11, 1848, at 2:30 in the afternoon.

Protocol of the dissection of the cadaver of the late maestro cav. Donizetti.

Present the *signori:*

Dr. Novati Girolamo, Director of the Hospitals
Dr. Cima Francesco, Prison Physician
Dr. Zendrini Andrea, Municipal Physician
Dr. Febo Ronzoni
Dr. Calvetti Luigi, Attending Physician of the Deceased
Dr. Giovanni Cassis, *idem*
Dr. Locatelli Gio. Maria, Dissectionist
Dr. Federico Maironi, *idem*

Denuded, the body was found extremely emaciated; the usual cadaveric suggillations were observed in the dependent parts; the abdominal parts presented a greenish discoloration, indicating that putrefaction already had begun, and this also extended to the integuments of the last ribs.

Dissection of the head—The integuments having been removed, a very great symmetry of the osseous parts, forming an ample and elevated dome, was revealed. The skull-vault having been sawed off all around, a diffuse venous infusion of the meninges was observed. In the hollow of the arachnoid was found a notable quantity of liquid, totaling approximately one ounce, a quantity that was increased further when the brain was lifted out; the basilar arteries were empty; the brain showed very highly developed circumvolutions corresponding to the locality of the organs of music, of mentation, and of genius [*meravigliosità*]; the corresponding bone was thinned down until no thicker than a fingernail. The base is regular, the prominences and the cavities [are] very well defined; only between the body of the sphenoid and the basilar apophysis was found a bony prominence on the right side, of irregular shape, in the form of a crest. The mass of the brain as weighed gave as a result 53½ local ounces, equal to 1.381 kilograms.

The mastoid cells almost entirely enveloped the petrosa. The pia mater was deeply infiltrated and adherent to the substance of the brain, so that pieces of brain tissue were torn away in attempting to detach it. The lateral ventricles were dilated by a copious serous effusion, to the quantity of about three ounces. The fourth ventricle similarly was found to be dilated by a serous effusion. There was slight, scattered dotting of the cerebral substance; the cerebellum is normal.

Dissection of the spinal cavity—Internal infiltration of the dura mater from the 5th dorsal [vertebra] to the 2nd lumbar. Internally [the dura mater] appears faintly reddish in this portion. At the beginning of the *cauda equina* was found a serous collection, to the quantity of one ounce; the spinal cord also was infiltrated with blood, especially in the region specified above, so that the redness grew more marked and diffuse toward the *cauda aquina*, which also was stained the same shade of red, signally in the inferior bulb of the spinal cord, which, when explored with the fingers, was harder than the rest of the spinal cord. The pia mater having been split open, the spinal substance appeared mashed, so that in the cervical portion it retained evidence of its proper structure, but little by little as one moved down, the substance itself gradually lost this evidence of its original structure.

Dissection of the thorax—The ribs are abnormally thin and brittle. The lungs are normal, the pericardium and the great vessels are normal, the heart appears moderately dilated.

Dissection of the abdomen—The viscera contained in this cavity all are perfectly normal. After which this protocol was made official by appending the signatures of the participants at 5 o'clock in the afternoon.

> Dr. Gir. Novati
> Dr. Cima
> Dr. L. Calvetti
> Dr. Andrea Zendrini
> Dr. Cassis Gio.
> Dr. Febo Ronzoni
> Dr. Locatelli
> Dr. Federico Maironi

I wish particularly to thank my friend Dr. Victor de Sabata, Jr., of Milan, for his valuable help in translating this document and for his comments on it. Some remarks may be helpful here:

1. The document demonstrates the Italian indifference to the order of "first" and "last" names.

2. Referring to the passage concerning "very highly developed circumvolutions corresponding to the locality of the organs of music, of mentation, and of genius," Dr. de Sabata wrote: "Of course, medically speaking, this is all sheer nonsense, for we know that there is no such thing as a localized center of mentation, let alone genius, which surely is an overall quality of the mind, made up of many components (insight, imagination, critical sense, richness of associations, memory—a lot of that—and others, all miraculously balanced and functioning in a genius). I am not aware that even a center of musical ability has been located, and I doubt that it could be, as musical

talent, again, is a manifold affair requiring the joint efforts of many widely separated parts of the brain. Just imagine: even the center of plain hearing is difficult to locate, being scattered in several complementary places. But then, this was more than a century ago, and the good doctors had to say something. They obviously knew that Donizetti was a composer. . . ."

3. Referring to the "bony prominence on the right side, of irregular shape, in the form of a crest," Dr. de Sabata wrote: "This is the basilar process of the occipital bone. The location of this bony excrescence, or crest, or swelling, or whatever it was, is very close to the medulla oblongata, and might explain why Donizetti's last easy chair had a special headrest, built to support his head *on the left side*," adding that the "crest" well may have been a "syphilitic gumma."

4. The weight of Donizetti's brain—given as 1.391 kilograms, or about 2.84393 pounds—is almost exactly the average weight of an adult male human brain.

5. Referring to the statement "The pia mater was deeply infiltrated and adherent to the substance of the brain, so that pieces of brain tissue were torn away in attempting to detach it," Dr. de Sabata wrote: "This looks very much like evidence of a chronic, probably luetic, meningitis."

6. Referring to the "slight, scattered dotting of the cerebral substance," Dr. de Sabata wrote: "These 'dots' might be hemorraghic petechiae, consistent with meningitis, or they might be post mortem capillary hemorrhages, or perhaps agonal."

7. Referring to the "internal infiltration of the dura mater from the fifth dorsal to the second lumbar," Dr. de Sabata commented: "That's a very long portion of the spine, and Donizetti certainly was very badly diseased."

8. Commenting generally on the autopsy report, Dr. de Sabata wrote: "There is definite evidence of a diffuse meningitis, very likely of considerable duration, involving the cerebral pia and the spinal dura, with damage to the underlying structures, and at least a suspicion of a localized bone lesion in the right spheno-occipital region. All of these findings are compatible with a diagnosis of quaternary syphilis, which is further supported by the testimony of Donizetti's symptoms—mainly general paresis and dementia, which also are typical of syphilis of the nervous system. . . .

"I would stress the fact that this famous autopsy was performed more than a century ago, when medical knowledge was especially primitive with regard to the structure of the central nervous system (witness the entirely imaginary 'center of genius' and other childishnesses of the same sort), and, above all, that the findings are unsupported by microscopic examination of the diseased parts and tissues, for which reason any interpretation of gross lesions must remain largely speculative. Nevertheless, a retrospective diagnosis of quaternary syphilis—based on clinical evidence *and* the autopsy—is almost overwhelmingly probable. In fact, there appears to be no other possibility."

Letter (*originally in French*)
to Margherita Tizzoni delle Sedie, Geneva,
from Giovannina Rota-Basoni, April 1848

My dearest friend,

I had thought to write you sooner, but my heart was too broken for me to be able to express to you the desolation in which I found myself and how unhappy I was. With time, I have been able to take hold of my sorrow and to prepare myself to write you a long letter.

By now, I think, you will have learned from the newspapers of Donizetti's death. An irreparable loss, not only for his friends, but also for all of Europe, which never will forget the operas of this great genius! To give you a complete notion of my desolation and that of my mother, I must tell you that for a long time there reigned between *signor* Donizetti and us a reciprocal friendship, and that his seven final months, which he came to pass with us, made that friendship closer and dearer. Despite his miserable malady, we were very happy to have him here.

The loss of him leaves a void in our house of which you can have no idea. His death surprised both us and his friends, in so far as the hopes based on the beautiful springtime days had begun to be realized in some way.

Signor Donizetti was cured of the fever that he had during the past February. Although that fever was independent of his miserable malady, his mind was further weakened and frequent sweats had much thinned the body of the poor invalid. But little by little he won back what the fever had made him lose, a fact that increased our persuasion that, with the help of the beautiful days of spring, the condition of the illustrious composer would have been, if not improved, at least rendered less dolorous. But that hope was cruelly crushed.

And here are the sad details.

On April 1, at five in the afternoon, while he was eating his supper, which he did with appetite, *signor* Donizetti was taken by an attack of apoplexy which disfigured his eyes and his mouth and paralyzed his arms and left leg! The poor invalid remained in that state all night though he was alternately given applications of a dozen mustard plasters on his feet and on his legs, and it was impossible to make him swallow anything, so tightly clenched were his teeth. It was not until toward seven o'clock in the morning that it was possible to have him swallow some spoonsful of broth, and the physiognomy of the celebrated maestro again became peaceful and his eyes intelligent.

At ten o'clock, a vesicant was applied to the nape of his neck. At noon, the fever announced itself and *signor* Gaetano's head became extremely hot. At two in the afternoon, sixteen leeches were placed behind his ears. The fever continued until the next morning, when he was able to take some spoonsful of broth with ease. We began to hope that the illustrious composer would emerge from this crisis . . . but, alas! that satisfaction was denied cruelly! Toward midday, the fever returned with greater strength than on the preceding day. At one o'clock, eighteen leeches were applied to his temples, and at the moment when the blood ceased to trickle, the unhappy invalid was seized by convulsions that twisted his members in a horrible manner. He breathed only through his nose, which was terribly clogged. Everyone believed that *signor* Gaetano had reached the final stage. We at once called the archpriest who lives near us, and that priest administered the holy oil. The convulsions lasted about three quarters of an hour, after which the fever increased with unexampled force. The poor invalid sweated so abundantly that the sweat penetrated everything that he had on him, and even the first mattress on the bed. At ten o'clock that evening, the sweating stopped. We changed *signor* Donizetti's bed and sheets, and despite his weak condition he stood all those movements very well.

On the morning of the fourth day, the poor invalid was indescribably emaciated. Notwithstanding the pains of his illness, after three days he had taken the quantity of one cup of broth. On the third and fourth days, we had Masses said in all the Madonna chapels and a High Mass at the Crucifixion altar in the Cathedral.

On the evening of the fourth day, the celebrated composer was in such great danger that the priest did not leave him all night. During the evening of the fifth day, the fever was very strong.

Up to that time we never had thought of having a portrait made of him, having the original near us. But on the fifth day of this illness, having lost all hope of being able to save the dear invalid, we hurried to call in a painter. And, a surprising thing (which could only be called a blessing from Providence, or as if the illustrious maestro had wanted to leave a faithful record of his pleasing physiognomy), his face, which during the preceding days had remained contracted by the malady, at once became calm again, the eyes expressive, in such a way that it would have been possible to believe that he was taking an interest in what was happening about him, so that the *signor* Rillosi was able to reproduce on the canvas all the inspiration of genius which the features of that great man diffused.

During the evening of the fifth day, the fever again became stronger. Early in the morning of the sixth day, they began to practice indirect feeding fortified with egg yolks. On the seventh and eighth, *signor* Donizetti was constantly sinking more and was at the point of death.

At five in the afternoon on April 8, the illustrious invalid breathed his last breath, attended by the priest and surrounded by my mother, me, his intimate friend Dolci, and his most affectionate domestic.

The funeral of the illustrious composer took place on April 11 at ten o'clock in the morning. It had been arranged by his most devoted friend, *signor* Dolci, who neglected nothing that could make it worthy of the glory of this great man. More than four thousand persons attended.[1] The cortege that accompanied him to the cemetery, made up of the numerous clergy

---

[1] The similarity of the rest of this paragraph of Giovannina Rota-Basoni's letter and the letter that Antoine Pourcelot, Donizetti's manservant, sent to Adolphe Adam (see p. 270) suggest strongly that she assisted Pourcelot in the task, perhaps unusual for him, of writing the letter to Paris.

of Bergamo, of the most important personalities of the city and its suburbs, of the Guardia Nazionale of the city and its environs—their muskets, encircled by three or four hundred torches—was a most beautiful sight.

The young *signori* of Bergamo insisted upon carrying the remains of their glorious townsfellow upon their shoulders, though the already great distance to the cemetery had been increased greatly because the inhabitants of the suburbs too wanted to give a final salute to the great Maestro, making it necessary for the cortege to pass through those streets, which, as you know, are almost three miles long. Over the whole course of the march, the streets and piazzas were full of people wanting to see the passing of that imposing cortege. Everything was animated by the bands of music and favored by a magnificent day.

By the testimony of the oldest inhabitants of Bergamo, no honors to equal these ever were paid to any personage of this city, and the two speeches pronounced over the tomb of the celebrated maestro were faithful interpreters of the glory of that great genius. . . .

The *signori* doctors of Bergamo had to perform an autopsy on *signor* Donizetti, they being obligated to render an account of his malady to all of Europe. Knowing our affection for the celebrated maestro—and even more the respect and care with which we had surrounded his last moments— these gentlemen understood what torment we would have suffered if that operation had been performed near us. It was only at the cemetery that the body was opened, the findings being: (1) that the strongest part of *signor* Donizetti's malady was in the spinal marrow, which had taken on the guise of coffee with milk; (2) that a liquid [*acqua*] had spread through the brain, being the cause of the attack that I spoke of at the beginning of this letter. The *signori* doctors, eleven in number, gathered together to perform the autopsy, have declared unanimously that if this malady had been taken care of from its inception, the celebrated maestro could have been entirely cured: his liver and his lungs were very healthy. (3) The celebrated composer's heart was much shriveled, certain proof that he had suffered a long time (through whose fault is not clear).

The testimony of the men of science has made very clear the immense loss that all of Europe has suffered through the death of *signor* Donizetti. These gentlemen said that God does not create such a brain every century, despite the fact that the brain of the illustrious maestro weighed one third more than the brain of ordinary men, and they found in it indications of the most marked sort for music, memory, and talent.[2]

What remorse (if they are culpable) must be with those who contributed to his loss (perhaps in an involuntary way)!

I shall not look for the causes of this loss! nor for its authors! Whether the poor invalid was the victim of inexperience or of the interests of this or that person, I leave to each one the remedy of consulting his own conscience. I want to give myself up only to sorrow, which renders bitterer the memory of the griefs that this great man experienced during the last years of his life.

[2] The good doctors evidently wrote one thing and told another to the doting Rota-Basoni women.

Operatic Documents and History

Lucrezia Borgia

*A Brief Acount of the Negotiations over
the Composition of this Opera among
Duke Carlo Visconti di Modrone,
Saverio Mercadante, Felice Romani, and Donizetti*

THE story of the negotiations leading up to Donizetti's composition of *Lucrezia Borgia* to a libretto by Felice Romani has been made needlessly complicated by reprintings and more or less accurate, uncredited adaptations of the account that Alphonse Royer published (*110*) in 1878. That account reads: "In 1833, the poet Romani had written the libretto of 'Lucrezia Borgia,' following the drama by Victor Hugo, requested from him by the impresario of La Scala, who then had commissioned Maestro Mercadante to compose the score. Mercadante, suffering from ophthalmia, interested Donizetti—who was in Milan at the time—and begged him to replace him in the contract he had already signed. Only forty days remained for staging an opera . . . of which not even one note had been written. Donizetti composed it in twenty-five days."

As Edoardo Clemente Verzino established (*132*, 68–74) as long ago as 1896, the facts were otherwise. In 1832, Duke Carlo Visconti di Modrone, director of La Scala, commissioned Romani to write a libretto. The poet, the contract having been signed on June 10, 1832, selected supposed incidents in the life of Lucrezia Borgia as a subject, planning to derive the outlines of his story from Victor Hugo's famous play, *Lucrèce Borgia*. He had begun to write the libretto in 1833 but put it aside: he had been requested to write a libretto to be set by Mercadante for the opening opera of the next Carnival season. For that purpose, he selected the subject of Sappho, which, it soon was discovered, did not meet with the approval of the prima donna for the coming season, Henriette-Clémentine Méric-Lalande. No suggestion was made that Romani should complete the Lucrezia Borgia libretto so that Mercadante could compose it instead. Visconti di Modrone, apparently not wishing to run counter to Méric-Lalande's wishes, did not press Romani to complete the libretto dealing with Sappho. Nor did he suggest that Romani write an entirely different libretto for Mercadante, perhaps because Mercadante was not known to be a swift composer.

At this juncture, Donizetti being in Milan and his reputation for speed having the proof of years, Visconti di Modrone sent for him. On October 10, 1833, they signed a contract by which Donizetti promised to provide La Scala with two *opere serie*, one of them to be a *Lucrezia Borgia* to a Romani libretto. Donizetti then called upon Romani, who understandably found himself confused among Lucrezia Borgia, Sappho, Visconti di Modrone, Mercadante, and Donizetti, and therefore wrote the following letter to Visconti.

Excellency,

At this moment Signor Maestro Donizetti has left me, who charges me, on your account, to write a *melodramma* for him to serve as the first spectacle of the coming Carnival.

Knowing that Signor Mercadante also is signed up for the same period, it is best to say that Your Excellency has settled with him in some other way, about which arrangement I beg you to tell me separately so that I may decide with knowledge of the cause. As far as my understanding with Signor Mercadante, these are the facts.

He, having been informed that, in order to acquiesce in the suggestions of Madame Lalande and Signor Gottardi,[1] I was replacing the subject of *Sappho*, which I already had started, with that of *Lucrezia Borgia*, he wrote me last Monday to hurry as much as I could in order to send him poetry; and I assured him by ordinary post that today, Friday, I should have sent him everything that I had been able to complete in so short a space of time. And today, to keep my word, I posted the introduction to him. If, I repeat, Your Excellency has arranged otherwise with Signor Mercadante,[2] my work will be useful to Signor Donizetti, and it will please him.

I should have come to see Your Excellency in person, but I am in such confusion because of changing my residence and of a rush of affairs that I find myself constrained to put off that act of duty to another day.

[1] Described as an *"incaricato,"* Gottardi appears to have been either Méric-Lalande's agent or an assistant at La Scala.

[2] This was exactly what Visconti di Modrone was in the process of ac- complishing: on October 12, writing from Novara, Mercadante agreed to compose an opera for 1834 rather than 1833. It turned out to be *La Gioventù di Enrico V*, a failure.

Eighteen days later, apparently after receipt from Visconti of a complaint that the libretto for *Lucrezia Borgia* was not being delivered quickly enough, Romani wrote him again, this time to defend himself against the charge of dilatoriness and to ask for formal contracts for the libretto for Donizetti and one for Luigi Ricci. His scruples about Mercadante having been dissolved, on November 18 he wrote Visconti to announce that two acts of *Lucrezia Borgia* were with a transcriber—and that he would deliver the third act the next morning. And on November 26, he sent the libretto off with the warning: "I can neither handle this story in a better way nor more prudently for the censorship."

Donizetti had not waited for the ironing-out of these practical and ethical problems. Visconti di Modrone had contracted with him for an opera to a Romani text, and the day after signing that contract (that is, on October 11), he had written to Visconti:

Excellency,

Signor Romani has sent me a note of the company [the singers available] for my opera *Lucrezia Borgia*. As I do not know all these personages whom I need, therefore I beg you to be willing to give me a list of the singers on the roster for the secondary parts so that I can assign one to each character:

Lucrezia Borgia	Madame Lalande
Alfonso d'Este	Mariani
Gennaro	Pedrazzi
Gubetta	Spiaggi
Maffio Orisini	Brambilla
Beppo Liveretto—secondary part	Vaschetti
Don Apostolo Gazzella	Visanetti
Ascanio Petrucci—secondary part	*basso secondo*
Oloferno Vitellozzo	Marconi
Rustighello	Pochini
Astolfo—secondary part	Petrazzoli
The Princess Negroni (first chorister)	
Cupbearers	

Two of these secondary parts we can choose from among the best choristers. But the others ought to be tenors and basses.

And so it turned out that Donizetti, who had the complete libretto in his hands on November 25 or 26, completed *Lucrezia Borgia* in time for it to open the season at La Scala on Santo Stefano (December 26), 1833. Romani went on writing librettos for Mercadante as well as for others, and all would have been well had not his fears about the meeting of the Borgias and the censors proved to be well founded.

Maria Stuarda

Contract Between Donizetti
and Duke Carlo Visconti di Modrone
for Its Production at the Teatro alla Scala, Milan

DURING the first days (and not later than January 4, 1836) of the open-
ing of the forthcoming Carnival season, the management of the Royal
Theaters will produce on the stage of La Scala the opera *Maria Stuarda* by
Maestro Signor Donizetti.

So that this may come out with the greatest possible success, the management wants to profit by Signor Maestro Donizetti's presence in Milan to
stage the said opera in a manner most convenient to the company named and
indicated below.

For which reason, the lauded Signor Maestro, responding to such a
desire, takes it upon himself to make in the score all those changes, ameliora-
tions, and other things which he conscientiously shall believe necessary and
useful to this common enterprise's good outcome, and also a *sinfonia*.

The rehearsals shall take place under the direction of the same
Signor Maestro

In return for which the management shall pay Signor Donizetti and anyone requested by him two hundred fifty bavare, I say No. 250 bavare.

Done and affirmed the day December 16, 1835.

Signed Gaet. Donizetti

Maria	Malibran
Leicester	Reina
Talbot	Marini
Cecil	Novelli
Anna	unnamed
Elisabetta	unnamed

Le Duc d'Albe

A Brief History of Donizetti's Unfinished Opera

ON August 16, 1838, and supplementarily on January 13, 1839, Donizetti,
Charles Duponchel of the Paris Opéra, and the librettists Eugène Scribe and
Charles Duveyrier formalized an agreement for the writing, composition,
and staging of a four-act grand opera in French to be completed by Janu-

ary 1, 1840. By the terms of these agreements, Scribe and Duveyrier were to receive four thousand francs and half of the income from authors' rights; exactly what Donizetti's remuneration was to be is not entirely clear, but it is likely to have been the same. The agreements specified that the Opéra was to be paid an indemnity of fifteen thousand francs by Scribe and Duveyrier if they did not present the libretto on time, and by Donizetti if he failed to deliver the score by January 1, 1840. In reverse, the Opéra was required to pay fifteen thousand francs as forfeit to Donizetti, fifteen thousand to Scribe and Duveyrier, if, having received the completed opera on time, it failed to stage the opera by the date specified. On November 27, 1839, Donizetti signed a contract with the Paris music publisher Schönenberger by which he ceded the publication rights to this opera, as well as certain proprietary rights in both it and *Les Martyrs,* for a promised payment of sixteen thousand francs for each opera, half of the payment for each to be made on the day of its *première,* the other half two months later.

The subject agreed upon for the libretto of the proposed opera involved an episode that occurred in 1573, during the Spanish occupation of Flanders, under Philip II. After this decision had been reached, a libretto dealing with much the same episode was written by Giovanni Peruzzi and Francesco Maria Piave[1] and composed by Giovanni Pacini as *Il Duca d'Alba.* Pacini's opera was only a mild success after its *première* at the Teatro La Fenice, Venice, during the Carnival season of 1842.[2] But even if it had become a spreading success throughout Italy, awareness of its existence probably would not have deterred Duponchel, Scribe, Duveyrier, or Donizetti from proceeding with another opera on the same subject for production in French at Paris.

During 1839, Donizetti worked at the composition of *L'Ange de Nisida,* to a libretto by Alphonse Royer and Gustave Vaëz, intending it for the Théâtre de la Renaissance. But a contract dated August 28, 1840, between Donizetti and Léon Pillet (Duponchel's temporary successor at the Opéra) provided that *L'Ange de Nisida,* metamorphosed into *La Favorite,* was to take the place of *Le Duc d'Albe* on the Opéra's future schedule—this with respect both to Donizetti's obligations under the 1838–39 agreements and to those of the Opéra management. This new arrangement specified that *Le Duc d'Albe,* which Donizetti then still halfheartedly hoped to complete, was

---

[1] This was the first libretto by the man who later was to supply Michael Balfe with that for *Pittore e duca;* Pacini with that of *Lorenzo de' Medici;* Achille Peri with that for *Vittore Pisani;* the brothers Ricci with that for *Crispino e la comare;* and Verdi with the texts of *Ernani, I Due Foscari, Macbeth, Il Corsaro, Stiffelio, Rigoletto, La Traviata, Simon Boccanegra,* and *La Forza del destino.*

[2] The cast at the Fenice included Fanny Goldberg, who would sing in

the *première* of Donizetti's *Caterina Cornaro;* Filippo Coletti, who also would sing in that disastrous failure; and Napoleone Moriani, who had sung in the *première* of Donizetti's *Maria di Rudenz* and would have a role in the brilliant first performance of his *Linda di Chamounix.* The Pacini opera also was heard at the Teatro San Carlo, Naples, in 1842, reconstituted to an anonymous libretto entitled *Adolfo di Warbel,* with Sophia Löwe, Coletti, and Gaetano Fraschini.

to be staged instead as the fourth new production at the Opéra after *La Favorite*, which was sung for the first time on December 2, 1840.

Rumors floated about Paris that the real reason for the delay in staging *Le Duc d'Albe* was that Rosine Stoltz, who was known to be Léon Pillet's mistress at the time, had refused to sing the relatively unimportant, though only female, role of Amélie d'Egmont. Pillet later denied this story, but his letters clearly show that he had become less than enthusiastic over the prospects of *Le Duc d'Albe*. Donizetti, however, continued desultorily to work at the opera, references to which are strewn through his letters of 1841 and 1842. In February 1843, writing to Antonio Vasselli, he said that *Le Duc d'Albe* would be staged at the Opéra the next spring. At some time during 1842, before Donizetti's return to Paris from Italy in September or October, Scribe, who appears to have been eager to propel *Le Duc d'Albe* into performance and who understood Pillet's doubts about its success, suggested that it be reduced to a *"petit ouvrage"* in three acts and staged at the Opéra-Comique during the summer season. Approached with this proposal, Donizetti rejected it angrily.

The three operas that were stipulated to intervene between the production of *La Favorite* (December 2, 1840) and that of *Le Duc d'Albe* turned out to be two by Fromental Halévy (*La Reine de Chypre* and *Charles VI*) and Meyerbeer's long-awaited *Le Prophète*. Halévy's operas duly were staged, *La Reine de Chypre* on December 22, 1841, and *Charles VI* on March 15, 1843. But the fussily perfectionist Meyerbeer handed in the score of *Le Prophète* only to retire it again and work over it for several more years.[3] So Pillet asked Donizetti to let him put on instead the still-unfinished *Duc d'Albe*. But now Donizetti considered the Opéra's roster of singers poorly adapted to the needs of that opera, and so chose instead to help Pillet out of his difficulty by composing another opera, *Dom Sébastien, roi de Portugal*, first heard at the Opéra on November 13, 1843.[4] In the interim, Pillet filled in the gap by staging Louis-Abraham Niedermeyer's opera *Marie Stuart* on December 6, 1844, Donizetti this time having refused to allow Pillet to produce *Le Duc d'Albe* immediately after *Dom Sébastien*, explaining that he thought it poor strategy to have two of his grand operas reach the stage of the Opéra in such quick succession.

In the midst of all these confusions, Scribe had suggested that he would provide Donizetti with an alternative text based on the life of Joanna the Mad. Donizetti merely said that he would set any libretto whatever which had been settled upon by Pillet, Scribe, and Michele Accursi. But Pillet would have nothing to do with the mad daughter of Ferdinand and Isabella, so Scribe searched vainly for another subject while all the existing contracts and all activity hung fire. In the spring of 1844, Scribe suddenly demanded

[3] *Le Prophète* was not staged until April 16, 1849, and it was one of the greatest operatic successes of the era.

[4] A very entertaining satire on the backings and fillings of Donizetti, Meyerbeer, and Pillet was published in Paris early in 1845. Its title page reads:

Donizetti et M. Léon Pillet/Indiscrétion/en trois scènes et en vers,/par l'un des trente-six auteurs/de la Tour de Babel. Running to fifteen pages of text, this pamphlet is illustrated with amusing woodcuts.

that Pillet pay him his half of the four thousand francs that he regarded as due him and Duveyrier under the 1838–39 agreements, as well as the librettists' half of the penalty provided in those contracts for nonproduction of the opera.

Pillet replied, reasonably enough, that he was willing to pay Scribe the two thousand francs[5] and that it was not his fault that the opera had not been staged. He added that he thus would have paid Scribe four thousand francs for "half of an opera," the rights in which Scribe could take back, if he wished to, so as to refashion it as a libretto for the Théâtre-Italien, a libretto to be used in the provinces or abroad, as a play or as an *opéra-comique* "if you persist in thinking the subject a happy one." Pillet commented wryly that this was not an indemnity to be despised.

Further, Pillet went on, he had paid Scribe four thousand francs for the libretto of *La Favorite*, though he had handed him the subject and, in fact, the libretto itself [meaning the text of *L'Ange de Nisida*] three quarters complete—in addition to which Scribe had acquired half of the authors' rights in that opera, just as he would have acquired them in *Le Duc d'Albe*. Finally Pillet said that he had offered to arrange for Scribe to collaborate with Donizetti on another opera, and it was not his fault that the project [for which Scribe had proffered Joanna the Mad] had fallen through.

But Scribe was a dogged opponent when money was involved. With Duveyrier, he decided to summon Pillet before the Paris business court. Pillet thereupon cut off all correspondence on the matter and remained deaf to suggestions for compromising the quarrel which were advanced by Théodore Anne, the librettist of Niedermeyer's *Marie Stuart*, Michele Accursi, Achille Scribe, Chaix d'Est-Ange, and Léon Duval. The court case was docketed for February 25, 1845—and then, on February 6, Pillet wrote to Scribe to suggest that they submit their differences to arbitrators. Scribe refused. But on the day when the trial was to begin, he changed his mind and accepted arbitration. The final result was that Pillet agreed to buy off Duveyrier by paying him five hundred francs and to let two arbitrators— Chaix d'Est-Ange and Achille Scribe—decide between Scribe's charges and his own defense.

Exactly what happened next or thereafter is not clear, but on August 13, 1847, Scribe wrote to Donizetti's Paris banker, Auguste de Coussy: "We entered upon and won two processes against the former director of the Opéra[6] with regard to the delay he caused in the performance of *Le Duc d'Albe*." As Alberto Cametti pointed out (27, 253), Scribe had not done badly from a financial point of view: he had received the not inconsiderable payment of eleven thousand five hundred francs [four thousand francs plus seven thousand five hundred francs of the indemnity]—and this was for his work on a libretto that he later was to recast and sell to Verdi as *Les Vêpres siciliennes*.

[5] Exactly what part in the libretto of *Le Duc d'Albe* had been played by Duveyrier is unclear. One detail that Pillet specified in his letter of May 13, 1844, was that if he paid Scribe, some of the payment was to be used to silence "Duveyrier's pretensions."

[6] In mid-1845, Pillet left the managership of the Opéra, turning it back to the man he had succeeded, Duponchel.

Donizetti too had gone to the Paris court. From Vienna, on June 29, he had written to his brother Giuseppe: "Four years ago, the agreement, and to me fell *Le Duc d'Albe* in four acts, with the penalty, if it failed to be performed, of paying fifteen thousand francs to Scribe and fifteen to me. Scribe has brought an action, he has won it! I want, too, to bring a second suit; with a copy of all of Scribe's reasons, and also my own, as the contract was signed by all three of us. . . . We shall see." And on August 21, 1845, he wrote Antonio Dolci from Paris: "Now I am here for the suit for fifteen thousand francs against the impresario for *Le Duc d'Albe*."[7]

The Opéra tried to discuss matters with Donizetti through Michele Accursi, but Donizetti either would not compromise or was too unwell to realize entirely what he was doing. Of his ethically questionable suit, Pillet said, in a letter to the *Gazette des tribunaux*: "As for Donizetti, I hasten to declare that if—at the moment when, in his name, a suit against me was projected to force me to pay the forfeit—his memory already had not undergone an alteration, to be followed so rapidly by that in his reason, he never would have authorized this action. By playing *Marie Stuart* instead of *Le Duc d'Albe*, I did nothing but carry out Donizetti's wish, and that by agreements that he himself accepted. The existence of these agreements was denied in the suit by his legal representative; a letter containing them, and which it seemed to me should be in his hands, was not found there! . . . I could make no useful appeal to a failing memory; the arbitrators, therefore, found themselves forced to condemn me. Today I have rediscovered the proof of the agreement, written in Donizetti's own hand. I am going by all possible means to appeal against a decision that rests upon an error."

But—probably because he ceased to be director of the Opéra—Pillet never instituted the threatened appeal. The suggestions that, in the meantime, the Opéra had sent Donizetti through Accursi were: (1) that the director of the Opéra join Donizetti in obtaining the libretto of *Le Duc d'Albe* from Scribe, with his permission that it be used abroad—and then have a writer of his own choice make the necessary changes in it; (2) that Donizetti have a completely new libretto fitted to the existing music, and that the resulting opera be staged immediately; (3) that the 1843 agreement be put into effect, Donizetti to compose a new opera for staging in 1846 or 1847; (4) that the Opéra share in the expense that Donizetti would incur in paying for a new libretto to be fitted to the music of *Le Duc d'Albe*.

Under ordinary conditions, Donizetti probably would have accepted one or another of these reasonable suggestions or some combination of them. But by the time they were made, his health had deteriorated so far that nothing useful could be accomplished. The Opéra paid the fifteen-thousand-franc forfeit, depositing the amount with Auguste de Coussy. A curious sidelight was cast on the entire affair when, in February 1847, Schönenberger in turn brought suit against Donizetti's representatives because of his failure to hand over, as provided in the contract of November 27, 1838, the complete score of *Le Duc d'Albe*. In this action the court decided that Donizetti's sale of proprietary rights had depended upon performance of the opera: the opera never had been performed, and Schöenberger therefore had no case.

[7] This was one of the series of "farewell" letters mentioned on p. 236.

When, in September, 1846, Andrea Donizetti left his uncle in the sanatorium at Ivry and stopped at Bergamo for a week or ten days en route to Constantinople, he deposited a bundle containing *Rita* and what there was of *Le Duc d'Albe* with Antonio Dolci.[8] By the time of Andrea's return to Bergamo in October, 1847, with Donizetti, Duponchel, as director of the Opéra, again was showing keen interest in staging *Le Duc d'Albe*, evidently believing it to have been advanced much nearer to completion than it had been. He announced his intention of staging it "with all the care and all the pomp that it demands." Learning of this intention, Scribe[9] had asked Auguste de Coussy to authorize delivery of the score to the Opéra. When nothing came of this request (De Coussy not having the score in his possession), the Opéra management announced to Andrea Donizetti that it still was planning to mount *Le Duc d'Albe* worthily, that Scribe would modify the libretto without altering the music, and that in view of the changed roster of singers, a renowned composer would be called in to supervise the entire process. Would Andrea please have the score forwarded to the Opéra?

Andrea went before the Tribunale di Bergamo for a decision as to what steps he should take. That court doubted its own jurisdiction in the matter and told him that such a decision probably would have to be made in Vienna. In January 1848, therefore, the Opéra asked the Austrian embassy in Paris to urge upon the Tribunale di Bergamo the speedy appointment of a trustee for the incompetent Donizetti, a trustee who could forward the score of *Le Duc d'Albe* to Paris. Duponchel was aware that the Opéra's profits on *La Favorite* up to that time had mounted to something like sixty thousand francs, and he evidently was dreaming of the gold locked up in the bundle in Bergamo. He feared, too, that if he did not get hold of the score quickly, commitments to other composers would intervene to delay its presentation.

After Donizetti's death at Bergamo on April 8, 1848, his brothers, Giuseppe and Francesco, became his equal heirs.[10] In May, the Opéra sent Louis Dietsch[11] to Bergamo in another attempt to get hold of *Le Duc d'Albe*. Still hesitant, the Tribunale di Bergamo would agree only that, in company with Antonio Dolci, Dietsch might examine the score to determine how nearly complete it was. This tardy examination—which, incredibly, seems then to have been made in detail for the first time—revealed that it was so

---

[8] See pp. 280–82, for Dolci's statement of August 15, 1847, to the Tribunale di Bergamo, interesting in many ways.

[9] In the letter of August 13, 1847, cited above.

[10] When Francesco Donizetti died on December 20, 1848, leaving his equity in Gaetano's estate to his mistress, the servant girl Elisabetta Santi Pesenti, she too began to interest herself in possible profits from *Le Duc d'Albe*. Somewhat later, she threatened to sue Giuseppe Donizetti to force the sale of Gaetano's scores. This dispute was settled out of court by an agreement signed on April 25, 1855, Giuseppe buying out most of her rights.

[11] Pierre-Louis-Phillippe Dietsch (1808–65) now is remembered chiefly because in 1842 he composed an opera, *Le Vaisseau fantôme*, the libretto of which was derived from Wagner's first sketch for the poem of *Der fliegende Holländer*, and because in 1861 he was the unfortunate and not very able conductor of the three renowned performances of *Tannhäuser* at the Opéra.

incomplete that the opera could not be staged unless drastically edited and completed by another composer. In view of Dietsch's subsequent report, the management of the Opéra wisely decided to abandon all plans to stage *Le Duc d'Albe*.

In October, 1849, the scores of *Rita* and *Le Duc d'Albe* still lay in Bergamo, by then in the custody of an accountant named Marco Peguzzi, appointed by the contending Donizetti heirs to arbitrate their own disputes. Assigned to Andrea Donizetti, the scores were sent to Teodoro Ghezzi in Naples, probably with the intention that something be done with them at one of the Neapolitan theaters. But somewhat later, a Bergamo lawyer named Campana was appointed to work out a final division of Donizetti's estate, and the bundle of manuscript was called back to Bergamo and returned to Peguzzi. In 1875, the city of Bergamo wanted to stage *Le Duc d'Albe* at the Teatro Riccardi as part of the solemn celebrations attending upon the reburial of Donizetti and Mayr in the Church of Santa Maria Maggiore. Consent for the performance having been obtained from the remaining heirs—Andrea Donizetti's two sons, Gaetano and Giuseppe, then still living in Constantinople—the city appointed three local musicians to examine the score. Alessandro Nini, Giovanni Bertuletti, and Bernardino Zanetti reported that the score of *Le Duc d'Albe* consisted of forty-eight pages of autograph music, some for each of the four acts. Completely orchestrated were only the first act, part of the second act, and a few other scattered passages. The rest existed only in indicated vocal lines and annotations about the orchestration. They also pointed out that, as Donizetti had transferred the aria *"Ange si pur"* to *La Favorite*, the possibility existed that other numbers from this score might have been inserted into that opera or other operas. Their sensible decision was that *Le Duc d'Albe* could not be staged. They opposed mounting the complete first act, which they described as no more than an introduction to the action, and suggested instead that a few of the best numbers be presented in concert.

Again nothing happened for a few years. Then, on September 18, 1881, the *Gazzetta musicale di Milano* stated that the incomplete autograph of *Le Duc d'Albe* had been offered to the Casa Ricordi, which had refused it, not wishing to damage the art and name of Donizetti by presenting publicly an incomplete, unpolished opera. At about that same time, the other prominent Milanese music publisher, Lucca, bought the score from the Donizetti heirs. Giovanna Lucca quickly announced that she would have it staged as completed by Donizetti's pupil and friend Matteo Salvi, who already had begun to work on it. The immediate result, as must have been foreseen, was a newspaper controversy led by defenders of Donizetti's reputation. Such a production, they said in ringing language, would be a desecration.

But Giovanna Lucca, a shrewd businesswoman, was ready. She asked the Milan Conservatory of Music to appoint a committee to re-examine the score and pass upon its playability. The Conservatory appointed Antonio Bazzini, Cesare Dominiceti, and Amilcare Ponchielli—all composers of opera —to this committee. The three men carefully reported the contents and condition of the manuscript, pointing out all the gaps and omissions. They concluded, however—as Giovanna Lucca seems to have been certain they would—that "despite this, the long line traced by the Maestro and the appreciable number of pieces completed entirely or in condition to be completed by small additions if confided to a sure, expert hand convince them that *Le Duc d'Albe* could be offered to the public as an undoubted work of Donizetti."

Published verbatim in the press, the committee's opinion led to another controversy. But Giovanna Lucca now had in hand all the justification for performance which she required. In the summer of 1882, Vincenzo Jacovacci having died, the new impresario of the Teatro Apollo at Rome was the ex-singer Filippo Tatti. He announced for the next season productions of three operas new to Rome: Meyerbeer's *L'Étoile du nord*, Karl Goldmark's *Die Königin von Saba*, and Donizetti's *Il Duca d'Alba*. He opened his season on December 26, 1882, with *L'Étoile du nord*, the cast of which aroused audience disapproval. Then he put on Halévy's *La Juive* and Verdi's *La Traviata*, the latter with the unpopular singers he had used in *L'Étoile du nord*. In *La Juive*, however, he introduced to Rome the soprano Abigaille Bruschi-Chiatti, and she, the tenor Capponi, and the bass Alessandro Silvestri delighted his audiences. *La Juive* was repeated until, on March 12, Goldmark was present for the successful Roman *première* of *Die Königin von Saba*, which in turn was played until the Donizetti-Salvi opera, adapted to Angelo Zanardini's translation of Scribe's text, finally reached its *première* on March 22, 1882, forty-four years after Donizetti first had begun to think about *Le Duc d'Albe*.

Salvi had been in Rome since early January. The rehearsals of *Il Duca d'Alba* had begun about the middle of that month. On February 13, the tenor Capponi having relinquished the role of Marcello because of a "serious vocal indisposition," Tatti had hired for the part a Spanish tenor named Julián Sebastián Gayarré, who was to achieve international fame.[12] Although the prices for seats were exorbitantly high,[13] the Apollo was sold out. Queen Margherita was in the royal box on the first night. The Milan Conservatory's committee—Bazzini, Dominiceti (who was said by some of the critics to have composed at least one of the numbers added to the score), and

[12] At about the time when these rehearsals began, Verdi wrote to Senator Giuseppe Pirolli regarding the imminent *première* of *Il Duca d'Alba:* "I never had known that Scribe had made use of *Le Duc d'Albe* to make *Les Vêpres siciliennes*, though it is true that Vasselli, Donizetti's brother-in-law, spoke to me about it *en passant* when I was in Rome for *Un Ballo in maschera* in '59. But I paid no attention, and probably believed that this was a suspicion, an idea of Vasselli. Now I understand and truly believe that *Les Vêpres* was taken from *Le Duc d'Albe*."

Verdi is rarely a target for a charge of disingenuousness, but certainly such a reasonable charge is hinted at in Alberto Cametti's comment on that letter: "This demonstrates that Verdi, going to Paris in 1855 [for the *première* of *Les Vêpres siciliennes* at the Opéra on June 13] did not read the periodicals of the time, which discussed this fact in detail."

[13] Cametti *(27)* stated that the prices were the same as those which had been set for the first Roman *Aïda* at the Apollo (February, 1875): thirty lire for a stall, ten lire for an ordinary seat, six lire for standing room.

Ponchielli—was on hand, as were uncounted publishers, impresarios, composers, critics, and correspondents of out-of-town and foreign periodicals.

The cast at the *première* of *Il Duca d'Alba* consisted of Abigaille Bruschi-Chiatti (Amelia d'Egmont), Julián Gayarré (Marcello di Bruges), Giovanni Paroli (Carlo), Romeo Sartori (Un Taverniere), Leone Giraldoni (Il Duca d'Alba), Alessandro Silvestri (Daniele), and Igalmer Frey (Sandoval); the orchestra was conducted by Marino Mancinelli; and the scenery was after designs by Carlo Ferrario. The success of the opera was instant and resounding. Few in that excited, enthusiastic audience had long enough memories to discover some "reminiscences" of the sort for which the living Donizetti so often had been criticized adversely, though, for example, a third-act baritone aria had been brought over from Donizetti's long-forgotten 1829 opera *Il Paria*. *Il Duca d'Alba* was repeated on March 25, 26, and 29, and on April 1. Two days later, the season at the Apollo closed with a repetition of *La Juive*.

That same month, however, witnessed a staging of *Il Duca d'Alba* at the Teatro San Carlo, Naples, with the role of Marcello di Bruges sung by Roberto Stagno.[14] The Neapolitan press turned up hostile almost to a man, and the public's reaction was little more favorable. On August 23, 1885, the opera reached the Teatro Riccardi, Bergamo, with Leone Giraldoni again in the title role, the noted Russian tenor Nikolai Figner as Marcello di Bruges. The Donizettians of Bergamo received the opera warmly. Other stagings of *Il Duca d'Alba* followed—at Barcelona on December 19, 1882, at Malta in 1884, and at the Teatro Regio, Turin, in February 1886. But after the Turin staging, *Il Duca d'Alba* seems to have lapsed for seventy-three years.

Then, in 1959, Gian-Carlo Menotti revived *Il Duca d'Alba* at Spoleto in his Festival of Two Worlds. The staging was assigned to Luchino Visconti, and the conductor, Thomas Schippers, undertook to prepare a version of the score preserving as little music as possible which was not Donizetti's. The opera was reduced to three acts; most of Matteo Salvi's handiwork was excised. The original scenery was located in a Roman theatrical warehouse, repainted, and used. Costumes were designed so that, to quote the Spoleto program, "with the sets they would form a coherent whole, evoking the atmosphere and the taste of an opera production of the 1880s," an intention that was carried out with complete success. The Zanardini translation was used. At the first Teatro Nuovo performance, June 11, 1959, the cast of *Il Duca d'Alba* (which was sung seven times that season) was: Ivana Tosini (Amelia d'Egmont), Renato Cioni (Marcello di Bruges), Enzo Tei (Carlo), Luigi Quilico (Il Duca d'Alba), Wladimiro Ganzarolli (Sandoval), and Franco Ventriglia (Daniele).

Ricordi, it will be recalled, was said to have refused to acquire the score of *Le Duc d'Albe* in 1881. In 1888, however, Ricordi & C. bought out

[14] Stagno (1836–97), whose wife was the noted soprano Gemma Bellincioni, was to sing Manrico in *Il Trovatore* the next year in New York —on October 26, 1883, the third night of the opening season of the Metropolitan Opera House.

the Lucca publishing firm—and the autograph score now forms part of the Ricordi archives in Milan.

Gli Innamorati

THIS two-page manuscript, unearthed in the Civic Library at Bergamo, is a scenario that Donizetti evidently prepared to present to a librettist. It was derived from Carlo Goldoni's *Gli Innamorati*, as Donizetti refers to its characters by the names Goldoni gave them. The libretto probably never was written; certainly the opera was not composed.

Eugenia	*prima donna*	*N. B.* Sometimes Lisetta seems nec-
Flaminia	*seconda donna*	essary, sometimes Tognino. The
Clorinda	*terza donna*	poet will know better than I know
Fulgenzio	*primo tenore*	which to suppress. The difficulty
Roberto	*baritono*	will be to introduce the choruses
Fabrizio	*buffo*	

N. B. Lisetta, or Tognino, or Succianespole; make them one or delete them.

ACT I. It can begin with the two *donne* on the stage, as scene I. Recitative for Flaminia. Love for the other—a short number. Only it must end with allegro for Eugenia and the other, two verses. Then contract the second, third, and fourth scenes in recitative until the entrance of Fabrizio and Roberto. Fabrizio should do all the talking at the beginning, not let Roberto speak more than monosyllables. Then, finally, Roberto should say: "But permit me, finally" (and here a short *adagio cantabile*), then a cabaletta, either in duet or solo, and while, in the meantime, Fabrizio speaks of his imaginary talents with the girls, etc., the *primo* talks constantly, so that the other scarcely can get a word in from time to time. But at the *stretta*, Roberto politely takes the lead and closes the cavatina while Fabrizio speaks under his breath to the girls and makes pompous compliments as in the *commedia*. (Recitative). He sends them all out into the arcade, remains alone, by himself takes all the dialogue of scene 7, with Succianespole at one side. Scene 8 could be a letter to Flaminia. Scenes 9 and 10 use for the cavatina of Fulgenzio the tenor. Scene 11, duet, end of Act I

ACT II. Air for Fabrizio, in which he talks about chickens, sauces, etc. Duet for Roberto and Eugenia, scene 6, second act, instead of three people, only two. Fulgenzio will enter with the other sister, Flaminia, and other people. The page or scene 9 seems to offer a place for an adagio (the irony for Eugenia of letting him go home, etc.). The finale then goes up to scene 11. The rest cannot be included. It can be spoken or recounted at the beginning of Act III.

Act III. The beginning as desired. At scene 13, ought to begin the duet with recitative of Fulgenzio and Eugenia.

Scene 15 could be played by the *buffo* alone, saying that Clorinda is in another room. Contract the rest. Scene 4 could be made either for the *buffo* or for the *buffo* with the sister. Scene 5, an ensemble piece, characters as desired until, in scene 8, they all accompany Clorinda, so that Fabrizio and Roberto remain alone (scene 9) without the women on the stage. Then the Count leaves. The tenth scene serves for the entrance of Eugenia alone (*romanza*), the twelfth scene for an aria for Fulgenzio, with a short number for Eugenia. The finale and the last allegro for Eugenia.

N. B. The poet must pay careful attention to the monotony of the situations between the two lovers, so that now one may shine, now the other.

Act I — 1 Cavatina Eugenia
      2 Entrance of Fabrizio and Roberto, with a short number, such as, for example, giving flowers . . .
      3 Cavatina tenor,
      4 Duet with Eugenia—first finale.

Act II — 1 Aria Fabrizio.
      2 Duet Roberto and Eugenia, beginning of the finale and what follows, etc.

Act III — 1 Duet Eugenia and Fulgenzio.
      2 Ensemble piece.
      3 Duet *buffo* Fulgenzio and Roberto.
      4 Romanza Eugenia (which could be suppressed)
      5 Aria tenor.
      6 Finale.

Some Details of

Giuseppi Donizetti's Career

(with a Note on Francesco Donizetti)

GIUSEPPE, the eldest child of Andrea and Domenica Donizetti, was born at Bergamo on November 7, 1788. He had some musical instruction from Giacomo Corini, who had married his aunt—Andrea Donizetti's sister—Angela. Although Giuseppe was refused admission to the newly instituted Lezioni caritatevoli di musica in 1805 because of his age (he was then seventeen), Giovanni Simone Mayr was sufficiently impressed with his musical ability to give him, without pay, nineteen private lessons. Giuseppe was at one time a choirboy in the Church of Santa Maria Maggiore, and his voice occasionally was heard in one or another of the Bergamese theaters.

In 1808, Giuseppe Donizetti was conscripted into the army of the Napoleonic Kingdom of Italy, becoming a member of the Seventh Italian Regiment. Having taken some part in the campaign against Austria, in 1809 he set out with the regiment for Spain, but was delayed by illness en route, and spent some time in a military hospital at Castelnaudary[1] in France. He saw service in Spain in 1811, 1812, and 1813, and is said to have been active during that siege of Saragossa which Byron romanticized in *Childe Harold*. When the army of the Kingdom of Italy was dissolved, Giuseppe returned briefly to Bergamo. After two months there, he went to Genoa, where he

[1] Almost forty-four years later, the Pasha Giuseppe Donizetti addressed the following to a high official of the Sultan's court: "Constantinople, November 22, 1854. *Mémoire* to His Highness Achmed-Fethy Pasha. Finding myself in a comfortable position thanks to the beneficences of Our August and Glorious Sovereign, I cede to the Hospital of Castelnaudary (Aude), in which I was ill in 1811, the portion coming to me of the legacy left by the Emperor Napoleon I to the Battalion of the Island of Elba. The papers establishing my right to participate in the credit opened up by the Decree of August 5, 1854, issued at Biarritz by His Imperial Majesty the Emperor Napoleon III, I have been obliged to send to France at the time when I was honored with a brevet as Chevalier of the Legion of Honor. Your Highness's Very Humble Servant, Joseph Donizetti."

enlisted in the French forces, becoming flutist in a military band stationed on Elba. In Portoferraio, chief town of the island, in 1815, he married a local girl named Angela Tondi.

Giuseppe Donizetti is said to have been on board the ship on which Napoleon, escaping from Elba, returned to France, landing near Antibes on March 1, 1815. He was with the Napoleonic troops during the Hundred Days and probably was at Waterloo. Later, in Paris, he was lodged for a time at the Caserne des Braves, opposite the Tuileries Palace. Leaving the French service, he returned to Italy and enlisted in the army of the Kingdom of Sardinia and Piedmont, becoming Musical Director of the Reggimento Provinziale di Casale on October 26, 1815, and being present at the battle of Novara in 1821. His regiment then was dissolved, having pronounced in favor of the Constitution of 1821, and he signed up as musical director of the Primo Reggimento della Brigata Casale. At Alessendria, on April 29, 1818, his only son had been born. Named Andrea, this child would grow up to become his uncle Gaetano's companion at Paris during his final illness. In 1825, Giuseppe was living at Genoa.

In 1827, events in remote Constantinople began to affect Giuseppe Donizetti's career. Mahmud II, Sultan of Turkey, desiring to put his armed forces into better order, detailed his grand vizier, Hosrev Pasha, to hire a first-rate musical director. The grand vizier turned to the Marchese Groppallo, minister of Sardinia and Piedmont to the Sublime Porte, who thereupon forwarded the request to the Sardinian Ministry of Foreign Affairs in Turin. A ministerial secretary named Grosson recommended Giuseppe Donizetti for the position, and a dispatch dated November 7, 1827, authorized him to become "*Istruttore generale delle musiche imperiali ottomane.*" The Donizettis embarked for Constantinople on a sailing ship and, after a turbulent voyage, reached there early in 1828, Giuseppe being received at once by the eager Sultan.

Donizetti's Turkish career prospered from the beginning. In 1829, he composed *Mahmudiè*, a march in the Sultan's honor, which was performed to everyone's delight by Giuseppe's military students. In 1831, he was decorated with the Order of Nicham-Iftihar. When Abdul Medjid succeeded to the imperial throne in 1830, Donizetti's star rose still higher, as he had been on friendly terms with the new Sultan, for whom he soon prepared a march entitled *Medjidiè*. This earned him a snuffbox with the imperial cipher in diamonds, one of many valuable gifts that came his way. He was made, in turn, an honorary colonel of the Imperial Guard, a pasha, and a brigadier general. In addition to the marches for his two imperial masters, he composed several "Algerian" and other marches, songs, and piano pieces—some of the last being published in Milan by Ricordi. He became sufficiently well known in European musical circles to be listed by François-Joseph Fétis in the *Biographie universelle des musiciens et bibliographie générale de la musique* (Paris, 1833–44). For his services to French music, he was awarded the Legion of Honor.

After some years in Turkey, Giuseppe Donizetti began the organization of an annual opera season at Pera (the section of Constantinople now called

Beyoglu), staging many Italian operas, including those of his brother Gaetano. Gérard de Nerval, visiting the Near East in 1843, met Giuseppe Donizetti just before the trip to Italy during which Gaetano was to say of his
brother: "Giuseppe is white-haired, but white and pink and as fat as a fool."
How highly Giuseppe was regarded in court circles at Constantinople was
indicated in October, 1844, when a destructive fire broke out near his house
there. Realizing that Donizetti's home was in peril, the Pasha Achmed-Fethy,
a brother-in-law to the Sultan, ordered the surrounding buildings razed
to save it.

Giuseppe Donizetti survived both of his brothers, dying at Constantinople on February 12, 1856, aged sixty-seven.

THE composer's other brother, Francesco, also was his senior. He was born
at Bergamo on February 7, 1802. Somewhat deficient mentally, Francesco
was torpid and of little practical intelligence, but he shared his brothers' musical bent. He volunteered for military service as a band musician, but soon was
back in Bergamo. There, for the rest of his life, he scraped together a meager
living, in time dependent upon gifts from his brothers. In 1821, he and fourteen other dilettantes and *professori di musica* living in Bergamo applied
to the local authorities for permission to form a town band. Thereafter, he
took childish pleasure in his uniform and in parading the streets as a drum-
mer. After his father's death in 1835, efforts were made to obtain for him the
porter's position that Andrea Donizetti had occupied in the local pawnshop
—and the free lodgings that went with it. He held this position from July
19, 1836, to his death, and even appears to have received some sort of promo-
tion in 1843. As he grew older, however, he became more and more of a
problem to both Gaetano and Giuseppe, showing himself less and less responsible.

Francesco Donizetti was generally a passive, good-natured man, but
was capable of irrational and destructive rages. He seemed to those who knew
him best a foolish, pompous, and at the same time timorous, man. Gaetano referred to him as his *"fratello scemo"*—witless brother. Writing from Vienna
on June 7, 1845, Gaetano told Antonio Dolci—who watched over Francesco
for the absent brothers, handing him the pension with which they filled out
his small wages: "My brother, where does he want to set up house? At San
Pellegrino? If he really needs the baths, *fiat*. But if it's for amusement, change
the thing." Francesco never married, but he had at least one illegitimate
child and a recognized mistress, a servant girl named Elisabetta Santi Pesenti,
who became his heir—a fact that complicated greatly the settling of that
part of Gaetano's estate in which Francesco (who outlived his famous
brother by little more than eight months) was a participant. After suffering
from dropsy for some years, Francesco Donizetti died of a pulmonary
hemorrhage resulting in *"soffocazione da ematorea"* (internal drowning)
on December 20, 1848.

A Note on Present-Day Values of Some

Currencies

Mentioned in This Book

THROUGH the kindness of my friend Signora Luisa Ambrosini of Rome (and indirectly through that of Dottoressa Maria Vismara of the Società per l'Organizzazione Internazionale, Rome), I am able to suggest here approximate present-day values for moneys mentioned by and in connection with Donizetti. The mathematics represents a consensus of several Italian and other economists and economic historians.

Column 1 below names the money; column 2 gives its value in the Italian lire of the unification (1861); column 3 attempts to account (multiplication by 210) for the increase since 1861 in the price of gold; column 4 similarly attempts to account (multiplication by 320) for the increase in the cost of living in Italy since 1861. The results of the latter calculation have been used to suggest approximate values in United States dollars, using an exchange figure of 620 lire to the dollar.

The coefficients were taken from *Coefficienti di trasformazione del valore della lira italiana, 1861–1955* (Rome: Istituto Centrale di Statistica, 1956). The lire values of the various moneys were found in pamphlets issued by the Archivio Economico dell'Unificazione Italiana.

These figures are approximations only. I believe that they are reasonably accurate, and therefore useful. But the coefficient of 320 was arrived at as of 1955—and, as the cost of living in Italy has increased materially since that year, the figures in the last two columns very probably should be somewhat higher.

MONEY	Value in 1861 lire	x 210	x 320	United States dollars
baiocco, Rome (pontifical)	0.053	11	17	.011291
bavaro[1]				
colonato[2]				
ducato, Kingdom of the Two Sicilies	4.24	890	1357	2.18841
” , Modena	2.80	588	896	1.445248
” , Parma	5.15	1081	1648	2.623224
franc: see *lira*, France				
lira, Austria	.84	176	268	.432284
” , France *(franc)*	1.00	210	320	.516160
” , Kingdom of the Two Sicilies	1.00	210	320	.516160
” , Lombardo-Veneto	.87	182	278	.448414
” , Parma	.20	42	64	.103232
” , Rome (pontifical)	1.00	210	320	.516160
” , Tuscany	.84	176	268	.432284
napoleona d'oro, France and the Kingdom of Sardinia and Piedmont	20.00	4200	6400	10.323
scudo, Austria	5.18	1087	1657	2.628741
” , France	5.00	1050	1600	2.5808
” , Milan	4.60	966	1472	2.374336
” , Piedmont (“old”)	7.10	1491	2272	3.664736
” , Piedmont (“new”)	5.00	1050	1600	2.5808
” , Repubblica italiana	3.85	808	1232	1.98721
” , Rome (pontifical)	5.32	1117	1702	2.745326
” , Sicily	5.21	1094	1667	2.687871
zecchino, Austria	11.48	2410	3673	5.924549
” , France	10.00	2100	3200	5.1616
” , Kingdom of the Two Sicilies	9.15	1921	2929	4.724477
” , Milan	11.84	2488	3792	6.116496
” , Rome (pontifical)	11.70	2457	3744	6.039072
” , Tuscany	12.00	2520	3840	6.19392
” , Venice	11.85	2488	3792	6.116496

NOTE: Donizetti's *"svansiche"* were Austrian lire. This was his phonetic rendition of *zwanzigste*. The *"piastre"* occasionally mentioned apparently had a value of about five Kingdom of the Two Sicilies *lire*.

[1] No such money known, perhaps a misnomer for the *bavaresa* of the Kingdom of Bavaria, with a present-day lira value of about 3500, a present-day dollar value of about 5.6455.

[2] Donizetti used this word as equivalent to *scudo* (specifically, the pontifical *scudo.*) Thus, Virginia Vasselli's dowry was two thousand *colonati* (Donizetti's letter of May 25, 1827, to his father; see p. 63n). On April 27, 1848, writing to Andrea Donizetti to ask that this dowry be refunded to him as the head of the Vasselli family, Antonio Vasselli referred to it as *"scudi 2000."* The word *colonato* remains a mystery: it may have been a vernacular persistence of either the Spanish *colonato* (late eighteenth century, with a present-day lira value of about 1600, a present-day dollar value of about 2.5708) or of the more remote *coronato*, a Neapolitan coin dating from 1458 and later the name of differing coins in circulation in Burgundy, Flanders, and Provence from the twelfth to the fifteenth centuries.

The Music

A Chronological List of Donizetti's Operas, with Commentary and Performance Data; A List of Donizetti's Nonoperatic Compositions

THESE lists are based on pages 169–218 of Guido Zavadini's monumental book (*138*), *Donizetti: Vita—Musiche—Epistolario* (Bergamo: Istituto d'Arti Grafiche, 1948). Credit for the original compilation belongs to Zavadini, but he is not to be blamed for any errors that I may have introduced while editing, translating, expanding—and, in a few places, contracting—his catalogues. Because I hope that later, amended editions of the present book may be published, I should appreciate the thoughtfulness of any reader who, detecting errors of commission or omission here, will send specific suggested corrections to me in care of my publisher. Zavadini found extensive causes for changes in the lists of Donizetti's compositions, which he had published first in (*139*), *Gaetano Donizetti: Vicende della sua vita artistica e catalogo delle musiche su documenti inediti* (Bergamo: Istituto Italiano d'Arti Grafiche, 1941). His considerable expansion of those lists in his later book resulted in large part from his examination and evaluation of evidence previously unavailable or overlooked. My hope is that passing years may bring me the additional knowledge and materials that would permit me to publish at a later date a similarly expanded and corrected catalogue of Donizetti's music. The present lists are as nearly complete and correct as I now am able to make them.

A Chronological List of Donizetti's

Operas

With Commentary and Performance Data

1816

Il Pigmalione; one act; librettist unknown (possibly Antonio Simone Sografi's version of Jean-Jacques Rousseau's *Pygmalion*); composed, 1816; autograph score (105 pages)—inscribed "Begun September 25, finished October 1, 1816, at almost 2 o'clock in the morning of Tuesday, arrival of the new Legate"—in Paris Conservatory Library.

First performance apparently October 13, 1960, in the series (1948 on) of stagings at the Teatro Donizetti, Bergamo, under the direction of Bindo Missiroli—which up to 1960 also had included *Poliuto, Betly, Il Campanello, Rita, La Figlia del reggimento, Linda di Chamounix, Anna Bolena, Maria di Rohan, Maria Stuarda, L'Ajo nell'imbarazzo, Lucia di Lammermoor, L'Elisir d'amore,* and *Don Pasquale.*

1817

L'Ira d'Achille; librettist unknown; composed 1817; autograph score in Paris Conservatory Library. Never performed.

(L')Olimpiade; librettist unknown (possibly Metastasio's *L'Olimpiade* was used unchanged); composed, 1817; score lost, but Museo Donizettiano, Bergamo, has a *scena e duetto* for characters named (as in Metastasio) Aristea and Megacle, with separate orchestral and vocal parts, not in Donizetti's autograph. Never performed.

1818

Enrico di Borgogna (opera semiseria); two acts; libretto by Bartolomeo Merelli; composed, 1818; autograph score lost.

Première: Teatro San Luca, Venice, November 14, 1818; cast included: Fanny Eckerlin, Adele Catalani, Antonio Fosconi, Giovanni Spech, Piero Verni, and Giuseppe Fioravanti.

(1818 Continued)

Una Follia (di Carnovale), perhaps also called *Il Ritratto parlante (farsa)*; one act; libretto by Bartolomeo Merelli; composed, 1818; Autograph score lost.

Première: Teatro San Luca, Venice, December 15, 1818.

1819

Piccioli Virtuosi ambulanti, sometimes called *Piccoli Virtuosi di musica ambulanti (opera buffa)*; one act; libretto attributed to both Bartolomeo Merelli and Gherardo Bevilacqua-Aldovrandini; composed, 1819; autograph score lost.

Première: summer 1819; cast—students of the Lezioni caritatevoli, Bergamo—included: Girolamo Forini, Gorini, Giacomo Cantù, and Carlo Trezzini.

Il Falegname di Livonia, o Pietro il grande, czar delle Russie (opera buffa): two acts; librettist unknown; composed 1819; autograph score in the Ricordi archives, Milan.

Première: Teatro San Samuele, Venice, December 26, 1819; cast included Amati, Giovanni Battista Verger, Pio Botticelli, and Luigi Martinelli. The first of Donizetti's operas to win performances at several other theaters after its *première*, it was staged at the Teatro Comunale, Bologna, during 1823–24 season; at Verona in September 1825; in Padua during the autumn of 1826; again at Venice (Teatro San Benedetto) during the Carnival season of 1827; and at Spoleto during that of 1829. When it was announced for the Bologna staging—the first Donizetti opera heard in that city—the composer was listed as "Maestro Donizetti Gaetano di Bergamo." The scenery for that production was by Domenico Ferri, who exercised an important influence on the evolution of scenic art in Paris. In view of a later comment by Donizetti that he was not popular in Bologna because the *bolognese* believed that he had refused to compose an opera specifically for them (whereas, in reality, no impresario had commissioned him to write one), it is interesting to note that *Il Falegname di Livonia* was succeeded at the Teatro Comunale by *Anna Bolena* (1832); *Fausta* 1834); *L'Elisir d'amore* and *Il Furioso all'isola di San Domingo* (1836); *Marin Faliero, Lucia di Lammermoor, Torquato Tasso,* and *L'Elisir d'amore* (1837); *Gemma di Vergy* (1837–38); *Roberto Devereux* and *Belisario* (1838); *Lucia di Lammermoor* and *Anna Bolena* (1839); *L'Elisir d'amore* (1839–40); *Gemma di Vergy* (1840–41); *Eustorgia da Romano* (i.e., *Lucrezia Borgia*, with Clara Novello and Napoleone Moriani, 1841); *L'Elisir d'amore* and *Lucrezia Borgia* (1842); *Marin Faliero, Le Convenienze ed inconvenienze teatrali,* and *Roberto Devereux* (1843, during which year *Linda di Chamounix* also was sung in Bologna, at the Casino dei Nobili); *Maria di Rohan* and *Lucrezia Borgia* (1844); *Linda di Chamounix* and *L'Elisir d'amore* (1844–45); *Maria di Rudenz* (1845–46); *Maria Padilla* (1847); *La Figlia del reggimento, Don Pasquale,* and *L'Elisir d'amore*—apparently Bologna's favorite

(*1819 Continued*)

among Donizetti's operas (1848–49). This does not look like unpopularity.

1820–21

Le Nozze in villa (opera buffa): libretto by Bartolomeo Merelli; composed 1820; autograph score lost.

Première: Teatro Vecchio, Mantua, Carnival season of 1820–1821; cast possibly included Fanny Eckerlin. Giuliano Donati-Petténi stated (*39*, 38), on what authority I do not know, that it failed after its second performance.

1822

Zoraide di Granata, (opera seria): two acts; libretto by Bartolomeo Merelli, perhaps based on a libretto on the same subject (after a story by Florian Gonzales) by Luigi Romanelli and set as an opera by Giuseppe Niccolini (La Scala, Milan, 1807); composed 1822; autograph score in the Ricordi archives, Milan.

Première: Teatro Argentina, Rome, January 28, 1822; cast included Ester Mombelli (Zoraide), Mazzanti (Abenamet), Gaetana Corini of Bergamo (Ines), Domenico Donzelli (Almuzir—given in some programs as Almuzio); Alberto Torri (Alj Zegri), and Gaetano Rambaldi (Almanzor); the conductor was the Argentina's first violinist, Gaspare Stabilini. When this opera was revived at the Argentina on January 7, 1824, Donzelli retained his original role; others in the new cast were Luigia Boccabadati-Gazzuoli (Zoraide), Rosmunda Pisaroni-

Carrara (Abenamet), Rosalinda Ferri (Ines), and G. Galassi (Almanzor). *Zoraide di Granata* also was staged in Lisbon in 1825.

La Zingara (opera seria): two acts; libretto by Andrea Leone Tottola; composed 1822; Nonautograph score in Naples Conservatory Library.

Première: Teatro Nuovo, Naples, May 12, 1822; cast included Monticelli (Ines), Francesca Checcherini (Amelia), Giacinta Canonici (Argilla), Clementina (?) Grossi (Ghita), Grossi *minore* (Manuelita), Giuseppe Fioravanti (Don Sebastiano), Carlo Moncada (Don Ranuccio), Carlo Casaccia (Pappacione), Marco Venier (Fernando), Alessandro Busti (Duca di Alziras), Raffaele Sarti (Antonio Alvares), and Raffaele Casaccia (Sguiglio). The *Giornale del Regno delle Due Sicilie* said on May 13: "Last evening the company at the Teatro Nuovo took up its series of performances again with an opera entitled *La Zingara*, written by the Maestro Signor Donnizzetti [*sic*] expressly for the company itself. This new work by our young composer was crowned with a success that sustains the reputation he acquired in the first tests of his music at Rome. The public awarded him the liveliest applause several times." *La Zingara* ran for twenty-eight consecutive performances; after an interval, it received twenty more.

La Lettera anonima (farsa): one act; libretto by Giulio Genoino; composed 1822; autograph score in the Ricordi archives, Milan.

Première: Teatro del Fondo, Naples, June 29, 1822; cast in-

(1822 Continued)

cluded Flora Fabbri (Contessa Rosina), Teresa Cecconi[1] (Melita), De Bernardis (Lauretta), Giovanni Battista Rubini (Filinto), De Franchi (Don Macario), Giovanni Pace (Giliberto), and Calvarola (Flageolet). The opera, received happily, was sung twenty times.

Chiara e Serafina, o I Pirati (opera semiseria): two acts; libretto by Felice Romani; composed 1822; autograph score in the Ricordi archives, Milan.

Première: Teatro alla Scala, Milan, October 26, 1822; cast included Rosa Morandi (Serafina), Isabella Fabbrica (Chiara), Maria Gioja-Tamburini (Lisetta), Carolina Sivelli (Agnese), Antonio Tamburini (Picaro), Carlo Pizzochero (Don Alvaro), Carlo Poggioli (Don Fernando and Gennaro), Savino Monelli (Don Ramiro), Nicola De Grecis (Don Meschino), and Carlo Donà (Spelatro). Tamburini, who just had married Maria Gioja, daughter of the noted choreographer Ferdinando Gioja, was to sing in eleven more Donizetti *premières,* the last that of *Don Pasquale* (1843). *Chiara e Serafina,* though received indifferently by its first audience and critics, was sung alternately with Saverio Mercadante's *Adele ed Emerico* and reached twelve performances by November 26. Romani's libretto

[1] Zavadini *(138),* probably following Florimo *(54),* assigns this role to Cecconi, though the *Giornale del Regno delle Due Sicilie* of July 1, 1822, said rather plaintively: "Why does Signora Cecconi never wish to sing"—perhaps thus indicating that she had not taken this role at the first performance.

for this opera was reused for Alberto Mazzucato's opera *I Corsari* (La Scala, February 15, 1840).

Alfredo il grande[2] *(opera seria):* two acts; libretto by Andrea Leone Tottola; composed 1823; autograph score in Naples Conservatory Library, nonautograph copy in Paris Conservatory Library.

Première: Teatro San Carlo, Naples, July 2, 1823; cast included Elisabetta Ferron (Amalia), Maria Anna Cecconi (Enrichetta), Gorini (Margherita), Andrea Nozzari of Bergamo (Alfredo), Pio Botticelli (Eduardo), Michele Benedetti (Atkins), Orlandi (Guglielmo), and Gaetano Chizzola (Rivers).

Il Fortunato inganno (opera buffa): one act; libretto by Andrea Leone Tottola; composed 1823; autograph score in Naples Conservatory Library.

Première: Teatro Nuovo, Naples, September 3, 1823; cast included Teresa Melas (Aurelia), Francesca Checcherini (Fulgenzia), D'Auria (Eugenia), Clementina Grossi (Fiordelisa), Carlo Casaccia (Lattanzio), Giuseppe Fioravanti (Colonnello), Marco Venier (Tenente), Carlo Moncada (Bequadro), Raffaele Casaccia (Vulcano), Giuseppe Papi (Biscaglino), and Raffaele Sarti (Ascanio).

1824

L'Ajo nell'imbarazzo, o Don Gregorio (opera buffa): two acts;

[2] Interestingly, an opera with this title by Giovanni Simone Mayr had received its *première* at the Teatro Sociale, Bergamo, in 1819.

(*1825 Continued*)

libretto by Jacopo Ferretti;[3] composed 1823–24; nonautograph score in Naples Conservatory Library.

Première: Teatro Valle, Rome, February 4, 1824; cast included Ester Mombelli (Gilda), Agnese Loyselet (Leonarda), Savino Monelli (Enrico), Giuseppe Fioravanti, Antonio Tamburini (Marchese), Nicola Tacci (Gregorio), Giovanni Puglieschi (Pippetto), and De Dominicis (Simone); the conductor was Giovanni Maria Pelliccia. *L'Ajo nell'imbarazzo* quickly spread to other Italian operas houses and abroad. Performances were staged at the Kärnthnertortheater, Vienna, April 2, 1827 (one week after Beethoven's death), with Henriette-Clémentine Méric-Lalande, Arcangelo Berettoni, and Luigi Lablache in leading roles (the first Donizetti opera sung in Vienna); at Dresden, April 9, 1828, as *Il Governo della casa;* Barcelona, June 3, 1828; Rio de Janeiro, July 14, 1829; Lisbon, December 4, 1837; Nice, Carnival, 1840; Berlin, Königsstädtischestheater, July 26, 1841; Corfu, autumn 1842; Copen-

hagen, spring 1844; Constantinople, spring 1844; London, Her Majesty's Theatre, July 28, 1846, as *Don Gregorio;* as well as in many Italian theaters. During the Carnival of 1829–30, *L'Ajo nell' imbarazzo* was heard at the Teatro della Società (or Sociale), Bergamo, under the direction of Pietro Rovelli, with Antonio Dolci —another of Donizetti's friends— as chorusmaster; the cast included Marietta Cantarelli, Rainiero Marchionni, Domenico Cossetti, and Antonio Cipriani; on this occasion, the opera seems to have been a failure. It was being sung as late as April 4, 1866, in Milan, and February 12, 1879, in Venice. With proper casting and stylish performance, it would repay revival today.

Emilia di Liverpool (also called *Emilia* and *L'Eremitaggio di Liverpool*) (*opera semiseria*): two acts; libretto by Giuseppe Checcherini; composed 1824; autograph score in Naples Conservatory Library.

Première: Teatro Nuovo, Naples, July 28, 1824; cast including Teresa Melas (Emilia), Francesca Checcherini, wife of the librettist (Candida), Clementina Grossi (Luigia), Carlo Casaccia (Don Romualdo), Giuseppe Fioravanti (Claudio di Liverpool), Zilioli (Federico), and De Nicola (Conte); it had eight performances, the last on November 2, 1824, and was revived briefly in 1828.

---

[3] Ferretti had based his libretto on a comedy by the Roman writer Count Giovanni Giraud which had been played at the Valle in 1807. The play previously had been adapted for at least four other operas: one by E. Guarnaccia (Teatro San Moisè, Venice, 1811, with libretto by Giulio Domenico Camagna); one by Giuseppe Pilotti, who had been Donizetti's counterpoint teacher at Bologna (Teatro della Pergola, Florence, 1811); one by Celli (Teatro San Benedetto, Venice, 1813, with libretto by Gaetano Gasparri); and one by either Giuseppe or Luigi Mosca (Naples, 1813). Later than Donizetti's opera was one by Count Nicelli (Piacenza, 1825), with libretto by Scribani.

1825

Alahor di Granata (*opera seria*): two acts; libretto by M. A.; composed 1825; autograph score lost.

(*1825 Continued*)

Première: Teatro Carolino, Palermo, January 7, 1826; cast including Elisabetta Ferron (Zobeida), Marietta Gioja-Tamburini (Muley-Hassem), Carlotta Tomasetti (Sulima), Berardo Winter (Alamar), Antonio Tamburini (Alahor), and (Ismaele) Salvatore Patti, future father of Adelina and Carlotta Patti. When *Alahor di Granata* was staged at the Teatro San Carlo, Naples, later in 1826, roles were taken by Henriette-Clémentine Méric-Lalande (Zobeida), Brigida Lorenzani (Muley-Hassem), either Almerinda or Eloisa Manzocchi (Sulima), Berardo Winter (Alamar), Luigi Lablache (Alahor), and Gaetano Chizzola (Ismaele).

[*Il Castello degli invalidi*] (*farsa*): one act; librettist unknown; composed 1825-26 (?); *première:* said to have taken place at the Teatro Carolino, Palermo, in spring 1826; cast unknown. Autograph score lost. See p. 47 for discussion of the existence of this opera.

1826

Elvida (*opera seria*): one act; libretto by Giovanni Federico Schmidt; composed 1826; autograph score in Naples Conservatory Library.

Première: Teatro San Carlo, Naples, July 6, 1826; cast included Henriette-Clémentine Méric-Lalande (Elvida), Brigida Lorenzani (Zeidar), either Almerinda or Eloisa Manzocchi (Zulima), Luigi Lablache (Amur), Giovanni Battista Rubini (Alfonso), and Gaetano Chizzola (Ramiro).

(*Gabriella di Vergy*): composed 1826; dated autograph score in Museo Donizettiano, Bergamo.

Première: see under 1869.

La Bella Prigioniera (*farsa*): one act; librettist unknown; probably composed (complete?) 1826; never staged. Autograph score lost, but Museo Donizettiano, Bergamo, has two autograph numbers for voices and piano: a recitative and duet for soprano and bass (Amina and Everardo)—*"Ella parlar mi vuole"* —and a recitative and duet for soprano and tenor (Amina and Carlo)—*"Olà . . . tosto discenda e a me si guida Amina."*

1827

Olivo e Pasquale (*opera buffa*): two acts; libretto by Jacopo Ferretti, after a comedy by Antonio Simone Sografi, with additional material from Sografi's comedy *Il Più Bel Giorno della Westfalia;* composed 1826; nonautograph score in Naples Conservatory Library.

Première: Teatro Valle, Rome, January 7, 1827; conducted by the Valle's first violinist, Giovanni Maria Pelliccia; cast included Emilia Bonini (Isabella), Anna Scudellari—Domenico Cosselli's wife—(Camillo), Agnese Loyselet (Matilde), Domenico Cosselli (Olivo), Giuseppe Frezzolini—whose daughter Erminia was to become an internationally famous soprano and to marry the tenor Antonio Poggi—(Pasquale), Giovanni Battista Verger (Le Bross), Luigi Garofolo (Columella), and Stanislao Prò (Un Servo). A staging of this opera at the Teatro della Società, Bergamo, on January 12, 1831, under the direction of Pietro Rovelli, was very well

(1827 Continued)

liked; the cast included the excelling French tenor Gilbert-Louis Duprez, then only twenty-four, and his wife, billed as Alessandrina Duprez, Vincenzo Galli, and Domenico Cosselli.

Among foreign stagings of *Olivo e Pasquale* during Donizetti's lifetime were: in Italian— London, March 3, 1832; Barcelona, February 6, 1833; Bastia (Corsica), autumn 1833; Lisbon, January 20, 1836; Nice, autumn 1839; Berlin, Königsstädtischestheater, January 8, 1845; Vienna, June 17, 1847; in German—Graz (translation by Georg Ott), April 10, 1830; Vienna, Theater in der Josefstadt, October 5, 1836. When *Olivo e Pasquale* was sung at the Kärnthnertortheater, Vienna, in Italian, on June 17, 1847, the Isabella was the Irish soprano Catherine Hayes; with her in the cast were Filippo Colini (Olivo) and Cesare Soares (Pasquale). The opera was sung at the Teatro Nuovo, Naples, in 1827, with Teresa Fischer (Isabella), Francesca Checcherini (Matilde), Filippo Galli (Olivo), Carolina Manzi (Le Bross), De Nicola (Columella), and Giuseppe Papi (Diego); at Palermo, in 1829; and at the Teatro della Canobbiana, Milan, summer 1830, this last with unusual success. During the winter of 1830–31, it was staged at Parma, Crema, and Brescia; later, it was repeated in Milan (Teatro Carcano); and during 1831 and 1832, it was sung in Genoa, Florence, Turin, Padua, Regio nell' Emilia, Leghorn, Trieste, Modena, and Verona. In 1833, stagings were put on at Cento, Bagna-

cavallo, Ascoli, and again at Naples. In 1834, *Olivo e Pasquale* was being sung at Ravenna and— unsuccessfully—at La Scala, Milan. Novara heard this opera in 1836, Pesaro in 1838. It was used to reopen the restored Teatro della Canobbiana, Milan, in 1844—fourteen years after its first performance in that theater.

Otto Mesi in due ore, ossia Gli Esiliati in Siberia (opera romantica): three parts; libretto by Domenico Gilardoni, after the *mélodrame La Fille de l'exilé, ou Huit Mois en deux heures,* by René-Charles-Guilbert de Pixérécourt; composed 1827; autograph score in Naples Conservatory Library.

Première: Teatro Nuovo, Naples, May 13, 1827; cast included Caterina Liparini, Francesca Checcherini, Servoli, Giuseppe Fioravanti, Gennaro Luzio, and Raffaele Scalese. When staged at La Scala, Milan, on September 4, 1831, as *Gli Esiliati in Siberia,* it chalked up only eight singings. When put on at Modena in 1831, it coincided with a rebellion that broke out at the home of the noted patriot Ciro Menotti, and its performances were suspended. The theater was kept closed for some days; then it reopened with Donizetti's opera. After Part I, the simmering audience shouted for an Italian hymn. As no national anthem was available, the orchestra obliged with a march, sonorous with trumpets, from Part III of the opera. This pleased the patriots so well that from that evening forward, Donizetti's *Otto Mesì* march became a sort of local revolutionary symbol. As Guglielmo

(1827 Continued)

Barblan pointed out *(12)*, this was one of the few occasions on which Donizetti's music played the role that Verdi's was to play so notably. *Otto Mesi in due ore* was sung some fifty times during its first run at Naples, was liked less well in Milan, and won an overwhelming reception at Rome, becoming the only success of the Carnival season of the Teatro Valle there in 1832, when it was sung by a cast including the great Hungarian contralto Caroline Ung(h)er, Celestino Salvatori, and Ferdinando Lauretti, running up about fifteen performances before Shrove Tuesday, March 6. Announced for performance at the Teatro Carignano, Turin, in the autumn of 1834, *Otto Mesi in due ore* actually was not heard in that city until February 18, 1835, at the Teatro Sutera, when the singers included Baletti, Gebaur, Fusari, Pani, Canetta, Antonio Benciolini, and Giovannini. Under a variety of titles, this opera also was sung: in Italian—at Lisbon, April 4, 1839; Barcelona, October 15, 1840; in German—at Graz, February 12, 1828 (translation by Georg Ott, billed as *Die Macht der kindlichen Liebe)*; Berlin, the Königsstädtischestheater, May 3, 1832; Vienna, August 3, 1832, as *Acht Monate in zwei Stunden*, the cast including Sebastian Binder (Peter the Great), Carl Josef Oberhofer (Grand Marshal), Bussmayer (Count Yorshy), Rosalie Schodel (Theodora), Anna Bondar (Marie), Eduard Weiss (Michael), Josef Staudigl, Sr. (Ivan), and Carl Wilhelm Just. After Donizetti's death, this opera was sung on December 31, 1853, at the Théâtre-Italien, Paris, in a French version by Adolphe de Leuven and Léon-Lévy Brunswick, as *Elisabeth, ou La Fille du proscrit*, the music having been "adapted" by Uranio Fontana. This curious gallimaufry, its text translated into Italian, was staged at the Teatro San Radegonda, Milan, on July 24, 1854.

Il Borgomastro di Saardam (opera buffa): two acts; libretto by Domenico Gilardoni, after a French play by Anne-Honoré-Joseph Mélesville, Jean-Toussaint Merle, and Eugène Cantiran de Boirie (1818); composed 1827; autograph score in the Ricordi archives, Milan.

Première: Teatro Nuovo, Naples, August 19, 1827; the cast was headed by Caroline Ung(h)er, whom Rossini once evaluated as "Fire of the south, energy of the north, a chest of bronze, a voice of silver, a talent of gold." Unger had studied with Mozart's sister-in-law and onetime infatuation, Aloysia Weber Lange, and had sung in the first performances of Beethoven's *Missa Solemnis* and Ninth Symphony. She was responsible for the prevalent story that deafness had kept Beethoven from hearing the applause until she prodded him into turning around, after which he saw the visible signs of the audience's enthusiasm. With Unger in the *première* of *Il Borgomastro di Saardam* were Almerinda Manzocchi (Carlotta), Salvadori (Lo Czar), Berardo Winter (Pietro Flimann), Carlo Casaccia (Timoteo), Raffaele Casaccia (Borgomastro), Giovanni Pace (Leforte), and

(*1827 Continued*)

Gaetano Chizzola (Ali-Makmed). Unger was to sing in two more Donizetti *premières:* those of *Belisario* (1836) and *Maria di Rudenz* (1838), and may have sung in that of *Parisina*, q.v. (1833). *Il Borgomastro di Saardam* was staged at La Scala, Milan, on January 2, 1828, and at the Teatro Valle, Rome, in June of that year, both times for a single unsuccessful performance. Foreign stagings included: Barcelona, December 16, 1829; Vienna, Theater in der Josefstadt, in German translation, September 16, 1838; Berlin, the Königsstädtischestheater, also in German, August 3, 1837; and Budapest, in a Hungarian translation by K. Lengey, in 1839.

Le Convenienze ed inconvenienze teatrali (farsa): one act; libretto by Donizetti, after Antonio Simone Sografi's comedies *Le Convenienze teatrali* (1794) and *Le Inconvenienze teatrali* (1800); composed 1827; autograph score in Paris Conservatory Library.

Première: Teatro Nuovo Naples, November 21, 1827, with Gennaro Luzio as Mamma Agata. It was staged at La Scala, Milan, on September 1, 1831, with Giulia Grisi, Domenico Reina, Vincenzo Galli, and Cesare Badiali. When it was mounted in Italian in Vienna at the Kärnthnertortheater on April 27, 1840, the cast included Luigia Abbadia (Corilla), Giuseppe Frezzolini (Mamma Agata), Elg Tuczek (Dorotea), Amalia Laroche (Luigia), Julius Pfister (Guglielmo), Antonio Benciolini (Prospero), Giuseppe Visanetti (Appoggiatura), Giacomo Roppa (Proculo), and Pietro Novelli

(Impresario); it was sung only once.

L'Esule di Roma, ossia Il Proscritto (sometimes billed as *Settimio il proscritto*) (*opera seria*): two acts; libretto by Domenico Gilardoni; composed 1827; autograph score in the Ricordi archives, Milan.

Première: Teatro San Carlo, Naples, January 1, 1828; cast included Adelaide Tosi (Argelia), Ricci (Leontina), Giovanni Battista Rubini (Settimio), Luigi Lablache (Murena), Giambattista (?) Campagnoli (Publio), Gaetano Chizzola (Lucio), and Capranica *figlio* (Fulvio); the singer of the role of Emilia is unknown. When this opera was staged at La Scala, Milan, on July 12, 1828, it instituted a run of ten consecutive nights. On April 3, 1830, the Accademia filarmonica romana, which had been founded in 1822, gave a concert performance of *L'Esule di Roma*, with leading singers listed by Alberto Cametti (*27*) as "Garofolini Mercuri (Argelia), the usual tenor (Pietro) Angelini (Settimio), and the baritone Miniato Ricci (Murena)." It was staged in Venice in spring 1831 as *Settimio, ossia L'Esule di Roma*. At the Teatro Valle, Rome, on October 20, 1832, it had a cast including Anna Delserre, Berardo Winter, and Giorgio Ronconi—all of whom were applauded wildly, particularly in the trio finale of Act I. At Bergamo on August 14, 1840, the Teatro Riccardi, Donizetti attended a performance of this opera. The conductor was his childhood friend Marco Bonesi, and the leading parts were assigned to Eugenia Tadolini, Do-

(*1827 Continued*)

menico Donzelli, and Ignazio Marini; the occasion provided the composer with his greatest triumph in his birthplace (see p. 154). He also heard it sung at Civitavecchia on February 20, 1841 (see p. 166).

Outside Italy, *L'Esule di Roma* was sung: in Italian—at London, February 3, 1832; Madrid, May 21, 1832; Corfu, autumn 1832; Cagliari, autumn 1833; Ragusa, Carnival 1838; Lisbon, June 13, 1839; Nice, Carnival 1840; Malta, summer 1841; in German—(translation by Georg Ott) at Graz, August 1, 1832; also in German, at Vienna, Theater in der Josefstadt, September 26, 1832, and at Prague, March 1837.

Alina, regina di Golconda (often called *La Regina di Golconda*) (*opera buffa*): two acts; libretto by Felice Romani, after a story by Stanislas-Jean de Boufflers used by earlier French librettists; composed 1828; autograph score in Naples Conservatory Library.

Première: Teatro Carlo Felice, Genoa, May 12, 1828; cast included Serafina Rubini, De Vincenti, Giovanni Battista Rubini, Antonio Tamburini, and Giuseppe Frezzolini. The opera was staged at the Teatro Valle, Rome, on October 29, 1833, in a revised version that included added numbers; the cast then included Annetta Fischer, Pietro Gentili, Federico(?) Crespi, the Roman *buffo* Spada, and Agnese Loyselet; the production was a success, though the first performance was greeted with coolness interrupted by bursts of applause. *Alina* was revived at Rome as late as February

1891, at the Teatro Drammatico Nazionale, when the cast included Svicher, Lombardi, Antonio Pini-Corsi, and Sottolana. On September 11, 1841, it began a run of twenty-one singings at La Scala, Milan; the role of Alina was sung by Pauline Viardot-García when the opera received three complete performances and one truncated one at La Scala between May 23, 1843, and June 4, 1846.

Derived ultimately from a *conte* by Stanislas-Jean de Boufflers (a military man and governor of Senegal who became a member of the Académie française largely because of his literary productions), the story of *Alina* first had been transmuted into a libretto by Jean-Michel Sedaine and set as an opera by Pierre-Alexandre Monsigny in 1766. With this libretto translated into Swedish by Cristofer Bogislaus Zibet, another opera was composed to it by Francesco Uttini (1776). Again using the French text, Johann Abraham Peter Schultz wrote still another opera on the subject (1787), as did François-Adrien Boieldieu (St. Petersburg, 1804). At least one more opera, also in French, had preceded that of Romani and Donizetti: this had been to a new libretto by Jean-Baptiste-Charles Vial and Edmond-Guillaume-François de Favières and had been composed by Henri-Montan Berton, a stylistic reactionary who had tried to stem Rossini's Parisian successes and whose death in 1844 was to be followed by an informal offer to Donizetti, under conditions that he found unacceptable, of his seat in the Académie des Beaux-Arts (see p. 217).

(*1827 Continued*)

Gianni di Calais (opera semiseria):
three acts; libretto by Domenico
Gilardoni; composed 1828; autograph score in Naples Conservatory Library.

Première: Teatro del Fondo,
Naples, August 2, 1828; cast included Adelaide Comelli-Rubini
(Matilde), Carraro (Adelina),
Giovanni Battista Rubini (Gianni), Michele Benedetti (Il Re),
Antonio Tamburini (Rustano),
Tatta [Tatti?] (Ruggiero) Giovanni Pace (Guido), and Gaetano
Chizzola (Corrado). When *Gianni di Calais* was staged at the
Théâtre-Italien, Paris, on January
3, 1834, Rubini remained from the
original cast; the leading female
role was sung by Caroline Unger.

*Il Giovedì grasso, o Il Nuovo Pour-
ceaugnac (farsa):* one act; libretto
by Domenico Gilardoni; composed 1828; autograph score in
Naples Conservatory Library.

Première: Teatro del Fondo,
Naples, autumn 1828; cast in-
cluded Adelaide Comelli-Rubini
(Nina), Carraro (Camilla), Ce-
cilia Grassi (Stefanina), Giovanni
Battista Rubini (Ernesto), Luigi
Lablache (Sigismondo), Arrigotti
(Teodoro), Giambattista(?) Cam-
pagnoli (Colonnello), and Gio-
vanni Pace (Cola).

1829

Il Paria (opera seria): two acts; libretto by Domenico Gilardoni;
composed 1828; autograph score
in Naples Conservatory Library.

Première: Teatro San Carlo,
Naples, January 12, 1829; cast
included Adelaide Tosi (Neala),
Ricci (Zaide), Giambattista(?)

Campagnoli (Akebare), Luigi La-
blache (Zarete), Giovanni Battista
Rubini (Idamore), and Gaetano
Chizzola (Empsaele).

Elisabetta al castello di Kenilworth
(sometimes called *Il Castello di
Kenilworth*) *(opera seria):* three
acts; libretto, after Sir Walter
Scott's *Kenilworth*, by Andrea
Leone Tottola; composed 1829;
autograph score in Naples Conservatory Library.

Première: Teatro San Carlo,
Naples, July 6, 1829; cast included Adelaide Tosi (Elisabetta
regina), Luigia Boccabadati-Gazzuoli (Amelia), Eden (Fanny),
Antonio David (Alberto, conte
di Leicester), Berardo Winter
(Warney), and Ambrosini (Lam-
bourne).

1830

I Pazzi per progetto (farsa): one act;
libretto by Domenico Gilardoni;
composed 1830; autograph score
in Naples Conservatory Library.

Première: Teatro del Fondo,
Naples, February 7, 1830; cast
included Luigia Boccabadati-Gazzuoli (Cristina), Carraro (Esta-
sia), Luigi Lablache (Darlemont),
Gennaro Luzio (Venanzio), and
Ambrosini (Frank). When this
brief *farsa* was given for one
night at the Teatro Valle, Rome,
on September 24, 1831, Prince
Agostino Chigi noted in his diary
that it had been hissed off the
stage. Nothing further seems to
have been heard of it.

*Il Diluvio universale (azione tragico-
sacra):* three acts; libretto by
Domenico Gilardoni (for sources,
see p. 68 *n*); composed 1830; autograph score in Naples Conservatory Library.

(1830 Continued)

Première: Teatro San Carlo, Naples, February 28, 1830; cast included Luigia Boccabadati-Gazzuoli (Sela), Carraro (Ada), Fabiani (Tesbite), Ricci (Asfene), Cecilia Grassi (Abra), Luigi Lablache (Noé), Ambrosini (Iafet), Arrigotti (Sem), Salvi (Cam), Berardo Winter (Cadmo), and Gaetano Chizzola (Artoo). During the succeeding Carnival season, this opera-oratorio was staged at the Teatro Carlo Felice, Genoa, and was sung there twelve times.

Imelda de' Lambertazzi (opera seria): two acts; libretto by Andrea Leone Tottola; composed 1830; autograph score in Naples Conservatory Library.

Première: Teatro San Carlo, Naples, August 23, 1830; cast included Antonietta Galzerani (Imelda), Berardo Winter (Lamberto), Antonio Tamburini (Ubaldo), Ambrosini (Bonifacio), and Gaetano Chizzola (Orlando) —this last, evidently a very useful *comprimario*, singing in his eighth and last Donizetti *première*.

Anna Bolena (opera seria): two acts; libretto by Felice Romani; composed 1830; autograph score in the Ricordi archives, Milan.

Première: Teatro Carcano, Milan, December 26, 1830; cast included Giuditta Pasta (Anna Bolena), Elisa Orlandi (Giovanna Seymour), Laroche (Smeton), Giovanni Battista Rubini (Riccardo Percy), and Filippo Galli (Enrico VIII). The opera soon was staged up and down the Italian peninsula. On July 6, 1832, it was mounted at the Teatro San Carlo, Naples, with a cast including Giuseppina Ronzi de Begnis (Anna Bolena), Toldi (Giovanna Seymour), Diomilla Santolini (Smeton), Giambattista(?) Campagnoli (Rochefort), Nicholas Ivanoff (Percy), Francesco Lombardi (Hervey), and Luigi Lablache (Enrico VIII). Six days later, Donizetti wrote to Count Gaetano Melzi: *"Anna,* on the sixth of the current month, had a happy success and (a rare thing on a gala evening) the court applauded four times and called out the actors and the poor Maestro. The next evening was the same."

On January 2, 1833, two Donizetti operas were sung in Rome: *Il Furioso all'isola di San Domingo,* in its *première,* at the Teatro Valle, and *Anna Bolena,* in a pirated version, at the Teatro Apollo. *Anna* had been staged without the composer's approval or participation, no legal recourse being available at the time. This performance included dances added by the choreographer, Giovanni Galzerani, and the cast was headed by Antonietta Galzerani (Anna Bolena), Schuster Placci (Giovanna Seymour), Chiara Gualdi (Smeton), Gennaro Ciolfi (Rochefort), Giovanni Basadonna (Percy), Giuseppe de Gregori (Hervey), and Giambattista(?) Campagnoli (Enrico VIII); the pirating impresario was the Modenese Pietro Camuri. Prince Agostino Chigi's diary records his impression that the performance was "absolutely unhappy." Four days later (January 6, 1833), at the Palazzo Lancellotti, Rome, Donizetti himself conducted the first of four performances of *Anna Bolena* given under the aegis of the Accademia

(*1830 Continued*)

filarmonica romana (commonly called the Filarmonici romani); this was a lovingly prepared semi-concert version; it was repeated (with Commendatore Vincenzo Costaguti conducting) on January 18 and 25 and February 8. The cast of amateurs and largely nonoperatic professionals included Orsola Corinaldesi (Anna Bolena), Elena Angelini (Giovanna Seymour), Orsola Aspri Uccelini (Smeton), Pietro Angelini (Percy), Leopoldo Eutizii (Rochefort), Luigi Quattrocchi (Hervey), and Annibale Fantaguzzi (Enrico VIII). The orchestra consisted of thirty-five musicians, the chorus of ten women and about thirty men. Two members of the cast were of special note: Orsola Aspri Uccelini, who as a very young girl had composed an opera, *L'Avventura di una giornata*, which had been produced successfully at the Teatro Valle in May 1827, and Orsola Corinaldesi, who, after a resounding personal success in Rossini's *Mosè* at Perugia in the summer of 1829, had sung to paeans of praise at Modena, Crema, Venice, and Rome.

On December 26, 1833, Rome heard an authorized public singing of *Anna Bolena* at the Teatro Apollo, when Gaetano Bruscagli conducted and the cast included Giuseppina Ronzi de Begnis, Giuseppina Merola, Gilbert-Louis Duprez (in his Roman debut), and, as Henry VIII, the renowned *basso* Carlo Porto. Basically, this was the company, now under the management of Alessandro Lanari, that had been touring the peninsula with a repertoire of operas highlighted by Bellini's *Il Pirata, Anna Bolena*, Mercadante's *I Normanni a Parigi*, and Rossini's *Il Conte Ory*. Almost eleven years later, during Donizetti's final visit to Rome, he attended a performance of *Anna Bolena* at the Teatro Argentina (September 18, 1844), especially admired because of its stage settings by Venier; the cast then included the soprano Marianna Barbieri-Nini and the tenor Francesco Ciaffei. Writing to August Thomas on September 23, 1844, Donizetti commented: ". . . at Rome, Ciaffei, young, handsome, with plenty of spirit, but his voice now tired. La Barbieri a good singer, but there is much to be corrected . . . *de minimis* . . ."

On December 26, 1833, the night of the first authentic Roman stage performance of *Anna Bolena*, the opera also was being sung in Bergamo, where Michele Racchele was the conductor and the cast included Antonia Vial, Giuseppina Fontana, Rosa Alessi, Timoleone Alexander, and Antonio Colla. When it was staged at Bergamo for the second time, at the Teatro Riccardi on August 31, 1843, Marco Bonesi conducted; leading roles were taken by Eugenia Tadolini, Paola Cattaneo, Carlo Guasco, and Camillo Fedrighini. A notable staging of *Anna Bolena* occurred at the Teatro La Fenice, Venice, during the Carnival season of 1833–34 (February 3, 1834), with a cast headed by Giuditta Pasta, Eugenia Tadolini, Domenico Donzelli, and Domenico Cosselli; Pasta repeated her

(*1830 Continued*)

Milanese triumph, and the opera was heard twelve times.

Among foreign mountings of *Anna Bolena* during Donizetti's lifetime were these: in Italian—London, Her Majesty's Theatre, July 8, 1831; Paris, Théâtre-Italien, the first Donizetti opera heard in Paris, September 1, 1831, with Giuditta Pasta, Eugenia Tadolini, Giovanni Battista Rubini, Amigo, and Luigi Lablache; Graz, April 27, 1832; Madrid, August 21, 1832; Brünn, February 24, 1833; Malta, September 15, 1833; Lisbon, February 23, 1834; Dresden, March 5, 1834; Havana, 1834; Berlin, the Königsstädtischestheater, July 1, 1841; Athens, autumn 1843; Constantinople, Carnival 1844; Smyrna, spring 1844; Copenhagen, spring 1844; Rio de Janeiro, 1844; St. Petersburg, Carnival 1845; Philadelphia, December 3, 1847; Santiago (Chile), 1847; in French —Le Havre (translation by Castil-Blaze), November 25, 1835; Antwerp, March 7, 1838; Brussels, March 29, 1838; Lyon, February 1839; Lille, February 24, 1839; New Orleans, November 1839; Geneva, autumn 1840; New York, August 2, 1843; Philadelphia, October 7, 1843; The Hague, 1844; in English—Philadelphia (translation by Joseph Reese Fry), April 11, 1844; New York, May 6, 1844; London, the Princess's Theatre (translation by Charles Jeffreys), January 12, 1847; in German—Vienna, Theater in der Josefstadt (translation by Josef Kupelwieser), January 3, 1833, and Kärnthnertortheater (translation by Johann Braun von Braunthal), February 26, 1833,

with a cast including Joseph Staudigl, Sr. (Henry VIII), Marianne Ernst-Seidler (Anne Boleyn), Rosalie Schodel (Jane Seymour), Carl Oberhofer (Rochefort), Hermann Breiting (Percy), Clara Heinefetter (Smeton), and Gustav Hölzel (Hervey); Budapest, August 29, 1833; Berlin, the Königsstädtischestheater, August 26, 1833; Prague, April 1834; St. Petersburg, spring 1838; in Hungarian—Budapest (translation by Rosa Schodel-Klein), 1840; in Swedish—Stockholm (translation by Niels Erik Wilhelm af Wetterstedt), June 17, 1844.

Alfred Loewenberg reported (77, I, column 729) of *Anna Bolena*: "The latest revivals in Italy were at Milan 20 January 1877; Brescia August 1879; and Leghorn 11 August 1881." But this opera rose into renewed life after the Second World War, being sung at Bergamo and then at La Scala, Milan, the latter (April 14, 1957) a triumphant revival conducted by a *bergamasco*, Gianandrea Gavazzeni, who had published a book on Donizetti (60); produced by Luchino Visconti; and magnificently set and costumed by Nicola Benois. The cast was headed by Maria Meneghini Callas (Anna Bolena), Giulietta Simionato (Giovanna Seymour), Gabriella Carturan (Smeton), Gianni Raimondi (Percy), Silvio Maionica (Rochefort), Plinio Clabassi (Hervey), and Nicola Rossi-Lemeni (Enrico VIII, a role taken later by Cesare Siepi). In 1955, the Soviet Government included in Vol. VI of its edition of Michael Glinka's works a piano piece entitled *Variazioni brillanti*

(1830 Continued)

> sul motivo dell'aria "Nel veder
> tua costanza" nell'Anna Bolena
> del M° Donizetti.

1831

Francesca di Foix (opera semiseria):
one act; libretto by Domenico
Gilardoni;[4] composed 1831; autograph score in Naples Conservatory Library.

> *Première:* Teatro San Carlo,
> Naples, May 30, 1831; cast includ-
> ing Luigia Boccabadati-Gazzuoli
> (La Contessa), Antonio Tambu-
> rini (Il Re), Giambattista(?)
> Campagnoli (Il Conte), Lorenzo
> Bonfigli (Il Duca), and Marietta
> Gioja-Tamburini (Il Paggio).

*La Romanziera e l'uomo nero (opera
buffa):* one act, libretto by Domenico Gilardoni; composed 1831;
autograph score in Naples Conservatory Library.

> *Première:* Teatro del Fondo,
> Naples, summer, 1831; cast in-
> cluded Luigia Boccabadati-Gaz-

---

[4] Rossini had considered this subject
in 1816, as is proved by a quotation
from Jacopo Ferretti (in *96*, 1, 268):
"It was only two days before Christmas
in 1816, when the peaceful impresario
Cartoni and Maestro Rossini invited me
to a meeting before the ecclesiastical
censor. It dealt with considerable modifications to be made in a libretto written
by Rossi for the Teatro Valle, and
which was to be composed by Rossini
as the second opera for Carnival. The
title read *Ninetta alla corte*, but the
subject was *Francesca di Foix*, one of
the least moral comedies of the French
theater at a time when it had begun to
transform itself into a renowned school
of libertinism, as later it showed itself
to be without tinsel and without a veil
of shame." It is interesting to notice
that Ferretti wrote this in 1835, four
years after the first appearance of
Donizetti's *Francesca di Foix*.

zuoli (Chiarina), Antonio Tam-
burini (Carlino), Gennaro Luzio
(Fedele), and Ambrosini (Il
Conte).

(Gianni di Parigi): composed 1831;
autograph score in Naples Conservatory Library.

> *Première:* see under 1839.

1832

Fausta (opera seria): two acts; libretto by Domenico Gilardoni;
composed 1831; autograph score
in Naples Conservatory Library.

> *Première:* Teatro San Carlo,
> Naples, January 12, 1832; cast in-
> cluded Giuseppina Ronzi de Beg-
> nis (Fausta), Eden (Beroè), Ricci
> (Licinia), Antonio Tamburini
> (Costantino), Giovanni Basa-
> donna (Crispo), Giambattista(?)
> Campagnoli (Massimiano), and
> Revalden (Albino). For a pro-
> duction at the Teatro alla Scala,
> Milan, December 26, 1832, Doni-
> zetti added to *Fausta* a *sinfonia*
> that became a popular concert
> excerpt; for a staging at the Tea-
> tro La Fenice, Venice, during the
> Carnival of 1834, he further
> added a duet ("*Vanne . . . ti
> scosta*") for the stars of the cast,
> Giuditta Pasta and Domenico
> Donzelli. The audience at one of
> the Fenice performances included
> two of the characteristic person-
> ages of French romanticism,
> George Sand and Alfred de Mus-
> set, then in the midst of their sad,
> tempestuous liaison. The staging
> at La Scala had not been wholly
> satisfactory to Donizetti; on De-
> cember 6, 1832, he wrote from
> Rome to Giovanni Ricordi: "I
> tremble for the poor *Fausta*, and
> not without reason. Santo Stefano

(1832 Continued)

[i.e., December 26, traditional gala opening night of the season] . . . [Carlo] Zucchelli, who in my view at least is not a baritone; [Antonio] Pedrazzi, who sings half a tone sharp according to the holy fathers. . . . The opera without cavatinas . . ." Pompeo Cambiasi stated (*26*, 276–77) that this performance was received coldly. During the rest of that season, nonetheless, *Fausta* seems to have been repeated at La Scala some thirty times. It had poorer luck when it was staged at Bergamo on August 1, 1843, at the Teatro Riccardi, conducted by Marco Bonesi and sung by a cast including Eugenia Tadolini, Carlo Guasco, and Gaetano Ferri; on that occasion, it definitely was not liked.

Outside Italy, during Donizetti's lifetime, *Fausta* was sung: in Italian—at Madrid, January 22, 1833; Lisbon, 1834; Havana, December 19, 1837; Vienna, April 25, 1841; London, May 29, 1841; Valparaiso, 1845; in German—at Berlin, the Königsstädtischestheater, February 26, 1835. No record of any performance in North America has come to my attention.

Ugo, conte di Parigi, opera seria; two acts; libretto by Felice Romani;[5] composed 1832; autograph score in Naples Conservatory Library.

Première: Teatro alla Scala, Milan, March 13, 1832; cast included Giuditta Pasta, Giulia

---

[5] Romani's libretto later was re-used by Alberto Mazzucato for his opera *Luigi V, re di Francia* (Teatro Re, Milan, February 25, 1843).

Grisi, Clorinda Corradi-Pantanelli, Domenico Donzelli, and Vincenzo Negrini. Edoardo Clemente Verzino also mentions (*132*, 59) a female singer named "Baillon-Hilaret," possibly Felicità Baillou-Hillaret. In the *Gazzetta privilegiata di Milano*, shortly after the Milanese *première* the critic Francesco Pezzi wrote of *Ugo, conte di Parigi:*

"Scattered voices among the public said that the new musical work by the composer of *Anna Bolena* had need—if it were to be appreciated at its true worth—of careful and repeated attention, a thing that has been modish since the moment at which musical genius ceded place to artistic efforts. But in general this opinion, though perhaps true only in part, has produced the most fortunate effect. Whether because the public has paid greater attention than usual precisely because it has heard about the need to do so, or whether because the opinion was not entirely correct, the music of Donizetti, generally speaking, pleases sufficiently at the first performance and has about equal success at the second.

"Time presses upon the composer of music. The singing actors scarcely have the time free to study their entire roles passably. They were visibly weary and, on the first night, the demands from the capacity audience were always the same, though we are in Lent; however, we repeat, the success was fortunate enough. A work of instrumentation revealing itself as fruit of a master hand; beautiful motives, not always new; reasonable conducting; the orchestra

(*1832 Continued*)

always occupied with beautiful division of parts—all this won Donizetti the most flattering applause.

"Beginning with a *sinfonia* in a new manner, and very effective, which has an admirable crescendo, it proceeds to the introduction, also a very highly praiseworthy labor.

"A quartet is distinguished by considerable worth, and though the motive that dominates it awakens some reminiscences, the ensemble is marvelous. The singers were applauded throughout, but at the end of this piece, the applause was not very lively. The cavatina sung by Pasta is a work in which vocal agility is displayed. But however masterfully performed, it did not produce any great effect upon the public. A duet between Pasta and Grisi, well enough sung by both of them, let one detect in the *stretta* a motive that was too common, for which reason applause was sparingly distributed.

"A quintet at the end of the first act proceeds with constantly greater beauties. The finale, in particular, is distinguished by a dramatic *cantabile* and great effectiveness. This piece too, admirably performed, earned the liveliest applause for the Maestro and the singers, who were called to appear on the proscenium several times. The second act, at least as far as can be judged up to now, does not seem to measure up to the first. A duet between Grisi and Donzelli, sung well enough, did not produce a big effect, much of it being *parlando*. Not so with

a greatly applauded quartet, which is beautiful, new in texture, and distinguished by its odd motives. We admired a beautiful trio, which merited the general suffrage from every point of view, having been well performed and musically well made.

"Another duet, between Bianca and Emma, was judged beautiful by the audience, and it is sad that the opera's finale, in which Pasta sings, did not merit that favor, which may have to await publication of the score. The audience remained cold and scarcely could rouse itself enough to acclaim all the singers and the Maestro anew.

"We do not wish to make comparisons or to give a hasty judgment on a work that seems commendable enough not only with respect to its art, but also very much with respect to that which generally pleases most, which is to say the inspiration, that electrifying movement which ordinarily is missing from music elaborated with too much science. We confine ourselves to the facts, and for that reason especially act as impartial historians, for which reason exactly we repeat that in this opera not a few reminiscences are to be discovered. We allow ourselves only to predict that this score, during the course of the performances, will obtain no smaller success than it has obtained now, and this the more probably because the performance on the part of the singers and the orchestra has need, in a particular way, of maturing. . . . The choristers of both sexes won applause, as not

(*1832 Continued*)

only was the music that they sang rich in values, but also it was performed in the most laudable manner."

L'Elisir d'amore (*opera comica*): two acts; libretto by Felice Romani, after Scribe's *Le Philtre,* first set by Auber (Opéra, Paris, 1831); composed 1832; Autograph score divided between Naples Conservatory Library (Act I) and Museo Donizettiano, Bergamo (Act II).

Première: Teatro della Canobbiana, Milan, May 12, 1832; cast included Clara Sabina Heinefetter[6] (Adina), Giuseppe Frezzolini (Dulcamara), Henry-Bernard Dabadie (Nemorino), and Giambattista Genero (Belcore). During Donizetti's lifetime, *L'Elisir d'Amore* became one of the most popular operas throughout the world. Then and since, it has been staged everywhere—in Italian, Spanish, German, Czech, English, Polish, Hungarian, French, Swedish, Russian, Croat, Danish, Finnish, Romanian, Portuguese, Bulgarian, Slovenian, and (at the Teatro Rossini, Turin, in the autumn of 1859) as "*tradot e ridot an dialet piemonteis*" (translated and edited in Piedmontese dialect) by Anaclet Como d'Alba. For a list of many of these stagings, see 77, 1, columns 743-44.

Through 1938, *L'Elisir d'amore* had been presented nineteen sep-

arate times at Bergamo alone— the first of them on January 1, 1833, at the Teatro Sociale, under the direction of Pietro Rovelli, with a cast including Elisa Edwig, Domenico Furroni (Furlani?), Paolo Barroilhet, and Girolamo Cavalli; the second time, January 3, 1836, at the same house, under the direction of Rovelli's successor, Michele Racchele, with a cast that included Teresa Melas, Francesco Regoli, Vincenzo Negrini, and Giuseppe Frezzolini. In the year of its centenary, it was revived at the Teatro Donizetti, Bergamo (September 25, 1932); the cast then included Mercedes Capsir, Beniamino Gigli, Gino Vanelli, and Ernesto Badini.

L'Elisir d'amore was sung at Rome for the first time on April 5, 1834, at the Teatro Valle, when the cast included Teresa Melas (Adina), Domenico Furlani (Nemorino), Pietro Gianni (Belcore), Antonio Desirò (Dulcamara), and Elena Fanny (Giannetta). This performance was a disaster. It was described this way by a writer in *Lo Spigolatore*:[7] "In Rome, *L'Elisir d'amore* has not been listened to, as between the dismay that reigned on the stage and the discontent that seethed in the theater, it seemed a piece of music performed by the artists of Babel on the day when the tongues were born. . . . Certain it is that we, in a moment that combined the confusion of the thunders on the stage and the unloosing of the hisses in the theater, believed that the impresario [Giovanni Paterni], though he had not changed com-

---

[6] One of six singing sisters—the others were Maria, Katinka, Eva, Fatima, and Nanette—Clara Sabina Stöckl-Heinefetter studied with Louis Spohr, had been a professional harpist, was renowned for her impersonation of Donna Anna in Mozart's *Don Giovanni*, and was to die insane at the age of sixty-three in 1872.

[7] Supplement to No. 6, April 5, 1834.

(1832 Continued)

posers, suddenly had changed operas—and instead of *L'Elisir d'amore*, was giving us *Il Diluvio universale*." The audience judged this performance so wretched that at its conclusion, Paterni was summoned to the stage, to be greeted by cries including "Stop, thief!" and "The impresario to prison!" Four days later, the government ordered the Teatro Valle closed until worthier performances could be offered. But when Paterni reopened it on April 30 with Bellini's *I Capuletti ed i Montecchi*, he offered his patrons little better.

L'Elisir d'amore was tried in Rome again in January 1837, but again in a poor production—and not until the Carnival season of 1838–39 did Vincenzo Jacovacci, having taken over the Teatro Valle, give it a worthy presentation there. His cast included Ferroni, Giovanni Basadonna, Ambrosini, and Carlo Cambiaggio, and on that occasion the opera won in Rome the popularity it meanwhile had been garnering almost everywhere else.

L'Elisir d'amore was sung in Naples for the first time at the Teatro del Fondo in the spring of 1834, when Fanny Tacchinardi-Persiani as Adina was supported by Teresa Zappucci (Giannetta), Lorenzo Salvi (Nemorino), Luigi Lablache (Dulcamara), and Ambrogi (Belcore). When the opera was put on at the Théâtre-Italien, Paris, on January 17, 1839, the cast included Persiani, Antonio Tamburini, Nicholas Ivanoff, and Lablache. The Kärnthertortheater, Vienna, presented it in Italian

on April 9, 1835, and then in German on December 2, 1838, when the cast included Jenny Setzer-Dinglestedt (Adina), Jetti Treffz—the future wife of Johann Strauss, Jr.—(Giannetta), Schmetzer (Nemorino), Johann Schober (Belcore), and Josef Staudigl, Sr. (Dulcamara). In Vienna, as elsewhere, *L'Elisir d'amore* became an established favorite;[8] between its first singing there and the opening of the new Kärnthnertortheater (May 25, 1869), it was heard there one hundred and seventy-eight times; between the opening of the new house and 1897, fifteen more performances were added. Michael Glinka wrote an *Impromptu en Galop sur la Barcarolle de Gaetano Donizetti dans l'Elisir d'amore*, for piano duet.

Francesco Pezzi, music critic of the *Gazzetta privilegiata di Milano*, praised *L'Elisir d'amore* unstintedly in 1832. After some slightly negative remarks about Romani's libretto, he said: "Still, let us leave the libretto to one side. It is worthy of Romani, though it cannot be called one of his best. Let us return to the Maestro, in praising whom there is no danger of being excessive. By little, by very little, the beginning of the introduction, when the curtain rises, and a chorus of women in the second act—by little, we would say, these two pieces suffer in comparison with the others. We note that fact, not

[8] When Adolph von Henselt, the notable German teacher and minor composer, published his opus 1, it proved to be *Variations de concert sur l'opéra L'Elisir d'amore de Donizetti*.

(1832 Continued)

out of excessive exigence, but only to give a little verisimilitude to our praise, so that it may shine in that light and shadow which is so necessary in all things. Arias, duets, trios, ensemble pieces, in both the first act and the second —everything is beautiful, very beautiful, and was well applauded. To say which piece is better than another piece is not any easy task. . . . Although it is now not necessary to say so, the composer was applauded for every piece, and when the curtain fell at the end of the acts, he was acclaimed more and more often on the stage with the singers, collecting his honorable and merited reward. The musical style of this score is lively, brilliant, truly of the *buffo* genre. The shading from *buffo* to *serio* can be observed taking place with surprising gradations, and the emotional is treated with that musical passion for which the composer of *Anna Bolena* is famous. Instrumentation that is always reasoned and brilliant, constantly adapted to the situations, an instrumentation that discloses the work of a great master, accompanies a vocal line now lively, now brilliant, now passionate. To lavish more praise on the Maestro would be to spoil the opera; his work has no need for hyperbolic encomia."

Sancia di Castiglia (opera seria): two acts; libretto by Pietro Salatino; composed 1832; autograph score in Naples Conservatory Library.
    Première: Teatro San Carlo, Naples, November 4, 1832; cast included Giuseppina Ronzi de Begnis (Sancia), Diomilla Santo-

lini (Garzia), Ricci (Elvira), Giovanni Basadonna (Rodrigo), and Luigi Lablache (Ircano). Not one of Donizetti's successes, it was not widely performed.

1833

Il Furioso all'isola di San Domingo (opera semisera): three acts; libretto by Jacopo Ferretti, after *Don Quixote* (Part I, chap. xvii *et seq.*); composed 1832; Autograph score in the Ricordi archives, Milan.
    Première: Teatro Valle, Rome, January 2, 1833; cast included Elisa Orlandi (Eleonora), Marianna Franceschini (Marcella), Lorenzo Salvi (Fernando), Giorgio Ronconi (Cardenio), Filippo Valentini (Bartolomeo), and Ferdinando Lauretti (Kaidamà). The opera was conducted by Giacomo Orzelli and had scenery by Luigi Ferrari. In published form, it was dedicated to Giacomo Pedroni, a Milanese associate of Giovanni Ricordi. Its story was not unfamiliar even to many Romans who had not read *Don Quixote*, as the Vestris-Venier troup, with Lombardi in the title role, had played an anonymous drama on the same episodes at the Valle in 1820. The diffusion and continual performances of Donizetti's opera became an amazing phenomenon. Well might Prince Agostino Chigi note in his diary after the Valle *première:* "The music has met with favor," for the opera was to be repeated many times before the season ended on February 19 —even being restored to the boards after two operas by other

(1833 Continued)

composers (Luigi Ricci's *Il Nuovo Figaro* and Rossi's *Il Disertore svizzero*) temporarily had replaced it.

The *Notizie del giorno*, in an article signed G. M., called *Il Furioso* "one of those operas whose spontaneously acquired success will endure for a long time," and added: "It can be said that the music as a whole is compounded of original beauties and is worthy of so distinguished a musician. The concourse of the public, which from the first evening on never has failed to attend in large numbers, is the most valid proof for demonstrating this universal approval." Other Roman periodicals were no less enthusiastic. And in the succeeding six years, *Il Furioso all'isola di San Domingo* was to be staged in some seventy other Italian theaters and re-presented several times in Rome.[9] The first Roman revival of the opera took place in the autumn of 1833; it was heard in Rome again in the autumn of 1835 and during the following Carnival season, still at the Valle. It was sung at the Teatro Argentina in 1839, with Felice Varesi in the title role; at the Teatro Metastasio in April 1842; at the Valle again in 1844, with Corradi-Setti; at the Argentina again in 1851 and January 1868, this last time with a cast including Parboni, Grosso, and Vincenzo Montanaro.

[9] The notable continuing popularity of the opera led to a revival of the anonymous play by the Colomberti troupe, again at the Teatro Valle, in the autumn of 1834.

The tally of performances of *Il Furioso* outside Rome is truly astonishing. The opera's extra-Roman career seems to have begun at the Teatro del Fondo, Naples, in the spring of 1833, when the cast included Anna Delserre (Eleonora), Teresa Zappucci (Giannetta), Lorenzo Salvi (Fernando), Crespi (Cardenio), Salvetti (Bartolomeo), and Gennaro Luzio (Kaidamà). The Neapolitans liked it so well that in the spring of 1834 it was to be heard at three Naples theaters: the Fondo, the Nuovo, and the Fenice. Donizetti wrote to its librettist, Ferretti, on May 20, 1834: "The three *Furiosi* had different fortunes: that is, at the Fondo, so-so. At the Nuovo, a great success; at the Fenice, almost none. I, however, say: the Fondo for the orchestra, the Nuovo for *Il Furioso*; the Fenice for nothing. For singing it, then . . . nowhere."

The Teatro Carignano, Turin, staged *Il Furioso* in August 1833, with a cast that included Luigia Boccabadati-Gazzuoli, Nicolini, Celestino Salvatori, and Lavaggi. At Padua in November 1833, it was staged with an inferior cast. During the Carnival season of 1834, it was produced at Lucca, Vicenza, Florence, Piacenza, Parma, Trieste, San Giovanni in Persiceto, Mirandola, Genoa, Varese, Cagliari, and Palermo. Performances of it were to be heard during 1835 at Modena, Fabriano, Foligno, Cremona, Terni, Pesaro, Fermo, Genoa (second time), Reggio nell'Emilia, Chieti, Alessandria, Bologna, Milan (Teatro della Canobbiana),

(1833 Continued)

Norcia, Verona, Viterbo, Bagna-cavallo, Trieste (second), Imola, Faenza, and Perugia. Italian towns and cities that heard *Il Furioso* in 1836 included Ancona, Florence (second), Spoleto, Sarzana, Mantua, Città della Pieve, Cremona (second), Narni, Genoa (third), Leghorn, Borgo San Sepolcro, Florence (third), and Perugia (second). To these were to be added: 1837—San Angelo in Vada, Pisa, Rimini, Ferrara, and Ascoli; 1838—Sinigaglia, Orvieto, Fermo (second), Jesi, and Parma (second); 1839—Macerata, Palermo (second), Forlì, and others. This opera was presented at Pisa in 1867 and at the Teatro Scribe, Turin, as late as 1885.

Especially noteworthy performances of *Il Furioso all'isola di San Domingo* were those at the Teatro alla Scala, Milan, on October 1, 1833, and at the Teatro della Società, Bergamo, on January 1, 1835. At La Scala, the opera had a first run of thirty-six performances; the first Milan cast included Eugenia Tadolini, Orazio Cartagenova, Berardo Winter, and Vincenzo Galli. Donizetti was paid seven hundred twenty Austrian lire for staging this performance and adding new numbers to the score. He actually changed three pieces, replacing tenor arias in the first and second acts and Eleonora's final aria with numbers that he adapted from *Elisabetta al castello di Kenilworth* and *Il Borgomastro di Saardam*. He was able to write Ferretti on October 9, 1833, that at the fourth Scala singing, nine hundred people in addition to the subscribers had bought tickets. In that letter, he also quoted some very adverse critiques from the periodicals *Il Eco* and *Il Barbiere di Siviglia*, which were notably hard on the libretto, though Francesco Pezzi—the usually severe critic of the *Gazzetta privilegiata di Milano*—had published an article bursting with praise:

"The score is dependent chiefly on the skill of the *basso*. Donizetti composed it at Rome for the young Giorgio Ronconi, and here his place is taken by the talented [Orazio] Cartagenova. The opera pleases very well on the banks of the Tiber, and it pleases equally in Milan. As far as we know, at Rome they found nothing but musical beauties; we, on the other hand, notice, in addition to those in very great abundance, some reminiscences, of which, further, the Maestro knows how to take full advantage with such fine tact. An instrumentation perhaps at times too noisy, but worked out with great wisdom; attractive, fresh motives; the musical character adapted to the subject; concerted pieces by a true master—here are the general judgments on this greatly applauded opera. After the introduction, which pleases a good deal, and after an aria by the *buffo* which pleases no less, the bass sings a *romanza*—and how beautiful and pathetic it is! A duet between the bass and the *buffo*, carried off as it could not be carried off better, was greatly applauded both for its musical excellences and for those of the performance. Then comes a beautiful chorus. Finally, the long and

(1833 Continued)

very beautiful finale of the first act (with six real parts), which was saluted with the liveliest acclamations, in sufficient supply for the singers and the extremely able Maestro. . . . The second act begins with another beautiful chorus. And rich in special beauties [is] a duet between the *donna* and the bass, a piece that was much applauded. An aria for the tenor, with chorus, pleases. A duet between the bass and the *buffo*, in which fine reminiscences are to be found, was much applauded, and nobody could have sung and acted it better. The score finally reached its conclusion amid general applause."

On May 30, 1840, Felice Romani was to publish in a supplement of the Turin *Gazzetta piemontese* (of which King Carlo Alberto had made him editor) a half-serious, half-jocular article in which he was to say of Ferretti's libretto for *Il Furioso:* "It is a somewhat faded copy of a sublime original, Paër's *Agnese*,[10] a fabric all of one color, which renders it sad and monotonous, a continuous repetition of, so to speak, little situations that, damaging the dramatic effect, consequently damage the musical

---

[10] The full title of this opera—once so famous, now so wholly neglected— was *Agnese di Fitz-Henry*. Its libretto, by Luigi Buonavoglia, had been based on *The Father and the Daughter*, a tale by Amelia Alderson, who became the wife and biographer of John Opie. *Agnese di Fitz-Henry* was sung for the first time in a private villa at Ponte d'Altaro, near Parma, in October 1809. Its tremendous international popularity endured until about 1840.

effect. The poet and the composer shaped this opera under the influence of a sad necessity, because there were not in the company [of singers] any people of value other than the fine Ronconi and a comic bass [Ferdinando Lauretti] whose name does not now come to me. To them alone were assigned the action and the song; the tenor used [Lorenzo Salvi] was a super; the prima donna [Elisa Orlandi] was used as a draught horse serving, in a certain way, to drag the drama along." As Romani was a man of superior intelligence and acuity, it is difficult to estimate how much of this apparently irrelevant criticism he really meant seriously. Hundreds of audiences did not agree with the opinions that he expressed either of the libretto or of the music.

Among foreign stagings of *Il Furioso* during and immediately after Donizetti's lifetime were: in Italian—Barcelona, May 3, 1834; Malta, 1834; Corfu, autumn 1834; Vienna, Kärnthnertortheater, April 22, 1835; Lisbon, 1835; Mexico City, spring 1836; Havana, 1836; London, Lyceum Theatre, December 17, 1836; Nice, spring 1837; Odessa, summer 1839; Brussels, May 1840; Lugano, 1840; Constantinople, spring 1842; Oran, autumn 1842; Alexandria, 1843; Rio de Janeiro, 1844; Bucharest, 1844; Buenos Aires, December 2, 1848; in German—Vienna, Kärnthnertortheater, March 29, 1835, with a cast including Marianne Ernst (Eleonora), Maria Ehnes (Marcella), Sebastian Binder (Fernando), Franz Wild (Cardenio), Josef

Scipell (Bartolomeo), and Antonio Forti (Kaidamà); Budapest, January 18, 1836; Graz, March 18, 1836; Berlin, Königsstädtischestheater, March 1, 1838; in Russian —St. Petersburg, February 1839; in French—Brussels (translation by Gustave Oppelt), March 14, 1844. *Il Furioso* was not heard in Paris until it was produced at the Théâtre-Italien on February 2, 1862, and it appears never to have been staged in the United States. It stands very high on the roster of Donizetti operas that should be revived.

Parisina (opera seria): three acts; libretto by Felice Romani, after the poem by Byron; composed 1833; autograph score in Museo Donizettiano, Bergamo.

Première: Teatro della Pergola, Florence, March 17, 1833; exactly who sang in the *première* is a matter of dispute. Guido Zavadini (*138*, 173, and elsewhere) gives the first Florence cast as Caroline Ung(h)er, Gilbert-Louis Duprez, Domenico Cosselli, and Carlo Porto—but this is the cast that sang the opera at the Teatro San Carlo, Naples, in the summer of 1834 (Unger as Parisina, Teresa Zappucci as Imelda, Duprez as Ugo, Coselli as Azzo, and Porto as Ernesto). Further, the next year (March 20, 1834), Unger wrote from Paris to the impresario Alessandro Lanari at Florence: "It gives me pleasure that I should sing at Florence [in] *Parisina* and I hope that this opera will also be that of my Naples debut." Eduardo Clemente Verzino (*132*, 65) gives the Pergola cast as Santina Ferlotti, Alexandrine Duperron-Duprez, Giuseppina Merola, Gilbert-Louis Duprez, and Carlo Porto, but that raises the problem of containing three female singers and two male singers, whereas the score calls for three male singers and two female. Yet in his book on Donizetti's operas (*138*, 123) he repeats this casting, which Alfredo Colombiani also underwrote (*36*, 118).

Parisina quickly was staged in other Italian cities. It opened the season at the Teatro Apollo, Rome—of which Pietro Camuri again was impresario—on December 31, 1834, when the cast included Unger (Parisina), Adelaide Gualdi (Imelda), Giovanni Battista Bottari (Folco—i.e., Azzo), Carlo Trezzini (Ugo), and Massimiliano Orlandi (Ernesto). The libretto had been shredded by the pontifical censor, Somai, who even had insisted that Azzo's name be changed to Folco. Only Unger was received enthusiastically by the audience, and the Roman fortunes of *Parisina* did not brighten until it was sung at the Valle again in 1836, this time with Giuseppina Ronzi de Begnis, Salvatore Patti, and Paolo Barroilhet. It was received well at La Scala, Milan, during the Carnival season of 1838–39, with Adelaide Moltini, Catone Lonati, and Orazio Cartagenova, and these singers were heard in it at the Teatro Riccardi, Bergamo, with Marco Bonesi conducting, on August 1, 1839.

Outside Italy during Donizetti's lifetime, *Parisina* was staged: in Italian—at Madrid, August 27, 1834; Lisbon, July 13,

(*1833 Continued*)

1835; Havana, 1836; Paris, the Théâtre-Italien, with Giulia Grisi, Giovanni Battista Rubini, and Antonio Tamburini, February 24, 1838; Dresden, July 27, 1839; Palma de Mallorca, October 9, 1839; Vienna, the Kärnthnertor-theater, with Caroline Unger (Parisina), Amalia Hoffman-Kunst (Imelda), Giorgio Ronconi (Azzo di Ferrara), Angelo Mariani (Ugo), and Novelli (Ernesto), April 25, 1840; Odessa, summer 1841; Berlin, Königsstädtisches-theater, November 5, 1841; Lima, spring 1843; Mexico City, 1843; Smyrna, spring 1844; Valparaiso, 1844; Budapest, January 25, 1847; in German—Bucharest, 1835; Graz, November 6, 1841. One of Franz Liszt's *Trois Valses-Ca-prices* (pub. 1847; partly rewrit-ten, 1852) is on a theme from *Parisina* (another theme is from *Lucia di Lammermoor*). Carl Czerny composed a *Grande Fan-taisie brillante* on themes from *Parisina*. On July 23, 1833, Doni-zetti wrote to Giovanni Ricordi: "I want to give you a waltz of mine on *Parisina* to publish," but I have found no trace of this piece.

The changes made in *Parisina* by the pontifical censor in 1834 border upon the hilarious. In the original libretto, the wife of Azzo, "*Signor di Ferrara*," entertains a purely friendly affection for Ugo —who suddenly is discovered to be Azzo's son by his first marriage (to Matilde, whom he had killed on suspicion of infidelity). Then Azzo finds out about what he supposes to be the guilty relation-ship between his wife and his son, kills the son, and shows the body to his wife, who dies of shocked grief. The censor ob-jected to both guilty love and parricide, at least as depicted on the opera stage. The dead Matilde therefore became Azzo's sister, Ugo his nephew, and Parisina his fiancée. This rendered preposte-rous the idea that Azzo (renamed Folco) should wax so fiercely jealous, and turned into something near farce the scene in which— now as Parisina's affianced rather than as her husband—Azzo goes to her bedchamber to ferret out the secret of her guilty love from her as she lies asleep and dream-ing aloud.

Torquato Tasso (sometimes played as *Sordello il trovatore* or *Sor-dello*) *(opera seria):* three acts; libretto by Jacopo Ferretti; com-posed 1833; autograph score in the Ricordi archives, Milan.

Première: Teatro Valle, Rome, September 9, 1833; cast included Adelina Spech (Eleonora d'Este), Angiolina Carocci (Eleonora di Scandiano), Giorgio Ronconi (Tasso), Antonio Poggi (Ro-berto), Ferdinando Lauretti (Don Gherardo), Antonio Rinaldi (Al-fonso II), and Luigi Garofalo (Ambrogio). Between the acts of the opera, the Mascherpa com-pany of dramatic actors enter-tained the audience. The applause for the opera was prolonged, and the audience demanded appear-ances by Donizetti, Ferretti, and the four chief singers. The press generally was enthusiastic, though some criticism was made of the libretto as causing the opera to seem overlong and the musical interest to wane from act to act.

Torquato Tasso was sung at the Valle more than fifteen times in three weeks, after which it made way for a reappearance of *Il Furioso all'isola di San Domingo*. It was heard at the Valle again in the spring of 1836, when many listeners thought Paolo Barroilhet as Tasso more effective than even Ronconi had been; a poor troupe repeated it again at the Valle in October 1840. In June 1844, at the Teatro Argentina, Rome, *Torquato Tasso* received a new lease on Roman attention when its title role was assumed by a very popular native son, Filippo Colini; the Argentina housed this opera again, but with a mediocre cast, in January 1851. It returned to the Valle during 1859 and again in 1864. (In November 1862, at the Argentina, the third act alone was part of the program for eight evenings, the title role being sung by Storti.) As late as 1896, at the Teatro Drammatico Nazionale, the baritone Corradetti chose the final scene of *Torquato Tasso*, with chorus, for his own benefit night.

Outside Rome, *Torquato Tasso* was staged: at the Teatro Carcano, Milan, and at the Teatro d'Angennes, Turin, both in the spring of 1834—and received a poor performance at Venice at about the same time. That fall, it was staged at Varese, Novara, Trieste, and Florence; in the Carnival season of 1834–35, it was heard at Palermo and Padua. In April 1835, it was mounted at Mantua and—providing Giorgio Ronconi with his Naples debut

role—at the Teatro del Fondo, where it was billed as *Sordello il trovatore*. A sentence in the review of this Fondo performance by the Naples correspondent of the Bolognese periodical *Teatro, Arti e Letteratura* reveals an amusing local attitude: "He [Ronconi] pleases very much; he produces the song of passion with great veracity, but is not free of the odious vice common to all those who *come down here from Italy* [italics mine], that is, he shouts too much, and in Naples it is necessary to sing properly." Others in that first Neapolitan cast were Anna Delserre (Eleonora d'Este), Teresa Zappucci (Eleonora di Scandiano), Lorenzo Salvi (Alfonso II), Luigi Fioravanti (Roberto), Raffaele (Don Gherardo), and Giacchini (Ambrogio).

Well launched on its long Italian careeer, *Torquato Tasso* was sung in the autumn of 1835 at Lucca (with Ronconi), Messina, and Padua (second time); in the spring of 1836 at Palermo (second), and that summer at Leghorn. In 1837, Ronconi sang in it at Florence (second), and it was heard in Milan (second, Teatro della Canobbiana) and Imola; during that autumn, it was staged at Bologna, Alessandria, Ferrara, and Parma, as well as at Bagnacavallo, where Ferdinando Paër conducted it. It finally reached La Scala, Milan (third time in that city), in March 1838 (and was repeated there during the Carnival season of 1840–41); during the 1838–39 Carnival, it was sung for the second time at the Teatro d'Angennes, Turin, and also was

(1833 Continued)

heard in Macerata, Siena, and Brescia. The opera was staged at Bergamo, the Teatro della Società, on January 1, 1839, conducted by Michele Racchele, with a cast including Anaide Castellan, Gaetano Fraschini, Giuseppe Paltrinieri, and Giuseppe Catalano (and was heard again at Bergamo, the Teatro Riccardi, on August 2, 1881). In 1840, *Torquato Tasso* was produced at Ancona; in 1841, at Como; in 1842, at Pesaro and Gorizia; and in 1847 at Vercelli. At some of these stagings, it was billed as *Sordello*.

Outside Italy, during Donizetti's lifetime, *Torquato Tasso* was staged: in Italian—at Barcelona, February 2, 1835; Lisbon, January 4, 1837 (with Filippo Coletti as Tasso); Dublin, April 19, 1838; Algiers, February 1839; Vienna, May 3, 1839; Odessa, spring 1839; Marseille, June 1839; London, March 3, 1840; Palma de Mallorca, Carnival 1841; Santiago (Cuba), 1841; Berlin, the Königsstädtischestheater, September 4, 1841; Agram, autumn 1841; Smyrna, 1842; Lugano, 1842; Rio de Janeiro, 1843; Copenhagen, spring 1847; in German—Vienna, the Kärnthnertortheater, April 10, 1837, with a cast including Johann Schober (Tasso), Carl Just (Alfonso II), Antonia Vial (Eleonora d'Este), Carolina Valesi, *née* Kunth (Eleonora di Scandiano), Franz Wild (Roberto), and Amerlahm (Don Gherardo), and at the Theater in der Josefstadt, January 13, 1837; Graz, March 31, 1837. No record of a performance in Paris or the United States has come to my attention.

Lucrezia Borgia (opera seria): pro-logue and two acts; libretto, after the drama by Victor Hugo, by Felice Romani; composed 1833; autograph score in the Ricordi archives, Milan.

Première: Teatro alla Scala, Milan, December 26, 1833; cast included Henriette-Clémentine Méric-Lalande (Lucrezia Borgia), Marietta Brambilla (Maffio Orsini), Francesco Pedrazzi (Gennaro), Luciano Mariani—who had created the role of Count Rodolfo in Bellini's *La Sonnambula* in 1831—(Alfonso d'Este), Domenico Spiaggi (Gubetta), Giuseppe Vaschetti (Beppo Liveretto), Giuseppe Visanetti (Apostolo Gazzella), Napoleone Marconi (Oloferne Vitellozzo), Raineri Pochini (Rustighello), Francesco Petrazzoli (Astolfo), and Coppiere (Principessa Negroni).

In the *Gazzetta privilegiata di Milano* for December 28, 1833, the critic Francesco Pezzi wrote: "Romani, the talented Romani, drew his *melodramma* from nothing less than a tragedy by Victor Hugo, by that *coryphée* of gross romanticism, by the most bizarre, haughtiest, most fanatic genius (and a great genius) of voluble France. The subject is that of Lucrezia Borgia, who was noted for her offenses and her adventures—and whom the French novelist has depicted in dark colors here. Romani has brightened the colors and, to put it briefly, has fashioned a libretto that perhaps will please the modern writers of *melodrammi*, but which as a work by him is weak, poor, and absolutely devoid of good poetry. Romani has rendered us demanding, and with him we simply tell the facts, however displeasing. But despite the indifference of the poetry, the action offers some points of interest; and where inspired verses are lacking, they can be replaced by inspired music. But inspiration is a gift granted to few, and does not always answer a summons, for which reason (generally speaking) even the extremely skillful Donizetti has let himself be borne away on the placid current, and where Romani said that the poet ought to conceal himself and let the characters speak their own language, the composer too has kept himself hidden, leaving the singers to fabricate the music, so empty is it of inspiration and novelty.

"We are far from employing excessive strictness with Donizetti; but it must be said, if we stick to the results, that the new score is little better than mediocre.

"The introduction of the Prologue, though not new as to melodies, nevertheless merited the flattering applause for a certain vivacity, a certain *brio* that distinguished it; and there was, also, the finale of the Prologue itself, very well planned and well enough carried out.

"In the first act, we had a chorus and a duet that ended in a trio, these of beautiful musical texture, and they met with the public's approbation.

"In the second act, we will note a *brindisi* sung by Brambilla which pleased though it was poor in novelty.

"It is only just to say that the talented Donizetti was called to the proscenium after the Prologue and at the end of the first act, along with the principal singers, to accept the signs of public gratitude.

"It is customary, when those who write theatrical criticism wish to criticize frankly the inspired, inventive side of the music, for them to praise the instrumentation; we therefore follow that usage, and not being able to praise greatly the vocal parts of the new opera by Donizetti, praise it for its instrumental parts. And here, to tell the truth, we believe that we are hitting the bull's eye, seeing that the talented composer's music is well elaborated, and we believe that we can congratulate ourselves that the score will acquire public favor through the best of the orchestra's musical harmonies. And those pieces which we have mentioned as winning applause—and perhaps some others—will emerge as of greater value with the passage of time."

Lucrezia Borgia swiftly garnered great popularity both in Italy and abroad. For some of its extremely numerous stagings throughout Europe, North and South America, Asia, and Africa, see 77, 1, columns 754-56. In Vienna, for example, it was sung first in Italian, at the Kärnthnertortheater, on May 9, 1839, when the cast included Caroline Unger (Lucrezia Borgia), Antonio Poggi (Gennaro), Domenico Cosselli (Alfonso d'Este), Marietta Brambilla (Maffio Orsini), Giuseppe Delverro (Apostolo Gazzella), Julius Pfister (Vitellozzo), Franz Winhops (Gubetta), and Antonio Benciolini (Rustighello); it

(1833 Continued)

was repeated there—its first singing in German—on November 28, 1843, with Clara Heinefetter (Lucrezia Borgia), Christina Dichl (Maffio Orsini), Josef Erl (Gennaro), Carl Kok (Apostolo Gazzella), Julius Pfister (Vitellozzo), Gustav Hölzel (Gubetta), and Alexander Reichard (Rustighello).[11] The first London staging of *Lucrezia Borgia*, June 6, 1839, at Her Majesty's Theatre, was in Italian, but the opera was also sung there in an English translation by J. M. Weston on December 30, 1843. The earliest performance in New York, in Italian, occurred on November 25, 1844, and was followed by one in German on March 18, 1856, and one in English on October 13, 1871. On December 5, 1904, the Metropolitan Opera, New York, gave its only singing of *Lucrezia Borgia* to date; the cast on that singular occasion included Maria de Macchi (Lucrezia Borgia), Edyth Walker (Maffio Orsini), Enrico Caruso (Gennaro), and Antonio Scotti (Alfonso d'Este). Stagings of *Lucrezia Borgia* throughout Italy during Donizetti's lifetime were too numerous to mention, but those at Rome and Bergamo require comment. In pontifical Rome, an opera about the Borgias, an opera in which a pope's daughter was a character, could be performed only after substantial recasting of the libretto. But early in December 1838, the Accademia fil-

armonica romana put on four semiprivate performances of this opera (December 11, 14, 22, 28) as prepared by Luigi Orsini and conducted by the violinist Achille de Nero. The cast included Orsola Corinaldesi (Lucrezia Borgia), Adele Henrich (Maffio Orsini), Pacifico Riccardi (Alfonso d'Este), and an eighteen-year-old Roman tenor named Enrico Tamberlik—for whom Verdi was to design the role of Don Alvaro in *La Forza del destino*—(Gennaro). In the audience for the last of these performances was the Tsarevich of Russia, the future Alexander II. When the music of *Lucrezia Borgia* at last was heard publicly in Rome—December 26, 1841, at the Teatro Apollo—the libretto had been rewritten and the opera was billed as *Elisa da Fosco*. The cast included Fanny Maray (Lucrezia Borgia), Antonio Poggi (Gennaro), Cesare Badiali (Alfonso d'Este), and Diomilla Santolini (Maffio Orsini). The critic of the *Rivista teatrale* commented: "About the secondary roles it is better to remain silent," and the prevalent opinion of the performance was that it was passable. Nonetheless, it established the Roman popularity of this opera, which thereafter was to be sung in Rome again and again.

Lucrezia Borgia, which was to be staged at Bergamo on nine separate occasions up to 1892, was heard there first at the Teatro della Società on December 26, 1840, under the direction of Marco Bonesi; the cast included Eugenia d'Alberti, Lorenzo Biacchi, and Giovanni Giordani, and

---

[11] For the curious story of *Lucrezia Borgia* in Paris, and for the many alternative titles under which it was sung, see p. 96.

the event was a triumph for the opera. A like success was won by the second Bergamo staging—at the Teatro Riccardi on April 2, 1842—when Bonesi again conducted, and the cast included Erminia Frezzolini, Carla Griffini, Lorenzo Salvi (by then Frezzolini's husband), and Raffaele Ferlotti. The opera was repeated at Bergamo in 1848, 1860, 1864, 1868, 1874, 1881, and 1892.

In 1841, Franz Liszt published for piano solo a two-part piece on themes from this opera: *Réminiscences de Lucrezia Borgia*.

1834

Rosmonda d'Inghilterra (opera seria): two acts; libretto by Felice Romani; composed 1834; autograph score lost, but it is known that the introductory *sinfonia* was borrowed from an earlier Donizetti score.

Première: Teatro della Pergola, Florence, February 27, 1834; cast included Fanny Tacchinardi-Persiani (Rosmonda), Anna Delserre (Leonora di Guienna), that Giuseppina Merola with whom Donizetti was said to have had a fleeting liaison (the travesty role of the young page Arturo), Gilbert-Louis Duprez (Enrico Secondo), and Carlo Porto (Clifford). Although described at the time as a success, this performance did not lead to many other stagings of *Rosmonda d'Inghilterra*. When it was sung at Naples, to an altered libretto, it was billed as *Eleonora di Gujenna*. The opera *Rosmonda d'Inghilterra* in which Giuseppina Strepponi sang

at the Teatro della Pergola, Florence, in 1840, was not, as sometimes stated, Donizetti's, but a then new opera by a twenty-six-year-old Mantuan composer Jules-Eugène-Abraham Alary, known as Giulio Eugenio Abramo Alari.

Maria Stuarda (opera seria): three acts; libretto by Giuseppe Bardari; composed 1834; nonautograph score in Naples Conservatory Library.

Première (as *Buondelmonte*, with libretto by Pietro Salatino and Donizetti): Teatro San Carlo, Naples, October 18, 1834; cast included Giuseppina Ronzi de Begnis (Elisabetta), Anna Delserre (Irene), Francesco Pedrazzi (Buondelmonte), Crespi (Mosca), Achille Balestracci (Lamberto), and Carlo Porto (Tebaldo). Relations between Ronzi de Begnis and Delserre were strained, and a description by Alberto Cametti (*27*, 148, n. 1) of what occurred when the strain broke out in public remarkably duplicates the scene at His Majesty's Theatre, London, on June 6, 1727, when a performance of Giovanni Battista Buononcini's *Astianatte* was turned into a shambles when its two leading sopranos, Faustina Bordoni Hasse and Francesca Cuzzoni Sandoni, flew at each other's elaborate coiffures: "Ronzi and Delsere [*sic*] figured in the opera as two enemies, and it is to be believed that they played their roles with much verisimilitude because they were equally enemies outside the theater. The malicious actions, the spiteful doings, the backbitings of the two *donne* had a large field

(*1834 Continued*)

for maneuvers during the rehearsals. But one fine day, Ronzi, exasperated by the behavior of her rival, grabbed Delsere by the hair, slapped her face, and struck her enough to force her to spend fifteen days in bed!" Donizetti referred to this fracas in a letter of October 8, 1834, to Ferretti, and the Bolognese periodical *Teatro, Arti e Letteratura* dealt with it at length in its issue of October 23.

Maria Stuarda was heard in its original form for the first time at La Scala, Milan, on December 30, 1835, with a cast that could boast Maria Malibran (Maria Stuarda), Giacinta Puzzi-Toso (Elisabetta), Teresa Moja (Anna), Domenico Reina (Roberto), Ignazio Marini (Giorgio Talbot), and Pietro Novelli (Guglielmo Cecil). But at Milan too it invited official meddling. On March 8 or 9, Donizetti wrote to Bardari: "*La Stuarda* was prohibited after six evenings in Milan, and at the happiest moment. They did not want 'bastard,' they did not want the [Order of the] Golden Fleece around the neck, they did not want kneeling for the confession to Talbot. La Malibran said: 'I don't trust myself to think about such things.' Then—forbidden. It will be given in London." Naples appears not to have heard *Maria Stuarda* pure until four years after Francesco II, last of the Bourbons there, had left for Gaeta and exile: it was staged at the Teatro San Carlo on April 8, 1865,[12] with a cast that

included De Ruda (Elisabetta), La Grua (Maria Stuarda), Carolina Cetronè (Anna), Raffaele Mirate (Roberto), Marco Arati (Talbot), and Giovanni Morelli (Cecil).

Gemma di Vergy (opera seria): two acts; libretto by Emmanuele Bidera, after the drama *Charles VII chez ses grands vassaux,* by Alexandre Dumas *père;* composed 1834; autograph score in the Ricordi archives, Milan.

Première: Teatro alla Scala, Milan, December 26, 1834; cast included Giuseppina Ronzi de Begnis, Felicità Baillou-Hillaret, Domenico Reina, Orazio Cartagenova, Ignazio Marini, and Domenico Spiaggi. The opera pleased enough so that it held the boards for twenty-six singings, after which it went on a round of successful mountings in Italy and abroad. *Gemma di Vergy* was repeated at La Scala in 1839, 1842, 1846, and 1864, this last time for fifteen performances. In a December 1843, issue of the *Gazzetta privilegiata di Milano,* Angelo Lambertini, its editor and critic, wrote of *Gemma di Vergy:* "And so? Will we not have forgotten the duet '*Giovin rosa*' from [Bellini's] *La Straniera,* the *cavatina* '*Dalla gioja e dal piacer*' by Bellini, the *ritornello* of the *cavatina* in [Rossini's] *Tancredi,* the trio in *La Gazza ladra,* the finale of *Norma,* that we should not applaud that which, in its time, we already have ap-

---

[12] Francesco Florimo (*54,* IV, 337), apparently not realizing that *Maria*

Stuarda was thirty-one years old when first sung under that title at the San Carlo, listed it as "*Opera postuma,*" though he had listed the original performance under *Buondelmonte* (p. 302).

(1834 Continued)

plauded? Some assert that if Donizetti does this, 'he does it with such grace as to deserve forgiveness,' and as for me, I grant it to him generously; but I could wish that, with such fecundity and such fertile imagination, Donizetti never should be found in need of it. Thus, there was no need of his deserving it—and therefore he was much appaluded —in the *sinfonia,* in the *cavatina* of Guido (well sung by the bass, Marini), in the *cavatina* of Gemma (except for the reminiscences), in full in the finale of the first act, in the Count's aria (which could be rendered more gratefully by [Orazio] Cartagenova), in a section of the well-paced quartet, in a big duet between Gemma and Tamas (Ronzi [de Begnis] and Reina), and in the very tender prayer that Ronzi uttered so well. It was for these things that, at the end, the Maestro was called out and there were also calls for the actors, among whom Ronzi was distinguished by the *evvivas* directed at her."

At Bergamo, *Gemma di Vergy* was given in the Teatro Riccardi twice before Donizetti's death in 1848: in August 1839, under the direction of Michele Racchele, with Adelaide Moltini, Catone Lonati, and Pietro Alberti; and in August 1845, with Marco Bonesi conducting and a cast that included Teresa Parodi, Pietro de Unaune, Felice Varesi,[13] and Antonio Solari. A pirated version

of *Gemma di Vergy* was given at the Teatro Valle, Rome, on April 28, 1836, by the impresario Luigi Marzi, winning such suffrage that the price of a pit ticket was raised from ten baiocchi to thirty. The cast for some of these performances (the opera was put on again at the end of the season, after other operas had intervened) included Giuseppina Ronzi de Begnis in the role that she had created (Gemma), Salvatore Patti (Tamas), Filippo Coletti (Conte), Angelo Alba (Rolando), Orsola Lanzi (Ida), and Carlo Dossi (Guido). *Gemma* was heard again at the Valle in October 1838; at the Teatro Apollo in April 1840, with Fanny Maray in the title role; back at the Valle in April 1842—and in July 1843, with Settimio Malvezzi as Tamas. As late as June 1881, it was heard in Rome at the Alhambra. It was presented at the Teatro del Fondo, Naples, in the winter of 1837, with a cast that included Caterina Barili-Patti, Angela Terraciani, Salvatore Patti, Luigi Lablache, and Pietro Gianni.

For a list of some performances of *Gemma di Vergy,* in Italian, Hungarian, German, and French, see 77, 1, columns 762–63. This opera was first heard in Vienna, in Italian, on May 28, 1838, at the Kärnthnertortheater, with Sophie Schoberlechner *née* Dall'Oca, in the title role; at Berlin, the Königsstädtischestheater, on May 6, 1841; at London on March 12, 1842; at New York on October 2, 1843; and at Paris, the Théâtre-Italien, on December 16, 1845,

---

[13] Varesi would create the title role in Verdi's *Macbeth* at Florence in 1847, that of *Rigoletto* at Venice in 1851.

(1834 Continued)

with a cast headed by Giulia Grisi and Settimio Malvezzi.

(Adelaide) (opera comica): librettist unknown; probably begun 1834; never completed.

The Paris Conservatory Library has more than one hundred pages of autograph orchestral fragments; these show characters named Adelaide, Gontier, Roberto, and Il Colonnello. Charles Malherbe stated (*78*, 8, 210) that the music for this incomplete opera was used in large part by Donizetti in *L'Ange de Nisida,* which later became *La Favorite.* He cited a quintet with chorus, *"Ah! sperdosi appieno,"* saying that, almost unaltered, it became the Act III finale of *La Favorite.*

(Dalinda): a version of *Lucrezia Borgia.* Charles Malherbe, who owned some of it in autograph, said (*78*, 8, 210) that its chief characters were named Dalinda, Ildamaro, and Ugo. He called it *"opéra en trois actes, avec paroles italiennes, inédit et non cité par les biographes,"* apparently not realizing what it was, but said quite properly that it appeared to have been composed (written out) about 1834.

1835

Marin(o) Faliero (opera seria): three acts; libretto by Emmanuele Bidera (with additions by Agostino Ruffini),[14] after a play by

---

[14] For these additions, see Alfonso Lazzari's *Giovanni Ruffini, Gaetano Donizetti e il "Don Pasquale,"* originally published in the *Rassegna nazionale* (October 1 and 16, 1915) and issued as a pamphlet under the same title (*75*).

Casimir Delavigne; composed 1835; autograph score in Naples Conservatory Library.

Première: Théâtre-Italien, Paris, March 12, 1835; cast included Giulia Grisi, Giovanni Battista Rubini, Antonio Tamburini, Luigi Lablache—the four members of the so-called *"Puritani* quartet"— and Santini. Billed as both *Marin Faliero* and *Marino Faliero,* it had an extensive history. The opera was staged at the Teatro Alfieri, Florence, in May 1836, with Pietro Romani conducting and a cast headed by Caroline Ung(h)er, Domenico Cosselli, Paolo Ferretti, and Napoleone Moriani. The impresario, Alessandro Lanari, wrote to Donizetti on May 19, 1836, that it had been received with "Furor! Fanaticism! Enthusiasm!" and judged to be his masterpiece. In 1837, *Marin Faliero* was heard at both Rome and Milan. The first Roman performance—April 4, 1837—was a semiprivate one by the Accademia filarmonica romana; little is known about it except that the principal singers in the three performances included Elena Franchi, Pietro Balzar, and probably Pietro Angelini. The first Milanese production, at the Teatro alla Scala, August 19, 1837, had a run of thirty-nine performances; the opera was repeated there in 1840, 1844, and 1856. The first professional performance in Rome took place after the opera had been sung in Florence, Milan, Bologna, Genoa, and Reggio nell' Emilia. This was at the Teatro Apollo, December 26, 1838, under the aegis of the impresario Pietro Camuri; the cast included Eugénie Mayer-García—sister-in-law of

(1835 Continued)

Maria Malibran and Pauline Viardot-García—(Elena), Domenico Cosselli (Marin Faliero), Domenico Reina (Fernando), Costantino Natale (Israele), Pietro Guidotti (Steno), Carlo Cortesi (Leoni), and Augusta Soccè (Irene). This was a much "edited" version of the score. For example, the tenor's *cavatina "Di mia patria il bel soggiorno,"* with which Rubini had stirred waves of applause in the original production, was replaced with a *cavatina* from Rossini's *Zelmira.* Like the other alterations, this one probably was dictated for political reasons by the pontifical censor. On the first night, only four numbers were applauded, and the chief enthusiasm appears to have been for a stage picture of a Venetian *campo* in moonlight. Subsequent singings, however, increased in popularity.

Marin Faliero opened another season at the Teatro Apollo on December 26, 1840, the season that was to include the *première* there of Donizetti's *Adelia.* The cast was to have included Giuseppina Strepponi (Verdi's future wife being something of a Donizetti specialist), but at the final hour she had to take to her bed, and the role of Elena was sung by Colleoni-Corti; with her were Lorenzo Salvi, Ignazio Marini, and Angelo Alba. What was judged the finest *Marin Faliero* at Rome was staged at the Teatro Apollo by Alessandro Lanari in November 1843, with augmented chorus and orchestra; the cast included Marianna Barbieri-Nini, Anaide Castellan, Giorgio Ronconi, and Dal Riccio. At the Teatro Ricardi, Bergamo, on August 1, 1841, under the baton of Marco Bonesi, *Marin Faliero* reaped a clamorous success for Donizetti and a cast including Giuseppina Strepponi, Lorenzo Salvi, and Filippo Coletti. It was staged in many other Italian opera houses including (1848, the year of Donizetti's death) the San Carlo at Naples. There the Elena was Teresa Brambilla Ponchielli, the wife of the composer of *La Gioconda;* she was to create the role of Gilda in Verdi's *Rigoletto* at Venice three years later. With Brambilla in the San Carlo cast of *Marin Faliero* were Salvetti Manzi (Irene), Raffaele Ferlotti (Marin Faliero), Gionfrida (Israele), Settimio Malvezzi (Fernando), Marco Arati (Steno), Domenico Ceci (Leoni), Michele Memmi (Vincenzo), Paduano (Beltrame), Michele Benedetti (Pietro), and Teofilo Rossi (Strozzi).

For a list of some performances of *Marin Faliero* outside Italy, in Italian, German, Hungarian, and French, see 77, 1, columns 768–69. On May 14, 1835, less than five weeks after its world *première*, it was staged in London in Italian, which also was the language when the opera was sung in Vienna at the Kärnthnertortheater, on April 20, 1839, with Caroline Unger (Elena) and Domenico Cosselli (Marin Faliero). When it was restaged there in German, March 6, 1841 (it had been heard there earlier in German at the Theater in der Josefstadt, on April 21, 1838), the cast was headed by Jenny Suta (Elena), and Josef Staudigl, Sr. (Marin Faliero); this singing initiated a sixteen-year

(*1835 Continued*)

stay in the repertoire which accounted for thirty-eight performances. Berlin heard *Marin Faliero* at the Königsstädtischestheater on May 27, 1843, and it was staged in New York on December 15 of that year.

Lucia di Lammermoor (opera seria): three acts; libretto by Salvatore Cammarano, after Sir Walter Scott's novel *The Bride of Lammermoor;* composed 1835; autograph score in the Museo Teatrale alla Scala, Milan.

Première: Teatro San Carlo, Naples, September 26, 1835; cast included Fanny Tacchinardi-Persiani (Lucia), Teresa Zappucci (Alisa), Gilbert-Louis Duprez (Edgardo di Ravenswood), Domenico Cosselli (Enrico Ashton), Achille Balestracci[15] (Arturo Bucklaw), Carlo Porto (Raimondo Bidebent), and Teofilo Rossi (Normanno). For a listing of some of this opera's thousands of extra-Italian performances during and since Donizetti's lifetime, see 77, I, columns 771–73.

Lucia di Lammermoor was

[15] That Balestracci sang this role at the *première* is no more than a careful guess. Florimo (*54*, IV, 302) assigns the role to "Gioacchini," whose name is missing from the index to his book. In a letter that Donizetti wrote to Innocenzo Giampieri on the day of the *première*, he assigned the role (according to the transcription in *43a*, 33) to "Balestrieri." But no singer named Balestrieri appears to have been singing at the San Carlo at this period, whereas Achille Balestracci sang roles in at least five other operas at the San Carlo in the year of the *Lucia première*. I therefore have guessed that Florimo simply was wrong, as so often elsewhere, and that difficulties with Donizetti's script transformed Balestracci into Balestrieri.

heard at Rome for the first time at the Teatro Valle on November 14, 1836, when the cast included Talestri Fontana (Lucia), Marianna Guglielmini (Alisa), Cirillo Antognini (Edgardo), Pietro Balzar (Enrico Ashton), Annibale Galucci (Normanno), and Carlo Dossi (Raimondo). Little more than two weeks after that first Valle performance, the opera was presented semiprivately by the Accademia filarmonica romana in several singings; the Lucia was Roberta Fauvet, and with her were Pietro Angelini (Edgardo), Pietro Balzar (Enrico Ashton), Annibale Statuti (Normanno), and Giovanni Albertoni (Raimondo). In the spring of 1838, Alessandro Lanari put *Lucia* on at the restored Teatro Argentina, assigning the title role to Giuseppina Strepponi, that of Edgardo to Napoleone Moriani, that of Enrico Ashton to Giorgio Ronconi—a trio that may never have been surpassed in these roles. On April 1, 1839, Bartolomeo Merelli presented the opera at La Scala, Milan, with his stars of the hour, Adelaide Kemble (sister of the more famous Fanny), Moriani, and Ronconi. The opera itself was praised, but the Milanese did not care for Kemble's anglicized Italian—and later that season she was replaced by Giuseppina Strepponi, whose Scala debut had been made on that April 20 as Elvira in Bellini's *I Puritani*. At Bergamo, where *Lucia* was heard in twenty-eight different singings between 1838 and 1941, the first cast (Teatro Riccardi, August 1, 1836) included Eugénie Mayer-García,

Antonio Poggi, Celestino Salvatori, and Giuseppe Catalano.

Outside Italy, *Lucia* was sung at Vienna for the first time, in Italian, on April 13, 1837, the cast including Fanny Tacchinardi-Persiani in the role she had created, Antonio Poggi (Edgardo), Vincenzo Negrini (Enrico Ashton), Luigi Rigamonti (Raimondo), and Elg Tuczek (Alisa); the first German performance at Vienna occurred on January 28, 1843, when the cast included Jenny Suta (Lucia), Joseph Erl (Edgardo), Julius Pfister, and Gustav Hölzel (Raimondo). Between April 13, 1837, and February 26, 1890, *Lucia di Lammermoor* was sung at Vienna's leading opera house 286 times—217 of them (to September 30, 1869) in the old Kärnthnertortheater, 69 of them (from January 3, 1870) at the new Opernhaus.

Lucia was first played in Paris, in Italian, at the Théâtre-Italien, on December 12, 1837, when the cast was headed by Fanny Tacchinardi-Persiani, Giovanni Battista Rubini, Antonio Tamburini, and Giovanni Morelli. Its first performance in French, in a translation by Alphonse Royer and Gustave Vaëz, took place at the Théâtre de la Renaissance on August 3, 1839, when Anna Thillon was the Lucia, supported by Achille Ricciardi (Edgardo), Hurteaux (Enrico Ashton), Gibert (Arturo Bucklaw), Zelger (Raimondo), and Joseph. It entered the repertoire of the Opéra on February 20, 1846, when Nau was the Lucia, Gilbert-Louis Duprez the Edgardo, and Paolo

Barroilhet the Enrico Ashton. So popular had this opera become in Paris by 1839 that on the night of October 1, it was being sung there both in Italian—as the opening night attraction of the season at the Théâtre-Italien—and in French at the Théatre de la Renaissance, which presented it forty-six times between August 6, 1839, and April 26, 1840.

Lucia was first heard in London, in Italian, at Her Majesty's Theatre, on April 15, 1838; in English at the Princess's Theatre on January 19, 1843; and in French at Drury Lane Theatre on July 16, 1845. It was given its two-hundredth performance at Covent Garden on June 4, 1902. *Lucia* was sung in French in New Orleans on December 28, 1841, and in Italian at New York on September 15, 1843. New York also heard it in an English translation by Michael Rophino Lacy and G. Bowes on November 17, 1845. It was heard at the Metropolitan Opera House on the second night of its opening season, October 24, 1883, with this cast: Marcella Sembrich (Lucia), Imogene Forti (Alisa), Italo Campanini (Edgardo), Giuseppe Kaschmann (Enrico Ashton), Vincenzo Fornaris (Arturo Bucklaw), Amadeo Grazzi (Normanno), and Achile Augier (Raimondo). Among notable later Metropolitan Lucias have been Lily Pons, Maria Meneghini Callas, and Joan Sutherland—the last of whom appeared, during the 1961-62 season, to be making an international career of singing nothing but this role. At the end of that season, *Lucia di Lammer-*

(*1835 Continued*)

moor had been heard at the Metropolitan 209 times.

1836

Belisario (*opera seria*): three acts; libretto by Salvatore Cammarano, after Jean-François Marmontel's *Bélisaire*; composed 1835–36; autograph score in the Ricordi archives, Milan.

Première: Teatro La Fenice, Venice, February 4, 1836; cast included Caroline Ung(h)er (Antonina), Antonietta Vial (Irene), Pasini (Giustiniano), and Celestino Salvatori—for whom Donizetti had designed the role of the Byzantine general, Belisarius, which later became a sort of Salvatori specialty. The day after the *première*, the *Gazzetta privilegiata di Venezia* said: "A new masterwork has been added to Italian music: *Anna Bolena* has found a worthy brother, and *Belisario*, produced last evening, not only pleased and delighted, but also conquered, enflamed, ravished the full auditorium. . . . The spectacle, from the first note to the last, was but a chain of applause and of calls for the Maestro and the singers. The *dramma* (for the beautiful composition of Signor Cammarano was not debased by the customary designation of libretto)[16] is worthy of the excellent musical work. . . . No first performance in memory has recorded a more splendid, fuller, more solemn suc-

cess. . . . The numbers that were most enthusiastically judged were the *donna's cavatina*, with its sublime *cabaletta*, a tenor-bass duet. . . . The handling of the finale and the scena and grand aria of the *donna* were other imaginative and graceful conceptions, and they will be enjoyed even more in time, when 'our ear, conquered by so much novelty, will have become a little accustomed [to it].' "

Belisario was successful enough at Venice so that other Italian opera houses took it up quickly. On August 20, 1836, it was staged both at La Scala, Milan—with a cast including Eugenia Tadolini, Marietta Brambilla, Francesco Pedrazzi, and (in "his" role) Celestino Salvatori—and in June 1836, at the Teatro San Carlo, Naples, with Giuseppina Ronzi de Begnis, Giulietta Borghese (Juliette Bourgeois), Angela Terraciani, Pietro Gianni, Paolo Barroilhet as Belisario, Giovanni Basadonna, Teofilo Rossi, Villanova, and Revalden. That this opera also grew into a considerable career abroad can be seen in the list of some extra-Italian performances in 77, I, columns 776–77, showing stagings in Italian, German, Russian, Hungarian, French, Czech, and Polish.

Belisario was first heard in London, in Italian, on April 1, 1837; at Berlin, the Königsstädt-ischestheater, in a German translation by Julius Hähnel, on April 10, 1838; at Philadelphia, in Italian, on July 29, 1843; at Paris, the Théâtre-Italien, in Italian, on October 24, 1843—with Giulia Grisi, Leone(?) Corelli, Fornasari, and

---

[16] Perhaps satirical, this strange little remark may equally well have been serious, referring to the fact that *libretto* literally means "*little* book."

(1836 Continued)

Giovanni Morelli; and at New York, in Italian, on February 14, 1844. Vienna heard it first in Italian, at the Kärnthnertortheater on June 16, 1836, with Eugenia Tadolini, Carlotta Villadini, Domenico Spiaggi, Ignazio Marini, Giovanni Genero, Luigi Asti, and Antonio Genero; it was produced there in German on November 12, 1839, with a cast including Wilhelmina von Hasselt-Barth, Cilli Kreutzer, Johann Schober, Theodor Schenk, Gustav Hölzel, and Franz Ulz. Its first performance at Bergamo, at the Teatro Riccardi, occurred on August 1, 1837, when Michele Racchele conducted and the cast was headed by Giuditta Grisi (Antonina), Ernestina Grisi (Irene), Domenico Reina (Alamino), and Cesare Badiali (Belisario).

Il Campanello (di notte or *dello speziale) (farsa):* one act; libretto by Donizetti; composed 1836; autograph score in Naples Conservatory Library.

Première: Teatro Nuovo, Naples, June 6, 1836; cast included Amalia Schütz, Giorgio Ronconi, and Raffaele Casaccia. For a list of some of its performances in Italy and elsewhere during and after Donizetti's lifetime, see 77, 1, columns 781–82. London heard it in Italian, at the Lyceum Theatre, on January 9, 1838; at the same theater in English on March 9, 1841; and at the Gaiety Theatre, again in English, on September 25, 1870. Philadelphia was the first city in the United States to perform this opera, in Italian, on October 25, 1861; what was very likely the same

production was heard in New York three days later. New York also had a production in an English translation by Sydney Rosenfeld on May 7, 1917. Paris first heard *Il Campanello* as *La Sonnette*[17] (French translation by Jules Ruelle), the opening attraction of the Fantaisies-Parisiennes, December 2, 1865.

Betly (sometimes *Bettly*), *ossia La Capanna svizzera (opera giocosa):* one act; libretto by Donizetti, after Augustin-Eugène Scribe's *Le Chalet,* first made into an opera by Adolphe Adam (*Le Chalet,* Opéra-Comique, Paris, September 25, 1834); composed 1836; non-autograph score in Naples Conservatory Library.

Première: Teatro Nuovo, Naples, August 24, 1836; cast included Toldi, Lorenzo Salvi, and Giuseppe Fioravanti. Revised as a two-act opera and staged at Palermo on October 29, 1837, with a cast including Irene Secci-Corsi, Ambrogio Danini, and Mazzotti. For a list of some performances of *Betly,* see 77, 1, columns 781–782. It was sung in Italian at the Lyceum Theatre, London, on January 9, 1838, and at the same house in English on March 9, 1841; it was heard at the Opéra, Paris, in a French translation by Hippolyte Lucas—and with the score arranged by Adam, whose version of Scribe's story by then was nineteen years old—on December 27, 1853, with Angiolina Bosio starred. *Betly* achieved

---

[17] The title of the vaudeville by Léon-Lévy Brunswick, Mathieu-Barthélemy Troin, and Victor Lhérie (1835) on which Donizetti had based his text had been *La Sonnette de nuit.*

(*1836 Continued*)

only five singings at the Opéra, clearly a house insufficiently intimate for it. *Betly* was mounted in Italian at Philadelphia on October 25, 1861, and at New York three days later.

L'Assedio di Calais (opera seria): three acts; libretto by Salvatore Cammarano; composed 1836; autograph score in Naples Conservatory Library.

Première: Teatro San Carlo, Naples, November 19, 1836; cast included Almerinda Manzocchi (Isabella), Caterina Barili-Patti[18] (Eleonora), Federico Lablache (Edoardo III), Nicola Tucci (Edmondo), Pietro Gianni (Un Incognito), Paolo Barroilhet (Eustachio), Ferdinando Cimino (Giovanni d'Aire), Revalden (Giacomo di Wisants), and Benedetti (Armando). Writing to Gilbert-Louis Duprez on May 21, 1837, to urge the production of *Lucia di Lammermoor* and *L'Assedio di Calais* in Paris, Donizetti said of the latter: "See that having given it in November, they still are giving it, and it is given especially at every gala as the best of the spectacles, and is billed now for July 6 [the birthday of the Queen Mother]." Outside Naples, however, this opera appears to have had a narrow career despite its obvious stageability and promise of much more.

Pia de' Tolomei (opera seria): two acts; libretto by Salvatore Cammarano; composed 1836–37; Non-autograph score in Naples Conservatory Library.

---

[18] Wife of Salvatore Patti, mother of Carlotta, and future mother of the great Adelina.

Première: Teatro Apollo, Venice; February 18, 1837; cast included Fanny Tacchinardi-Persiani (Pia), Rosina Mazzarelli, Antonio Poggi, and Giorgio Ronconi. The opera seems never to have been revived in Venice or (almost certain proof that it did not become one of Donizetti's successes) to have been staged at Bergamo. It was mounted at the Teatro Argentina, Rome, in the spring of 1838 with a cast that included Giuseppina Strepponi and the "tenor of the beautiful death" (who incidentally was the father of Strepponi's two illegitimate children), Napoleone Moriani, as well as Giorgio Ronconi—who, according to Franco Abbiati (*1*), expressed the fear that his powerful high notes might shatter the windows of the Argentina. Strepponi, following upon her success as Lucia di Lammermoor at the same theater, was much admired as the unhappy Pia, criticism going so far as to compare her "beautiful death in Pia's costume" to the renowned final agonies of Moriani, of whom it was written that "his leave-taking from life is expressed by singing that has the tints and capriciousness of death; he is a Narcissus who submits brokenheartedly and in whose breast the dying, vanishing echo of sorrow weeps." Not even the conjunction of two such experienced expirers and Ronconi won an enduring Roman career for *Pia de' Tolomei*. It was, however, staged at the Teatro San Carlo, Naples, also in 1838, with a cast including Giuseppina Ronzi de Begnis (Pia), Buccini (Rodrigo),

(*1836 Continued*)

Rizzati (Bice), Paolo Barroilhet (Nello), Giovanni Basadonna (Ghino), Giuseppe Benedetti (Piero), Teofilo Rossi (Lamberto), and Barattini (Ubaldo).

Roberto Devereux, ossia Il Conte di Essex (opera seria): three acts; libretto by Salvatore Cammarano, after François Ancelot's tragedy *Elisabeth d'Angleterre* and Lescène Desmaison's *Historie secrète des amours d'Elisabeth d'Angleterre et du comte d'Essex;* composed 1837; autograph score in Naples Conservatory Library.

Première: Teatro San Carlo, Naples, October 29, 1837; cast included Giuseppina Ronzi de Begnis (Elisabetta), Almerinda Granchi[19] (Sara), Paolo Barroilhet (Nottingham), Giovanni Basadonna (Roberto), Barattini (Cecil), and Teofilo Rossi (Gualtiero). A very considerable success, *Roberto Devereux* soon spread across Italy and traveled abroad. For a list of some of its numerous stagings outside Italy —in Italian, German, French, Hungarian, and Russian—see 77, 1, columns 789-90. A pirated version of it was sung at the Teatro Re, Milan, late in 1837 or early in 1838. On May 5, 1838, in a letter to Count Gaetano Melzi, Donizetti complained: "I know that my poor *Roberto* at the Re was orchestrated by others. Oh! musical piracy! Oh! degraded art! There is no one to protect you in Italy." The opera was presented at the Teatro La Fenice, Venice, in the autumn of 1838. At La Scala, Milan, it was sung on September 21, 1839, with a cast including Rosina Mazzarelli, Giuseppina Armenia, Lorenzo Salvi, and Ignazio Marini. The criticism of this performance in the *Gazzetta privilegiata di Milano* of September 24, 1839, indicated that, as on other occasions, the critic had joined members of the audience in objecting to the opera's containing "graftings" and "adaptations" from earlier Donizetti scores: "It seems to me that some operas benefit the singers, others acquire value and fame from the singers. Among the former there was, at La Scala (after the younger Ricci's *Il Duello* had been played), Rossini's *L'Italiana in Algeri*, in which the Marini couple especially won praise and applause; among the latter there would now be counted Donizetti's *Roberto Devereux* (for it is good to remain silent about *Gianni di Parigi*,[20] both for the Maestro's sake and for that of the singers, who gave unflattering accounts of themselves in it). It cannot be doubted that Mazzarelli, Armenia, Salvi, and Marini effectively contributed toward the pleasure afforded by several pieces in a score that is not among the celebrated Maestro's best, and, in the bargain, contains the usual graftings and recastings, against which the public and the journals waste the breath of their lungs."

Roberto Devereux was received better at the Teatro della

---

[19] Donizetti told Alessandro Lanari that he had composed this opera for Granchi.

[20] The first performance of Donizetti's 1831 opera had taken place at La Scala exactly two weeks before this article appeared.

(*1836 Continued*)

Società, Bergamo, on January 19, 1841, when Marco Bonesi conducted a cast including Eugenia d'Alberti, Lorenzo Biacchi, and Giuseppe Paltrinieri. When it was staged, in Italian, at the Kärntnertortheater, Vienna, on June 22, 1844, with a cast including Antonietta Montenegro (Elisabetta), Nicholas Ivanoff (Roberto), Felice Varesi, and Giorgio Ronconi, Donizetti wrote to Giacomo Pedroni: "I inform you of the enormous [*piramidale*] fiasco of *Roberto d'Evereux* [*sic*]." He composed a *sinfonia* especially for a performance of this opera at the Théâtre-Italien, Paris, on December 27, 1838, when it was sung by, among others, Giulia Grisi, Giovanni Battista Rubini, Antonio Tamburini, and Emma Albertazzi. It was heard at the Théâtre des Arts, Rouen, on February 15, 1841, in a French translation by Étienne Monnier; at Berlin, the Königsstädtischestheater, in Italian, on June 12, 1841; and at New York, still in Italian, on January 15, 1849.

1838

Maria di Rudenz (opera seria): three acts; libretto by Salvatore Cammarano; composed 1837; nonautograph score in archives of the Teatro la Fenice, Venice.

Première: Teatro La Fenice, Venice, January 30, 1838; cast included Caroline Ung(h)er (Maria di Rudenz), Napoleone Moriani, and Giorgio Ronconi. The opera won relatively few stagings. Donizetti regarded it as a fiasco. For

a short list of its performances during and just after his lifetime, see 77, I, column 794—a list that significantly includes no stagings in Paris, Vienna, Berlin, London, or New York. It was heard at the Teatro Valle, Rome, on October 3, 1841, under the aegis of Vincenzo Jacovacci, with a cast including Maria Napoleona Vellani-Albini (Maria), Francesco Luigi Morini (Enrico), Pietro Balzar (Corrado), Elisabetta Sonderegger (Matilde), Giuseppe Bien (Rambaldo), and Giuseppe Vergani (Cancelliere); Balzar found the role of Corrado, originally composed for Ronconi, too high for comfort, and some of it had to be transposed down for him. Although neither the public nor the critics reacted enthusiastically —reminiscences of other Donizetti scores, notably that of *Lucia di Lammermoor*, were disliked— *Maria di Rudenz* ran up a total of fourteen performances. The formidable Belgian musicologist François-Joseph Fétis was present at one of these performances; in a letter giving his impressions of the state of music in Italy,[21] he said: "My surprise was even greater at Rome, as there the singers, choristers, orchestral musicians, all were mediocre or bad, and nonetheless I could not help admiring the animation of all these people in the finale of the first act of *Maria di Rudenz*."

Alessandro Lanari tried *Maria di Rudenz* on a Roman audience again at the Teatro Apollo on October 10, 1843, with Teresa Brambilla in the title role, sup-

---

[21] *Gazzetta musicale*, Milan, July 2, 1843, p. 113.

(*1838 Continued*)

ported by Giorgio Ronconi and the tenor Giacomo Roppa. The excellent production and superior singing this time won vigorous approval for the opera. Five years later (1848), it was put on at the Teatro Nuovo, Naples, with a cast including Agresti del Fante (Maria di Rudenz), Tucci (Matilde), the younger Lablache (Corrado Valdorf), Agresti (Enrico), and Grandilli (Rambaldo); this same cast appears also to have sung it again at the Teatro San Carlo in 1851. The title of this opera was kept somewhat familiar throughout the rest of the nineteenth century by the favor with which baritones in concert regarded its *romanza* "*Ah! non avea più lagrime.*" Donizetti raided the score of *Maria di Rudenz*, transferring to *Poliuto* (*Les Martyrs*) the first act *concertato* finale that had impressed Fétis.

1839

Gianni di Parigi (*opera comica*): two acts; libretto by Felice Romani, perhaps influenced by the libretto (by Claude Godard d'Aucour de Saint-Just) for François-Adrien Boieldieu's *Jean de Paris*, Opéra-Comique, Paris, April 4, 1812; composed 1831, for Giovanni Battista Rubini, who never sang in it; autograph score in Naples Conservatory Library. *Première:* Teatro alla Scala, Milan, September 10, 1839; cast included Antonietta Marini-Raineri (Principessa di Navarra), Ignazio Marini (Gran Siniscalco), Lorenzo Salvi (Gianni), Agostino

Rovere (Fedrigo Locandiere), Felicità Baillou Hillaret (Oliviero Paggio), and Marietta Sacchi (Lorezza). Having been staged without Donizetti's personal supervision, it was received badly, taking up only the first three nights of the season and making way for Rossini's *L'Italiana in Algeri*, being heard again on September 18, and then being retired in favor of Donizetti's *Roberto Devereux*, which ran out the rest of the season until November 17, the day of the first, badly received performance of Verdi's first opera, *Oberto, conte di San Bonifacio*.

When *Gianni di Parigi* was staged at the Teatro San Carlo, Naples, in 1846, the cast was recorded as Gabussi or Gabuzzi[22] (Principessa della Rocca), Salvetti Manzi (Lorezza), Buccini (Oliviero Paggio), Baillou (Siniscalco della Principessa), Flavio (Gianni di Parigi), and Salvetti (Fedrigo Locandiere).

(*Poliuto*): composed 1839, rewritten as *Les Martyrs*, q. v. (1840) for data on both the French opera and later stagings of the original Italian version, which was heard for the first time at the Teatro San Carlo, Naples, on November 30, 1848. The original Italian libretto was by Salvatore Cammarano, and the year after its announced production at the San Carlo in 1839 was forbidden, he borrowed verses from it for the text he wrote for Saverio Mercadante's opera *La Vestale*.[23]

---

[22] Could this have been the Giuseppina Gabuzzi whom Donizetti's unhappy nephew Andrea married in 1858?

[23] Franco Schlitzer, "*Mercandante e Cammarano,*" in *S. Mercadante* (*Numero Unico*, Bari, 1945).

(1839 Continued)

When, after Donizetti's death, *Poliuto* was staged at Naples and a piano score published by Francesco Lucca, Giovanni Ricordi became interested in it and asked Cammarano for information on it. On March 14, 1850, Cammarano wrote Ricordi: "Here is what you asked me for concerning *Poliuto*. The book was written by me for Barbaja, to whom I also ceded the proprietary right; Barbaja transmitted it to Donizetti and Donizetti to an old friend, Signor Teodoro Ghezzi; this man has sold the music and the book to Signor [Francesco] Lucca,[24] retaining for himself the proprietary right only for the Kingdom of Naples. . . . I did not answer sooner because I wasn't able sooner to see Signor Ghezzi, from whom I wanted to get a clarification of his right, which is revealed by the original score of *Poliuto*, where Donizetti wrote [of] the gift that that notable man made [of it] to the abovementioned Ghezzi." The original autograph score of *Poliuto* in the Naples Conservatory Library has this inscription by Donizetti on its title page: "*Donato a Teodoro 1844 Donizetti*" ("Given to Teodoro 1844 Donizetti").

(L'Ange de Nisida): incomplete opera; never performed, but transformed into *La Favorite*, q. v. (1840).

(Le Duc d'Albe): worked at in 1839 and later; never completed; for *première* as completed by Matteo Salvi and translated into Italian

---

[24] Ghezzi appears to have acted as Lucca's representative at Naples.

by Angelo Zanardini (*Il Duca d'Alba*), see under 1882.

1840

La Fille du régiment (opéra-comique): two acts, libretto by Jules-Henri Vernoy de Saint-Georges and Jean-François-Alfred Bayard; composed 1839–40; nonautograph score in Naples Conservatory Library.

Première: Opéra-Comique, Paris, February 11, 1840; cast included Juliet(te) Bourgeois, also known as Giulietta Borghese (Marie), Marie-Julienne Boulanger[25] (Marquise), Blanchard (Duchesse), Henry (Sulpice), Mécène Marié de l'Isle[26] (Tonio). The fact that his last singer noticeably sang off pitch throughout the first performance did not help *La Fille* to win its eventual public immediately. But by 1950, this opera had been sung 1,044 times at the Opéra-Comique. Its fiftieth singing occurred at the Salle Favart on January 12, 1841, with the original cast; its one-thousandth at a matinee on March 8, 1914. On December 6, 1914, the Favart was opened for the first of the Comique's wartime performances—with the 1,020th singing of *La Fille du régiment*,

---

[25] If the documents are to be trusted, this was Marie-Julienne Halligner, known as Mme Boulanger, born *ca.* 1784. She did not retire until about 1845.

[26] Some nine months later, Marié de l'Isle became the father of a girl who was named Célestine and who was to become one of the most admired mezzo sopranos of her age: as Célestine Galli-Marié, she would create the title roles of both Ambroise Thomas's *Mignon* and Bizet's *Carmen*.

which always has exerted special appeal during wars. For a list of some of the extremely numerous other stagings of this opera—in French, Danish, Italian, Finnish, Croat, Slovenian, and Estonian— see 77, 1, columns 804–6.

As *La Figlia del reggimento,* in an Italian translation by Calisto Bassi, this opera soon became popular not only in Italy, but also elsewhere—including Paris, where its title role was sung at the Théâtre-Italien by, among others, Jenny Lind and Henriette Sontag. *La Figlia* evoked enthusiastic response when it first was sung at the Teatro alla Scala, Milan, on October 3, 1840, a few months before the single disastrous performance there of Verdi's second, comic opera, *Un Giorno di regno.* Donizetti's opera was first heard in Vienna, in Italian, on May 11, 1841; at Berlin, the Königliches Opernhaus, in German, on July 29, 1842; at New Orleans, in French, on March 6, 1843; at New York, in French, on July 19, 1843; at London, Her Majesty's Theatre, in Italian, on May 27, 1847; and at San Francisco, in English, in April 1854.

The apparently delicious Angiolina Zoja became a renowned specialist in the drum-playing and other antics of Maria's role in *La Figlia del reggimento* after (January 9, 1846) the *basso comico* Carlo Cambiaggio, acting as impresario, staged the opera at the Teatro Valle, Rome. Others in that highly appreciated cast were Cambiaggio himself (Sergente), Adelindo Vietti (Tonio), Assunta Balelli (Marchesa),

Domenico Prò (Ortensio), and Vincenzo Gobbetti (Caporale). This opera was almost sixty-two years old when, in French, it finally occupied the stage of the Metropolitan Opera House, New York, on January 6, 1902, sharing a double bill with *Cavalleria rusticana;* the cast that evening was Marcella Sembrich (Marie), Marie van Cauteren (Marquise), Thomas Salignac (Tonio), Charles Gilibert (Sulpice), Eugène Dufriche (Hortensius), and Lodovico Viviani (Corporal). When *La Fille du régiment* was revived at the Metropolitan at a matinee on December 28, 1940, Lily Pons was the Marie, supported by Irra Petina (Marquise), Maria Savage (Duchesse), Raoul Jobin (Tonio), Salvatore Baccaloni (Sulpice), and Louis D'Angelo (Hortensius). Reviewing that performance, Virgil Thomson said of the opera that it "has gaiety and melodic eloquence; it is good Donizetti all right. Only it isn't the best Donizetti. It lacks occasions for the grander flights of feeling, and most especially for those magnificently theatrical and expressive concerted numbers that he could write as no other composer ever did, excepting Mozart." *La Fille du régiment* opened the 1942–43 season at the Metropolitan on November 23, 1942, with Pons, Petina, Jobin, and Baccaloni; it was repeated on January 2, 1943— and then left the Metropolitan, having been heard there twenty-seven times.

Les Martyrs (grand opéra): four acts; libretto by Augustin-Eugène Scribe, in part derived

(1840 Continued)

directly from Corneille's *Polyeucte* and in part an adaptation of Salvatore Cammarano's Italian libretto *Poliuto*, itself derived from *Polyeucte*; autograph score of original Italian version in Naples Conservatory Library, that of *Les Martyrs* in the Ricordi archives, Milan.

Composed (as *Poliuto*) 1839, revised as *Les Martyrs* 1840; *premières:* as *Les Martyrs*, Opéra, Paris, April 10, 1840, with a cast including Julie Dorus-Gras (Pauline), Gilbert Louis-Duprez (Polyeucte), Jean-Étienne Massol (Sévère), Nicholas-Prosper Derivis (Félix), Pierre-François Wartel, Serda, Molinier, and Wideman; as *Poliuto*, Teatro San Carlo, Naples, November 30, 1848, with a cast including Eugenia Tadolini (Paolina), Carlo Baucardé (Poliuto), Filippo Colini (Severo), Teofilo Rossi (Felice), Marco Arati (Callistene), and Domenico Ceci (Nearco). Enrico Tamberlik became a noted Poliuto. The role of Pauline in the French version originally had been intended for the great dramatic soprano Cornélie Falcon.

For a list of some stagings of *Les Martyrs* and *Poliuto* in various languages and versions, including the Italian original as *Paolina e Poliuto* and *Paolina e Severo*, see 77, I, column 807.[27] The opera first was heard in Vienna, in a German translation by Karl August, Freiherr von Lichtenstein, as altered by Josef

Kupelwieser, under Donizetti's supervision, on June 6, 1841, at the Kärnthnertortheater; at New Orleans, in French, in 1846; at Naples, Teatro San Carlo, in Italian, on November 30, 1848 (see above); at London, Covent Garden, in Italian, on March 20, 1852, with a cast including Dejean Jullienne, Enrico Tamberlik, and Giorgio Ronconi; and at New York, in Italian, on May 25, 1859. At Bergamo, where this opera was sung as early as August 31, 1850, it was produced for the ninth time on November 16, 1907, to inaugurate the Teatro Rubini. Gino Marinuzzi conducted, and the cast included Elvira Magliulo, José García, Tegani, and Contini. The most spectacular revival of later years, as *Poliuto*, was presented at La Scala, Milan, on December 7, 1960, with a cast including Maria Callas, Franco Corelli, and Ettore Bastianini.

Poliuto (apparently as *Paolina e Severo*) was heard at the Teatro Apollo, Rome, on December 26, 1849, with the Contessa Gigliucco—i.e., Clara Novello—(Paolina), Emilio Naudin (Poliuto), and Filippo Colini (Severo), and was a disaster. Repeated in Rome in 1852, 1860, and January 1881—this last time as the final offering of the veteran impresario Vincenzo Jacovacci, who died two months later—it continued not to please. At the Teatro Costanzi in April 1883, however, it won a success, largely because of the performance of the role of Poliuto by Francesco Tamagno, thus making his Roman debut, and that of Paolina by Teresa Brambilla-Ponchielli. As

---

[27] Alfred Loewenberg's statement (77) that *Les Martyrs* was not a great success in Paris needs interpretation. See p. 150.

(1840 Continued)

late as April 1904, Pietro Mascagni conducted the second and third acts of a Tamagno *Poliuto* during a benefit performance at the Costanzi.

La Favorite (grand opéra): four acts; libretto by Alphonse Royer and Gustave Vaëz, possibly with additions by Scribe; adapted to the partially completed score of *L'Ange de Nisida,* with an added act; composed, as *L'Ange de Nisida,* 1839; rearranged and composed as *La Favorite* 1840; nonautograph score in Naples Conservatory Library.

Première: Opéra, Paris, December 2, 1840; cast included Rosine Stoltz (Léonore), Elian or Eliam (Inès), Gilbert-Louis Duprez (Fernand), Paolo Barroilhet (Alphonse XI), Nicholas-Prosper Levasseur (Balthasar), Pierre-François Wartel (Don Gaspard). When the original settings for *La Favorite* were destroyed in an Opéra storehouse fire in 1894, new scenery was built, and by 1897 *La Favorite* had been sung at the Opéra some 660 times. Renowned Léonores there, after the sensational Stoltz, included Adelaide Borghi-Mamo, Pauline Viardot-García, Guéymard, Rosina Bloch, Figuet, Richard, and Blanche Deschamps-Jéhin. For a list of some of the very numerous stagings of *La Favorite* throughout the world— in French, German, Italian, Hungarian, Russian, English, Swedish, Polish, Croat, Czech, and Slovenian—see 77, I, 811–12.

La Favorite reached Vienna— in German, as *Richard und Matilde* (later billed as *Leonore*)

—on December 26, 1841, when the cast included Jenny Suta (Mathilde, Countess Ecluse), Joseph Erl (Richard), Johann Schober (Ippolito), and Josef Staudigl, Sr. At the Teatro San Carlo, Naples, in 1848, Eugenia Tadolini sang the role of Leonora in *La Favorita,* with Salvetti Manzi (Ines), Felice Varesi (Alfonso XI), Carlo Baucardé (Fernando), Antonio Selva (Baldassare), and Domenico Ceci (Don Gasparo). The opera was first heard in Berlin, the Königsstädtischestheater, in Italian, on October 15, 1842; at New Orleans, in French, on February 9, 1843; at London, Drury Lane Theatre, in an English translation by Edward Fitzball, on October 15, 1843; and at New York, in French, on June 25, 1845. Fifty years later (November 29, 1895), *La Favorita,* being sung at the Metropolitan Opera House, New York, for the first time, could boast a cast consisting of Eugenia Mantelli (Leonora), Mathilde Bauermeister (Ines), Mario Ancona (Alfonso), Giuseppe Cremonini (Fernando), Pol Plançon (Baldassare), and Roberto Vanni (Don Gasparo).

La Favorite was revived at the Teatro alla Scala, Milan, on January 4, 1962, with the *bergamasco* Gianandrea Gavazzeni conducting. The cast consisted of Fiorenza Cossotto (Leonora), Edith Martelli (Ines), Gianni Raimondi (Fernando), Ettore Bastianini (Alfonso XI), Nicolai Ghiaurov (Baldassare), Piero de Palma (Don Gasparo), and Walter Gullino (Un Cavaliere).

Of the critical reaction to *La Favorite* when it was sung for the

(*1840 Continued*)

first time in 1840, Maurice-Pierre Boyé wrote (*22*): "For what did the habitués of the Opéra reproach this score, received by them without enthusiasm? In it were to be found, according to [Théophile] Gautier, 'facility (always!), fortunate melodies, passages well composed for the voice, a certain éclat,' but equally one met trumpery melodies, worn and trivial phrases, and that negligence, owing to the hasty conception of the work, which the Italian melomanes accepted, but which our dilettantes could not allow. In truth, Donizetti's weakness resided there, in that acceptance of the unfinished, in that lack of taste and of the need for perfection. His entire impetuous nature was against it."

1841

Adelia, o La Figlia dell'arciere (opera seria): three acts; libretto by Felice Romani and Girolamo Maria Marini;[28] composed 1840–1841; autograph score in the Ricordi archives, Milan.

Première: Teatro Apollo, Rome, February 11, 1841; cast included Giuseppina Strepponi (Adelia), Clementina Baroni (Odetta), Filippo Valentini (Carlo), Lorenzo Salvi (Oliviero), Ignazio Marini (Arnoldo), Pietro Gasperini (Comino), and Luigi Fossi (Uno Scudiere); the orchestra was conducted by Emilio Angelini, who later was to win considerable praise from

---

[28] See p. 158 for discussion of this refashioned libretto, originally composed by Carlo Coccia in 1834.

Verdi. Although *Adelia* was considered a success at Rome, Alfred Loewenberg (*77*, I, column 813) listed only these stagings outside Italy: Lisbon, March 28, 1842; Malta, 1842; Madrid, September 23, 1842; London, March 11, 1843. Clearly, *Adelia* won no extended career.

(Rita, ou Le Mari battu): composed 1841; autograph score, with Italian text (*Due Uomini ed una donna*), in Naples Conservatory Library

For *première*, etc., see under 1860.

Maria Padilla (opera seria): three acts; libretto by Gaetano Rossi, after a play by François Ancelot; composed 1841; autograph score in the Ricordi archives, Milan.

Première: Teatro alla Scala, Milan, December 26, 1841; cast included Sophie Löwe (Maria Padilla), Luigia Abbadia (Ines Padilla or Francesca), Giorgio Ronconi (Don Pedro), and Domenico Donzelli (Ruiz de Padilla). For a brief listing of this opera's performances outside Italy, see *77*, I, column 817. It was staged at the Teatro San Carlo, Naples, in 1842, with Eugenia Tadolini (Maria Padilla), De Varny (Ines), Chiara Gualdi (Francesca), Filippo Coletti (Pedro Mendez), Marco Arati (Don Ramiro), Giovanni Basadonna (Don Ruiz de Padilla), Teofilo Rossi (Don Luigi d'Aguilar), and Domenico Ceci (Don Alfonso de Pardo). *Maria Padilla* was presented at the Kärnthnertortheater, Vienna, on May 18, 1847, again with Tadolini in the title role, supported by Felice Varesi (Don Pedro Mendez),

(1841 Continued)

Koch (Don Ramiro), Maria Coridori (Ines), Elisa Friedbay (Francesca), Luigi Bottagisi (Conte d'Aguilar), C. Herberth (Alfonso de Pardo), and Raffaele Mirate (Ruiz de Padilla). At the Teatro Apollo, Rome, on January 10, 1852, *Maria* had a Ruiz—Gaetano Fraschini—whom the periodicals reported as having been coached in the role some years earlier by Donizetti. Others in that Roman cast were the Sicilian soprano Carolina Alajmo (Maria Padilla), Calista Fiorio (Ines), Filippo Colini (Don Pedro Mendez), Achille Biscossi (Don Ramiro), Mariano Conti (Don Luigi d'Aguilar), and Luigi Fani (Don Alfonso de Pardo). After these performances at the Apollo, *Maria Padilla* in effect disappeared altogether from the boards.

1842

Linda di Chamounix (opera semiseria): three acts; libretto by Gaetano Rossi;[29] composed 1842; autograph score in the Ricordi archives, Milan.

Première: Kärnthnertortheater, Vienna, May 19, 1842; cast included Eugenia Tadolini (Linda), Marietta Bambilla (Pierotto), Napoleone Moriani (Carlo, Visconte di Sirval), Felice Varesi (Antonio), Prosper Derivis (The Prefect), and Agostino Rovere (Marchese di Boisfleury). For a listing of the very numerous

---

[29] Donizetti himself wrote the text of "*O luce di quest'anima.*" Rossi appears to have derived his libretto from the melodrama *La Grâce de Dieu,* by Adolphe-Philippe d'Ennery (called Dennery) and Gustave Lemoine.

stagings of *Linda di Chamounix* outside Italy—in Italian, German, Hungarian, English, French, Czech, Russian, Romanian, Polish, Swedish, Finnish, and Slovenian —see 77, I, columns 820–22.

Linda di Chamounix was sung at the Teatro Carignano, Turin, on August 24, 1842; at Rome, the Teatro Valle, on November 5, 1842, when Emilio Angelini conducted a cast including Schieroni-Nulli (Linda), Eugenio Musich (Visconte), Felice Varesi in the role he had created at Vienna (Antonio), Teresa Ceci (Pierotto), Giovanni Pallelli (Prefetto), Giuseppe Scheggi (Marchese), Gerardo Caruso-Lenzi (Intendente), and Teresa Massia (Maddalena); at Venice, the Teatro La Fenice, in the Carnival season of 1843;[30] at Naples, the Teatro San Carlo, in the winter of 1843, with Tadolini in the role she had created, Salvetti Manzi (Maddalena), Maria Taglioni (Pierotto), Salvetti (Marchese di Boisfleury), Gaetano Fraschini (Visconti di Sirval), Giuseppe Beneventano[31] (Remigio), Filippo Coletti (Antonio), and Domenico Ceci (L'Intendente); at Milan, the Teatro alla Scala, March 2, 1844; at Bergamo (the first of many stagings there), the Teatro della Società, January 8, 1846, when the cast included Luigia Schierani, Achille Balestracci, and Domenico

---

[30] "What a fiasco, *Linda* at Venice," Donizetti wrote to Giovanni Ricordi from Vienna on January 20, 1843.

[31] Francesco Giuseppe Federico del Bosco Beneventano, Barone della Piana, later became the first London Giorgio Germont and the first New York Nabucco.

(*1842 Continued*)

Donzelli, with Marco Bonesi conducting. The first Bergamo performance was a failure, but seven months later, with Bonesi again at the helm, this time at the Teatro Riccardi, *Linda* scored a success as sung by a cast including Tadolini, Gaspare Pozzolini, Francesco Gnone, Cesare Soares, and Beneventano. It was first heard in Paris at the Théâtre-Italien, in Italian, on November 17, 1842, with a cast that included Fanny Tacchinardi-Persiani, Marietta Brambilla, Mario, Luigi Lablache, and Antonio Tamburini—surely one of the most remarkable troupes of the era;[32] at London, Her Majesty's Theatre, in Italian, on June 1, 1843, and, in an English translation by Michael Desmond Ryan, at Drury Lane Theatre on January 12, 1848, during a season managed there by the eccentric Louis-Antoine Jullien, its conductor being Hector Berlioz. Later that month, Berlioz wrote: "They are playing *Linda* . . . I have the good luck to be ill"; and at New York, in Italian, on January 4, 1847, and—in English—August 4, 1847, the occasion on which Anna Bishop, who was almost as eccentric as Jullien, made her United States debut.

[32] To about the period of this Paris *Linda* must belong an undated note from Alexandre Dumas *père* to Donizetti: "*Mon cher* Maestro, Write four measures of *Linda di Chamounix* at the place indicated, and receive my benediction. All good things to you. Alex. Dumas. I'll pass by tomorrow to pick up this album." It was, of course, the heyday of the autograph album, a contrivance that intensely annoyed famous men and against which Rossini in particular inveighed in irritation.

1843

Don Pasquale (opera buffa): three acts; libretto by Giovanni Ruffini[33] and Donizetti; composed

[33] Almost all references to the libretto of *Don Pasquale,* including a book published in 1962 of which I was co-author, misattribute it to Michele Accursi, sometimes with the added misinformation that "Michele Accursi" was a pseudonym of Giovanni Ruffini. The fact that Ruffini wrote the libretto, with considerable interference from Donizetti, was established in 1915, when Alfonso Lazzari published in the *Rassegna nazionale* (Florence) an article entitled "*Giovanni Ruffini, Gaetano Donizetti e il 'Don Pasquale.'*" Lazzari's facts were made available to English-speaking readers in an article by the late Frank Walker (*136*), "The Librettist of 'Don Pasquale,'" in *The Monthly Musical Record* (London), November-December, 1958. It began: "Strictly speaking, there is nothing new in this article." Giovanni Ruffini and Michele Accursi were two very different men, both for a time exiles, both for a time living in Paris—Ruffini because at the time he was a dedicated Mazzinian; Accursi because, though he too had been a Mazzinian, he had sold out and was continuing to pose as one while actually spying on the Italian exiles for the Vatican. In 1836, in fact, charges that Accursi was a spy were made by Antonio Ghiglione to the Ruffini brothers, who believed them at first. As a result of Ghiglione's charges, in fact, Agostino Ruffini and Mazzini withdrew their support from Accursi's Paris literary periodical, *L'Italiano,* which shortly thereafter ceased publication. Accursi, an extremely vivacious and talkative man, was far from being the attractive character he seemed. But the Ruffinis fell under his spell again. Donizetti, who saw through the pettier of Accursi's dealings and small dishonesties, found him useful as a factotum. And it was Accursi who persuaded Giovanni Ruffini to revise the Angelo Anelli libretto of Stefano Pavesi's *Ser Marc 'Antonio,* making it over into the text of *Don*

(*1843 Continued*)

1842; autograph score in the Ricordi archives, Milan.

Première: Théâtre-Italien, Paris, January 3, 1843; cast included Giulia Grisi (Norina), Mario (Ernesto), Antonio Tamburini (Dottor Malatesta), Luigi Lablache, singing in his tenth and last Donizetti *première* (Don Pasquale), and Lablache *figlio*—Federico Lablache—(Notario). The immediate popularity of *Don Pasquale* in Paris is attested by the production at the Gymnase-Dramatique on the following March 14 of a parody listed as *Don Pasquale, Opéra buffa mêlé de couplets*, the work of Paul-Aimé Chapelle, known as M. Laurencin, who later wrote librettos for Jacques Offenbach.

For a list of some of the very numerous performances of *Don Pasquale* outside Paris—in Italian, German, English, French, Spanish, Hungarian, Polish, Swedish, Czech, Romanian, Finnish, Croat, Slovenian, Bulgarian, and Lithuanian—see 77, 1, columns 827–29. The opera was first heard in Italy at the Teatro alla Scala,

Milan, on April 17, 1843—ten weeks after its Paris *première*—and shortly later was staged at the Teatro d'Angennes, Turin, and at the Teatro Nuovo, Naples, this latter with a cast headed by Rebussini (Norina), Laboccetta (Ernesto), Filippo Coletti (Dottor Malatesta), and Giuseppe Fioravanti (Don Pasquale). It was sung at the Kärnthnertortheater, Vienna, in Italian, on May 14, 1843, with a cast including Eugenia Tadolini, Lorenzo Salvi, Giorgio Ronconi, and Agostino Rovere, and in German on October 4, 1879, when the leading roles were taken by Clementine Schuch-Prosha, Gustav Walter, Ludwig von Bignio, and Carl Mayerhofer. Its first London performance occurred at Her Majesty's Theatre, in Italian, on June 29, 1843; it was staged at Berlin, the Königsstädtisches-theater, in Italian, on February 24, 1845; and at New York, in English, on May 9, 1846.

The first of many mountings of *Don Pasquale* at Bergamo took place at the Teatro Sociale, under Marco Bonesi's direction, on January 17, 1844, when the four principal roles were assigned to Anna Gambardella, A. Biacchi, Gaetano Maspez, and Napoleone Rossi. An especially notable cast sang *Don Pasquale* at the Teatro Donizetti, Bergamo, on October 11, 1933: Mercedes Capsir, Tito Schipa, Mariano Stabile, and Salvatore Baccaloni. Curiously, *Don Pasquale* seems not to have been sung in French until 1864, when the translation by Alphonse Royer and Gustave Vaëz was heard at the Théâtre-Lyrique, Paris.

Pasquale. Because Ruffini disapproved of much in the libretto after Donizetti had tampered with it, and for that reason withheld his name from it, it was published (like the libretto of *Alahor di Granata*, 1826) as by "M. A." Those initials started the trail of errors about its authorship. Donizetti or Accursi may have thought that, lacking Ruffini's name, the authorship might as well be assigned to Accursi's initials as to a pseudonym. But the facts are incontestable: Michele Accursi persuaded Giovanni Ruffini to prepare the libretto, which, as we know it, is largely Ruffini's and in part Donizetti's. See also pp. x–xii, 188.

(*1843 Continued*)

Rome heard *Don Pasquale* for the first time on December 26, 1843, at the Teatro Valle, conducted by Tullio Ramacciotti, with a cast including Amalia Scalese (Norina), Giovanni Confortini (Ernesto), Luigi Corradi-Setti (Dottore Malatesta), and Raffaele Scalese—father of the Norina—(Don Pasquale). This production failed to attract audiences, and in fact *Don Pasquale* did not establish itself in enduring popularity at Rome until November 27, 1850, at the Teatro Argentina, when the Norina was Virginia Boccabadati-Carignani, Scalese again was the Don Pasquale, the Ernesto was Corrado Miraglia, and the Dottore Malatesta was Felice Varesi. In the 1850s, Marietta Piccolomini made a specialty of the role of Norina.

Maria di Rohan (*opera seria*): three acts; libretto by Salvatore Cammarano, originally derived for Vincenzo Bellini, from Lockroy's *Un Duel sous le cardinal de Richelieu* but set instead by Giuseppe Lillo in 1839 as *Il Conte di Chalais* (Naples) and in that same year by Federico Ricci as *Un Duello sotto Richelieu* (Milan); composed 1843; autograph score in the Ricordi archives, Milan.

Première: Kärnthnertortheater, Vienna, June 15, 1843; cast included Eugenia Tadolini (Maria di Rohan), Carlo Guasco (Riccardo, conte di Chalais), Giorgio Ronconi (Enrico, duca di Chevreuse), Friedrich Becher (Visconte di Suze), Michele Novaro (Armando di Gondì), Gustav Hölzel (Di Fiesco), Anton Müller (Aubry), and Friedrich Baldewern (Un Famigliare di Chevreuse). For a list of some others of the numerous stagings of *Maria di Rohan*—in Italian, French, German, Czech, Polish, and Rumanian—See 77, 1, columns 832–33.

Maria di Rohan was first heard in Paris at the Théâtre-Italien on November 14, 1843, when the role of Armando di Gondì, composed for a second tenor, was sung by Marietta Brambilla, a contralto, for whom Donizetti had revised the music.[34] To a letter that Donizetti wrote on November 15 to the Marchese A. Ricci, chargé d'affaires at Lisbon for the Kingdom of Sardinia and Piedmont, he attached an unidentified clipping of one of the first reviews: "Théâtre-Italien—*Maria di Rohan* has done the honors of the week at this theater, which now more than ever is the vogue in high Parisian society. The new pieces that had been announced were sung, and gave the greatest pleasure. In the first act, there are *couplets* of exquisite freshness for Salvi which the singer rendered with perfect taste; in the second act, a little aria for La Brambilla which will obtain the same success in the salons as in the theater; finally, in the closing duet of this same act, an andante for Salvi and Madame Grisi, bearing the im-

---

[34] The translation into French probably was that made in collaboration with Edmond Badon by the man who, eleven years before, had written *Un Duel sous le cardinal de Richelieu*, the drama on which the libretto was based: Joseph-Philippe Simon, called Lockroy. The Badon-Lockroy translation certainly was used when *Maria di Rohan* was sung at Brussels on January 7, 1845.

(*1843 Continued*)

print of a touching melancholy. *Maria di Rohan* now is a complete work of the first order. Ronconi had to repeat his third-act aria; at this moment, the enthusiasm reached its climax. Grisi sang admirably the prayer and the brilliant aria that follows it, and it was only the fear of causing her too great fatigue which prevented its being called for again."

At Naples, the Teatro San Carlo, November 11, 1844, *Maria di Rohan* was sung as *Il Conte di Chalais*, with Tadolini again in the role of Maria, Gaetano Fraschini (Chalais), Filippo Coletti (Chevreuse), Benedetti (Suze), Luciani (Gondì), Marco Arati (Di Fiesco), and Teofilo Rossi (Aubry); Donizetti was present. The opera was mounted at Bergamo, the Teatro Riccardi, on August 9, 1837, with Marco Bonesi conducting and a cast that included Catherine Hayes, Enrico Calzolari, and Giovanni Bencich. It was first heard in London, Covent Garden, in Italian, on May 8, 1847, with Michael Costa conducting a cast that included Marietta Alboni and Giorgio Ronconi; at Berlin, the Königsstädtischestheater, in Italian, on September 4, 1847; and at New York, in Italian, on December 10, 1849. The first German performance at Vienna took place on August 2, 1849. During the 1880s and later, the affection of the great Roman baritone Mattia Battistini for *Maria di Rohan* won it many performances in Rome, beginning at the Teatro Costanzi in November 1885, and

elsewhere; Battistini continued to sing the role of the Duke of Chevreuse for decades. On March 24, 1962, *Maria di Rohan* was revived at the Teatro San Carlo, Naples. Fernando Previtali conducted, and the cast consisted of Virginia Zeani (Maria, contessa di Rohan), Anna Maria Rota (Armando di Gondì), Enzo Tei (Riccardo, conte di Chalais), Mario Zanasi (Enrico, duca di Chevreuse), Mario Rinaudo (Il Visconte di Suze), Silvano Pagliuca (De Fiesque), Luigi Paolillo (Aubry), and Antonio Rubino (Un Famigliare di Chevreuse).

Dom Sébastien, roi de Portugal (*grand opéra*): five acts; libretto by Augustin-Eugène Scribe; composed 1843; copy of published Paris edition in Biblioteca comunale, Naples.

Première: Opéra, Paris, November 11, 1843; cast included Rosine Stoltz (Zaida), Gilbert-Louis Duprez (Dom Sébastien), Nicholas-Prosper Levasseur (Don Juan), Jean-Étienne Massol (Abayaldo), Ferdinand Prevôt (Don Enrique), Paolo Barroilhet (Camoëns), Octave (Don Antonio), and Brémont (Ben-Selim). For a list of some performances of *Dom Sébastien*—in French, Italian, German, and Czech—see 77, I, columns 833–34.

Because most of the Parisian critics and reviewers were unfavorable toward *Dom Sébastien*, it often has been said that the opera was a failure with the public. That this was not the case —and that not all the criticisms were unfavorable—is proved by an unidentified clipping that

(*1843 Continued*)

Donizetti sent to the Marchese A. Ricci, chargé d' affaires at Lisbon for the Kingdom of Sardinia and Piedmont, on November 15, 1843: "Opéra—*Dom Sébastien* has reached its twelfth presentation in four weeks, and its success has been increasing constantly. For a long time, the public has lost the habit of applauding, but now it is not only from the parterre, but from all parts of the hall that the manifestations in favor of Donizetti's new score arise. This result says more than all the eulogies can. Barroilhet's prophecy, the duet of Madame Stoltz and Massol, Madame Stoltz's *romance,* Duprez's aria, Barroilhet's *cavatina,* the funeral march, the fourth act, and the entire fifth act excited, at each performance, real and merited enthusiasm. The performance of *Dom Sébastien* is as remarkable in detail as in ensemble. There is success for everyone—for Duprez, for Barroilhet, for Massol, for Levasseur and Madame Stoltz. In the dances, the biggest applause goes to Adèle Dumilâtre, whom the intelligent feelings of the public have elevated so quickly to the first ranks of our dancers."

Another proof that *Dom Sébastien* was a public success is the fact that performances of it soon were presented in the French provinces. On January 26, 1844, writing to Antonio Vasselli, Donizetti said: "Did you know that at Lille, in France, so that the impresario should mount *Dom Sébastien* (which is not for Italy) quickly, the city granted him an additional eight thousand francs?" On September 23 of that year, writing to August Thomas from Rome, Donizetti mentioned a staging at Lyon. The French original was also to be heard outside France, during Donizetti's lifetime, at Antwerp, January 16, 1848, and at Brussels on April 5, 1848, three days before his death. Franz Liszt wrote a *Fantaisie sur des motifs de Dom Sébastien,* to which Donizetti referred in a letter of March 15, 1845, to Vasselli: "Buy the march arranged by Liszt; it's frightening!"

Dom Sébastien reached Vienna, in a German translation by Leo Herz, on February 6, 1845, when the cast included Clara Stöckl-Heinefetter (Zaida), Joseph Erl (Sebastian), Joseph Drawbe (Juan), Franz Wild (Abayaldo), Friedrich Becher (Enrique), Eduard Seithner (Camoëns), Carl Wolf (Antonio), Gustav Hölzel (Ben-Selim), Carl Reinhold (Luis), and Johann Bender (Muley Bey); Donizetti conducted. *Don Sebastiano,* the Italian translation by Giovanni Ruffini, apparently first heard at Lisbon on May 4, 1845, was staged at the Teatro San Carlo, Naples, in 1856, with a cast including Tedesco (Zaida), Ludovico Graziani (Sebastiano), Luigi Brignoli (Don Giovanni di Silva), Benedetti (Abajaldo), Garito (Enrique), Domenico Ceci (Camoëns), Filippo Coletti (Antonio), Teofilo Rossi (Ben-Selim), and Marco Arati (Luigi). This opera appears never to have been sung in London, but was heard in New York, in Ruffini's Italian translation, on November 25, 1864.

1844

Caterina Cornaro (opera seria): prologue and two acts; libretto by Giacomo Sacchèro, originally called *La Regina di Cipro;* composed 1842–43; autograph score in Naples Conservatory Library.

Première: Teatro San Carlo, Naples, January 12, 1844; cast included Fanny Goldberg (Caterina), Salvetti (Matilde), Marco Arati (Andrea Cornaro), Gaetano Fraschini (Gerardo), Filippo Coletti (Lusignano), Teofilo Rossi (Strozzi), Nicola Beneventano (Mogenico), and Domenico Ceci (Un Cavaliere del re). *Caterina Cornaro* seldom was staged after its unsuccessful Naples *première*. One of its scarce productions occurred at Parma on February 2, 1845, with Nicola di Giovanni conducting. Happily received, the opera was sung on four evenings. Writing from Vienna on February 21 to Antonio Vasselli, Donizetti said: "*La Caterina* at Parma has given me great pleasure. I've never been blind about my labors, and I always said: *Caterina* won't be a masterwork. But it didn't deserve that ruination by the singers [at Naples] or those criticisms from the journalists."

1860

Rita, ou Le Mari battu (also known as *Deux Hommes et une femme*) *(opéra-comique):* one act; libretto by Gustave Vaëz; composed 1841; autograph score in Naples Conservatory Library.

Première: Opéra-Comique, Paris, May 7, 1860; cast consisted of Mme Faure-Lefebvre (Rita), Warot (Beppe), and Barrielle (Gasparo). When *Rita* was staged at the Palazzo Cassano, Naples, in 1876, by the Società filarmonica, the roles were distributed as follows: Emma Nascio (Rita), Vincenzo Montanaro (Beppe), Alessandro Polonini (Gasparo). For a list of some other stagings of *Rita*, see 77, I, column 947. The little opera often has been staged in recent years, both in Italy (notably since a revival at the Teatro Ristori, Verona, on March 2, 1924) and elsewhere.

Writing to Antonio Vasselli on October 10, 1841, Donizetti said: "Do me the favor of writing to [Tommaso] Persico by the same courier that Barbaja has written me to instruct Persico himself to pass the *farsetta* [*Rita*] on to him." This would seem to indicate that Barbaja had intended to perform the opera at the Teatro del Fondo, Naples. But he died that year before taking action on *Rita*, which waited almost nineteen years more for its first hearing.

1869

Gabriella di Vergy (opera seria): two acts; libretto by Andrea Leone Tottola, originally written for Michele Carafa, whose opera of the same name was heard at the Teatro del Fondo, Naples, on July 3, 1816, with Isabella Colbran in the title role; composed 1826; dated autograph score in Museo Donizettiano, Bergamo; nonautograph score, differing in many details, in the Ricordi archives, Milan.

Première: Teatro San Carlo, Naples, November 22, 1869; cast

(*Operas Continued*)

included Marcellina Lotti della Santa (Gabriella), Carolina Cetronè (Almeide), Marco Arati (Filippo Augusto), Villani (Fayel), Gottardo Aldighieri[35] (Raul), and Memmi (Armando). See p. 49 for the dubiousness of this score as performed.

Of *Gabriella di Vergy*, Guglielmo Barblan wrote (*12, 27*): "In this fable of love and death one identifies the fundamental themes of the Donizettian opera, which are pure love as victimized by rivalry and perfidy; feminine virtue misunderstood and brutalized by accusation of treachery (Gabriella facing Raul will become Lucia facing Edgardo and, in *Poliuto*, Paolina facing Severo); the inexorability of misfortune; the contrast between conjugal duty and the impulse of love."

1882

Le Duc d'Albe (incomplete *grand opéra*): five acts; libretto by Augustin-Eugène Scribe and Charles Duveyrier;[36] composition begun 1839, never completed; finished by Matteo Salvi, to an Italian four-act version of the libretto by

---

[35] Aldighieri was to create the role of Barnaba in Ponchielli's *La Gioconda* in 1876. He also wrote the lyric that Luigi Arditi made into an incredibly popular song as "*Il Bacio.*"

[36] The autograph libretto, with marginal notations by Donizetti, was left by Andrea Donizetti to his sons, Gaetano and Giuseppe. The catalogue (*42*) of their collection as exhibited at Bergamo in 1897 lists as No. 129 a libretto of *Le Duc d'Albe* of which Act I is in Scribe's autograph; this appears to be the libretto that later found its way to the musical archives of the Accademia Chigiana, Siena.

Angelo Zanardini (autograph score in the Ricordi archives, Milan).

Première: the Teatro Apollo, Rome, March 22, 1882; cast including Abigaille Bruschi-Chiatti (Amelia d'Egmont), Julián Gayarré (Marcello di Bruges), Giovanni Paroli (Carlo), Romeo Sartori (Un Taverniere), Leone Giraldoni (Duca d'Alba), Alessandro Silvestri (Daniele), and Igalmer Frey (Sandoval). Marino Mancinelli conducted. For further details concerning this opera and its performances, see p. 305.

Undated, Unperformed, Projected, and Possibly Spurious Operas

Circé: otherwise unidentified work mentioned by Francis Saltus[37] as an opera that Donizetti considered composing and of which fragments might survive.

La Fidanzata (farsa): never completed. The Paris Conservatory Library has an aria, "*Sì, colpevol' son'io,*" bearing the title of this projected opera.

Francesca da Rimini: on April 18, 1963, Maestro Marcello Ballini published in *L'Eco di Bergamo* photographs of a recently recovered letter of Donizetti's to Prince Giovanni Lanza e Ventimiglia of Palermo in which Donizetti says that he has begun *Francesa da Rimini*, "but God knows if the cholera will allow me to finish it . . ." Nothing further is known of this projected opera.

Gli Illinesi: Donizetti signed a contract with the Turinese impresario Giuseppe Consul to compose this opera to a libretto by Felice

---

[37] According to *78*, 211.

(Operas Continued)

Romani,[38] but it never was composed. In a letter of July 21, 1835, when negotiations over *Gli Illinesi* were proceeding, Donizetti wrote to Consul about the libretto: "I want love, without which the stories are cold—and violent love."

Gli Innamorati: a manuscript found in the Bergamo Civic Library presents Donizetti's ideas about the construction of a possible libretto, to be derived from Carlo Goldoni's comedy of the same title, on this subject.[39] The characters are named Eugenia, Flaminia, Clorinda, Fulgenzio, Roberto, Fabrizio, Lisetta, Tognino, and Succianespole, with the suggestion that the last three be deleted or telescoped.

Jeanne la folle: subject proposed by Donizetti as a libretto that Scribe might prepare for him (1844); never composed. Scribe eventually wrote a *Jeanne la folle,* which was set as an opera by Antoine-Louis Clapisson and produced on November 6, 1848, after Donizetti's death.

Lara: a subject after Byron's sequel to *The Corsair,* discussed by Donizetti with a would-be librettist, Count Giulio Pullé of Verona, in a letter written at Venice in February 1837 (*43a,* 38) and by Count Pullé in a long letter

(*43a,* 125) setting forth the story and including the verses of the first two scenes. Nothing came of this project. As Donizetti wrote Pullé, an opera entitled *Lara,* Henri de Ruolz's setting of a libretto by Bidera, had been staged at the Teatro San Carlo, Naples, on November 22, 1835; the presence of Fanny Tacchinardi-Persiani, Gilbert-Louis Duprez, and Giorgio Ronconi in its first cast apparently did not save it. No more success accrued to another operatic version, with libretto by Leopoldo Tarantini and score by Matteo Salvi (La Scala, Milan, November 4, 1843).

Mlle de la Vallière: according to Guido Zavadini, (*138,* 179), an opera that Donizetti projected but never composed.

Ne m'oubliez-pas: projected *opéra-comique* in three acts to a libretto by Jules-Henri Vernoy de Saint-Georges, intended for the Opéra-Comique, Paris; discussed and begun 1842; never completed. The Paris Conservatory Library has seven orchestrated numbers from the score, some for each of its three acts.

Onore vince amore: projected opera to a libretto by Giovanni Ruffini, intended for performance at the Théâtre-Italien, Paris, with Fanny Tacchinardi-Persiani, Mario, Georgio Ronconi, and Luigi Lablache; discussed 1845; never composed. Donizetti believed the original drama to be the work of Giovan Carlo, Barone di Cosenza, but Ruffini wrote his mother on July 21, 1845, that Cosenza merely had imitated a play by August Wilhelm Iffland, giving its title in Italian as *Il Tutore e la pupilla.*

---

[38] Romani's libretto had been written for Francesco Basilj, whose *Gl'Illinesi* was staged at the Teatro alla Scala, Milan, on January 26, 1819. It was used again, as revised, by Pier' Antonio Coppola, whose *Gli Illinesi* was staged at the Teatro Regio, Turin, on December 26, 1835, the seasonal opening for which Consul had sought the opera from Donizetti.

[39] See p. 306 for text of this manuscript.

(Operas Continued)

Il Pascià di Scutari: this *melodramma* in three acts, librettist unknown, has been attributed to Donizetti without good reason. The Naples Conservatory Library has a copy of the libretto, published at Messina in 1832 by Michelangelo Nobolo.

Il Ritratto parlante: possibly the title of an opera by a composer other than Donizetti, this equally well may have been a subtitle or alternative title for Donizetti's *Una Follia (di carnovale)*, 1818.

Ruy-Blas: Donizetti considered composing an opera on this subject, to a libretto by Salvatore Cammarano, but dropped the idea to compose instead *Caterina Cornaro* (1842–43).

Sganarelle: Donizetti in 1845 considered the possibility of composing for Luigi Lablache an opera to a libretto to be based on Molière's *Sganarelle*. But he never composed another opera.

L'Ultima parte del comico: According to Alborghetti-Galli (5, 176), Donizetti in 1843 contributed some numbers to a *pasticcio* by this title performed in Vienna, the other contributing composers being "Muller, Panseron, Herold." Panseron would have been the French singing-teacher and composer Auguste-Mathieu Panseron, who spent some time in Vienna; Muller probably was the Austro-Hungarian opera composer Adolf Müller, Sr., who conducted at the Theater an der Wien. "Herold" possibly referred to Louis-Joseph-Ferdinand Hérold, the composer of *Zampa:* though he had died in 1833, his music might have been drawn upon for the *pasticcio,* especially as some of it had been popular in Vienna, where he had visited in 1815.

NUMBERS AND SECTIONS FROM UNIDENTIFIED OPERAS

Chorus, scena, and *trio,* for two sopranos and tenor, the characters identified as Lesbia, Alpino, and Pastore, together with a recitative for two sopranos (Lesbia and Alpino): this manuscript score, for voices and orchestra, is in Museo Donizettiano, Bergamo.

Duet for tenor and bass, the characters identified as James and Woender (?), *"Scrivi, obbedisci, insano":* manuscript for voices and orchestra—with which is included another piece in the same tonality for the same characters—in Museo Donizettiano, Bergamo.

Recitative and *duet* for soprano and bass, for characters identified as Deidamia and Don Achille, *"Mi lasci . . . come?"*—with piano accompaniment, apparently for an *opera buffa,* this autograph is in Museo Donizettiano, Bergamo.

Scena and *cavatina* for tenor (identified as Enrico) and chorus, *"Che pensi, Enrico, riedi al campo":* lengthwise across the first side of the autograph score in Museo Donizettiano, Bergamo, appears in Donizetti's script: "Donizetti to his friend Mariani, 1838."

Scena and *cavatina* for tenor (identified as Enrico) and chorus, *"Già dell'avita gloria":* autograph score, for voices and orchestra, in Museo Donizettiano, Bergamo.

A List of Donizetti's

Nonoperatic Compositions

The following list is divided into these categories:
Oratorios
Cantatas
Hymns
Religious Music
Instrumental Music
    Orchestra
    Chamber Groups
        Quartets
        Quintets
        Miscellaneous
    Piano, Two Hands
    Piano, Four Hands
Vocal Compositions
    Solo Voice
    Two Voices
    More than Two Voices
Miscellaneous Vocal Pieces and Student Exercises

Oratorios

DONIZETTI composed no true oratorios, though the *azione tragico-sacra* entitled *Il Diluvio universale* (see pages 68–70 and 324–25) partakes as much of oratorio character as of operatic. Additionally, two oratorios, with scores arranged by others from Donizetti's compositions, often are listed among his works. They are:

Oratorio sacro: performed at Acireale, Sicily, in July, 1841. The Zelantea Library at Acireale has a libretto entitled *"Oratorio Sacro* with music of Cavaliere Gaetano Donizetti, to be performed during

(*Oratorios Continued*)

the imminent feast of the Trimartire S. Venera, citizen and chief patron of Acireale, during the days July 23-24 of the year 1841."

Le Sette Chiese: "*Azione sacra per musica,* to be sung in the Oratorio of the *Rev. P. P. della Congrega-*

zione di San Filippo Neri. Music of Maestro Cavaliere Gaetano Donizetti, words by Cesare Sernicoli." The libretto, with the names of the singers, was published in 1842 at Rome by the Tipografia Cannetti.

Cantatas

A Silvio amante (little cantata): for tenor voice and orchestra. Autograph lost; copy in Museo Donizettiano, Bergamo, dated 1823, but this probably is a juvenile work composed much earlier.

Aci e Galatea (cantata): undated, included in the Albinati list (1897).

Angelica e Medoro (cantata): composed at Naples in May, 1822, for Anna Carnevali(?). Autograph lost.

Aristea (azione pastorale): text by Giovanni Federico Schmidt, for three female voices (Aristea, Filinto, Corinna) and three male voices (Liciseo, Comone, Erasto). Performed at the Teatro San Carlo, Naples, May 30, 1823, the singers being Elisabetta Ferron, Girolama Dardanelli, De Bernardis, Andrea Nozzari, Michele Benedetti, and Gaetano Chizzola. Autograph in Naples Conservatory Library.

L'Assunzione di Maria Vergine, ossia Gli Apostoli al sepolcro della medesima (cantata): text by Giovanni Battista Rusi(?), Rome, 1822. Autograph in Museo Donizettiano, Bergamo.

Cantata for the birth of Maria Carolina Augusta, daughter of Leopoldo, Prince of Salerno, and

Maria Clementina of Austria, Naples, April 6, 1822: for two sopranos (Genio di Partenope and Genio dell'Istro), with piano accompaniment. Autograph in Museo Donizettiano, Bergamo.

Cantata for the birthday of the King of Naples (Francesco I): for voices and orchestra, performed at the Teatro Carolino, Palermo, August 14, 1825.

Cantata for the happy delivery of Her Majesty the Queen of Naples: for voices and orchestra, text by the composer. Performed at the Teatro San Carlo, Naples, August 1838, with these singers: Almerinda Granchi (Partenope), Buccini (Genio Siculo), Giovanni Basadonna (Genio Borbonico), Paolo Barroilhet (Il Sebeto). Autograph in Naples Conservatory Library.

Cantata for the marriage of Ferdinand of Austria and the Princess Maria Anna Carolina of Savoy (February 27, 1831): for voices and orchestra. Autograph vocal and orchestral parts in Museo Donizettiano, Bergamo.

Cantata for the saint's day of the excellent mother, Anna Carnevali: written for her daughters Edvige and Clementina (Rome, July 26, 1833). In 1948, the autograph be-

(*Cantatas Continued*)

longed to Dr. Heinrich Steger, Vienna.

Cantata in honor of Maestro Giovanni Simone Mayr on the occasion of his seventy-eighth birthday (*"Dalla Francia un saluto t'invia"*): for voices and orchestra, Paris, May 1841. Autograph in Museo Donizettiano, Bergamo; reproduced in facsimile, with interpolated letter (as mailed from Paris on May 20, 1841), in 5.

Canto accompagnatorio for the funeral eulogies of the late Marchese Giuseppe Terzi: for two sopranos, tenor, bass, and orchestra, in B-flat. Autograph in Bergamo Civic Library.

Il Canto XXXIII della Divina Commedia (Il Conte Ugolino—"La bocca sollevò dal fiero"): for *basso cantante* with piano accompaniment, dedicated to Luigi Lablache (January-February, 1828). Published by Ricordi, Milan, in *Antologia musicale*, 1843, No. 2.

Cristoforo Colombo (cantata): for baritone and orchestra, sung by Paolo Barroilhet at the Théâtre de l'Opéra, Paris, on the occasion of his benefit, March 1834. A *scena* and *cavatina* in autograph are in the Library of the Conservatorio di Santa Cecilia, Rome.

Il Fato (little cantata): text by Jacopo Ferretti; performed in the house of Count Antonio Lozano on the occasion of his saint's day (Rome, June 13, 1833). According to Alberto Cametti (27, 128), both text and music were improvised in a few hours.

Il Fausto Ritorno, o anche Il Ritorno desiderato (cantata or *azione allegorico-melodrammatica*): f o r voice and orchestra, text by Domenico Gilardoni; written on the occasion of the return of Their Majesties from Spain; performed at the Teatro San Carlo, Naples, in the summer of 1830, with Antonietta Galzerani (Partenope), Luigia Boccabadati-Gazzuoli (L'Armonia), Sedlacek (La Pace), Antonio Tamburini (Genio Tutelare), and Berardo Winter (Genio Guerriero). Autograph in Naples Conservatory Library.

La Fuga di Tisbe (cantata): for soprano with piano accompaniment; dedicated to the Marchesa Sofia de' Medici di Marignano; composed on October 15, 1824. Autograph in Paris Conservatory Library.

Il Genio dell'armonia (collaborative cantata): for three solo singers, chorus, and orchestra; prepared in honor of the exaltation to the papacy of Pius VIII; first sung December 20, 1829, by Paolina Mancinelli Testa, Pietro Angelini, and Sardi, with chorus (fifty voices) and orchestra of the Accademia filarmonica romana. The Marchese Vincenzo Costaguti composed the *sinfonia*, the introduction, the finale of Part I, and the introduction to Part II; Donizetti composed the finale of Part II, including a trio and the closing chorus; the rest was composed by the Marchese Domenico Capranica; text by Cavaliere P. E. Visconti. Published by Mercurj e Robaglia, Rome, 1829.

Gloria a Dio di nostri padri (cantata): for bass and orchestra, undated. Autograph in Naples Conservatory Library.

Licenza (cantata): for voices and orchestra; composed for an evening

(*Contatas Continued*)

gala at the Teatro Carolino, Palermo, 1825.

Niso e Violetta: undated autograph sketch of a cantata for voice and orchestra in the Ricordi archives, Milan.

La Partenza (cantata): for voices and orchestra; for the departure of Lieutenant General the Marchese Ugo delle Favare; performed at the Teatro Carolino, Palermo, August 14, 1825.

Per il nome di Francesco I (cantata): undated, but included in the Albinati list (1897); possibly the same as Cantata for the birthday of the King of Naples, listed above.

Il Ritorno desiderato: see *Il Fausto Ritorno.*

Il Ritorno di primavera (cantata): for three voices and full orchestra; text by Gaetano Morandi (April, 1818). Autograph in the Library of the Liceo Musicale, Bologna.

Saffo (cantata): for solo voice, chorus, and orchestra; dedicated to "*Madamigella Virginia Vasselli*"—and therefore composed before 1828. Autograph in Museo

Donizettiano, Bergamo; published with piano accompaniment.

Teresa e Gianfaldoni (cantata): for two voices and orchestra (1821); dedicated to ex-Queen Maria Luisa, Infanta of Spain, Duchess of Lucca. Francesco Florimo wrote (54, IV, 248) that it was performed at Mantua in 1821. Autograph lost; published by Ratti e Cencetti, Rome, with piano accompaniment.

Uno Sguardo (cantata): to words by Felice Romani; performed at the home of Paolo Branca, Milan; undated, but included in the Albinati list (1897).

I Voti dei sudditi (cantata, *azione pastorale,* or *melodramma pastorale*): for four voices and orchestra; text by Giovanni Federico Schmidt; for the occasion of the succession of the new king of Naples, Francesco I; performed at the Teatro San Carlo, Naples, May 5, 1825, with Adelaide Tosi (Lesbia Pastorella), Signora Cesari (Alpino Pastore), Michele Benedetti (Euriso), and Andrea Nozzari, the renowned Rossinian tenor from Bergamo (Un Pastore.) Published by the Tipografia Flautina, Naples, 1825.

Hymns

Inno: for the marriage of King Ferdinando II of Naples and Maria Cristina of Sardinia (Voltri, near Genoa, November 21, 1832).

Inno: for the saint's day of Don Pietro Pangrati. Autograph in Naples Conservatory Library.

Inno reale: for voices and orchestra;

text by Felice Romani; composed for the inauguration of the Teatro Carlo Felice, Genoa, April 7, 1828.

La Preghiera d'un popolo (hymn): for four voices and orchestra; for His Majesty Ferdinand II; words by "N. C."; performed at the

(*Hymns Continued*)

Teatro San Carlo, Naples, July 31, 1837,[1] in honor of the birthday of Maria Teresa, Queen of the Two Sicilies; cast consisted of Toldi (Una Ninfa), Buccini (Un'altra Ninfa), Paolo Barroilhet (Un Pastore), and Giovanni Basadonna (Un'altro Pastore). Autograph in Naples Conservatory Library.

Sacro è il dolore (inno): for two voices and orchestra. Autograph in Naples Conservatory Library.

Religious Music[2]

*Asperges me: for soprano, contralto, tenor, and bass, with orchestra, in B-flat; dated April 8, 1820. Autograph score in Paris Conservatory Library.

Ave Maria (Offertorio): for soprano, contralto, and string orchestra; on lines by Dante; composed at Vienna late in January, 1844, and performed at the first Lenten *concert spirituel* of the Musikfreunde. Manuscript score for voices and strings in Naples Conservatory Library. Published by Lucca, Milan, undated, and in a version with piano accompaniment "under the aegis of Commendatore G. Donizetti" by the Stamperia Zollich, location and date unspecified.

Ave Maria: for two voices in the violin clef, with piano, in F major; Latin text. Autograph, inscribed "Donizetti to the friend who does not climb the stairs to see me," in Museo Teatrale alla Scala, Milan.

Ave Maria: for five voices, see *Offertorio (Ave Maria)* below.

Beatus vir: for tenor and small orchestra, with oboe and clarinet *obbligati,* F major; dated 1819. Autograph in Paris Conservatory Library.

Canzoncine sacre (three): for two voices and piano; "*Questro cor, quest' alma mia*"; *L'Amor di Maria Santissima:* "*T'amo potessi adergere*"; *Preghiera a Maria Vergine:* "*Fa che d'amarti impari.*" Autographs in the Noseda Collection, Milan Conservatory Library.

Christe: tenor solo in B-flat, with orchestra; appears in an 1848 listing in the Library of the Bergamo Musical Institute. Same as next item?

Christe eleison: for tenor, two violins, clarinet, and contrabass. Autograph in the Library of the Conservatorio di Santa Cecilia, Rome. Same as *Christe* listed above?

*Confitebor: for three voices (soprano, tenor, bass) *a cappella,* in C major, with figured bass for organ. Autograph score and parts.

*Credidi: for three voices (soprano, tenor, bass) *a cappella* in D major, with figured bass for organ. Autograph score and parts.

Credo: for three voices and orches-

---

[1] In a letter of July 22, 1837, to Agostino Pedrotti, Donizetti said: "I have written a hymn for the 31st, birthday of the new Queen."

[2] In this section, an asterisk before a title indicates that the Museo Donizettiano, Bergamo, has either an autograph or a manuscript copy of the piece so marked.

(*Religious Music Continued*)

tra, in C major. Autograph score, dated April 17, 1819, in Paris Conservatory Library.

Credo: for three voices (soprano, tenor, bass), and orchestra, in C major. Autograph score, dated "Almenno, October 18, 1820," consists of seventeen separate parts, two of them signed.

Credo: for four voices (soprano, contralto, bass), and orchestra, in D major; composed for the St. Cecilia's Day celebration instituted by Giovanni Simone Mayr. In Mayr's autograph, on first page of which, in another script, appears "*Credo di Donizetti 1824.*"

Credo: for three voices (soprano, tenor, bass) and orchestra, with instruments *obbligati.* Twenty-seven-page autograph in Naples Conservatory Library.

Credo: for four voices and orchestra, in E-flat. Autograph in Naples Conservatory Library.

Credo, for four voices with orchestra, in C major.

Credo (breve), in C major, and *Crucifixus,* in F major: for voices and orchestra. Autograph of orchestral parts only; score and vocal parts lost.

Crucifixus: see *Credo (breve)* above.

Cum Sancto Spiritu: for voices and orchestra. Autograph, signed "Bergamo, July 16, 1817," in Paris Conservatory Library.

Cum Sancto Spiritu: for voices and orchestra, in C major. Autograph score in Naples Conservatory Library; first page inscribed "For Giuseppe" and last page "May the Lord be praised that this too is done."

Cum Sancto Spiritu: for four voices and orchestra, in C minor. Auto-

graph score in Naples Conservatory Library.

Cum Sancto Spiritu: for three and four voices and orchestra, in D major. Autograph (1819) in Paris Conservatory Library.

De torrente: for soprano and tenor with orchestra, in F major. Autograph, dated "Bergamo, June 1819," in Paris Conservatory Library.

Dies irae: incomplete sketch, lacking beginning and end, for voices and orchestra, in C minor.

Dixit: for soprano, tenor, and bass, with orchestra, in C major. Autograph, dated 1819, in Naples Conservatory Library.

Dixit Dominus (1820): for three voices (soprano, tenor, bass) and orchestra, in C major. The eighteen separate parts are autograph, but the score is not.

Docebo: for bass solo and small orchestra with organ bass, in D major. Score missing; soloist's part and three of the thirteen orchestral parts are autograph.

Domine (ad adjuvandum): for three voices (soprano, tenor, bass) with wind instruments and organ, in C major. Autograph in Paris Conservatory Library.

Domine (ad adjuvandum) (breve): for three voices (soprano, tenor, bass) and orchestra, in C major, 1819. Autograph in Paris Conservatory Library.

Domine Deus (versetto): for bass solo and orchestra, with clarinet *obbligato,* in E-flat major; 1820. Autograph in Naples Conservatory Library.

Domine Deus: bass solo, in D major. Autograph in Naples Conservatory Library.

Domine Deus: bass solo with small orchestra, in D major. Autograph

(*Religious Music Continued*)
in Naples Conservatory Library.

Dominus a dextris: bass solo with orchestra, in D minor. Autograph, dated 1819, in Naples Conservatory Library.

Dominus a dextris: tenor solo with orchestra, with violin obbligato, in D minor. Autograph, dated "Bergamo, August 1820," in Paris Conservatory Library.

Et vitam: for four voices *a cappella* (with fugue in C major). Autograph in Naples Conservatory Library.

Gloria in excelsis: for four voices and orchestra, in C major. Autograph in Naples Conservatory Library.

Gloria in excelsis (1814): for three voices (soprano, tenor, bass) and small orchestra (violins, horns, organ), in D major. Score, vocal parts, and orchestral parts all autograph.

Gloria in excelsis (May 28, 1818): for three and four voices and orchestra, in C major. Twenty of the twenty-seven orchestral parts are autograph, but the other seven and the score are not.

Gloria in excelsis: for three voices and orchestra. Autograph, dated "July 16, 1819, Bergamo," in Naples Conservatory Library.

Gloria in excelsis (May 20, 1820): for three and four voices and orchestra, in C major. Autograph in Naples Conservatory Library.

Gloria in excelsis: for four voices and orchestra. Autograph in Naples Conservatory Library.

Gloria Patri (May 28, 1820): for soprano and orchestra, with violin *obbligato*, in F major. Autograph in Paris Conservatory Library.

Gloria Patri: for four voices and orchestra. Autograph, dated "Paris, 1843," in Naples Conservatory Library.

Gloria Patri and *Sicut erat:* for three voices (soprano, tenor, bass) and orchestra, in C major. Nine of the twenty-three vocal and orchestral parts are autograph, but the score and the other fourteen parts are not.

Gratias agimus: for soprano solo and orchestra, with flute *obbligato*, in G major, dated July 6, 1820. Autograph score and parts in Paris Conservatory Library.

In convertendo: for bass solo and orchestra, in C major. Autograph score and parts in Paris Conservatory Library.

In gloria Dei Patris: four-voice fugue, in C minor. Autograph dated "Bologna, September 17, 1816."

Inno (Hymn to St. Peter): for tenor solo and small orchestra, in C major. Autograph in Naples Conservatory Library.

Inno (*Iste confessor*): for three voices and orchestra, in C major; dated "Alzano, August 6, 1819." Autograph in Naples Conservatory Library.

Iste confessor: see preceding item.

Judica me Deus (Psalm XLII): for two children's voices with or without organ; text a versified vulgarization of the Latin text by Samuele Biava. Manuscript copy.

Kyrie: for four voices; composed at Bologna in 1816 under the direction of Padre Stanislao Mattei. Autograph in Naples Conservatory Library.

Kyrie: for four voices, in D major; dated "Bolgare, August 1, 1817." Autograph in the Paris Conservatory Library.

Kyrie: for chorus and orchestra, in D major; for the feast of St.

378) *The Music*

(*Religious Music Continued*)

Cecilia; dated "Bologna, August 7, 1817"; sung at the Church of San Giacomo there on November 23, 1817. Autograph in Library of the Liceo Musicale, Bologna.

Kyrie: for three voices, in C minor; dated "Bergamo, August 8, 1818." Autograph in Paris Conservatory Library.

Kyrie: for four voices and orchestra. Autograph, dated "May 20, 1820," in Naples Conservatory Library.

Kyrie: for four voices; dated May 26, 1821. Autograph in Paris Conservatory Library. See next item, bearing same date.

Kyrie: for four voices, in F major; dated May 26, 1821. Autograph in the Naples Conservatory Library. See preceding item, bearing same date.

*Kyrie: for three voices, two oboes, two horns, and organ, in C minor. Score and parts in autograph.

*Kyrie: for three voices, two oboes, two horns, and organ, in C minor. Score only in autograph.

*Kyrie: for three voices and small orchestra, in C minor. Twenty of the parts are autograph, but the score and the other ten parts are not.

*Kyrie: for four voices, chorus, and orchestra, in D minor. Score lost; eighteen of the thirty-three vocal and orchestral parts are autograph.

*Kyrie: for four voices and orchestra, in D minor. Score lost; fourteen of the eighteen vocal and orchestral parts are autograph.

*Kyrie, in E minor, *Christe*, second *Kyrie:* for voices and orchestra. Neither score nor parts autograph.

*Kyrie, in F major, *Christe*, in B flat, second *Kyrie*, in F major: for four voices and orchestra. Fifteen of

the eighteen parts of the second *Kyrie* are autograph, but the score and the other parts are not.

Laudamus (andante) and *Gratias* (allegro): for tenor and orchestra, with clarinet *obbligato*, in F major. Formerly on sale by a New York dealer in autographs. Present location unknown.

*Laudamus and *Gratias:* for tenor or soprano and orchestra, with oboe or clarinet *obbligato*, in G major. Autograph, inscribed "*3 luglio 1819 il 4 detto cantò Brighella Donizetti*," in Paris Conservatory Library.

*Laudamus and *Gratias:* for voices and orchestra, with clarinet *obbligato*. Score and vocal parts lost; four of the fourteen orchestral parts are autograph.

Laudamus and *Gratias:* for four voices and orchestra, in A major. Appears in a listing from about 1848 in the Library of the Bergamo Istituto Musicale.

*Laudamus te: for four voices and orchestra, in A major. Autograph, dated "Bergamo, July 6, 1820," in Naples Conservatory Library.

*Laudate pueri: for four voices and orchestra, in D major. Autograph, dated "Bergamo, October 8, 1819," in Naples Conservatory Library.

Laudate pueri: for three voices and orchestra, C major. Appears in a list from about 1848 in the Library of the Bergamo Istituto Musicale.

Libera me de sanguinibus: for soprano and orchestra, with violin *obbligato*. Autograph, dated "Almenno [San Salvatore], October 30, 1820," in Paris Conservatory Library.

Luge qui legis ("*Marcia funebre*"):

(*Religious Music Continued*)

with voices, on words from the Requiem aeternam; composed 1842 in Milan for the sculptor Pompeo Marchesi. Published with piano accompaniment by the Stabilimento Partenopeo di T. Cottrau, Naples, undated.

*Magnificat: for three voices and orchestra, in D major. Autograph, dated "Bergamo, May 1819," in Paris Conservatory Library.

*Messa di gloria and Credo: for three or four voices, chorus, and large orchestra, in C minor; performed in the Church of Santa Maria Nova, Naples, on November 28, 1837. Autograph in Naples Conservatory Library.

*Messa da Requiem: for soloists, chorus, four separate voices, and orchestra; composed for the funeral services for Vincenzo Bellini, dedicated to his memory (1835). Autograph in Naples Conservatory Library; published by Ricordi, Milan.

Messa da Requiem: on the death of Maestro Nicolò Zingarelli, May 1837. Autograph lost.

Messa da Requiem: for the funeral of the Abbé Fazzini, Naples, November 7, 1837. Autograph lost.

Miserere: for four voices (contralto, tenor, bass); composed at the request of the "filarmonici Grassi e Orlandini," Venice, January, 1820. Manuscript in Naples Conservatory Library.

Miserere: for four unequal voices and chorus (the first four verses). Autograph, dated April 4, 1820, in Vatican Library.

Miserere: for four voices and orchestra, in C minor. Autograph score and parts in Paris Conservatory Library, with this inscription in autograph on page 1: "*1822, 18 gennaio, il compositore stava a Roma in gran pensieri per la Zoraide [di Granata], ol franguel orb gemeba a Bergamo. Otello[3] ordinava la musica, la Teresa rideva. Evviva noi; Miserere.*"

Miserere: for first and second tenor and two basses concertante, with chorus, organ, two violas, two cellos, and two contrabasses. Autograph in Paris Conservatory Library.

*Miserere: for four voices and orchestra, in D minor. The score is lost; four of the twenty-one vocal and orchestral parts are in autograph; that for the flute is signed.

Miserere: for three male voices, chorus, string orchestra, and organ; offered to His Holiness Gregory XVI in July 1841. Autograph in Vatican Library. An early version of the next Miserere listed here.

Miserere (Offertorio): for voices, chorus, and orchestra; composed for the Imperial Chapel, Vienna, in December 1842; performed for the first time on Good Friday, April 14, 1843. A revised version of the preceding Miserere listed here. Autograph in the Ricordi archives, Milan.

Motet: for tenor and small orchestra, with clarinet obbligato. Autograph, dated "March 29, 1820," in Paris Conservatory Library.

Ne proicias me: for bass and orchestra, with horn obbligato, in E major. Autograph, dated "Almenno [San Salvatore], November 29, 1830," in Naples Conservatory Library.

*Nisi Dominus: for tenor and or-

---

[3] Donizetti's nickname for his music-loving friend Antonio Quarenghi.

(*Religious Music Continued*)

chestra, in D major. Twelve of the thirteen vocal and orchestral parts are autograph, but the thirteenth and the score are not.

*Offertorio *(Ave Maria):* for five voices, soprano solo (Angel) and four-voice chorus (the Church), with two violins, two violas, cello, and contrabass. The frontspiece of the autograph score bears this autograph inscription: "Done for the Imperial Royal Chapel. Dedicated to His Majesty Ferdinand I, Emperor of Austria, by Gaetano Donizetti of Bergamo, 1 8 4 2, Vienna"; published with piano accompaniment by Ricordi, Milan. Donizetti described this piece in detail in a letter of May 9, 1842, to his friend Antonio Dolci.

Offertorio *(Miserere):* for voices and orchestra; see *Miserere (Offertorio)* above.

Offertorio *("Quoniam ad te"):* for soprano and small orchestra. Autograph, dated 1844, in Naples Conservatory Library.

Offertorio *("Domine, Dominus noster"):* for bass and orchestra. Nonautograph score, dated "Vienna 1845," with autograph title, in Naples Conservatory Library.

Oro supplex: for bass and orchestra, with horn *obbligato,* in E major; composed for the funeral of the Marchese Giuseppe Terzi (1819). Autograph in Bergamo Civic Library.

Pange lingua: for a procession, in F major. Included in a list of about 1848 in the Library of the Bergamo Istituto Musicale.

Parafrasi del *"Christus":* for soprano contralto, and string orchestra; on text by Serafino Gatti. Autograph in Naples Conservatory Library.

On February 29, 1844, Donizetti wrote to Antonio Vasselli: "I have delivered to His Majesty [the Emperor of Austria] the required annual piece: the *Parafrasi del 'Christus.'* I did it in 1829 at Naples. In 1844, cleaned up, recast, washed, and well attired, it shines in the Imperial and Royal Library at Vienna."

Preces me: for tenor and four-voice chorus. Autograph in the Civic Library, Bergamo.

Psalm XLII: see *Judica me Deus* above.

*Qui sedes and *Quoniam:* for tenor and orchestra, with violin *obbligato,* in C major. Autograph in Paris Conservatory Library.

*Qui sedes and *Quoniam:* for soprano and orchestra, with violin *obbligato,* in A minor. Eleven of the fourteen vocal and orchestral parts are autograph, but the score and the other three parts are not.

*Qui tollis: for tenor and orchestra, with clarinet *obbligato,* in F major; dated "September 7, 1814." The score is lost; six of the ten vocal and orchestral parts are autograph, the others not.

*Qui tollis: for tenor and orchestra, with chorus, in E-flat major, dated "May 24, 1820." Thirteen of the twenty-four vocal and orchestral parts are autograph; the other eleven and the score are not.

*Qui tollis: for tenor and orchestra, with horn *obbligato,* in E major, The score is lost; the solo part and eleven of the sixteen orchestral parts are autograph, the others not.

*Qui tollis: for three voices and orchestra, in E-flat major. Eighteen of the twenty-four vocal and

(*Religious Music Continued*)

orchestral parts are autograph; the score and the six other parts are not.

Qui tollis: for tenor and small orchestra, in B-flat major. The score is lost; the part for the tenor and one of the eleven orchestral parts are autograph, the others not.

Qui tollis–Miserere: for three voices and orchestra, dated "July 8, 1819." Nonautograph score property of the Donizetti heirs.

Requiem: for three voices and orchestra, composed for the benediction of the tomb of Alfonso della Valle di Casanova. Published with piano accompaniment by Cottrau, Naples, undated.

Rex Christi: details unobtainable; in the library of the cathedral at Cracow, Poland.

Salve Regina: for tenor and orchestra, in F major. Autograph, dated "Bergamo, August 5, 1819," in the Paris Conservatory Library.

Salve Regina: for three voices and wind orchestra (oboes, clarinets, horns, trombones, cellos, and violins), in F major. Autograph in the Paris Conservatory Library.

Sic transit gloria mundi: for eight voices and organ. Autograph, signed and dated "G. Donizetti, Milano, 1844," in the Paris Conservatory Library.

Sicut erat: for four voices and orchestra, in C major. Autograph in the Paris Conservatory Library. For another (?) *Sicut erat*, see *Gloria Patri* and *Sicut erat* above.

Sicut erat: for three voices, "*per campagna*," in C major. Autograph, dated "September 9, 1819," in the Paris Conservatory Library.

Tantum ergo: for two tenors, bass, and orchestra, performed in the Church of San Giacomo, Bologna, for the Feast of Saint Cecilia. Autograph, dated "Bologna, November 8, 1816," in the Library of the Bologna Liceo Musicale.

Tantum ergo: for tenor and orchestra, F major. Autograph in Naples Conservatory Library.

Tantum ergo: for soprano and organ, in D major. Nonautograph score in Milan Conservatory Library.

Tantum ergo: for tenor, wind instruments, and contrabass, in E-flat major. The score is lost; the eight vocal and orchestral parts are autograph.

Tecum principium: for soprano or tenor and orchestra, with oboe or clarinet *obbligato*. Autograph, dated 1819, in Naples Conservatory Library.

Te Deum: for two children's voices, with or without organ, with bass, in B-flat major; text a versified vulgarization of the Latin words by Samuele Biava. Manuscript copy.

Tibi solo peccavi: for soprano and orchestra, with bassett horn *obbligato*, in F major. Autograph, dated "April 6, 1820," in Paris Conservatory Library.

Tuba mirum: for bass and orchestra, in E-flat major. Nonautograph score, dated "Bergamo, January 5, 1821."

Tunc acceptabis: for four voices and full orchestra, in D major; dated "April 6, 1820." Vocal and orchestral parts in autograph in Paris Conservatory Library.

Instrumental Music

ORCHESTRA

I: DATED COMPOSITIONS

Grand Imperial Military March: dedicated to the Sultan Abdul Medjid Khan, 1840. Published in solo piano transcription by Bernard Latte, Paris, undated. In 1847, Franz Liszt published a *Paraphrase de la Marche d'Abdul Medjid Khan,* for piano solo; Ferruccio Busoni played this in recitals.

Introduction: for string orchestra; dated 1829. Autograph in Naples Conservatory Library.

March: composed for Francesco Donizetti in August, 1840. Autograph in Paris Conservatory Library.

Sinfonia: in C major. Autograph, dated "Bologna, June 12, 1816," in the Library of the Bologna Liceo Musicale.

Sinfonia concertata: in D major; composed in Bologna on September 17, 1816, and performed during the 1817 examinations at the Liceo Musicale there. Autograph in the Library of the Bologna Liceo Musicale; published by Carisch, Milan, undated.

Sinfonia: in C major; "Done at the Casino dei Filarmonici in Bologna, November 24, 1816. Autograph in Museo Donizettiano, Bergamo.

Sinfonia: D major; "For the Casino dei Filarmonici in Bologna, March 29, 1817." Autograph in Paris Conservatory Library.

Sinfonia: for wind instruments, in G minor; "Dedicated to Signor 'Nebbia' [Luigi] Deleidi by his servant G. D., Bologna, April 19, 1817." Nonautograph score in Museo Donizettiano, Bergamo.

Sinfonia "originale": in D major. Autograph, dated "September 10, 1817," in Paris Conservatory Library.

Sinfonia ("La Partenza"): dated "Bologna, October 25, 1817." Autograph in Paris Conservatory Library. The Museo Donizettiano, Bergamo, has a photographic copy of the piano version belonging to the Ghilardi family, Faenza.

Sinfonia: autograph dated "Bergamo, December 17, 1817," in Paris Conservatory Library.

Sinfonia: D minor; on the death of Antonio Capuzzi (March 28, 1818). Autograph in Paris Conservatory Library. The Museo Donizettiano, Bergamo, has autograph parts for this piece, some of them in Donizetti autograph, others in autograph by Giovanni Simone Mayr.

Sinfonia ("L'incendio"): on text from an ode by Ferdinando Arrivabene; performed at a benefit concert at Bergamo on March 19, 1819. Autograph in Paris Conservatory Library.

Sinfonia: on motives by Vincenzo Bellini, 1836. Autograph in Paris Conservatory Library.

Sinfonia: for the cantata "On the death of Maria F. Malibran," performed at the Teatro alla Scala, Milan, on March 17, 1837.

(Instrumental Music Continued)

Autograph in the Ricordi archives, Milan.

II: UNDATED COMPOSITIONS

Preludio, intended for insertion into an unpublished opera. Autograph in the Paris Conservatory Library.

Rataplan. Autograph in the Ricordi archives, Milan.

Sinfonia, in D major. Twenty-five nonautograph parts in the Museo Donizettiano, Bergamo.

Sinfonia, in D major. Autograph, lacking a conclusion, in the Museo Donizettiano, Bergamo. In this score, completely worked out, are to be found a motive used in the *sinfonia* for *Il Furioso all' isola di San Domingo* and one used in the trio of Act II of *L'Elisir d'amore.*

Sinfonia, in four movements, of which only an *adagio non troppo* and a *minuetto* survive. Autograph in the Paris Conservatory Library.

Instrumental Music

CHAMBER GROUPS

I: QUARTETS *(for first and second violin, viola, and cello)*

1. *Quartet:* in E-flat major. Autograph, inscribed "First Quartet of G. Donizetti, December 26, 1817," in Paris Conservatory Library.
2. *Quartet:* in A major; undated. Autograph, inscribed *"Quartetto II,"* in Paris Conservatory Library.
3. *Quartet:* in C minor; undated. Autograph, inscribed *"Quartetto III,"* in Museo Donizettiano, Bergamo.
4. *Quartet:* D major. Autograph, inscribed *"Quartetto IV"* and with the violin and viola parts dated "July 27, 1818," in Museo Donizettiano, Bergamo.
5. *Quartet:* in E minor. Autograph, inscribed *"Quartetto V,"* undated, in Museo Donizettiano, Bergamo.
6. *Quartet:* in G minor. Autograph score and parts, undated, inscribed

"Originale del Quartetto VI di Donizetti," in Paris Conservatory Library.

7. *Quartet:* in F minor. Autograph score, inscribed "Bergamo, May 6, 1819, the death of the Marchese [Giuseppe] Terzi in quartet, dedicated to Alessandro Bertoli," in Paris Conservatory Library; autograph parts in Museo Donizettiano, Bergamo. It is in four movements: 1. *Allegro vivace* (his illness and the prayer of his wife and children for his recovery); 2. *Adagio ma non troppo* (his death); 3. *Presto* (despair of his wife and weeping); 4. *Marcia lugubre.*
8. *Quartet:* in B-flat major. Autograph score, inscribed "Quartet done for my friend [Marco] Bonesi. Donizetti, May 26, 1819," in Paris Conservatory Library; autograph parts in Museo Donizettiano, Bergamo.
9. *Quartet:* in D minor. Autograph

(*Instrumental Music Continued*)

score and parts, dated "The 22nd, 1821," in Paris Conservatory Library.

10. Quartet: G minor. Autograph score and separate parts (the fourth movement missing), dated "January 26, 1821," in Paris Conservatory Library.

11. Quartet: in C major. Autograph score and parts, dated "March 12, 1821," in Paris Conservatory Library.

12. Quartet: C major. Autograph score, dated "March 15, 1821," in Museo Donizettiano, Bergamo.

13. Quartet: in A major. Autograph score and parts, dated "April 19, 1821," in Paris Conservatory Library.

NOTE from *138*, 195: "The succeeding four quartets carry no indication of date, but by various indications, especially in the handwriting, they can be assigned securely to the three years 1819–1821."

14. Quartet: in D major. Autograph score and parts in Paris Conservatory Library.

15. Quartet: C major. Autograph score and parts (final movement missing), in Paris Conservatory Library.

16. Quartet: in F major. Autograph score of the first two movements and the four parts complete in Museo Donizettiano, Bergamo.

17. Quartet: B minor. Autograph score in Paris Conservatory Library. With it is a sketch in A minor, also in autograph; apparently a first movement, it stops at measure 122.

18. Quartet: in D major. Autograph signed score, dated 1825, in Museo Donizettiano, Bergamo.

19. Quartet: in E minor. Nonautograph score, dated 1836, in Naples Conservatory Library.

II: QUINTETS

Quintet (two violins, two violas, cello): in C major. First movement only; undated. Autograph score and parts in Museo Donizettiano, Bergamo.

Quintet (two violins, viola, cello, doublebass): *Introduzione* and *Largo affettuoso* only. Autograph property of the Donizetti heirs.

Quintet (two violins, viola, cello, guitar): *Larghetto, allegretto* in C major; *Andante* in D major; *Largo* in E-flat major; *Larghetto* in A major; *Andante* and *Allegro* in C major. Autograph, undated, in Naples Conservatory Library.

III: MISCELLANEOUS PIECES

Concerto: for English horn; dedicated to "Giovanni Catolfi, pupil at the Liceo Filarmonico di Bologna, Bologna 1816." Autograph in Paris Conservatory Library.

Concerto: for clarinet; with varied theme, in E-flat major. Autograph property of Professore Alessandro Marinelli, Bergamo.

Concerto: for violin and cello. Autograph in Paris Conservatory Library.

Concerto: for unspecified instrument. Sixty pages of autograph score in Paris Conservatory Library.

(*Fragment*): for oboe solo, partly accompanied, partly with bass only. Autograph in Paris Conservatory Library.

Larghetto: for violin and harp, in G minor. Autograph in Museo Donizettiano, Bergamo.

(*Instrumental Music Continued*)

Larghetto: for flute and bassoon, with piano accompaniment. Autograph in Museo Donizettiano, Bergamo.

Larghetto and *Polonaise:* for violin, unaccompanied except in the first twenty-six measures of the *Polonaise.* Autograph in Paris Conservatory Library.

Largo: for cello, with piano accompaniment. Autograph in Museo Donizettiano, Bergamo.

(*Scherzo*): for violin with piano accompaniment; composed on twenty-seven motives selected from the operas that Donizetti had composed through 1826. The operas from which the motives were taken are listed on the last page of the autograph in Museo Donizettiano, Bergamo; under that listing this autograph inscription appears: "*Alla Signora Virginia Vasselli, Roma.*"

Sextet: for two violins, viola, cello, flute, and two horns. Listed in Marco Bonesi's autograph catalogue in Museo Donizettiano, Bergamo; the autograph belonged to Bonesi.

Suonata: for oboe; dedicated to Severino degli Antonj (Bologna). Autograph in Paris Conservatory Library.

Suonata: for piano and cello; *Allegro, Larghetto, Finale allegro.* Nonautograph manuscript in Museo Donizettiano, Bergamo.

Suonata: for flute and piano; in C minor; for use by the Signora Marianna Pezzoli-Grattaroli. Autograph, dated "Bergamo, May 15, 1819," in Museo Donizettiano, Bergamo.

Suonata: for violin and piano; in F minor; dedicated to Madame P[ezzoli-] G[rattaroli]. Autograph, dated "Bergamo, October 26–27, 1819," in Museo Donizettiano, Bergamo.

(*Untitled piece*): for clarinet and small orchestra; in B-flat major. Autograph in Museo Donizettiano, Bergamo.

(*Untitled piece*): for wind instruments and organ; in B-flat major. Autograph in Museo Donizettiano, Bergamo.

Variations (6): in D-flat major; for piano and violin; dedicated to the Noble Signor Alessandro Zineroni. Autograph property of Professore Alessandro Marinelli, Bergamo.

Variations (18): in D minor and F major; for piano and violin. Nonautograph score property of Professore Alessandro Marinelli, Bergamo.

Instrumental Music

PIANO, TWO HANDS

Adagio and *Allegro:* in G major. Autograph, undated, in Museo Donizettiano, Bergamo.

Allegro: in F minor. Autograph, undated, in Museo Donizettiano, Bergamo.

Allegro: in C major. Autograph, undated, in Museo Donizettiano, Bergamo.

Allegro vivace: in C major. Autograph, undated, in Museo Donizettiano, Bergamo.

(Instrumental Music Continued)

Allegro vivace: in G major. Autograph, undated, in Museo Donizettiano, Bergamo.

Un Capriccio in sinfonia: in E minor. Autograph, inscribed "In half an hour, between 4:30 and 5, Bologna, August 15, 1817," in Museo Donizettiano, Bergamo.

Fugue: in G minor. Autograph, undated, in Museo Donizettiano, Bergamo.

Giuseppina (polka-mazurka): published posthumously by Girard, Naples.

(Incomplete sketch): in E-flat major. Autograph, undated, in Museo Donizettiano, Bergamo.

Invito (waltz): autograph, undated, in Museo Donizettiano, Bergamo.

Largo (theme and variations): in E-flat major. Autograph, undated, in Museo Donizettiano, Bergamo.

Larghetto: in C major. Autograph, signed and dated "Donizetti, December 30, 1834," in Milan Conservatory Library.

Pastorale: in E major; for piano or organ. Autograph, dated 1813, in Museo Donizettiano, Bergamo.

Presto: in F major. Autograph, undated, in Museo Donizettiano, Bergamo.

La Ricordanza: adagio sentimentale: in E-flat major. Autograph in Museo Donizettiano, Bergamo.

Rondo: in D major; dedicated to the Marchesa Sofia [de' Medici] di Marignano. Autograph, dated "Naples, February 1825," in Museo Donizettiano, Bergamo.

Sinfonia: dated at Bologna on November 19, 1816, with the inscription "Done in an hour and a quarter by order of Padre Maestro Mattei and finished at the dinner hour." Autograph (4 pages, 220 measures) in the Library of the Bologna Liceo Musicale.

Sinfonia: in A major. Autograph, dated "Bergamo, October 13, 1831," in Museo Donizettiano, Bergamo.

Sinfonia: in D major. Autograph, undated, in Museo Donizettiano, Bergamo.

Sinfonia: in D major. Autograph (four pages), undated, in Naples Conservatory Library.

Two Motives of the Celebrated Maestro Paër: put into a *suonata.* Autograph, dated "Bologna, October 7, 1817," in Museo Donizettiano, Bergamo.

Variations: on a theme from a duet in Mayr's opera *La Rosa bianca e la rosa rossa* (1815); listed by Zavadini (*138*, 199), but existence doubtful, possibly an error for the next item.

Variations: on a theme from the "*Canzon del bardo*" in Mayr's opera *Alfredo il grande.* Published in 1820 by Ricordi, Milan (catalogue number 789), probably Donizetti's first published composition.

Variations: for cembalo; in G major. Autograph, undated, in Museo Donizettiano, Bergamo.

Variations: in E major. Autograph, undated, in Museo Donizettiano, Bergamo.

La Vénitienne (waltz): autograph, undated, in Museo Donizettiano, Bergamo.

Waltz: signed "*Donizetti qui vous aime . . .*" Autograph in Paris Conservatory Library.

Waltzes (two): Autograph, undated, in Museo Donizettiano, Bergamo.

Instrumental Music

PIANO, FOUR HANDS

Allegro: in C major. Autograph, undated, in Museo Donizettiano, Bergamo.

Allegro moderato: in A major. Autograph, undated, in Museo Donizettiano, Bergamo.

Il Capitan Battaglia (suonata): in E-flat major (1819). Autograph in Museo Donizettiano, Bergamo.

Il Genio di G. D.: in G major; "*Pour Madame P[ezzoli] G[rattaroli].*" Autograph in Museo Donizettiano, Bergamo.

L'Inaspettata: in E-flat major; dedicated to Madame P[ezzoli-] Grattaroli. Autograph in Museo Donizettiano, Bergamo.

L [rest of title erased]: in C major; dedicated to Madame Pezzoli-Grattaroli. Autograph, dated "February 25, 1821," in Museo Donizettiano, Bergamo.

La Lontananza: in E minor. Autograph, undated, in Museo Donizettiano, Bergamo.

Marcia lugubre: in E minor. Autograph, undated, in Museo Donizettiano, Bergamo.

Polacca: in D major; 1819. Autograph, signed in French "By the mad Donizetti," in Museo Donizettiano, Bergamo.

Sinfonia (second): in D minor; dedicated to the Signora M[arianna] P[ezzoli-] Grattaroli. Autograph,

dated "Almenno [San Salvatore], March 28, 1820," in Museo Donizettiano, Bergamo.

La Solita Suonata: in F major. Autograph, undated, in Museo Donizettiano, Bergamo.

Suonata: in C major; dedicated to M[arianna] P[ezzoli-]Grattaroli. Autograph, dated "March 31, 1819," in Museo Donizettiano, Bergamo.

Suonata: in D major; dedicated to the Noble Signora Marianna Pezzoli-Grattaroli. Autograph, dated "October 12, 1819," in Museo Donizettiano, Bergamo.

Suonata "a 4 sanfe": dedicated to the pianoforte of Madame Pezzoli-[Grattaroli]. Autograph in Museo Donizettiano, Bergamo.

Suonata: in B-flat major; "For [Antonio] Dolci and Donizetti." Autograph, undated, in Museo Donizettiano, Bergamo.

Suonata: in D major; dedicated to M[arianna] P[ezzoli]G[rattaroli]. Autograph, undated, in Museo Donizettiano, Bergamo.

Suonata (third): in F major. Autograph, undated, in Museo Donizettiano, Bergamo.

Waltz: dedicated to the Marchesa Adelaide de Sterlich. Autograph, dated 1844, in Museo Donizettiano, Bergamo.

Vocal Compositions

IN addition to the many unpublished compositions by Donizetti for solo voice, two voices, and three and more voices, and those which were published individually, many collections of them were issued during and immediately after his lifetime. The titles of eleven of the most important of these collections (which often were issued by two or three different publishers in Italy and France under different titles and with varying contents) are: *Collezione di canzonette, Dernières Glânes musicales, Donizetti per camera* (the title of both a small collection and of a publisher's extensive series), *Fiori di sepolcro, Un Hiver à Paris, Inspirations viennoises, Matinées musicales, Nuits d'été à Pausilippe, Rêveries napolitaines, Soirées d'automne à l'Infrascata,* and *Tre Melodie postume.* Three of these collections certainly were posthumous: *Dernières Glânes musicales, Fiori di sepolcro,* and *Tre Melodie postume.* In the following list, I have indicated, wherever possible, the collection or collections in which a given individual song was published. Among the editions of which I have personal knowledge are the following:

Collezione di canzonette: five solo songs, three duets, and an unaccompanied quintet; Edizione Litografia e Calcografia di Ricci e Negri, Naples, undated.

Dernières Glânes musicales: eight solo songs and two duets; Bernardo Girard, Naples, undated.

Donizetti per camera: twelve solo songs and four duets; Bernardo Girard, Naples, undated. Girard's successor, the Stabilimento T. Cottrau, Naples, also used this title for an undated collection of eight solo songs—and for a series that included individual publication of fifty-nine solo songs, seven duets, and two quartets.

Fiori di sepolcro, subtitled *Melodie postume:* nine solo songs; Cottrau, Successori della Ditta Girard, Naples, undated.

Un Hiver à Paris: four solo songs and a duet; Bernardo Girard, Naples, undated; also five solo songs and a duet published by Stabilimento Musicale di Ferdinando Lorenzi, Florence, undated. See also *Rêveries napolitaines* below.

Inspirations viennoises: five solo songs and two duets, all to texts by Carlo Guaita; Bernardo Girard, Naples, undated; also the Stabilimento T. Cottrau, Naples, un-

dated. The same songs and duets were issued by Tito di G. Ricordi, Milan, undated, as *Ispirazioni viennesi.*

Matinées musicales (Italian: *Mattinate musicale*): six solo songs, two solo songs, six duets, two quartets; "Dedicated to Her Majesty the Queen of England"; F. Lucca, Milan, undated; also Bernardo Girard, Naples, undated; also, in a rearranged order of songs, by the Stabilimento T. Cottrau, Naples, undated.

Nuits d'été à Pausilippe (Italian: *Notti d'estate a Posilippo*): six solo songs and six two-voice nocturnes; Ricordi, Milan, undated (but 1836?); also Bernard Latte, Paris, undated (but 1840?).

Rêveries napolitaines: a revised edition of *Un Hiver à Paris;* including the four solo songs and duet of that collection, plus *L'Ultima Notte di un novizio* and the same song in French as *La Dernière Nuit d'un novice;* Bernardo Girard, Naples, undated; also, as *Ricordi napoletani,* Ricordi, Milan, undated.

Soirées d'automne à l'Infrascata:[4] four

---

[4] Infrascata was the name of a rural district adjoining the Vomero hill in Naples; in Donizetti's day it was outside the city, of which it now forms an indistinguishable part.

(*Vocal Compositions Continued*)

solo songs and a duet; Bernardo Girard, Naples, undated; also, the same plus the duet *L'Incostanza d'Irene*, Ricordi, Milan, undated.

Tre Melodie postume: as the three songs in this collection also appear in *Fiori di sepolcro*, it probably is a partial republication of the larger collection; T. Cottrau, Naples, undated.

Vocal Compositions

Solo Voice[5]

A Mezzanotte (French: *Á Minuit*) ("*Quando notte sarà oscura*"), (*arietta*): text by "N. N."; included in *Nuits d'été à Pausilippe*.

"*A piè del mesto salce*" (*canzonetta*): unpublished; autograph property of the Marchesa Medici, Rome.

Addio ("*Ah! tu mi fuggi . . . addio!*") (*romanza*): text a translation from the French of G. Vitali; included in the collections. *Rêveries napolitaines* and *Dernières Glânes musicales*.

"*Addio brunetta, son già lontano,*" (*allegretto scherzoso*): given by Donizetti to Raffaele D'Auria. Autograph later belonged to Verdi.

"*Adieu, tu brise et pour jamais*" (*romance*): unpublished; autograph in Paris Conservatory Library.

"*Ah, che miro o sventurato*" (*aria*): autograph in the Ricordi archives, Milan (from an opera?).

"*Ah! ingrato m'inganni*": see *La Tradita*.

"*Ah, non lasciarmi, no, bell'idol mio*" (*romanza*): unpublished; autograph in Paris Conservatory Library.

"*Ah, rammenta, o bella Irene*" (*cav-*

atina): composed for the Signora M. P. de Sévigny.

"*Ah, si tu voulais, toi que j'aime*" (*canzone*): for soprano; unpublished; autograph in Museo Donizettiano, Bergamo.

"*Aimer ma Rose est la sorte de ma vie*" (*romance*): included in the collection *Donizetti per camera*.

"*Al campo della gloria*": see *La Partenza del crociato*.

L'Amante spagnuolo ("*Corri destrier, deh celeri*") (*arietta*): for soprano; text by Leopoldo Tarantini; included in the collection *Soirées de l'automne à l'Infrascata*; autograph in Paris Conservatory Library.

Amiamo ("*Or che l'età ne invita*"): unpublished; autograph in the Ricordi archives, Milan.

"*Amis, courons chercher la gloire*" (*canzone*): unpublished; autograph in Paris Conservatory Library.

"*Ammore!*": Popular song to a Neapolitan text.

"*Amor che a nulla amato*" (Dantesque *terzina*; album leaf): unpublished; autograph, signed and dated "Paris, 1843," in Museo Donizettiano, Bergamo.

Amor corrisposto ("*Bei labbri che amore formò*") (*canzonetta*): composed 1822; included in the collection *Donizetti per camera*.

---

[5] Unless otherwise specified, these have piano accompaniment.

(*Vocal Compositions Continued*)

Amor marinaro ("*Me voglio fà na casa*") (*canzonetta napoletana*): for soprano; included in the collection *Soirées d'automne à l'Infrascata*; autograph in Paris Conservatory Library.

L'Amor mio ("*Amo, sì, ma l'amor mio*"): text by Felice Romani; included in the collections *Tre Melodie postume* and *Fiori di sepolcro*.

Amore e morte ("*Odi d'un uom che muore*") (*arietta*): included in the collection *Soirées d'automne à l'Infrascata*.

Amor tiranno ("*Perchè due cori insieme*") (*romanza*): included in the collection *Fiori di sepolcro*.

Amour jaloux ("*Dans un salon si quelqu'un vous regarde*") (*romance*): unpublished; autograph in Paris Conservatory Library.

"*Anch'io provai le tenere smanie*" (*arietta*): unpublished.

Antonio Foscarini ("*Quando da te lontano*"): text by Giovanni Battista Niccolini.

L'Attente ("*La mère, ma toute belle*") (*mélodie*).

Au Pied d'une crois ("*Voyez-vous cette femme*") (*romance*): unpublished; autograph in Paris Conservatory Library.

"*Au tic-tac des castagnettes*" (*canzonetta* or aria): included in the collection *Donizetti per camera*.

Il Barcajuolo ("*Voga, voga, il vento tace*"): text by Leopoldo Tarantini; included in the collection *Nuits d'été à Pausilippe*.

"*Bedda Eurilla*": see *La Vendetta*.

"*Bei labbri che amore formò*": see *Amor corrisposto*.

Berceuse ("*Questo mio figlio*"): unpublished.

Les Billets doux (*romance*): French version of *La Corrispondenza amorosa*.

La Bohémienne ("*La zingara, sur l'herbe arrosée*") (*ballade*): autograph in the Malherbe Collection, Paris.[6]

Canzone dell'ape: Italian version of *La Chanson de l'abeille*.

I Capelli ("*Questi capelli bruni*") (*romanza*): included in the collection *Donizetti per camera*.

Il Cavallo arabo ("*O corridor più ratto assaï*") (French: "*Léger coursier plus léger que le daim*") (*romanza*): included in the collection *Matinées musicales*.

Cavatina ("*Ella riposi alcuni istanti almeno*"): composed for Prince Joseph Poniatowski; autograph in the Museo Teatrale alla Scala, Milan.

La Chanson de l'abeille (Italian: *Canzone dell'ape*) ("*Sur les fleurs voltige une abeille*"): text by Hippolyte Lucas; included in the collection *Dernières Glânes musicales*.

"*Che cangi tempra mai più non spero*" (*andante*): for soprano; unpublished; autograph, with dedication "*Per Adele Appiani, Caietanus De Donizectis faciebat,*" in Museo Donizettiano, Bergamo.

Cifre d'amore: see *La Corrispondenza amorosa*.

Combien la nuit est longue ("*Hélas, j'entend sonner une heure*") (*romance*): unpublished; autograph in Paris Conservatory Library.

"*Come volgeste rapidi, giorni de' miei primi anni*" (*romanza*): unpublished; autograph in Paris Conservatory Library.

La Conocchia ("*Quann'a lo bello mio vojo parlare*") (*arietta* or *canzone*

---

[6] With other text, this became the final rondo of Act III of *Don Pasquale*.

(*Vocal Compositions Continued*)
napoletana): included in the collection *Nuits d'été à Pausilippe*.

La Corrispondenza amorosa ("*O dolce righe, pittura del core*") (*romanza*): included in the collection *Matinées musicales*. Also called *Cifre d'amore* (French: *Billets chéris*).

Le Crépuscule ("*L'aube naît e la porte est close*"): text by Victor Hugo; included in the collection *Nuits d'été à Pausilippe*.

Il Crociato ("*Colle piume sul cimiero*") (*arietta* or *romanza*): text by Carlo Guaita: included in the collection *Nuits d'été à Pausilippe*.

"*Dell'anno novello—nel giorno primero—un voto sincero—accetta per me*" (*canzonetta*): unpublished; autograph in the Lucchesi-Palli Library, Naples.

"*Del colle in sul pendio*" (*canzonetta*): for soprano; included in the collection *Donizetti per camera*.

Le Départ pour la chasse ("*Voici la trace du cerf*") (*aria*): for baritone or bass, horn in F; text by P[aul] L[acroix]; autograph in Naples Conservatory Library.

"*Depuis qu'un autre a su te plaire*" (*mélodie*): for soprano; see *Malvina*.

Le Dernier Chant du troubadour (*romance*): unpublished.

Doux Souvenirs, vivez toujours ("*Pourquoi toujours avoir dans ma pensée*") (*mélodie*): text by Émile Barateau.

D'un genio che m'accende: for soprano; included in the collection *Donizetti per camera*.

"*Elle n'existe plus*" (*mélodie*): unpublished.

È morta (French: "*Morte! et pourtant hier*") ("*Morta! e ieri ancor*") (*scena*): text by Carlo Guaita; included in the collection *Inspirations viennoises*.

"*E più dell'onda instabile*" (*arietta*): autograph in Naples Conservatory Library.

"*Eterno amore e fè ti giuro umile al piè*": see *Giuro d'amore*.

L'Etrangère (*romance*): autograph property of the Marchesa Medici, Rome.

La Farfalla ed il poeta ("*Io son farfalla e volo, per quanto volar*"): unpublished; autograph in Paris Conservatory Library.

"*Fausto sempre*" (*aria*): for Signora [Luigia] Boccabadati-[Gazzuoli]; unpublished; autograph in Paris Conservatory Library.

"*Faut-il renfermer dans mon âme*" (*mélodie*): unpublished; autograph in Paris Conservatory Library.

La Fiancée du timballier ("*Monseigneur le duc de Bretagne*"): text by Victor Hugo; unpublished; autograph, with dedication "To the Gayard couple, January 14, 1843, Munich," in Paris Conservatory Library.

La Fidanzata ("*No, tu non m'hai tradita*") (*romanza*): "for Belluccia and Rosuccia of the Vasselli household"; included in the collection *Fiori di sepolcro*; signed autograph property of the Vasselli-Gabrielli heirs, Rome.

La Folle de Sainte-Hélène (Italian: *La pazza di Sant'Elena*) ("*Ils disent tous*"—Italian: "*Stolta ognor me il mondo chiama*") (*ballade*): text by Adolphe Nourrit; included in the collection *Donizetti per camera*.

"*Garde tes moutons*" ("*Gentille fillette*") (*romance*).

(*Vocal Compositions Continued*)

"*Già presso al termine de' suoi martiri*" (*cavatina*): for soprano; with the dedication "For . . . I know whom it's for"; unpublished; autograph in the Museo Donizettiano, Bergamo.

Il Giglio e la rosa ("*Non sdegnar vezzosa Irene*") (*canzonetta*): included in the collections *Dernières Glânes musicales* and *Donizetti per camera*.

Giovanna Gray ("*Io morrò, sonata è l'ora*") (*romanza*): included in the collections *Tre Melodie postume* and *Fiori di sepolcro*.

Giuro d'amore ("*Eterno amore e fè ti giuro umile al piè*") (*arietta*): included in the collection *Donizetti per camera*.

La Gondola ("*Meco in barchetta*") (*canzone*).

Le Gondolier de l'Adriatique ("*La brise plaintive*") (*nocturne*): text by Crevel de Charlemagne.

La Gondoliera or *Oh vieni al mare* ("*Vieni, la barca è pronta*") (*barcarola*): included in the collection *Matinées musicales*.

Gran Dio, mi manca il cor ("*Ah, madre, se ognor lontan vissi al materno sen—che a te pietoso Iddio—mi unisca in morte almen*"): unpublished; autograph in Paris Conservatory Library.

La Hart ("*Non loin de Montfaucon*") (*chant diabolique*): for bass; text by "The Bibliophile Jacob."

L'Heure du retour ("*Lise, écoute, voici l'heure*"): text by Crevel de Charlemagne. French version of *L'Ora del ritorno*, q.v.

"*Heureuse qui près de toi*": for soprano; text a French version of lines from Sappho, accompaniment lines blank; unpublished; autograph in Museo Donizettiano, Bergamo.

"*Il m'aime encore, doux rêve de mon âme*" (*mélodie*): unpublished; autograph, with the inscription "Two hours after midnight you sleep," in Paris Conservatory Library.

"*Il mio ben m'abbandonò*" (*melodia*): for soprano; unpublished; autograph in Museo Donizettiano, Bergamo.

"*Il mio grido getto ai venti*" (*romanza moresca*): for soprano; unpublished; autograph, with the dedication "*Alla Marchesina Caterina Sterlich, D. D. Donizetti, 1844,*" in Museo Donizettiano, Bergamo.

"*Il Sorriso è il primo vezzo*": for soprano; included in the collection *Donizetti per camera*.

L'Ingratiude ("*Tu n'aimes plus*") (*romance*): French version of *Non m'ami più*, q.v.

Io amo la mestizia (*romanza*): consists of vocal line and text without accompaniment, written by Donizetti in a musical autograph album belonging to Sofia de' Medici, Marchesa di Marignano, with this inscription: "*Vous étez priée d'y faire l'accompagnement, ainsi nous serons deux auteurs.*" It was not dated, but Franco Schlitzer noted (*114, 55*)[7] that other musicians appearing in the album included Antonio Bazzini, Sigismond Thalberg, Niccolò Vaccaj, Pierantonio Coppola, Franz Schoberlechner, Ferdinand Hiller, and Verdi, and he appears to have believed that the Donizetti *romanza* was written in it during the composer's stay at the Appiani home in Milan between September 1841, and March

---

[7] The autograph is reproduced in part by Schlitzer on pp. 56–57.

(*Vocal Compositions Continued*)

1842. The text of the *romanza* breaks off with the lines: "*È l'ora, è l'ora . . . Elvira,/A te pensando io sento*" ("It is the hour, it is the hour . . . Elvira,/Thinking of you, I feel")—after which Donizetti wrote: "*Indovinate cosa sento. Donizetti*" (You guess what I feel. Donizetti).

"*Io son pazza capricciosa*" (*arietta*).

"*Io te voglio* [or *vojo*] *bene assaje e tu non pienze a me*" (*canzonetta napoletana*): text by Raffaele Sacco; see "*Te voglio bene assaje.*"

J'attends toujours ("*Dans la course rapide*") (*romance*): text by Eugène de Lonlay.

"*Je vais quitter tout ce que j'aime*" (*romance*): autograph, with the dedication "*À messieurs les frères Escudier, editeurs de 'La France musicale,'*" in Paris Conservatory Library.

Lamento in [or *per la*] *morte di V. Bellini* ("*Venne sull'ale ai zeffiri*"): 1836; text by Andrea Maffei; dedicated to Maria Malibran; included in the collection *Donizetti per camera*.

Lamento di Cecco di Varlungo (album leaf): unpublished; autograph property of Donebauer, Prague.

Leonora (French: *Léonore*) ("*Partir conviene, Leonora, addio*"—French: "*Il faut partir*") (*romanza*): text by Marie Escudier; included in the collection *Dernières Glânes musicales*.

La Longue Douleur ("*Dieu qui d'un signe appaise*") (prayer).

La Lontananza ("*Or ch'io sono a te rapita*") (*arietta*): included in the collecton *Soirées d'automne à l'Infrascata.*

Malvina (Italian: "*Dal dì che un altro ti fu più bello*") ("*Depuis qu'un autre a su te plaire*") (*scène dramatique*): text by G. Vitali; sung at Paris in October 1845 by Mme Banussire; unpublished; autograph, dedicated to the Marchesina Giovanna de Sterlich, "1844," in Museo Donizettiano, Bergamo.

"*Marie enfin quitte l'ouvrage*" (*romance*): unpublished; autograph in Paris Conservatory Library.

M'è Dio il tuo Signore (French: *Ton Dieu est mon Dieu*) ("*Il tuo pensier è il mio*"—French: "*Connais sur mon âme asservie*"): included in the collection *Matinées musicales*. Sometimes referred to as "*Oh quanto in me tu puoi.*"

"*Mentre del caro lido*" (*canzonetta*): autograph property of the Marchesa Medici, Rome.

La Mère au berceau de son fils: French version of *La Ninna-Nanna*, q.v.

La Mère et l'enfant ("*Un voile blanc couvrait la terre*") (*mélodie*): included in the collection *Dernières Glânes musicales*; nonautograph score, with dedication to Mme [Zélie] de Coussy, in Museo Donizettiano, Bergamo.

"*Me voglio fà na casa*": see *Amor marinaro*.

La Mia Fanciulla ("*Ah! se d'amore un palpito*"): included in the collection *Fiori di sepolcro*.

Minvela ("*Quando verrà sul colle*") (*canzonetta*): included in the collection *Donizetti per camera*.

Le Miroir magique ("*Ninette, celle que j'aime*") (*chansonette*): text by Édouard Plouvier.

Mon Enfant, mon seul espoir ("*Mon enfant, mon sang, ma vie*") (*ro-*

(*Vocal Compositions Continued*)

mance): unpublished; autograph in Paris Conservatory Library.

"*Morte! et pourtant hier*": French version of *È morta*; autograph in Paris Conservatory Library.

La Musulmane ("*Si tu m'aimais, o musulmane*"): text by Maurice Bourges.

La Negra (French: *La Nouvelle Ourika*) ("*Fin dalla culla intrepida*"—French: "*Dès le berceau*") (*romanza*): included in the collection *Matinées musicales*.

"*Nel tuo cammin fugace*": see *T'aspetto ancor.*

"*Nice, st'occhiuzzi càlali*" (*canzonetta*): unpublished; autograph property of the Marchesa Medici, Rome.

La Ninna-Nanna (French: *La Mère au berceau de son fils*) ("*Dormi, fanciullo mio*"—French: "*Dors, enfant de ta mère*") (*ballata*): text by Achille de Lauzières; included in the collection *Un Hiver à Paris.*

Noé, Scène du Deluge ("*Dieu terrible, Dieu redoutable*"): text by J. de Boutellier (February, 1839).

Il Nome ("*Voi vorreste il nome amato* [or *accanto*]") (*arietta*): included in the collection *Donizetti per camera.*

"*No, tu non m'hai tradita*": see *La Fidanzata.*

"*Non amerò che te*" (*romanza*): text a translation from the French of G. Vitali.

"*Non amo che te*" (*romanza*), G major.

"*Non giova il sospirar*" (*canzonetta veneziana*): for soprano; C major; composed 1822.

Non m'ami più ("*Non m'ami più, rimira*"): text by Carlo Guaita; included in the collection *In-*

spirations viennoises; autograph in Paris Conservatory Library.

"*Non priego mai nè piano le parche impietosì*": see *Una Prece sulla mia tomba.*

"*Non v'è più barbaro di chi non sente*" (*canzonetta*): autograph property of the Marchesa Medici, Rome.

"*Non v'è nume, non v'è fato*" (*romanza*): dedicated to Signora Emilia Branca.

"*N'ornerà la bruna chioma*" (*scena* and *cavatina*): composed for Signora Lina Freppa Cottrau.

La Nouvelle Ourika: French version of *La Negra*, q.v.

"*O anime affannate, venite a noi parlar*": text from the Francesca da Rimini episode of the *Divina Commedia*, Canto V; unpublished; autograph in Paris Conservatory Library.

"*O fille que l'ennui chagrine*" (*romance*): unpublished; autograph in Paris Conservatory Library.

"*Occhio nero incendiator*" (*canzonetta*): included in the collection *Donizetti per camera.*

"*Oh, Cloe, delizia di questo core*" (*canzonetta*): autograph property of the Marchesa Medici, Rome.

"*Oh* [*Ah*], *ingrato, m'inganni*:" see *La Tradita.*

"*Oh, je rêve d'une étrangère plus douce que l'enfant qui dort*": unpublished; manuscript in Paris Conservatory Library.

Oh vieni al mar: see *La Gondoliera.*

"*On vous a peint l'amour*" (*romance*): text by "Docteur [the Bibliophile] Jacob" (pseudonym of Paul Lacroix); unpublished; autograph in Paris Conservatory Library.

"*Or che la notte invita*" (*canzonetta*): for soprano; for Signora Teresina

(*Vocal Compositions Continued*)

Spadaro [del Bosch]; unpublished; autograph in Paris Conservatory Library.

L'Ora del ritorno ("*Odi, Elisa, questa è l'ora*") (*arietta*): text by Carlo Guaita; included in the collection *Inspirations viennoises.*

"*Oui, je sais votre indifférence*": unpublished; autograph in Paris Conservatory Library.

"*Oui, ton dieu c'est le mien*" (*romance*): text by M. Michonne; unpublished; autograph in Paris Conservatory Library.

"*Ov'è la voce magica*" (*melodia*): for soprano; unpublished; autograph, with the dedication "*Alla marchesina Caterina Sterlich nel giorno del suo onomastico* [November 25] *offriva benchè lontano,*" in Museo Donizettiano, Bergamo.

La Partenza del crociato ("*Al campo della gloria*") (*arietta* or *romanza*): text by Puoti; included in the collection *Donizetti per camera.*

"*Pas d'autre amour que toi*" (*mélodie*): text by Émile Barateau.

La Passeggiata al lido ("*Che bel mar, che bel sereno*"): included in the collection *Donizetti per camera.* See also this title on page 400.

Le Pauvre Exilé ("*Faut-il, hélas! sans espérance*") (*romance*): text by Adolphe de Leuven.

La Pazza di Sant'Elena: see *La Folle de Sainte-Hélène.*

Il Pegno (*canzonetta*): autograph property of the Marchesa Medici, Rome.

"*Perchè due cori*" (*romanza*): unpublished; manuscript in Naples Conservatory Library.

"*Perchè mai, Nigella amata, insensibile tu sei?*" (*romanza*): for soprano; unpublished; autograph in Paris Conservatory Library.

"*Perchè se mia tu sei, perchè se tuo son io, perchè temer, ben mio, ch'io manchi mai di fè*" (*romanza*): unpublished; autograph, with the dedication "*A S. E. la contessa Ludolf, Donizetti,*" in Paris Conservatory Library.

Il Pescatore ("*Batte il bronzo, il ciel s'imbruna*"): text by Achille Ricciardi; included in the collection *Fiori di sepolcro.*

Il Pescatore ("*Era l'ora che i cieli*") (*ballata*): text by Schiller as translated by Achille de Lauzières; included in the collection *Un Hiver à Paris.*

Le Petit Joueur de la harpe ("*O ma harpe, seul héritage*"): text by Paul Lacroix; unpublished; autograph in Naples Conservatory Library.

Le Petit Montagnard ("*Ouvre-moi, bonne mère*"): text by "Mme X."; included in the collection *Fiori di sepolcro.*

"*Philis plus avare que tendre*" (*romance*): unpublished; autograph in Paris Conservatory Library.

"*Più che non m'ama un angelo*" (*romanza*): with cello or horn; written for Prince Metternich in 1842; Nonautograph manuscript in Museo Donizettiano, Bergamo. For another version, see the duet *L'Amor funesto,* page 400.

"*Plus ne m'est rien*" (*romance*): unpublished; autograph in Paris Conservatory Library.

"*Pourquoi me dire qu'il vous aime*" (*romance*): unpublished; autograph in Paris Conservatory Library.

Una Prece sulla mia tomba ("*Non*

(*Vocal Compositions Continued*)
priego mai nè pianto le parche
impietosì") (*canto elegiaco* or
romanza): for soprano; text by
Redaelli; included in the collection *Donizetti per camera*;
autograph in Paris Conservatory
Library.

Preghiera ("*Dio! Dio! che col cenno
moderi*"): included in the collection *Matinées musicales*. Also
called *Una Lagrima*.

La Prière ("*Voici le jour qui va
paraître*"): text by B. Jacob [the
Bibliophile Jacob?]

"*Quand un soupçon mortel*" (*romance*): unpublished; signed autograph in Paris Conservatory
Library.

"*Quand je vis que j'étais trahie*"
(religious *scène*): with piano and
organ accompaniment; unpublished; autograph in Paris Conservatory Library.

"*Quando da te lontano*": see *Il
Rimprovero*.

"*Quando il mio ben io rivedrò*"
(*canzonetta*): autograph property
of the Marchesa Medici, Rome.

"*Quando morte coll'orrido artiglio*"
(prayer): unpublished; autograph
in Paris Conservatory Library.

"*Quando verrà sul colle la dolce
primavera*": see *Minvela*.

"*Quanto mio ben t'adoro*" (*canzonetta*): autograph property of the
Marchesa Medici, Rome.

"*Questi capelli bruni*": see *I Capelli*.

"*Qui sospirò, là rise*" (*aria*): for
soprano; unpublished; copy with
autograph notations in Naples
Conservatory Library.

"*Rendimi il core, o Barbara*" (*canzonetta*): composed 1822.

Le Renégat (Italian: *Il Rinnegato*)
("*J'ai renié ma foi*"—Italian: *Io
rinnegai ma fè*) (*scène*): text by

Émielien Pacini; dedicated to M.
[Nicholas-Prosper] Levasseur.

Le Retour au désert: French version
of *Il Cavallo arabo.*

Les Revenants ("*Un soir à l'heure où
finit la veille*") (*aria*): text by
The Bibliophile Jacob; unpublished; autograph in Paris Conservatory Library.

Il Rimprovero ("*Quando da te lontano*") (*romanza*): included in
the collection *Donizetti per camera*.

Il Rinnegato: Italian version of *Le
Renégat.*

*Il Ritorno del trovatore da Gerusa-
lemme:* unpublished; autograph in
Paris Conservatory Library.

Il Ritratto ("*Son due stelle i cari
occhietti*") (*impromptu*): text by
Felice Romani; words and music
were improvised one evening at
the home of Paolo Branca in
Milan, where the autograph remained; unpublished.

"*Rose che un dì spiegaste*" (*romanza*): unpublished; autograph
in Paris Conservatory Library.

La Savoiarda (French: *La Savo-
yarde*) ("*Lasciata ho la montagna,
madre de' miei bei dì*"—French:
"*Je quitte la montagne*") (*romanza*): text by A. Broffeni; included in the collections *Tre
Melodie postume* and *Fiori di
sepolcro*.

La Schiava africana: see *La Negra.*

"*Se talor più nol rammento*" (*cava-
tina*): sung by Signora [Giuditta]
Pasta at the Società del Giardino,
Milan.

"*Seul sur la terre, en vain j'espère*"
(album leaf or *romance*): unpublished; autograph property of
Commendatore Carlo Lozzi, Bologna.

Sì o no ("*Tutte le femmine fanno*

(*Vocal Compositions Continued*)
così") (*canzonetta giocosa*): included in the collection *Dernières Glânes musicales.*

"*Si tanto sospiri, ti lagni d'amore*" (*romanza*): unpublished; autograph in Paris Conservatory Library.

"*Si tu m'as à ton image*" (*romance*): unpublished; autograph in Paris Conservatory Library.

Sombres pensées ("*Femme coupable et téméraire*"): text by Crevel de Charlemagne. A French version of *Il Sospiro.*

"*Sorgesti alfin, aurora desiata*" (*aria*): unpublished; autograph in Naples Conservatory Library.

"*Il sorriso è primo vezzo*" (*canzonetta*): included in the collection *Donizetti per camera;* autograph property of the Marchesa Medici, Rome.

"*Sospiri, aneliti che m'opprimete*" (*canzonetta*): unpublished; autograph property of the Marchesa Medici, Rome.

Il Sospiro ("*Donna infelice, stanca d'amore*") (*melodia*): text by Carlo Guaita; included in the collection *Inspirations viennoises.*

Il Sospiro del gondoliere (*barcarola*): unpublished; autograph in Naples Conservatory Library.

"*Sovra il campo della vita, sono pianta abbandonata*" (*larghetto*): for soprano; unpublished; autograph, with the dedication "*À Mademoiselle Catherine Marquise Sterlich, Donizetti*," in Museo Donizettiano, Bergamo.

La Speranza ("*Parto, parto*").

"*Spunta il dì l'ombra sparì*" (*romanza*) for tenor; unpublished; autograph in Paris Conservatory Library.

"*Su l'onda tremula ride la luna*": for soprano; included in the collection *Donizetti per camera.*

La Sultana ("*Là sedeva sull'erto verone*"): text by Leopoldo Tarantini ("*imitazione dal francese*"); included in the collection *Un Hiver à Paris.*

Su questi allor (*canzonetta*): autograph property of the Marchesa Medici, Rome.

"*Taci invan, mia cara jole*" (*romanza*): unpublished; at the bottom of the one-page autograph appears "Donizetti a De Martino, 1835."

T'aspetto ancor! ("*Nel tuo cammin fugace*") (*romanza*): included in the collection *Dernières Glânes musicales.*

Te dire adieu ("*Tu pars, il faut te dire adieu*"): text by Gustave Vaëz.

"*Te voglio* [or *vojo*] *bene assaje*": No documentary proof survives that this once-famous and long very familiar song was composed by Donizetti. Giuliano Donati-Pettèni, however wrote (*39, 202*): "Michele Scherillo attributes it to the *guaglioni*, who in turn would have taken it from a phrase in *La Sonnambula.* No, the music of this song is Donizetti's own. Not only is this affirmed by the tradition recorded by Bernardino Zendrini, but also it is testified to by Salvatore di Giacomo, a poet peculiarly versed in these studies. He wrote the history of this famous song, and said textually: 'I have forgotten, by the way, to tell you that "*Te voglio bene assaie*" was set by Donizetti; I could swear it to you—and if necessary furnish the proofs, if I am still alive.'" Donati-Pettèni then implies that the song might

(*Vocal Compositions Continued*)

have been one of the "twelve *canzonette*" that Donizetti (letter of September 12, 1837, to Antonio Vasselli) said he must write in order to earn twenty ducati. The song is Neapolitan in character—and September is the time of the Neapolitan *festa di Piedigrotta*, then as now the time to launch new songs.

"*Tengo no n'namurato, faccia d'empiso*" (*canzonetta napoletana*): included in the collection *Donizetti per camera*.

Ton Dieu est mon Dieu: French version of *M'è Dio il tuo Signore*.

La Torre di Biasone ("*Vedi là, sulla collina*") (*ballata*): text by Leopoldo Tarantini; included in the collection *Nuits d'été à Pausilippe*.

Lu Trademiento ("*Aje, tradetore, tu m'haje lassata*") (*canzone napoletana*): included in the collection *Donizetti per camera*.

La Tradita ("*Oh* [or *Ah*], *ingrato, m'inganni*") (*romanza* or *arietta*): included in the collection *Donizetti per camera*; autograph in Paris Conservatory Library.

"*Troppo vezzosa è la ninfa bella*" (*canzone*): for soprano; unpublished; autograph in Museo Donizettiano, Bergamo.

Le Troubadour à la belle étoile ("*Chaque lumière éteinte*") (*scène bouffe*): a French version of *Il Trovatore in caricatura*, q.v.

"*Trova un sol mia bella Clori*": for soprano; autograph property of Count Giovanni Battista Camozzi-Vertova, Bergamo; the Museo Donizettiano, Bergamo, has a manuscript copy. See next item.

"*Trova un sol mia bella Clori*"; for tenor; same text as the preceding item, but with different music; unpublished; autograph property

of Walter Toscanini, New York; the Museo Donizettiano, Bergamo, has a manuscript copy.

Il Trovatore ("*Del Giordano in sulle sponde*"): for soprano; unpublished; autograph, signed and dedicated "*À Mad. Thérèse Spadaro* [*del Bosch*]," in Museo Donizettiano, Bergamo.

Il Trovatore in caricatura (French: *Le Troubadour à la belle étoile*) (*scène bouffe*) ("*Era notte e la campana dava un tocco ogni secondo*"—French: "*Chaque lumière éteinte*") (*ballata*): text by Borsini; included in the collection *Un Hiver à Paris*.

"*Tu me chiedi se t'adoro*" (*arietta*): unpublished; autograph, with the dedication "*Pour Mad.* [*Zélie*] *de Coussy, 1840, Donizetti*," in Paris Conservatory Library.

"*Il tuo pensiero è il mio*": see *M'è Dio il tuo Signore*.

L'Ultima notte di un novizio (French: *La Dernière nuit d'un novice*) ("*Doman quando la squilla*"—French: "*Demain quand sonnera*") (*ballata*): text by Adolphe Nourrit; included in the collection *Un Hiver à Paris*.

L'Ultimo dì (*melodia*): according to Zavadini (*138*, 211, song 513), published in *I dodici album*.

L'Ultimo rimprovero: see this title in list of duets, page 401.

Un Bacio di speranza (French: *Un Baiser pour éspoir*) (*romanza-romance*): text in Italian and French.

Un Coeur pour abri ("*Sur des bords inconnus*") (*scène*): text by Auguste Richomme.

Un Detto di speranza ("*Abbandonar ogni speranza*") (*romanza*): for mezzo soprano or baritone; included in the collection *Dernières Glânes musicales*.

Una Lagrima: see *Preghiera*.

(*Vocal Compositions Continued*)

Una Tortora innocente (romanza): for soprano; dedicated to Virginia Vasselli; unpublished; signed autograph in Museo Donizettiano, Bergamo.

"Una vergine donzella per amore sospirò" (romanza): unpublished; autograph in Paris Conservatory Library.

Uno Sguardo ("Oh di quegli occhi teneri") (romanza): text by Felice Romani; unpublished; text and music were improvised one evening at the home of Paolo Branca, Milan, where the autograph remained.

"V'era un dì che il cor beato" (romanza): for tenor; unpublished; autograph in the Museo Teatrale alla Scala, Milan.

La Vendetta ("Bedda Eurilla") (canzonetta): included in the collection *Donizetti per camera.*

"Venne sull'ale ai zeffiri": see *Lamento in* [or *per la*] *morte di V. Bellini.*

"Vien ti conforta, o misera": unpublished; autograph in Paris Conservatory Library.

Le Violon de Crémone ("Cet instru-

ment silencieux renferme l'âme de ma fille") (romance): text by E. T. A. Hoffmann; unpublished; autograph in Paris Conservatory Library.

Vision ("Quand descend la nuit sombre") (mélodie): text by Édouard Plouvier.

Viva il matrimonio ("Se tu giri tutto il mondo") (cavatina buffa): for bass; text by Leopoldo Tarantini; "For the occasion of the very happy wedding of Baron Luigi Compagno with Signorina Maria del Carretto"; included in the collection *Donizetti per camera.*

"Voi vorreste il nome amato": see *Il Nome.*

La Voix d'espoir ("Une voix douce et pure") (romance): text by M. Cimbal.

Les Yeux noirs et les yeux bleus ("Ah! quelle embarras extrême") (romance): text by Étienne Monnier.

La Zingara ("Fra l'erbe cosparse" or "La zingara, la zingara") (arietta): text by Carlo Guaita; included in the collection *Inspirations viennoises.*

Vocal Compositions

Two Voices[8]

L'Addio ("Dunque addio, mio caro amore") (duettino): text by Felice Romani; included in the collection *Un Hiver â Paris.* Sometimes called *Le Pèlerinage.*

L'Addio (French: *L'Adieu*) *("Io resto fra le lagrime"*—French: *"Je reste abandonée"):* Italian text and

French translation by Émile Deschamps; included in the collection *Matinées musicales.*

"Ah, non lasciarmi, no" (duettino): unpublished; manuscript in Naples Conservatory Library.

L'Alito di Bice ("O profumo delicato") (notturno): for two voices; text by F. Puoti; included in the collection *Nuits d'été à Pausilippe.*

[8] Unless otherwise specified, these have piano accompaniment.

(*Vocal Compositions Continued*)

L'Amor funesto ("*Io d'amore, oh! Dio, mi moro*"): for soprano and tenor. See also, "*Più che non m'ama un angelo*", page 395.

Amor, voce del cielo ("*Sì t'amo, a te nascondere*") (*notturno*): for two voices; text by Leopoldo Tarantini; included in the collection *Nuits d'été à Pausilippe*.

Armida e Rinaldo (*duetto*): text from Tasso; unpublished; autograph in Paris Conservatory Library; the Bergamo Civic Library has a photographic copy.

L'Aurora ("*Vedi come in sul confine*") (*notturno*): for two voices; text by Leopoldo Tarantini; included in the collection *Nuits d'été à Pausilippe*.

I Bevitori ("*Mesci, mesci e sperda il vento*") (*notturno* or *brindisi*): for two voices; text by Leopoldo Tarantini; included in the collection *Nuits d'été à Pausilippe*.

Canzonetta con l'eco ("*Per valli, per boschi, cercando vò Nice, l'eco mi dice che Nice non v'è*": for two sopranos; composed at Bologna, August 27, 1817; unpublished; autograph in Museo Donizettiano, Bergamo.

C'est le printemps ("*On entend dans les brises*") (*chansonette-valse*): for two voices; text by Édouard Plouvier.

"*Che bel mar, che bel sereno*": see *La Passeggiata al Lido*; see also this title, page 395.

"*Che cangi tempra mai più non spero*": for two unaccompanied voices; unpublished; autograph in Museo Donizettiano, Bergamo.

"*Che vuoi di più? non splenda*" (*duettino*): text by Carlo Guaita; included in the collection *Inspirations viennoises*.

"*Da me che vuoi, che brami?*": see *I Fervidi Desiri*.

I Due Carcerati ("*Via dimmi due parole*") (*duetto*): for soprano and bass; unpublished; manuscript in the Noseda Collection, Milan Conservatory Library.

Duettino: for two sopranos; unpublished; autograph in Naples Conservatory Library.

Duetto: for two sopranos; unpublished; autograph, with the dedication "*Alla Marchesa Medici, Donizetti,*" in Paris Conservatory Library.

Duetto: composed for Clementina Carnevali and Nicola Cartoni, December 19, 1822; unpublished; autograph property of Commendatore Carlo Lozzi, Bologna.

I Fervidi Desiri ("*Da me che vuoi, che brami?*") (*duettino*): included in collection *Donizetti per camera*.

Il Fiore ("*Qui dove mercè negasti*") (*duettino pastorale*): for soprano and tenor; included in the collection *Soirées d'automne à l'Infrascata*; autograph in Paris Conservatory Library.

La Gelosia (French: *Querelle d'amour*) ("*Non giova il sospirar*" —French: "*Tu n'aura rien*") (*scherzo*): for soprano and bass; included in the collections *Matinées musicales* and *Donizetti per camera*.

Il Giuramento ("*Tuo finchè il sol rischiara*") (*notturno*): for two voices; text by Palazzolo; included in the collection *Nuits d'été à Pausilippe*.

"*Godi diletta ingrata nell'ingannarmi tu*" (*canzone*): for two voices; unpublished; autograph in Paris Conservatory Library.

"*Ha negli occhi un tale incanto*" (*duetto*): for two sopranos; in-

(*Vocal Compositions Continued*)
cluded in the collection *Donizetti per camera.*

Héloïse et Abélard ("*Quittons nous*") (*duo historique*): text by Crevel de Charlemagne.

"*Ho perduto il mio tesoro*" (*duettino*): for two sopranos; included in the collection *Donizetti per camera.*

L'Incostanza di Irene ("*Sarà più fida Irene*") (*duettino*): for two sopranos; included in the collections *Soirées d'automne à l'Infrascata* and *Donizetti per camera;* autograph, with the dedication "*Per la Sig. Virginia Vasselli, Donizetti nell' anniversario suo D. D. D.— Sono 29—30 Nov. 1826,*" in Museo Donizettiano, Bergamo.

"*Io d'amor, o Dio, mi moro*" (*duettino*): for soprano and tenor; included in the collection *Donizetti per camera.*

"*Lumi rei del mio martire*" (*canzonetta*): for two voices; autograph property of the Marchesa Medici, Rome.

Les Napolitains ("*En main les mandolines*") (*nocturne*): for two voices; text by Crevel de Charlemagne.

"*Non mi sprezzar licori*" for two sopranos; autograph in Museo Donizettiano, Bergamo.

"*O crudel che il mio pianto non vedi*": see *L'Ultimo rimprovero.*

La Passeggiata al lido ("*Che bel mar, che bel sereno*"): included in the collection *Dernières Glânes musicales;* see also this title, page 395.

Le Pèlerinage: see *L'Addio.*

Predestinazione ("*Qual colomba che fugge*") (*duettino*): text by Carlo Guaita; included in the collection *Inspirations viennoises.*

"*Quegli sguardi e quegli accenti*":

for two sopranos; unpublished; autograph in Museo Donizettiano, Bergamo.

Querelle d'amour: see *La Gelosia.*

"*Qui dove mercè negasti*": see *Il Fiore.*

"*Sarà più fida Irene*": see *L'Incostanza di Irene.*

"*Se mal turbo il tuo riposo*" (*duettino*): for two sopranos; unpublished; autograph in Naples Conservatory Library.

"*Sempre più t'amo, mio bel tesoro*" (*duetto*): unpublished; autograph in the Malherbe Collection, Paris Conservatory Library.

"*Sempre sarò costante* (*duettino*): for two sopranos; dedicated to the Countess Ravizza-Botti.

"*Se tu non vedi tutto il mio cor*" (*canzonetta*): for two voices; unpublished; nonautograph signed manuscript in Paris Conservatory Library; another manuscript in Naples Conservatory Library.

"*Si soffre una tiranna*" (*duetto*): for two sopranos; unpublished; autograph in Museo Donizettiano, Bergamo.

I Sospiri ("*Ti sento, sospiri*") (*duettino*): included in the collection *Donizetti per camera.*

"*Sull'onda cheta e bruna*" (*barcarola*): for two voices; unpublished; autograph in the Library of the Conservatorio di Santa Cecilia, Rome.

"*T'intendo mio cor*": see *La Voce del core.*

"*Ti sento, sospiri*": see *I Sospiri.*

L'Ultimo rimprovero ("*O crudel che il mio pianto*"): included in the collection *Dernières Glânes musicales;* see also this title, page 398.

Un Guardo ed una voce ("*Un guardo di nera pupilla*") (*not-*

(*Vocal Compositions Continued*)
turno): for two voices; text by
Palazzolo; included in the collection *Nuits d'été à Pausilippe;* see
also next item.

Une Nuit sur l'eau ("L'air est pure")
(*nocturne*): for two voices; French
version of *Un Guardo ed una
voce.*

"Vedi là sulla collina" (duettino): unpublished; autograph in the
Noseda Collection, Milan Conservatory Library.

*La Voce del core ("T'intendo, sì
mio cor") (duettino):* included in
the collection *Donizetti per camera;* autograph in Paris Conservatory Library.

Vocal Compositions

More than Two Voices

"Ah che il destino": for two sopranos and tenor (can be sung by
two sopranos alone); unpublished;
autograph in Museo Donizettiano,
Bergamo.

La Campana (French: *La Cloche*)
(*"Il sole discende"*—French:
*"Déjà le jour baisse") (quartet-
tino):* for two tenors and two
basses; included in the collection
Matinées musicales.

*"Cedè la mia costanza, Irene, al tuo
rigor"* (quartet): A minor; for un
accompanied soprano, contralto,
tenor, and bass; unpublished; autograph, signed "Donizetti 1820,"
in Paris Conservatory Library.

Clori infidel: for soprano, contralto,
and bass; unpublished; manuscript
in the Library of the Conservatorio di Santa Cecilia, Rome.

*"Di gioja di pace la dolce sper-
anza,"* for soprano, tenor and bass;
unpublished; manuscript in the
Moldenhauer Archive, Seattle,
Washington.

*"Finchè fedele tu mi sei stata" (can-
zonetta):* for four voices; unpublished; autograph, dated "Bologna,
May 5, 1817," in Paris Conservatory Library.

"Io morrò, sonata è l'ora": for three

voices; unpublished; autograph in
Paris Conservatory Library.

*Madrigale ("Lumi rei del mio mar-
tire"):* unpublished; autograph,
signed and dated "Bologna, June
12, 1817," in Museo Donizettiano,
Bergamo; see also *"Lumi rei del
mio martire,"* page 401.

"Qui sta il male" (terzetto): unpublished; autograph in Naples Conservatory Library.

Rataplan or *La Partenza del reggimento ("Rataplan, rataplan, ecco
grato ognor col gentil fragor"* or
*"Rataplan, convien partir") (quar-
tettino):* for two tenors and two
basses; included in the collections
Matinées musicales and *Fiori di
sepolcro.* Also called *Canto marziale.*

*"Se schiudi il labbro, o Fillide" (di-
vertimento):* for five voices; included in the collection *Donizetti
per camera.*

Strofe di Byron: for four solo voices
(soprano, tenor, two basses); (a)
"Sien l'onde placide," (b) *"Per
noi la vita,"* (c) *"Ma poi passati
stragi e orror;"* unpublished;
manuscript in the Noseda Collection, Milan Conservatory Library.

Miscellaneous Vocal Pieces and Student Exercises

L'Amor materno (recitative and aria), for solo voice, dedicated "To Countess Amélie Taaffe, 1844"; unpublished; manuscript in the Moldenhauer Archive, Seattle, Washington.

Anacreontic ("Guarda che bianca luna"): for voice and orchestra; text by Jacopo (Giacopo) Vittorelli; autograph in Paris Conservatory Library; inscribed "Set to music by me, Gaetano Donizetti, for Signor Gian Batt. Capitanio on the day March 30, 1815."

Aria ("Amor mio nume, eccomi a' piedi tuoi"): composed for the 1816 examinations at Bologna.

Aria ("Ognun dice che le donne"): for bass and orchestra; autograph with inscription "*Quant mai l'ò tirada a mà/ Bergamo a dì 20 Marzo 1815 ad uso di G. D.*" in Paris Conservatory Library.

Aria ("Ti sovvenga amato bene, che fedel ti serbo il cor"): for soprano and orchestra; autograph with inscription "*Addì 10 Maggio 1817 in una mattina*" in Naples Conservatory Library.

Aria: for soprano and orchestra, horn *obbligato*; composed for the singer Carolina Magni; performed for her benefit evening, September 11, 1820, at the Teatro Riccardi, Bergamo, when it was inserted into Melara's opera *Berengario;* autograph lost.

Cabaletta ("Pietosa all'amor mio"): inserted into the second-act duet of Pamira and Maometto in Rossini's opera *L'Assedio di Corinto* as performed at the Teatro Carlo Felice, Genoa, in April, 1828; autograph lost.

Canto marziale: see *Rataplan (La Partenza del reggimento),* page 402.

Duetto ("Perchè quell'alma ingrata"): for soprano, tenor, and small orchestra; autograph, dated September 27, 1816, in Naples Conservatory Library.

Duetto ("Se bramate che vi sposi"): for "Lisetta and Procolo"; autograph property of the Donizetti heirs.

Duetto ("Taci, tu cerchi invano"): for two sopranos and orchestra; autograph in Naples Conservatory Library.

Fugue: for four voices; autograph in Naples Conservatory Library (catalogue No. 63746).

Fugue: for four voices; autograph in Naples Conservatory Library (catalogue No. 63861).

Fugues (eleven): for four, five, and six voices; student exercises, most of them dated Bologna 1817; autographs in Museo Donizettiano, Bergamo.

Fugues (three): for four voices; student exercises; autographs in Naples Conservatory Library (catalogue Nos. 64003, 64004, 64005).

Grande Offertorio: for organ or pianoforte; published in the collection *Raccolta periodica* (L. Bertuzzi, Milan).

Recitative and Duet ("Sposo lo so, lo so . . . Da quel piano difende-

(*Miscellaneous Pieces Continued*)

temi, o Dei"): for soprano and bass, with small orchestra; autograph in Naples Conservatory Library.

Recitative and Romanza ("Che avvenne che fu . . . Solo per te sospiro"): for tenor and small orchestra; autograph in Museo Donizettiano, Bergamo.

Sextet ("Ah! quel Guglielmo, qual sorpresa, o ciel, che miro"): for two sopranos, two tenors, two basses, and orchestra; autograph, dated 1812, with inscription "Done before the studies at Bologna followed in 1816–1817," in Naples Conservatory Library.

Sketches (of parts and scores): four pages of autograph manuscript in Naples Conservatory Library (catalogue Nos. 63855, 63856, 63857).

Sketches (pencil; various pieces): autograph in Naples Conservatory Library (catalogue Nos. 63855 to 63893 inclusive).

Sketches and studies: five pages of autograph manuscript in Naples Conservatory Library (catalogue Nos. 63866 to 63872 inclusive).

Sketches and studies (various pieces): autograph manuscript in Naples Conservatory Library (catalogue Nos. 63894 to 63909 inclusive).

Sketches and studies (various pieces): prevalently, sketches of orchestral scores; autograph manuscript in Naples Conservatory Library (catalogue Nos. 63910 to 63923 inclusive).

Solfeggi: for mezzo-soprano and piano; written at Paris; thirty-four pages of two notebooks in Naples Conservatory Library (catalogue No. 63590).

Study: for clarinet; B-flat; autograph, with dedication "For my friend Begnigni [Benigni], 1821" in Museo Donizettiano, Bergamo.

Studies (in counterpoint and fugue): a large book containing twenty-two studies in counterpoint and forty in fugue for two, three, and four voices. The autograph contains this inscription on its first page: "Study of Counterpoint made by Gaetano Donizetti of Bergamo under the direction of the Celebrated Signor Maestro Don Stanislao Mattei. In Bologna, the years 1815 and 1816, begun on the day November 22, 1815." Copy of the autograph in Museo Donizettiano, Bergamo.

Terzetto ("Isabella ormai mi rendi"): for two tenors, bass, and orchestra; autograph, dated 1818, in Naples Conservatory Library.

Vocalizzi or *gorgheggi:* two pages of oblong folio, written on paper ruled in twenty-four pentagrams; an example of the *solfeggi* and vocal exercises that Donizetti wrote out for friends, interpreters, and pupils; autograph in Paris Conservatory Library.

Bibliography

1. Abbiati, Franco. *Giuseppe Verdi*. 4 vols. Milan, 1959.
2. ———. *"La Musica in Turchia con Giuseppe Donizetti, pascià,"* in *Bergomum* (November 1928).
3. Acton, Harold. *The Last Bourbons of Naples (1825–1851)*. London and New York, 1961.
4. Adam, Adolphe. *Derniers Souvenirs d'un musicien*. Paris, 1859.
5. Alborghetti, Federico, and Galli, Michelangelo. *Gaetano Donizetti e G. Simone Mayr, Notizie e documenti*. Bergamo, 1875.
6. Amore, Antonino. *Vincenzo Bellini: Vita, studi e ricerche*. Catania, 1894.
7. Antonini, D. G. *"Un Episodio emotivo di Gaetano Donizetti,"* in *Rivista musicale italiana* (Turin), VII (1900), 3.
8. Appelius, Elda. *"Il Centenario dell'Elisir d'amore,"* in *Rivista di Bergamo*, 11 (1932).
9. Barbiera, Raffaelo. *Vite ardenti nel teatro (1700–1900)*. Milan, 1931.
10. Barblan, Guglielmo. *"Donizetti nel passato e nel presente,"* in *Rivista musicale italiana* (Milan, July–December 1948).
11. ———. *"La 'Messa di requiem' di Gaetano Donizetti,"* in *Rassegna musicale* (July 1948).
12. ———. *L'Opera di Donizetti nell'età romantica*. Bergamo, 1948.
13. Bellotti, Antonio. *Donizetti e i suoi contemporanei*. Bergamo, 1866.
14. Bennati, Nando. *Quattro lettere inedite di G. Donizetti e una lettera di Giacomo Meyerbeer*. Ferrara, 1908.
15. Berlioz, [Louis-]Hector. *Mémoires*. Paris, 1870.
16. ———. *Voyage musical en Allemagne et en Italie. Études sur Beethoven, Gluck et Weber. Mélanges et nouvelles*. 2 vols. Paris, 1844.
17. Berri, Pietro. *"Il Librettista del Don Pasquale: Leggende, ingiustizie, plagi,"* in *La Scala: Rivista dell'opera*, 110 (January 1959).
18. Bettòli, Parmenio (ed.). *Gaetano Donizetti. Numero Unico nel Primo Centenario della sua nascita, 1797–1897*. Bergamo, (n.d., but) 1897?
19. Bienenfeld, Elisa. *"Donizetti und Verdi,"* in *Musik*, 22 (1930).
20. Boigne, Charles de. *Petits Mémoires de l'opéra*. Paris, 1857.
21. Bossi, Lea. *Donizetti*. Brescia, 1956.
22. Boyé, Maurice-Pierre. *"Donizetti et l'opéra italien,"* in *Revue de la Méditerranée*, 73–83 (May–June 1956 through January–February 1958).

23. Branca, Emilia. *Felice Romani ed i più riputati maestri di musica del suo tempo.* Turin, Florence, and Rome, (n.d., but) 1882?

24. Brockway, Wallace, and Weinstock, Herbert. *The World of Opera, The Story of Its Development and The Lore of Its Performance.* New York, 1962.

25. Calzado, Adolfo. *Donizetti e l'opera italiana in Spagna.* Paris, 1897.

25a. Cambi, Luisa. *Bellini: La Vita, Epistolario.* 2 vols. Milan, 1934.

26. Cambiasi, Pompeo. *La Scala, 1778–1889.* 4th (enlarged) edn. Milan, (n.d., but) 1889?; rev. ed., covering period 1778–1906, with an account of the Teatro della Canobbiana, Milan, 1906.

27. Cametti, Alberto. *Donizetti a Roma.* Milan, Turin, and Rome, 1907.

28. ———. "*La Musica teatrale a Roma,*" in *Annuario dell'Accademia di Santa Cecilia* (1931–34).

29. ———. *Un Poeta melodrammatico romano, Appunti e notizie sopra Jacopo Ferretti e i musicisti del suo tempo.* Milan, 1898.

30. Cappelli, Dr. G. "*La Calotta cranica di Donizetti,*" in *Archivio italiano per le malattie nervose e più particolarmente per le alienazioni mentali, Organo della Società freniatrica italiana* (1887).

31. Caversazzi, Ciro. *Gaetano Donizetti: La Casa dove nacque, La Famiglia, L'Inizio della malattia.* Bergamo, 1924.

32. Chilesotti, Oscar. "*Gaetano Donizetti,*" in *I Nostri Maestri del passato.* Milan, n.d.

33. Cicconnetti, Filippo. *Vita di Gaetano Donizetti.* Rome, 1864.

34. Clayton, Ellen Creathorne. *Queens of Song.* London and New York, 1865.

35. Codignola, Arturo. *I Fratelli Ruffini.* Genoa, 1925–31.

36. Colombiani, Alfredo. *L'Opera italiana nel secolo XIX.* Milan, 1900.

37. Cottrau, Guglielmo. *Lettres d'un Mélomane pour servir de document à l'histoire musicale de Naples de 1829 à 1847.* Naples, 1885.

38. Daub-Mohr, Marie. "*Ein Meister der italischen Oper: Zum 100 Todestag von Donizetti,*" in *Neue Musikzeitschrift* (July 1948).

39. Donati-Pettèni, Giuliano. *Donizetti.* 3rd edn. Milan, 1940.

40. ———. *L'Istituto musicale Gaetano Donizetti. La Cappella musicale di Santa Maria Maggiore. Il Museo donizettiano.* Bergamo, 1928.

41. ———. *Studi e documenti donizettiani.* Bergamo, 1929. Contains articles originally published in *Bergomum* and *Revista di Bergamo.*

42. [Donizetti]. *Ricordi di Gaetano Donizetti esposti nella mostra centenaria tenutasi in Bergamo nell'agosto–settembre 1897.* Collected and arranged by the brothers Giuseppe and Gaetano Donizetti. 2nd (enlarged) edn. Bergamo, 1897.

43. ———. *Mostra donizettiana: Catalogo del Regio Conservatorio di Napoli.* Bergamo, 1897.

43a. ———. *Studi Donizettiani: Contributo all'Epistolario di Gaetano Donizetti, Lettere inedite o sparse raccolte da Guglielmo Barblan e Frank Walker.* Bergamo, 1962.

44. ———. "*Prospetto cronologico delle opere di Gaetano Donizetti,*" in *Rivista musicale italiana* (Turin), 4 (1897).

45. ———. *Alcune Lettere di Gaetano Donizetti pubblicate per nozze Sigis-mondi-Scotti.* Bergamo, 1873.

46. Dragoni, Aristide. *L'Arte in Bergamo e l'Accademia Carrara.* Bergamo, 1897.

47. Duprez, Gilbert-Louis. *Souvenirs d'un chanteur.* Paris, 1880.

48. Eisner-Eisenhof, Baron Angelo de. *Lettere inedite di Gaetano Doni-zetti a Diversi e Lettere di Rossini, Scribe, Dumas, Spontini, Adam, Verdi a Gaetano Donizetti.* Bergamo, 1897.

49. Engel, Louis. *From Mozart to Mario: Reminiscences of Half a Cen-tury.* 2 vols. London, 1886.

50. Escudier, Léon. *Mes Souvenirs.* Paris, 1863.

51. Ferrari, P. E. *Spettacoli in Parma dal 1828 al 1883.* Parma, 1883.

52. Ferrarini, Mario. *Parma teatrale ottocentesca.* Preface by Carlo Gatti. Parma, 1946.

53. Florimo, Francesco. *Bellini: Memorie e lettere.* Florence, 1882.

54. ———. *La Scuola musicale di Napoli e i suoi conservatorii, con uno sguardo sulla storia della musica in Italia.* 4 vols. Naples, 1880–84.

55. Fraccaroli, Arnaldo. *Donizetti.* (No p. or d., but) Milan, 1945? A novel.

56. Francavilla, Luigi Maria Majorca Mortillaro, Conte di. *Il Real teatro S[anta] Cecilia e le sue vicende, MDCXVII–MCMVIII.* Pa-lermo, 1909.

56a. Fumagalli, Camillo. *"Memoria riguardante la riesumazione delle ossa di Gaetano Donizetti avvenuto in Santa Maria Maggiore la sera del 26 luglio 1951,"* in *Bergomum* (October–December 1951).

57. Gabrielli, Annibale. *"La Casa di Donizetti a Napoli,"* in *Fanfulla della domenica,* 53 (Rome, 1893).

58. ———. *Gaetano Donizetti.* Rome and Turin, 1904.

59. Galesti, P. (ed.). *Lettere inedite di G. Rossini e G. Donizetti, per nozze Tozzoni-Torrigiani.* Imola, 1889.

60. Gavazzeni, Gianandrea. *Donizetti: Vita e musiche.* Milan, 1937, XV.[1]

61. ———. *Il Suono è stanco: Saggi e divertimenti.* Bergamo, (n.d., but) 1950?

62. Geddo, Angelo. *Donizetti.* Preface by Giuseppe Bonandrini. Bergamo, 1938, XVII.

63. ———. *Donizetti (l'uomo—le musiche).* Bergamo, 1956.

64. ———. *Donizetti: "Ordine fra i suoi quartetti,"* in *La Scala: Rivista dell'opera,* 77 (April 1956).

65. ———. *"Donizetti e la sua casa natale,"* in *Rivista di Bergamo,* 19, (1940).

66. Gennari, Aldo. *Il Teatro di Ferrara: Cenni storici.* Ferrara, 1883.

67. Ghezzi, Teodoro. *"Ricordi su Donizetti,"* in *Omnibus* (Naples, March 7, 1860).

68. Giulini, Maria Ferranti Job. *Giuditta Pasta e i suoi tempi.* Milan, 1935.

[1] A Roman numeral following the publication date refers to the year of the Fascist regime in Italy.

69. Grout, Donald Jay. *A Short History of Opera.* 2 vols. New York, 1947.

70. Jarro (Iarro) [Giulio Piccini]. *Memorie di un impresario fiorentino.* Florence, Rome, and Turin, 1892.

71. ———. *Storia Aneddotica dei Teatri Fiorentini. 1.—Il Teatro della Pergola.* Florence, etc., 1912.

72. Klein, John W. "Gaetano Donizetti, 1797–1848: A Centennial Tribute," in *Musical Opinion* (1948).

73. Kolodin, Irving. *The Story of the Metropolitan Opera 1883–1950: A Candid History.* New York, 1953.

74. Láng, Paul Henry. *Music in Western Civilization.* New York, 1941.

75. Lazzari, Alfonso. *Giovanni Ruffini, Gaetano Donizetti e il "Don Pasquale."* Florence, 1915. Reprinted from *Rassegna nazionale* (October 1915).

76. Lianovosani, Luigi. *La Fenice, Gran teatro di Venezia: Serie degli spettacoli dalla primavera 1792 a tutto il carnovale 1876.* Milan, (n.d., but) 1876?

77. Loewenberg, Alfred. *Annals of Opera 1597–1940, with an Introduction by Edward J. Dent.* 2 vols. 2d. edn., rev. and corr. by Frank Walker. Geneva, 1955.

78. Malherbe, Charles. *Centenaire de Gaetano Donizetti, Catalogue bibliographique de la Section Française à L'Exposition de Bergame.* Paris, 1897.

79. ———. *"Le Centenaire de Donizetti et l'exposition de Bergame,"* in *Rivista musicale italiana* (Turin), 4 (1897).

80. Marchetti, Filippo, and Parisotti, Alessandro (eds.). *Lettere inedite di G. Donizetti.* Rome, 1892.

81. Mazzatinti, G., and Manis, F. and G. *Lettere di Gioacchino Rossini.* Florence, 1902.

82. Mazzini, Giuseppe. *Scritti letterari di un italiano vivente (Filosofia della musica),* Vol. 2. Lugano, 1897.

83. Micca, Cesare Betto. "Giovanni Ruffini e il libretto del 'Don Pasquale,'" in *Rivista di Bergamo,* 10 (1931).

84. Mocenigo [M. Nani-Mocenigo]. *Il Teatro La Fenice.* Venice, 1926.

85. Monaldi, Marchese Gino. *G. Donizetti.* Turin, 1938.

86. ———. "Pel centenario di Gaetano Donizetti," in *Rivista d'Italia,* Supplement VI (1898).

87. Morazzoni, G. *[Donizetti] Lettere inedite.* Milan, 1930.

88. Pacini, Giovanni. *Le Mie Memorie artistiche.* Synthetic autobiography prepared by Ferdinando Magnani. Florence, 1875.

89. Pannain, Guido. *Ottocento musicale italiano: Saggi e note.* Milan, 1952.

90. Pasolini-Zanelli, G. *Il Teatro di Faenza dal 1788 al 1888.* Faenza, 1888.

91. Pastura, Francesco. *Bellini secondo la storia.* Parma, 1959.

92. ———. *Le Lettere di Bellini.* Catania, 1935.

93. Pinetti, Giambattista. *Le Opere di Donizetti nei teatri di Bergamo.* Bergamo, 1942, XX.

94. Pizzetti, Ildebrando. *La Musica italiana dell'ottocento.* Turin, 1947.

95. Prout, Ebenezer. "Auber's *Le Philtre* and Donizetti's *L'Elisir d'amore*: A Comparison," in *Monthly Musical Record* (1900).

96. Radiciotti, Giuseppe. *Gioacchino Rossini, Vita documentata: Opere ed influenza su l'arte.* 3 vols. Tivoli, 1927–29.

97. ———. *Teatro, Musica e musicisti in Sinigaglia.* Milan, 1893.

98. Raggi, Alessandro and Luigi. *Il Teatro Comunale di Cesena: Memorie cronologiche (1500–1905).* Cesena, 1906.

99. Regli, Francesco. *Gaetano Donizetti e le sue opere.* Turin, 1850.

100. Rinaldi, Mario. "*Antonio e Pasquale,*" in *La Scala: Rivista dell'opera* (July 1950).

101. Riva, Ubaldo. "*Un Bergamasco (Giuseppe Donizetti pascià) riformatore della musica in Turchia,*" in *Rivista di Bergamo,* I (1922).

102. Rinieri, Ilario. *Le Cospirazioni Mazziniane nel carteggio di un trasfugo.* Milan, 1923–28.

103. Rizzi, Aldo and Giuseppe. *Gaetano Donizetti nel primo centenario della morte.* Bergamo, (n.d., but) 1948?

104. Roberti, Giuseppe. "*Donizettiana,*" in *Rivista musicale italiana* (Milan), II (1895).

105. Rolandi, Ulderico. *Il Libretto per musica attraverso i tempi.* Rome, 1951.

106. Roncaglia, Gino. "*Ricuperato anche 'Il Furioso all 'isola de San Domingo' di Gaetano Donizetti,*" in *La Scala: Rivista dell'opera,* 115 (June 1959).

107. ———. *Rossini l'olimpico.* 2d. edn. Milan, 1953.

108. Rosenthal, Harold. *Two Centuries of Opera at Covent Garden.* London, 1958.

109. Rovani, Giuseppe. "*Gaetano Donizetti,*" in *Storia delle lettere e delle arti in Italia,* IV, ed. C. Nicolini. Milan, 1958.

110. Royer, Alphonse. *Histoire universelle du théâtre—Histoire du théâtre contemporain en France et à l'Étranger.* Paris, 1878.

111. Ruggeri da Stabello, Pietro. *Oda enfatica bartoliniana.* Bergamo, 1842.

112. Schlitzer, Franco. "*Curiosità epistolari inedite nella vita teatrale di G. Donizetti,*" in *Rivista musicale italiana* (Milan, July–December 1948).

113. ———. *L'Eredità di Gaetano Donizetti. Quaderni dell'Accademia Chigiana,* XXX. Siena, 1954.

114. ———. *Mondo teatrale dell'ottocento.* Naples, 1954.

115. ———. *L'Ultima Pagina della vita di Gaetano Donizetti. Quaderni dell'Accademia Chigiana,* XXVIII. Siena, 1953.

116. Scotti, Baroness Ginevra Rota-Basoni. "*Le Memorie donizettiane della Baronessa Basoni Scotti,*" in *Rivista di Bergamo,* 8 (1929).

117. Scudo, Paul. *L'Art ancien et l'art moderne.* Paris, 1854.

118. ———. *Critique et littérature musicales.* Paris, 1852.

119. ———. *Critique et littérature musicales,* 2d series. Paris, 1859.

119a. Seltsam, William H. *Metropolitan Opera Annals.* New York, 1947.

119b. ———. *Metropolitan Opera Annals. First Supplement, 1947–1957.* New York, 1957.

119c. ———. [*Metropolitan Opera Annals*], annual supplements published in *Opera News* (1958–59), thereafter separately.

120. Stendhal (Henri Beyle). *Rome, Naples et Florence en 1817.* Paris, 1817; tr. Richard N. Coe (London and New York, 1959), an annotated translation of the enlarged 1926 version.

121. ———. *Vie de Rossini.* Paris, 1824; tr. Richard N. Coe (London and New York, 1957), an annotated translation of the 1922 Paris edition (ed. Henry Prunières).

122. [Teatro alla Scala, Milan]: "*La Scala nei centocinquant'anni della sua vita artistica, 1778–1928,*" in *La Scala & Il Museo teatrale*, II (Nos. 2, 3, and 4 combined) (June–December 1928, VI).

123. [Teatro di San Carlo, Naples]: *Cento Anni di Vita del Teatro di San Carlo, 1848–1948.* Naples, (n.d., but) 1948?

124. Tiby, Ottavio. *Gaetano Donizetti a Palermo, estratto dall'Annuario dell'Accademia di Santa Cecilia, 1949–1951.* Rome, 1951.

125. Toye, Francis. *Rossini, A Study in Tragicomedy.* London and New York, 1934.

126. Trebbi, Oreste. *Il Teatro Contavalli (1814–1914).* Bologna, 1914.

127. Trevisani, Cesare. "*Come un grand'uomo fosse perseguito da uno piccolo,*" in *Fanfulla della domenica*, 41 (Rome, 1890).

128. Valetta, Ippolito [Giuseppe Ippolito Alessandro Desiderato Pio Maria Franchi-Verney, Conte della Valetta]. *Donizetti.* Rome, 1897.

129. "Vecchio Dilettante, Un." *Cenni biografici su Donizetti.* Milan, 1874.

130. "Vecchio Ottuagenario Dilettante, Un." *Cenni biografici di Donizetti e Mayr.* Bergamo, 1875.

131. "Vecchio Teatrofilo, Un." *Memorie del Teatro Comunale di Trieste dal MCCCI al MDCCCLXXVI.* Trieste, (n.d., but) 1877?

132. Verzino, Edoardo Clemente. *Contributo ad una biografia di Gaetano Donizetti.* Bergamo, 1896.

133. ———. *Le Opere di G. Donizetti: Contributo alla loro storia.* Bergamo and Milan, 1897.

134. Vittadini, Stefano (compiler). *Catalogo del Museo Teatrale alla Scala.* Milan, 1940, XVIII. With preface by Renato Simoni.

135. Walker, Frank. "Donizetti, Verdi and Mme. Appiani," in *Music and Letters* (January 1951).

136. ———. "The Librettist of 'Don Pasquale,'" in *Monthly Musical Record*, No. 990 (November–December 1958).

137. ———. *The Man Verdi.* London and New York, 1962.

137a. Wolff, Stéphane. *Un Demi-Siècle d'Opéra-Comique, 1900–1950.* Paris, 1953.

137b. ———. *L'Opéra au Palais Garnier, 1875–1962.* Paris, (n.d., but) 1962?

138. Zavadini, Guido. *Donizetti: Vita—Musiche—Epistolario.* Bergamo, 1948.

139. ———. *Gaetano Donizetti: Vicende della sua vita artistica.* Bergamo, 1941, XIX.

140. ———. *Museo Donizettiano di Bergamo: Catalogo generale.* Bergamo, 1936, XIV.

141. Zendrini, Bernardino. *Donizetti e Simone Mayr.* Bergamo, 1875; also included in his *Prose*, Vol. III, Milan, 1881.

Index

* Nonoperatic works are indexed here only if mentioned in the body of the text or in the appendix. A complete list of them will be found on pages 371–404.